Second Canadian Edition

P9-CRO-929

Issues and Controversies
SPORTS IN SOCIETY

Jay Coakley
University of Colorado
Colorado Springs

Peter Donnelly
University of Toronto

**McGraw-Hill
Ryerson**

Toronto   Montréal   Boston   Burr Ridge, IL   Dubuque, IA   Madison, WI   New York
San Francisco   St. Louis   Bangkok   Bogotá   Caracas   Kuala Lumpur   Lisbon   London
Madrid   Mexico City   Milan   New Delhi   Santiago   Seoul   Singapore   Sydney   Taipei

McGraw-Hill Ryerson

Sports in Society: Issues and Controversies
Second Canadian Edition

ISBN-13: 978-0-07-097184-4
ISBN-10: 0-07-097184-6

5 6 7 8 9 QFR 1 9 8 7 6 5 4 3 2

Printed and bound in the United States of America.

Care has been taken to trace ownership of copyright material contained in this text; however, the publisher will welcome any information that enables them to rectify any reference or credit for subsequent editions.

Vice President and Editor-in-Chief: Joanna Cotton
Publisher: Cara Yarzab
Sponsoring Editor: Nick Durie
Marketing Manager: Michele Peach
Managing Editor, Development: Kelly Dickson
Developmental Editor: Sara Braithwaite/Jennifer Oliver
Editorial Associate: Marina Seguin
Senior Supervising Editor: Joanne Limebeer
Copy Editor: Evan Turner
Production Coordinator: Sharon Stefanowicz
Cover Design: Greg Devitt Design
Cover Image: Grant Faint/The Image Bank/Getty Images
Page Layout: SR Nova Pvt Ltd, Bangalore, India
Printer: Quad/Graphics Fairfield

Library and Archives Canada Cataloguing in Publication Data

Coakley, Jay J.
    Sports in society: issues and controversies / Jay Coakley, Peter Donnelly.—2nd Canadian ed.
    Previous eds. published under title: Sport in society.

    Includes bibliographical references and indexes.
    ISBN 978-0-07-097184-4

    1. Sports—Sociological aspects—Textbooks. I. Donnelly, Peter II. Coakley, Jay J. Sport in society. III. Title.
    GV706.5.C63 2009   306.4'83   C2008-907101-8

About the Authors

Jay Coakley

Jay Coakley is currently a professor of sociology at the University of Colorado in Colorado Springs. He was born in Chicago and used an athletic scholarship to fund his undergraduate degree in sociology and psychology. In 1966 he went to the University of Notre Dame where he completed his M.A. and Ph.D. degrees. In 1970, he moved to Arizona to teach at the University of Northern Arizona before moving on to Colorado Springs in 1972. He was the founding editor of the *Sociology of Sport Journal* (1984–89), and he served as Chair of the Sport Sociology Academy of the National Association of Sport and Physical Education (1983) and the North American Society for the Sociology of Sport (1991). His research interests include youth sports, socialization, deviance, gender, and race and ethnicity. He has published many articles and book chapters and consults widely with journalists writing about social issues in sports. His text, *Sports in Society: Issues and Controversies* has been revised nine times since it first published in the United States in 1978, and there are now adaptations for students in Australia/New Zealand and the United Kingdom. Other books include the *Handbook of Sport Studies*, edited with Eric Dunning (2000), and *Inside Sports*, edited with Peter Donnelly (1999). He stays active by spending time with three granddaughters and traveling to new places whenever possible.

Peter Donnelly

Peter Donnelly is currently Director of the Centre for Sport Policy Studies, and a professor in the Faculty of Physical Education and Health, at the University of Toronto. He was born in Chester, England, studied physical education as an undergraduate, and taught school for several years. In 1969, he moved to the United States where he completed undergraduate studies in New York City, and then received Master's and Ph.D. degrees in Sport Studies from the University of Massachusetts. In 1976, he moved to Canada, where he taught at the University of Western Ontario from 1976–79 and at McMaster University from 1980–98. He was the second editor of the *Sociology of Sport Journal*, interim editor of the *International Review for the Sociology of Sport* (2003–06), and served as President of the North American Society for the Sociology of Sport in 2000. His research interests include sport politics and policy issues (including the area of children's rights in sports), sport subcultures, and mountaineering (history). He has published numerous scholarly articles on those and other topics. Recent books include: *Taking Sport Seriously: Social Issues in Canadian Sport* (1997; 2nd edition, 2000), and *Inside Sports* (with Jay Coakley, 1999). His current sporting interests include rock climbing/mountaineering (continually proving the inverse relationship between age and risk-taking) and hiking.

Contents

15 Sports in the Future: What can we expect?   487

Preface

"My name is Joe, and I am Canadian!"

The well-known Molson commercial from several years ago emphasizes that it is a mistake to assume that Canada and the United States are the same. Our societies are different, but not completely different; and our sports are different, but not completely different. These differences were enough to warrant an experiment four years ago.

Sociology of sport courses in Canada had often used U.S. sociology of sport text books when no viable Canadian alternatives were available. Canadian instructors often supplemented those texts – the most popular of which was Jay Coakley's *Sports in Society*—with Canadian readings and lecture materials. In 2003, Jay Coakley generously agreed to support a Canadian adaptation of his book, then in its seventh edition. The success of that experiment is now evident. The first Canadian edition was widely used, and that success now creates the need for a new and updated second Canadian edition.

PURPOSE OF THE TEXT

The second Canadian edition of *Sports in Society: Issues and Controversies* has a threefold purpose. First, it is designed to show students the ways that sociology can be used to study sports in society. Second, it is written to evoke critical questions from students as they think about sports in their lives and the world around them. Third, it is organized to facilitate the use of research, theory, and everyday experiences to learn about sports in society.

The chapters, organized around controversial and curiosity-arousing issues, present current research and theory in the sociology of sport so that readers may discuss and analyze those issues. Although popular sources are used in addition to sociological materials, the content of the book is grounded in sociological research and theoretical approaches. Therefore, the emphasis is clearly on sport as it influences and is influenced by social and cultural contexts.

FOR WHOM IS THIS BOOK WRITTEN?

Sports in Society is written for those taking their first look at the relationships between sports, culture, and society. Each chapter is accessible to university and college students who have not taken courses in sociology or kinesiology. Discussions of issues do not presume in-depth experience in sports or a detailed knowledge of sport jargon and statistics. The primary goal is to assist students in identifying and exploring critical issues related to sports in their lives, families, schools, communities, societies, and the world as a whole. To achieve this goal, we use concepts, theories, and research as tools that enable us to visualize sports as activities that are inseparable from everyday life, at the same time that they are more than mere reflections of the world in which we live.

Since so few books are written about Canadian sociology of sport, this adaptation is also useful for people interested in sports in Canadian society, and for students and scholars taking a comparative approach to studying issues and controversies in sports in Canada and other societies.

The emphasis on issues and controversies makes the content of all chapters useful for people who are concerned with sport-related policies and programme administration. Our purpose is to assist those who wish to make sports more democratic and sport participation more accessible, especially to those who continue to be excluded or marginalized.

WHAT'S NEW IN THE SECOND CANADIAN EDITION

The second Canadian edition is an adaptation of the ninth U.S. edition, and has been substantially rewritten from start to finish so that it is easier to read and understand. Information, including the content of tables and figures, has been updated. New substantive materials and examples have been added to maximize the timeliness of the text, and to incorporate feedback received from readers of the first Canadian edition.

Each chapter has been revised to be more concise and to take into account new research and theoretical developments in the field. There are more than 250 new references cited in this edition; about 1,000 references in all. Most of the new references identify materials published since the first Canadian edition went to press.

The most important addition is a series of Breaking Barriers boxes—one in each chapter. These boxes present issues and controversies associated with sports for people with a disability.

Their purpose is to provide the vocabulary and examples needed to think critically about the exclusion of people with a disability from sports, and to creatively consider the ways that inclusion might occur now and in the future. Being able-bodied is a temporary condition for most of us; if we continue to play sports through our lives, nearly all of us will eventually participate with some form of disability.

This edition continues to highlight current issues and controversies in Reflect on Sports boxes, which are designed to provoke student interest and stimulate critical thinking. Many of these boxes have been updated or replaced with new topics for the second Canadian edition.

A major challenge faced when rewriting this edition was to identify topics and references that would not be included. The sociology of sport has expanded so much, even in the past few years, that *Sports in Society* is an introduction to the field rather than an overview. Fully integrating this edition with the Online Learning Centre (www.mcgrawhill.ca/olc/coakley) enabled us to move additional material online.

Revision Themes and New Material

This second Canadian edition continues to emphasize the cultural, interactional, and structural dimensions of sports and sport experiences. It also continues to emphasize Canadian material. Canadian research and data, where available, have been used widely, but not exclusively.

Chapter 1 is reorganized so that readers are introduced to definitions of sports as they begin thinking about the connections between sport and their lives and social worlds.

The chapter on theories (Chapter 2) is condensed and revised to more clearly explain the usefulness of theory, as well as the differences between theories widely used by those who study sports in society.

The chapter on history (Chapter 3) provides additional material on the growth of organized sports in Canada, and on recent history—including the selection of Canada's national sport(s)—to illustrate more clearly the ways that changes in sports are connected with changes in culture and society.

The chapters on socialization and youth sports (Chapters 4 and 5) now include discussions of health and obesity in connection with sports in society, and explain why parents have become so concerned about the sport involvement of their children. Chapter 5 also contains a new box about child trafficking in sport.

The chapter on deviance in sports (Chapter 6) includes a new section that compares an absolutist approach with a constructionist approach to deviance. This section emphasizes that theories influence popular definitions of deviance and the policies that people use to control deviance in sports. This chapter also contains an updated analysis of performance-enhancing substances and technologies in sports, including a new box on blood boosting.

The chapter on violence (Chapter 7) presents new material on player–fan violence, celebratory violence, criminal violence, and sexual misconduct by coaches. Two new boxes have also been added, about terrorism, and injuries in children's hockey, respectively.

The chapter on gender and gender relations (Chapter 8) presents an updated discussion of gender equity, including a new box on the differences between equality and equity. New information has been added about gender relations in alternative and informal sports, and women in university coaching in Canada. This chapter now highlights the ways that gender ideology influences the culture and organization of sports.

The chapter on race and ethnicity (Chapter 9) is revised to clarify the concepts of race and racial ideology, and to develop the discussion on changing racial relations in sport.

The chapter on social class and class relations (Chapter 10) contains updated material on the ways that social class and life chances have become increasingly apparent and influential in

sport participation at all levels of competition and involvement. Updated and new information is also included on health and social class, global social inequalities, and the democratizing effects of public funding for sports.

The chapter on economics (Chapter 11) contains an expanded discussion of corporate influence in sports and updated materials on stadium funding. All data on salaries in professional sports are updated, and labour relations are discussed in connection with the full-season (2004–2005) lockout in the National Hockey League.

The media chapter (Chapter 12) includes new material on selling and buying media rights, as well as updated coverage of the Internet and sport video games and the ways in which ideologies influence media coverage of sports. New discussions have also been added about racial and gender ideology in sport media, the relationship between viewing sports and participation in sports, and the relationship between media coverage and rule changes in the NHL.

The chapter on government, global processes, and politics in sports (Chapter 13) is revised to highlight connections between sports, capitalist expansion, and global relations. New material is included on the sport for development and peace movement, on player migration, and on the manufacture of sporting goods.

The chapter on education and sports (Chapter 14) summarizes new issues and recent research on interschool and interuniversity sports, and uses this research as a foundation to discuss current problems at both the high school and university levels. This chapter also includes a new box on the privatization of school sport and physical education.

The chapter on the future (Chapter 15) has been shortened and revised to emphasize the role of human agency in creating the future of sports. There is new information on trends (including the development through sport movement), as well as factors that influence those trends.

INSTRUCTOR RESOURCES

*i*Learning Sales Specialist

Your *Integrated Learning Sales Specialist* is a McGraw-Hill Ryerson representative who has the experience, product knowledge, training, and support to help you assess and integrate any of the below-noted products, technology, and services into your course for optimum teaching and learning performance. Whether it's how to use our test bank software, helping your students improve their grades, or how to put your entire course online, your *i*Learning Sales Specialist is there to help. Contact your local *i*Learning Sales Specialist today to learn how to maximize all McGraw-Hill Ryerson resources!

*i*Learning Services Program

McGraw-Hill Ryerson offers a unique *i*Services package designed for Canadian faculty. Our mission is to equip providers of higher education with superior tools and resources required for excellence in teaching. For addition information, visit www.mcgrawhill.ca/highereducation/eservices.

Teaching, Technology and Learning Conference Series

The educational environment has changed tremendously in recent years, and McGraw-Hill Ryerson continues to be committed to helping you acquire the skills you need to succeed in this new milieu. Our innovative Teaching, Technology & Learning Conference Series brings faculty together from across Canada with 3M Teaching Excellence award winners to share teaching and learn best practices in a collaborative and stimulating environment. Pre-conference workshops on general topics, such as teaching large classes and technology integration, are also offered. We will also work with you at your own institution to customize workshops that best suit the needs of your faculty at your institution.

Course Management

Content cartridges are available for the course management systems **WebCT** and **Blackboard**. These platforms provide instructors with user-friendly, flexible teaching tools. Please contact your local McGraw-Hill Ryerson *i*Learning Sales Specialist for details.

Primis Online

Primis Online gives you access to our resources in the best medium for your students: printed textbooks or electronic e-books. There are over 350,000 pages of content available from which you can create customized learning tools from our online database at www.mhhe.com/primis.

CourseSmart

CourseSmart brings together thousands of textbooks across hundreds of courses in an eTextbook format providing unique benefits to students and faculty. By purchasing an eTextbook, students can save up to 50 percent off the cost of a print textbook, reduce their impact on the environment, and gain access to powerful Web tools for learning including full text search, notes and highlighting, and e-mail tools for sharing notes between classmates. For faculty, CourseSmart provides instant access to review and compare textbooks and course materials in their discipline area without the time, cost, and environmental impact of mailing print examination copies. For further details contact your *i*Learning Sales Specialist or go to www.coursesmart.com.

Online Learning Centre (OLC)

The password-protected Instructor's site of the Online Learning Centre (www.mcgrawhill.ca/olc/coakley) offers a wealth of supplementary material to aid instructors teaching *Sports in Society* in university or colleges, including an Instructor's Manual, Computerized Test Bank, and PowerPoint Presentations.

- The **Instructor's Manual** contains chapter outlines, quick overviews of the topics covered in each chapter; and discussion/ essay questions, designed to encourage students to synthesize and apply materials in one or more of the sections in each chapter.
- The **Computerized Test Bank** contains more than 630 multiple choice questions. Available for Macintosh or Windows users, the computerized test bank using EZ Test—a flexible and easy-to-use electronic testing program—allows instructors to create tests from book-specific items. EZ Test accommodates a wide range of question types and allows instructors to add their own questions. Test items are also available in Word format (Rich text format). For secure online testing, exams created in EZ Test can be exported to WebCT, Blackboard, and EZ

Test Online. EZ Test comes with a Quick Start Guide, and once the program is installed, users have access to a User's Manual and Flash tutorials. Additional help is available online at www.mhhe.com/eztest.
- **PowerPoint Presentations** summarize and illustrate material from each chapter with photos, cartoons, and tables.

The Instructor's OLC also offers ideas for group and class projects, as well as discussion questions and worksheets relating to each chapter.

STUDENT RESOURCES

Online Learning Centre (OLC)

The Student's site of the Online Learning Centre (www.mcgrawhill.ca/olc/coakley) offers links to supplemental materials associated with each chapter, including:

- Supplementary material from past Canadian and U.S. editions that add depth and background to current chapter topics
- Hyperlinks to websites that are useful sources of information about key topics
- Suggested Readings, updated and expanded for this edition
- A bonus chapter on *Sports and Religion*

ACKNOWLEDGMENTS

A great many people are involved in adaptations such as this, but particular thanks must again go to Jay Coakley for his generosity and integrity. In addition to this second Canadian edition, the first British, and the first Australia/New Zealand adaptations of *Sports in Society* are about to be published. By allowing others to become involved in this project that he has nurtured so carefully through ten editions, Professor Coakley has not only demonstrated his commitment to the democratization of knowledge, but also shared both the material and intellectual rewards of working on this project.

Thanks go to students in our sociology of sport courses, and others who have provided constructive criticisms over the years. Students regularly open our eyes to new ways of viewing and analyzing sports as social phenomena. Special thanks go to friends and colleagues who influence our thinking, provide valuable source materials, and willingly discuss ideas and information with us.

For this second Canadian edition, thanks go to friends and colleagues who have helped with this adaptation in more ways than they may realize: Louise Donnelly for her continuing love and support, and her ongoing tolerance of my use of the dining room table; Michele Donnelly for her diligent work fact-checking, and for continually raising critical questions; Alison Donnelly for the "Blackpool breaks," where the brisk Irish Sea air helped to clarify my thinking on a number of issues; Gilbert Leduc, and the late Pat Townsend-Leduc, for sharing the tranquility of their cottage on Little Bob Lake, where much of the final editing for this edition was completed; Graham Knight, James Gillett, and Phil White for their stimulating discussions over "Friday afternoon beers" at the Phoenix; my colleagues at the University of Toronto—Bruce Kidd, Margaret MacNeill, and Caroline Fusco—who have been supportive of this project in every possible way; colleagues across Canada and internationally who have helped in ways they may not realize—Jean Harvey, Nancy Theberge, John Loy, Susan Birrell, Rob Beamish, Kevin Young, Brian Wilson, Mike Atkinson, Barrie Houlihan, Parissa Safai, and many others too numerous to mention; and to the graduate students at "40 Sussex," who keep me "on my toes" and never cease to amaze me with their enthusiasm and capacity for intellectual work. No acknowledgements that I could write at this time would be complete without mentioning the debt owed to the late Alan Ingham. His work was an ongoing reminder that the sociology of sport has the capacity to challenge our parent disciplines in the social sciences; his absence leaves that burden to us.

My appreciation also extends to the reviewers whose suggestions helped to plan this revision:

Anna Lathrop, *Brock University*
Ann Oishi, *College of New Caledonia*
Robert Lewis, *Memorial University of Newfoundland*
Gary Koroluk, *Mount Royal College*
David Erickson, *Trinity Western University*
Monika Schloder, *University of Calgary*

Thanks also go to the team at McGraw-Hill Ryerson—Sara Braithwaite and Jennifer Oliver, Developmental Editors; Nick Durie, Sponsoring Editor; Joanne Limebeer, Supervising Editor; and Evan Turner, Copy Editor.

Peter Donnelly
Burlington, ON
November 2008

[CP(Steve White)]

The Sociology of Sport

What is it and why study it?

Sport is all hoke and hype, but I find it outrageous and wonderful.

—**Dick Beddoes, Canadian sportswriter (1975)**

Sport is no longer just sport for individual expression. Rather, it has become spectacle, with a jaundiced eye on the profit margin.

—**Robert Rinehart, author,** *Players All* **(1998)**

The rituals of sport engage more people in a shared experience than any other institution or cultural activity today.

—**Varda Burstyn, author,** *The Rites of Men* **(1999)**

ABOUT THIS BOOK

Most of you reading this book have experienced sports personally, as athletes or spectators or both. You probably are familiar with the physical and emotional experiences of playing sport, and you may know the rules and strategies used in certain sports. You may even follow the lives of high-profile athletes in your community or country. Most of you have watched sports, read about them, and participated in discussions about them.

This book assumes you are interested in some facet of sports, but it is written to take you beyond the scores, statistics, and personalities in sports. The goal is to focus on the "deeper game" associated with sports, the game through which sports become part of the social and cultural worlds in which we live.

Fortunately, we can draw on our emotions and experiences as we consider this deeper game. Let us use our experiences with community sports in Canada as an example. When young males play junior hockey, we know that team membership may affect their status in school and the way teachers and fellow students treat them. We know it may have implications for their prestige in the community, for their self-images, and for their self-esteem. We know that it may affect even their future relationships, their opportunities in education and the workforce, and their overall enjoyment of life.

Building on this knowledge enables us to move further into this deeper game associated with sports. For example, we might ask why Canadians place such importance on professional sports and high-performance athletes, and what this says about Canadian values. We might study how sport programmes are organized and how they are connected with ideas about masculinity and femininity, achievement and competition, pleasure and pain, winning and fair play, and other important aspects of our culture. We might ask how sports influence the status structure that exists in our institutions, our communities, and our society, and how athletes fit into that structure. We also might ask if the organization of sports is influenced by corporate sponsorships and examine athletes' ideas about the corporations whose names and logos are on their uniforms and on the surfaces of their sport facilities.

The assumption underlying these questions is that sports are more than just games and meets; they are also important parts of our social lives that have meanings and influence that go far beyond scores and performance statistics. Sports are integral parts of the social and cultural contexts in which we live. They provide the stories and images that many of us use to explain and evaluate these contexts, our experiences, and our connections to the world around us.

People who study sports in society are concerned with the deeper meanings and stories associated with sports. They carry out research to understand (1) the cultures and societies in which sports exist, (2) the social worlds created around sports, and (3) the experiences of individuals and groups associated with sports.

Sociology is helpful when it comes to studying sports as social phenomena. This is because **sociology**[1] *is the study of social life, including all forms of interactions and relationships*. The concepts, theories, and research methods that have been developed by sociologists enable us to study and understand sports as they exist in our lives and as they are connected with history, culture, and society. Sociology helps us to examine social life *in context* and see connections between our lives and the larger social world. In this book, we use sociology to see sports as part of social and cultural life and understand social issues as we study sports.

---

[1]Important concepts used in each chapter are identified in **boldface**. Unless they are accompanied by a footnote that contains a definition, the definition is given in the text itself. This puts the definition in context rather than separating it in a glossary.

Finally, as with the previous edition, the goal is to accurately represent research in the sociology of sport as we discuss issues central to current students in the courses we teach. As we consider those issues, we seek information primarily from scholarly research published in journal articles and books. The "gold standard" for evaluating scientific evidence is the peer review process that results in the publication of research in "refereed journals." We also use newspaper articles, certain Internet sites, and other media sources for examples, but we depend on "gold standard" research findings when making substantive points and drawing conclusions. This means that statements about sports and sport experiences are based, as much as possible, on data from studies that use surveys, questionnaires, interviews, observations, content analyses, and other accepted research methods in sociology. Other sources are used with extreme caution, and we always use the maxim, "consider the source" of "non-refereed" materials, which may have been written without concern for accuracy or by unreliable individuals, and which have never been reviewed and evaluated by other experts in the field before they were published or uploaded.

The material in this book is different than material presented on blogs, talk radio, television news shows, game and event commentaries, and in everyday conversations about sports. We critically examine sports as they exist in people's lives and the social contexts where people live, play, and work. We use research findings to describe and explain as accurately as possible the important connections between sports, society, and culture. We try to be comprehensive and fair when using research to make sense of the social aspects of sports and sport experiences. This is why there are approximately 1,000 books and articles listed as sources in this book. Of course, we want to hold your attention as you read, but we do not exaggerate, distort, purposely withhold or present information out of context to impress you and boost our "ratings."

ABOUT THIS CHAPTER

This chapter focuses on five questions:

1. What are culture and society?
2. What are sports and how might we distinguish them from other activities?
3. What is the sociology of sport?
4. Why study sports in society?
5. Who studies sports in society, and what are their goals?

The answers to these questions will be our guides for understanding the material in the rest of the book.

DEFINING CULTURE AND SOCIETY

As we use sociology to study sports, it is important to know the definitions of *culture* and *society*. **Culture** *consists of the ways of life people create as they participate in a group or society*. These ways of life are complex. They are created and changed as people struggle over what is important in their lives, how to do things, and how to make sense of their experiences. Culture encompasses all of the socially invented ways of thinking, feeling, and acting that emerge as people try to survive, meet their needs, and achieve a sense of meaning and significance in the process. Of course, some people have more power and resources than others in the culture creation process, and sociologists study how people use power and resources in the social world.

As parts of cultures, sports have forms and meanings that vary from one group to the next, and vary over time as groups and societies change. For example, traditional martial arts and sumo wrestling in Asia have different meanings and purposes than combat sports such as boxing and wrestling in Canada. The meaning, organization, and purpose of basketball have changed considerably since 1891, when it was developed at a YMCA in Massachusetts as an indoor exercise activity for young men who did not want to play football outside during winter. Canadian James Naismith, who invented basketball as part of an assignment in a physical education course, would not recognize his game if he were to see Yao Ming slam dunk during the Olympics while a billion people watch on television and thousands of others pay up to hundreds of dollars per ticket to see the game in person. It is important to know about these cultural and historical differences when we study sports as parts of social life.

The term **society** refers to *a collection of people living in a defined geographical territory and united by a political system and a shared sense of self-identification that distinguishes them from other collections of people*. Canada, China, Nigeria, and the Netherlands are societies. Each has a different culture and different forms of social, political, and economic organization. It is important to know about these characteristics of society as we study the meaning and social significance of sports from one social context to another.

DEFINING SPORTS

Most of us have a good enough grasp of the meaning of sports to talk about them with others. However, when we study sports, it helps to define what we are talking about. For example, can we say that two groups of children playing road hockey in an Alberta town and a pickup game of soccer on a Mexican beach are engaged in sports? Their activities are quite different from what occurs in connection with World Junior Hockey Championship games and World Cup soccer matches. These differences become significant when parents ask if playing sports is good for their children, when community leaders ask if they should use tax money to pay for sports, or when school officials ask if sports contribute to the educational missions of their schools.

Students ask us if jogging and skipping are sports. How about weight lifting? Hunting? Scuba diving? Darts? Automobile racing? Ballroom dancing? Chess? Professional wrestling?

Skateboarding? The X Games? Paintball? A piano competition? Should any or all of these activities be called sports? In the face of such a question, some scholars use a precise definition of sports so that they can distinguish them from other types of social activities.

A Traditional Definition of Sports

Although definitions of *sports* vary, many scholars agree that **sports** *are institutionalized competitive activities that involve rigorous physical exertion or the use of relatively complex physical skills by participants motivated by internal and external rewards*. Parts of this definition are clear, but other parts need explanations.

First, sports are *physical activities*. Therefore, according to the definition, chess probably is not a sport, since playing chess is more cognitive than physical. Are darts and pool physical enough to qualify as sports under this definition? Making this determination is arbitrary because there are no objective rules for how physical an activity must be to qualify as a sport. Pairs ice dancing is considered a sport in the Winter Olympics, so why not add ballroom dancing to the Summer Games? Members of the International Olympic Committee (IOC) asked this question, and ballroom dancing was included in the 2000 Sydney Olympic games as a demonstration sport.

Second, sports are *competitive activities*, according to this definition. Sociologists realize that competitive activities have different social dynamics from cooperative or individualistic activities. They know that when two girls kick a soccer ball to each other on the grass outside their home, it is sociologically different from what happens when the Canadian women's soccer team plays the U.S. national team in the World Cup tournament, so it makes sense to separate them for research purposes.

Third, sports are *institutionalized activities*. **Institutionalization** is a sociological term referring to *the process through which actions, relationships, and social arrangements become patterned or* *standardized over time and from one situation to another*. Institutionalized activities have formal rules and organizational structures that guide people's actions from one situation to another. When we say that sports are institutionalized activities, we distinguish what happens when two skiers decide to race each other down their favourite ski slope while vacationing at Mont Tremblant from what happens when skiers race each other in a World Cup giant slalom event, which has been highly organized according to strict rules laid down by the Fédération Internationale de Ski (FIS). In specific terms, institutionalization involves the following:

1. *The rules of the activity become standardized.* Sports have official rules applied whenever and wherever they are played.
2. *Official regulatory agencies take over rule enforcement.* Representatives of recognized "governing bodies"—such as a local rules committee for a children's soccer league, a provincial high school athletics association, Canadian Interuniversity Sport (CIS), and the International Olympic Committee (IOC)— enforce the rules.
3. *The organizational and technical aspects of the activity become important.* Sports occur under controlled conditions in which there are specific expectations for athletes, coaches, and officials so that results can be documented, certified, and recorded. Furthermore, equipment, technologies, and training methods are developed to improve performance.
4. *The learning of game skills becomes formalized.* Participants must know the rules of the game, and coaches become important as teachers; participants may also consult others—such as trainers, dieticians, sport scientists, managers, and team physicians—as they learn skills.

> What disqualifies war from being a true game is probably what also disqualifies the stock market and business— the rules are not fully known nor accepted by all the players.
>
> —Marshall McLuhan, author, *Understanding Media* (1964)

The fourth point in the definition of sport is that sports are *activities played by people for internal and external rewards.* This means that participation in sports involves a combination of two sets of motivations. One is based in the internal satisfactions associated with expression, spontaneity, and the pure joy of participation. The other motivation is based in external satisfactions associated with displaying physical skills in public and receiving approval, status, or material rewards in the process.

When we use a precise definition, we can distinguish sports from both play and dramatic spectacle. **Play** is *an expressive activity done for its own sake*. It may be spontaneous or guided by informal norms. An example of play is three four-year-olds who, during a recess period at school, spontaneously run around a playground, yelling joyfully while throwing playground balls in whatever directions they feel like throwing them. Of course, it makes sociological sense to distinguish this type of behaviour, motivated almost exclusively by personal enjoyment and expression, from what happens in sports.

Dramatic spectacle, on the other hand, is *a performance that is intended to entertain an audience.* An example of dramatic spectacle is four professional wrestlers paid to entertain spectators by staging a skilled and cleverly choreographed tag-team match in which outcomes are prearranged for audience entertainment. It also makes sociological sense to distinguish this physical activity, motivated almost exclusively by a desire to perform for the entertainment of others, from what happens in sports. Sports are distinguished from play and spectacle in that they involve combinations of *both* intrinsic enjoyment and extrinsic rewards for performance. This means that all sports contain elements of play and spectacle. The challenge faced in some sports is to preserve a relatively even balance between these two elements.

Many sociologists define *sports* in precise terms, so they can distinguish sports from other activities, such as informal play and dramatic spectacle. Interschool wrestling is sociologically different both from wrestling that might occur in a backyard or in the televised spectacle "Raw Is War." We used "action figures" to represent dramatic spectacle, partly because pro wrestling organizations exercise restrictive control over the images of their events and "personalities." [Jay Coakley]

This is a practical approach to defining sports, but it has potentially serious problems associated with it. For example, when we focus our attention only on institutionalized competitive activities, we may overlook physical activities in the lives of many people who have neither the resources to formally organize those activities nor the desire to make their activities competitive. In other words, we may spend all our time considering the physical activities of relatively select groups in society, because those groups have the power to formally organize physical activities and the desire to make them competitive. If this happens, we privilege the activities of these select groups and treat them as more important parts of culture than the activities of other groups. This, in turn, can marginalize people who have neither the resources nor the time to play organized sports or who are not attracted to competitive activities.

Most people in the sociology of sport are aware of this possibility, so they use this definition cautiously. However, some scholars reject the idea that sports can be defined once and for all time, and they use an alternative approach to identifying and studying sports in society.

An Alternative Approach to Defining Sports

Instead of using a single definition of *sports*, some scholars study sports in connection with answers to the following two questions:

1. What activities do people in a particular group or society identify as sports?
2. Whose sports count the most in a group or society when it comes to obtaining support and resources?

Asking these questions does not limit the analysis of sports in ways that might happen when a precise definition is used. In fact, asking these questions leads researchers to dig into the social and cultural contexts in which people form ideas and beliefs about physical activities. The researchers must explain how and why some physical activities are defined as sports and become important activities in the social and cultural life of a particular society.

Those who use this alternative approach do not describe sports with a single definition. When they are asked, "What is sport?" they say, "Well, that depends on whom you ask, when you ask, and where you ask." They explain that not everyone has the same way of looking at and defining *sports* and that ideas about sports vary over time and from one place to another. For example, they would

note that people in England who raced horses and went for hunting during the 1870s would be horrified, confused, or astonished by what Canadians today consider to be sports. Similarly, the people who watch CFL football games today would look at many activities that were considered sports in nineteenth-century England and say they were not "real" sports because participants did not train, compete according to schedules, play in leagues, or strive to set records and win championships. Maybe people in the year 2100 will play virtual sports in virtual environments and see our sports today as backwards, overorganized, and funless activities that do not allow participants to combine movements with fantasies in ever-changing environments.

Those who use this alternative approach to defining *sports* also understand that there are cultural differences in how people identify sports and include them in their lives. For instance, in cultures that emphasize cooperative relationships, the idea that people should compete with one another for rewards might be defined as disruptive, if not immoral. For people in cultures that emphasize competition, physical activities and games that have no winners may seem pointless. These cultural differences suggest that we should not let a definition of *sports* shape what is studied. Those who use this alternative approach do research based on what the people in particular cultural settings think is important in their own lives (see Bale and Christensen, 2004; Rail, 1998; Newberry, 2004; Rinehart and Syndor, 2003).

The assumption underlying this approach is that sports are *contested activities—that is, activities for which there are no universal agreements about meaning, purpose, and organization.* This means that in the case of sports there are varying ideas about who will participate, the circumstances under which participation will occur, and who will sponsor sports for what reasons. The most important sociological issue to recognize when we use this approach is that people in particular places at particular times struggle over *whose* ideas about sports will count as *the* ideas in a group or society. A guide for thinking about these issues is in the Reflect on Sports box titled "Sports as Contested Activities."

Struggles over whose ideas count when it comes to the meaning, organization, and purpose of sports are much more common than you might think. To illustrate this, consider the different ways *sports* might be defined as people make decisions related to the following questions:

- Should children younger than six years old be allowed to play sports? If so, how should those sports be organized and what will be their meaning and purpose?
- Should money from a local youth sports budget be given to a programme in which young girls are taught skipping or to a programme in which boys and a few girls compete in a roller hockey league at a local arena?
- Should the provincial high school athletic associations include cheerleading as an official high school sport?
- Should skateboarding and hacky sack be supported through a university intramural sport programme?
- Should tenpin bowling, darts, and men's synchronized swimming be recognized as Olympic sports in 2012?
- Should a permit to use a sport field in a public park be given to an informal group of Frisbee players or to an organized softball team that plays in an official community league?
- Should synchronized swimming events be covered in the sports section of a city newspaper, or in the lifestyle section?
- Should wrestler "Edge" be nominated for a "sports person of the year" award?

How these questions are answered depends on what activities are counted as sports in a society at a given time. These questions also remind us to be cautious in how we use a single definition of sports. For example, if sports are institutionalized, competitive physical activities played to achieve internal and external rewards, then why are competitive dancing, aerobics, skipping, and cheerleading not counted as sports? They fit the definition. The fact that they are not considered sports when it comes to important issues such as sponsorships, funding, and formal recognition raises two questions: (1) What activities are defined as sports in a society, and (2) Whose ideas and interests are represented most in those definitions?

Answering these questions requires a careful analysis of the cultural context in which decisions are made in everyday life. Asking what activities are identified as sports raises critical issues. These issues force us to look at the cultures in which people live, work, and play together, and struggle over what is important and how they will set collective priorities in their lives.

What is sport? This question cannot be answered without considering cultural values and power in a society. In the Olympics, synchronized swimming is a sport although people in some societies believe that "real" sports must reflect "manly" attributes. [CP(Brendon Dlouhy), *Edmonton Sun*]

REFLECT ON SPORTS   Sports as Contested Activities

When sociologists say that sports are contested activities, they mean that, through history, people have regularly disagreed about what sports could and should be. These disagreements have led to struggles over three major questions about sports and a number of related questions.

As you read the following questions, remember that there are many possible answers to each. Sociologists study how and why people in different places and times answer these questions in different ways.

1. WHAT ARE THE MEANING, PURPOSE, AND ORGANIZATION OF SPORTS?

The struggles related to this question have raised other questions such as the following:

- What activities are defined as "official" sports?
- How are sports connected with social values and people's ideas about one another, social relationships, and the social worlds in which they live?
- What physical skills are valued in sports—are strength, size, and speed, for example, more important than flexibility, balance, and endurance?
- How are sport experiences evaluated—is emotional enjoyment more important than competitive success?
- What types of performance outcomes are important, and how is success defined, measured, and rewarded?
- How is excellence defined—in terms of one's ability to dominate others, all-around athletic abilities, or one's abilities to maximize everyone's enjoyment in sports?

2. WHO WILL PARTICIPATE IN SPORTS, AND UNDER WHAT CONDITIONS WILL THIS PARTICIPATION OCCUR?

The struggles related to this question have raised other questions, such as the following:

- Will females and males play the same sports, at the same time on the same teams? On what basis will people make such decisions? Should rewards for achievement be the same for females and males?

- Will sports be open to people regardless of their social class and wealth? Will wealthy and poor play and watch sports together or separately? Will people from different racial and ethnic backgrounds play together or in segregated settings? Will the meanings given to skin colour or ethnicity influence participation patterns or access to participation?
- Will age influence eligibility to play sports, and should sports be age integrated or segregated? Will people of different ages have the same access to participation opportunities?
- Will able-bodied people and people with disabilities have the same opportunities to play sports, and will they play together or separately?
- What meanings will be given to the accomplishments of athletes with disabilities compared to the accomplishments of able-bodied athletes?
- Will gay men and lesbians play along side heterosexuals?
- Will athletes control the conditions under which they play sports, and have the power to change those conditions to meet their own needs and interests? Will athletes be rewarded for playing, and how will rewards be determined?

3. HOW WILL SPORTS BE SPONSORED, AND WHAT WILL BE THE REASONS FOR SPONSORSHIP?

The struggles related to this question have raised other questions, such as the following:

- Will sports be sponsored by public agencies for the sake of the "public good"? If so, who will determine what the public good is?
- Will sports be sponsored by nonprofit organizations? If so, how will organizational philosophies influence the type of sports that are sponsored?
- Will sports be sponsored by commercial organizations? If so, how will the need for profits influence the types of sports that are sponsored?
- To what extent will sponsors control sports and athletes? What are the legal rights of the sponsors relative to those of the athletes and others involved in sports?

Continued

Sports as Contested Activities
continued

As you can see, many aspects of sports are contested. Sports change depending on how people answer these questions. Furthermore, answers to these questions are never permanent. New answers replace old ones as interests change; as power shifts; as the meanings associated with age, skin colour, ethnicity, gender, and disability change; and as economic, political, and legal forces take new and different forms.

This means that the definition of *sports* always reflects the organization of a society at a particular time. A precise definition of sports is helpful, but it should always be used with caution because truths about sports rest in people's lives, not sociological definitions. *What do you think?*

....

WHAT IS THE SOCIOLOGY OF SPORT?

This question is best answered at the end of the book instead of the beginning. However, you should have a clear preview of what you will be reading for the next fourteen chapters.

Most people in the sociology of sport agree that the field is a subdiscipline of sociology that studies sports as parts of social and cultural life. Much research and writing in this field focuses on "organized, competitive sports," although researchers also study other physical activities that involve goals and challenges (Martin and Miller, 1999; Rinehart, 2000; Rinehart and Sydnor, 2003). The people who carry out this research and writing use sociological concepts, theories, and research to answer questions such as the following:

1. Why have some activities rather than others been selected and designated as sports in particular societies?
2. Why have sports in particular societies been created and organized in certain ways?
3. How do people include sports and sport participation in their lives, and does participation affect who we are and our relationships with others?
4. How do sports and sport participation affect our ideas about bodies, masculinity and femininity, social class, race and ethnicity, work, fun, ability and disability, achievement and competition, pleasure and pain, "deviance" and conformity, and aggression and violence?
5. How are the meaning, purpose, and organization of sports connected with culture, organization, and resources in societies?
6. How are sports related to important spheres of social life, such as family, education, politics, the economy, and the media?
7. How do people use knowledge about sports as they go about their everyday lives?
8. How can people use sociological knowledge about sports to understand and participate in society as agents of progressive change?

Understanding the sociology of sport is easier if you learn to think of sports as **social constructions**—that is, as *aspects of the social world that are created by people as they interact with one another under the social, political, and economic conditions that exist in their society*. To stress this point, we generally use the term *sports* rather than *sport*. We do this to emphasize that the forms and meanings of sports vary from place to place and time to time. We want to avoid the inference that "sport" has an essential and timeless quality apart from the contexts in which people create, play, and change sports in society. Figure 1.1 illustrates that this approach may make some people uncomfortable because they have vested interest in sports as they are currently organized and played. They

FIGURE 1.1 If sports are social constructions, it means that we create them and that we can change them. The sociology of sport helps people to identify things about sports that could or should be changed; other people, including those associated with sports, may resist this notion because they benefit from sports as they are currently organized.

are not anxious for people to see sports as social constructions that are subject to change if people wish to organize and play them differently.

Differences between the Sociology of Sport and the Psychology of Sport

An additional way to understand the sociology of sport is to contrast it with the psychology of sport. Psychologists study behaviour in terms of attributes and processes that exist *inside* individuals. They focus on motivation, perception, cognition, self-esteem, self-confidence, attitudes, and personality. They also deal with interpersonal dynamics, including communication, leadership, and social influence, but they usually discuss these things in terms of how they affect attributes and processes that exist inside individuals. Therefore, they would ask a research question such as: "How is the motivation of athletes related to personality and the perception of their physical abilities?"

Sociologists study actions and relationships in terms of the social conditions and cultural contexts in which people live their lives. They focus on the reality *outside and around* individuals and deal with how people form relationships with one another and create social arrangements that enable them to control their lives. Sociologists ask questions about the ways that actions, relationships, and social life are related to characteristics that are defined as socially relevant by people in particular groups. This is why they often deal with the social meanings and dynamics associated with age, social class, gender, race, ethnicity, (dis)ability, sexuality, and nationality. A sociologist would ask a question such as: "How do prevailing ideas about masculinity and femininity affect the organization of sport programmes and who participates in sports?"

When applying their knowledge, psychologists focus on the personal experiences and problems of particular individuals, whereas sociologists focus on group experiences and the social issues that have an impact on entire categories of people. For example, when studying burnout among adolescent athletes, psychologists look at factors that exist *inside* the athletes themselves. Because stress has been identified as a key "inside factor" in human beings, psychologists focus on stress experienced by individual athletes and how it affects motivation, performance, and burnout (Smith, 1986). When applying their knowledge, they help athletes to manage stress through goal setting, personal skill development, and the use of relaxation and concentration techniques.

Sociologists, on the other hand, study burnout in connection with the social reality that surrounds adolescent athletes. They focus on the organization of sport programmes and the relationships between athletes and other people, including family members, peers, and coaches. Because athletes are influenced by the social context in which they play sports, the application of sociological knowledge emphasizes that to control burnout we must change the organization of youth sport programmes and the dynamics of athletes' relationships so that athletes have more control over their lives and more opportunities to have experiences and relationships outside sports.

Both approaches have value, but some people may see a sociological approach as too complex and disruptive. They feel that it is easier to change individual athletes and how they deal with stress than it is to change the social conditions in which athletes live their lives. This is why many people who control sport programmes prefer psychological over sociological approaches. They do not want to change patterns of organization and control in their programmes. Similarly, many parents and coaches also prefer a psychological approach that focuses on stress management rather than a sociological approach that focuses on changing their relationship with athletes and the organization of sport programmes.

Using the Sociology of Sport

The insights developed through sociological research are not always used to make changes in favour of the people who lack power in society. Like any science, sociology can be used in various ways. For example, research findings can be used to assist powerful people as they try to control and enhance the efficiency of particular social arrangements and organizational structures. Or they can be used to assist people who lack power as they attempt to change social conditions and achieve greater opportunities to make choices about how they live their lives.

Science is not a pure and objective enterprise. Therefore, sociologists, like others who produce and distribute knowledge, must consider why they ask certain research questions and how their research findings may affect people's lives. Sociologists cannot escape the fact that social life is complex and characterized by conflicts of interests between different groups of people. Like the rest of us, sociologists must deal with the fact that some people have more power and resources than others. Therefore, using sociology is not a simple process that always leads to good and wonderful conclusions for all humankind. This is

why we must think critically about the potential consequences of sociological knowledge when we study sports.

As a result of our thinking about sports in society, we have written this book to help you use sociology to do the following:

1. Think critically about sports, so you can identify and understand social problems and social issues associated with sports in society.
2. Look beyond issues of physical performance and scores to see sports as social constructions that influence how people feel, think, and live their lives.
3. Learn things about sports that you can use to make informed choices about your own sport participation and the place of sports in the communities and societies in which you live.
4. Think about how sports in schools and communities might be transformed so they do not systematically disadvantage some categories of people while privileging others.

Controversies Created by the Sociology of Sport

Research in the sociology of sport sometimes creates controversy. This occurs when research findings suggest that there should be changes in the organization of sports and the structure of social relations in society as a whole. The recommendations may threaten some people, especially those who control sport organizations, benefit from the current organization of sports, or think the current organization of sports is "right and natural." These people have the most to lose if changes are made in the way that sports and social life are organized. People in positions of power and control know that changes in society could jeopardize their positions and the privilege that comes with them. Therefore, they prefer approaches to sports that blame problems on the weaknesses and failures of individuals. When theories put the blame for problems on individuals, solutions will generally call for better ways to control people and teach them how to adjust to society as it is, rather than calling for changes in how society is organized (Donnelly, 1999).

The potential for controversy that results from a sociological analysis of sports can be illustrated by reviewing research findings on sport participation among women around the world. Research shows that women, especially women in poor and working-class households, have lower rates of sport participation than other categories of people. Research also shows that there are many reasons for this, including the following: (1) women are less likely than men to have the time, freedom, and money to play sports regularly; (2) women have little or no control of the facilities where sports are played, or the programmes in those facilities; (3) women have less access to transportation and less overall freedom to move around at will and without fear; (4) women are often expected to take full-time

responsibility for the social and emotional needs of family members—a job that is never completed or done perfectly; and (5) many sport programmes around the world are organized around the values, interests, and experiences of men. As a result of these reasons, many women do not see sports as appropriate activities for them to take seriously.

It is easy to see the potential for controversy associated with such research findings. For example, sociologists might use them to suggest that opportunities to play sports should be increased for women, that women and men should share control over sports, and that new sports organized around the values, interests, and experiences of women should be developed. Other suggestions would call for changes in gender relations, family structures, and child care responsibilities, the organization of work, the distribution of resources in society, and ideas about femininity and masculinity.

Sports are part of everyday life in wealthy countries, when and where people have the time, energy, and resources to organize and play physical games. Local youth sports are a rich site for studying sports in society because social dynamics revolve around issues related to gender, social class, race and ethnicity, family, and community.
[Peter Donnelly]

When sociologists say that increasing sport participation among women or achieving gender equity in sport programmes requires such changes, they threaten those who benefit from sports and social life as they are currently organized. In response, these people see the sociology of sport as too critical and idealistic and often claim that these changes would upset the "natural" order of things.

However, good research always helps people to think critically about the social conditions that affect our lives. Studying sports with a critical eye is easier if we have informed visions of what sports and society could and should be in the future. Without such visions, often born of idealism, what would motivate and guide us as we participate in our communities, societies, and world? People who make a difference and change the world for the better have always been idealistic. (This is illustrated in "Breaking Barriers" on pages 15–16.)

Different Approaches in the Sociology of Sport

Some scholars who study sports in society are more interested in learning about sports than society. They focus on understanding the organization of sports and the experiences of athletes and spectators. Their goal, in most cases, is to improve sport experiences for current participants and make sport participation more attractive and accessible. They also may do research to improve athletic performance, coaching effectiveness, and the efficiency and profitability of sport organizations. These scholars often refer to themselves as *sport sociologists*, and see themselves as part of the larger field of *sport sciences*.

Scholars concerned primarily with social and cultural issues usually refer to themselves as sociologists who study sports or as cultural studies scholars. Their research on sports in society is often connected with more general interests in

leisure, popular culture, social relations, and social life as a whole. They use sports as windows into culture, society, and social relationships, and they study sports as the stories that people tell themselves about themselves thereby revealing their values, ideas, and beliefs.

Differences between scholars are not unique to the sociology of sport. They occur in every discipline as researchers make decisions about the questions they will ask and the knowledge they seek to produce. Knowledge is a source of power, so our knowledge in the sociology of sport has practical and political implications. It influences the ways that people view sports, integrate them into their lives, and make decisions about the organization and place of sports in society.

WHY STUDY SPORTS IN SOCIETY?

This is a serious question for people in the sociology of sport. The answer that most of us give is that we study sports because they are given special meaning by particular people in societies, they are tied to important ideas and beliefs in many cultures, and they are connected with major spheres of social life such as the family, religion, education, the economy, politics, and the media.

Sports Are Given Special Meaning in People's Lives

We study sports in society because they are important parts of everyday social life around the world. As we look around us, we see that the Olympic Games, soccer's World Cup, the Tour de France, the tennis championships at Wimbledon, and American football's Super Bowl are now worldwide events capturing the interest of billions of people. As these and other sport events are viewed in person or through the electronic media by people in over two hundred countries, they produce vivid images and lively

Cultural Barriers
Aren't We Athletes?

Randy Snow is a ten-time U.S. Open Wheelchair Tennis Champion. Today he is a film producer and social activist who has received national citizenship awards. Asked about the Paralympics for elite athletes with physical disabilities, he has this to say:

> Paralympians are better athletes than our able-bodied counterparts. We work just as hard, do it for a lot less money, carry education to our venue as well as competition, and have overcome [physical challenges to do our sports]. Our stories display... true resiliency ... therefore better matching us with the way life really exists. (in Joukowsky and Rothstein, 2002b, p. 39)

Snow's comment, plus the relative invisibility of sports for athletes with a disability, raises a sociological question: Whose sports count in society? The answer is that ideas and decisions about sports are based on multiple interactions that occur under particular cultural, political, and economic conditions. For sociologists, this raises three additional questions: Who is involved in and excluded from these interactions? Whose interests are represented or disadvantaged by the decisions made? How can cultural, political, and economic conditions be changed so that decisions are more representative of all people in a social world?

Most readers of this book have never had friends whose physical or intellectual impairments made them "disabled," and never met an athlete from the Paralympic Games or the Special Olympics. This means that if we asked you to close your eyes and imagine five different sport scenes, few of you would picture a scene involving athletes with an amputated limb, in wheelchairs, blind, with cerebral palsy, or with intellectual or developmental disabilities.

Are these athletes? Their times in the 100- and 200-metre sprints are better than all but a handful of sprinters worldwide. Why are some sports defined as more real or more important than others? Who determines the standards? These three sprinters run on Ossur's Cheetah Flex-Foot. Does this matter in terms of a definition of sport? [David Biene; photo courtesy of Ossur]

Continued

stories that entertain and inspire people and provide them with the words and ideas that they use to make sense of their experiences and the world around them. Even when people do not have an interest in sports, their family and friends may insist on taking them to games and talking with them about sports to the point that they are forced to make sports a part of their lives. Sport images are so pervasive today that many young people are more familiar with the tattoos and

---

Breaking Barriers   **Cultural Barriers**
continued

This imagination exercise is not meant to evoke guilt. Our views of the world, including the authors' views, are based on personal experiences; and our experiences are influenced by the meanings that people give to age, gender, race, ethnicity, social class, sexuality, (dis)ability, and other characteristics that are defined as socially significant in our lives. Neither culture nor society forces us to think or do certain things, but the only way to mute their influence is to critically examine social worlds and understand the ways that cultural meanings and social organization create constraints and opportunities in people's lives, including people with disabilities.

In each of the following chapters, a "Breaking Barriers" box presents the voices and experiences of people with disabilities. If you are *currently* able-bodied, each box alerts you to social and cultural barriers that constrain the lives of people with disabilities. If you have a disability, each box acknowledges the barriers that you, Randy Snow, and millions of others face in the pursuit of sport participation.

These barriers, according to many people, are "just the way things are." Eliminating them is impossible or unrealistic because they require changes in the organization of relationships, schools, communities, and societies. However, we are not victims of culture and society. If we have informed and idealistic visions of what sports could and should be, it is possible to identify and eliminate barriers. Fung Ying Ki, a triple gold medal winner in the 2000 Sydney Paralympics, knew that it was possible to break barriers when she said, "I hope that, in the future, there will no longer be 'disabled athetes' in this world, only 'athletes'" (in Joukowsky and Rothstein, 2002b, p. 115).

••

body piercings of their favourite sport celebrities than they are with political leaders who make policies that have a significant impact on their lives.

People worldwide increasingly talk about sports—at work, at home, in bars, on dates, at dinner tables, in school, with friends, and even with strangers at bus stops, in airports, and on the street. Sports provide nonthreatening conversation topics with strangers. Relationships often revolve around sports, especially among men, and increasingly among women. People identify with teams and athletes so closely that what happens in sports influences their moods, identities, and sense of well-being. People's identities as athletes and fans may be more important to them than their identities related to education, career, religion, or family.

Overall, sports and sport images have become a pervasive part of our everyday lives, especially for those of us living in countries where resources are relatively plentiful and access to the media is widespread. For this reason, sports are logical topics for the attention of sociologists and anyone else concerned with social life today.

Sports Are Tied to Important Ideas and Beliefs in Many Cultures

We also study sports in society because they are closely linked with how people think about and see the world. Sociologists try to understand these links by studying connections between sports and cultural ideologies.

Ideologies *are webs of ideas and beliefs that people use to give meaning to the world and make sense of their experiences.* Ideologies are important aspects of culture because they embody the principles, perspectives, and viewpoints that underlie our feelings, thoughts, and actions. However, ideologies seldom come in neat packages, especially in highly diverse and rapidly changing societies.

Different groups of people in society often develop their own ideas and beliefs for giving meaning to the world and making sense of their experiences, and they do not always agree. These groups may struggle over whose ideologies provide the most accurate, useful, or moral ways of giving meaning to and explaining the world and their experiences in it.

As various groups use and promote their ideologies in society, sports become socially relevant. Because they are social constructions, sports can be organized to reinforce or challenge important ideas and beliefs. People create and organize sports around their ideas and beliefs about bodies, relationships, abilities, character, gender, race, social class, and other attributes and characteristics that they define as important in their lives. Usually, the most popular forms of sports in a society reinforce and reproduce the ideologies favoured and promoted by people with the most power and influence in that society. In the process, those ideologies often become dominant in that most people learn to use them as they make sense of the world and their experiences in it. When this occurs, sports serve as cultural practices that support and solidify particular forms of social organization and power relations.

Gender Ideology We can use gender ideology to illustrate these points. **Gender ideology** consists of *a web of ideas and beliefs about masculinity, femininity, and male–female relationships.* People use gender ideology to define what it means to be a man or a woman, evaluate and judge people and relationships, and determine what they consider to be natural and moral when it comes to gender. It also is used as people create, play, and give meaning to sports.

Dominant gender ideology in most societies has traditionally emphasized that men are naturally superior to women in activities that involve strength, physical skills, and emotional control. Through most of the twentieth century, this idea was used to establish a form of "common sense" and a vocabulary that defined female inferiority in sports as "natural." Therefore, when a person threw a ball correctly, people learned to say that he or she "threw like a boy" or "like a man." When a person threw a ball incorrectly, they learned to say that he or she "threw like a girl." The same was true when people were evaluated in terms of their abilities to run or do sports in general. If sports were done correctly, they were done the way a boy or man would do them. If they were done incorrectly, they were done the way a girl or woman would do them.

> **Hockey is our national glue. It defines Canada and Canadians. We have so few people in such a large land...But hockey holds us together.**
>
> —Roy Green, host of a Toronto talk radio programe (1996)

The belief that doing sports, especially sports that are physically demanding, would make boys into men has long been consistent with dominant gender ideology in many cultures. Consequently, when women excelled at these sports, many people claimed that they were "unnatural." Dominant gender ideology led them to assume that femininity and athletic excellence, especially in physically demanding or heavy-contact sports, could not go together. As they tried to make sense of strong, competent women athletes, they concluded that such women must be malelike or lesbians. When this conclusion was combined with related ideas and beliefs about nature, morality, and gender, many people restricted opportunities for girls and women to play sports.

This gender ideology was so widely accepted by people in sports that coaches of men's teams even used it to motivate players. They criticized men who made mistakes or did not play aggressively enough by "accusing" them of "playing like a bunch of girls." As they made sense of sports and gender, these coaches inferred that being female meant being a failure. This ideology clearly served to privilege males and disadvantage females in the provision of opportunities and the allocation of resources to play sports. Although it has been challenged and discredited in recent years, the legacy of this gender ideology continues to privilege some boys and men and disadvantage some girls and women.

Fortunately, ideology is always subject to change. People may question and struggle over it, and some people organize challenges that produce changes in deeply felt and widely accepted ideas and beliefs. In the case of gender ideology, sports have occasionally been sites or "social places" for challenging dominant ideas about what is natural and feminine. The history of struggles over the meaning and implications of gender in sports is complex, but recent challenges by both women and men who do not accept traditional ideas and beliefs have led to important changes in gender ideology.

Women athletes have illustrated clearly that females can be physically powerful and capable of noteworthy physical achievements surpassing those of the vast majority of men in the world. Furthermore, the accomplishments of women athletes have raised serious questions about what is "natural" when it comes to gender. We discuss issues related to gender ideology in sports in nearly every chapter, but especially chapter 8. The box "A Sociological Look at Bodies in Sports," which is available on the Online Learning Centre at www.mcgrawhill.ca/olc/coakley, presents issues related to another ideological issue in our lives: What do we consider to be natural when it comes to the body?

Racial Ideology Sports are sites for important ideological struggles. For example, in Canada, they have been sites for either reproducing or challenging dominant ideas about race and the connections between skin colour and abilities, both physical and intellectual. **Racial ideology** consists of *a web of ideas and beliefs that people use to give meaning to skin colour and to evaluate people in terms of racial classifications*. Racial ideologies vary around the world, but they are powerful forces in the social lives of many people. They are used to place people into racial categories, and they influence important social practices and policies that affect people's lives.

The connections between sports and racial ideologies are complex. Racial ideology is often used as a basis for evaluating athletic potential or explaining athletic success. The notion that light-skinned people cannot jump and that dark-skinned people are natural athletes are expressions of dominant racial ideology in certain cultures—an issue discussed in chapter 9.

Class Ideology **Class ideology** consists of *a web of ideas and beliefs that people use to understand economic inequalities and make sense of their own position in an economic hierarchy in society*. In Canada, for example, class ideology is organized around the idea of a **meritocracy** *where deserving people become successful and success is achieved by those who deserve it*. Sports provide many stories and slogans emphasizing that people can achieve anything through discipline and hard work and that failure awaits those who are lazy and undisciplined. By extension, this ideology leads people to make positive conclusions about the character and qualifications of wealthy and powerful people and negative conclusions about the character and qualifications of those who are poor and powerless. Winners are assumed to have strong character, whereas losers are assumed to have weak character. This way of thinking connects sports positively with capitalism and its competitive system of economic rewards in that it explains and legitimizes class inequality. This is discussed in chapter 10.

Sports and Ideologies: Complex Connections

As we think about sports and ideologies, it is important to know that ideology is complex and sometimes inconsistent, and that sports come in many forms and have many meanings associated with them. Therefore, sports are connected with ideologies in various and sometimes contradictory ways. We saw this in the example showing that sports are sites for simultaneously reproducing *and* challenging dominant gender ideology in society. Furthermore, sports can have many social meanings associated with them. For example, baseball is played by similar rules in Japan and Canada, but the meanings associated with baseball and with athletes' performances are different in the two cultures because of ideological differences. Team loyalty is highly prized in Japan, and emotional displays by players or coaches are frowned upon, whereas in Canada individualism is emphasized and emotional displays are accepted and defined as entertaining. Japanese baseball games may end in ties, but games in Canada must have clear winners and losers, even if it means playing extra innings and overtime or "sudden death" periods.

The complex connections between sports and ideologies make it difficult to generalize about the consequences of sports in society. Sports have the social potential to do many things. This is another reason for studying them as social constructions.

Sports Are Connected to Major Spheres of Social Life

Another reason to study sports in society is that they are clearly connected to major spheres of social life, including the family, the economy, the media, politics, education, and religion. We discuss many of these connections in various chapters in this book, but it is useful to highlight them at this point.

In terms of cultural ideology, and the relationships between sports and the economy, we have become so accustomed to the commercialization of sport that when Nike buys the surface of an entire building to advertise sport shoes, we are no longer surprised. This one was in Sydney, during the 2000 Olympic Games. [M. MacNeill]

Sports and the Family Sports are closely related to the family. In Canada, for example, hundreds of thousands of children are involved in a variety of organized sport activities. It is primarily their parents who organize leagues, coach teams, attend games, and serve as "taxi drivers" for child athletes. Family schedules are altered to accommodate practices and games. These schedules also may be affected by sport participation by adult family members. The viewing of televised sport events sometimes disrupts family life and at other times provides a collective focus for family attention. In some cases, relationships between family members are nurtured and played out during sport activities or in conversations about these activities. Two of these situations are represented in figure 1.2. Family issues are discussed in chapters 4 and 5.

Sports and the Economy The economies of most countries, especially wealthy postindustrial countries, are affected by the billions of dollars spent every year for game tickets, sports equipment, participation fees, athletic club membership dues, and bets placed on favourite teams and athletes. Sport teams affect the economies of many local communities. Some countries use public monies (taxes) to subsidize teams and events. Sports and commerce have fused together so that corporate logos are linked with sport teams and athletes and displayed prominently in universities, arenas, parks, stadiums, and other places where sports are played and watched.

Some athletes make a great deal of money from various combinations of salaries, appearance fees, and endorsements. Corporations have paid as much as US$100 million to be international Olympic sponsors and have their corporate names associated with the Olympic name and symbol for four years. Sport stadiums, arenas, and teams are now named after corporations instead of people or images with local cultural or historical relevance. Sponsorships and commercial associations with sports are so common that people now believe that, without Adidas, Coca-Cola, McDonald's, Panasonic, Nike, and other transnational corporations, sports could not exist.

This indicates that sports are cultural practices deeply connected with the material and economic conditions in society. These issues are discussed in chapters 10 and 11.

Sports and the Media Television networks and cable stations pay billions of dollars for the rights to televise major games and events. As U.S. television networks drive these rights fees ever higher, even public broadcasters such as the Canadian Broadcasting Corporation and its counterparts in countries such as the U.K. and Australia have been obliged to pay increased fees, or lose the rights to broadcast events such as the Olympics and the World Cup of soccer. People in sport organizations that depend on spectators are keenly aware that without the media their lives would be different.

The images and messages presented in media coverage of sports also emphasize particular ideological themes, and they influence how people see and think about sports and social life. The media have converted sports into a major form of entertainment witnessed by billions of people. Athletes are global celebrities, and the corporations that sponsor sports inscribe their logos in people's minds as they promote lifestyles based on consumption. These issues are discussed in chapter 12.

Sports and Politics People in many societies link sports to feelings of national pride and a sense of national identity. Despite frequent complaints about mixing sports and politics, most people around the globe have no second thoughts about displaying national flags and playing national anthems at sporting events.

Political leaders at various levels of government promote themselves by associating with sports as participants and spectators. Former athletes have even been elected or appointed to powerful political positions because of their name recognition and reputation from sports.

In Canada, the state is central to the amateur sport system, and has even intervened at the professional sport level. Since the 1960s, the federal government and, to a lesser extent, provincial governments have developed laws and policies that have a major impact on the conduct of sports.

International sports have become hotbeds of political controversy in recent years, and many countries around the world have used sports actively to enhance their reputations in global political relationships. Furthermore, sports involve political processes associated with issues such as who controls sports and sport events, the terms of eligibility and team selection, rules and rule changes, rule enforcement, and the allocation of rewards and punishments. Sports and sport organizations are political because they involve the exercise of power over people's lives. These issues are discussed in chapter 13.

Sports and Education Sports are integral parts of school life in many countries. They are taught and played in physical education classes, and schools in a few countries have interschool sport teams. Some of these teams attract more attention among students than academic programmes. However, the interschool sports sponsored by schools in most countries take the form of low-profile, club-based teams that emphasize participation and student control. As many Canadian scholarship athletes know, some U.S. universities may use their interuniversity teams to promote

the quality of their academic programmes while the athletes come to recognize the difficulties of being a serious student in these "big time" programmes. Athletic scholarships have been a significant and divisive issue in Canadian Interuniversity Sport (CIS). These issues are discussed in chapter 14.

Sports and Religion Although formal organized religion has far less significance in Canada than in the United States, with significantly fewer Canadians attending religious services regularly, and a great deal less likelihood that politicians will be identified by their religion or use it in their work, there are still some associations between sports and religion. For example, local churches and church groups may sponsor athletic teams and leagues, and the YMCA and other community centres with religious affiliations are widely associated with physical fitness activities. Also, following the U.S. lead, some athletes in Canada have become increasingly likely to display religious beliefs in connection with their sport participation, and may define

[Peter Donnelly]

FIGURE 1.2 Families and family schedules often are influenced by sport involvement. Sometimes this involvement disrupts family life and interferes with family relationships (left); sometimes it brings family members together in enjoyable ways, as in this "just married" couple on a tandem bicycle (right).

their sport participation in religious terms (see *Sports in Society* Online Learning Centre [www.mcgrawhill.ca/olc/coakley] for a bonus chapter on "Sports and Religion").

WHAT IS THE CURRENT STATUS OF THE SOCIOLOGY OF SPORT?

Prior to 1980, very few people studied sports in society. Scholars were not concerned with physical activities and thought that sports were unrelated to important issues in society. However, a few sociologists and physical educators in North America and Europe began to think outside the box of their disciplines. They decided that sports should be studied because they were becoming increasingly important activities in many societies. During the last two decades of the twentieth century, the sociology of sport gradually came to be recognized as a legitimate subfield of sociology, and physical education/kinesiology/sport science.

Research and interest in the sociology of sport has increased significantly in recent years.

Table 1.1   Publication sources for sociology of sport research

Journals Devoted Primarily to Sociology of Sport Articles	**Journals in Related Fields That Sometimes Include Articles on or Related to Sociology of Sport Topics**
International Review for the Sociology of Sport (quarterly) *Journal of Sport and Social Issues* (quarterly) *Sociology of Sport Journal* (quarterly) *Sport in Society* (quarterly)	*Adolescence* *Aethlon: The Journal of Sport Literature* *The British Journal of Sport History* *The European Sports History Review* *International Journal of the History of Sport*
Sociology Journals That Sometimes Include Articles on or Related to Sports	*International Journal of Sport Psychology* *Journal of Human Movement Studies* *Journal of Leisure Research*
Body & Society *British Journal of Sociology* *Canadian Journal of Sociology* *Canadian Review of Sociology* *Sociology of Education* *Theory, Culture and Society*	*Journal of the Philosophy of Sport* *Journal of Popular Culture* *Journal of Sport and Exercise Psychology* *Journal of Sport History* *Leisure Sciences* *Leisure Studies*
Interdisciplinary, Sport Science, and Physical Education Journals That Sometimes Include Articles on or Related to Sociology of Sport Topics	*Olympika: The International Journal of Olympic Studies* *Soccer and Society* *Loisir et Societé/Society and Leisure* *The Sport Psychologist*
CAHPER Journal *European Physical Education Review* *Journal of Physical Education, Recreation & Dance* *Journal of Sport Behavior* *Quest* *Research Quarterly for Exercise and Sport* *Sport, Education and Society* *Sport Science Review* *Women in Sport & Physical Activity Journal*	*Sport History Review* *Sport in History* *Sporting Traditions* *The Sports Historian* *Youth & Society*

For example, Amazon.ca has nearly nine hundred books listed in the "Sociology of Sport" categories. In 2000, only a third of that number of books were listed. Recent growth has been fuelled by the formation of professional associations and academic journals devoted to the field. These associations and journals enable scholars studying sports in society to meet with each other and present and publish their ideas and research. The journals related to the field are listed in table 1.1. Sociology of sport organizations include the following:

1. *The International Sociology of Sport Association (ISSA).* This is the first organization in the field, formed in 1964 and originally known as the International Committee for the Sociology of Sport. ISSA meets annually, attracting scholars from all over the world. Since 1965, it has sponsored publication of the *International Review for the Sociology of Sport.*
2. *The North American Society for the Sociology of Sport (NASSS).* This is the principal organization for scholars in the sociology of sport in Canada and the United States. It was formed in 1978, and has held conferences every year since 1980. NASSS has sponsored publication of the *Sociology of Sport Journal* since 1984.
3. *Other organizations.* Many countries and regions have their own sociology of sport organizations. Sometimes, these are informal groups of scholars who meet occasionally, but more often they form national organizations in countries such as Japan, Korea, and Spain. There are also regional organizations such as the European Sociology of Sport Association, (ESSA) and language-based organizations such as the Société de Sociologie du Sport de la Langue Française. Sociology of sport scholars also meet and present their research at a variety of physical education, sport sciences, and social sciences conferences around the world.

Growth in the sociology of sport will continue to occur if scholars in the field can conduct and publish research that people find useful for understanding social life, and participating effectively as citizens in their communities and societies.

SUMMARY

WHY STUDY THE SOCIOLOGY OF SPORT?

Sociology is the study of social life, including all forms of social interaction and relationships. Sociologists are concerned with social issues, social organization, and social change. Their goal is to enable people to understand, control, and change their lives so that human needs are met at both individual and group levels.

Sociologists study sports as parts of cultures and society. They look at sports in terms of their importance in people's lives, and their connections to ideology and major spheres of social life. Research in the sociology of sport helps us to understand sports as social constructions created by people for particular purposes. As social constructions, sports are related to historical, political, and economic factors. Some scholars in the field define *sports* as activities involving (1) the use of physical skill, prowess, or exertion; (2) institutionalized com-petition; and (3) the combination of intrinsic and extrinsic reasons for participation. Such a definition is problematic if it leads us to ignore or devalue the lives of people who do not have the resources and the desire to develop formally organized and competitive physical activities. For this reason, many scholars now recommend that, instead of using a single definition of *sports*, we should ask what activities are counted as sports in different groups and societies at different points in time. This question forces us to recognize that sports are contested activities, which focuses our attention on the relationship between sports and power and privilege in society, and leads more directly to concerns for transforming social life so that more people have access to the resources they need to control their lives and make them meaningful.

When sociologists study sports in society, they often discover problems based in the structure and organization of either sports or society. When this happens, the recommendations that sociologists make may threaten those who want sports and sport programmes to remain as they are now. Therefore, sociology sometimes creates controversies. Continued growth of the sociology of sport depends primarily on whether scholars in the field do research and produce knowledge that makes meaningful contributions to people's lives.

Visit *Sports in Society*'s Online Learning Centre at www.mcgrawhill.ca/olc/coakley for additional information, website resources, and study tools for this chapter.

[CP(Ryan Remiorz)]

Using Social Theories

How can they help us to study sports in society?

Hockey is the Canadian metaphor, the rink is this country's vast stretches of water and wilderness, its extremes of climate, the player a symbol of our struggle to civilize such a land. Some people call it our national religion. Well, what better?

—Bruce Kidd and John Macfarlane, authors, *The Death of Hockey* (1972)

[S]port provides a structured, organized world that satisfies some of our need for meaning.

—Robert Fulford, *journalist* (2006)

Those of us who study sports in society want to understand four things: (1) the social and cultural contexts in which sports exist, (2) the connections between those contexts and sports, (3) the social worlds that people create as they participate in sports, and (4) the experiences of individuals and groups associated with those social worlds. We are motivated by various combinations of curiosity, interests in sports, and concerns about social life and social issues. Most of us also want to use what we know about sports in society to promote social justice, expose and challenge the exploitive use of power, and empower people so they might resist and transform oppressive social conditions.

As we study and apply knowledge about sports, we use social and cultural theories. Theories provide frameworks for asking research questions, interpreting information, and uncovering the deeper meanings and stories associated with sports. They also enable us to be more informed citizens as we apply what we learn in our research to the world in which we live. Because those of us who study sports in society come from diverse academic backgrounds, and because social life is so complex, we use multiple theories to guide our work.

The three goals of this chapter are to

1. Identify and describe the theories used most widely to study sports in society
2. Explain the ways that theories help us to understand sports and the society in which we live
3. Demonstrate how theories influence our view of sports and the practical actions we take in connection with sports.

WHAT ARE THEORIES AND WHY DO WE NEED THEM?

Whenever we ask why our social world is the way it is and then imagine how it might be changed, we are "theorizing" (hooks, 1992). **Theorizing** involves *a combination of description, analysis, reflection, and application*. When we theorize, it is not necessary to use complex terminology. In fact, the best theories are those we understand so clearly that they help us to make sense of our experiences and the social world.

When we study sports in society, the best theories are those that describe and explain aspects of social life in logical terms that are consistent with systematic observations of the social world. Theories enable us to see things from new angles and perspectives, understand more fully the relationship between sports and social life, and make informed decisions about sports and sport participation in our lives, families, communities, and societies.

Many people think that theories do not have practical applications, but this is not true. Most of our decisions and actions are based on our predictions of their possible consequences, and those predictions are based on our "personal theories" about social life. Our theories may be incomplete, poorly developed, based on limited information, and biased to fit our needs, but we still use them to guide our behaviour. When our theories are accurate, our predictions help us to relate more effectively with others and control more directly what happens in our lives. When people make decisions about sports, formulate policies, or decide whether to fund or cut money from sport programmes, they base decisions on their personal theories about sports and society.

The theories discussed in this chapter are different from our personal theories about social life. This is because they are based on a combination of systematic research and deductive logic. They have been presented in books and articles so that others may evaluate, test, use, and revise them. When logic or evidence contradicts them, theories are revised or abandoned.

People who study sports in society have used many theories to guide them as they ask questions and interpret research findings. However, most

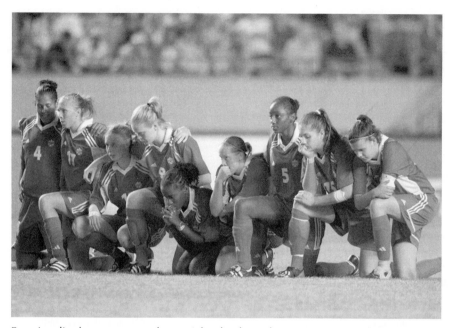

Functionalist theory assumes that social order depends on maintaining solidarity through established social institutions, including the institution of sport. [CP(Adrian Wyld)]

scholarly work over the past half century has been based on one or a combination of five major theories[1]:

- Functionalist theory
- Conflict theory
- Interactionist theory
- Critical theory
- Feminist theory

Although there are important differences between these five theories, there are many points at which two or more of them converge and overlap. This is because people read and respond to the ideas of others as they do research and develop new explanations of society and social life. Therefore,

theories are *emerging* explanations of what we know about social worlds at this time.

Each of the five theories discussed in this chapter provides a different perspective for understanding the relationship between sports and society. This will be highlighted through the following: (1) a brief overview of each theory, (2) examples of the ideas and research that have been inspired by the theory, (3) explanations of how the theory can be used as we take actions and make policies about sports in our everyday lives, and (4) an overview of the major weaknesses of the theory.

Table 2.1 provides a summary of each theory and how it helps to understand sports in society. The table contains a large amount of material, but as you read through the chapter you will find it to be a useful reference guide to each theory. Most important, it will help you to identify and understand similarities and differences between the theories.

---

[1]Figurational theory, widely used to guide research on sports in Europe, and to some extent in Canada, is explained and discussed in the Online Learning Centre at http://mcgrawhill.ca/olc/coakley.

Table 2.1   Using social theories to study sports in society: a summary and comparison

Functionalist Theory	Conflict Theory

I. ASSUMPTIONS ABOUT THE BASIS FOR SOCIAL ORDER IN SOCIETY

Social order is based on consensus and shared values, which hold the interrelated parts of society together. All social systems operate efficiently when each part of the system stays "in synch" with other parts.	Social order is based on economic interests and the use of economic power to exploit labour. Social class shapes social structures and relationships.

II. MAJOR CONCERNS IN THE STUDY OF SOCIETY

How do the parts of social systems contribute to the satisfaction of "system needs" and the efficient operation of the system?	How is economic power distributed and used in society? What are the dynamics of social class relations? Who is privileged and exploited in class relations?

III. MAJOR CONCERNS IN THE STUDY OF SPORT

How does sport fit into social life and contribute to social stability and efficiency? How does sport participation teach people important norms in society?	How does sport reflect class relations? How is sport used to maintain the interests of those with power and wealth in society? How does the profit motive distort sport and sport experiences?

IV. MAJOR CONCLUSIONS ABOUT THE SPORT–SOCIETY RELATIONSHIP

Sport is a valuable social institution that benefits society as well as individuals in society. Sport is a source of inspiration on both personal and social levels.	Sport is a form of physical activity that is distorted by the needs of capital. Sport is an opiate that distracts attention away from the problems that affect those without economic power.

V. SOCIAL ACTION AND POLICY IMPLICATIONS

Develop and expand sport programmes that promote traditional values, build the type of character valued in society, and contribute to social order and stability.	Raise class consciousness and make people aware of their alienation and powerlessness. Eliminate the profit motive in sports thereby allowing them to foster expression, creativity, and physical well-being.

VI. MAJOR WEAKNESSES

It does not acknowledge that sports are social constructions. It overstates the positive consequences of sport. It ignores that sport serves the needs of some people more than others.	It ignores that sport can be a site for creative and liberating experiences. It tends to overstate to the influence of economic forces in society. It assumes that people who have economic power always shape sports to meet their interests.

Critical Theory	Feminist Theory	Interactionist Theory
Social order is negotiated through struggles over ideology, representation, and power. Social life is full of diversity, complexities, and contradictions.	Social order is based primarily on the values, experiences, and interests of men with power. Social life and social order is gendered and based on patriarchal ideas.	Social order is created by people as they interact with each other. Social life is grounded in social relationships and the meanings people give to social reality.
How is cultural ideology produced, reproduced, and transformed? What are the conflicts and problems that affect the lives of those who lack power in society?	How is gender ideology produced, reproduced, and transformed? How do dominant forms of gender relations privilege men over women and some men over others?	How are meanings, identities, and culture created through social interaction? How do people define the reality of their own lives and the world around them?
How are power relations reproduced and/or resisted in and through sports? Whose voices are/are not represented in the narratives and images that constitute sports?	How are sports gendered activities, and how do they reproduce dominant ideas about gender in society? What are the strategies for resisting and transforming sport forms that privilege men?	How do people become involved in sports, become defined as athletes, derive meaning from participation, and make transitions out of sports into the rest of their lives?
Sports are social constructions. Sports are sites at which culture is produced, reproduced, and transformed. Sports are cultural practices that repress and/or empower people.	Sports are grounded in the values and experiences of powerful men in society. Sports reproduce male power and distorted ideas about masculinity. Sports produce gendered ideas about physicality, sexuality, and the body.	Sports are forms of culture created through social interaction. Sport participation is grounded in the decisions made by people in connection with their identities and relationships.
Use sports as sites for challenging and transforming exploitative and oppressive forms of social relations. Increase the range and diversity of sport participation opportunities. Challenge the voices and perspectives of those with power.	Use sports as sites for challenging and transforming oppressive forms of gender relations. Expose and resist homophobia and misogyny in sports. Transform sports to emphasize partnership over competition and domination.	Allow individuals to shape sports to fit their definitions or reality. Make sport organizations more open and democratic. Focus on the culture and organization of sports when controlling "deviance" in sports.
It does not provide guidelines to assess the effectiveness of particular forms of resistance as strategies for making progressive changes in social worlds. It often uses confusing vocabularies making it difficult to merge critical ideas and theories.	It does not provide guidelines to assess the effectiveness of particular forms of resistance as strategies for making progressive changes in social worlds. It sometimes uses confusing vocabularies making it difficult to merge critical ideas and theories.	It does not clearly explain how meaning, identity, and interaction are related to social structures and material conditions in society. It generally ignores issues of power and power relations in society.

FUNCTIONALIST THEORY: SPORTS PRESERVE THE *STATUS QUO*

Functionalist theory is based on the assumption that society is an organized system of interrelated parts held together by shared values and established social arrangements that maintain the system in a state of balance or equilibrium. The most important social arrangements are social institutions such as the family, education, the economy, the media, politics, religion, leisure, and sport. If these social institutions are organized around a core set of values, functionalists assume that a society will operate smoothly and efficiently.

When sociologists use functionalist theory to explain how a society, community, school, family, sport team, or other social system works, they study the ways that each part in the system contributes to the system's overall operation. For example, if Canadian society is the system being studied, a person using functionalist theory wants to know how the Canadian family, economy, government, educational system, media, religion, and sport are related to one an other and how they work together in contributing to the smooth operation of the society as a whole. An analysis based on functionalism focuses on the ways that each of these social institutions helps the larger social system to operate efficiently.

According to functionalist theory, social systems operate efficiently when they are organized to do four things: (1) socialize people so that they learn and accept important cultural values, (2) promote social connections between people so that they can cooperate with one another, (3) motivate people to achieve socially approved goals through socially accepted means, and (4) protect the overall system from disruptive outside influences. Functionalists assume that if these four "system needs" are satisfied, social order will be maintained and everyone will benefit. The first column in table 2.1 on page 28 summarizes functionalist theory.

Functionalist Theory and Research on Sport

Functionalist theory leads people to ask research questions about the ways that sport contributes to the organization and stability of organizations, communities, societies and other social systems. Using functionalist theory, researchers have studied some of the questions and issues that are discussed in the following chapters. Examples include the following:

1. Do sports and sport participation influence social and personal development? This issue is discussed in chapters 4 through 7, and 14.
2. Do sports and sport participation foster the development of social bonds and relationships in groups, communities, and societies? This issue is discussed in chapters 9, 10, 13, and 14.
3. Does playing sports have a positive impact on academic and occupational success, and does it teach people to follow the rules as they strive for success? This issue is discussed in chapters 4, 6, 7, 10, and 14.
4. Do sports contribute to personal health and wellness and the overall strength and well-being of society? These issues are discussed in chapters 4, 7 and 13.

Functionalist theory focuses on the ways that sports contribute to the smooth operation of societies, communities, organizations, and groups. This is why a functionalist approach is popular among people interested in preserving the *status quo* in society. They want sociologists to tell them how sports contribute to the smooth operation of the social systems in which they have been successful. Many people connected with organized competitive sports also prefer functionalist theory because it emphasizes the "functions" of sports and supports the conclusion that sports are a source of inspiration for individuals and societies.

Using Functionalist Theory in Everyday Life

Popularized forms of functionalist theory often are used when people in positions of power make decisions about sports and sport programmes at national and local levels. For example, a functionalist analysis of sports in society would support the following actions: promoting the development and growth of organized youth sports (to build values), funding sports programmes in schools and communities (to promote organizational loyalty and attachments to schools and communities), developing sport opportunities for girls and women (to increase achievement motivation among girls and women), including sports in military training (to increase military preparedness and the fitness of soldiers), and staging the Olympic Games (to build international goodwill and unity).

Functionalist theory generally leads to the conclusion that sports are popular in society because they maintain the values that preserve stability and order in social life. For example, in Canada it is assumed that sports are popular because they teach people to feel comfortable in tasks that involve competition, goal achievement, and teamwork under the supervision of an authority figure. Sports are also considered to be tools of integration in a society with two official languages and a high level of immigration. Furthermore, because functionalist theory leads to the conclusion that sports build the kind of character valued in society, it supports policies that recommend the growth of competitive sport programmes, the development of coaching education programmes, the establishment of training centres for top-level athletes, and increased surveillance and drug testing to supervise and control the actions of athletes. In the case of youth sports, functionalist theory supports actions to expand developmental sport programmes for children, establish criminal background checks and certification requirements for coaches, and build a sport system that trains young people to become elite athletes. Overall, functionalist theory inspires research questions about the ways that sports contribute to the development of individuals and society as a whole.

Many people reading this book are attracted to functionalist theory because they like its emphasis on the positive aspects of sports in society. People in positions of power in society also favour functionalist theory because it is based on the assumption that society is organized for the equal benefit of all people and therefore should not be changed in any dramatic ways. The notion that the system operates effectively in its present form is comforting to people with power because it discourages changes that might jeopardize their privilege and influence. Because the functionalist approach is popular, it is important to know its weaknesses.

Weaknesses of Functionalist Theory

Functionalist theory has three major weaknesses. First, it does not acknowledge that sports are social constructions that take diverse forms as they are created and defined by people interacting with one another. Functionalists see sport as a relatively stable social institution that always serves specific functions in societies. Such an approach overlooks the diversity of sports, the extent to which sports promote the interests of powerful and wealthy people, and the possibility that sports may sometimes produce or reproduce social outcomes that actually disrupt the smooth functioning of society.

Second, functionalist theory leads to overstatements about the positive effects of sport in society and understatements about its negative effects. For example, it does not help us to understand that women in society are disadvantaged when sports are organized in ways that legitimize the use of physical power to dominate others. Nor does it help us understand how sport teams in some schools and communities may actually undermine social integration when status systems favour athletes and lead others to feel marginalized.

Third, functionalist theory is based on the assumption that the needs of all groups within a society are the same. This overlooks the existence

"Ya know, I can't relate to these kids' music anymore, but at least i know we'll always have sports in common."

FIGURE 2.1 Functionalists overlook the fact that sports can create divisions in society as well as unifying people.

of real differences and conflicts of interest in society and cases when sports benefit some groups more than others (see figure 2.1). This limits our understanding of difference, conflict, and the dynamics of change in societies.

CONFLICT THEORY: SPORTS ARE TOOLS OF THE WEALTHY

Conflict theory focuses on the ways that sports are shaped by economic forces and used by economically powerful people to increase their wealth and influence. It is based on the assumption that every society is a system of relationships and social arrangements that are shaped by economic factors. In capitalist societies, relationships and social arrangements are organized around money, wealth, and economic power.

Conflict theorists assume that all aspects of social life revolve primarily around economic interests and that people who control the economy use their power to coerce and manipulate workers and their families to accept the existence of economic inequality as a natural feature of social life. Conflict theorists often focus their research on **class relations**—that is, *social*

processes that revolve around who has economic power, how that power is used, and who is advantaged or disadvantaged by the economic organization of society. Studies of class relations focus on the consequences of social inequality in all spheres of social life.

The primary goal of conflict theory is similar to the goal of functionalist theory: to develop a general theory that explains the organization and operation of all societies. Conflict theory emphasizes that economic power in capitalist societies is entrenched so deeply that progressive changes are possible only if workers become aware of the need for change and take action to make major changes in the organization of the economy. Sports focus the attention and the emotions of the have-nots in society on escapist spectator events that distract them from the economic issues and policies that reproduce their own powerlessness in society. Therefore, sports, especially mass spectator sports, are organized and sponsored by wealthy people and large corporations because they perpetuate capitalist values and a lifestyle based on competition, production, and consumption. When people accept capitalist values without question, sport becomes an opiate in society—an aspect of culture that deadens their awareness of economic exploitation and perpetuates the privilege and positions of people who control wealth and the economy.

Conflict Theory and Research on Sport

Conflict theory is often used by people who ask questions and do research on the connection between sports and the dynamics of power and privilege in society. This research will be used in subsequent chapters as we discuss the following issues:

1. Why do athletes become so alienated from their bodies that they will risk injury and physical well-being to play sports? This issue is discussed in chapters 4–7.

2. How are sports related to socioeconomic inequality in society? This issue is discussed in many chapters—especially chapters 8–11.
3. What happens to sports when they become commercialized? This issue is discussed in chapters 10–13.
4. How do wealthy and economically powerful people use sports to further their interests? This issue is discussed in chapters 10–13.

Like functionalist theory, conflict theory is based on the assumption that society is a social system. However, it focuses on "needs of capital" rather than "general system needs." Therefore, conflict theorists explain that a capitalist society cannot survive and grow without exploiting workers for the sake of boosting financial profits. Conflict theorists also focus on the ways that sports perpetuate the unequal distribution of power and economic resources in societies. Therefore, they often identify the negative consequences of sports and conclude that radical changes are needed in sports and society if fairness and justice are to prevail. Only when those changes are made will sports become sources of expression, creative energy, and physical well-being.

Many people in countries with capitalist economies are not comfortable with the assumptions and conclusions of conflict theory. They say that the negative tone of conflict theory does not fit with their ideas about sports or society, and they are uneasy with conclusions that call for radical changes in the current structure and organization of sports and society. However, conflict theory calls attention to important economic issues in sports and to forms of inequality that create conflict and tensions in society as a whole.

Using Conflict Theory in Everyday Life

Conflict theory focuses on the need to change the organization of sports and society. The goal of these changes is to give workers, including athletes, control over the conditions of their work. Problems in society and sports are attributed to the lack of power possessed by workers. Therefore, conflict theorists support policies and programmes that regulate or eliminate profit motives in sports and increase the control that athletes have over the conditions of their own sports participation. They also support policies that increase the element of *play* in sports and decrease the element of *spectacle* because it is designed to generate commercial profits. More play and less spectacle, they argue, would turn sport participation into a liberating and empowering experience for the masses of people in society.

In terms of specific issues, conflict theorists favour players' unions, organizations that represent the interests of people in communities where tax money is being used to subsidize wealthy pro-sport team owners, and radical changes in the overall organization of sports. Ideally, public resources would be used to sponsor sports designed to promote fun, fitness, and political awareness; spectator sports would exist for enjoyment in local communities rather than as tools for creating celebrity athletes and financial profits for a few wealthy people.

Weaknesses of Conflict Theory

Conflict theory has three major weaknesses. First, it tends to ignore the possibility that sports in capitalist societies may involve experiences that empower individuals and groups. Conflict theorists talk about sports being organized to maximize the control that wealthy people have over everyone else in capitalist societies. They see sports as activities through which athletes learn to define their bodies as tools of production, becoming alienated from their bodies in the process. This approach does not acknowledge that sport can take forms that could serve the interests of the have-nots in society, and it denies that sport participation can be a personally creative and liberating experience that inspires people to make economic changes that promote equality and eliminate the vast income and power gaps that currently exist in capitalist societies.

Second, conflict theory assumes that all aspects of social life are economically determined—that is, shaped by the profit motive and the needs of capital in society. It focuses on the inherent conflict between the economic haves and have-nots, and assumes that the haves always use their power to control and exploit the have-nots who live in a state of powerlessness and alienation. These assumptions lead conflict theorists to focus exclusively on economic factors when they study sports. However, many sports, especially those emphasizing recreation and mass participation, are not completely shaped by economic factors or the interests of wealthy people in society.

Third, conflict theory underestimates the importance of gender, race, ethnicity, age, sexuality, disability, and other factors when it comes to explaining how people identify themselves, relate to others, and organize the social worlds in which they live. Therefore, it often leads people to overlook the possibility that power and inequalities in society are based on factors other than social class and economic differences.

> Today, sports has come to pit race against race, men against women, city against city, class against class, and coach against player.
>
> —Frank Deford, sportswriter (1998)

Beyond the Needs of Society

Functionalist theory and conflict theory both focus on societal needs and how sports are related to the satisfaction of those needs. They give us a view of sports in society from the top down, but they do not tell us about sports in everyday life or the ways that people are active agents who participate in the processes through which sports and society are organized and changed. They ignore a view of society from the bottom up—from the perspectives of people who "do" sports and give meaning to them in their everyday lives. They also ignore the complexities of everyday social life and that sports and society are social constructions that emerge as people struggle over what is important in their lives and determine how their collective

lives should be organized. The theories that focus attention on these issues are critical, feminist, and interactionist theories.

CRITICAL THEORY: SPORTS ARE SITES WHERE CULTURE AND SOCIAL RELATIONS ARE PRODUCED AND CHANGED

Critical theory exists in a variety of forms, and it offers a useful alternative to functionalist and conflict theories.[2] It is based on the following three assumptions: (1) Groups and societies are characterized by shared values *and* conflicts of interest, (2) social life involves continuous processes of negotiation, compromise, and coercion because agreements about values and social organization are never permanent, and (3) values and social organization change over time and from one situation to another as there are shifts in the power balance between groups of people in society. Forms of critical theory were developed as people realized that societies are too messy, complex, and fluid to be described as "systems" and that it is

---

[2]This chapter is a basic introduction to using theories, and the goal is to provide a general explanation and overview of the valuable work done by scholars using forms of critical theories to study sports in society. We attempt to pull together major ideas from the following theories and theoretical frameworks: *neo-Marxist theories*, *traditional critical theory* (combining ideas of Marx and Freud), *hegemony theory* (based on the ideas of Antonio Gramsci), *cultural studies* (as it focuses on cultural production, power relations, ideology, and identity), *poststructuralism* (based on cultural studies, semiotics, and forms of literary analysis dealing with language and the construction of power, meaning, representation, and consciousness under the unstable, fluid, fragmented, and often contradictory conditions of postmodern life), and *queer theory* (combining feminist cultural studies and poststructuralism). None of these frameworks is specifically identified, but we highlight issues raised by people using these approaches.

not possible to develop a general explanation of social life that is applicable to all societies at all times in history.

Instead of focusing on society as a whole, critical theory focuses on the diversity, complexity, contradictions, and changes that characterize social life as it is lived and experienced by people who interact with one another and struggle over how to organize their lives together. Although critical theory comes in many forms, it focuses primarily on the following topics: (1) the processes through which culture is produced, reproduced, and changed, (2) the ways that power and social inequalities are involved in processes of cultural production, reproduction, and change, and (3) the ideologies that people use as they make sense of the world, form identities, interact with others, and transform the conditions of their lives.

People using functionalist and conflict theories often say that "sport is a reflection of society," but critical theorists explain that, in addition to reflecting society, sports are sites where culture and social organization are produced, reproduced, and changed. This makes sports much more than mere reflections of society. This issue is discussed in the box "Sports Are More Than Reflections of Society."

Unlike functionalists or conflict theorists, critical theorists realize that there are many vantage points from which to study and understand social life and that the relationship between sports and society is always subject to change. Therefore, they study sports in connection with changes in (1) the organization of government, education, the media, religion, the family, and other spheres of social life, (2) cultural definitions of masculinity and femininity, race, ethnicity, age, sexuality, and physical (dis)ability, and (3) the visions that people have about what sports could and should be in society.

Critical theory also encourages action and political involvement. It has been developed by scholars dedicated to identifying issues and problems for the sake of eliminating oppression and seeking justice and equity in social life. Critical theory is a valuable tool when identifying and studying specific social problems. People who use it assume that social relationships are grounded in political struggles over how social life should be defined and organized. They study sports to see if they are organized to systematically privilege some people over others. Their goal is to explain how sports have come to be what they are and to inspire new ways to discuss, define, organize, and play sports.

Critical Theory and Research on Sports

Those who use critical theory to study sports generally focus on one or more of the following issues:

1. Whose ideas about the meaning and organization of sports are used to determine funding priorities for sports, who will participate in them, how they will be covered in the media, and how they will be used for social, political, and economic purposes?
2. How are sports and sport experiences influenced by the dynamics of power in social life, and how do sports reproduce patterns of privilege in society?
3. How are sports related to people's ideas about economic success or failure, work and fun, physical health and well-being, gender and sexuality, race and ethnicity, and physical ability and disability, and what is "natural" or "deviant" in society?
4. What are the ways that people struggle over the meaning, purpose, and organization of sports in their lives?
5. When do sports become sites where people challenge, resist, and change prevailing ideas and the organization of social life?
6. What are the narratives and images that people use to give meaning to sports and their sport experiences?
7. Whose voices and perspectives are represented in the media coverage of sports?

REFLECT ON SPORTS   Sports Are More Than Reflections of Society

When people study the social aspects of sports, they often say that "sports are reflections of society." This is true in that many aspects of society are represented in its sports. However, sports also are social constructions that have an impact on relationships and social organization in society as a whole. For example, sports in Canada are organized in ways that represent outdated ideas and beliefs about masculinity and gender relations. Therefore, they do not reflect the forms of masculinity and gender relations that are increasingly accepted by many people. At the same time, sports have been a social arena in which women athletes have displayed physical strength and skills that have long been defined as unacceptable in most spheres of life. As a result, new ideas about femininity and body image have become widely accepted in the rest of society.

The notion that sports are more than a reflection of society can be demonstrated by shifting our attention to another sphere of social life, such as the family. Like sports, families are reflections of society, but our personal experience tells us that everyday family life is more than that. Families are created by particular groups of people as they interact with one another in their own ways, depending on their abilities, resources, and definitions of family life. Of course, the opportunities and choices available to the members of any particular family are influenced by factors in the larger society, including laws, economic conditions, government policies, and cultural beliefs about the actions and interactions of husbands, wives, parents, and children.

This means that similarities will exist between families in the same society, but it does not mean that all families are destined to be the same or to be mere reflections of society. Society serves as a context in which individuals produce, define, and reproduce specific family practices. But real families are sets of relationships produced by people as they determine how they want to live with one another. This is why your family is different from many other families. At times, families even become sites (social locations) where people raise questions about the meaning and organization of family life.

These questions often force people to rethink larger issues related to cultural values and the organization of society as a whole. In this way, what we do in our families becomes part of a general process of cultural production, the impact of which goes far beyond family life. For example, between 1960 and 1980 some

....

8. What strategies can be used to empower people who are regularly excluded from the processes through which sports are organized and played?

One or more of these issues are discussed in each of the following chapters. Critical theories inspire interesting and provocative research on sports in society. This research is based on the assumptions that sports are complex and sometimes internally contradictory activities and that there are no simple or general rules for explaining them as social phenomena. The intent of research based on critical theories is to understand the structure, organization, and meaning of particular sports in connection with changing relationships in and between groups that possess different amounts of power and resources over time and from one place to another.

Critical theorists also study how sports affect the processes through which people develop and maintain **cultural ideologies**—that is, *the webs of ideas and beliefs that they use to explain and give meaning to the social world and their experiences in it.* They want to know how and when sports become sites for questioning and changing dominant ideologies related to social class, gender, sexuality, race and ethnicity, age, and (dis)ability. One of the mottos of critical theorists is a statement made by C. L. R. James, a native of Trinidad in people in Canadian families asked questions about the rights of women within the legal structures of marriage and family. These questions fostered discussions that ultimately led to changes in divorce laws. These changes encouraged people to rethink other ideas about intimate relationships, gender, gender equity, parent–child relationships, children's rights, and even the organization and delivery of community-based social services. In other words, families have always been much more than mere reflections of society. They are the creations of human beings and sites for producing and changing social worlds and the ways of life that constitute culture.

This means that human beings are active agents in the construction of social worlds—not just in their immediate family lives but also in the larger social settings in which they live. Through the things they do in their families, people reproduce and occasionally change the culture and society of which they are a part. So it is with sports and all the people associated with sports. People construct sports as they interact with each other. No voice comes out of the sky and says, "I am society, and sports shall reflect my image." Social conditions clearly influence the structure and dynamics of sports, but within the parameters set by those conditions, people can change sports or keep them as they are. It is even possible for people to create and define sports in ways that differ from or even defy dominant ideas and norms and, in the process, to turn sports into activities that contradict the culture and society of which they are a part.

This way of thinking about sports in society recognizes that sports can have both positive and negative effects on participants, that people define and create sports in many different ways, and that sports are involved in reproducing and changing culture. This makes sports important in a sociological sense. Instead of being mirrors that simply reflect society, they are the actual "social and cultural stuff" out of which society and culture come to be what they are. When we understand this, we become aware of our capacity as agents of cultural production and social change. This helps us realize that we are not victims of society, nor are we destined to do sports as they are portrayed in the images promoted by Nike or Kokanee. We can create new and different forms of sports if we think critically about the contexts in which we live, and learn how to work with others to change them. *What do you think?*

the West Indies, who learned to play cricket after the British colonized his homeland. James said, "What do they know of cricket who only cricket know?" (James, 1984, preface). Critical theorists would answer this question by saying, "We know nothing about sports if sports is all we know." This means that if we want to know about and understand sports, we must also know about the social and cultural contexts in which sports are created, maintained, and changed.

Using Critical Theory in Everyday Life

Critical theory is based on a desire to understand, confront, and transform aspects of social life that involve exploitation and oppression. Critical theorists emphasize that changes in sports depend on more than simply shifting the control of sports to the participants themselves, because many of those participants accept sports as they are and know little about sport forms that have different meanings, purposes, and organizational structures. Therefore, critical theorists emphasize the need for multiple and diverse forms of sport participation in society. This, they claim, would increase participation, diversify the stories told about sports, and add to the voices represented in those stories. As a result, sports would become more humane and democratic, and less subject to the exclusive control of any particular category of people. This is exciting or threatening, depending on one's willingness to view and experience sports in new and different ways.

Critical theory calls attention to the possibility that sports can be sites for transforming social life. When Alwyn Morris, and his kayak partner Hugh Fisher, won a gold medal for Canada at the 1984 Los Angeles Olympics, Morris raised an eagle feather on the victory podium: "I raised the feather to… identify the fact that I was a Mohawk person, and I was very proud of that aspect; of being able to share that experience of being an aboriginal person, share that aspect of my grandfather, and the honour that I wanted to bestow on him…." Morris had obtained prior permission from the IOC (and his partner) to make what was clearly a political statement in support of aboriginal rights. It is interesting to compare the support for his political statement with the reaction 18 years earlier to Tommy Smith and John Carlos (see page 511). [CP(Crombie McNeil)]

Weaknesses of Critical Theory

There are three general weaknesses associated with most forms of critical theory.

First, most critical theory does not provide clear guidelines for determining when sports reproduce culture and social organization and when they become sites for resisting and transforming them. Although research has identified cases when sports were believed to be sites for resistance, critical theorists do not outline the criteria they use to determine when resistance occurs and the conditions under which it is most likely to create enduring changes in sports and the organization of social life. This is partly because most critical theorists focus on specific problems and do not think in terms of changing social systems as much as creating the processes through which previously underrepresented people can participate in social life. They explain that all knowledge is situation specific; therefore, there is no single way to explain or solve all social problems. This is a useful approach when dealing with a particular problem, but it does not provide guidelines for determining when oppositional actions are most effective and when they are most likely to produce changes that go beyond particular situations and problems.

Second, because critical theory emphasizes the need for actions that disrupt current forms of social organization, there is a tendency among those who use it to see value in all actions that violate prevailing norms or oppose prevailing ideas; this is especially true when critical theorists study the actions of marginalized or powerless people in society. However, prevailing norms are not always unfair or oppressive, and the interests of marginalized or powerless people are not always based on concerns about fairness and justice. It is important to respect the voices and creative potential of people who are marginalized or oppressed, but it is not politically wise to assume that the disruptive actions of all people and groups have equal value when it comes to making progressive changes in social life. Critical theorists do not often provide the criteria needed to identify the characteristics of effective forms of resistance. Therefore, they are often not able to assess the value of change-producing strategies from one situation to the next.

Third, some critical theories use vocabularies that are confusing and make it difficult to merge different critical ideas into theoretical frameworks that expand our knowledge of the strategies that, under certain conditions, are most likely to produce progressive change.

FEMINIST THEORY: SPORTS ARE GENDERED ACTIVITIES

Feminist theory is based on the assumption that knowledge about social life requires an understanding of gender and gender relations. It has grown out of a general dissatisfaction with intellectual traditions that base knowledge on the values, experiences, and insights of men and do not take seriously the values, experiences, and insights of women. Feminist theory explains the ways that women have been systematically devalued and oppressed in many societies, and emphasizes that gender equity is a prerequisite for social development and progress.

Many scholars in the sociology of sport use critical feminist theory as they study issues of power and the dynamics of gender relations in social life.[3] Critical feminists focus on issues of power and seek to explain the origin and consequences of gender relations, especially those that privilege men over women and some men over other men (see figure 2.2). They study the ways that gender ideology (that is, ideas and beliefs about masculinity and femininity) is produced, reproduced, resisted, and changed in and through the everyday experiences of men and women.

---

[3]There are many forms of feminist theory, including liberal, radical, gynocentric, socialist, Marxist, black, and postmodern, among others. However, critical feminist theory focusing on issues of ideology, power, and change is most commonly used in the sociology of sport today.

"Feminists say that sports are organized around an ideology that emphasizes domination, conquest, and make superiority. Isn't that ridiculous?!"

FIGURE 2.2 Refusing to acknowledge the contributions of feminist theories leads people to overlook important and sometimes obvious aspects of sports.

Critical feminist research has shown that sports are *gendered activities*, in that their meaning, purpose, and organization are grounded in the values and experiences of men and celebrate attributes associated with dominant forms of masculinity in society (Birrell, 2000; Burstyn, 1999). Therefore, in the world of sports, a person is defined as "qualified" as an athlete, a coach, or an administrator if he or she is tough, aggressive, and emotionally focused on competitive success. If a person is kind, caring, supportive, and emotionally responsive to others, he or she is qualified only to be a cheerleader, a volunteer worker, or an assistant in marketing and public relations. These latter qualities, often associated with femininity and weakness, are not valued in most sport organizations.

Critical Feminist Theory and Research on Sports

Critical feminist theory emphasizes the need to critique and transform the culture and organization of sports, so that they represent the perspectives and experiences of women as well as men in society. Critical feminists argue that ideological and organizational changes are needed before there can be true gender equity in sports or society as a whole.

Studies based on critical feminist theory generally focus on one or more of the following research questions (see Birrell, 2000):

1. In what ways have girls and women been excluded from or discouraged from participating in sports, and how might gender equity be achieved without promoting sports that jeopardize the health and physical well-being of girls and women who play sports?
2. How are sports involved in producing and maintaining ideas about what it means to be a man in society, and forms of gender relations that privilege tough and aggressive men over everyone else?
3. How are women and men represented in media coverage of sports, and how do those representations reproduce or resist dominant gender ideology?
4. What strategies effectively resist or challenge the male-centred gender ideology that is promoted and reproduced through most competitive sports?
5. How are sports and sport participation involved in the production of gendered ideas about physicality, sexuality, and the body?

When critical feminists do research, they often focus on whether sports are sites for challenging and transforming oppressive forms of gender relations, including expressions of sexism and homophobia. For many critical feminists, the goal is to change the meaning, purpose, and organization of sports so that caring for and competing *with* others is more important than dominating and competing *against* others (Duquin, 2000).

Using Critical Feminist Theory in Everyday Life

Critical feminist theory has had a major impact on the sociology of sport. It has increased our understanding of sports as a part of culture, and made us aware of gender-related issues in sports. For example, critical feminists focus on questions such as these: Why do many men around the world continue to resist efforts to promote gender equity in sports? Why do some women fear being called lesbians if they become strong and powerful athletes? Why are some men's locker rooms full of homophobia, gay-bashing jokes, and comments that demean women? Why are people not more concerned about the 40,000 young men who incur serious knee injuries every year in North America as they play football? Why do church-going mothers and fathers take their children to football games and cheer for young men charged and sometimes convicted of physical and sexual assault? Why do many people assume that men who play sports must be heterosexual? Why has there never been an openly gay, active male athlete featured on the cover of *Sports Illustrated*? Why are so many women's high school and university teams called "Lady so-and so's" and "Something-ettes"? These questions, inspired by critical feminist theory, deal with issues that affect our lives every day. In fact, if we do not have thoughtful answers to these questions, we really do not know much about sports in society.

Weaknesses of Critical Feminist Theory

Critical feminist theory has some of the same weaknesses of critical theory. Although critical feminists have become increasingly aware of the connections between gender and other categories of experience related to age, race and ethnicity, social class, disability, religion, and nationality, they have been slow to theorize these connections. Furthermore, there is an urgent need for more research on the sport-related experiences of women of different ages, abilities, religions, and nationalities (Nakamura, 2002; Walseth and Fasting, 2003).

INTERACTIONIST THEORY: SPORTS ARE GIVEN MEANING AS PEOPLE INTERACT WITH ONE ANOTHER

Interactionist theory focuses on issues related to meaning, identity, social relationships, and subcultures in sports. It is based on the idea that human beings, as they interact with one another, give meanings to themselves, others, and the world around them, and use those meanings as a basis for making decisions and taking action in their everyday lives.

According to interactionist theory, we humans do not passively respond to the world around us. Instead, we actively make decisions about our actions as we consider their potential consequences for us, the people around us, and the social world in which we live. Culture and society, according to interactionists, are produced as patterns emerge in our actions and relationships with others.

According to interactionist theory, our ability to reflect on our actions and relationships with others enables us to develop **identity**—that is, *a sense of who we are and how we are connected to the social world*. Identities are key factors as people interact with one another and construct their social worlds. They are the foundation for self-direction and self-control in our lives. Identities are never formed once and for all time; they change over time as our actions and relationships change, as we meet new people, and as we face new situations.

Research based on interactionist theory helps us to understand how people define and give meaning to themselves, their actions, and the world around them. It also helps us to understand human beings as choice makers and creators of identities and relationships. Interactionists generally carry out in-depth research that involves observations of and interviews with people who are members of particular groups or identifiable cultures. The goal of this research is to understand social worlds from the inside—through the perspectives of the people who create, maintain,

and change them. Unlike functionalists and conflict theorists, interactionists view culture and society from the bottom up rather than the top down.

Interactionist Theory and Research on Sports

Interactionist theory is often used in research on the experiences of athletes and the ways that athletes define and make sense of their sport participation. A common goal of interactionist research is to reconstruct and describe the reality that exists in the minds of athletes, coaches, spectators, and others involved in sports.

The data collection methods used in this research are designed to gather information about the ways that people define and give meaning to their experiences as they form identities and interact with others. Those who use interactionist theory to study sports focus on the following issues:

1. What are the social processes through which people become involved in sports?
2. How do people come to define themselves and be identified by others as athletes?
3. How do people give meaning to and derive meaning from their sport experience?
4. What happens when athletes retire and make the transition into the rest of their lives?
5. What are the characteristics of sport cultures, how are they created, and how do they influence people's lives on and off the field?

One or more of these issues are discussed in all chapters. This is because interactionist research provides vivid descriptions of sports experiences and the social worlds in which they occur.

Using Interactionist Theory in Everyday Life

Interactionist theory focuses on the meanings and interaction associated with sports and sport participation. It emphasizes the complexity of human action and the need to understand action in terms of how people define situations and give meaning to their experiences as they interact with others. Interactionists generally recommend changes that represent the perspectives and identities of those who play sports. In many cases, this would involve restructuring sport organizations so that participants are given opportunities to raise questions and discuss issues related to the meaning, purpose and organization of the sports they play. Therefore, interactionists would support changes that make athletes more responsible for organizing and controlling their sports.

In the case of youth sports, for example, interactionists would support organizational changes that would give young people opportunities to create games and physical challenges that would more closely reflect their needs and interests, rather than the needs and interests of adults. Interactionists would caution parents and coaches about problems that occur when young people develop sport-related identities and relationships to the exclusion of other identities and relationships, and to the point that burnout is likely.

In the case high-performance sports, interactionists would support changes that discourage athletes from defining pain and injury as normal parts of the sport experience. Because the use of performance-enhancing substances is connected with issues of identity and the norms that exist in sport cultures, interactionists argue that the use of these substances can be controlled only if there are changes in the norms and culture of sports; identifying substance users as "bad apples" and punishing them as individuals will not change the culture in which athletes learn to sacrifice their bodies for the sake of the team and their sport.

Weaknesses of Interactionist Theory

Interactionist theory has inspired many informative studies of meaning, identity, interaction, and cultures in sports. However, it has two primary weaknesses. First, it focuses our attention almost exclusively on relationships and definitions of reality without explaining the ways that interaction and the construction of meaning in sports are influenced by social organization, power, and material conditions in society. Therefore, interactionist research often ignores power dynamics and inequality in connection with sports and sport experiences.

Second, interactionist theory does not provide critical visions of the ways that sports and society could and should be organized. However, many people who use interactionist theory now combine it with critical and critical feminist theories to provide a basis for developing such visions (Coakley and Donnelly, 1999).

IS THERE A BEST THEORETICAL APPROACH TO USE WHEN STUDYING SPORTS?

Each theory discussed in this chapter has made us aware of questions and issues that are important to us, to the people with whom we work and play, and in the social worlds in which we live. In most of our research, we have used combinations of *interactionist, critical, and feminist theories* because we wanted to view sports from the inside, from the perspectives of those who make decisions to play or not to play and who integrate sport participation into their lives in various ways. As we view sports from the inside, we also want to be aware of the social, economic, political, and historical factors that influence access to sport participation and the decisions that people make about sport participation. Critical and critical feminist theories have also helped us to think about very practical issues, such as how to become politically involved in proposals to fund new parks, or a new stadium for a professional football team. They have helped us to assess policies related to sport programmes for at-risk youth and to evaluate candidates for coaching jobs at our universities. More recently this combination of theories has guided much of our thinking about sports for people with a disability, as is shown in the "Breaking Barriers" box on page 44.

Interactionists study meanings associated with sports and sport participation. Meanings vary from one culture to another. Players in Japanese youth sports give meanings to sports that differ from meanings given to youth sports in other cultures. [Jay Coakley]

Social life is complex and is best understood when viewed from multiple perspectives. Each theory in this chapter can be used to ask sociological questions about this scene. Afghan boys (no girls) are playing baseball organized by U.S. ground troops after the U.S. military had bombed Afghanistan. Adult male refugees watch as the soldiers teach the rules and the skills involved in the game. [Wally Santana, AP/Wide World Photo]

Breaking Barriers	**Language Barriers**

Language Barriers
We're Not Handicapped; We Just Can't Hear

Len Gonzales is deaf. But more important, he is head football coach at the California School for the Deaf at Riverside (CSDR). When his team capped its season by winning the 2004 regional high school championship, a reporter asked Gonzales what other teams thought when they lost to CSDR. Gonzales explained that "teams hate to lose to us because they think we're a handicapped team. But we're not handicapped. We just can't hear" (in Reilly, 2004, p. 144).

Coach Gonzales is sensitive to the barriers created when people use the word *handicapped* to refer to physical and mental impairments and disabilities. Clear definitions of these words are necessary to understand and evaluate theories of disability.

An **impairment** *exists when a person has a physical, sensory, or intellectual condition that potentially limits full participation in social and/or physical environments.* Many people have impairments and, as we get older, impairments generally increase in number and severity. This is part of normal, everyday life. None of us is physically or mentally perfect, and we regularly make personal adjustments to limit the impact of impairments on our lives. If we are lucky, we have access to technologies that make adjustments more effective. For example, we wear eyeglasses that "correct" our impaired vision.

An impairment becomes a **disability** only *when accommodations in social or physical contexts are not or cannot be made to allow the full participation of people with functional limitations.* This means that disabilities are created when relationships, spaces, and activities present barriers that limit the opportunities and experiences of people with particular impairments. For example, prior to the late-1990s, if an athlete's leg was amputated below the knee and he wore a prosthetic leg and foot, he could not have been a member of the Canadian Powerlifting Team because the International Powerlifting Federation rules stated that "Lifters without two real feet cannot compete in regular contests." This rule created a barrier making the athlete disabled. However, after the rule was changed, the barrier was eliminated and the prosthetic leg and foot no longer disabled the athlete as a powerlifter. This shows that disability often has less to do with

impairment and ability than with social, environmental, attitudinal, and legal factors (Brittain, 2004; Hargreaves, 2000; Higgins, 1992; Morris, 1996; Oliver, 1996). Therefore, a person may be (dis)abled in one context but not in another (Friedman et al., 2004). Only when there are barriers that exclude or limit people with impairments do disabilities exist.

People become **handicapped** *when others define them as inferior and "unable" due to perceived impairments.* For example, when opposing players defined the football team from CSDR as handicapped, they hated losing to them because it meant that they lost to players who they defined as inferior and unable.

These three definitions are based on critical and interactionist theories. They locate handicaps and disabilities in the social processes through which (a) environments are organized to meet the needs of temporarily able-bodied people, (b) norms (rules) are created that disadvantage people with impairments, and (c) people learn to equate particular impairments with inferiority and inability.

Other definitions, based on medical and psychological theory, explain disability as a characteristic of individuals. Medical–psychological theories locate disability in the physical and cognitive "abnormalities" of individuals and they lead to interventions emphasizing personal coping strategies and assistive technologies. Critical interactionist theories, on the other hand, locate disability in social and cultural barriers that limit participation; they lead to interventions emphasizing the elimination of cultural, organizational, legal, and environmental barriers.

Both approaches are needed, but people too often overlook the need to eliminate barriers. Coping strategies and assistive technologies are crucial for individuals, but eliminating barriers makes disability less relevant for entire categories of people (DePauw, 1997). Leslie Little, a sailor with muscular dystrophy, helps us to understand what this means when she says, "Every day is a new adventure when I'm sailing… Plus, I'm not disabled when I'm on the water" (www.mdausa.org/publications/Quest/q82water.cfm). The goal therefore is to create social and physical worlds that are like being on the water for Leslie Little.

Although we have not used *functionalist theory* and only occasionally used *conflict theory*, in our research, we have used them to inform our general understanding of sports in society. For example, functionalist theory helps us to understand how other people think about sports in society, even though it does not help to identify the social issues and controversies connected with sports in our communities and in the sport organizations in which we work with coaches and administrators. Conflict theory alerts us to issues related to social class and economic exploitation as we use *critical theories* to help understand the dynamics of power in sports and society; the ways that power is related to gender, race, ethnicity, disability, and sexuality; and the ways that people use ideologies as they explain and give meaning to the world and their experiences. This use of a combination of theories to better understand social worlds, often termed "theoretical pluralism," is increasingly being advocated in the sociology of sport (e.g., Giulianotti, 2005).

Overall, our preference for a combination of interactionist, critical, and critical feminist theories is based on our interest in making sport participation more accessible to a wider range of people in society. We are much more interested in increasing choices and alternatives for people in sports than we are in making sports a more efficient means of maintaining the *status quo* in society (a goal of functionalist theory). We think that many aspects of the *status quo* in Canada and other societies are in need of change, and that sports are sites at which we can learn strategies for effectively making creative and progressive changes.

Creating alternative ways of doing sports requires an awareness of contemporary sports culture as well as a vocabulary for thinking critically about the future. A combination of interactionist, critical and critical feminist theories provides a guide for developing that awareness and vocabulary, and for creating new sport forms that offer human beings additional possibilities for physical and social experiences.

Our theoretical preferences often conflict with the preferences expressed by some students and people who work for sport organizations. Students who want to work in sport organizations know that most people in those organizations see sports in functionalist terms, so they sometimes prefer functionalist theory. However, we remind them that it is important to understand issues related to power and culture so that they can critically assess organizational policies in terms of their impact on people in the organization and the surrounding community. When we work with coaches and sports administrators, they often tell us that our critical approach has helped them to see things in their lives in new and helpful ways.

Finally, we have learned that true empowerment involves enabling people to be critically informed actors so that they can effectively "challenge and change unequal power relationships" (Mahiri, 1998). As we participate in social worlds, we find that critical, feminist, and interactionist theories can be combined in ways that are especially helpful.

SUMMARY

HOW CAN SOCIAL THEORIES HELP US STUDY SPORTS IN SOCIETY?

Theories are tools that enable us to ask questions, identify problems, gather information, explain social life, prioritize strategies to deal with problems, and anticipate the consequences of our actions and interventions. Different theories help us to understand sports from different angles and perspectives. In this chapter, we discussed functionalist, conflict, critical, feminist, and interactionist theories.

The purpose of the chapter is to show that each theory provides a framework that we can use as we think about sports in society and make decisions in our own lives. For example, functionalist theory offers an explanation for positive consequences associated with sports and sport involvement. Conflict theory identifies factors related to class relations and economic exploitation in sports. Critical theory shows that sports are connected with culture and social relations in complex ways and that sports change as power and resources shift in social, political, and economic relations in society. Critical feminist theory emphasizes that gender is a primary category of experience and that sports are sites for producing, reproducing, and transforming gender ideology and power relations in society. Interactionist theory helps us to understand the meanings, identities, and social relationships associated with sport involvement.

As we use these theories it is important to know their weaknesses. Functionalist theory exaggerates the positive consequences of sports and sport participation because it is based on the assumption that there are no conflicts of interest between groups within society. Conflict theory tends to overstate the importance of social class and economic factors in society, and focuses most attention on top-level spectator sports, which

make up only a part of sports in any society. Critical theory provides no explicit guidelines for determining when sports are sites where resistance leads to progressive transformations in society. Critical feminist theory has not sufficiently explained connections between gender and other categories of experience, including age, race, religion, nationality, and disability. Interactionist theory does a poor job of relating issues of meaning, identity, and experience in sports to general social conditions and patterns of social inequality in society as a whole.

Despite their weaknesses, social theories are helpful as we explore issues and controversies in sports and assess research and ideas about sports in society. We do not have to be theorists to use theory as we organize our thoughts and become more informed citizens in our social worlds.

Visit *Sports in Society*'s Online Learning Centre at <u>www.mcgrawhill.ca/olc/coakley</u> for additional information, website resources, and study tools for this chapter.

Studying the Past

Does it help us to understand sports today?

There is no game as Canadian as lacrosse. Hockey is really an ice version of bandy, played by the English years before it was adapted for Canada. Basketball was invented by a Canadian, but he invented it in the United States. Lacrosse was the natives' game. Its origins are unclear, but it was played long before the Europeans arrived.

> —William Humber, Canadian sports historian (1989)

They who laid the intellectual foundations of the western world were the most fanatical players and organizers of games that the world has ever known.

> —C.L.R. James, West Indian writer and cricket player (1963)

Sports have been revered by fascists and communists, by free-marketers and filibusters. They have also been, paradoxically, reviled by all those political factions. Sports may be among the most powerful human expressions in all history.

> —Gerald Early, Professor of Modern Letters, Washington University, St. Louis (1998)

Hockey transforms the immobility of winter, the hardness of the earth and the suspension of normal life into a buoyant, vigorous and passionate sport.

> —Roland Barthes (1997)

To understand sports today, we need a sense of what physical games and sport activities were like in past times. This chapter presents brief overviews of sport activities in different cultural and historical settings. Our intent is *not* to provide an integrated overall history of sports. Such a history would look at the development and organization of games and sports across all continents from one cultural group to another over time. This is an ambitious and worthy project, but it is far beyond the scope of this chapter.

This chapter focuses on (1) the ancient Greeks, (2) the Roman Empire, (3) the Middle Ages in parts of Europe, (4) the Renaissance through the Enlightenment in parts of Europe, and (5) the Industrial Revolution through recent times, with special emphasis on Canada. These times and places, often covered in history courses, are familiar to many of us, and they illustrate the way that sports are connected with the social and cultural contexts in which they exist.

The goal of this chapter is to show that our understanding of sports depends on what we know about the social lives of the people who created, defined, played, and integrated them into their everyday experiences. As critical theory suggests, it is important to study the ways that people use their power and resources as they create and participate in physical activities.

When we view sports history in this way, dates and names are less important than what we can learn about social life by studying sport and physical activities at particular times and places.

UNDERSTANDING HISTORY WHILE STUDYING SPORTS IN SOCIETY

Many people think about history as a chronological sequence of events that gradually lead to a better and more "modern" society. Many historical accounts are full of references to societies that are traditional or modern, primitive or civilized, underdeveloped or developed, preindustrial or industrial. This terminology implies that history

is always moving forward so that societies are improving and becoming more developed.

This approach to history enables some people to feel superior as they assume that they are the most modern, civilized, and developed people in the world. However, this conclusion is not historically accurate. In the case of sports, there are literally thousands of "histories" of physical activities among thousands of human populations in different places around the world. These histories sometimes involve patterns of changes that do not provide evidence of becoming more civilized or highly developed.

Research shows that physical activities and games have existed in all cultures. The specific forms of these activities and games, along with the meanings that people gave to them, were shaped through struggles over the meaning, purpose, and organization of the activities; over who should play them; and over the ways that they were to be integrated into people's lives. To say that physical activities and games over the years have evolved to fit a pattern of progress, or modernization is to distort the life experiences of people all over the world (Gruneau, 1988). There may be fewer contrasts among the sports and games that different people play today, but this does not mean that sports are evolving to fit a grand scheme for how physical activities *should* be organized or what they *should* mean in people's lives (Maguire, 1999). Instead, it means that certain nations and corporations now have the power to define, organize, and present through the media particular sport forms for the entire world to see.

When beach volleyball was included as a new sport in the 1996 Summer Olympics in Atlanta it was an example of wealthy countries and corporations using their power to promote a sport through international travel, social connections, and access to resources. When beach volleyball became commercially attractive to the International Olympic Committee, it was not part of the general pattern of progress in the history of sports.

Therefore, this chapter is not a story of progress. Instead, it is a sample of stories about people at different times and places struggling over and coming to terms with what they want their physical activities to be and how they wish to include them in their lives. There is historical continuity in these processes and struggles, but continuity does not mean that history follows some grand plan of progress. Progressive changes do occur, but they are the result of actions taken by collections of people with the power to make them happen and then keep them from returning to what they were in the past.

SPORTS VARY BY TIME AND PLACE

People in all cultures, past and present, have used human movement in their ritual life. As we study history, we see that few cultures have had physical games that resemble the highly organized, rule-governed competitive games that we describe as sports today.

In prehistoric times, for example, there were no sports as we know them today. Physical activities were tied to the challenge of survival and the expression of religious beliefs (see figure 3.1). People hunted for food and sometimes used their physical abilities to defend themselves, establish social control and power over others, and appease their gods. These activities involved acting out events that had important meaning in their lives, and even though they were organized games, they were inseparable from sacred rituals and ceremonies. They often were performed as religious worship, and their outcomes were determined by religious necessity as much as the physical abilities of the people involved (Guttmann, 1978).

The first forms of organized games among humans probably emerged from this combination of physical challenges and religious rituals. From what we can tell, these games were connected closely with the power structures and belief systems of the societies in which they existed, and

they usually re-created and reaffirmed dominant cultural practices in those societies. On rare occasions, they served as sources of protest or opposition to the *status quo* in particular groups or societies.

Historical and cultural variations in physical activities remind us that all cultural practices, even sports, serve a variety of social purposes. This raises the question of how the definition and organization of sports in any society promote the interests of various groups in that society. People create sport activities within the constraints of the social world in which they live. Therefore, everyone does not have an equal say in how those activities are defined and organized. People with the most *power* generally have the greatest impact on how sports are defined, organized, and played in a group or society. Sport activities do not totally reflect their desires, but sports represent the interests of the powerful more than they represent the interests of others.

SIDELINES

©1982 M.T.F.-T.W.S.-Lakewood, CO

"You weren't playing soccer last night—it won't be invented for another 10 million years!"

FIGURE 3.1 In early human history, there were no sports as we define them. Physical activities occasionally were included in community and religious rituals, but their purpose probably was to appease the gods, rather than to entertain or build character.

This approach to studying sports in history is based on critical theory. It calls attention to the existence and consequences of social inequality in societies. Inequalities related to wealth, political power, social status, gender, age, (dis)ability, and race and ethnicity have always had a significant impact on how sport activities are organized and played in any situation. We pay special attention to these in the following discussions of times and places. (John McClelland (2006), of the University of Toronto, has covered the Roman to Renaissance periods in much greater detail in a recent book.)

CONTESTS AND GAMES IN ANCIENT GREECE: BEYOND THE MYTHS (1000 B.C.E. To 100 B.C.E.)[1]

The games played by the early Greeks (circa 900 B.C.E.) were grounded in mythology and religious beliefs. They usually were held in conjunction with festivals that combined prayer, sacrifices, and religious services, along with music, dancing, and ritual feasts. Competitors in these games were from wealthy and respected Greek families. They were the only people who had the money to hire trainers and coaches and the time and resources to travel. Sports and events were based on the interests of able-bodied young males. They usually consisted of warrior sports, such as chariot racing, wrestling and boxing, javelin and discus throwing, foot racing, archery, and long jumping. Violence, serious injuries, and even death were commonplace, in comparison with today's sport events (Elias, 1986; Kidd,

1984, 1996b; Mendelsohn, 2004). Greek women, children, and older people occasionally played sports in these festivals, but they never played in the games held at Olympia.

The locations and dates of the Greek festivals also were linked to religious beliefs. For example, Olympia was chosen as one of the festival sites because it was associated with the achievements and activities of celebrated Greek gods and mythological characters. In fact, Olympia was dedicated as a shrine to the god Zeus in about 1000 B.C.E. Although permanent buildings and playing fields were not constructed until 550 B.C.E., the games at Olympia were held every four years. Additional festivals involving athletic contests were also held at other locations throughout Greece, but the Olympic Games became the most prestigious of all athletic events.

Women were prohibited from participating as athletes or spectators in the Olympic Games. However, women held their own games at Olympia. These games, dedicated to the goddess Hera, the sister-wife of Zeus, grew out of Greek fertility rites. When women participated in sports it was often to demonstrate their strength, sexually attract men, and eventually bear strong warrior children (Perrottet, 2004). In general, physical prowess was inconsistent with dominant definitions of femininity among the Greeks and women were seen as inferior to men—they could neither vote nor be Greek citizens,[2] wives were the property of their husbands and often isolated in their homes, and women did not participate in political or economic affairs.

The men's games at Olympia took on political significance as they grew in visibility and popularity. Winning became connected with the glory of city-states, and physically skilled slaves and young men from lower-class backgrounds were forced to become athletes, or wealthy

---

[1]The terms C.E. (common era) and B.C.E. (before the common era) are used here rather than the more traditional A.D. (*anno Domini*—the year of our Lord) and B.C (before Christ) because such usage is now becoming the norm in the academy. This is in recognition of the fact that Christian traditions should no longer predominate in a secular, multicultural society. As is traditional, however, when there is no designation (e.g., 1922), it refers to the common era.

[2]It should be remembered that, until 1929 ("the Persons case" of 1927–29), women were not recognized as "persons" in the *British North America Act*, which was the Canadian constitution until 1982.

patrons and government officials hired them to train for the Olympics and other games. Victories brought cash prices and living expenses for many of the slaves and hired athletes. Contrary to widely believed myths about the amateur ideals held by the Greeks, many male athletes saw themselves as professionals. During the second century B.C.E., they even organized athletic guilds enabling them to bargain for rights, gain control over the conditions of their sport participation, and enjoy material security when they retired from competition (Baker, 1988).

Greek athletes were so specialized in their physical skills that they made poor soldiers. They engaged in warrior sports, but they lacked the generalized skills of warriors. Furthermore, they concentrated so much on athletic training that they ignored intellectual development. This evoked widespread criticism from Greek philosophers, who saw the games as brutal and dehumanizing and the athletes as useless and ignorant beings.

> Of the thousands of evils... in Greece there is no greater evil than the race of athletes....Since they have not formed good habits, they face problems with difficulty. They glisten and gleam like statues ... when they are in their prime, but when bitter old age comes...they are like tattered and threadbare old rugs.
>
> —Euripides, Greek dramatist (fifth century B.C.E.)

Representatives of the modern Olympics have romanticized and perpetuated myths about Greek games to connect the modern Olympics to a positive legacy. However, the ancient games were not tributes to mind–body harmony. Athletes were maimed and killed in the pursuit of victories and the rewards that came with them (Mendelsohn, 2004; Perrottet, 2004); fairness was not as important as honour, violence was common, and athletic contests were connected with a cultural emphasis on warfare.

Physical contests and games in Greek culture influenced art, philosophy, and the everyday lives of people wealthy enough to train, hire professionals, and travel to games. However,

Greek contests and games were different from the organized competitive sports of today (see the box "Dominant Sport Forms Today," pp. 63–64). First, they were grounded in religion; second, they lacked complex administrative structures; third, they did not involve measurements and record keeping from event to event. However, there is one major similarity: They often reproduced dominant patterns of social relations in the society as a whole. The power and advantages that went with being wealthy, male, young, and able-bodied in Greek society shaped the games and contests in ways that limited the participation of most people. The definitions of excellence used to evaluate performance even reflected the abilities of young males. This meant that the abilities of others were substandard by definition—if you could not do it as a young, able-bodied Greek man could do it, then you could not do it the right way.

ROMAN CONTESTS AND GAMES: SPECTACLES AND GLADIATORS (100 B.C.E. To C.E. 500)

Roman leaders used physical contests and games to train soldiers and provide mass entertainment spectacles. They borrowed events from Greek contests and games, but they focused athletic training on preparing obedient soldiers. They were critical of the Greek emphasis on individualism and specialized physical skills that were useless in battle. Because Roman leaders emphasized military training and entertainment, the contests and games during the first century C.E. increasingly took the form of circuses and gladiatorial combat. Chariot races were the most popular events during Roman spectacles.

Wealthy Romans recruited slaves as charioteers. Spectators bet heavily on the races and, when they became bored or unruly, the emperors passed around free food to prevent outbreak of violence. This strategy pacified the crowds and allowed the emperors to use the events to celebrate themselves and their power. Government officials throughout the Roman Empire used similar events to control people in their regions.

As the power and influence of the Roman Empire grew, spectacles consisting of contests and games, became increasingly important as diversions for the masses. By C.E. 300, half of the days on the Roman calendar were public holidays because slaves did most of the work. Many Romans held only part-time jobs, if they worked at all. Activities other than chariot races and boxing matches were needed to attract and distract people. Bearbaiting, bullbaiting, and animal fights were added to capture spectator interest. Men and women were forced into the arena to engage in mortal combat with lions, tigers, and panthers. Condemned criminals were dressed in sheepskins to battle partially starved wild animals. Gladiators, armed with various weapons, were pitted against each other in gory fights to the death. These spectacles achieved two purposes for Roman rulers: They entertained an idle populace, and disposed of socially "undesirable" people such as thieves, murderers, unruly slaves, and Christians (Baker, 1988).

Some Romans criticized these spectacles as tasteless activities, devoid of value. However, the criticisms were not based on concerns for human rights, but on their objections to events where wealthy people and peasants mingled together. Other than some outspoken Christians, few people criticized the spectacles on moral or humanitarian grounds. The spectacles continued until the Roman economy went into a depression, and wealthy people moved from cities, taking their resources with them. As the Roman Empire deteriorated, there were not enough resources to support the spectacles (Baker, 1988).

Women were seldom involved in Roman contests and games. They were allowed in the arenas to watch and cheer male athletes, but few had opportunities to develop athletic skills. Within Roman families, women were legally subservient to and rigidly controlled by men. As in ancient Greece, few women pursued interests outside the household.

Although local folk games and other physical activities existed in the Roman Empire, we know little about how they were organized and played and what they meant in people's lives. The gladiatorial spectacles did not capture everyone's interest, but they attracted considerable attention in major cities. Roman contests and games differed from organized sports today because they sometimes were connected with religious rituals, and they seldom involved quantifying athletic achievements or recording outstanding accomplishments (review the box "Dominant Sport Forms Today," pp. 63–64).

TOURNAMENTS AND GAMES IN MEDIEVAL EUROPE: SEPARATION OF THE MASTERS AND THE MASSES (500 TO 1300)

Sport activities in Medieval Europe consisted of folk games played by local peasants, tournaments staged for knights and nobles, archery contests, and activities in which animals were brutalized (Dunning, 1999). The folk games, often violent and dangerous, and sometimes organized to maim or kill animals, emerged in connection with local peasant customs. The tournaments and archery contests were linked with military training and the desire for entertainment among the feudal aristocracy and those who served them.

Some of the local games of this period have interesting histories. As Roman soldiers and government officials travelled around Europe during the fourth and fifth centuries, they built bathing facilities to use during their leisure time. To loosen up before their baths, they engaged in various forms of ball play. Local peasants during the early medieval period used the Roman activities as models and developed their own forms of ball games. They often integrated these games into local religious ceremonies and cultural events. For example, tossing a ball back and forth sometimes represented the conflict between good and evil, light and darkness, or life and death. As the influence of the Roman Catholic Church spread through Europe during the early years of the medieval period, these symbolic rituals were redefined in terms of Catholic beliefs. In these cases, sports and religion were closely connected with each other.

During most of the medieval period, the Roman Catholic Church accepted peasant ball games, even though they occasionally involved violence. Local priests encouraged games by opening church grounds on holidays and Sunday afternoons. As games became part of village life, people played them during festive community gatherings that also involved music and dancing. These local ball games contained the roots for many contemporary games such as soccer, field hockey, football, rugby, bowling, curling, baseball, and cricket. However, the games in peasant villages had little structure and few rules. Local traditions guided play, and traditions varied widely from one community to the next.

The upper classes in medieval Europe paid little attention to and seldom interfered in the leisure of peasants. They saw peasant games and festivities as safety valves defusing mass social discontent. The sport activities of the upper classes were distinctively different from those of the peasants. Access to specialized equipment and facilities allowed them to develop early versions of billiards, shuffleboard, tennis, handball, and jai alai. Ownership of horses allowed them to develop forms of horse racing, while their stable hands developed a version of horseshoes. On horseback, they also participated in hunting and hawking. Owning property and possessing money and servants clearly influenced their sports.

Through the medieval period, the popular sporting events among upper-class males were tournaments consisting of war games to keep knights and nobles ready for battle. Some tournaments resembled actual battlefield confrontations. Deaths and serious injuries occurred, victors carried off opponents' possessions, and losers often were taken as prisoners and used as hostages to demand ransoms from opposing camps. Later versions of tournaments were not quite so serious, but they still involved injuries and occasional deaths. Toward the end of the medieval period, colourful ceremonies and pageantry softened the warlike tournaments, and entertainment and chivalry took priority over military preparation and the use of deadly violence.

Women during this time seldom participated in physical games and sport activities. Gender restrictions were grounded in a male-centred family structure and Catholic teachings that women were inferior to men. A woman's duty was to be obedient and submissive; however, peasant women were involved in some of the games and physical activities that occurred during village festivals.

Among the aristocracy, gender relations were patterned so that men's activities and women's activities were clearly differentiated. Aristocratic women did little outside the walls of their dwellings, and their activities seldom involved rigorous physical exertion for fun. They sometimes engaged in "ladylike" games, but, because women were subject to men's control and often viewed as sex objects and models of beauty, their involvement in active pursuits was limited. Feminine beauty during this time was defined in passive terms: the less active a woman, the more likely she was perceived as beautiful.

Even though some sports in Europe and North America today can trace their roots back to the medieval period, the contests and games of that time were not much like today's organized sports. They lacked specialization and organization, they never involved the measurement or recording of athletic achievements, and they were not based on a commitment to equal and open competition among athletes from diverse backgrounds (review the Box "Dominant Sport Forms Today," pp. 63–64.). Historian Allen Guttmann has vividly described this last point:

> In medieval times, jousts and tournaments were limited to the nobility. Knights who sullied their honor by inferior marriages—to peasant girls, for instance—were disbarred... Peasants reckless enough to emulate the sport of their masters were punished by death. (1978, p. 30)

Although some characteristics of medieval sport activities may be seen in the games and contests of the Renaissance, Reformation, and Enlightenment, these later periods involved important transformations which shaped the forms and meanings of physical activities and games.

THE RENAISSANCE, REFORMATION, AND ENLIGHTENMENT: GAMES AS DIVERSIONS (1300 TO 1800)

The Renaissance

Wars throughout Europe during the fourteenth and fifteenth centuries encouraged some monarchs, government officials, and church authorities to increase their military strength and prohibit popular peasant pastimes. Those in authority believed that the peasants should spend less time playing games and more time learning to defend the lands and lives of their masters. But, despite the pronouncements of bishops and kings, the peasants did not readily give up their games. In fact, the games sometimes became rallying points for opposition to government and church authority.

At the time that peasants were subjected to increased controls in many locations, the "scholar-athlete" became the ideal among the affluent. This "Renaissance man" was "socially adept, sensitive to aesthetic values, skilled in weaponry, strong of body, and learned in letters" (Baker, 1988, p. 59).

Throughout the Renaissance period, women had relatively few opportunities to be involved in tournaments and sport activities. Although peasant women sometimes played physical games, their lives were restricted by the demands of work in and out of the home. They often did hard physical labour, but they were not encouraged to engage in public games and sports that called attention to their physical abilities.

Upper-class women sometimes participated in bowling, croquet, archery, and tennis, but involvement was limited because women during this time were seen as "naturally" weak and passive. Some of these "Renaissance women" may have been pampered and placed on "pedestals," but men maintained their power by tightly controlling the lives of women, partly by promoting the idea that women were too fragile to leave the home and do things on their own. The code of chivalry, popular during this time, had less to do with protecting women than with reproducing patriarchy and privileging men.

The Reformation

During the Protestant Reformation, growing negative attitudes about games and sports discouraged participation, especially where Calvinist or Puritan beliefs were popular. For example, between the late 1500s and the late 1600s, English Puritans tried to eliminate or control leisure activities, including physical contests and games. They were devoted to the work ethic and, according to Robert Malcolmson, a social historian at Queen's University:

> [Sports] were thought to be profane and licentious—they were occasions of worldly indulgence that tempted men from a godly life; being rooted in pagan and popish practices, they were rich in the sort of ceremony and ritual that poorly suited the Protestant conscience; they frequently involved a desecration of the Sabbath and an interference with the worship of the true believers; they disrupted the peaceable order of society, distracting

men from their basic social duties—hard work, thrift, personal restraint, devotion to family, [and] a sober carriage. (Malcolmson, 1984, p. 67)

The primary targets of the Puritans were the pastimes and games of the peasants. Peasants did not own property, so their festivities occurred in public settings and attracted large crowds. This made them easy for the Puritans to condemn and control. The Puritans did their best to eliminate festivities—especially those scheduled on Sunday afternoons. They objected to the drinking and partying that accompanied the games and disapproved of physical pleasure on the Sabbath. The physical activities and games of the affluent were less subject to Puritan interference. Activities such as horse racing, hunting, tennis, and bowling took place on the private property of the wealthy, making it difficult for the Puritans to enforce prohibitions. As in other times and places, power relations had much to do with who played what activities under what conditions. Despite Puritan influence and social changes affecting the economic structure and stability of English village life, many peasants maintained their participation in games and sports.

During the early 1600s, King James I formally challenged Puritan influence in England by issuing *The King's Book of Sports*. This book, reissued in 1633 by Charles I, emphasized that Puritan ministers and officials should not discourage lawful recreational pursuits among English citizens. Charles I and his successors ushered in a new day for English sporting life. They revived traditional festivals and actively promoted and supported public games and sport activities. Consequently, cricket, horse racing, yachting, fencing, golf, and boxing, became highly organized during the late 1600s and the 1700s, although participation patterns reflected and reproduced social class divisions in society.

In colonial Canada, British and French influences were strong in the Maritimes and Upper and Lower Canada. Many of the colonists were not necessarily playful people; hard work

was necessary for survival. However, as the lifestyles of the colonists became established, and as free time became available, there was a growing desire to introduce games from the past into life in the new colonies. Voyageurs engaged in the fur trade and troops garrisoned in Canada also found time to play. As the colonies became more established, the class structures of Europe, especially Britain, began to be re-created in the playing styles of landowners and workers (Bouchier, 2003).

During this period, although there was extensive contact between native peoples and colonists, there is little evidence that the games of colonists were affected by the influence of natives, or vice versa. However, the widespread adoption of the canoe as a means of transportation by colonists certainly meant that informal races occurred; and a later fascination with baggataway led to its incorporation as lacrosse.

Native peoples continued to play the games that had been a part of their cultures for centuries. In fact, sports and sport participation have many histories across North America. This reminds us to keep in mind whose voices and perspectives are represented in various historical accounts of games, contests, and sports. The box, "Lessons from History," on pages 57–58 emphasizes that most historical accounts do not represent the experiences and perspectives of those who lack the power to tell their stories and make them a part of dominant culture.

The Enlightenment

During the Enlightenment period (1700 to 1800), many games and sport activities in parts of Europe and North America began to resemble sport forms that we are familiar with today. With some exceptions, they were no longer grounded in religious ritual and ceremony; they involved a degree of specialization and organization; achievements sometimes were measured; and records occasionally were kept. Furthermore, the

SIDELINES

"Why don't we settle this in a civilized way? We'll charge admission to watch!"

FIGURE 3.2   Dominant sport forms in many societies have been organized to celebrate a particular form of masculinity, emphasizing aggression, conquest, and dominance.

idea that events should be open to all competitors, regardless of background, became increasingly popular. This commitment to equality and open participation, along with other forces and ideas, gave rise to world-changing revolutions in France and the United States.

However, sport activities during the Enlightenment period were different from the dominant sport forms of today in at least one important respect: they were defined strictly as diversions—as interesting and often challenging ways to pass free time. People did not see them as being useful for athletes in particular or society in general. No one thought that sports and sport participation could change how people developed or acted, or how social life was organized. Therefore, there were no reasons for people to organize sport activities for others, or create organizations to govern sports. A few people formed clubs, and they occasionally scheduled contests with other groups, but they did not form leagues or national and international associations. All this changed during the Industrial Revolution.

THE INDUSTRIAL REVOLUTION: THE EMERGENCE OF ORGANIZED COMPETITIVE SPORTS (1780 TO 1920)

It is an oversimplification to say that the organized competitive sports of today are simply a product of the Industrial Revolution. They clearly emerged during the process of industrialization, but they were actually social constructions of people themselves—people who played games and sports while they coped with the realities of everyday life in rapidly changing families, communities, and societies. Of course, the realities of everyday life included economic, political, and social forces that either enabled or constrained people, depending on their position in society.

The development of factories, the mass production of consumer goods, the growth of cities, and increased dependence on technology marked the industrial revolution. It involved changes in the organization and control of work and community life and was generally accompanied by an increase in the number of middle-class people in the societies where it occurred. The Industrial Revolution first began in England around 1780, and became a part of life after 1800 in other European countries, Canada, and the United States.

The Early Years: Limited Time and Space For Sports

During the early years of the Industrial Revolution, few people had regular opportunities to play games and sport activities. Farm, resource, and factory workers had little free time. The workdays, even for many child workers, were often long and tiring. People who lived in cities had few open spaces where they could play sports. Production took priority over play. Industrialists and politicians were not concerned with providing parks and public play spaces. Working people were discouraged from gathering in large groups outside the workplace. The authorities perceived such gatherings as dangerous because they wasted time that could be used for work. Additionally, they provided

Lessons from History
Who Tells Us About the Past?

History is much more than a chronological series of events. Historical research should take us inside the lives of people who lived before us. It should give us a sense of how people lived and gave meaning to their experiences and the events of their times. Therefore, when we study sports, it is important to be aware of whose voices and perspectives are used to construct historical accounts, as well as whose voices and perspectives are missing. This is the case when it comes to the physical activities, games, and sports of native peoples in North America.

Prior to the arrival of Europeans, the histories of aboriginal peoples were kept in oral rather than written form; they were local and personal histories. It was not until the late eighteenth century that accounts of the lives and cultures of aboriginal peoples were recorded in English, French, or Spanish. However, those accounts were written by Europeans with limited knowledge of the diverse languages, cultures, and complex social arrangements in the lives of nearly 500 unique cultural groups of aboriginal peoples in North America. This diversity was obscured by general accounts describing the lives and customs of "Indians,"

> **Just as the dominant class writes history, so that same class writes the story of sport.**
>
> James Riordan, social historian and former soccer player (1996)

as if all native cultures were the same. These accounts provide limited information about the diverse games and sports played by aboriginal peoples. In many cases, accounts were written after the lives of aboriginal people had been disrupted and influenced by European explorers and settlers. This history provides little information about the ways that traditional games and sports were played and integrated into the diverse cultures that existed in North America.

Europeans were seldom able to observe authentic expressions of traditional native cultures. When they did make observations, it was often under strained circumstances during which aboriginal peoples were unwilling to reveal their customs while being watched by outsiders who often viewed them as "oddities." Because most important games were connected with religious rites, it was even less likely that Europeans would be allowed to observe them in authentic, traditional forms or be able to understand the meanings associated with them. By the time aboriginal peoples provided their own historical accounts, their cultures had changed in appreciable ways, and few people were willing to listen to their stories and publish them in

Continued

opportunities for workers to organize themselves and challenge the power of factory owners (Gruneau, 1999; Metcalfe, 1987; Palmer, 1979).

In most industrializing countries, the clergy also endorsed restrictions on popular games and gatherings. Ministers preached about the moral value of work and the immorality of play and idleness. Many even banned sports on Sundays and were supported by the government in the notorious "blue laws." Anyone who was not totally committed to work was accused of being lazy. Work, they preached, was a sign of goodness. Not everyone agreed, but working people had few

choices. For them, survival depended on working long hours, regardless of what they thought about work, and they had little power to change the conditions of these lives. The so-called blue laws, which in some Canadian jurisdictions lasted well into the twentieth century, prohibited play, sports, and commercial entertainment on Sundays, and obliged taverns to close. Since Sunday was the only free day for workers, the laws were regularly disregarded by the latter part of the nineteenth century, and Metcalfe (1978) describes a widespread "Sunday subculture" of sports and gambling that developed in Montréal.

REFLECT ON SPORTS   Lessons from History
continued

forms that were considered "real history." In the meantime, experiences and meanings were lost forever.

That we know so little about the many histories of games and sports among aboriginal peoples demonstrates that social, political, and economic forces influence our knowledge of sport history. For example, if we wish to understand the importance of an event, such as the establishment of the Iroquois National Lacrosse Team in 1983, we must know the following:

- The histories and cultures of specific native societies and the six nations of the Iroquois Confederation
- The formal and informal political relationships between native societies and the Canadian and U.S. governments
- The experiences of aboriginal peoples in North America as they struggled to maintain their cultures while others tried to strip them of their dignity, language, religion, and customs (e.g.,

through mandatory attendance at the residential schools set up throughout Canada for the "education" of aboriginal children)

This knowledge enables us to begin an investigation of the significance of the Iroquois National Lacrosse Team in terms of those who formed it, participated on it, and followed its games.

The scarcity of information from the perspectives of those who lack power diminishes our awareness of sports history around the world (see the quote from Riordan). Therefore, when our knowledge of the past does not go beyond the experiences and perspectives of those with the power to tell their own stories, it is always incomplete. In the worst case, such stories reproduce stereotypes and justify discrimination against those with little power. This is why some people support cultural diversity in the content of courses taught in high schools and universities. *What do you think?*

In most countries, games and sport activities during this period existed *despite* the Industrial Revolution, *not* because of it. People in small towns and farm communities still had opportunities to play games and sport activities during their seasonal festivities, holidays, and public ceremonies (Bouchier, 2003). Most city people had few opportunities to organize their own games and sports, although very wealthy people lived highly publicized "lives of leisure" (Veblen, 1899). Among the working classes, sport involvement seldom went beyond being spectators at new forms of commercialized sport events. These events varied by nations, but urban workers tended to watch a combination of cricket, horse racing, boxing and wrestling, footraces, rowing and yachting races, cockfighting, bullbaiting, and circus acts, among other events.

Rules prohibiting crowds were suspended when people participated in controlled commercialized

spectator events. Local neighbourhood events that attracted crowds were often defined as illegal, but organized commercial events were approved in most industrial societies, even when they attracted large crowds. These events were controlled and organized to benefit the interests of those with power and money in society.

Some sport participation did occur among urban workers, but it was relatively rare during the early years of the Industrial Revolution. In Canada, for example, it usually was limited to various tavern games, played mostly by men. The constraints of work and the lack of money and facilities made it difficult for working-class people to engage in anything but informal games and physical activities. Exceptions to this pattern were rare.

By the middle of the nineteenth century, reformers were beginning to express concern about the physical health of workers. This concern was based, in part, on the awareness that workers were being exploited, but was also motivated by the recognition that weak and sickly workers could not be productive. Similar concerns were also expressed during times of war, when the health and fitness of the men who were expected to fight also became a concern. As a result, there were growing calls for new open spaces for recreation, and for the funding of "healthy" leisure pursuits in the limited free time available to poorer people.

The emergence of formally organized competitive sports would require more than increased freedom and limited support for healthy leisure activities, but this was the time during which the foundations for organized sports were established.

The Later Years: Changing Interests, Values, and Opportunities

From the second half of the nineteenth century until today there has been a growing emphasis on rationality and organization in Canadian society. For example, during the mid-1800s, common interests in sport activities led to the establishment of organized clubs, which sponsored and controlled sport participation. Club membership usually was limited to wealthy men, and sometimes women, in urban areas. Metcalfe (1989) notes, for example, that there were 32 sports clubs in Montréal in 1861, mostly for wealthy anglophones in the sports of cricket, curling, lacrosse, and snowshoeing. However, the clubs did sponsor competitions, which often attracted spectators from all social classes.

The rapidly expanding middle classes during this time, particularly in the major cities such as Halifax, Montréal, and Toronto, were a key element in the development and spread of organized sports. As Hall, et al., point out with regard to the significant increase in the number of urban sports clubs between the 1860s and the end of the century (table 3.1 outlines the rapid increase in Montréal):

[A]s the mercantile middle class (businessmen, merchants, storeowners, bookkeepers, clerks, and sales personnel) grew, so did the sports clubs, particularly in team sports like lacrosse, baseball, hockey, and football. The original political and commercial elite who had dominated the earlier clubs retreated to their socially oriented golf, tandem, and hunt clubs, leaving the organization and administration of the more competitively focused clubs to the middle class. (1991, p. 57)

The expanding middle classes sought to bring a new cultural logic to sports—order, seriousness, new meanings, and regulation (see following sections on character and gender). The reformers of the "rational recreation" movement were from the middle classes, and, in addition to parks, playgrounds, public libraries, and museums, they developed organizations such as the YMCA, founded in 1844 in England. The YMCA did much to change the popular notion that physical conditioning through exercise and sports was anti-Christian and to promote recreational physical activity to lower-middle-class and working-class males. The games and sport activities of working-class people did not usually occur under the sponsorship of clubs or organizations, and they seldom received any publicity.

As sport activities became more organized, they generally reinforced existing class distinctions in society. Upper-class clubs emphasized achievement and "gentlemanly" involvement—an orientation that ultimately provided the basis for definitions of amateurism (which originated in England). Definitions of the "amateur" then became tools for excluding working-class people from the sport events organized to express the interests of upper-class participants (Bouchier, 2003; Gruneau, 1999; Metcalfe, 1987). In at least one case in Canada, the definition of amateurism also excluded native peoples. An amateur was: "One who has never competed in any open competition for public money, or for admission money, nor has ever taught, or assisted in the pursuit of Athletic exercise as a means of livelihood *or is a labourer or an Indian*" (Constitution

Table 3.1   The growth of sport clubs in Montréal, 1840–1894*

Club	1840	1861	1871	1877	1881	1887	1891	1892	1893	1894
Curling	1	3	3	3	4	3	5	5	5	5
Hunting	1	1	1	1	1	1	1	1	2	1
Snowshoe	1	10	7	15	20	16	17	17	16	22
Cricket	1	6	6	6	3	8	13	14	16	21
Lacrosse	–	9	15	31	25	45	36	53	56	49
Skating	–	1	1	1	1	2	2	2		1
Football	–	–	1	9	8	5	12	16	15	15
Baseball	–	–	6	14	14	21	11	14	19	10
Rowing	–	–	1	–	4	7	1	8	11	7
Hockey	–	–	–	4	2	18	23	19	28	46
Bicycle	–	–	–	–	1	1	2	2	4	4
Tennis	–	–	–	–	1		3	6	3	5
Quoits	–	–	–	–	1	3	3	3	5	7
Soccer	–	–	–	–	–	4	9	19	30	29
Others	3	2	1	1	4	8	7	10	12	23
TOTAL	7	32	42	85	88	142	145	189	222	245

*Adapted from Metcalfe (1989)

and By-Laws of the Montréal Pedestrian Club,[3] Article XII, 1873 (from Morrow, 1988, p. 23), emphasis added). The activities of the working classes, by contrast, were much more likely to involve folk games and commercialized sports—a combination that ultimately led to professionalization. This two-phased development of amateurism and professionalization occurred in slightly different ways in different countries (Dunning, 1999).

The Seeds of New Meanings Not only were sports being organized into clubs, but also the clubs were establishing agreements to form leagues and the first national and provincial sport organizations to govern the way that sports were played. Table 3.2 outlines the development of these clubs and organizations in Canada for various sports. Similarly, before the development

of multi-sport organizations such as the Canadian Olympic Committee, the Canadian Paralympic Committee, and Commonwealth Games Canada, clubs were amalgamating by the end of the nineteenth century to form the first multi-sport organizations (see table 3.3).

Underlying the growing organization of sports activities during the second half of the nineteenth century were two factors. First was the growing struggle to *control* sports—to determine who played sports, and how they were played, to turn *a way* of playing a sport into *the way* of playing a sport (Gruneau, 1999). Second, instead of defining sports simply as enjoyable diversions, people gradually came to see them as tools for achieving what were now defined as important goals such as economic productivity, national loyalty, and the development of admirable character traits, especially among males. This new way of viewing sports was fuelled by changes in every segment of industrial society: the economy, politics, family life, religion, education, science, philosophy, and technology.

[3]Pedestrian Clubs "were organized as the summer equivalents to snowshoe clubs and were prompted by the prevailing popularity of snowshoeing. They were weak efforts to bring organization to track and field and passed out of existence within a few years" (Morrow, 1988, p. 23).

Table 3.2   Growth and development of organized sports in Canada*

Sport	First Club(s)	National Association(s) Formed
Baseball	Burlington, Hamilton, Barton, Toronto (1854)	Canadian Baseball Association (1864, then 1876)
Basketball	Montréal, St. Stephens, NB (1892)	Canadian Basketball Association (1923)
Bowling		Canadian Bowling Association (1901)
Canoeing	Point St. Charles (1875)	Canadian Canoe Association (1900)
Cricket	St. John's, NF (1828)	Canadian Cricket Association (1892)
Curling	Montréal (1807)	"Canadian Branch" of the Royal Caledonian Curling Club (1852)
Cycling	Montréal, Halifax (1876)	Canadian Wheelmen's Assoc. (1882) Canadian Cyclists Assoc. (1900)
Football**		
Golf	Montréal (1873)	Royal Canadian Golf Assoc. (1894) Canadian Ladies Golf Union (1913)
Gymnastics	Montréal (1843, then 1860)	Canadian Gymnastic Assoc. (1899)
Harness racing	Québec (1864)	National Trotting Association (1889) Canadian Trotting Assoc. (1914)
Horse racing	Québec (1789, then 1817)	Canadian Jockey Club (1895)
Ice hockey	Montréal (1877)	Amateur Hockey Association (1886) Canadian Amateur Hockey Association (1914)
Lacrosse	Montréal (1842, then 1856)	National Lacrosse Assoc. (1882) Nat'l. Amateur Lacrosse Ass. (1892) Canadian Lacrosse Assoc. (1887) Canadian Amateur Lacrosse Association (1914)
Lawn tennis	Toronto (1876)	Canadian Lawn Tennis Ass. (1895)
Mountaineering		Alpine Club of Canada (1906)
Rowing	Bytown (1839)	Canadian Association of Amateur Oarsmen (1880)
Rugby	Montréal (1868) Halifax (1870)	Canadian Rugby Football Union (1887) Rugby Union of Canada (1929)
Shooting	Montréal (1850) Québec (1862)	Dominion of Canada Rifle Assoc. (1868)
Skating	Montréal (1850)	Amateur Skating Association of Canada (1888)
Snowshoeing	Montréal (1840, then 1843)	Canadian Snowshoe Union (1900)
Soccer	Montréal (1865)	Dominion Football Assoc. (1912)
Squash		Canadian Squash Racquets Association (1913)
Swimming	Montréal (1850, then 1876) Toronto (1875)	Canadian Amateur Swimming Association (1909)
Yachting	Kingston (1826)	Canadian Yachting Assoc. (1931)

*Adapted from Redmond (1989) and Kidd (1997)—Redmond also includes first international competitions in his table.

**The origins of Canadian football lie in soccer ("football") and rugby ("rugby football"); conflict and negotiations over the preferred rules of the game of "football" occurred during the 1870s and 1880s, and a Canadian version of the game began to emerge at McGill University and the University of Toronto by the early 1880s.

Table 3.3   Multi-sport governing bodies in the nineteenth century*

Organization	Year	Brief Description
Montréal Amateur Athletic Association (MAAA)	1881	Established by several clubs—(Montréal) Snowshoe, Lacrosse, Bicycle, and Football clubs, and the Tuque Bleue Toboggan Club—into one association (incorporated under the Québec Act).... excellent indoor and outdoor facilities for several sports; soon joined by chess, debating, drama, hockey, music, and skating clubs. Still on Peel Street in downtown Montréal; recently renovated as Club Sportif MAA.
Amateur Athletic Association of Canada (AAAC)	1884	Although primarily concerned with track and field, the AAAC was formed also to regulate all sports not under the control of other associations (gymnastics, handball, fencing, boxing, and wrestling). The AAAC (renamed Canadian Amateur Athletic Union in 1898, and the Amateur Athletic Union of Canada in 1909) became the authoritative body on the question of *amateur status*—an issue of growing concern with the increasing desire to maintain separation between the social classes in the 19th century, and the growth of professional sports in the 20th century.
Association Athlétique d'Amateurs le National (AAAN)	1894	Formed by Francophone businessmen to emulate the MAAA model. The mission of the AAAN was to encourage Québecois to become more involved in sport; there were also nationalistic reasons for creating the AAAN. Sports included hockey, lacrosse, gymnastics, and track and field (Harvey, 2006; Janson, 1995).

*Adapted and amended from Redmond (1989)

The Growth of Organized Sports in Canada: 1880 to 1920

POWER AND WEALTH IN ACTION The years between 1880 and 1920 were crucial for the development of organized sports in Canada (Howell, 2001; Kidd, 1996b, 1997; Metcalfe, 1987). Wealthy people developed lives of leisure, that often included sports, and they used participation in certain sports to prove that they were so successful that they could "waste" time by playing nonproductive games (Veblen, 1899). Although the wealthy often used sports to reinforce status distinctions between themselves and other social classes, they also influenced how sports were played and organized by others, especially middle-class people whose status aspirations led them to emulate the rich and powerful.

In this way, the upper and upper-middle classes influenced the norms for many players and spectators, the standards for facilities and equipment, and the way in which people in lower social classes defined and integrated sports into their lines. Gruneau and Whitson (1993) identify two different trajectories to their influence. The first they term "moral entrepreneurs," who were promoting the reformist and positive recreational aspects of sports and physical activity—strict amateurism, and the idea that participation would make you a "better" person (in terms of both health and character). The second were the "economic entrepreneurs," who saw sports both as commercial

REFLECT ON SPORTS

Dominant Sport Forms Today
What Makes Them Unique?

The organized competitive sports so popular today are very different from the physical activities and games played in the past. Allen Guttmann's study of sport activities through history shows that *dominant sport forms (DSFs)* today have seven interrelated characteristics, which have never before appeared together in physical activities and games. These characteristics are:

1. *Secularism.* DSFs today are not directly linked to religious beliefs or rituals. They are sources of diversion and entertainment, not worship. They are played for personal gains, not the appeasement of gods. They embody the immediacy of the material world, not the mysticism of the supernatural.

2. *Equality.* DSFs today are based on the ideas that participation should be open to everyone regardless of family or social background and that all contestants in a sport event should face the same competitive conditions.

3. *Specialization.* DSFs today involve athletes dedicated exclusively to participation in a single event or position within an event. Excellence is defined in terms of specialized skills, rather than all-around physical abilities.

4. *Rationalization.* DSFs today consist of rules that regulate the conditions of participation and rationally controlled strategies and training methods guided by "sport sciences."

5. *Bureaucratization.* DSFs today are governed by complex organizations, and officials who control athletes, teams, and events; enforce rules; organize events; and certify records.

6. *Quantification.* DSFs today involve precise timing and measurements and statistics in the form of scores and performance data that are recorded and used as proof of achievements.

7. *Records.* DSFs today emphasize setting and breaking records. Performances are compared over time to determine personal, national, and world records.

Dominant sport forms today emphasize quantification. Performances are timed, measured, and recorded. The clock is crucial, and digital scoreboards now show times in hundredths of seconds. [David Biene; photo courtesy of Ossur]

Continued

REFLECT ON SPORTS

Dominant Sport Forms Today

continued

One or more of these characteristics have been present in the physical activities and games of previous historical periods, but not until the nineteenth century did all seven appear together in *modern* sports (Dunning, 1999; Dunning and Sheard, 1979; Guttmann, 1978). This does not mean that today's organized competitive sports are superior to the games and activities of past times and other places. It means only that they are different in the way they are organized and integrated into people's lives. Sociologists study these differences in terms of their connections with culture and society.

Table 3.4 summarizes Guttmann's comparison of games, contests, and sports activities in each of the places and time periods discussed in this chapter. The table shows that the dominant sport forms that exist in many postindustrial societies today are different from the "sports" played by people in times past. However, it does not explain why the differences exist or the social implications of the differences.

The seven characteristics identified by Guttmann are not found in all sports today. Sports are social constructions. They change as social, economic, and political forces change and as people seek and develop alternatives to dominant sport forms. The DSFs played fifty years from now are likely to have characteristics that are different from these seven characteristics. *What do you think?*

Table 3.4   Historical comparison of organized games, contests, and sport activities*

Characteristic	Greek Contests and Games (1000 B.C.E. to 100 B.C.E.)	Roman Contests and Games (100 B.C.E. to C.E. 500)	Medieval Tournaments and Games (500 to 1300)	Renaissance, Reformation, and Enlightenment Games and Sport Activities (1300 to 1800)	"Modern" Sports
Secularism	Yes and no**	Yes and no	Yes and no	Yes and no	Yes
Equality	Yes and no	Yes and no	No	Yes and no	Yes
Specialization	Yes	Yes	No	Yes and no	Yes
Rationalization	Yes	Yes	No	No	Yes
Bureaucratization	Yes and no	Yes	No	No	Yes
Quantification	No	Yes	No	Yes and no	Yes
Records	No	No	No	Yes and no	Yes

*Modified version of table 2 in Guttmann (1978).

**This characteristic existed in some sports during this time, but not in others.

opportunities and as ways to promote one's community. Sports became part of the entertainment industry with the emergence of professional leagues and barnstorming teams, and the promotion of events such as boxing matches. Having a representative team in one's community was an aspect of civic boosterism that was characteristic of the newly developed towns growing all over Canada. These two views of sports clashed continually over the issue of amateurism and professionalism, eventually coming to a head in what came to be known as "the athletic war" in 1906–08 (Morrow, 1986; Metcalfe, 1987).[4]

---

[4]This war continued to be fought, on and off, and in various ways, through most of the twentieth century. It only came to an end as the Olympics began to embrace Western notions of professionalism at the 1984 Los Angeles Games (see Grunean, 2006).

The two forms of entrepreneurialism came together in an interesting way as wealthy people used their economic resources to encourage others to define sports as *consumer activities* to be played in *proper* attire, using the *proper* equipment in a *proper* facility, and preceded or followed by *proper* social occasions separated from employment and the workplace. Through this process of "encouragement," and the development of consensus about the forms and meanings of sports (described as *hegemony* by sociologists; see chapter 4, page 102), sports became connected with the economy. The connection was subtle because sports involved both consumption and worklike orientations, while being popularly defined as "nonwork" activities, separate from the economy.

The emergence of these ideas about how sports "should be" played was important. It enabled people with power to reproduce their privilege in society without overtly coercing workers to think and behave in certain ways. Instead of maintaining their privilege by force,

The leisure activities of the wealthy at the turn of the twentieth century included sports. However, physical activities and sports for girls and women often stressed balance and coordination, which were defined as "ladylike" qualities, and they often included nets or other barriers, so that there would be no physical contact between female players. [McGraw-Hill]

people with economic power promoted forms of sports that were entertaining, and supported the values and orientations that promoted capitalist business expansion. Critical theorists have noted that this is an example of how sports can be political and economic activities, even though most people see them as sources of excitement and enjoyment (Gramsci, 1971, 1988; Gruneau, 1999; Rigauer, 2000).

From 1880 to 1920, middle- and working-class people, especially white males, had new opportunities to play sports. Labour unions, progressive government legislation, and economic expansion combined to improve working and living conditions. The efforts of unions and social reformers gradually led to more free time and material resources available to many working-class people. As the middle class expanded, more people had resources for leisure and sport participation. The spirit of reform at the turn of the twentieth century also led to the development of parks, recreation programmes, and organized playground activities for urban residents, especially boys and young men (Kidd, 1996b).

IDEAS ABOUT SPORT PARTICIPATION AND "CHARACTER DEVELOPMENT" Early in the twentieth century, opportunities for sport involvement increased, but the kinds of opportunities available to most people were shaped by factors beyond the interests of the participants themselves. Important new ideas about human behaviour, individual development, and social life led to an emphasis on organized competitive sports as "character-building" activities.

Until the latter part of the nineteenth century, most people believed that the actions and development of human beings were unrelated to social factors. They assumed that fate or supernatural forces dictated individual development and that social life was established by a combination of God's will, necessity, and coincidence. However, these ideas changed as people discovered that the social environment influenced people's actions and that it was possible to change patterns of individual growth and development by changing the organization of society.

This new way of thinking was a crucial catalyst in the growth of modern sports. It made sports into something more than enjoyable pastimes. Gradually, sports were defined as potential educational experiences—experiences with important consequences for individuals, communities, and society. This change, based on behaviourist and evolutionary theories, which were popular at the time, provided a new basis for organizing and promoting sport participation. For the first time in history, people saw sports as tools for changing behaviour, shaping character, creating national loyalty, and building unity in an ethnically diverse population.

People began to think about the meaning and purpose of sports in new and serious terms. For example, some religious groups, referred to as "muscular Christians" (see the "Sports and Religion" chapter on the Online Learning Centre), suggested a link between physical strength and the ability to do good works; therefore, they promoted sport involvement as an avenue for spiritual growth. Others saw sports as tools for teaching immigrant children lessons that would turn them into contributing members of a corporate-bureaucratic-democratic society. These people also promoted organized playground programmes that used team sports to undermine traditional ethnic values and replace them with an emerging Canadianized way of looking at the world. People interested in economic expansion saw organized sports as tools for generating profits by introducing untrained workers to tasks emphasizing teamwork, obedience to rules, planning, organization, and production. They thought that sports could create good workers who could tolerate stressful working conditions, obey supervisors, and meet production goals through teamwork on factory assembly lines.

In large part, organized sports became important because people with power and money believed that sport participation could be used to train loyal and hardworking people dedicated to achievement and production for the glory of God and country. Sports were socially constructed and defined in ways that were believed to promote this type of character development.

ORGANIZED SPORTS AND IDEAS ABOUT MASCULINITY AND FEMININITY The new belief that sports built character was applied primarily to males. The people who organized and sponsored new programmes thought they could use organized sports, especially team sports, to tame what they perceived as the savage, undisciplined character of young, lower-class males. Their intent was to create obedient citizens and productive workers. At the same time, they used sports for young males from upper- and middle-class backgrounds to counteract what many believed was the negative influence of female dominated home lives. Their goal was to turn "overfeminized"

Table 3.5 Women's participation in organized sports in the nineteenth century*

Sport	First/early participation, and Associations
Archery	Montréal Ladies** Club (1858)
Baseball	Reports of girls playing in Newcastle and Chatham, NB (1890)
	Women's club formed in Nanaimo, BC (1890)
Basketball	Women playing in Toronto and Whitby, ON (1895)
Bicycling	Many women members in bicycle clubs in the 1880s
	In 1890s (from 1894), women formed their own clubs
	"Ladies" half-mile race in Goderich, ON (1895)
Curling	First women's club, Montréal (1894)
Equestrian sports	First Dominion Championships for women (1895)
Fencing	Toronto Club included women members (1895)
	University College, Toronto, formed women's club (1895)
Field hockey	First women's club, Vancouver (1896)
Figure skating	60 women demonstrated "Fancy Skating" in Halifax (1863)
	Women members of Rideau Club, Ottawa, held figure skating competition (1890)
Fox hunting	Women participated in Montréal (1873)
Golf	Clubs in Hamilton, Montréal, Niagara, Oshawa, Ottawa, Québec, Sherbrooke, Toronto, Winnipeg, and Victoria had women members (1890s)
	First women's interclub match: Toronto vs. Rosedale (1896)
	First women's interprovincial match: Toronto vs. Montréal and Québec (1897)
Ice hockey	Women's team organized in Barrie, ON (1892)
	Women students at McGill hold interclass games (1894)
Lawn tennis	Tournaments for women organized in Ottawa and Montréal (1881)
	First Dominion Championships for women at Toronto Club (1883)
Rowing	Many regattas in 1870s included events for women
	One mile girls' single sculls race in Grand Trunk Regatta, Montréal (1880)
Snowshoeing	Ladies' Prince of Wales Club, Montréal (1861)
Squash	First Dominion Championships for women, Ottawa (1881)
Swimming	Women granted privileges (3 days a week) at Montréal club (1889)
Tobogganing	First competitions of Tuque Bleue Club, Montréal, included a "combined lady-and-gentleman" race (1885)

*Adapted from Redmond (1989)

**The term "ladies" was in common use in the 19th century for middle- and upper-class women, precisely the classes of women who were most likely to participate in organized sports at the time.

boys into assertive, competitive, achievement-oriented young men, who would become effective leaders in business, politics, and the military. In these ways, contemporary sports were heavily grounded in the desire of those in the dominant social classes to control the working classes, while preparing their own sons to inherit their positions of power and influence (Burstyn, 1999; Kidd, 1996b).

Although an increasing number of women participated in sport activities between 1880 and 1920, many sport programmes ignored, or actively opposed, females (see table 3.5, and the quotation on this page). Organizers and sponsors did not see sport participation as important in the character development of girls and women. They sometimes included girls with boys in the organized games at playgrounds, but they discouraged sex-integrated sports for children nearing the age of puberty. It was widely believed that if boys and girls played sports with one another, they would become good friends and lose their interest in being married, having children, and maintaining beliefs in male superiority and female inferiority.

When boys were taught to play sports on playgrounds in the early 1900s, girls were told to sit in the shade and preserve their energy. Helen Lenskyj (1986), of the University of Toronto, and Patricia Vertinsky (1990), of the University of British Columbia, have both documented the ways in which the medical profession was involved in preventing girls and women from becoming involved in sports and physical activity, warning that involvement would sap the energy needed to conceive and bear healthy children. However, despite a continuous barrage of warnings from physicians women became increasingly involved:

> There is no reason to think that a healthy woman can be injured [cycling]… provided she does not over-exert herself by riding too long a time, or too fast, or up too steep hills, and provided she does not ride when common sense and physiology alike forbid any needless exertion. (Dr. J. West Roosevelt, 1895; cited by Lenskyj, 1986, pp. 24–25)

In the same year as Roosevelt's warning, Dr. Grace Ritchie, writing in the *National Council of Women of Canada Yearbook, 1895*, pointed out that:

> Every year, some new avenue, some new form of physical exercise is being opened to women. What was once frowned down upon as unladylike, trivial and shocking, is now done openly and with the approval of the beholders. Perhaps nothing illustrates this so much as the riding of the bicycle. (1896, p. 117; cited by Lenskyj, 1986, pp. 24–25)

Ann Hall (1999, 2002), of the University of Alberta, has pointed out the importance of cycling in the political and cultural emancipation of women.

Still, organized activities for girls often consisted of domestic science classes designed to make them good wives, homemakers, and mothers. When playground organizers provided opportunities for girls to play games and sports, they designed activities that would cultivate "ladylike" traits, such as poise and body control. This is why so many girls participated in gymnastics, figure skating, and other "grace and beauty" sports (Burstyn, 1999; Hart, 1981). Another goal of the activities was to

> …we, the members of the Queen's College Snowshoe Club after much anxious thought, do hereby seriously but heartily resolve, that owing to the dire and disastrous effects of co-education, at the Royal College, that no 'female woman' whatsoever, be allowed, no matter in what capacity to participate in any manner in our tramps. That we shall not peril the prosperity of this Club by subjecting it to their baleful influences.
>
> —*Queen's University Journal*, 1883; (cited by Cochrane, et al., 1977, p. 26)

make young women healthy for bearing children. Competition was eliminated or controlled, and the activities emphasized personal health, the dignity of beauty, and good form. In some cases, the only reason games and sports were included in girls' activities was to provide the knowledge they would need in the future to introduce their sons to active games.

Limited opportunities and a lack of encouragement did not stop women from participating in sports, but they certainly restricted the extent of their involvement (Vertinsky, 1994). Some middle- and upper-class women engaged in popular physical exercises and recreational sport activities such as cycling but, apart from limited interuniversity games and private tournaments,

they had few opportunities to engage in formal competitive events. The participation of girls and women from lower-income groups was restricted to informal street games, a few supervised exercise classes, and play days in public schools. Ideas about femininity changed between 1880 and 1920, but traditional gender ideology and numerous misconceptions about the physical and mental effects of strenuous activities on females prevented the "new woman" of the early twentieth century from enjoying the same participation opportunities and encouragement males received (Lenskyj, 1986). In fact, medical beliefs did more to subvert the health of women during these years than to improve it (Vertinsky, 1987).

Although hockey did not meet the "ladylike" criteria for girls' and women's sports, it has been played by girls and women since the earliest days of organized hockey. [City of Toronto Archives, Fonds 1244, item 477]

ORGANIZED SPORTS AND IDEAS ABOUT SKIN COLOUR AND ETHNICITY The previous sections have focused primarily on anglophone sport development in Canada. By this time, however, clubs and teams were beginning to be formed around various ethnic affiliations as new waves of immigrants reached Canada. Of the "two" colonizing nations of Canada, the Montréal anglophone community figures prominently in Canadian sport history, but, as Harvey (1999, p. 31) notes, "Although they took longer to get organized, a modernist and liberal faction of the French Canadian community also decided to use sport as a means for the promotion of its nationalist interests with the creation, in 1894, of the Association Athlétique d'Amateurs Le National" (see table 3.3). However, while sports remained a major interest of francophones in larger communities, where they were well represented in organized sports, several researchers have pointed out that the major influence of the Catholic Church (especially in smaller communities) resulted in a somewhat different pattern of sport development in francophone Québec (Bellefleur, 1986, 1997; Harvey, 1988). Indeed, for the francophone Catholic hierarchy in Québec, sports under the control of anglophones posed a danger of assimilation. Unable to prevent the growing interest of francophones in sports, the clergy took the initiative to create a separate sport system with a less competitive set of values. This was to have interesting consequences for the development of sports in Québec until the "Quiet Revolution."

The first nations/aboriginal Canadians, fared less well. Native sports such as snowshoeing and baggataway were incorporated and transformed into precisely the types of DSFs outlined in the Reflect on Sports box, "Dominant Sport Forms Today," on pages 63–64, and aboriginal peoples were prevented from joining the clubs where competitions took place. Pointing out that native Canadians were usually "excluded from white competitions [or] held up to ridicule," Morrow (1988) also noted that sometimes "efforts were made to push Indians (sic) to the limits of their endurance for reasons of pure spectacle and wagering" (p. 23). At one point, all native Canadians were designated as "professionals" in order to prevent them from competing against the amateur clubs. Eddington (2000) points out that it took twenty years, until 1887, before the Iroquois Nationals became the first native team to join the International Lacrosse Federation. Native skill at running was also exploited, and Bruce Kidd (1980, 1983) documented the vicious racist treatment experienced by one of the best-known native Canadian runners, Tom Longboat.

Other visible minorities in Canada received similar treatment at this time, with few opportunities for participation for, for example, Asian immigrants. And, despite a different history of race relations, African Canadians fared no better than African Americans at this time. Following a period of emancipation after the Civil War, the segregation of African Americans was reinstated at the end of the nineteenth century with the "Jim Crow laws." These laws were imitated in Canada, leading to the appearance of a number of segregated baseball and hockey teams. The stories of these black teams and leagues has almost "disappeared" from the history of sport in Canada (see Reflect on Sports box, "Lessons from History," pp. 57–58) and, as a result of new and more inclusive sport histories, we are only now beginning to learn of examples such as the "Coloured" Hockey League in Nova Scotia at the beginning of the twentieth century (Fosty and Fosty, 2004), and the short-lived all-Black baseball leagues (Humber, 2004). The treatment of francophones, native Canadians, and visible minorities by the anglophone majority was a manifestation of the prevailing race and ethnic relations at the time. Non-Europeans and non-anglophones were considered to be inferior, and it was undignified to be beaten at sports by one's social "inferiors."

ORGANIZED SPORTS AND IDEAS ABOUT AGE AND DISABILITY Aging involves biological changes, but the connection between aging and sport participation depends on the social meanings given to those changes. Developmental theory in the early 1900s emphasized that all growth and character formation occurred during childhood and adolescence. Therefore, it was important for young people to play sports, but older people were already "grownups" and no longer needed the character-building experiences provided by sports.

Medical knowledge at the time also discouraged older people from engaging in sports. Strenuous activities were thought to put excessive demands on the heart and organs in aging bodies. This did not prevent older people from playing certain sports, but it did prevent the establishment and funding of organized sport programmes for older people. Furthermore, when older people were physically active, they participated by themselves or in age-segregated settings.

People with observable physical or mental disabilities were denied opportunities to play sports and often told that strenuous physical activities were bad for their well-being. Widely accepted definitions of mental and physical disability often gave rise to fears and prejudices that led many people to think it was dangerous to allow people with a disability to become physically active or excited. Therefore, programmes to build their bodies were discouraged. This meant that people born with certain disabilities were isolated and destined to be physically inactive; obesity and other problems caused by a lack of physical activity shortened their life expectancy. People with an "acquired disability," usually those injured in war or accidents, were treated with physical therapy in the hope of some degree of rehabilitation. As explained in the Breaking Barriers box (p. 72), sports for most people with a disability did not exist until after World War II.

1880 TO 1920—A KEY PERIOD Although opportunities for participation in organized, competitive sports between 1880 and 1920 were not equally distributed by social class, gender,

skin colour, ethnicity, age, or ability, participation among most categories of people increased dramatically. This was the case in most industrializing societies. In most Western cultures, the organizational attributes that we associate with today's high-profile organized sports became clearly established during this time. The games people played featured a combination of secularism, a growing commitment to participation among competitors from all socioeconomic backgrounds, increased specialization, rationalization, bureaucratization, quantification, and the quest for records. (See "Dominant Sport Forms Today," pages 63–64.) These are some of the sociologically relevant characteristics that have become the foundation of what many people define as sports today.

Since 1920, the resources devoted to organized, competitive sports have increased in many societies around the world. Technology has been used to change sport experiences for participants and spectators, and tremendous growth has occurred in sport-related industries and the government sponsorship of sports. Many of today's struggles about the organization, meaning, and purpose of sports, and how sports should be integrated into people's lives, were visible in some form ninety years ago.

Since 1920: Struggles Continue

By 1920, major connections had been established between sports and Canadian society. Sports were a growing part of people's everyday lives, and they were linked to major social institutions such as the family, religion, education, the economy, the government, and the media. But the major divisions in Canadian society were also evident in sports: "amateur and professional, east and west, male and female, 'bourgeois' and 'workers' organizations" (Kidd, 1997). Since 1920, the rate of change and the expansion of the visibility and importance of sports in people's lives have intensified. The last nine decades have

Breaking Barriers

"Other" Barriers
They Found It Hard to Be Around Me

Danny was twenty-one years old, a popular and able-bodied rugby player. Then came the accident, the amputation of his right arm just below the shoulder, the therapy, and eventually, getting back with friends. But reconnecting with friends after suddenly acquiring a disability is not easy. Danny describes his experience with these words: "A lot of them found it very difficult . . . to come to terms with it . . . And they found it hard to be around me, friends that I'd had for years" (in Brittain, 2004, p. 437).

Chris, an athlete with cerebral palsy and one of Danny's teammates on the British Paralympic Team, explains why his friends felt uncomfortable: "They have very little knowledge of people with a disability and [they think that] if I leave it alone and don't touch them and don't get involved, then it's not my problem" (in Brittain, 2004, p. 437). Chris raises a recurring issue in the history of disability: What happens when people define physical or intellectual impairments as "differences" and use them to create "others" who are distinguished from "us normals" in social worlds?

Throughout history, people with disabilities have been described by words inferring revulsion, resentment, dread, shame, and a world of limitations. In Europe and North America, it took World War II and thousands of returning soldiers impaired by injuries before there were widespread concerns about the words used to describe people with disabilities. Language has changed so that people with intellectual disabilities now have opportunities to participate in the Special Olympics, and elite athletes with physical disabilities may qualify for the Paralympics ("para" meaning *parallel with*, not *paraplegic*). Words like *retard*, *spaz* (spastic), *cripple*, *freak*, *deaf and dumb*, *handicapped*, *gimp*, and *deformed* have largely been abandoned. However, they are not gone, and people with disabilities are still described as "others"—such as "she's a quad," "he's a CPer," "they're amputees," and "what a retard!"

Improvements have occurred, but when people with disabilities are defined as "others," encountering disability raises questions about personal vulnerability, aging, and mortality. It also highlights the faulty assumptions of normalcy around which we construct social worlds. Therefore, those identified as "normal" often ignore, avoid, or patronize people with disabilities, and this subverts the possibility of ever seeing the world through their eyes.

The fear of "otherness" is powerful, and people in many cultures traditionally restrict and manage their contact with "others" by enlisting the services of experts. These include doctors, mental health workers, psychiatrists, healers, shamans, witchdoctors, priests, exorcists, and all professionals whose assumed competence gives them the right to examine, test, classify, and prescribe "normalizing treatments" for "others." Therefore, the history of disability is also the history of giving meaning to difference, creating "others," and using current knowledge to treat "otherness" (Foucault, 1961/1967; Goffman, 1963).

As noted in Breaking Barriers in chapter 2, cultural traditions in North America have long emphasized treatment-oriented approaches to fix impairments or help people adjust to living with disabilities. Only recently have these approaches been complemented by transformational approaches focused on creating barrier-free social spaces in which disabilities become irrelevant and "others" are no longer created. This is an idealistic project, and it requires actions that disrupt the "normal" order of social worlds. But Jean Driscoll, eight-time winner of the Women's Wheelchair Boston Marathon, has experienced such worlds, and she says that "when sports are integrated, the focus turns from the person with a disability to the guy with a great shot or the gal with a fast 800-meter time. Integration provides the perfect venue where 'actions speak louder than words'" (in Joukowsky and Rothstein, 2002b, p. 28). And we would add that interactionist theory helps us to understand that words are the foundation for action.

also been a time for continuing struggles over the following:

1. The meaning, purpose, and organization of sports
2. Who plays sports under what conditions
3. How and why sports are sponsored

As explained in chapter 1, sports are social constructions *and* contested activities. Therefore, we can outline social trends and patterns in recent history by focusing on issues and events related to these three realms of struggle. In fact, so fundamental are these struggles to understanding the development of sport, that Bruce Kidd (1997) titled his history of sport during this period, *The Struggle for Canadian Sport*. The struggles serve as useful reference points for discussing social history, and we use them to guide our choice of materials in the following chapters. They also provide a useful framework for understanding patterns and trends during the twentieth century.

Of course, the timing, dynamics, and outcomes of these struggles and changes are related to larger historical events and trends such as wars, economic recessions, suburbanization, the growth of universities, the various human and civil rights movements, the development and expansion of electronic media and other technologies, globalization, and the growing concentration of corporate power. (For a list of specific events and trends affecting U.S. sports, see the OLC at www.mcgrawhill.ca/olc/coakley.)

Connections between the recent history of sports and these trends and events are too complex and extensive to discuss in this chapter. But it is possible to briefly outline some of the major struggles that have occurred since 1920.

Struggles over Meaning: Is Hockey "the Canadian Specific"?

British Columbia poet, Al Purdy, referred to hockey as "the Canadian specific;" others have called it "Canada's national sport," "our common passion," and "the most Canadian of metaphors"

(Roch Carrier). These are indications of two interconnected struggles regarding the meaning of hockey: first, the struggle to understand what a national obsession with hockey means about us as Canadians; second, the struggle to impose a specific meaning on "the Canadian game."

In the nineteenth century, popular team sports reflected both the British and U.S. influences on Canada—they included cricket, baseball, lacrosse, rugby, soccer, and hockey. While other countries of the British Commonwealth adopted the British games of cricket, rugby, and soccer, by the turn of the twentieth century U.S. influence in Canada led to baseball beating out cricket as the summer sport, to a North American form of football being adapted from rugby, and to the growth of the "Canadian" sports of lacrosse and hockey on both sides of the Canadian border. Because of the socially constructed and contested nature of sports, any one of these could have come to be considered as the national sport. Just as Kidd (1997) describes how the National Hockey League became the dominant league for that sport in North America, it is also worth considering how hockey became the dominant sport in Canada. Climate, commercial entrepreneurs of the game, and U.S. sponsorship (four of the original six teams of the NHL were American owned and based, and a number of other professional hockey leagues played on both sides of the border) all combined to make hockey the dominant sport in Canada.

National sports are supposed to carry all kinds of meanings about a country, and to be a part of national identity. As William Humber points out in the quote on page 47, lacrosse has far more claim than hockey to be Canada's national sport, and even basketball was invented by a Canadian. For much of the last century, both lacrosse and hockey claimed to be Canada's national sport. However, it was not until 1994 that an NDP MP from British Columbia, Nelson Riis, introduced a private member's bill (Bill C-212) to the House of Commons to recognize hockey as the national sport. Considerable lobbying and support for lacrosse resulted in an amendment that represents a truly Canadian compromise. Bill C-212, Canada's National Sport Act, received Royal Assent in May, 1994, when it became law *"To recognize Hockey as Canada's National Winter Sport and Lacrosse as Canada's National Summer Sport."*

Hockey is certainly the most popular sport in terms of spectatorship in Canada, but how meaningful is the game to all Canadians. As the "whitest" of the four major professional team sports in North America, many Canadians do not see themselves represented in the game. Also, until recently, very few women have played the game in Canada. Many Canadians have found other reasons to ignore or dislike hockey—the high salaries of players, the dilution of talent resulting from league expansion, the high incidence of injuries, fighting, and unruly behaviour by players, coaches, and parents.

Despite this, hockey continues as the dominant sport, slowly becoming less "white" and less male-dominated. It has also carried various meanings for Canadians, as shown in the following examples:

- Francophone/anglophone relations have often been represented in Canada by the Toronto Maple Leafs/Montréal Canadiens rivalry. Rick Salutin captured this in his play, *Les Canadiens* (1977). In the opening scene, a French soldier lies dying on the Plains of Abraham. With a last effort he throws his rifle. As it flies across the stage, it turns into a hockey stick, and is caught by his son who is wearing a Habs shirt. Thus, the game came to represent much larger issues involved in the struggles for rights and independence in Québec.
- International political struggles were represented in sport, especially at the Olympics, during the Cold War years of the 1960s and 1970s. Canada's involvement in this struggle followed a period of declining success in international hockey. Canadian men had not won an Olympic gold medal in ice hockey since 1952, and had little success in the world championships. Arguing that the

International Ice Hockey Federation obliged them to play amateur players against the best players in other countries, a "summit series" was eventually organized in 1972 to match the "best" Canadian players (NHL players) with the Soviet national team in an eight-game series. Canada finally won the series in the last minute of the final game, having been surprised by the strength and skill of the Soviet players. Despite the closeness of the series, victory was frequently taken to symbolize a Cold War success indicating the superiority of democratic and capitalist systems of government over communist systems. [However, it was 50 years before Canadian men won an Olympic gold medal in hockey—Salt Lake City, 2002.]

As is often the case with national sports, the sport is far more meaningful than just a game.

Struggles over Purpose: Is Winning the Only Thing?

Meaning and purpose are closely aligned. On a general level, the central purpose of most sports between 1920 and the 1960s was to develop fitness and encourage fair play. However, as career success and social mobility became more important in a growing capitalist economy during the 1950s, there was a gradual turn toward an emphasis on competitive success and winning in sports. In this shift from a participation orientation to an outcome orientation, competitive sports came to be seen as a way to build the kind of character that many felt was essential to Canadian prosperity.

As sports teams and sports events were linked to educational institutions, communities, and the nation, the primary purpose of sports continued to shift from participation and fair play to victories that brought prestige to sponsors. By the 1960s, many Canadians had adopted a slogan from the U.S.—they felt that "winning is not the most important thing, it is the *only* thing." With the 1970s and the dramatic growth of media coverage, entertainment became an increasingly important purpose of sports. As this occurred, the styles and personas of athletes took on new meanings, and teams built public relations profiles around values and identities that resonated with audience segments or mass audiences. It was during this period that Canada was most polarized in terms of supporting the Montréal Canadiens or the Toronto Maple Leafs.

There is never complete agreement on the purpose of sports. Physical educators and health educators may emphasize fitness and health, whereas advertisers and people associated with the commercial media emphasize entertainment. This and other disagreements occur today as people struggle to define the purpose of sports in their schools and community youth sport programmes.

Struggles over Purpose: Can We Play Without a Coach and Referee?

Since 1920 there has been a clear trend towards organizing sports in formal and "official" ways. Mainstream sports are increasingly organized around standardized rules enforced by official governing bodies. Some people have resisted increased organization and rationalization, but resistance has not slowed or reversed this trend. Even many alternative and recreational sports have become increasingly organized in attempts to make them safer (e.g., the so-called "extreme sports"), more accessible, and/or more commercially pro-fitable. Even shinny, street hockey, and pick-up basketball have their organized versions.

Hundreds of sports organizations have come and gone in recent years, but the emphasis on organization has become more prevalent. As this has occurred, classic and sometimes bitter struggles have taken place over who controls sports so that they will be organized consistently over time (recent examples include curling and volleyball). In the process, governing bodies, coaches, and other officials have become key "players" in sports at all levels. In fact, many children today grow up thinking that sports cannot exist without coaches and referees.

The Conditions of Sport Participation: Can Everyone Play?

Some of the most contentious struggles in sports since 1920 concern who participates in formally organized mainstream sport programmes. Most sports were initially organized around various forms of exclusion and segregation based on race, ethnicity, religion, gender, age, and (dis)ability. For example, men from middle- and upper-class white families have consistently had the greatest access to sport participation opportunities throughout their lives.

There have been constant struggles to expand participation opportunities for women, people from low-income families and neighbourhoods, ethnic minorities, people with a physical or intellectual disability, and people labelled as gay or lesbian. Complex histories are associated with each of these struggles, but the general trend since 1920 has been to open sport participation to more people, especially through sports receiving public funding and being played in public facilities. Private clubs and organizations maintained exclusionary membership criteria over the years, and many continue to do so today. However, increased privatization and the increasing implementation of user fees for public facilities and programmes since the 1980s has made it more financially difficult for many people to initiate or maintain regular sport participation, and this trend suggests that sports will be characterized by increased socioeconomic segregation in the future.

Struggles over who participates under what conditions have been further complicated by the diversity of goals among the people involved. Some groups of people have fought to be inte-grated fully into organized mainstream sports, whereas others have fought to have separate opportunities that meet their specific needs and interests. For instance, not everyone wishes to play sports developed and organized around the interests and experiences of young, able-bodied, white, heterosexual males.

Struggles over the conditions of participation have occurred when professional athletes formed players' associations to bargain with team owners and leagues over issues related to the organization and rules of their sports. University students have struggled to obtain recognition and funding for club teams with the hope of eventually becoming official interuniversity teams. Women's teams have struggled to achieve similar funding, facilities, practice times, and equipment to their male counterparts. And many struggles have arisen over eligibility, the allocation of rewards, and the funding of new or alternative sport participation opportunities.

Sport Sponsors: Who Needs Them?

The major economic recession in the 1930s generally interfered with the funding and sponsorship of many sports. However, as government policies and programmes were developed to cope with the consequences of the depression (e.g., Jan Eisenhardt's Pro-Rec (Provincial Recreation) programme for the homeless in British Columbia), there was an emphasis on the public sponsorship of sports, especially for children, adolescents, and young adults. After World War II, most Canadian communities embraced the idea that tax money should be used to provide a range of sport participation opportunities, especially for boys and young men.

Since the 1980s and 1990s, the growth of anti-government and anti-tax sentiments, combined with the growth of corporate power and influence, led to a shift in sponsorship patterns. After more than 30 years of increased sponsorship of sports by all levels of government, public programmes began to lose their funding. This led to an increase in non-profit (fee-paying) organizations, and the widespread introduction of user fees in school sports and municipal recreation programmes. Some public programmes were replaced with programmes funded by private money and corporate sponsors. This new form of sponsorship had a major impact on the types of sports that have become popular and who has the opportunities to participate in them.

Instead of being based on ideas about "the common good"—such as improvements in public health[5]—sports today are often sponsored in connection with the commercial interests of corporations. Struggles over sport sponsorships have recently involved corporations that sell tobacco, alcohol, fast foods, products made in sweatshops, and services defined by some people as immoral (e.g., gambling). These struggles will continue as long as the sports that people want to play and watch require large amounts of capital and as long as people do not approve of their tax money being used to sponsor public sports and sport facilities. Eventually, this could raise the question of whether people want to play and watch sports that require external sponsors. There is some evidence that people are beginning to realize that they can have fun playing and watching sports and participating in physical activities that they can organize and maintain by themselves, if there are accessible public spaces available.

USING HISTORY TO THINK ABOUT THE FUTURE

As we study the past, we learn that struggles over the meaning, purpose, and organization of sports always occur in particular social, political, and economic contexts. Sport history does not just happen; it always depends on the actions of people working with one another to construct sports to match their visions of what sports could and should be in their lives. Many people in recent history have ignored what others say is practical or realistic, and they have pursued idealistic notions of what sports could be. These are the people who have inspired racial desegregation in sports, new opportunities for girls and women,

---

[5]Even at this time of major public concern about health and healthy weight, Health Canada still invests significantly more money in anti-smoking programmes than it does in fitness and physical activity programmes.

During the twentieth century, sports clearly were linked to political and racial ideologies. During the 1936 Olympic Games in Berlin, Hitler and the Nazi Party used the games to promote their ideas about the superiority of the "Nordic race." This historic photo shows a German official giving the Nazi salute and Jesse Owens, the African American sprinter who won four gold medals during the games, giving the U.S. salute. The success of Owens had challenged Hitler's ideas about Nordic—that is, white—supremacy in sports. [USOC Archives]

new programmes for people with a disability, and the recognition and acceptance of lesbian and gay athletes. Each of those struggles has its own history, and those of us who choose to be actively involved in creating future histories will shape them.

SUMMARY

CAN WE USE HISTORY TO UNDERSTAND SPORTS TODAY?

Our selective look at different times and places shows that physical games and sports are integrally related to social contexts in which they exist. As social life changes and power shifts in any society, the meaning, purpose, and organization of games and sports also change.

In ancient Greece, games and contests were grounded in mythology and religious beliefs. They focused on the interests of able-bodied young men from wealthy segments of society. As the outcomes of organized games took on political and social implications beyond the events, athletes were recruited from the lower classes and paid to participate. The existence of professional athletes, violence, and an emphasis on victory shows us a side of sports in ancient

Greece that contradicts many popular beliefs. It also demonstrates that sports may not represent the interests of everyone in a society.

Roman contests and games emphasized mass entertainment. They were designed to celebrate and preserve the power of political leaders and to pacify masses of unemployed and underemployed workers in Roman cities and towns. Many athletes in Roman events were slaves or "troublemakers" coerced into jeopardizing their lives in battle with one another or with wild animals. These spectacles faded with the demise of the Roman Empire. Critically assessing the contests and games of this period makes us more aware of the interests that powerful people may have in promoting large sport events.

Folk games and tournaments in medieval times clearly reflected and reproduced gender and social class differences in European cultures. The peasants played local versions of folk games in connection with seasonal events in village life. The knights and nobles engaged in tournaments and jousts. Other members of the upper classes often used their resources to develop games and sport activities to occupy their leisure time. Studying the history of sports during this time period shows that gender and class issues should not be ignored as we analyze sports and sport experiences today.

Patterns from the medieval period continued through the Renaissance in parts of Europe, although the Protestant Reformation generated negative attitudes about any activities that interfered with work and religious worship. Peasants were affected most by these attitudes because they did not have the resources to resist the restrictive controls imposed by government officials inspired by Calvinist or Puritan orientations. The games and sports of the wealthy generally occurred in the safe confines of their private grounds, so they could avoid outside control. The Enlightenment was associated with increased political rights and freedom to engage in diversionary games and physical activities.

Studying these historical periods shows us the importance of cultural ideology and government policies when it comes to who plays sports under what conditions.

During the early days of the Industrial Revolution, the demands of work and the absence of spaces for play generally limited sport involvement to the wealthy and to people in rural areas. This pattern began to change in Canada from the mid-1800s to the early 1900s, when the combined influence of labour unions, progressive legislation, and economic expansion led to the creation of new ideas about the consequences of sport participation and new opportunities for involvement. However, opportunities for involvement were shaped primarily by gender ideology and the needs of an economy emphasizing mass production and consumption. It was in this context that people developed organized competitive sports. Studying this period shows us that the origins of today's sports are tied closely to complex social, political, and economic factors.

Sports history since 1920 involves continuing struggles over (1) the meaning, purpose, and organization of sports, (2) who participates in sports under what conditions, and (3) who sponsors sports and why. These struggles occur in connection with major historical events, trends, and patterns. In most cases, powerful economic and political interests have prevailed in these struggles but, in a few cases, people motivated by idealistic visions of what sports could and should be like have prevailed. The visions of idealists have sometimes become reality, but struggles continue while there are competing interests involved. As we study current issues and controversies in sports, our awareness of past struggles is useful.

Visit *Sports in Society*'s Online Learning Centre at <u>www.mcgrawhill.ca/olc/coakley</u> for additional information, website resources, and study tools for this chapter.

[Anne-Marie Webber/Taxi/Getty Images]

Sports and Socialization

Who plays and what happens to them?

Athletics taught me so much about life that it's
hard to know where to begin.

—Elaine Tanner, Canadian swimmer (1979)

I love the self-discovery. Life off ice is so
complicated, its outcomes smudged, its
motivations rationalized and finessed, the picture
you get of yourself so unclear. On the ice, you
see your elemental self, whether you like it or
not—do you try hard? do you quit? are you fair?
are you selfish? do you give? are you willing to
take risks? do you care too much or too little? do
you fit in with a team on the ice, and off?

**—Ken Dryden, hockey player, author, *Home
Game* (1989)**

Socialization is a popular topic in discussions about sports. We deal with socialization issues whenever we discuss the following questions:

- Why are some people fanatically interested in playing and/or watching sports, while others do not seem to care about sports?
- How and why do some people see themselves as athletes and dedicate themselves to playing sports?
- When and why do people stop playing competitive sports, and what happens to them when they do?
- What impact do sports and sport participation have on people's lives?

Many of us in the sociology of sport have carried out research to find answers to one or more of these questions. The search for answers has taken us in different directions, depending on the theories that we use to guide our thinking about sports and sport participation. The influence of theoretical perspectives is discussed in the first section of this chapter. Then we consider three topics that are central to most discussions of sports and socialization:

1. The process of becoming involved and staying involved in sports
2. The process of changing or ending sport participation
3. The impact of being involved in sports.

As these topics are discussed, we provide tentative answers to the socialization questions that have been asked by researchers in the sociology of sport. As you read the chapter, you will see that most of the answers are incomplete and many others are so complex that discussions about them will carry over into other chapters.

The chapter closes with information about new approaches to socialization. These approaches are based on critical, feminist, and interactionist theories that emphasize socialization as a community and cultural process as well as an individual and personal process.

WHAT IS SOCIALIZATION?

Socialization is a *process of learning and social development, which occurs as we interact with one another and become acquainted with the social world in which we live.* It involves the formation of ideas about who we are and what is important in our lives. We are *not* simply passive learners in the socialization process. We actively participate in our own socialization as we influence those who influence us. We actively interpret what we see and hear, and we accept, resist, or revise the messages we receive about who we are, about the world, and about our connection with the world. Therefore, socialization is *not* a one-way process of social influence through which we are moulded and shaped. Instead, it is an interactive process through which we actively connect with others, synthesize information, and *make decisions* that shape our lives and the social world around us.

This definition of *socialization*, which we use to guide our research, is based on a combination of *critical* and *interactionist* theories. Therefore, not all sociologists would agree with it. Those using functionalist or conflict theory, for example, would define *socialization* in slightly different terms. Their definitions have an impact on how they do research and the questions they ask about sports and socialization.

A Functionalist Approach to Socialization

Scholars using *functionalist theory* to guide research view socialization as a process through which we learn what we must know to fit into society and contribute to its operation. This approach to socialization is based on an *internalization model* (see Coakley, 1993, 2007). In other words, as we grow up in our families, attend school, interact with peers, and receive images and messages from the media, we learn the rules we should follow and the roles we should play in society.

When researchers use an internalization model to guide their studies, they focus on four things: (1) the characteristics of those being socialized, (2) the people who *do* the socializing, (3) the contexts in which socialization occurs, and (4) the specific *outcomes,* or results, of socialization. In studies of sports and socialization, researchers focus on athletes as the people being socialized and on the *agents of socialization* who exert influence on athletes. Agents, or "socializers," generally include fathers, mothers, brothers, sisters, teachers, coaches, peers, and people used as role models. The most central and influential socializers are described as **significant others** a term used to describe *the most central and influential socializers.* In some cases, contexts in which socialization occurs, such as the family, education, and the media, are also studied in connection with sport participation. The socialization outcomes, or results, that are studied include the personal attitudes, values, and skills, and behaviour patterns, especially those that are seen as contributing to the operation of society as a social system.

Research guided by functionalist theory has focused on who influences the sport participation patterns of children. Fathers and other family members have usually been identified as *significant others* who influence when, how, and where children will play sports.

Those who use a functionalist approach also study what *causes* people to participate in sports and how participation influences them and the patterns of their lives. This research generally uses surveys to collect data. Researchers have carried out literally hundreds of studies by sending questionnaires to people, especially high school students. Their analyses compare those who do and do not play organized sports, and their goal is to discover the socialization experiences that lead to and result from sport participation (see figure 4.1).

Until recently, this research has provided us with inconsistent and contradictory findings about why people play sports and what happens to them when they do. However, more research using large data sets collected through well-funded regional

FIGURE 4.1   "I know this is starting early, but I can't let him get too far behind the other kids if he's ever going to make a team in high school."

and national studies, has begun to provide more consistent and detailed analyses of the complex connections between sport participation and the processes of socialization (Curtis, et al., 1999, 2003; Guest and Schneider, 2003; Loveless, 2002; Marsh & Kleitman, 2003; Miller, et al., 1999; President's Council on Physical Fitness and Sports, 1997; Sabo, et al., 1998, 2005; Spreitzer, 1995; Stempel, 2006; Tracy and Erkut, 2002; Videon, 2002). These studies provide us with many snapshots rather than videos of socialization as it occurs over the course of people's lives. But multiple snapshots can be used to identify general patterns and guide further research that is designed to study the specific details of socialization processes. These patterns are discussed in the pages of this chapter.

A Conflict Theory Approach to Socialization

Scholars using conflict theory also view socialization in terms of an internalization model. However, they focus primarily on the ways that economic factors influence sport participation and the consequences of sport participation on the economic organization of society. For example, studies based on conflict theory investigate questions such as these: (1) Does participation in organized competitive sports reproduce capitalist economies by creating conservative, militaristic, sexist, and racist orientations among players and spectators? (2) Are people from low-income and working-class backgrounds systematically denied opportunities to play sports on their own terms and in their own ways? (3) Are athletes, especially those from poor, minority backgrounds, victims of a profit-driven, win-at-all-cost sport system in which they have no rights? (4) Do people with money and power control the conditions of sport participation and exploit others to make money and maintain their own interests?

Although there are fewer studies based on conflict theory than functionalist theory, they suggest that rigidly structured programmes controlled by autocratic, military-style coaches attract and produce people who are politically conservative and supportive of the status quo. But the samples in these studies have been so small that research findings provide only fuzzy snapshots telling us little about the details of sport-related socialization. In general terms they do show us that economic resources are related to the organization of sports and the dynamics of sport participation, and that the people who control economic resources often use them to promote their own interests.

Unfortunately, the large data sets that enable scholars to examine questions based on functionalist approaches seldom include information about the ways that economic resources and power influence who does and does not play sports and what happens to them when they do play. Fortunately, new approaches to socialization help us to understand some of these issues.

New Approaches to Socialization

Sociologists today are unlikely to view socialization as a process through which culture is passively internalized as it is transmitted from one generation to the next. Instead of using an internalization model they prefer an **interactionist model** *based on the idea that socialization involves participatory learning through which people are involved in larger processes of cultural production, reproduction, and change.* Researchers who use an interactionist model generally use qualitative research methods. Instead of using questionnaires to obtain statistical data from large numbers of people, they use in-depth interviews and field observations. Their goal is to obtain detailed descriptions of sport experiences as they occur in people's lives. They seek information about the processes through which people make decisions about their sport participation and give meanings to their sport experiences. Finally, they seek to connect those decisions and meanings with the larger cultural context in which sports and sport participation exist. This approach, they argue, captures the complexity of processes related to becoming and staying involved in sports, changing or ending sport participation, and incorporating sports into people's lives. The rest of this chapter draws on both old and new approaches in an effort to outline what we know about sports and socialization today.

BECOMING INVOLVED AND STAYING INVOLVED IN SPORTS

Research based on functionalist theory indicates that sport participation is related to three factors: (1) a person's abilities, characteristics, and resources; (2) the influence of significant others, including parents, siblings, teachers, peers, and role models; and (3) the availability of opportunities to play sports in ways that are personally satisfying. These are the snapshots that we have of *socialization into sports.* However, a fuller description of the ongoing process of becoming and staying involved in sports emerges when we obtain detailed stories from people about their sport participation. These stories are more like videos than snapshots.

Studies using in-depth interviews, fieldwork, participant observations, and strategic conversations indicate that sport participation is connected with multiple and diverse processes that make up people's lives, and it occurs as people make decisions about and give meaning to sports. In other words, people continually make decisions about sport participation; they do not make decisions once and for all time. As social conditions change, so do sport-related decisions and meanings. Furthermore, as people stay involved in sports, their reasons for participating on one day may be different from the reasons for participating on the next day. When there is no reason, they may discontinue or change their sport participation.

To understand how and why people become and stay involved in sports, it is helpful to review research on these issues. The following studies provide three sociological videos of the decision-making processes related to playing sports.

Example 1: The Process of Becoming a High-Performance Athlete

Chris Stevenson, from the University of New Brunswick, is interested in how people become athletes. Using interactionist theory to guide his research, he interviewed and collected stories from high-performance athletes about how they were introduced to their sports and became committed to sport participation. As he analyzed the stories, he noticed that they sounded much like descriptions of careers. In other words, they had identifiable beginnings, followed by a process of development, and ultimately an end. Stevenson felt that he could understand these careers in terms of the decisions that people made about sport participation and about how those decisions were related to important issues and relationships in their lives over time.

In one of his studies, Stevenson (1999) interviewed twenty-nine Canadian and British international athletes. At first he was struck by the diversity of the stories the athletes told him. But

then he detected two processes that were common in nearly all the stories. First, there was a process of *introduction and involvement*, during which young people received support as they tried certain sports. His interviewees talked about being introduced to sports bit-by-bit over time through important relationships in their lives. Gradually, they chose to specialize in a particular sport based on an evaluation of their

Participation in sports is usually sponsored through important social relationships. This boy's participation in skiing is likely to be influenced by both his mother and father, agents of socialization and significant others in his life. However, continued participation requires a combination of developing a commitment to the sport, receiving material and emotional support, and establishing social relationships and an identity related to the sport. [Photomondo/Taxi/Getty Images]

potential for success and their sense of being personally connected with the people associated with the sport. Second, there was a process of *developing a commitment* to sport participation. This process occurred as the athletes formed a web of personal relationships connected with their participation and gradually established personal reputations and identities as athletes in their sports. Their relationships and identities figured prominently in how they set priorities and made decisions about sport participation. Staying involved in their sport depended on active and thoughtful efforts to develop identities as athletes. This occurred as people who were important in their lives recognized and defined them as athletes. Over time, this social recognition led them to become more deeply committed to their sports and their lives as athletes.

Stevenson found that these processes did *not* occur automatically. The young people themselves helped them happen. Becoming and staying involved in sports was a complex process. The young people realized that they could not take for granted the social support they received for playing sports and being athletes. They knew that the resources needed for participation could disappear and that changes in other parts of their lives could force them to alter the importance of sport participation. Therefore, they made decisions to stay involved in sports day after day, and as they stayed involved, they impressed and influenced those who supported and influenced them.

Stevenson's research shows that the socialization process is *interactive* and that each of us participates in our own socialization as we make decisions and become committed to particular identities.

Example 2: The Process of Being Accepted as an Athlete

Peter Donnelly, from the University of Toronto, and Kevin Young, from the University of Calgary, are sociologists who have studied sports as social worlds, or subcultures in which people develop ways of doing things and relating to one another. In their research, they paid special attention to how people become accepted members of those subcultures. Consequently, they have taken a closer look at some of the process studied by Stevenson (Donnelly and Young, 1999).

On the basis of data that Donnelly collected from rock climbers in the U.S. and U.K., and that Young collected from rugby players in Canada, they concluded that playing sports occurs in connection with complex processes of identity formation. They explain that entering and becoming an athlete in a particular sport subculture occurs through a four-phase process:

1. Acquiring knowledge about the sport
2. Associating with people involved in the sport
3. Learning how those people think about their sport and what they do and expect from each other
4. Becoming recognized and fully accepted into the sport group as a fellow athlete

These details of sport socialization indicate that becoming involved in a sport depends on learning to "talk the talk and walk the walk," so that one is identified and accepted as an athlete by others who are athletes. This process of identification and acceptance does not happen once and for all time; it is continuous. When we lose touch and are no longer able to talk the talk and walk the walk, acceptance wanes, our identities become difficult to maintain, and overall support for our participation becomes weak. We are not athletes forever.

To understand what Donnelly and Young found in their study, just observe a sport group such as skateboarders, in-line skaters, snowboarders, beach volleyball players, or basketball players. Each group has its own vocabulary and its own way of referring to its members and what they do. The terms they use are not found in dictionaries. They also have unique ways of thinking about and doing their sports, and they have special understandings of what they can expect from others in their groups. New participants in these sports may be tested and "pushed" by the "veterans" before being accepted and defined as true skaters, riders, volleyball players, or ballers. Vocabularies may change over time, but this process of becoming accepted and gaining support for participation exists in all sports. Many people have discovered that, if they do not establish social connections and acceptance in a sport, their sport participation may be difficult to maintain over time. Becoming involved in sports clearly is part of a complex, *interactive* socialization and identity formation process.

Example 3: To Participate or Not to Participate

Anita White is a sport sociologist and former director of sport development at Sport England. Before she began working at Sport England, White and Jay Coakley carried out a study of sport participation among British adolescents in a working-class area east of London (Coakley and White, 1999). Their goal was to provide coaches and programme organizers with information about why some young people participated in government-sponsored sport programmes, while most did not.

In-depth interviews indicated that participation was the result of decisions based on a combination of factors, including the following:

1. Their ideas about how sport participation was related to other interests and goals in their lives
2. Their desires to develop and display competence so that they could gain recognition and respect from others
3. Social support for participation and access to the resources needed for participation (time, transportation, equipment, and money)
4. Memories of past experiences with physical activities and sports
5. Sports-related cultural images and messages that they had in their minds

They found that young people decided to play sports when it helped them extend control over their lives, achieve development and career goals, and present themselves to others as competent. They also found that the young women were less likely than the young men to imagine that sport participation could do these things for them. Therefore, the young women participated in organized sports less often and less seriously.

The young people in the study did not simply respond to the world around them. Instead, they actively thought about how sports might be positively incorporated into their lives and they made decisions based on their conclusions. Their sport participation patterns shifted over time, depending on their access to opportunities, changes in their lives, and changes in their identities. Therefore, socialization into sports was a *continuous, interactive process* grounded in the social and cultural contexts in which the young people lived.

The interviews also indicated that people make decisions to participate in sports for different reasons at different points in their lives. This fits with theories telling us that developmental tasks and challenges change as we move through childhood, adolescence, young adulthood, and adulthood. Therefore, the issues considered by seven-year-olds who make decisions about sport participation are different from the issues considered by fourteen-year-olds, forty-year-olds, or sixty-year-olds (Porterfield, 1999; Stevenson, 2002). Furthermore, when seven-year-olds make decisions about sport participation today, they do so in a different cultural context than the context in which seven-year-olds lived in 1970 or will live in 2020.

Sport participation decisions at all points during the life course and through history also are tied to the perceived cultural importance of sports and the links between playing sports, gaining social acceptance, and achieving personal goals. Therefore studies of socialization into sports must take into account the ways in which sport participation is related to individual development, the organization of social life, and the ideologies that are prevalent in a culture (Ingham et al., 1999).

In summary, these studies provide three videos about becoming involved and staying involved in sports. They show that sport participation is grounded in decision-making processes involving self-reflection, social support, social acceptance, and cultural factors. People do not make decisions about sport participation once and for all time. They make them day after day as they consider how sports are related to their lives. In fact, they sometimes make them moment by moment when coaches are making them run wind sprints and they are sucking air at the starting line! These decisions are mediated by the social and cultural contexts in which the people live. Therefore, the social meanings attached to gender, class, skin colour, ethnicity, age, and physical (dis)abilities influence sport participation decisions and these meanings are influenced by political, economic, social, and cultural forces.

> In gym, when we start basketball or volleyball, most of the girls go to the benches and just talk. All the guys are on the court...That's why I think most of the guys from my school figure the girls can't play sports.
>
> —David, high school student (1996)

CHANGING OR ENDING SPORT PARTICIPATION

Questions about becoming and staying involved in sports often are followed by questions about changing or ending involvement. Much of the research on this latter issue has been guided by "role theories" inspired by functionalist theory, or "alienation theories" inspired by conflict theory (see Coakley, 1993).

Researchers using *functionalist theory* have been concerned with identifying who drops out of sports and what can be done to keep them in sports so that they can learn the positive lessons taught through participation. This was a popular research topic when millions of baby boomers were flooding playgrounds and elementary schools, and parents wanted to know how to control and build character in their children. Research based on functionalist approaches also focuses on how to make sport programmes more efficient in developing skills and preparing young people to move to higher levels of competition. This remains a popular topic among people who have an interest in creating successful athletes and sport teams.

Researchers using *conflict theory* generally focus on the ways that rigidly organized, win-oriented programmes discourage many children from participation. They have hypothesized that these programmes, along with autocratic, command-style coaches, alienate many young athletes and cause them to drop out. Similarly, older athletes drop out because of injuries or alienation caused by years of being exploited. Their studies explore the ways that athletes are victims of exploitation and alienating experiences that damage their bodies and leave them unprepared for life after sport.

Studies grounded in functionalist and conflict theories tell us the following important things:

- When people drop out of particular sports, they do not drop out of all sports forever, nor do they cut all ties with sports; many play different and less competitive sports as they grow older or they move into other sport roles, such as coach, administrator, or sports businessperson.
- Dropping out of sports is usually connected with development changes and transitions in the rest of a person's life (changing schools, graduating, getting a job, getting married, having children, and so on).
- Dropping out of sports is not always the result of victimization or exploitation although injuries and negative experiences can and do influence decisions to change or end participation.

- Problems may occur for those who end long careers in sports, especially those who have no identities apart from sports and lack social and material resources for making transitions into other careers and social settings.

Recent studies, especially those using qualitative research methods and based on critical theory and interactionist models of socialization, have built on these findings and extended our understanding. Following are three examples of these studies.

Example 1: Burnout among Young Athletes

Jay Coakley's work with coaches combined with his interest in identity issues led him to carry out a study of young people who, after being age-group champions, had decided to quit playing their sports (Coakley, 1992). Since people described these young athletes as "burned out," Coakley decided to interview former elite athletes identified by themselves or others as cases of burnout; all were adolescents.

Data from in-depth interviews indicated that burnout during adolescence was grounded in the organization of the high-performance sports. It occurred when young athletes felt they no longer had control over their lives and could not explore, develop, and nurture identities apart from sports. This led to increased stress and decreased fun in their sports. Burnout occurred when stress became so high and fun declined so much that athletes no longer felt that playing their sport was worth their effort.

The data also indicated that stress increased and fun decreased when sport programmes were organized so that successful young athletes felt that they could not accomplish important developmental tasks during adolescence. Coakley concluded that burnout could be prevented only if sport programmes were reorganized so that athletes had more control over their lives. Stress management strategies could be used to delay burnout, but they would not change the underlying organizational and developmental causes of burnout. Overall, the study indicated that ending sport participation during late adolescence sometimes occurs when young people feel that staying in sport prevents them from developing the autonomy and multiple identities that mark people as adults in North American culture.

Example 2: Getting Out of Sports and Getting On with Life

Derek Swain (1999) is a psychologist in Vancouver who joined a number of other researchers (e.g., Coakley, 1983; Curtis and Ennis, 1988) in critiquing the view that retirement from sports was always a traumatic experience. Swain conducted multiple in-depth interviews with ten men who were former professional athletes in Canada (hockey players, jockeys, football players, and racquetball players). All were accomplished athletes in their sports, although none held million-dollar contracts. Swain's research emphasizes the idea that retirement from high-performance sports is often a process that occurs gradually over a long period of time. Thus, retirement is not an *event* but a *process*—starting soon after they became involved in their professional careers for many of the athletes interviewed. These athletes initiated the process when they realized that they could not play forever, and that there was life after sports. They anticipated problems as they ended their careers, but they were often ready for retirement because they had become increasingly tired of training and competition, and concerned about the toll that sport participation was taking on their bodies. They began to seek new careers and plan for the future. They all viewed retirement with mixed feelings, but gradually accepted it as it became a reality, and settled into their new lives after sports. (For another example of the *process* of retirement, see the Koukouris [1994] example on the Online Learning Centre.)

Swain reports that these former athletes did experience a strong sense of loss as their careers ended. On the one hand, they felt alienated and worried about their futures, and it was difficult for them to give up the celebrity status they had as athletes. On the other hand, they appreciated the new opportunities and improved health that came with retirement, and enjoyed the chance to connect in new ways with their families. Overall, the former athletes were ready to move on in their lives, but they also made efforts to stay connected with sports at a recreational level or in supporting roles in sport organizations. This enabled them to retain part of their sport-related identities as they developed additional ones through new relationships and activities.

Swain also found that the athletes' wives, girlfriends, and other family members sometimes had problems adjusting to their loss of celebrity status when the athletes retired. This reminds us that athletes often receive emotional and social support from others during their playing careers and through the retirement process. The experiences of those who provide this support has seldom been acknowledged (McKenzie, 1999).

Example 3: Changing Personal Investments in Sport Careers

Garry Wheeler from the University of Alberta is concerned with the careers of athletes with disabilities and what happens when their playing careers end. Building on a study with Canadian Paralympic athletes (Wheeler et al., 1996), Wheeler and his fellow researchers gathered data through interviews with forty athletes from Israel, the United Kingdom, Canada, and the United States (Wheeler et al., 1999). Data indicated that athletes in each of the countries became deeply involved in playing sports, and often achieved a high level of success in a relatively short time. Through sports they developed a sense of personal competence and established identities as elite athletes.

Withdrawing from active participation and making the transition into the rest of life often presented challenges for these athletes. Retirement

Although people may drop out of sports at one point in the life course, they may return at a later point. [Robert E. Daemmrick/Stone/Getty Images]

often came suddenly and forced them to reinvest time and energy into other spheres of their lives. As they reconnected with family members and friends, returned to college or university, and resumed occupational careers, some individuals experienced emotional problems. However, most stayed connected with sports and sport organizations as coaches, administrators, or recreational athletes. Those few who hoped they might compete again often experienced serious difficulties during the retirement transition, whereas those who accepted the end of their competitive careers had fewer adjustment problems.

In summary, research shows that ending or changing sport participation often involves the same interactive and decision-making processes that occur when becoming and staying involved in sports. Just as people are not simply socialized into sports, neither are they simply socialized out of sports. Changes in participation are grounded in decisions associated with other life events, social relationships, and cultural expectations related to development. This means that theories explaining why people play sports and change their participation over time must take into account identity issues and developmental processes that are part of the social and cultural contexts in which people make decisions about sports in their lives (Dacyshyn, 1999; Drahota

Many factors influence the decisions to drop out of sports or shift their participation from one sport to another. Identity changes, access to resources, and life course issues are involved. As our circumstances change, so do our ideas about ourselves and about sports and sport participation. [CP(Preston Brownschlaigle), *Edmonton Sun*]

and Eitzen, 1998; Swain, 1999). Furthermore, the theories must consider the personal, social, and material resources that athletes have as they make transitions to other relationships, activities, and careers. Some people have problems when they retire from sports, but to understand those problems, we need information about the ways that sport participation has been incorporated into their lives and the resources that can be used as changes occur and challenges are faced. Research suggests that, if sport participation expands a person's identity, experiences, relationships, and resources, changes and retirement transitions will be smooth. Difficulties are most likely to occur when a person has never had the desire or the chance to live outside the culture of high-performance or professional sports (Messner, 1992; Murphy et al., 1996).

BEING INVOLVED IN SPORTS: WHAT HAPPENS?

Beliefs about the consequences of sport participation vary from culture to culture, but the beliefs that playing sports builds character and improves health and well-being are widely accepted in many cultures. These beliefs are used as a basis for encouraging children to play sports, for funding sports programmes in school, building stadiums, promoting teams and leagues, and for sponsoring international events such as the Olympic Games, the Paralympics, and the Special Olympics.

Do Sports Build Character?

For over fifty years, researchers have examined the validity of the belief that "sport builds character." Many of the studies involved comparisons of the traits, attitudes, and behaviours of people who play organized sports with people who do not play. These comparisons usually focused on differences between members of U.S. high school teams and other students who are not on teams. The snapshot comparisons produced inconsistent and confusing findings. This is because there are many different definitions of "character," and researchers have used inconsistent measures of *character* in their studies (Stoll and Beller, 1998). Furthermore, many researchers based their studies on two faulty assumptions (McCormack and Chalip, 1988). First, they mistakenly assume that *all* athletes have the same or similar experiences in *all* organized competitive sports. Secondly, they mistakenly assume that organized sports provide learning experiences that are not available to people in any other activities.

A third characteristic of such studies is the assumptions made by researchers about what are valuable character traits. Characteristics that are likely to lead an individual to be a "team player" and to be obedient were highly valued—especially by coaches who rated individuals in terms of their "coachability." Character traits such as independence, stubbornness, and creativity tend to be less valued if they might lead athletes to question or reject certain practices. In the character building assumptions of some outdoor education courses, "[t]hose individuals who refuse to engage in certain activities in the face of enormous social pressures may actually be showing more courage [and character] than those who comply. But they are never made to feel that way" (Donnelly, 1981, p. 23).

These faulty assumptions cause researchers to overlook the following important points when they study sports and socialization:

> What do kids know about us? They only know that we play sports. They don't know who we are as people. You don't learn the important things about life by watching a person play football.
> —Emmitt Smith, NFL player (1996)

1. Sports offer many *different experiences*, both positive and negative, to participants because sport programmes and teams are organized in vastly different ways. Therefore, we cannot make general statements about the consequences of sport participation. This point is explained in the Reflect on Sports box, pages 92–93.

2. People who choose or are selected to participate in sports may have different traits than those who do not choose or are not selected to participate. Therefore, sport may not *build* character as much as they are organized to *select* people who already have certain character traits that are valued by coaches and compatible with highly organized, competitive activities.

3. The meanings given to sport experiences vary from one athlete to the next, even when they play in the same programmes and on the same teams. Therefore, the lessons that athletes learn and the ways they apply those lessons to their lives vary greatly.

4. The meanings that people give to their sport experiences change over time as they grow older and view themselves and the world in new ways. Therefore, people revise their evaluation of past sport experiences as they develop new ideas and values.

5. Socialization occurs through the social interaction that accompanies sport participation. Therefore, the meaning and importance of playing sports depend on a person's social relationships and the social and cultural contexts in which participation occurs.

6. The socialization that occurs in sports may also occur in other activities. Therefore, people who do not play sports may have the same development experiences as athletes.

Due to these oversights, studies that have compared "athletes" with "nonathletes" produce inconsistent and sometimes misleading evidence about sports and socialization.

Our review of these studies leads us to conclude that sport participation is most likely to have positive socialization consequences for people when it provides the following:

- Opportunities for exploring and developing identities apart from playing sports
- Knowledge-building experiences that go beyond the locker room and the playing field
- New relationships, especially with people who are not connected with sports and do not base their interaction on a person's status or identity as an athlete
- Explicit examples of how lessons learned in sports may be applied to specific situations apart from sports
- Opportunities to develop and display competence in nonsport activities that are observed by other people who can serve as mentors and advocates outside of sports

Research also suggests that when playing sports *constricts* a person's opportunities, experiences, relationships, and general competence apart from sports, it is likely to have negative consequences for overall development. Therefore, we cannot make a general statement that sports build *or* undermine character development. Neither positive nor negative character is automatically developed in sports. This is because sport experiences are defined and incorporated into people's lives in various ways depending on the social and cultural contexts in which they live.

This conclusion *does not mean* that sports and sport participation are irrelevant in people's lives. We know that the discourses, images, and experiences associated with sports are vivid and powerful. Sports do have an impact on our lives and the world around us. However, we cannot separate that impact from the meanings we give to sports and the ways we integrate sport experiences into our lives. Therefore, if we want to know what happens in sports, we must study sport experiences in the social and cultural contexts in which they occur.

This type of research is exciting and provides insights into the complex connections between sports and socialization. Unfortunately, the uncritically accepted belief that "sports build character" has prevented this research from being taken seriously. Additionally, this belief has prevented some people from recognizing that if we want sports to build character we must critically examine sports and determine the types of sport experiences that are sites where positive socialization outcomes are most likely to occur.

Do Sports Improve Health and Physical Well-Being?

If something is said often enough, many people accept it as true. This has certainly been the case with the statement, "sports are healthy activities." Therefore, many people were surprised when a list of healthy physical activities identified in a report by the U.S. Surgeon General (USDHHS, 1996) included only two competitive sports: fifteen to twenty minutes of playing basketball and forty-five minutes of playing volleyball. No other sports were on the list because the surgeon general reviewed research on sport participation and health and determined that the injury risks associated with nearly all competitive sports were so high that participation often created more health costs than benefits (White, 2004; Young, 2004a).

The Sport–Health Connection The relationship between sports, exercise, and health is complex. However, people who list the health benefits of sports when they are really talking about the benefits of regular physical exercise, often ignore this complexity. After reviewing dozens of studies on this topic, sociologist Ivan Waddington (2000a, 2000b, 2007) explains that the healthiest of all

Power and Performance versus Pleasure and Participation
Different Sports, Different Experiences, Different Consequences

Sport experiences are diverse. It is a mistake to assume that all sports are defined in the same way, organized around the same goals and orientations, and played in the same spirit. In North America, for example, there are highly organized competitive sports, informal sports, adventure sports, recreational sports, extreme sports, alternative sports, cooperative sports, folk sports, contact sports, artistic sports, team sports, individual sports, and so on. However, at this time, it seems that the dominant sport form in many societies is organized around a *power and performance model*.

Power and performance sports are highly organized and competitive. Generally, they emphasize the following:

- The use of strength, speed, and power to push human limits and dominate opponents in the quest for victories

- The idea that excellence is proved through competitive success and achieved through dedication, hard work, sacrifices, risking personal well-being, and playing in pain
- The importance of setting records and using technology to control and monitor the body
- Tryouts and selection systems based on physical skills and competitive success
- Hierarchical authority structures in which athletes are subordinate to coaches and coaches are subordinate to owners and administrators
- Defining opponents as enemies to be conquered, especially when they are confronted on "home turf."

These points exaggerate the characteristics of power and performance sports, but our purpose is to show that experiences in such sports are very different from experiences in sports with other characteristics.

Power and performance sports involves the use of strength, speed, and power to dominate opponents in the quest for competitive victories. [CP(Adrian Wyld)]

Pleasure and participation sports may involve competition, but the primary emphasis is on connections between people and on personal expression through participation. [CP(Jeff Stokoe), *Red Deer Advocate*]

Pleasure and participation sports generally emphasize the following:

- Active participation revolving around connections between people, mind and body, and physical activity and the environment
- A spirit of personal expression, enjoyment, growth, good health, and mutual concern among teammates and opponents
- Personal empowerment created by experiencing the body in pleasurable ways
- Inclusive participation based on accommodating differences in physical skills among players
- Democratic decision-making structures characterized by cooperation and sharing power, even in coach–athlete relationships
- An emphasis on competing *with* others and defining opponents as partners who test skills

Again, these points exaggerate the characteristics of pleasure and participation sports, but they show that experiences in these sports would be very different from experiences in power and performance sports.

These two sport forms do *not* encompass all the ways that sports might be defined, organized, and played. Many people play sports that contain elements of both forms and reflect diverse ideas about what is important in physical activities. However, power and performance sports remain dominant today in the sense that they receive the most attention and support.[1] When people play or watch these sports, their socialization experiences are likely to be different from their experiences when playing or watching pleasure and participation sports. Not all sports are the same when it comes to socialization. *What do you think?*

Although the power and performance model has become the standard for defining "real" sports in North American culture, some people have maintained or developed other forms of sports. Some of these are revisions of dominant forms, while others represent alternative or even oppositional sport forms. The sports that are the most oppositional are organized around a *pleasure and participation model*.

---

[1]On the Online Learning Centre (www.mcgrawhill.ca/olc/coakley), you will find a feature suggesting why power and performance sports are dominant today. Also, since one of the distinguishing characteristics between power and performance sports and pleasure and participation sports is the intensity of and meaning attached to competition, you will also find additional information specifically on competition and cooperation.

physical activities are rhythmic, noncompetitive exercises in which individuals control and regulate their own body movements. Health benefits decline when there is a shift from self-controlled exercise to competitive sports; in fact, the health costs of competitive sports are relatively high, due primarily to injuries. This benefit–cost ratio becomes even less favourable when there is a shift from noncontact to contact sports and from mass sports to elite sports in which players train intensely, put their bodies at risk, and play while injured. Overall, Waddington concludes the following:

> The health-related arguments in favor of regular and moderate physical activity are clear, but they are considerably less persuasive in relation to competitive, and especially contact, sport and very much less persuasive in relation to elite, or professional sport. (Waddington, in press)

Other scholars in the sociology of sport have made similar points. For example, Mike Messner (1992) explains that in heavy-contact sports, male athletes routinely turn their bodies into weapons and use them in ways that injure themselves and opponents. According to research by Kevin Young (1993), of the University of Calgary, this orientation has made men's heavy-contact professional sport a hazardous workplace with a higher injury rate than construction sites, oil drilling rigs, or underground mines— the three most dangerous workplaces apart from professional sports. Jennifer Waldron and Vikki Krane (2005) also explain that female athletes often participate in contexts where there are group pressures to engage in risky and unhealthy actions as they seek success and live up to the expectations of coaches and teammates.

Although risks are highest in high-performance sports, they also exist in mass sports where injury rates are regularly higher than in other everyday activities.

> **Athletic participation at the elite level is an egoistic, self-centered activity, as athletes must continue to hone their bodies.**
>
> —George J. Bryjak, sociologist, University of San Diego, 2002

Philip White (2004, p. 312), of McMaster University, cites two emergency room physicians working at a hospital near a Canadian ski resort:

> If the number of injuries seen on the ski hills occurred on a section of highway, that section of highway would be closed down. (Dr. Harry O'Halloran)
>
> If ski injuries were caused by a virus, they would be viewed as a major public health issue. (Dr. John McCall)

Researchers in England found that when they compared the health benefits and costs of exercise and sports, the health benefits outweighed costs for people forty-five years old and over. However, the costs outweighed benefits for people fifteen to forty-four years old. In financial terms, this meant that every young adult who regularly participated in exercise and sports "created" $45 per year of costs more than if they had not participated regularly (Nichol et al., 1993). In other words, the "disease prevention benefits" were lower than the medical costs of treating exercise and sport-related injuries in younger adults.

These findings about benefits and costs do not consider the difficult-to-measure social and psychological benefits of being active and having "good workouts" in competitive sports. But they clearly indicate that we cannot say that "sports improve health and physical well-being" without qualifying what we mean. In fact, pointing out that the more you exercise the more likely you are to be injured, Jones, et al. note that "the strongest and most consistent association exists between total amounts of exercise and higher risks of injury" (1994, pp. 202–203). White's (2004) review of "The costs of injury from sport, exercise and physical activity," points out that current policies aimed at increasing the number of people who engage in physical activity, and the amount of physical activity, are based "on the relatively untested assumption that the benefits of participation in physical activity out-weigh the costs" (p. 310).

The Sport–Obesity Connection Obesity is the most publicized health issue today, and nearly every discussion of this issue ends with the conclusion that healthy nutri-tion and exercise are the best way to avoid unhealthy weight gains. This is of course true, for the most part, and research consistently supports the value of exercise in controlling body weight.

But, can we say that as sports become increasingly popular in society, obesity rates go down? The data suggest otherwise: Obesity rates have increased at the same time and in the same cultures that competitive sports, especially those organized around the power and performance model, have become increasingly popular. This does not mean that playing sports causes obesity, but it does mean that the popular-ity of sports in a society does not inspire more than a few people to embrace forms of exercise that enable them to avoid gaining weight.

Like the connection between sports and health, the connection between sports and weight is complex.[1] Some sports emphasize extreme forms of weight control; wrestling and gymnas-tics are prime examples of this. Other sports em-phasize weight gain for some or all the athletes involved. For example, many football players are encouraged to gain weight to the point that over

> Neglecting ... rules of health, [athletes] spend their lives like pigs—over-exercising, over-eating and over-sleeping .... Athletes rarely live to old age, and if they do, they are crippled by diease.
>
> —Galen, Greek physician, A.D. 180

half of the nearly 2,200 NFL players during the 2003–2004 season were classified as obese, and one-half of the obese players were in the severely obese range on the BMI-body mass index (Harp and Hecht, 2005). Although the BMI is probably not a good measure to use when studying the relationship between weight and health, the way that it is used in this study suggests that NFL play-ers are not good athletes to use if one is arguing that playing sports is a way to control weight. Expec-tations in football now demand excessive eating and/or taking nu-tritional supplements to gain size. In 1988 there were only 17 NFL players over 136 kilograms (300 lbs.), but in 2005 there were over 350, with some close to 181 kilo-grams (400 lbs.), and they claimed to have gained weight by overeat-ing. This takes a serious toll on life expectancy as well as overall health (Briggs, 2002).

How Do Sports Affect Our Lives?

Sports and sport participation do have an impact on people's lives. We are learning more about this impact through three types of studies based on a combination of critical, feminist, and inter-actionist theories:

1. Studies of sport experiences as explained through the voices of sport participants
2. Studies of social worlds, or subcultures, that are created and maintained in connection with particular sports
3. Studies of sports as sites, or "social locations," where dominant ideas and ideologies are expressed and sometimes challenged and changed

Taken together, these studies have helped many of us who are concerned with sports in society to rethink socialization issues. Now we view sports as *sites for socialization experiences*, rather than as *causes*

---

[1]Australian physical educators Michael Gard and Jan Wright (2005) have raised serious questions about the social basis of the so-called "obesity epidemic" in their recent book. Heather-jane Robertson (2004), an Ottawa researcher, points out that it is not surprising that fast- and junk-food companies have been quick to blame inactivity for rising obesity levels among children, rather than an unhealthy diet.

of specific socialization outcomes. This is an important distinction. It highlights two things. First, sports are social locations rich in their potential for providing memorable and meaningful personal, social, and cultural experiences. Second, sports *by themselves do not cause particular changes in the character traits, attitudes, and actions of athletes or spectators.* Therefore, when positive or negative socialization outcomes occur in connection with sports, we do not simply say that they were caused by sports; instead, we view sports as sites for influential experiences and then search for and explain the specific social processes through which particular socialization outcomes occur.

The following summaries of selected studies illustrates how this approach to socialization helps us to understand what happens in sports, and how sports are connected with social issues and forces in society.

Real-Life Experiences: Sport Stories from Athletes

The following examples provide three socialization videos. They illustrate what happens in sports from the perspectives of the participants themselves, and they show us how people give meaning to sport experiences and integrate them into their lives on their own terms.

Example 1: The Moral Lessons of Sports Chris Stevenson, at the University of New Brunswick, spent a number of years conducting in-depth interviews with Christian athletes in various settings—current and former professional and university athletes who are members of Athletes in Action in western Canada (Stevenson, 1991, 1997), and members of a church-sponsored hockey league in New Brunswick (Dunn and Stevenson, 1998). These individuals had been socialized as both Christians and athletes, and Stevenson was interested in how they resolved any conflicts that may exist between their participation in **power and performance sports** and their Christian beliefs and values. (Hoffman

[1992, 1999] has argued convincingly that such conflicts exist.) Dilemmas such as these, described as *role conflict* in interactionist theory, are important because the ways humans attempt to resolve them provide insights into human behaviour and the processes of socialization.

The resolutions took various forms. Players in the church-sponsored hockey league adopted many aspects of a **pleasure and participation** approach to sports in an attempt to play hockey in a way that reflected their Christian values:

- There was a stated commitment in the league to fair play.
- The players agreed to ban body contact, fights, swearing on the ice, and beer in the locker room.
- There was public prayer before each game.
- There were no official league standings, although scores were kept in games.

The players were not always successful in the attempt—especially when they became caught up in the action—but, in general, they managed to maintain their values in sport.

The Athletes in Action resolved their *role conflict* in three distinct ways:

- One response was to completely *segregate* the two roles: when you are in a sporting context, you are only an athlete, with athletes' values; when you are in other settings, you are a Christian.
- The majority were *selective* in the way they accommodated the two roles, giving preference to the athlete role in athletic settings, but maintaining some of their religious values to the extent that they were able.
- The smallest group remained *committed* to their Christian values even in the sports setting, although in practice they admitted to some aspects of *selectivity*.

Stevenson's studies highlight the strong influence of power and performance sports, and the way that they oblige athletes to find ways to accommodate and resolve their religious beliefs and value systems.[2]

Example 2: Lessons in the Locker Room Sociologist Nancy Theberge (1999, 2000b) spent two years studying an elite women's ice hockey team in Ontario. As she observed and interviewed team members, she noted that their experiences and orientations were related to the fact that men controlled the team, the league, and the sport itself. Within this overall sport structure, the women developed a professional approach to participation. They focused on hockey and were serious about being successful on the ice. In the process, they developed close connections with each other. The team became a community with its own dynamics and internal organization. Within this constructed community, the athletes learned things about hockey, themselves, and teammates. The meanings that the players gave to their hockey experiences and the ways they integrated them into their lives emerged as they interacted on and off the ice.

The locker room was a key place for the interaction through which the team members bonded with each other and gave meanings to their experiences. The emotional climate of the locker room, especially *after* a practice or game, encouraged talk that focused on the athletes as people and their experience apart from hockey. This talk gave shape and meaning to what they did on the ice. It also served as a means for expressing feelings and thoughts about men, sexuality (male partners and female partners), and families. The women talked and joked about men but did not degrade or reduce them to body parts in their comments. They made references to sex and sexuality in their conversations, but the substance of these references inferred inclusiveness rather than hostility or stereotypes. This was

very different from what has reportedly occurred in many men's locker rooms where women have been routinely derogated and objectified, and homosexuality has been vilified if it has been discussed at all (Curry, 1993).

Theberge's study shows us that playing sports is a social as well as a physical experience. Hockey was a site for experiences, but it was *through social relationships* that those experiences were given meaning and incorporated into the women's lives. Theberge focused on relationships between the athletes, but also important were their relationships with coaches, managers, trainers, friends, family members, sport reporters, and even fans. If we want to know what happens in sports, we must understand what happens in all those relationships. It is through them that athletes are socialized.

Example 3: Stories of Gay Male Athletes The meanings given to sport experiences emerge in connection with social relationships. Meanings vary from one person to another because social relationships are influenced by social definitions given to age, gender, social class, ethnicity, skin colour, (dis)abilities, and sexuality. Dan Woog (1998) reinforces this point in his book about gay male athletes in the United States. Using data collected in interviews, Woog tells twenty-eight stories about athletes, coaches, referees, administrators, and others in sports.

The stories indicate that gay men are especially cautious about coming out in sports. Successfully combining a gay identity with an athlete identity was a challenging process for nearly all the interviewees. Woog observed that the social contexts and relationships associated with individual sports, such as running and swimming, generally were more gay-friendly than team sports, although a cosmopolitan sport such as soccer provided a more gay friendly context than "a mechanized, play-by-rote game like football." Being out was liberating for most of the gay men, but it was also dangerous for some of them. These men cared deeply about sports, and they feared that being out could lead them to be

---

[2]On the Online Learning Centre, you will find Coakley's full chapter on "Sports and Religion." It includes a figure outlining a model of conflict, doubt, and resolution that demonstrates the conflict between Christian beliefs and power and performance sports.

excluded from sport teams and programmes. Positive experiences for the gay athletes were enhanced when there were organizations that supported them on and off the field, when there was overt support from family and friends, and when someone in their sport, such as a teammate or coach, served as their advocate and showed others that sexuality should not undermine acceptance and friendship.

Brian Pronger's (1990a, 1990b) interviews with gay male athletes in Canada produced some different results. While the primary concern of U.S. athletes seems to be coming out, the Canadian athletes were also likely to be struck by the irony of "passing" as a heterosexual athlete when naked in a locker room with other males. While the athletes interviewed by Pronger have the same concerns about coming out, and recognize the potential danger of passing, they are also conscious of the humour of the situation. Being a gay male athlete on a heterosexual team, or in a social world of sports in which "compulsory heterosexuality" appears to be the norm, represents another situation where *role conflict* may occur. As with the Christian athletes noted previously, gay athletes may employ different strategies to resolve the conflict. For those interviewed by Woog, the ideal strategy seems to be coming out, although most gay athletes have not chosen this route. Pronger's interviewees seem to have opted to keep the two roles separate, while also finding humour in the assumption of heterosexuality made by heterosexual teammates. (See Fusco [1995] for some stories of lesbian athletes in Canada.)

Despite similarities between the experiences of gay men and straight men in sports, the meanings given to those experiences and how they are integrated into people's lives differ because of how *heterosexuality* and *homosexuality* are defined by many people. Those definitions influence the meanings and impact of sport experiences; as those definitions change, so will the meanings given to the experiences that people have in sports (see also Anderson, 2000, 2002, 2004).

Social Worlds: Living in Sports

Although sociologists study sports mostly as parts of the societies and cultures in which they are played and watched, some studies focus on sports as **social worlds**, a term used in interactionist theory to refer to *a way of life and an associated mindset that revolve around a particular set of activities and encompass all the people and relationships connected with the activities.* These studies are based on the assumption that we cannot understand who athletes are, what they do, and how sports influence their lives unless we view them in the context of the social world in which they give meaning to sport experiences. Unless we know about these contexts, we have difficulty making sense of sport experiences and their impact on socialization. This is especially the case when we study people whose lives revolve completely around a particular sport, i.e., when the social world of their sport is their entire world.

Studies of social worlds that are created in connection with specific sports provide useful information about socialization processes and experiences. Following are three examples.

Example 1: Learning to Be a Pro Sociologist Michael Robidoux, at the University of Ottawa, spent a season travelling with and studying an American Hockey League (AHL) team. The AHL is now the primary farm system for NHL teams, and the majority of the professional players in the AHL aspire to play in the NHL; only a few actually do. Robidoux (2001) documented the daily lives of the players and the team: practices, games, initiation ceremonies for rookies, the training room, and travel. He was struck by three significant, and interconnected, features of working life at this level of professional sports as these players—mainly from the Canadian junior system, but also from U.S. universities and Europe—learned to be pros.

The first is what Robidoux terms "homogenized masculinity." Rookie players must endure an initiation ceremony that, if successful, permits them to be a part of the team as a professional player. But a second, and more implicit, part of the process is that players must adopt a very limited view of what it is to be a man. While the job itself, particularly given the style of play that is expected in the AHL, involves adopting a physically dominant style of masculinity, that demand is repeated also for off-ice behaviour. Adopting that style is rewarded with acceptance by established players and management; but it means that players must abandon other aspects of their identity and their personal development.

Once the players have accepted this limited view of themselves as human beings, they must face the second significant feature of life—becoming a "commodity." This is a relatively standard critique of professional sports—many players are highly rewarded, but they are bought and sold (drafted and traded) just like commodities. However, this notion takes on much greater significance in the farm system for the NHL: "[t]he players are literally cultivated on the farm; only those with suitable qualities are 'picked' to be used in the NHL market. The cultivation period, moreover, is limited, and those who do not develop sufficiently are eventually replaced with new 'stock'" (p. 190).

The third feature is the players' powerlessness in the face of a totally controlling, continually demanding management. The players are living out their dream, and the dream of many Canadian boys—they are professional hockey players, about as close as you can get to the NHL. They are totally committed (on an average salary of about US$55,000 a year), and their commitment is easy to exploit. Robidoux (p. 193) lists the price that players pay for such commitment:

- They deprive themselves of occupational and other experiences outside of hockey, limiting their employment opportunities when their careers end.
- They deprive their families of their presence, and themselves of family support.

- They endure injuries on a regular basis, and often suffer from more long-term disability as a consequence of their injuries.
- Their education is limited, with many not having completed high school.
- They have difficulties in finding meaningful relationships outside hockey.

Robidoux's study takes us into the heart of professional sports, where players are attempting to live out their dreams. But they cannot even point to the million-dollar salaries as justification for the costs incurred.

Example 2: Realizing Image Isn't Everything Anthropologist Alan Klein studied the social world of competitive bodybuilding for seven years. In his book *Little Big Men* (1993), he explains that much of the lives of the bodybuilders revolved around issues of gender and sexuality. The bodybuilders, both male and female, learned to project public images of power and strength although privately they experienced serious doubts about their identities and self-worth. The social world of bodybuilding seemed to foster a desperate need for attention and approval from others, especially other bodybuilders. Ideas about masculinity within the social world of bodybuilding were so narrow and one-dimensional that the male bodybuilders developed homophobic attitudes and went to great lengths to assert their heterosexuality in public. Also, the focus on body size and hardness created such insecurities that the men learned to present and even define themselves in terms of exaggerated caricatures of masculinity—like comic-book depictions of manly men. Overall, bodybuilding was a site for powerful socialization experiences in their lives. However, due to gender relations in the culture at large, these experiences took on different meanings for the women bodybuilders than they did for the men (see the Reflect on Sports box, "Female Bodybuilders," on the OLC at www.mcgrawhill.ca/olc/coakley).

Example 3: Working in the LPGA Two sociologists carried out studies—almost twenty years apart—of the golfers on the LPGA tour. Nancy Theberge (1977, 1981), at the University of Waterloo, conducted observations, interviews, and surveys in the mid-1970s, and was struck by the *structured uncertainty* faced by women golfers as a result of their work, especially on a tour which was struggling for recognition, and on which the prizes were significantly less than those available today. Their work routines were characterized by "extreme variability and indeterminacy": financial (since most golfers could not win enough to support their careers, they were obliged to find other sources of income); courses and competition (every week, golfers have to contend with new courses and must learn course management); relationships (with other golfers, caddies, coaches, and spectators); and lifestyle (constant travel, living in hotels, etc.). Theberge cites golfer Amy Alcott: "In professional golf, you have to stay on top every week, adjust to travel, to practice schedules; you learn to deal with people, with weather. It's all a big mystery at first, but if you want to remain on tour, you learn to cope." Theberge (1981) documents the ways in which professional golfers learned to cope with this *structured uncertainty* as they were socialized into the culture of the LPGA tour. The surviving golfers learned to resolve the uncertainty by attempting in every way possible to standardize their work situation. They establish routines, attempt to develop a stable source of income, develop course management skills, and standardize as much as possible their relationships with those with whom they must interact.

Todd Crosset (1995) focuses more specifically on gender relations in the LPGA. He spent fourteen months travelling and living in his pickup truck while studying the social world of women's professional golf. Crosset found that being on the LPGA tour created and, in fact, required a mindset focused on using physical competence as a basis for evaluating self and other golfers.

He described this mindset as "an ethic of prowess," and explained that it existed partly because the women wanted to neutralize the potentially negative effects that dominant ideas about gender could have if they entered the social world of women's professional golf. One golfer he interviewed said that much of what she did in her life was a response to the notion that "*athlete* is almost a masculine noun" in this society. The impact of being a pro golfer was summarized by one woman, who said, "We are different than the typical married lady with a house full of kids in what we think and do." Both studies emphasize that we can understand the meaning of this statement only in the context of the social world of the LPGA and that we can understand the social world of the LPGA only in the context of gender relations in North American culture at the turn of the twenty-first century.

Ideology: Sports as Sites for Struggling Over How We Think and What We Do

Socialization research has focused mostly on what occurs in the lives of individuals or small groups. However, as researchers have combined critical theories with cultural studies and poststructuralism,[3] they have carried out creative

---

[3]Poststructuralism is a theoretical and methodological perspective based on the assumption that culture today revolves around language and rapidly changing media representations. Functionalists and conflict theorists consider material production and empirical reality to be the foundation of culture and society; poststructuralists focus on language and media representations because they assume that social life in today's postmodern culture is constantly negotiated, constructed, challenged, and changed through language and images that represent people, ideas, and things. Research carried out by poststructuralists often deals with the media and focuses on how images, identities, symbols, and meanings are fabricated through media representations that constitute the contexts of our lives. Poststructuralists often engage in scholarly work that is intended to disrupt meanings and representations that oppress some people and privilege others.

Sports in many cultures are no longer seen as exclusively masculine activities. However, traditional gender definitions and associated clothing may still keep some girls out of the action. [Jay Coakley]

studies of *socialization as a community and cultural process*. Their research goes beyond looking at the experiences and characteristics of athletes. Instead, it focuses on sports as sites where people in society collectively create and learn "stories," which they use to give meaning and make sense of the world and their lives. The stories that revolve around sports and athletes have their own vocabularies and images; their meanings shift, depending on who tells and hears them, and they often identify important cultural issues in everyday life. Researchers identify these stories and study how they fit into the culture and how people use them in connection with what they think and do.

Researchers also are concerned with whose stories about sports become dominant in the culture, because so many stories could be told about sports. These stories are culturally important because they identify what is natural, normal, and legitimate and therefore give priority to ideas and orientations that privilege some people more than others, some interests more than others. For example, the stories and vocabulary frequently associated with sports revolve around heroic figures who are big, strong, aggressive, record-setting champions. Canadian writer Varda Burstyn (1999, p. 23) says that these stories celebrate the notion of "higher, faster, stronger" that today serves the interests of capitalist expansion and traditional manly values associated with conquest. This is an important way in which comprehensive forms of socialization occur in connection with sports.

Researchers are also concerned with whose stories are not told and whose voices are silenced or even "erased" from the stories that are told in the dominant culture. For example, media coverage of sports might be studied to learn what is *not* contained in narratives and images as much as what is contained in them. This is because we can learn about culture by seeing what *is not* represented in narratives and images as well as seeing what is represented.

This type of research is difficult to do because it requires a knowledge of history and a deep understanding of the settings in which sports and sport stories come to be a part of people's lives. But it is important to do this research because it deals with the influence of sports in the culture as a whole, rather than just in the lives of individuals and small groups.

The Politics of Socialization as a Community and Cultural Process

Research on socialization as a community and cultural process is partly inspired by the ideas of Italian sociologist, Antonio Gramsci. When fascists in Italy imprisoned Gramsci for speaking out against their oppressive policies, he used his time in prison (1928–35) to think about why people had not revolted against exploitive forms of capitalism in Western societies. Gramsci concluded that it was important to understand how people in society form their notions of common sense and ideas about how society ought to be organized socially, politically, and economically. He explained that powerful people could influence and win the support of the people over whom they exercised power by providing them with exciting and pleasurable experiences.

Gramsci suspected that most people use the cultural messages associated with the sources of excitement and pleasure in their lives to inform their notions of common sense and their ideas about the organization and operation of society as a whole. Therefore, existing forms of power relations in society could be maintained if people with power organized and sponsored exciting and pleasurable activities that promoted their perspectives and interests.

Gramsci's analysis helps us to understand why large corporations spend billions of dollars every year to sponsor sports and to advertise in connection with sports. For example, Coca-Cola, Panasonic, and McDonald's have each spent hundreds of millions of dollars sponsoring and presenting advertising messages during the 1996, 2000, 2004, and 2008 Olympic Games. These expenditures were made to promote sales but, more important, they were made to use the Olympics as vehicles for delivering cultural messages that corporate executives wanted people in the world to hear. They wanted people watching the Olympics to agree that competition is the best way to allocate rewards and that wealthy and powerful people (and corporations) deserve what they have because they are the best at what they do.

The people who run Coca-Cola and Panasonic want people to drink Coke and buy DVD players, but they also want people to develop lifestyles in which excitement and pleasure are associated with consumption, and social status associated with corporate brands and logos. They want people to say, "These large companies are important to us because without them we would not have the sports we love so dearly." They want people to believe that their excitement and pleasure depends on large corporations and their products. They want to establish consumption as the foundation for measuring progress and defining prosperity. Their profits and power depend on it, and their marketing people use sports to promote an ideology of competition and consumption. To the extent that people in society accept this ideology, corporate interests gain more power in society.

Many sociologists refer to this process of forming consent around a particular ideology as the process of establishing hegemony. In political science and sociology, **hegemony** is a *process of maintaining leadership and control by gaining the consent of other groups, including those who are being led or controlled.* For example, U.S. hegemony in the world exists when people worldwide accept

U.S. control as legitimate. Hegemony is never permanent, but it can be maintained in a society as long as most people feel that their lives are as good as can be expected and that there is no strong reason to change the way social worlds are currently organized. Similarly, corporate hegemony is maintained as long as most people accept a view of the world that is consistent with corporate interests.

People in corporations know that their interests depend on establishing "ideological outposts" in people's heads. Sports, because they are exciting and pleasurable activities for so many people, are important tools for building such outposts. Once established, these outposts are useful to corporations because they serve as terminals through which a range of corporate messages can be delivered into people's minds. To paraphrase Gramsci's conclusion about hegemony, it is difficult to fight an enemy that has outposts in your head.

Research on Socialization as a Community and Cultural Process

It is difficult to understand socialization as a community and cultural process unless we see it in action. The following examples of research highlight this informative approach to sports and socialization.

1. U.S. sociologist David Riesman, an early supporter of the sociology of sport, commented: "The road to the boardroom leads through the locker room." In other words, characteristics of sports provide valuable socialization for the corporate world. Even before Riesman made this comment, a classic Canadian sociological study, *Crestwood Heights* (Seeley, Sim, and Loosley, 1956) identified the importance of sports in an upper-middle-class community (now widely acknowledged to be Forest Hill in Toronto). The importance of sports was in socializing boys into a career.

"[E]ven in recreational activity, the youth of the community do not engage in sport or games as activities to be participated in for enjoyment only. Sport provides an enculturative [socializing] milieux that prepares boys to become executives, or more broadly, upwardly mobile *career competitors*" (Gruneau and Albinson, 1976, p. 298). The importance of sports, especially football, baseball, and hockey, was that they encouraged competition and teamwork, allowed stars to emerge, and created bonding and networking opportunities.

Although this idea seems to make sense for males from a particular social class—after all, most elite private schools require sport participation of their students—there are few studies in the sociology of sport that explore the socializing path from the locker room to the board room. Only Gai Berlage has focused on the issue, particularly with regard to the "glass ceiling" experienced by many women in business and politics: "Several organizational studies of women in corporations suggest . . . women's lack of experience with team sports as one reason they have not been more successful in the corporate world" (Berlage, 1982, p. 310; see also, Nelson, 1994). Harvard sociologist Orlando Patterson reiterated this idea in an essay on social inequality:

" … women's exclusion from male bonding practices seriously impedes their access to vital tacit knowledge for successful entrepreneurial activity" (2002, p. 33). There are serious ideological implications of such socialization practices.

2. Brian Pronger's reflections on his undergraduate experiences in the anatomy laboratory studying human cadavers led him to sound some warnings about the type of education that physical educators and kinesiologists receive in Canada (Pronger, 1995). As with most physical education and kinesiology students in Canada, Pronger

took a required course in anatomy as part of his physical education degree at the University of Toronto. The lab instructor told him: "The only way you really learn anatomy is to get your hands inside and manipulate the parts of the body." Given the amount of discussion that takes place among students afterwards, this is an extremely vivid experience; but it is also an experience that is controlled in a very precise way. Students "are told explicitly what to see and implicitly how to relate to it" (p. 441).

Pronger adapts and develops a critique that has been made more generally about medical education. Students are not encouraged to see the subjectivity and humanity of the human body; emotional responses such as joy, sadness, fear, and awe are strongly discouraged; and even an empirical sense of exploration and discovery is discouraged. Students are encouraged to see and experience the cadaver as a mechanical object, as a "technological body." This objectification of the body is also encouraged and developed in other required courses such as biomechanics and physiology, and just as in medicine, it has distinct consequences.

Pronger argues that the "objectification of the body in the gross anatomy lab is transposed into the practices of physical education which reproduce the body as an object: high performance sport, the fit body, and so on" (p. 442). Supposedly professional attitudes also encourage abuse of the body for the purposes of high-performance sports and physical appearance. How many times have you heard an athlete objectify his or her own injured body part—referring to "the ankle" or "the shoulder," rather than "my ankle" or "my shoulder"? Physical education and kinesiology students are socialized into this particular ideology of the body, and alternative views are not encouraged: "[s]tudents who would refuse

to see the body technologically…would fail physical education" (p. 441). The hegemony of this ideology is extremely powerful, but, as with all hegemonies, it is vulnerable, and Pronger suggests some ways in which the objectification of the body may be resisted.

3. Susan Birrell and Diana Richter's (1994) observations of softball teams and in-depth interviews with players showed that feminist orientations can alter the way that women play sports. As the women organized their games around the pleasure and participation

Just as Nike and other corporations worked hard to sever the Michael Jordan persona from connections with African-American experiences (Andrews, 1996b), the search now continues for replacements—other visible minorities that allow people to comfortably ignore the legacies of colonialism and racism, while at the same time promoting corporate products. Here, NBA players Yao Ming and Vince Carter are on a Nike promotional tour of China. [CP/AP(Ng Han Guan)]

model, their experiences became sources of personal empowerment and a commitment to supporting each other. This made their sport experiences very different from the experiences of people who play power and performance sports. Additionally, it demonstrated that sports may be played in ways that challenge dominant ideas. When this happens, socialization in sports may involve changes in how entire groups of people think about what is important in life and how social relationships can and should be organized.

These and other studies emphasize that *none of us lives outside the influence of ideology* (Andrews, 1996a,b; Burstyn, 1999; Foley, 1999a; Messner, 1992; Paraschak, 1997). This research is based on the premise that sports, because they are popular sources of excitement and pleasure in people's lives, are significant sites at which people learn and sometimes raise questions about ideology. Such research holds the promise of showing us how sports influence widely held ideas in a culture and how people can disrupt that influence when it promotes stereotypes and exploitation (see Andrews and Jackson, 2001).

WHAT SOCIALIZATION RESEARCH DOES NOT TELL US

Existing research does not tell us all we want to know about sports and socialization. We have many research snapshots and a few videos to help us understand parts of socialization processes related to sports. But we lack information on how these processes operate in the lives of people from various ethnic groups and social classes. In Canada, research on South and East Asians, First Nations Canadians, African Canadians, and Francophones in sports is especially needed. We also need studies of sport participation in high-income and low-income communities, as well as among wealthy and poor individuals and families.

Clearly we need to know more about variations in sport experiences and how people from different social and cultural backgrounds give sport experiences meaning and integrate them into their life course. We cannot talk about the socialization consequences of sports without putting sport experiences into real-life contexts (see figure 4.2). That is why your sport participation has had a different impact on you than other people, and that is why it is senseless to argue about whether all sports build character or whether all athletes are role models. Neither socialization nor sports are that simple, and research cannot give us unconditional yes or no answers about what sports do to us or to our communities and societies.

We also need research on sport participation careers among children, and on how those careers are linked to overall social development, especially among girls, children with a disability, and children from ethnic minority backgrounds.

"I don't think these guys agree about the meaning of boxing."

FIGURE 4.2 Meanings given to sports vary from one person to another. However, many power and performance sports are organized to encourage orientations that emphasize domination over others. Those who do not hold this orientation may not fit very well in these sports.

Breaking Barriers   Socialization Barriers
Living in the Empire of the Normal

Popular images of bodies embedded in our culture, the media, and our minds are images of able bodies. Seldom do we see images of impaired bodies, except in notices for fund-raising events to "help the disabled." Images that represent disability as an embodied form that is valuable, beautiful, healthy, fit, or athletic are practically nonexistent (Seeley and Rail, 2004). This is because we live in an "Empire of the Normal" where productive, healthy, fit, beautiful, and ideal bodies are *able bodies* (Couser, 2000).

In the Empire of the Normal, the existence of a disabled body causes people to ask, *"What happened to you?"* People in the empire demand an explanation for a disabled body—a story that accounts for its difference from normal bodies. As people with disabilities are asked incessantly to tell their stories, their identities come to be organized around their accounts of "why my body is different from your body" (Thomson, 2000, p. 334).

This information helps us understand socialization and sports in more detail. For example, when people with disabilities make decisions to play sports, the *significant others* in their lives include physical therapists, physical educators, athletes with disabilities, sport scientists, and doctors as well as family members and peers (Schilling, 1997). In fact, the origin of today's Paralympics was in a British medical centre for war veterans with spinal cord injuries. Ludwig Guttmann, the neurosurgeon in charge of the centre, was convinced that sports could be used as therapy for patients. His idea to schedule public games for people with disabilities at the same time as the 1948 Olympics in London was radical. People in the Empire of the Normal became uncomfortable when they were confronted with disabled bodies. "Out of sight, out of mind" has always been a norm in the empire.

After a person with a disability becomes involved in sports, decisions to stay involved are related to how other people define their bodies and treat them as athletes. Also important are participation opportunities, resources for transportation and adapted equipment, knowledgeable coaches, and programmes that inspire achievement and success.

When people see a body with a disability, they often want to hear the story that accounts for its difference from "normal" bodies. Over time this may lead to the development of an identity organized around a person's account of "why my body is different from your body." [David Biene; photo courtesy of Ossur]

Changing or ending sport participation occurs in connection with many of the same factors that lead able-bodied athletes to disengage from sports. Injuries, a sense of reaching one's goals or hitting one's limits, responsibilities related to work and family, a

Continued

lack of resources, and new opportunities to coach or work in sports influence decisions to alter or end sport participation.

The issue of what happens to people with disabilities when they play sports has seldom been studied. As with able-bodied athletes, socialization experiences among athletes with disabilities depend on their relationships, the general social and cultural context in which participation occurs, and the meanings given to participation.

In societies where power and performance sports predominate, people with disabilities seldom play with or alongside able-bodied athletes. Power and performance sports are exclusive: Only able bodies may try out. This forces athletes with disabilities to play in segregated or "special" programmes or leads them to prefer those programmes, and influences the meanings given to their sport participation.

Among many athletes with disabilities, sports are perceived as sites for challenging body images in the Empire of the Normal. Among a few, sports are sites for planning how to break through the empire's walls, open gates for others, and rebuild its foundation so that people no longer see disabled bodies as needing to be cured, fixed, regulated, or separated from other bodies (Thomson, 2002, p. 8).

Road and track cyclist, Pam Fernandez, speaks from experience when she says "if we could somehow bring the respect, dignity, and camaraderie of the Paralympic Village to the rest of the world, we could teach a lifetime of lessons in a single day" (in Joukowsky and Rothstein, 2002a, p. 93). These lessons just might hasten the fall of the Empire of the Normal.

Similarly, we need research on older people, especially those considering or trying sports for the first time or resuming participation after decades of not playing.

We need research on how people make participation decisions about different types of sports. Sports come in many forms, and the socialization processes related to power and performance sports are different from experiences related to pleasure and participation sports.

If we knew more about each of these topics, we could provide sport participation opportunities that fit into the lives of a greater number of people. This would help to make sports more democratic and less subject to the commercial forces that make them exclusive and elitist (Donnelly, 1993a, 1996b). This is the focus of the Breaking Barriers box on pages 106–107.

We also need research on the emotional dimensions of socialization processes. Few sociologists have considered emotions in their research, but most of us know that decisions about sport participation are clearly connected with our feelings, fears, and anxieties. For example, some decisions may be linked with "psyching up," the emotional experience of forming expectations about what a person will encounter in sports. These expectations are based on memories and the stories about sports that exist in the culture as a whole. Stories about the emotional side of sports have been collected by social psychologists who have studied "flow experiences" among athletes (Jackson and Csikszentmihalyi, 1999). Flow occurs when we face a challenge that requires us to use all of our skills and, in the process lose track of time and are carried along by the activity itself. The runner's high, peak experiences, and "that game when everything just seems to click" are examples of flow in action. Even though flow is a personal experience, it is tied to sociological issues such as how activities are organized and the amount of control that participants have over their involvement in those activities.

Finally, we need more research on the ways that vocabulary used in certain sports influences sport participation decisions and the meanings given to sport experiences. When sports constantly refer to opposition, hostility, rivalries, confrontations, domination, and mastery over others, they set the stage for memories, fantasies, and identifications that serve as powerful sources of personal identity and social dynamics. This vocabulary tells us much about the organization and spirit of sports. For example, given the words that many people use when they talk about sports, it is not surprising that young women in high schools are less likely than their male counterparts to be interested in or try out for and stay on school teams. If the language of sports is based on traditionally masculine images and orientations, many girls and women may not find certain sports very appealing. Furthermore, what types of boys and men are likely to be attracted to sports described as forms of "warfare," requiring aggression, toughness, and the desire to dominate others? Sociologists, especially those interested in gender equity and gender relations, are interested in these questions.

In practical terms, when we learn more about sports and socialization, we can become wiser parents, coaches, teachers, managers, and sport administrators. Then we are able to create sports that offer a wider array of challenging and satisfying experiences.

SUMMARY

WHO PLAYS AND WHAT HAPPENS?

Socialization is a complex, interactive process through which people form ideas about themselves and the social worlds in which they participate. This process occurs in connection with sports and other activities and experiences in people's lives. Research indicates that playing sports is a social experience as well as a physical one.

Becoming involved and staying involved in sports occur in connection with general socialization processes in people's lives. Decisions to play sports are influenced by the availability of opportunities, the existence of social support, processes of identity formation, and the cultural context in which decisions are made.

Studies of socialization into sports show that sport participation decisions are related to the processes of individual development, the organization of social life, and cultural ideology. People do not make decisions about sport participation once and for all time. They make them day after day as they set and revise priorities for their lives. Research on sport-related decisions helps us to understand the social dynamics of early experiences in sports and who influences those experiences. The reasons for staying in sports change over time as people's lives change, and it is important to understand the complexities of these processes.

Changing or ending active sport participation also occurs in connection with general socialization processes. These processes are interactive and influenced by personal, social, and cultural factors. Changes in sport participation are usually tied to a combination of identity, developmental, and life course issues. Ending sport participation often involves a transition process, during which athletes disengage from sport, redefine their identities, reconnect with friends and family members, and use available resources to become involved in other activities and careers. Just as people are not socialized into sports, they are not simply socialized out of sports. Research shows that changing or ending a career as a competitive athlete occurs over time and is often tied to events and life course issues apart from sports. These connections are best studied by using research methods that enable us to identify and analyze long-term transition processes.

Socialization that occurs as people participate in sports has been widely studied, especially by people wanting to know if and how sports build character. Much of this research has produced inconsistent findings because it has been based on oversimplified ideas about sports, sport experiences, and socialization. Reviews of this research indicate that studies of sports and socialization must take into account variations in the ways that sports are organized, played, and integrated into people's lives. This is important because different sports involve different experiences and produce different socialization patterns. For example, the experience of playing power and performance sports is different from the experience of playing pleasure and participation sports. The visibility and popularity of power and performance sports are related to issues of status and ideology: these sports fit the interests of people who have the power and wealth to sponsor and promote sports.

We know that sports have an impact on people's lives. The most informative research on what happens in sports deals with (1) the everyday experiences of people who play sports, (2) the social worlds created around sports, and (3) community and cultural processes through which ideologies are created, reproduced, and changed. As we listen to the voices of those who participate in sports,

study how they live their lives in connection with sports, and pay special attention to the ideological messages associated with sports, we learn more about sports and socialization.

Most scholars who study sports in society now see sports as sites for socialization experiences, rather than as causes of specific socialization outcomes. This distinction recognizes that powerful and memorable experiences may occur in connection with sports, but it emphasizes that these experiences are given meaning through social relationships, and these meanings are influenced by the social and cultural contexts in which sports are played. Therefore, the most useful research in the sociology of sport focuses on the importance of social relationships and the contexts in which sports are given meaning by a wide and diverse range of people who play and watch sports in some form or another.

Visit *Sports in Society*'s Online Learning Centre at www.mcgrawhill.ca/olc/coakley for additional information, website resources, and study tools for this chapter.

[Ron Chapple/Taxi/Getty Images]

Sports and Children

Are organized programmes worth the effort?

Somewhere along the way we developed a mistrust of idle time. Children became an investment; it cost money to join the classes and courses and sports that are supposed to turn them into well-rounded little human beings. It took adult time to drive and wait, and, well, if you have to be there anyway, you may as well get involved. Time is money, money is time. And if the child is the investment, what, then, is the return on that investment? Certificates, badges, trophies—perhaps even a professional career. There is simply no time for play in such a serious undertaking.

—**Roy M acGregor, author,** *The Seven AM Practice: Stories of Family Life* **(1996)**

Unless we pay attention to poverty-stricken children, our culture will fall apart. We already see the beginning of it. If we are not careful, the children who have never played games will inherit the earth, and that will be a joyless earth.

—**Les McDonald, president of the International Triathlon Union**

It's a huge reason we don't have enough kids playing sports, because they get too competitive too soon. At this age, everyone should get to play…. The only way you learn the skills and get better…is to play.

—**Penny Werthner**

When, how, and to what end children play sports are issues that concern families, community leaders, and child advocates in national and internationalorganizations. When sociologists study youth sports, they focus on the experiences of children and how those experiences vary depending on the organization of programmes and the social contexts in which the programmes exist. Since the early 1970s, research carried out by sociologists and others has influenced the ways that people think about and organize sport programmes for children. Parents, coaches, and programme administrators are increasingly aware of the issues they should consider when evaluating youth programmes.

This chapter deals with five major topics:

1. The origin and development of organized youth sports
2. Problems in adult-organized youth sports, and "made in Canada" solutions
3. Children in high-performance sports
4. Commonly asked sociological questions about youth sports, including
   - When are children ready to play organized competitive sports?
   - What are the dynamics of family relationships in connection with organized youth sports?
   - How do social factors influence youth sport experiences?
5. Trends in children's sports, and recommendations for change

An underlying question that guides our discussion of these topics is this: Are organized youth sports worth all the time, money, and effort put into them? We first asked this question as our children played sports during childhood, and we continue to ask it as we talk with parents and work with coaches and policymakers who have made extensive commitments to youth sports.

ORIGIN AND DEVELOPMENT OF ORGANIZED YOUTH SPORTS

During the latter half of the nineteenth century, people in Europe and North America became aware that the social environment influenced child development. This led many people to organize the contexts in which children grew up. Their goal was to ensure that boys and girls would become productive adults in rapidly expanding capitalist economies.

A part of this organization involved sports for boys, sponsored by schools, communities, and church groups. The organizers hoped that sports, especially team sports, would teach boys from working-class families to work together productively, and help to assimilate the children of immigrants into North American values. Also, with the increasing industrialization and urbanization of cities, and before compulsory secondary education for children from low-income families, unemployed working-class youth came to be labelled as a "social problem." Working from the assumption that "the Devil makes work for idle hands," sport programmes were organized to occupy their "leisure" time. Critical theorists refer to this as a social control response since it was developed to deal with a perceived social problem; and there are still some aspects of organized youth sports that meet this definition (e.g., "Midnight basketball"—Pitter, 2004).[1]

The organizers also hoped that sports would turn middle- and upper-class boys into tough competitive men, who would become leaders in business, government, and the professions, by providing them with learning experiences that would offset the "feminized" values learned from stay-at-home mothers. At the same time, girls were provided with activities that would teach them to be good wives, mothers, and homemakers. The prevailing belief was that girls should learn domestic skills, and this is what they were taught in schools and playground activities.

There were exceptions to these patterns. For example, the influence of the clergy in rural

---

[1]Assimilation and social control are also considered, by critical sociologists, to be a part of the motivation for introducing organized sports to youth in First Nations and immigrant communities (see chapter 9).

Québec resulted in a somewhat different pattern of development (Bellefleur, 1997; Harvey, 1988). But in most industrial nations until World War II, youth sport programmes were organized in these ways.

The Postwar Baby Boom and the Growth of Youth Sports

The baby-boom generation was born between 1946 and 1964. Young married couples during these years were optimistic about the future and eager to become parents. As the first wave of the Baby Boomers moved through childhood during the 1950s and 1960s, organized youth sports grew dramatically. Parents entered the scene, eager to have the characters of their sons built through organized competitive sports. Fathers became coaches, managers, and league administrators. Mothers did laundry and became chauffeurs and fast-food cooks, so that their sons were always ready for practices and games.

Most programmes were for boys eight to fourteen years old and emphasized competition as preparation for future occupational success. Until the 1970s, girls' interests in sports were largely ignored. Girls were relegated to arena seats and bleachers during their brothers' games. Then the women's movement, the fitness movement, and government legislation prohibiting sex discrimination all came together to stimulate the development of new sport programmes for girls (see chapter 8). During the 1980s, these programmes grew rapidly to the point that, in some sports, girls had nearly as many opportunities as boys. However, their participation rates have remained lower than rates for boys—for reasons we discuss later in this chapter (and in chapter 8).

Participation in organized youth sports is now a valued experience in the process of growing up in Canada, especially among the middle and upper classes where family and community resources enable adults to sponsor, organize, and administer programmes for their children. Parents now encourage both sons and daughters to participate in sports. Some parents question the benefits of programmes in which winning seems to be more important than overall child development, while others look for the win-oriented programmes, hoping their children will become the winners. Some parents also encourage their children to engage in noncompetitive physical activities outside of organized programmes, and many children participate in these activities as alternatives to adult-supervised organized sports. Research shows that a variety of so-called alternative sports have become increasingly popular in the lives of children in many countries (Beal, 1999; Midol and Broyer, 1995; Rinehart and Grenfell, 2002; Rinehart and Syndor, 2003).

Social Changes Have Influenced the Growth of Organized Youth Sports

Since the 1950s, an increasing amount of children's free time and sport participation has occurred in organized programmes supervised by adults. This growth is related to a whole series of changes that occurred in Canadian society, in Canadian families and relationships between parents and their children, and in Canadian sports after World War II. For example, in Canadian society:

- The return of troops from the various theatres of war led to the Baby Boom, and a large population of young people in Canada from the late 1940s through the 1960s. This was complemented by a significant increase in immigration during this period (Donnelly, 2000, p. 170);
- The housing needs of young families led to a massive growth in the development of suburbs which, with their new sport and recreation facilities, became one of the major sites of adult-organized youth involvement (Donnelly, 2000, p. 170);
- There was a period "of unprecedented prosperity in Canada," and that prosperity was used in the provision of sport and

recreation facilities in the new suburbs and in urban areas (Hall et al., 1991, p. 198).

In terms of family life and parent–child relations, there were significant changes that are especially relevant for the growth of adult-organized youth sports.

First, the return of (primarily male) troops led to restructuring of work, with jobs that had been carried out by women during the war being reclaimed by men. While this helped to create what was considered the "typical" family (working father, stay-at-home mother, children), it was also connected with the new interest in child development (cf., Dr. Spock), and created, for middle-class and more affluent working-class families, available time for volunteer work, which often involved children's (especially boys') activities (Donnelly, 2000, p. 170).[2]

Second, the number of families with both parents working outside the home increased dramatically since the early 1970s. This created a growing demand for organized and adult-supervised after-school and summertime programmes.[3] Organized sports are especially popular because many parents believe they offer their children opportunities to simultaneously have fun, learn adult values, become physically fit, and acquire status among their peers. In many cases in Canada, parents were more involved in the lives of their children during this period

because they were concerned about giving children opportunities that had not been available during their own childhoods—in Europe during the War, or in Canada during the Depression. They promoted social mobility for their children in various ways, from education to sports (Hall et al., 1991, pp. 198–99).

Third, since the early 1980s, there have been significant changes in what it means to be a "good parent." Good parents, in the minds of many people today, are those who can account for the whereabouts and actions of their children twenty-four hours a day every day. This expectation is a new component of parenting ideology, and in recent years it has led many parents to seek organized, adult-supervised programmes for their children. Organized sports are favoured because they involve adult leadership, have predictable schedules, and provide parents with measurable indicators of their children's accomplishments. When their children succeed, parents can make the claim that they are meeting their responsibilities. In some cases, parents feel that they are making provision for the long-term physical health of their children, especially with the growing concerns about inactivity and obesity. In other cases, some mothers and fathers feel that their moral worth as parents is associated with the visible achievements of their children in sports—a factor that further intensifies parental commitment to youth sports (Coakley, 2006; Dukes and Coakley, 2002).

Fourth, there has been a growing belief that informal, child-controlled activities often provide occasions for children to cause trouble. In its extreme form, this belief leads adults to view children as threats to social order. This leads them to see organized sports as ideal activities because they keep active children occupied, out of trouble, and under the control of adults.

Fifth, many parents have come to see the world outside the home as dangerous for their children. They regard organized sports as safe alternatives to informal activities that occur away from home. This belief is so strong that it often persists in

---

[2]This 1950s–60s period of the "typical" family was short-lived for some, and non-existent for many others. However, it was enshrined by a number of U.S. television series (also seen in Canada). The growth of the women's movement in the late 1960s and 1970s, combined with changes in the economy that made it more difficult for families to thrive on a single income, led to the end of this era of the "typical" family. Note also that Spock's *Baby and Child Care* was first published in 1945 and, despite many imitators, had sold 28 million copies by 1977.

[3]For example, in a recent trend in some communities, martial arts academies have made arrangements to pick up children directly from school and to drive them to the *dojo* for lessons. This service frees parents from an additional chauffeuring responsibility.

the face of information about declining activity levels, coercive coaching methods, the predatory behaviour of some coaches, and high injury rates in organized youth sports (Donnelly, 2006; Gorman, 2005; Pennington, 2005).

Sixth, an increasingly educated population of parents developed a growing belief in the value of sports for health and physical fitness, and adopted the elite private school belief that sports promoted the development of important values, attitudes, and habits that would carry over into other aspects of children's lives (Hall et al., 1991, p. 188). Both parents and educators developed an increasing belief in the benefits of coaching and teaching for more rapid development of skill and for safety (and as a necessity to reach the high-performance or professional levels of sports). They were supported in this by "conventional wisdom in psychology, spread not only through schools but through the popular media and self-help books, [which] emphasized the

benefits of an early introduction to skill development and learning" (Hall et al., 1991, p. 200).

Seventh, the visibility of high-performance and professional sports increased people's awareness of organized competitive sports as a valued part of culture. As children watch sports on television, listen to parents and friends talk about sports, and hear about the wealth and fame of popular athletes, they often see organized youth sports, especially those modelled after professional sports, as attractive activities. And when children say they want to be gymnasts or soccer players, parents often look for the best-organized programmes in those sports (see figure 5.1). Therefore, organized youth sports have become popular because children see them as enjoyable and culturally valued activities that will gain them acceptance from peers and parents alike.

Together, these social changes, have boosted the popularity of organized youth sports in recent decades. Knowing about these changes

FIGURE 5.1 When children have schedules that are full of organized youth sports, they have little time to be with their parents. The irony is that many parents spend more time making it possible for their children to play sports than they spend with their children.

helps us to understand why parents are willing to invest so many family resources into the organized sport participation of their children. The amount of money that parents spend on participation fees, equipment, travel, personal coaches, high-performance training sessions and other things defined as necessary in many programmes has increased significantly in recent years (Ferguson, 1999; Giordana and Graham, 2004; King, 2002; Moore, 2002; Poppen, 2004; Sokolove, 2004a; Wolff, 2003). For example, when Jay Coakley and his students interviewed the parents of elite youth hockey players who travelled to Colorado for a major tournament, they discovered that the families spent at least US$5,000 to US$20,000 per year to support their sons' hockey participation. As they added up their expenses, many of them shook their heads and said, "I can't believe we're spending this much, but we are." And then they quickly explained that it was worth it because their son would benefit from the experience.

One of the negative consequences of these changes is that mothers and fathers in working-class and lower-income households are increasingly defined as irresponsible or "bad" parents because they are unable to pay the financial price to enrol their children in supervised after-school sport programmes. Furthermore, they are not as likely to have the time and other resources needed to serve as volunteers and coaches for youth sport programmes. (See chapter 10 for data on sport participation and social class.) In this way, organized sports for children become linked to political issues and debates about "family values" and the moral worth of parents in lower income households.

PROBLEMS IN ADULT-ORGANIZED YOUTH SPORTS AND "MADE IN CANADA" SOLUTIONS

The growth of adult-organized children's sports in Canada—estimated at approximately 2 million children in 1978 and 2.5 million in 1991—initially coincided with an important period of social criticism. Social movements in the 1960s such as the women's movement, the civil rights movement, and the anti-[Vietnam] war movement adopted an anti-authoritarian stance that involved critiques of the military, education, government, and even sports. Recognition that children's sports were being run by adults in a particularly joyless way, often in exactly the same authoritarian manner as adult high-performance and professional sports, made children's sports a target of criticism. In democratic terms, there was also a recognition that if there were positive aspects of participation in sports—ranging from benefits to physical and mental health to the pleasures of participation—then such benefits should be available to all children.

Michael Smith, who taught at York University, identified four assumptions that appeared to dominate children's organized programmes in the early 1970s (1975, pp. ix–x):

- Children play sports to entertain adults.
- Games and sports for kids must be organized and controlled by adults if they are to be of real value.
- Kids are miniature adults.
- The real value in sports lies in learning to be a winner, people can be divided into winners and losers, and sport[s are vehicles] to make sure you (or your kids) end up in the right group.

Each of these four assumptions is considered in more detail here, together with the steps taken in Canada in an attempt to solve the issues. It is striking, however, to note the extent to which many of these issues persist over 30 years later.

Assumption 1: Children Play Sports to Entertain Adults

This is a continuing issue, and is clearly a double-edged sword. In our research, many young athletes that we have talked with expect their parents to attend every game or competition, and feel disappointed or neglected if they are not there. However, a few told us that they are sometimes embarrassed by one or both of their parents, who yell at them and at referees, coaches, and other players, especially when the parents say inappropriate things. A few others told us that the constant presence of one or more parents, even at practices, became a problem as they grew older and wanted to have time with friends away from their parents. And others noted that their parents (one or both) were hypercritical or judgmental, and used their presence at competitions, and sometimes practices, to generate a list of mistakes made by the young athletes, which would all be pointed out to them on their way home.

Why do parents attend their children's games? Certainly, practices are sometimes seen as a "babysitting" opportunity by parents, who may

"Have you ever considered that maybe I'd like this to remain a repressed childhood memory?"

FIGURE 5.2 Many children who play sports do not enjoy videotapes of their games, meets, and matches. They would rather remember their experiences in their own terms. Too often, the tapes are used to identify mistakes and make youth sports more important than children want them to be.

use the time to carry out errands or chores, but attendance at community and club level games and competitions has become a ritual.[4] By attending, parents are able to demonstrate to other parents and to their children that they are "good" parents (see preceding section on new demands on parents) who are prepared to support their children's activities and spend "quality time" with their children. They are also able to "look out" for their children, to ensure their safety and protect them from potential unfairness (see the section, "Major Trends in Youth Sports Today," later in this chapter). Most will cheer for their children and/or their child's team, and they have the opportunity to socialize with other parents. There is nothing wrong with this behaviour—it is a social occasion for parents who meet in the bleachers or the stands, or line their lawn chairs along the touch line, but it is not necessarily entertaining. There may be little excitement in watching the ninth game of "beehive" soccer for the season, although most parents agree that the children "look cute."

But while there are positive and supportive aspects to the behaviour, there are also some mixed messages being sent, and some alternatives to consider.

First, in a society increasingly concerned about sedentary behaviour, the messages implicit in parents sitting down to watch their children play are significant. Is participation just for children? This is less an issue for parents who do participate in sports, and/or who spend time playing with their children. Parents' games, or parents' exercise programmes (e.g., a brisk hike around the playing fields) during the children's game may be healthy alternatives for organizers of children's sports to consider.

Second, watching your child is supportive, but it is not necessarily "quality time" since there is little time to interact. A recent report from the

---

[4]This is less the case for interschool sports in Canada, which are often played during working hours.

American Academy of Pediatrics provides an estimate that "by the time they are six years old, the average child will have spent more time watching television than they will talking to their fathers during their entire lifetimes" (Kesterton, 2002, p. A24). We have heard both positive and negative reports from young athletes about "quality time." Looking back, some see the time spent with one or both parents travelling to and from competitions, or in informal practices and pick-up games together, as enormously rich, fun, and rewarding time. Others grew to dread those times, which they remember as endlessly directive and judgmental.

Third, we wonder how children would feel if their parents were always present, sitting in lawn chairs around the school playground at recess, or standing at the back of the classroom. Time spent with children is extremely important; time spent watching children while they are doing something else may be less so, and some parents are now beginning to question whether they should be at every possible occasion in their children's lives (see quote on this page).

> **Sometimes I think that by being so involved in our kids' sports, we dilute their experience. After all, it's not *their* win, it's *our* win. Do all the valuable lessons—losing, striking out, missing the winning shot—have the same impact when Mom and Dad are there to immediately say it's okay?…As parents, we know that at some point we need to make it *their* game, *their* recital, *their* grades. If we share every element of their lives, we're cheating them out of part of it….As hard as it is to risk missing her first home run, or not being there to comfort him after the missed foul shot, at some point we need to take ourselves out of their ball game. Because that is what good parents do.**
>
> —(Keri, 2000, p. 55)

Assumption 2: Sports for Kids Must Be Organized and Controlled by Adults If They Are to Be of Real Value

Adults have a number of appropriate concerns about children's informal and/or unsupervised play. They are concerned about safety and want to protect children from bullying and accidents (see section, "Major Trends in Youth Sports Today," later in this chapter). They are concerned about instruction—that children will learn sport skills in an appropriate and safe manner. (After all, who would want their children to learn to swim without supervision and instruction?) And they hope that their children will receive messages about character development as a result of their participation.

However, since the early 1970s, many critics of adult-organized sports for children have agreed with Bill L'Heureux, then a professor at the University of Western Ontario: "The only problem with kids' sports is adults." Two solutions to this problem have usually been offered: *ban the adults* or *educate the adults*.

Proposals to *ban adults* from children's games may be traced to Devereaux (1976a), and to a somewhat romanticized view of children's play that does not take into account the fact that supervision and guidance may sometimes be appropriate and necessary. Devereaux's film, *Two Ball Games* (1976b), provides a direct and unfavourable comparison between an informal game of baseball in a public park and a Little League game. His argument, that adult involvement removes both fun and important educational experiences from children's play, was widely supported. Jay Coakley, who has carried out the most systematic comparison between the two variations of children's sports (see the Reflect on Sports box, "Different Experiences: Informal Player-Controlled Sports versus Organized, Adult-Controlled Sports," pp. 135–136) points out that each has advantages and disadvantages.

Apart from pick-up ball hockey and basketball games played in driveways and neighbourhood streets and playgrounds, there are now fewer opportunities for children to interact, learn, and play sports in contexts other than those directly supervised by adults. These opportunities have decreased, at least for middle-class children, since the 1970s (cf., Elkind, 1981), with one obvious exception. (See the section on alternative sports in "Major Trends in Youth Sports Today," later in this chapter.)

The majority of children enjoy their participation in adult-organized sports, and proposals to ban adults were never pursued except in the case of particularly unruly individuals. However, the problems remained, and proposals to *educate adults* came to be seen as a more realistic alternative to banning adults. In addition to the points made above about when it is appropriate to have adult supervision and instruction, it also became apparent that the structures of adult-organized children's sports were too well-established to dismantle them easily. Once this was recognized, academics, educators, and other policymakers set about devising ways of providing appropriate information to adults involved in youth sport programmes. It should be pointed out that Canada was among the first countries to formally recognize that problems existed, and to start to develop policies and procedures for their resolution. Several national conferences in the 1970s began to identify problems, and made a number of recommendations about adult involvement (Orlick and Botterill, 1975, pp. 161–63, 173–75).

One of the most significant "made in Canada" solutions was the development of coaching education. The Coaching Association of Canada (CAC) was formed in 1971 during a significant period of development in Canadian sports as the country geared up to host the 1976 Montréal Olympic Games. Its establishment coincided with the emerging critique of children's

organized sport programmes, and the CAC, with its mission to "enhance the experiences of all Canadian athletes through quality coaching" (www.coach.ca), was seen as a key to resolving some of the problems. The National Coaching Certification Programme (NCCP), started by the CAC in 1974, established five levels of accomplishment in coaching—Level 1 (novice) to Level 5 (national)—and provided training programmes at each level based on theoretical, technical, and practical elements of coaching.[5] For the purposes of children's sports, the parent volunteers who form the backbone of children's organized sports programmes, were encouraged to achieve at least NCCP Level 1 certification. After struggling with a number of grandparenting issues (e.g., should a coach who has been coaching for fifteen years be obliged to take a novice coaching course), the certification became more and more accepted, recommendations to enrol for the courses became stronger, and holding NCCP Level 1 has now become mandatory for volunteer coaches in many youth sport organizations. Certification is intended to ensure that coaches have at least a minimal knowledge about medical, physiological, psychological, and social issues regarding child development and participation. Of course, not all coaches change their coaching style as a result of certification, and attempts to evaluate or mandate continuing education for coaches in a volunteer system are quite problematic. However, anecdotal reports suggest that the increasing numbers of women coaches in children's sport programmes are benefiting more than males from the certification programmes.

Various programmes and publications were developed to further the education of parents and coaches: for example, Orlick and Botterill's widely read *Every Kid Can Win* (1975), and the Canadian Council on Children and Youth's extremely popular pamphlet and poster series, "Fair

---

[5]The NCCP has recently been reorganized to include three streams of coaching (community, competition, and instruction) with training in up to eight coaching contexts.

Play Codes for Children in Sport" (1979), which listed appropriate behaviour for all involved in children's sports—parents, coaches, officials, spectators, and players. Spink's *Give Your Kids a Sporting Chance* (1988), and the Bylsmas' *So Your Son Wants to Play in the NHL?* (1998) attempted to bring a note of caution to parents with NHL ambitions for their sons.

The second significant "made in Canada" solution to educating adults, and resolving some of the issues of adult-organized sports for children, was the re-invention of "house leagues." Although minor hockey had been organized before the 1970s into house leagues and the more elite "travel leagues," the house leagues became a target of criticism in the early 1970s. Conducting what was called "change agent research," Dick Moriarty and Jim Duthie at the University of Windsor videotaped parents and coaches at house-league hockey games, then interviewed those parents and coaches about the values of youth sports; they then confronted them with the often contradictory videotape evidence. At the same time, the researchers began to identify what we now call "best practices" to ensure that children have quality experiences in youth sports: making sure that teams were created with relatively equal levels of skill (i.e., make sure that one or two teams do not draft all the best players), ensuring that all players have approximately equal amounts of playing time (recognizing that all parents pay the same registration fee to have their children play in a league, and that children do not learn skills when they are sitting on the bench), and encouraging leagues to begin to emphasize skill development and to de-emphasize the outcome of games.

The Windsor and Essex County Leagues in southwestern Ontario began to introduce these changes in hockey, and the changes slowly began to spread across Canada and to other sports. Baseball, basketball, lacrosse, and soccer introduced this new concept of house leagues, emphasizing enjoyment and activity for young players. The change was not a complete success. Anecdotal

evidence suggests that some house-league coaches attempt to manipulate the player draft or give their best players more playing time (especially during playoffs and finals), and our observations of house-league parents suggest that some do not behave as well as might be expected. However, in general, the changes have greatly improved the involvement and experience of less-talented players, and the philosophy has even spread to individual sports. There are now many recreational programmes in swimming, skating, martial arts, gymnastics, and so on, which encourage skill learning and fun rather than competition.

Another "made in Canada" solution to educating adults emerged during the 1980s when there was a significant decline in participation by boys in hockey. Between 1983 and 1989, boys' registration declined 17.4 percent.[6] The decline was even more marked in é where registrations dropped by 47 percent between 1974 and 1990, from a high of 111,960 to a low of 57,340 (Scanlan, 2002). While there were many reasons for the decline (e.g., the cost of hockey, demographic changes in Canadian society), violence was a growing concern of parents together with the related fear of injury.[7] The response in Québec was to begin to introduce "fair play" leagues (leagues that reward fair play, by awarding additional points for fewer penalties, and punish illegal play) and non-contact leagues. These forms of hockey have also spread across Canada. The solution to this issue started with "educated" parents, concerned about their children's safety, but led to the education of other parents and adults involved in organizing youth hockey. Safety issues also led to concerns about

---

[6]A small part of this loss was taken up by girls, whose registration in hockey increased 400 percent between 1989 and 1999 (from 10,000 to 40,000), and continues to increase.

[7]The 1974 McMurtry Report in Ontario highlighted the growing concerns about violence in the game. As a result of all of these changes, and because of a massive increase in girls' participation, soccer passed hockey as the sport with the highest participation rate in Canada in 1990 (Scanlan, 2002).

skill development—especially recognition of the declining number of Canadian players in the NHL, and the fact that few Canadian players are among the scoring leaders in the NHL. The Open Ice Summit, chaired by Wayne Gretzky in Toronto in 1998, addressed the issue of practice time versus competition, and its recommendations are slowly leading to more emphasis on skill development in minor hockey.

Finally adults who organize sports in Canada (and especially hockey) have had to respond to two major child sexual abuse crises: the Graham James case and the Maple Leaf Gardens scandal (sexual abuse and sexual harassment in sports are discussed in more detail in chapter 7). Police checks and a number of educational programmes (e.g., STOP, "Speak Out," and "Respect" programmes) were developed in response to this problem.

Educating the adults is an ongoing issue in children's sports programmes. The steps taken in Canada have helped to ameliorate some of the problems, but anyone who follows children's sports is aware that we have a long way to go. A number of children's sport organizations have introduced parent education programmes, encouraged parents to sign agreements and charters regarding their behaviour, and even gone so far as to ban parents from hockey arenas, figure skating practices, and so on. But still there are problems. In hockey, 10,000 referees quit every year in Canada (one-third the total number of referees), partly as a result of the abuse received from parents, coaches, and players.[8]

Assumption 3: Kids Are Miniature Adults

Problems occur when adults fail to take into account that the athletes involved at this level of sports are children. Some problems are associated with the fact that children are smaller and

not as strong as adults; others result when adults fail to consider children's stages of cognitive and physical development. Many of these problems are addressed in the following sections on "Children in High-Performance Sports," and "Sociological Questions about Youth Sports," but two points are worth considering here.

First, how are children treated during their participation? Is there enough quality practice time to develop the skills necessary to participate? (Does hockey have too many competitions and too little practice? Does diving have too much practice and not enough competitions?) Do referees see educating children about the rules of the game (written and unwritten) as a part of their duties? Do league and sport administrators try to deal fairly with children with regard to transfers, sanctions, appeals, and so on, while also having to deal with their parents? Do coaches see it as their task to yell criticism about the mistakes young players invariably make, or to be supportive and explain how mistakes can be rectified? And do parents know that it is inappropriate to yell the same types of things at children's games as they do at Calgary Stampeders or Montréal Canadiens games?

Second, when children are playing, are the equipment and rules adapted to their age and ability levels? Are they playing with a small-size soccer ball or basketball? Is the net lower and the basket bigger than it is for adults in basketball? Are goalies in hockey and soccer expected to protect the same size goals as adults? Is the playing area smaller to encourage more action and involvement?

Many creative changes in equipment and playing areas have been made for children, but more need to be made. With regard to rules, are children playing by the same rules as adults, and is this appropriate? The answers will vary depending on the sport and the level of competition. Despite many progressive moves, sports sometimes take a step backwards. In 2002, Hockey Canada reintroduced bodychecking for nine-year-old players (Atom)—it had previously been

---

[8]In Dartmouth, Nova Scotia, "[T]he dropout rate among officials is . . . one third of the national average," as a result of the introduction of a fair play league (Scanlan, 2002, p. 256).

limited to peewee divisions (12–13-year-olds, reduced to 11–12-year-olds in 2002). The decision was intended to encourage players to begin to learn the skill of checking as early as possible, but it was extremely controversial (Robidoux and Trudel, 2006), based on erroneous research claiming no difference in injury levels between checking and non-checking leagues. The majority of studies show that there are more injuries in checking leagues at these age levels (e.g., Macpherson et al., 2006; see the box on "Injuries in Children's Hockey," in chapter 7). Hockey Canada did not revoke the new regulation, but left it up to each minor league to decide.

Some sports have been more creative than others with rule adaptations. For example, baseball created T-ball to overcome the problem of young children pitching and hitting pitched balls, introduced pitching machines into games, and is currently working on a number of modified and more active forms of baseball to attract participants at a time of declining registrations in the sport.[9]

Assumption 4: The Real Value in Sports Lies in Learning to Be a Winner, People Can Be Divided into Winners and Losers, and Sport[s Are Vehicles] to Make Sure You (or Your Kids) End Up in the Right Group

Michael Smith's final assumption points to a struggle that is still alive in the field of children's sports and physical activity. On one side of the struggle, there are those, often educators, who advocate children's involvement in a variety of healthy forms of physical activity because of the established mental, physical, and social benefits that result. They advocate both competitive and non-competitive forms of activity, but sometimes emphasize the non-competitive and cooperative forms of activity because of the social benefits of cooperation (cf., Kohn, 1992). They also point

out the "exclusive" nature of competition and the disturbing dropout rate in many competitive organized sports. As Canadian sport psychologists Terry Orlick of the University of Ottawa and Cal Botterill of the University of Winnipeg point out: "It's ridiculous to promote participation on the one hand, and then to cut interested individuals from the team, or to in any way limit their participation" (1975, p. 17). If children are being cut from programmes because of their lack of size or skills (instead of being taught those skills), and no alternatives are available, participation is reduced.

On the other side of the struggle, there are those who support the view that "people can be divided into winners and losers" and who want their children to participate in organized competitive sports because they believe it will give them a competitive advantage in life. Primary school teachers often hear from such parents advocating this view when they attempt to run cooperative educational programmes in their classrooms; and some analysts have argued that the growth in community sports, especially for younger males, occurred precisely because professional educators tended to discourage or de-emphasize competition in primary schools, and to play down the intensity of interschool competitions in high school.

Both sides in this struggle have seen some successes and failures. On the participation side, the development of house leagues and the widespread use of cooperative games have helped to promote participation; and interschool sports have, in general, managed to maintain an emphasis on participation and education rather than just competition. However, in the mid-1970s, many municipal Parks and Recreation Departments in Canada stopped organizing competitive sport programmes, ostensibly because of the criticism of and problems in such programmes, but cutting them was also a cost-saving move for municipalities. The loss of these low-cost opportunities to participate (which still exist in a number of U.S. cities) forced non-school organized competitive

---

[9]These issues of adaptation can be controversial, and some adults argue that children need to play with full-size equipment and formal rules in order to become used to them.

sports for children into the non-profit and private sectors where it became more difficult to control the problems that existed. Organized competitive sport programmes emphasizing competition are now an important part of most communities in Canada, and the introduction of house leagues has resulted in the provision of a wide range of participation and competition opportunities. But the problems outlined above still exist at the competitive levels—poor coaching, problem parents, high injury rates, and so on. As noted in the Reflect on Sports box, "Informal, Player-Controlled Sports versus Organized, Adult-Controlled Sports" on pages 135–136, children themselves often de-emphasize competition, both in alternative sports and in other informal, player-controlled sports.

CHILDREN IN HIGH-PERFORMANCE SPORTS

At the Montréal Olympic Games in 1976, a 14-year-old Romanian gymnast named Nadia Comaneci completed a number of amazing routines and was awarded the first ("perfect") scores of 10.0 ever recorded in the sport. She, and the large number of medals that were won by East German athletes, drew attention in the West to the sport system that had been developed in Eastern Europe and the Soviet Union. Doug Gilbert (1976), a sportswriter for the *Montréal Gazette*, described the system:

- Early exposure of children to physical education and a wide range of physical activities
- A broad base of participants in sports and physical activity
- Early identification of athletic talent
- Intensive and specialized training for those identified

East European and Cuban success in Montréal, combined with Canada's hurt pride as the first Olympic host not to win a gold medal, triggered interest in the new system. Sport scientists began

to conduct research into talent prediction and early specialization in sports, and sport organizations began to recruit younger and younger athletes. After the fall of the GDR, top-secret documents revealed that East Germany's Olympic success was due in large part to the biggest government-sponsored doping program the sports world has ever known (*Doping for Gold*, 2008). The early success of the female gymnasts, and victories for young female athletes in sports such as figure skating and swimming, provided an additional incentive for early involvement and specialization. Such a system was not completely new to Canada since it existed to some extent in hockey, but early intensive involvement was new to most other sports, and problems began to emerge.

By the early 1980s, commentators such as Hart Cantelon of Queen's University (1981) were beginning to identify the new participants as "child athletic workers," and their participation as "child labour," and as a social problem. Following Cantelon's lead, in 1985, Peter Donnelly began collecting data on these problems. He conducted a series of retrospective interviews with retired high-performance athletes in Canada. The 45 former athletes (16 male, 29 female) represented a variety of sports and claimed to have had successful careers; all had intensive involvement in the sport during their childhood and adolescence; all were given every opportunity to address both positive and negative aspects of their careers; and each spent approximately ten times more time on the negative than the positive.

They reported a variety of problems that they connected directly to their early intensive involvement and specialization. These included:

- Family concerns—problems such as sibling rivalry and parental pressure
- Social relationships—missed important occasions and experiences during childhood and adolescence
- Coach–athlete relationships—authoritarian and abusive (emotional, physical, sexual) relationships, especially in male coach/female athlete relationships

- Educational concerns—any achievements were earned in spite of the sport and education systems, not because of them
- Physical and psychological problems— injuries, stress, and burnout
- Drug and dietary problems—some experiences of drug use, concern about eating disorders
- Retirement—adjustment difficulties, especially when retirement was not voluntary

These findings have been confirmed by additional informal interviews in Canada (including athletes who had heard or read about the research and approached Donnelly with their own stories) and other countries that adopted the early involvement and specialization model, and have been supplemented by reports in more popular sources (e.g., Ryan, 1995).

Donnelly also asked the former athletes whether they would repeat their careers (10 percent said no, and 65 percent gave a qualified yes—knowing what they know now); and whether they would permit their own children to become involved in intensive training in their sport (40 percent said no, and many of the 60 percent who said yes suggested that their experiences and knowledge would help them to protect their own children from the problems and provide them with a more positive experience).

As a result of these types of critiques, and especially following an intensive period of criticism about the U.S. women's gymnastics team following the 1992 Barcelona Olympic Games (their youth, small bodies, and stress fractures gave rise to numerous concerns about eating disorders), three sport organizations made rule changes. The Women's Tennis Association (WTA) raised the age for turning professional to sixteen because of the well-publicized burnout of young players such as Tracy Austin, Jennifer Capriati, and Andrea Jaeger; and both women's gymnastics and women's figure

> Last summer I was skating five hours a day, five days a week. I really wanted to try something else. I just . . . got sick of it. My parents . . . felt bad because I'd spent so much time and money on it.
>
> —Megan, age 13, Grosse Point Woods, MI (1999)

skating organizations raised the minimum age for international competition to sixteen. [Concerns that the age limit had been violated by Chinese gymnasts were widespread at the Beijing Olympics.] However, we argue that the new age limits are only token changes, and, particularly in gymnastics and figure skating, they have done little to resolve the problems, and may even have made them worse. Extending the age of international competition without changing judging criteria, or introducing regulations about health, nutrition, or bone density, could force adolescent girls to attempt to maintain a pre-pubescent body type until they are even older.

The widespread concerns, together with critical and medical research, appear to have had some impact in gymnastics where a range of body types is now apparent in international competitions. (For an example of a current problem involving children in high-performance sport, see the Reflect on Sports box on "The New Slave Trade? Child Trafficking in Sports," pp. 124–125).

Canadian children from all backgrounds, but now most commonly from the middle classes, who have shown talent in hockey, swimming, figure skating, tennis, gymnastics, and so on—all the sports that are invested in an early specialization developmental track—may experience the types of problems outlined above. Gabriela Tymowski, of the University of New Brunswick, also recognized these problems (2001a, 2001b). Solving the problems created by early intensive involvement and specialization raises a question of balance. (See the Reflect on Sports box, "Solving the Problems in Children's High-Performance Sports" on the Online Learning Centre.) But that balance is difficult to maintain when we consider all of the adults who may have a vested interest in a child's success in sports—parents, coaches, sport administrators, educators, sport scientists, sports medicine staff, agents, and even media personnel (Donnelly, 1997;

REFLECT ON SPORTS

The New Slave Trade?
Child Trafficking in Sports

> **Amazingly, the selling of minors [in sports] is not an offence.**
>
> —*Straits Times*, 2000

Children are bought and sold on national and international markets, usually for the purposes of physical labour or sexual exploitation. This is a lucrative business for the traffickers, involving an estimated one million children each year. However, one rarely discussed aspect of child trafficking is the trade in young athletes.

Perhaps the most heinous aspect of this involves the purchase or kidnap of young boys from Pakistan or Bangladesh to become jockeys in the camel racing industry on the Arabian Peninsula. The sport, centred in the United Arab Emirates, involves large amounts of money in camel breeding and gambling. Small boys, as young as five or six years of age, are preferred as jockeys because of their low weight. There are many accidents, widespread reports of abuse, and the children are abandoned or returned to their homes when they reach the age of eleven or twelve, and are too heavy to be of value as jockeys (Donnelly and Petherick, 2004). Pressure from organizations such as Anti-Slavery International, and Lawyers for Human Rights and Legal Aid, led the Camel Jockey Association to change its rules in 1993 to prohibit the use of boys under fourteen years of age and under 45kg; however, it appears that these rules are widely ignored, with evidence of six-year-olds who weigh less than 20kg still participating.

The most widespread aspect of child trafficking is in soccer/football. Young players, mainly from Africa and South America, are recruited by agents for professional soccer clubs in Western Europe. Recent data regarding this "muscle drain" (Poli and Ravenel, 2006) indicate that there are some 316 African players in the first division clubs in the eleven major European soccer nations, and many more at the lower division clubs. Because of widespread examples of exploitation

---

V. INTERNATIONAL TRANSFERS INVOLVING MINORS
Article 19: Protection of Minors

1. International transfers of players are only permitted if the player is over the age of 18.
2. The following three exceptions apply to this rule:
   a) The player's parents move to the country in which the New Club is located for reasons not linked to football; or
   b) The transfer takes place within the territory of the European Union (EU) or the European Economic Area (EEA) and the player is aged between 16 and 18. In this case, the New Club must fulfill the following minimum obligations:
      i. It shall provide the player with an adequate football education and/or training in line with the highest national standards.
      ii. It shall guarantee the player an academic and/or school and/or vocational education and/or training, in addition to his football education and/or training, which will allow the player to pursue a career other than football should he cease playing professional football.
      iii. It shall make all necessary arrangements to ensure that the player is looked after in the best possible way (optimum living standards with a guest family or in club accommodation, appointment of a mentor at the club, etc.).
      iv. It shall, on registration of such a player, provide the relevant Association with proof that it is complying with the aforementioned obligations; or
   c) The player lives no further than 50km from a national border, and the club for which the player wishes to be registered in the neighbouring Association is also within 50km of that border. The maximum distance between the player's domicile and the club's quarters shall be 100km. In such cases, the player must continue to live at home and the two Associations concerned must give their explicit consent....
4. Each Association shall ensure the respect of this provision by its clubs.

FIFA: Regulations for the Status and Transfer of Players (2003)

Continued

(e.g., agents stealing money from the young players, players being abandoned on the streets of European cities when they fail to make the professional club's youth team—often becoming child prostitutes in order to survive), the Fédération Internationale de Football Association (FIFA) introduced new regulations for the "protection of minors" in 2003 [see inset box]. However, in what has been termed a "modern version of the slave trade" (Lindberg, 2006), it seems that the regulations are widely ignored by a large number of unofficial agents. For example, in what Mbvoumin (www.footsolidare.org) calls "player laundering," documents (including passports) are often changed to make the players older.

The organization, Culture Foot Solidaire, estimates that there are 7,000 African youths across France, originally brought to the country by football agents—98 percent are illegal immigrants, and 70 percent are below eighteen years of age (www. footsolidaire.org). The situation is similar in a number of European countries, and the reason for recruiting such large numbers is because it is so inexpensive (children often have to pay their own fares to Europe, their families borrowing the money), and because the rewards from discovering a star player are so high. For example, in the case of Michael Essien, the French team SC Bastia paid 50,000 euros to Liberty Accra, his team in Ghana; Olympique Lyonnais paid SC Bastia 8 million euros for his contract; and Chelsea FC paid Olympique Lyonnais 36 million euros (Bennhold, 2006). The slavery analogy continues with European clubs establishing soccer training schools in countries such as South Africa and Senegal—these are sometimes referred to as "football plantations."

How is trafficking in young athletes relevant in Canada? The early talent identification and recruitment systems for high-performance and professional sports are now well-established in North America, and in the globalized market for talented athletes North American teams now send scouts to all countries where there are likely players. Perhaps the best example in Canada is Major Junior hockey. The "midget" draft of the best 14-, 15- or 16-year-old players, many who already have agents, represents a form of trafficking, and most of those drafted will have to leave home in order to play. The Major Junior clubs also maintain their quota of young European players. These clubs are not technically professional (although the players are considered to be professional, and therefore not eligible for scholarships by U.S. universities), but spectators must pay to attend games, the clubs "trade" players, and they are still considered to be the major avenue of recruitment to National Hockey League teams.

As with the other forms of trafficking, there are many examples of exploitation (Allain, 2004; Cantelon, 2006) and some notorious examples of abuse (Kennedy, 2006; Robinson, 1998). There are few regulations governing this traffic in young hockey players, and numerous examples of the regulations not being enforced or monitored. There are a great many policies and regulations that govern the treatment of children in education, the workplace, and other areas of their lives, but not in sports. The introduction, and enforcement, of a set of regulations similar to FIFA's Article 19 (*Protection of Minors*) could lead to a widespread reconsideration of our treatment of children as economic commodities in sports. *What do you think?*

••

Donnelly and Petherick, 2004). For some of these adults, their careers and incomes may depend on a child's success, and there are even cases of parents who have taken out a second mortgage in order to finance their talented child's sport development. Parents, coaches, and other interested parties are concerned that an overemphasis on the child having

a "normal" life may lead to failure to fully develop his/her talent (and miss a chance at the Olympics and/or a career as a highly paid professional athlete), but it is apparent that an overemphasis on the talent can also lead to a variety of problems, from exploitation to burnout. It is precisely this lack of balance that led Donnelly (1993b, p. 120) to suggest that Canadian national team athletes were the survivors, rather than the products, of our high-performance development system, and that we had to find a way to stop "sacrific[ing] children on the altar of international and professional sport success." (See Reflect on Sports box "Solving the Problems in Children's High-Performance Sports," on the Online Learning Centre.)

SOCIOLOGICAL QUESTIONS ABOUT YOUTH SPORTS

Dozens of questions could be raised in this section, and we have chosen three that people who work with children ought to be able to answer as they plan programmes and make policies related to youth sports.

When Are Children Ready to Play Organized Competitive Sports?

Parents ask readiness questions often. They wonder: should I sign my four-year-olds up for T-ball teams, put my six-year-olds on a competitive swim team, and let my ten-year-olds participate in provincial skating competitions? Some want to give their children an early start on an imagined path to athletic glory; some do not want their children to fall behind peers in skills development; and some just want their children to have healthy fun and a positive body image.

Scholars in physical education, motor learning, exercise physiology, psychology, and sociology provide answers to readiness questions. Sociological answers often reflect interactionist research carried out by researchers who study social development during childhood. This work indicates that children begin, at about eight years of age, to develop the cognitive and social abilities they must have to understand the complex relationships in competitive sports. Among most children these abilities are not fully developed until about twelve years of age.

Anyone who has watched two teams of seven-year-old soccer players knows about these developmental issues. Most children younger than twelve play "beehive soccer": After the opening kick, there are twenty bodies and forty legs surrounding the ball, and they follow the ball around the playing field like a swarm of bees. Everyone is out of position, and most players usually stay that way for the entire game. Meanwhile, the coaches and parents loudly plead with them to "Stay in position!" and "Get back where you belong!" However, determining where you belong in most sports is difficult. Positions change, depending on the placement of teammates and opponents relative to the location of the ball. Understanding the concept of position requires the ability to do three things simultaneously: (1) mentally visualize the ever-changing placements of teammates and opponents over the entire field, (2) assess their relationships to each other and to the ball, and (3) then decide where you belong. The ability to think through these three things and accurately determine where you should be on the field develops gradually in connection with social experience and individual maturation.

Parents and coaches become frustrated when children fail to understand positions and strategies. When adults do not take into account the cognitive and social development patterns during childhood, they mistakenly think that children are not concentrating or trying hard. This frustrates children who *are* doing the best they can at their level of psychosocial development.

"Beehive soccer" and its equivalents in other sports are avoided in two ways. *First*, the games children play can be altered to focus on skills and expression rather than competition and team strategies. In other words, games can be revised to fit the children's needs and abilities (Morris and Stiehl, 1989; Orlick, 1978; Torbert, 2004, 2005). This is a preferred strategy.

Second, children can be systematically conditioned to respond in certain ways to certain situations during competitive games and matches. This requires that coaches create game situations during practices so that each player can rehearse individual tactical responses to each situation, over and over, again and again. This makes practices boring, but it generally helps teams to win games. However, in the long run it is not a preferred strategy because it often destroys much of the action and personal involvement that children value in sports.

Children are not born with the ability to compete or cooperate with others. Nor are they born with the ability to visualize complex sets of social relationships between teammates and opponents. They must learn these things, and the learning occurs in connection with a combination of social experiences and the development of abstract thinking abilities. This learning cannot be forced. It occurs only as children move from a stage in which they see the world from an egocentric viewpoint to a stage in which they can see the world through the eyes of many others at once. (Donnelly, 2002). This ability gradually emerge between the ages of eight and twelve years in most children. Therefore, organized sports for children younger than twelve should be controlled and modified to accommodate this gradually emerging ability. In the meantime, the main emphasis should be on developing physical skills and basic cooperation. After all, children must learn to cooperate before they can compete with each other in positive ways. If they do not know how to cooperate, competitions often degenerate into chaos.

Finally, those of us who ask the question "When should children play organized competitive sports?" generally live in cultures in which scientific approaches to childhood development are popular, and people have the time and resources to organize children's activities. *Youth sports are a luxury.* They cost money and take time; therefore, many people cannot afford them. This is true even in wealthy countries among families with few resources. Many children around the world simply include movement and physical play in their lives as they grow up in their cultures. Deciding when to begin organized sports is not an issue for them or their parents because their lines are seriously constrained by a lack of resources. Therefore, it is important to be aware of poverty and its impact on children's lives as we discuss questions related to youth sports.

What Are the Dynamics of Family Relationships in Connection with Organized Youth Sports?

Organized youth sports require time, money, and organizational skills, and these usually come from parents. Therefore, playing organized sports is often a family affair. However, few sociologists have carried out research on how youth sport participation affects family relationships.

Anecdotal information indicates that youth sports can bring family members together in supportive ways or create problems in family relationships. Parents may become so emotionally involved with sports that they put pressure on their children or fail to see that their children perceive their encouragement as pressure to play well and stay involved in sports. When children feel such pressure, they face a triple dilemma: (1) if they quit sports, they fear that the parents may withdraw support and attention; (2) if they play sports but do not perform well, they fear the parents will criticize them; (3) if they perform well, they fear that their parents will treat them like "little pros" and never let them do other things.

Studies by Coakley (2001), Donnelly (1993), and Kay (2000) all highlight the stresses experienced by parents and siblings in families where at least one of the children is involved in sports at a high-performance level. When a great deal of the family's time and resources are directed to the sport participation of one individual, it can become all-consuming, and Kay (2001) noted that, in the U.K., the divorce rate in such families was higher than the national average. The widely reported father–son bonding through sports may also have limitations. Messner's (1992) interviews with former elite male athletes showed that the father–child togetherness they had in sports did not involve real intimacy and did not carry over into their lives away from sports. This can occur with daughters as well.

Organized youth sports have an impact on families and family relationships in other ways as well. Studies in the United States (Chafetz and Kotarba, 1999) and Australia (Thompson, 1999a, 1999b) highlight the fact that organized sport programmes for children could not exist without the volunteer labour of parents, especially mothers. Mothers drive children to practices and games, fix meals at convenient times, launder dirty training clothes and uniforms, and make sure that equipment is ready. They raise funds for teams and leagues; purchase, prepare, and serve food during road trips and at postgame get-togethers; form and serve on committees that supervise off-the-field social activities; and make phone calls about schedules and schedule changes. Mothers also manage the activities of brothers and sisters who are not playing in the programmes, and they provide emotional support for their child-athletes when they play poorly or when coaches or fathers criticize how they play. Fathers also provide labour, but it is devoted primarily to on-the-field and administrative matters, such as coaching, field maintenance, and

league administration (although mothers increasingly are taking on these tasks as well).

When parental labour occurs in this pattern, youth sports reproduce a gendered division of labour in families, communities, and the minds of children, especially the boys who are treated as "son-gods" as they play organized sports. More research is needed on this and other aspects of family dynamics that exist in connection with youth sports. For example, we know little about fatherhood and sports, a topic that is important to consider as expectations for parents become more demanding and wives demand more assistance from their husbands (Kay, 2006).

How Do Social Factors Influence Youth Sport Experiences?

Children make choices about playing sports, but they have little control over the context in which they make their choices. Many factors, including parents, peers, and the general social and cultural context in which they live, influence the alternatives from which they choose and how they

There is an interesting parental division of labour associated with youth sports. Mothers provide a wide range of off-the-field support, while fathers do the coaching and league administration. [M. MacNeill]

define and give meaning to their choices. For example, children from low-income backgrounds generally have fewer sport participation opportunities than other children. Children with able bodies have more opportunities and receive more encouragement to play sports than children with a disability. Choosing to play a contact sport, such as football, is seen by most people to be more appropriate for boys than for girls. Boys who want to figure skate generally do not receive the same encouragement from peers as girls receive. Racial and ethnic stereotypes often influence the sport participation choices made by people who learn to associate certain sports and physical skills with various skin colours and cultural backgrounds (Coakley, 2002; Harrison and Lawrence, 2004; L. Harrison, 1995; Harrison et al., 1999; Harrison et al., 2004; Lewis, 2003).

None of these statements is earthshaking. People know these things. They know that, as children make sport choices and give meaning to their experiences, they and the people around them are influenced by the prevailing cultural beliefs about age, gender, sexuality, race and ethnicity, ability and disability, and social class. This is how social forces influence youth sport experiences. (See the Breaking Barriers box on pages 130–131.)

For example, research shows that sport choices and experiences are influenced by dominant definitions of gender in society. These definitions influence early childhood experiences when it comes to physical activities (White et al., 1992). In the United States, research has shown that fathers play with their sons more often and in more physically active ways than they play with their daughters. Furthermore, the physical activity messages that most young boys receive differ from the messages many young girls receive, both inside and outside family settings (Beal, 1994; Greendorfer, 1993; Hargreaves, 1994; Hasbrook, 1999; Lenskyj, 1986; Nelson, 1991).

Because of these messages, most children have definite ideas about their physical skills and potential before they even think about playing sports. For example, boys are more likely, than girls to *think* they are better than they actually are as athletes. This affects their self-confidence and willingness to be physically active and express an interest in playing youth sports. Overall, girls learn to minimize the physical space they occupy, sexualize their bodies through modifying their appearance and movement, and accept the notion that boys are physically superior to them. And boys learn to present themselves as physically big and strong, act in ways that claim physical space around them, and assume power and control over girls in sports (Hasbrook, 1999; Hasbrook and Harris, 1999).

Gender-related expectations may be one of the reasons boys' ball games often dominate the space on elementary school playgrounds and in other public places. This pattern extends through the life course. For instance, observe the playing fields and gyms on a Canadian campus and measure the amount of time that young men or young women appropriate those spaces for themselves. It is often difficult to change these male-dominant patterns because they are deeply rooted in the culture as a whole.

The influence of social forces on youth sports has been identified in many studies. Research by Ingham and Dewar (1999) shows how dominant ideas about masculinity influence the meanings that boys give to their experiences in a youth hockey programme. Jay Coakley's research shows how dominant ideas about ethnicity and social class influence the funding and programme orientations of youth sport programmes in minority areas in inner cities and in white suburban areas in the U.S. (Coakley, 2002). Howard Nixon (2000) discusses the exclusion and the participation barriers faced by children with certain disabilities. As we read these studies, it is important to focus on variations in the experiences of children rather than simply looking for differences by gender, ethnicity, ability, and social class. As we see how experiences vary, we learn how social forces interact with each other and influence children's lives on and off the playing field.

Breaking Barriers

Mainstreaming Barriers
Will They Let Me Play with My Brace?

Ally was born with a physical impairment—no fine motor movement in her left hand and a left leg that was stabilized by a brace as she learned to walk. Ally did not see her impairments as problems because she never experienced life without them. In her eyes, her body was simply a fact of life. Like other children, she developed physical skills and learned about her limits. After playing soccer with her parents and sisters and watching her older sister play on a team, she said she wanted to be on a team, and asked, "Will they let me play with my brace?"

Ally's brace had never been an issue in her family. But Ally observed sports on television, went to high school and university volleyball and basketball games, and watched her parents and sister play in local leagues. Not seeing athletes with braces caused her to wonder if people would let her play with one. Growing up in a society where images of athletes reflect a "cultural fantasy" of bodies that conform to ideal standards of beauty and ability (Thomson, 2002), Ally wondered if there was space for a girl who deviated from those standards enough to need a brace.

The public, community-sponsored youth soccer programme where Ally lived was covered by the Americans with Disability Act (ADA).[1] When

applied to youth sports, this law states that public programmes and private programmes open to the public cannot exclude children with disabilities unless there are direct threats to the health and safety of able-bodied participants. The threats must be real, based on objective information, and unavoidable even after reasonable efforts are made to eliminate them. In Ally's case, it was easy to follow the law: Pads were put on her brace, and the soccer league did not have to make accommodations that would cause "undue burden" or a "fundamental alteration of the programme" (Block, 1995).

According to the ADA, if there were tryouts for a team, the coach *could* not cut Ally because she had a disability, but Ally could be cut for skills-related reasons. Her coaches could not say that all players must be able to run without a limp to play on the team, but they could say that any child who could not run the length of the field would be cut.

As youth sports programmes increasingly stress a performance ethic, children with disabilities lack the requisite skills to play on mainstream organized teams. This is why few children with disabilities are mainstreamed in youth sports, even though they are routinely mainstreamed in classrooms.

Although most people define this approach as reasonable, it leaves children with disabilities two options if they wish to play sports: Find an adapted programme, or play informal games in which peers are willing and able to develop adaptations. Unfortunately, many communities lack public programmes adapted for children with disabilities, and local peer groups

[1]Mental and physical disability rights were included, after some struggle, in the Canadian Charter of Rights and Freedoms, and in many provincial Human Rights Acts. However, although accommodations are frequently made in sport and physical education for children with a disability, there is no federal or provincial legislation yet that carries the force of the ADA.

Continued

MAJOR TRENDS AND RECOMMENDATIONS

Major Trends in Youth Sports Today

In addition to their growing popularity, youth sports are changing in at least five other socially significant ways. *First*, organized programmes have become increasingly privatized. This means

that more youth sports today are sponsored by private, non-profit, and commercial organizations, or are increasingly subject to user fees.

Second, organized programmes increasingly emphasize the "performance ethic." This means that participants in youth sports, even in house leagues and recreational programmes, are encouraged to evaluate their experiences in terms seldom have experiences that enable them to quickly or easily include a child with disabilities in their informal games.

Research indicates that in light of these two options most children with disabilities are relegated to the sidelines. Without someone to advocate their interests, they become observers rather than participants. This is noted by a ten-year-old boy with cerebral palsy who explains that his peers "like me but . . . if I'm trying to get in a game without a friend, it's kind of hard" (in Taub and Greer, 2000, p. 406). Without a friend who has enough power with peers and enough experience with disabilities to facilitate a process of adaptation and inclusion, this ten-year-old does not play sports. Other children describe their experiences in these terms: "[Kids] try and shove me off the court, tell me not to play," "they just don't want me on their team," and "there's a couple of people that won't let me play" (in Taub and Greer, 2000, p. 406). Such experiences deny

children with disabilities access to contexts in which friendships are formed and nurtured, and to activities that have "normalizing" effects for children growing up in a culture where sports are defined as socially and self-validating activities.

As we consider how to eliminate barriers that prevent mainstreaming in sports, think of these statements made by children with cerebral palsy:

> [Playing games] makes me feel good 'cause I get to be with everybody, . . . and talk about how our day was in school while we play.
>
> Playing basketball is something that I can do with my friends that I never thought I could do [with them], but I can, I can! (in Taub and Greer, 2000, pp. 406 and 408)

Eliminating barriers to mainstreaming is challenging. But we can if we use our abilities creatively and compassionately.

- -

of developing technical skills and progressing to higher personal levels of achievement. Linking this with the first trend, there has also been an increase in the number of private, elite sport-training facilities that are dedicated to producing highly skilled and specialized athletes who can move up to higher levels of competition.

Third, parents have become more involved in and concerned about the participation and success of their children in organized youth sports. This has made youth sports into serious activities for adults and children, and adults are more likely to act in extreme ways as they advocate the interests of their children.

Fourth, there seems to be an increasing culture of caution surrounding youth sports and physical activity, with increased supervision and surveillance, legislation in the face of concerns about injuries, sexual abuse, and other safety concerns.

Fifth, participation in alternative action sports has increased. This means that many young

people prefer unstructured, participant-controlled sports, such as skateboarding, in-line skating, snowboarding, BMX biking, and various other physical activities that have local or regional relevance for children.

These five trends have an impact on who participates in organized youth sports and what kinds of experiences children have when they do participate.

Privatization and User Fees in Organized Programmes

Privatization, and the introduction of user fees, are interesting and sometimes alarming trends in youth sports today. Although organized sports and physical activity have become more popular, there has been a decline in the number of publicly funded programmes with free and open participation policies. When local governments face budget crises, various social services, including recreation programmes, often are cut back. In the face of cutbacks, local parks and recreation departments have tried to maintain physical activity and instructional programmes by imposing participation fees to cover expenses (Slack, 2003). (See chapter 10, pp. 315–316, for an example of how this impacted the City of Toronto.) There are now user fees in interschool sport programmes as provincial government cutbacks have also affected education budgets.

When municipalities stopped funding youth sport leagues in the mid 1970s, community non-profit organizations (e.g., the Burlington Youth Soccer Association) began to offer them. All involved fees, although commercial sponsors from the community and favourable public facility rental rates often helped to keep the fees fairly low. However, fees do depend on facility rental costs, the amount of travel, and the number of practices and competitions. Thus, a "travel team" in hockey usually involves significant costs for the parents of children involved—not just in terms of equipment and ice time but also travel and tournament costs. In many parts of Canada, it appears that only middle-class children are now able to participate easily at the higher levels of hockey. In fact, concerns about costs are now widespread in youth sports. For example, a recent report from Swim B C stated: "As the government cuts back significantly in their contributions to sport... *the primary issue facing the administration of swimming in B.C. is the rising cost of participation* (Swim B C, 2005, p. 39, emphasis added).

Commercial sport providers also have entered the youth sport scene in growing numbers. In Canada, these often take the form of private clubs for skiing, skating, golf, and other sports, or summer sport specialist camps providing intensive training in a sport. The camps are often owned by celebrity athletes and coaches, and are usually run on a commercial (for profit) basis. The private commercial programmes are usually selective and exclusive, and they provide few opportunities for children from low-income households. The technical instruction in these programmes often is good, and they provide

regulated skills training for children from wealthier families. Through commercial programmes, some parents hire private coaches for their children at rates of $35–$150 per hour.

Two negative consequences are associated with this trend. *First*, privatized programmes reproduce the economic and ethnic inequalities that exist in the larger society. Unlike public programmes, they depend on the resources of participants rather than entire communities. Low-income and single-parent families often lack money to pay various expenses. This, in turn, creates or accentuates ethnic segregation and social class divisions in communities. *Second*, as parks and recreation departments cease to offer programmes, they often become brokers of public parks and facilities, and rent them out for private and non-profit sport programmes. The private programmes that use public parks and facilities may not have commitments to gender equity or other policies of inclusion, which are mandated in public programmes. For example, if 83 percent of the participants in these programmes are boys, and 17 percent are girls, taxpayers face a situation in which they directly subsidize the perpetuation of gender inequity. (See the B.C. human rights case in chapter 8, p. 237.) There are obvious problems associated with privatization and user fees, and they disproportionately affect poor people with little political power; therefore they receive little attention.

Emphasis on the Performance Ethic The performance ethic has become increasingly important in youth sport programmes. This means that performance becomes a measured outcome and an indicator of the quality of the sport experience. *Fun* in these programmes comes to be defined in terms of becoming a better athlete, becoming more competitive, and being promoted into more highly skilled training categories. Often, the categories have names that identify skill levels, so there may be gold, silver, and bronze groups to indicate a child's status in the programme. Many parents like this because it enables them to judge their child's progress and to prove to themselves and others that they are "good" parents (see the quote from MacGregor on the first page of this chapter).

Private and commercial programmes emphasize the performance ethic to a greater degree than public and non-profit programmes, and many market themselves as "centres of athletic excellence." This approach attracts parents willing and able to pay high fees for membership, participation, and instruction. Another way to sell a private programme to parents who can afford the cost is to highlight successful athletes and coaches who have trained or worked in the programme.

Parents of physically skilled children are attracted to programmes emphasizing the performance ethic. They sometimes define high fees and equipment expenses as *investments* in their children's future. They are concerned with skill development and, as their children grow older, they use performance-oriented programmes as sources of information about scholarships, as well as networks for contacting coaches and sport organizations. They approach their children's sport participation rationally and see clear connections between participation and their children's future development, educational opportunities, and success in adult life.

Of course, the application of the performance ethic is not limited to organized sports; it influences a range of organized children's activities (Mannon, 1997). Childhood in some segments of wealthy societies has been changed from an age of exploration and freedom to an age of preparation and controlled learning. Children's sports reflect this longer trend (Elkind, 1981; Sokolove, 2004a; Wolff, 2003).

Increased Involvement and Concerns Among Parents

Youth sports have become a serious business in many families. The notion that good parents today must control the actions of their children 24 hours a day, and carefully promote and monitor their children's development has changed parents' lives over the past two generations. Many parents now feel compelled to find the best organized youth sport programmes for their children and to ensure that their children's interests are being met in those programmes.

Even though various factors influence child development today, many people attribute the success or failure of children entirely to their parents. When children are successful in sports, their parents are seen to be doing the right thing as parents. When Wayne Gretzky began to set NHL records, everyone labelled Walter Gretzky, his father, as a good and wise parent. When children succeed, parents are labelled "good parents" and even asked by other parents how they did it. When a child fails, people question the moral worth of the parents.

Under these conditions, a child's success in sports is especially important for many parents. Youth sports are highly visible activities and become sites where fathers and mothers can establish and prove their moral worth as parents. This increases the stakes associated with youth sports, and the link between parents' moral worth and their children's sports achievements leads many parents to take youth sports seriously.

The stakes associated with youth sports are increased even further among parents who hope that their children might earn a U.S. athletic scholarship, a contract as a professional athlete, or social acceptance and popularity in school and among peers. When parents think in these terms, the success of their children in youth sports is linked to expected social and financial payoffs.

As the moral, financial, and social stakes associated with youth sport participation have increased, youth sports have become sites for extreme actions among some adults (Engh, 1999; Nack and Munson, 2000). Parents may be assertive and disruptive as they advocate the interests of their child with coaches and youth sport programme administrators. Some are obnoxious and offensive as they scream criticisms of coaches, referees, players, and their own children. A few have even attacked other people over sport-related disagreements.

In one of the most extreme cases, a father from Reading, Massachusetts (U.S.A.), attacked and beat to death another father in connection with events that occurred at an open skating session at an arena. This case was defined as an example of "rink rage" and covered by the media in terms of one hockey dad killing another hockey dad. Subsequent media coverage of extreme, disruptive, or belligerent actions by parents has led many people to think that there is a general epidemic of out-of-control youth sport parents.

This case and others have led to calls for the type of parent education outlined previously, combined with new rules and enforcement procedures to control adults associated with youth sports (e.g., the introduction of video surveillance cameras at Hamilton, Ontario arenas; and the implementation of zero-tolerance policies in some municipalities). These are appropriate strategies, but to be successful they must be administered with an understanding of the context in which parenting occurs today. As long as parents' moral worth is linked with the achievements of children in youth sports, and as long as financial and social payoffs are associated with success in sports, parents will be deeply concerned about their children's sport participation. Furthermore, if people continue to believe that it takes only a family to raise a child, parents will not receive more support from community institutions. This leaves them in a position where they must advocate the interests of their children. If they do not, who will? Under this condition, many parents feel that it is their moral obligation to confront anyone they perceive as standing in the way of their child's happiness and success in sports.

The Culture of Caution We often claim that play and sports are where children learn to take risks, have adventures, and generally prepare in a relatively safe way for the world that they will enter as adults. And, as we argue in subsequent chapters, those risks—particularly the risk of

injury—are still there. But, in a rather contradictory way, there is growing evidence of increasing concern about safety of children, and a growing distrust of those parents pay and/or entrust to look after them. This involves growing surveillance—hidden cameras in children's nurseries and webcams in daycare centres to monitor child care, "black boxes" in cars to check the location and driving behaviour of teenage children, and parental presence at all games and practices to monitor children's safety and coaches' behaviours.

It also involves other concerns about safety, and about lawsuits. The Children's Society and the Children's Play Council in the U.K. recently surveyed children to find out what types of behaviour were being controlled in schools and playgrounds. Their findings (www.the-childrens-society.org.uk) were startling. For example:

- Yo-yos were banned from school playgrounds because they may cause injury.
- Tag and running games were banned in case children fell over.
- In one school, handstands were banned because one student had injured her elbow doing a handstand.
- Children were prevented from picking wildflowers at a kindergarten because they may pick up germs from the ground.
- One school banned the use of a climbing frame in case children fell.

Playgrounds in Toronto, and in some British cities, were closed because the equipment did not meet new safety standards and, at a time of tax cuts and restricted municipal budgets, the equipment was not immediately replaced. A research report prepared for the Play Safety Forum in the U.K. ("Playgrounds: Risks, Benefits and Choices"—www.the-childrens-society.org.uk) calls for a balance between safety and some controlled risk and excitement: "Play provision is first and foremost for children and if it is not exciting and attractive to them, then it will fail, no matter how 'safe' it is."

REFLECT ON SPORTS

Different Experiences: Informal Player-Controlled Sports versus Organized, Adult-Controlled Sports

Jay Coakley and his students have observed children in sports, and interviewed the participants, since the 1970s. They found that the experiences are quite different depending on the type of organization:

- Sports informally organized and controlled by the players tend to be "action-centred."
- Sports formally organized and controlled by adults tend to be "rule-centred."

INFORMAL, PLAYER-CONTROLLED SPORTS

Players in informal and pick-up games of all kinds are interested in four things:

1. Action, especially action leading to scoring
2. Personal involvement in the action
3. A challenging or exciting experience (e.g., a close score in a competitive game)
4. Opportunities to reaffirm friendships during games

Games usually had two to twelve players who often knew each other from previous games. Usually, they formed teams quickly using skill differences and friendship patterns. Starting games, and keeping them going and full of action, was a complex operation and depended on how good the players were at managing interpersonal relationships and making effective decisions.

While rules were similar to formal game rules, there were many modifications to maximize action, scoring, and personal involvement while keeping the scores close. For example, basketball free throws were eliminated, there were no yardage penalties in football, soccer throw-ins were limited, and pitchers moved close enough to batters for them to be able to hit the ball. The games usually had very high scores.

Personal involvement was maximized with clever rule qualifications, such as imposing handicaps on highly skilled players, permitting "do-overs" and other chances for less skilled players, and having every player eligible to receive a pass in football. Children almost always claimed that the biggest source of fun in their games was hitting, catching, kicking, scoring, and any other form of action in which they were personally involved, and which kept the scores close.

Players tolerated a great variety of performance styles and moves, and even joking around and ignoring rules, so long as these did not interfere with the action. Older and more skilled players were involved in settling disputes, and arguments were usually handled in creative ways. Friendships were reaffirmed as children played together often, and they became more skilled at solving conflicts.

A word of caution: Problems in informal games do occur. Bigger and stronger children may exploit or even bully smaller and weaker ones, girls may be patronized or dismissed if they try to play with boys, and those excluded from games often feel rejected by their peers. Limited availability of play space or equipment can also cause problems.

FORMAL, ADULT-CONTROLLED SPORTS

Even though children still value action and personal involvement in formal sports, they are more likely to be serious and concerned with performance quality and game results. Action, personal involvement, and behaviour are strictly regulated by formal rules enforced by adults—coaches, managers, referees, scorekeepers, timekeepers, and so on. Children are also concerned with formal positions, and are likely to refer to themselves by their position—left winger, right fielder, goalie, and so on. Coaches and spectators continually emphasize the importance of these by encouraging children to "stay in position."

Playing time is often determined by a player's level of skill, and those spending more time on the bench may be bored or less interested in the game. Adult control also decreases the number of arguments and overt hostility between players, and more conflict has been observed between adults than between players on the same team. There were also fewer displays of affection among players, making it difficult to determine which players were friends.

Rules standardize competition and control player behaviour. Their enforcement regularly causes breaks in the action that are not usually resented by the players

Continued

Different Experiences: Informal Player-Controlled Sports versus Organized, Adult-Controlled Sports
continued

(unless it is a penalty against their team). Adults usually apply the rules universally, seldom making exceptions even when there are differences in players' abilities and characteristics, and when the sanctions do not have an effect on game action or outcome. Games are played until the end regardless of quality of play or player satisfaction. Rules applied by coaches restrict players' freedom, but compliance is high.

Children in organized sports want to win, but are not usually obsessed by winning. Skilled players and those on successful teams are more concerned with winning. Most players want to have fun, but usually know their win–loss records and league standings. Status on teams is largely based on coaches' assessments of players' skills. Status also leads to more playing time, which is highly valued, and more latitude during games.

ANALYSIS OF DIFFERENCES

Which of these experiences is more valuable in the development of children? The answer is important to both the children involved and the adults who invest so much time, money, and energy into organized sports. Each experience makes different contributions to the lives of children, and people generally overrate the contributions of participation in organized sports and underrate the contributions of participation in informal sports (Schultz, 1999).

Informal sports clearly require creativity and interpersonal and decision-making skills. Children encounter dozens of unanticipated challenges requiring on-the-spot decisions and interpersonal abilities. They learn how to organize games, form teams, cooperate with peers, develop rules, and take responsibility for following and enforcing rules. They provide experiences involving cooperation, planning, organizing, negotiating, problem solving, flexibility, and improvisation (Adler and Adler, 1998). We do not know how much of this learning carries over to other settings, but we can assume that children are influenced by their experiences.

Organized sports help children learn to manage relationships with adult authority figures. They learn the rules and strategies of activities defined as important in the culture, and they may gain status that carries over to other parts of their lives. They learn about formal structures, rule-governed teamwork, and adult models of work and achievement (Adler and Adler, 1998).

However, it is possible that too much participation in organized sports may lead children to view the world in passive terms, as something that is given rather than created. If this occurs, children grow up thinking they are powerless to change the world in which they live. *What do you think?*

....

When children are involved in informal, player-controlled sports and alternative sports, they take risks and create excitement, but adults often have legitimate concerns about safety. It will take some creative thinking, and perhaps a return to an old view that sometimes children hurt themselves during play, and it is often nobody's fault, in order to produce a balance between the culture of risk and the culture of caution.

Increased Interest in Alternative Sports As organized programmes have become increasingly

exclusive, structured, and performance oriented, some young people have sought alternatives that allow them to engage freely in physical activities on their own terms. Because organized youth sports are the most visible settings for children's sport participation, unstructured and participant-controlled activities are referred to as alternative sports—alternatives to organized sports. Alternative sports, or "action sports" as many now refer to them, encompass a wide array of physical activities practiced individually or in groups. Their popularity is based in part on children's reactions against the highly structured character of adult-controlled, organized sports.

When we observe children in action sports, we are regularly amazed by the physical skills they have developed without adult coaches and scheduled practices and contests. Although we are concerned about the injury rates, and about the sexism that is often a part of these activities, we are impressed by the discipline and dedication of children who seek challenges apart from adult-controlled sport settings, and by the cooperation often shown as they help each other, applaud each other's successes, and give advice to each other as they develop their skills. However, the norms in these participant-controlled activities are complex, and they vary from one location to another.

Mark Shaw, winner of the first International Mountain Board Championships in 2000, explains a widely accepted norm that has made many of these activities attractive to children. He says that, when he goes to areas where there are other skateboarders and mountain boarders, he feels that it is important to be "a positive influence as a skater." He teaches tricks, gives helpful hints to less experienced board riders, and values the friendships and sense of community created around the sports. He explains, "I look forward to helping young skaters... at the park each weekend almost as much as I look forward to skating and my own progression on the board (2002, p. 3). Many children find this orientation more engaging that what they perceive or experience in competitive youth sport programmes.

Increased participation in alternative sports is so widespread that media companies and corporations wishing to turn children into consumers have invented competitive forms of these sports and now hype them as high-risk and "extreme" sports. These sponsored events, such as the X Games, Gravity Games, and Dew Action Sports Tour provide exposure and material support for athletes willing to display their skills in a televised format that is, or at least appears to be, highly organized and competitive. Although the participants in these events are teens and young

adults, many spectators are children. Children use the images from these media events to inform what they do when they play action sports, but we need research on the ways that this occurs and its implications in the lives of young people. Adult intervention in these activities has been limited to the provision of facilities such as skateboard parks, and occasional words of advice regarding safety (Merrill, 2002). But will the future bring adult skateboard coaches and organized programmes? We would bet on it, but we would also bet that children will continue to seek opportunities to play sports on their own terms. (See the Reflect on Sports box, "Different Experiences," on pages 135–136.)

Recommendations for Improving Youth Sports

In previous sections, we have examined how problems appear as adults become involved in organized sports for children, and how people in Canada have attempted to deal with the problems. We have also looked at the special problems presented by the early involvement and specialization model of involving children in high-performance sports, and outlined some possible solutions. In this final section, we return to the issue of resolving problems, making recommendations for both informal and adult-organized sports, and return to the issue of education with recommendations for coaching certification programmes.

Improving Informal, Alternative, and Action Sports Informal, alternative, and action sports are unique because they are not controlled directly by adults. Many children opt for these sports because they seek activities without organized structures and adult control. However, it is possible for adults to become indirectly involved in ways that increase safety and participation opportunities for children interested in action sports.

For example, instead of passing laws to prohibit skateboarding or BMXing, adults can work with young people to design and provide safe settings for them to create their own activities. If adults are not supportive of alternative sport forms, their children will use the extreme models of the X Games, Gravity Games, and other made-for-TV spectacles as sole sources of inspiration.

The challenge for adults is to be supportive and provide guidance without controlling alternative sports. Children need their own spaces in which they can be creative and expressive while they engage in physical activities. Sometimes it is necessary to be as persistent, flexible, and innovative as the participants. In London, Ontario a group of parents and children, who had unsuccessfully lobbied the city council and various sponsors to create a skate park, were finally successful when they approached and received the help of a local construction workers' union. Adult guidance is crucial in making those spaces safe and open for as many children as possible—boys and girls as well as children with a disability and those from various ethnic and social class backgrounds.

We could institute a "life guard" or "school recess" model of supervision. A responsible adult is there to ensure safety, prevent bullying, and mediate disputes if called on, but not to direct the activity. Even competitive sports could be run on this model, which is, in many ways, a revival. In the 1920s, in the state of New York, Frederick Rand Rogers insisted that teachers and other adults should remain in the bleachers during school sports. He argued that the players could not learn to make decisions if adults always made them (Kidd, 1997, p. 128).

Improving Organized Sports When considering improvements for organized youth sports, most people agree that programmes should meet the needs of the children who participate in them. This means that the children are valuable sources of information about possible changes. If children seek fun emphasizing action, involvement, close scores, and friendships in their informal games, it makes sense that organized programmes also should emphasize these things.

The following recommendations are based on this assumption.

INCREASING ACTION Children emphasize *action* in their games. Much activity occurs around the scoring area, and scoring is usually so frequent that it is difficult to keep personal performance statistics. Organized sports, although they contain action, strongly emphasize rules, order, standardized conditions, and predictability. The strategy of many organized teams is to prevent action, rather than stimulate it. Parents and coaches sometimes describe high-scoring games as undisciplined free-for-alls caused by poor defensive play. The desired strategy in the minds of many adults is to stop action: Strike out every batter (baseball and softball), stall the game when you are in the lead (soccer and basketball), and use a safe running play for a 4-yard gain (football). These tactics may win games, but they limit the action and scoring—the things that children define as the most exciting aspects of playing sports.

It is usually easy to increase action and scoring in organized sports, as long as adults do not view game models as sacred and unchangeable. Bigger baskets, smaller playing areas, and fewer rules are the best means to increase action. Why not make all players eligible to receive passes and carry the ball in football, and use a 2-metre basket in a half-court basketball game?

Many adults resist changes they think will alter game models—that is, the models used in elite, adult sports. They want children to play "the real thing," even though adults are often prepared to make all kinds of modifications in their own recreational and pick-up games to achieve action and scoring. They forget that children are more interested in having fun than mimicking adults following institutionalized rules.

INCREASING PERSONAL INVOLVEMENT Children do not sit on the bench in informal games. They use rule qualifications and handicap systems to maximize personal involvement and promote action. Smaller or less skilled players may not contribute to the action as much as others do, but they play the whole game. If they are treated badly or excluded, they leave without being branded as quitters, or given lectures on commitment by their parents.

In organized games, playing time is often limited for all but the most skilled players, and the substitution process creates problems for coaches and pressure on players. Specialization by position further restricts involvement by limiting the range of experiences for players. Improvements would involve rotating players to different positions and coordinating group substitutions with opposing teams. Team size could be reduced (as already done in many leagues for very young children) to create more opportunities for players to be involved in the action. Batting lineups for baseball and softball could include all team members, regardless of which ones were playing the nine or ten positions in the field. In ice hockey, games could be played across the width of the rink, thereby allowing three times as many teams to compete at the same time. In basketball, first-string teams could play a half-court game at one basket, while the second-string teams played each other at the other basket, and a combined score would determine the winner. These and many other versions of games would increase personal involvement.

CREATING CLOSE SCORES "Good games" are those for which the outcomes are in doubt until the last play; double overtime games are the best. Lopsided scores destroy the excitement of competition. Children realize this, so they keep their informal games close.[10] Because motivation depends on perceived chances for success, a close game usually keeps children motivated and satisfied. Just like adults who use handicaps to keep the competition interesting in bowling, golf, and

other sports, children adjust their games to keep them close.

In organized games, lopsided scores are common and team records are often uneven. Keeping players motivated under these circumstances is difficult. Coaches are forced to appeal to pride and respect to motivate players in the face of lopsided scores and long, losing seasons. Ironically, when coaches urge players to develop a "killer instinct" by taking big leads during games it often undermines motivation among all players in the long run.

Many adults hesitate to make changes that affect the outcomes of games, but some possibilities are worth consideration. For example, they could encourage close scores by altering team rosters or by using handicap systems during games. The underdog could be given an advantage such as extra players or the right to use four downs, five outs, or a smaller goal. Many changes could keep games close; however, when game models are viewed as unchangeable, possibilities are not discussed, even though children makes such changes when they play informal games.

MAINTAINING FRIENDSHIPS When children play informal and alternative sports, the reaffirmation of friendships is important. Friendships influence processes of selecting teams (see footnote 10) and the dynamics of problem-solving processes during games. Organized sports provide contexts for making friends, but players need more than adult-controlled practices and games to nurture relationships with teammates and peers on other teams.

To foster friendships, coaches could help groups of players to plan game strategies or coach practices. They could enable players to interact with opponents in supportive ways during games. Too often, relationships between opposing players are impersonal or hostile, and players do not learn that games have a human component that is central to having fun in competitive relationships. Most important, players should be expected to enforce game rules so that

---

[10]Close scores may be sacrificed when close friends want to be on the same team; playing with friends is sometimes more important than having evenly balanced teams.

they understand why rules are necessary and how collective action depends on cooperation related to following rules. Many people claim that self-enforcement would never work (although it does in tennis). However, if organized programmes do not teach young people how to cooperate to the extent needed to play games with their friends, then those programmes are *not* worth our time and effort.

If young people do not learn how to play games without coaches and referees, how can adults claim that sports teach young people leadership, discipline, decision-making skills, or character? (See the quote from Les McDonald on the first page of this chapter.)

PROSPECTS FOR IMPROVING YOUTH SPORTS

Many youth sport programmes have made changes that reflect a concern for the needs and well-being of children. Research identifies many excellent models for making creative and progressive changes in youth sports (Chalip and Green, 1998; Morris and Stiehl, 1989; Murphy, 1999; Torbert, 2004; 2005). However, the approach most often used to guide changes in youth sport programmes is grounded in functionalist theory and focuses primarily on increasing the efficiency and organization of existing programmes and maximizing the physical skills of athletes.

A functionalist orientation often leads to an emphasis on coaching education programmes and formal rules regulating the actions of parents, spectators, players, and coaches. But at the same time, it leads to increased emphasis on the performance ethic and more tournaments, playoffs, and championships that take children around the country for the sake of creating sport "résumés." Furthermore, as local organizations align with national organizations and sport governing bodies, the people who run these

Many sport programmes for younger children have decreased the size of playing fields and teams. This soccer programme has three-on-three teams, there are no goalies, and no scores are recorded although some parents keep track of scores and team records. The four- and five-year-olds in the league are most interested in running around and kicking the ball somewhere, even if it's in the wrong direction. [Jay Coakley]

organizations decide how to define "improvement" and what should be changed in youth sports. Most of these organizations run programmes that are commercial and "excellence oriented," and they appeal to parents who mistakenly equate excellence in sports with overall child development. Even parents who do not make this mistake find themselves in a bind because the national organizations that now control many local programmes also monitor the "feeder" process leading onto teams at higher competitive levels. And parents know that if their children drop out at eleven years old, they will fall behind and never get back into the feeder tracks through which players are chosen for high school or junior teams, provincial and national teams, U.S. university scholarships, and even professional contracts.

"How many times have I told you to practise your basketball before you even think about homework!"

FIGURE 5.3 The fame and fortune of some professional athletes may encourage some parents to overemphasize youth sports in the lives of their children. Might this turn young athletes into "child workers"?

Changes are also slow to come because many adults who administer and support organized sport programmes have vested interests in keeping them as they are. They know the programmes are not perfect, but they are afraid changes in them will eliminate many of the good things they have accomplished in the past. In fact, one of the few triggers for progressive change seems to be a drastic decline in youth registrations in a sport, as noted previously with regard to hockey in Québec, and as is currently occurring in youth baseball.

Coaching Education as a Means of Producing Changes

Coaching education programmes could be a tool for changing these trends to impose complete adult control in youth sports. Earlier in this chapter, we wrote about the National Coaching Certification Programme as one of the "made in Canada" solutions to the problems that were recognized in youth sports. The NCCP provides coaches with information on how to (1) deal with young people responsively and safely and (2) be more effective in organizing their practices and in teaching skills to young people. Most coaching education programmes emphasize putting athletes' needs ahead of winning, but none of them teaches coaches how to critically assess the sport programmes in which they work with young people. None presents information on how to make structural changes in the programmes themselves or on how to create alternatives to existing programmes. Even with two former NHL players as assistant coaches, Arnold (2002) notes the difficulties involved in introducing progressive changes to the way that they coached one minor hockey team in Peterborough, Ontario. Coaching education materials generally are based on the functionalist assumption that existing sport programmes are pretty good, but they could be better if coaches were to use more applied sport science as they work with child athletes.

Although coaching education is important, we worry that it may foster what we might call a "technoscience approach" to youth sports. A technoscience approach emphasizes issues of control and skill development, rather than an overall understanding of young people as human beings. If this happens, coaches are better defined as "sport efficiency experts," rather than teachers who provide young people with opportunities to become autonomous and responsible decision makers who control their own lives.

At this point, the NCCP has made a contribution to responsible coaching in youth sport programmes. But, as we examine coaching education and critically assess its place at all levels of sports, it would be good to remember that the former East Germany had one of the most efficient and highly respected coaching education programmes in the world. However, history has now shown that its programme was based on a technoscience approach, and did little to contribute to the overall development of young people as human beings (*Doping for Gold*, 2008). Unfortunately, we know of no organized youth sport programme or coaching education programme with a mission statement declaring that the goal is to help child athletes become decision makers who control their sport lives and the context in which they play sports. Such a mission statement would be based on critical rather than functionalist theory.

SUMMARY

ARE ORGANIZED YOUTH SPORT PROGRAMMES WORTH THE EFFORT?

Although physical activities exist in all cultures, organized youth sports are a luxury. They require resources and discretionary time among children and adults. They exist only when children are not required to work and only when adults believe that experiences during childhood influence overall growth and development. Youth sports have a unique history in every society where they exist. However, they characteristically emphasize experiences and values defined as important in the societies in which they exist.

The growth of organized sports in North America and much of Europe is associated with the changes in the family that occurred during the last half of the twentieth century. Many parents now see organized sports as vehicles to control children and ensure that boys and girls have access to important developmental experiences.

In Canada, academics and some individuals involved in sports began to recognize quite early that adult-organized sport programmes for children led to a number of problems resulting from the particular set of values that have come to be associated with them: that children's play is entertainment for adults, that only games organized and controlled by adults are of any value, that children are miniature adults, and that the real value of sport lies in learning to be a winner. We discuss a number of "made in Canada" attempts to resolve these problems: the development of house leagues, the introduction of a coaching education programme for volunteers in youth sports, the development of "fair play" leagues in hockey, and the introduction of child protection schemes. Developments in high-performance sports for children since the mid-1970s provide even more reason for concern, and, although there have been attempts to resolve some problems—for example, eating disorders—change has been very slow because some adults stand to profit from the *status quo*.

Interactionist research in the sociology of sport helps us to understand that, prior to eight years old, children do not have the developmental abilities to fully participate in organized competitive sports, especially team sports in which complex strategies are used. Such abilities are not fully developed until twelve years of age in most children. Research also describes and helps us to understand some of the family dynamics associated with organized youth sports, especially in terms of how they affect family relationships, family schedules, and the lives of mothers and fathers. Studies guided by critical theories illustrate how social factors influence youth sport experiences, including the participation choices available to children and the meanings given to various sport experiences.

Major trends in youth sports today include increased privatization of, and user fees for, organized programmes, a growing emphasis on the performance ethic in most programmes, more involvement by and concern among parents, and growing evidence of a culture of caution that limits the excitement and occasional risks associated with children's play and sport experiences. In response to these trends, some children have turned to informal, alternative, and action sports.

Children's sport experiences vary with levels of formal organization and with the extent to which they are participant-controlled or adult-controlled. The dynamics of sport participation, and the lessons learned are different in informal games than in organized youth sports. Involvement across a range of participation settings is best for the overall development of children.

Recommendations for improving organized youth sports emphasize action, involvement among all participants, exciting competition, and opportunities for children to form and nurture friendships with peers—just as there are in many informal games.

Adults inhibit the prospects for change because they often have vested interests in maintaining programmes as they are currently organized. This is especially true in high-performance sport programmes, even though those are the ones in which improvements are most needed. Coaching education programmes could facilitate critical thinking among those who work most directly with children in these programmes, but coaching education is usually based on functionalist rather than critical approaches to sports.

No sports programme can guarantee that it will make children into models of virtue, but the adults who control youth sports can make improvements to existing programmes. This means that organized sports for children *are* worth the effort—when the adults put children's interests ahead of the programmes' organizational needs and their own needs to gain status through their association with successful and highly skilled child athletes.

Visit *Sports in Society*'s Online Learning Centre at <u>www.mcgrawhill.ca/olc/coakley</u> for additional information, website resources, and study tools for this chapter.

6

[CP(Jonathan Hayward)]

"Deviance" in Sports

Is it out of control?

You don't go from 10.17 to 9.83 on Petro-Canada unleaded gas.

> **—Jamie Astaphan, physician who provided steroids to Ben Johnson (1989)**

You grow up getting special treatment because you're an athlete, then you get millions of dollars thrown at you. Shady people gravitate toward money.

> **—Lew Lyons, sports psychologist (2000)**

Athletes have to speak out louder about the importance of clean sport. Cheaters cannot be allowed to shame those thousands of athletes who have been honest to the game.

> **—Viacheslav Fetisov**

My definition of a pro is a guy who plays even when he's hurting.

> **—attributed to Angelo Mosca, former Hamilton Ti-Cat football player**

Note: This chapter was written with the assistance of Robert Hughes.

Although this chapter is called "Deviance in Sports," using the sociological term "deviance" raises a number of problems for authors who have stated their preference for a sociological approach that combines interactionist and critical theories in order to study sports in society. As we note below, the terms "norms" and "deviance" are derived from functionalist theory and are based on the assumption that there is a widespread consensus in society about what is "normal" (norms, normative), and therefore what is non-normative or "deviant." If we think of these concepts in terms of who has the *power* to define what is "normal" and what is "deviant," we can see how they raise concerns for critical theorists.[1]

Actions defined as "normal" at one time or in one place can be re-defined as "deviant" in another time and/or another place, and vice versa. Thus, for example, protests against injustice or inequality are often seen as "deviant" in a functionalist theoretical approach. In the nineteenth century, slaves escaping, and those helping them to escape, the United States to travel the underground railroad to Nova Scotia or southern Ontario were seen as "deviant" because slavery was normative in the U.S. In the early part of the twentieth century, women who engaged in passive resistance and other forms of protest in an attempt to win the right to vote were seen as "deviant" since it was not "normal" for women to have the right to vote. And, until Prime Minister Pierre Trudeau declared in the 1970s that "the state has no business in the bedrooms of the nation," there were laws against homosexuality in Canada. Nowadays, it is normal for the mayors of many major cities to march in annual "Gay Pride" parades. When Trudeau made his remarks he was giving voice to a changing attitude in society—there was no consensus, there

was never a consensus, and, of course, there still is no consensus.[2] When a basketball player at Manhattan College turns her back on the U.S. flag during the pre-game national anthem to protest the impending invasion of Iraq, whether her action is defined as "normal" or "deviant" depends on who is making the definition.

We approach the issue from the position that there is often no such consensus in society about what is "deviant"; and this lack of consensus extends to the discipline of sociology. University courses on this topic are sometimes called "social problems" or "social issues," and may be covered in "criminology." When courses are called "Deviant Behaviour" or "Deviance," they very often begin precisely with the qualification that we are making here about the socially constructed nature of "deviance." This chapter and the following chapter also make it quite clear that there is little consensus about social problems and social issues in sport.

We use the term "deviance" in this chapter, but to underline our point, and, to emphasize these qualifications, we use the term "deviance" in quotation marks. We intend the term to be understood with all of the cautions noted above, and the quotation marks are a reminder that "deviance" is a problematic term. This does not mean that we think that immoral or illegal actions or actions designed to gain an unfair advantage over an opponent, or actions likely to lead to injuries to an athlete or his/her opponents, are acceptable. It means that we need to explore and understand such actions from the perspectives of, and in the context of, those involved; we do not need to accept mainstream definitions of what is "normal" and what is "deviant."

"Deviance" among athletes, coaches, agents, and others connected with sports have attracted widespread attention in recent years. Daily media reports of on-the-field rule violations and

---

[1]In fact, one of the first theoretical attempts to combine interactionist and critical theories involved precisely this issue. Labelling theory argued that the power of an individual, or an institution such as the police, to label a person or action as "deviant," and to have that label widely accepted, was as important as the action itself.

[2]Some Canadians still do not accept equal rights for women, and some Canadians still believe that homosexuality should be illegal.

off-the-field criminal actions lead some people to conclude that such behaviour in sports is out of control. News about widespread drug and substance use among athletes has intensified this perception. Because many people believe that sport builds character, every case of "deviance" in sports leads them to be disappointed and believe that the moral fabric of society itself is eroding. They often conclude that money and greed, combined with a lack of discipline and self-control, have destroyed the purity of sport and the existence of sportsmanship.

Because many people have come to this conclusion, the purpose of this chapter is to examine "deviance" in sports. We focus on four questions as we deal with this issue.

1. What problems do we face when we study "deviance" in sports?
2. What is the most useful way to define "*deviance*" when studying sports in society?
3. Are rates of "deviant" actions of athletes (on and off the field), coaches, and others connected with sports out of control?
4. Why do some athletes use performance-enhancing substances, and is there a way to control substance use in sports?

These questions direct our attention to important issues in the study of sports in society.

PROBLEMS FACED WHEN STUDYING "DEVIANCE" IN SPORTS

Studying "deviance" in sports presents special problems for five reasons. First, *those involved in sports, especially the athletes, are governed by many different sets of regulations.* For example, there are the rules of the sport that determine actions that are permitted and those that are not. These rules are enforced by the various governing bodies of the sport. Then there are the laws of the land, the criminal and civil codes of a country that also apply to athletes. Sometimes there is confusion about who has jurisdiction in certain cases,

particularly cases of doping or violence—is it the governing body of the sport, or is it the police?

However, there are two additional sets of rules that may be called on to determine the behaviour of those involved in sports. The first apply on a team, usually established by a coach and other team administrators: dress codes, curfews, punctuality, diet, and so on. The second are often called the "unwritten rules of sport." These govern the moral behaviour of athletes in terms of fair play (e.g., not running up the score on an opponent, not taking advantage of an opponent's misfortune). These rules are the most ambiguous, and the most frequently violated in modern sports.

Soccer and tennis have clear examples of playing by "the spirit of the rules." In soccer, when a player is injured, a player on the opposing team kicks the ball out of play in order to stop the game and allow the injured player to be treated. To resume, the player taking the throw-in throws the ball to an opponent. These off-setting courtesies have become *normal* because referees no longer stop play for an injury—a consequence of actions that are the exact opposite of fair play (i.e., faking injuries). In tennis, even in high-level matches, a player may recognize a judge's mistaken call in his/her favour or against his/her opponent by deliberately giving the next point to his/her opponent. But what if the fair play from tennis was applied to soccer—a mistaken call by a linesman means that you refuse the goal kick and give your opponents a corner (or they refuse a corner and give you a goal kick)! Players attempting such actions would probably be defined as "deviant," and referees would probably not know how to respond. It is possible to think of many more examples to highlight the ambiguous, contested, and sometimes conflicting nature of such rules. Determining "deviant" behaviour depends on both context, and which set(s) of rules are being enforced.

Second, these different sets of rules, and some of the confusion about jurisdiction, results in *actions being accepted in sports that may be "deviant" in other spheres of society, and actions accepted in society that may be "deviant" in sports.* Athletes are

It is difficult to study "deviance" in sports because athletes often engage in actions that would not be accepted in other settings. For example, actions that are acceptable in boxing, hockey, football, and other sports would get you arrested or sued if you were to engage in them off the field. [*Colorado Springs Gazette*]

allowed and even encouraged to behave in ways that are prohibited or defined as criminal in other settings. For example, the actions of athletes in contact sports would be classified as felony assault if they occured on the streets; boxers would be criminals outside the ring; ice hockey players would be arrested for actions they define as normal during their games; race car drivers would be ticketed for speeding and careless driving; speed skiers and motocross racers would be defined as irresponsible, if not "deviant," outside their sports. However, even when serious injuries or deaths occur in sports, criminal charges usually are not filed, and civil lawsuits asking for financial compensation are generally unsuccessful.

The use of anger as a source of motivation in sports clearly deviates from the norms most people use to guide their behaviour in families, religious congregations, classrooms, and work settings. On the other hand, male teammates may embrace one another, touch each other supportively, hold hands, and cry with each other in sports, while the same actions in other settings violate traditional western norms about masculinity.

Coaches treat players in ways that most of us would define as "deviant" if teachers treated students, or managers treated employees similarly. Team owners in North American professional sports clearly violate the anti-combines legislation that apply to other business owners. Fans act in ways that would quickly alienate friends and family members in other settings, or lead people to define them as mentally disturbed.

On the other hand, if athletes take the same drugs or nutritional supplements used by millions of nonathletes, they may be banned from their sports and defined as "deviant," even by people using those drugs and supplements. Athletes who miss practices or games due to sickness or injury often are defined as "deviant" by coaches and teammates. Youth league players may be benched for a game if they miss practice to attend a family picnic.

Norms in sports are often different from norms in other social worlds, and responses to "deviance" by athletes may be different from responses to others who engage in "deviance." For example, athletes often are praised for their extreme actions that risk health or well-being and inflict pain and injury on others, whereas non-athletes would be defined as "deviant" for doing the same things. We tend to view the motives of people in sports, especially athletes, as positive because their actions are directed toward the achievement of success for their team, school, community, country, or corporate sponsor. Therefore, those actions, even when they clearly overstep generally accepted limits in society, may be tolerated or even praised, rather than condemned. Athletes often are seen as different and "deviant" in ways that evoke fascination and awe rather than repulsion and condemnation. Most sociological theories about "deviance" do not adequately explain many actions that occur in sports and the meanings given to them.

Third, *the types and causes of "deviance" in sports are so diverse that no single theory can explain all of them.* For example, consider the forms of "deviant" behaviour that have been engaged in by at least some male junior hockey players. The "letter" and the "spirit" of the rules of hockey may be routinely violated; players may break established curfews; they may use recreational and/or performance-enhancing drugs; they may accept illegal payments; they may engage in under-age drinking and get into fights in local bars; they may engage in the sexual harassment or sexual abuse of women; they may become involved in the abuse of rookie players at team initiations (hazing); they may ask others to do their high school homework; and they may engage in the vandalism of hotel or bus company property. This diverse list includes only a sample of cases reported for one group of athletes at one level of competition over the past decade. The list would be more diverse if we included all athletes and if we were to list types of "deviance" among coaches, administrators, team owners, agents, and spectators.

Fourth, *training and performance in sports are now based on such new forms of science and technology that people have not yet developed norms to guide and evaluate the actions of athletes and others in sports.* Science and medicine once used only to treat people who were ill are now used regularly in sports. The everyday challenge of training and competition in sports often pushes bodies to such extremes that continued participation requires the use of new medical treatments and technologies just to stay on the field. For example, the use of nutritional supplements has become a standard practice in nearly all sports. Ingesting substances thought to enhance performance is simply part of being an athlete today. Athletes buy supplements online and at local stores, not because they want to take shortcuts, but because they want to be all they can be in sports.

Count the ads for performance-enhancing substances in any recent issue of the magazines *Muscle Media and Muscle and Fitness.* The motto for these ads seems to be "Strength and high performance are just a swallow away"! Of course, corporations encourage this approach when they use athletes' bodies to promote products and corporate images in terms of strength and machine-like efficiency (Hoberman, 1995). In the meantime, it has become much more difficult to determine just what actions are "deviant" and what actions are accepted parts of athletic training.

Fifth, *"deviance" in sports often involves an unquestioned acceptance of norms, rather than a rejection of norms.* Much of the "deviance" in sports does not involve a rejection of commonly accepted norms and expectations for action. Sports involve exciting experiences and powerful social processes, which encourage extreme actions among athletes. These actions, even when they are tolerated or seen as entertaining, are also seen as falling outside the range of normal acceptance in society. However, they may not be punished because they exaggerate ideals such as commitment, sacrifice, dedication, and a desire to achieve goals. Ironically, this leads many people to see athletes as role models, even as they push or exceed normative limits.

Unlike "deviance" in other settings, "deviance" in sports often involves an unquestioned acceptance of and extreme conformity to norms and expectations. For example, most Canadians see playing hockey as a positive activity. Young men, and increasingly young women, are encouraged to "be all they can be" as hockey players and to live by slogans such as "There is no *I* in t-e-a-m," and "No pain, no gain." They are often encouraged to increase their weight and strength so that they can play more effectively and contribute to the success of their teams. When young men go too far in conforming to expectations and use banned substances to become bigger and stronger, they become "deviant" (Neyer, 2000).

This type of "overdoing it" is dangerous, but it is based on a desire to fit in and maintain an athlete identity through excessive dedication and commitment. This is sociologically different from *antisocial "deviance"* grounded primarily in alienation and a rejection of norms. Athletes usually accept without question the norms that define what it means to be an athlete, and their "deviance" often involves overconformity to those norms, not a rejection of them. Therefore, taking a drug to meet expectations in sports is very different from taking a drug to escape reality and expectations. The athlete overconforms when taking a drug to improve performance and gain acceptance from teammates; the alienated youth underconforms when mainlining heroin. This difference is important when we study and try to explain the origins of "deviance" in sports.

DEFINING AND STUDYING "DEVIANCE" IN SPORTS: THREE APPROACHES

Approaches to identifying, defining, and controlling "deviance" in sports vary depending on the theoretical framework used. We focus here on three approaches—functionalist theory, conflict theory, and a combination of interactionist and critical theories.

Using Functionalist Theory: "Deviance" Disrupts Shared Values

As noted above, "deviance" is a functionalist concept, and it is worth outlining in a little more detail how the concept fits the theory.

According to functionalist theory, social order is based on shared values. Shared values give rise to shared cultural goals and shared ideas about how to achieve those goals. "Deviance" occurs when actions demonstrate a rejection of cultural goals and/or the accepted means of achieving them. In other words, "deviance" involves a departure from cultural ideals: the greater the departure, the more disruptive the action, the greater the "deviance." Conversely, conformity to cultural ideals reaffirms the social order and is seen as the foundation of ethics and morality.

Most functionalists see "deviance" as resulting from faulty socialization or inconsistencies in the organization of society. "Deviance" occurs because people have not learned and internalized cultural values and norms or because there are conflicts and strains built into the structure of society. Therefore, reforming socialization processes and eliminating structural conflicts, strains, and inconsistencies in social systems is the best control for "deviance."

In sports, according to a functionalist approach, "deviance" occurs when an athlete rejects the goal of improving skills or the expectations that the means to achieve goals is to work harder than others.

A problem with this approach is that it becomes difficult to identify "deviance" when there is a lack of agreement about the importance of various goals. For example, if we think the goal in sports is to play fair but you think that it is to win, then we will see any violation of the rules as "deviant," whereas you will see some violations as "good fouls" if they contribute to winning. If we regard sports as a form of play in which intrinsic satisfaction is the reason for participation but you regard sports as "war without weapons" fought for external rewards such as trophies and cash prizes, then we will see violent actions as "deviant," whereas you will see them as signs of courage and commitment. Because we do not share beliefs about the ideals of sports, we will not define "deviance" in the same way.

Another problem with a functionalist approach is that it leads many people to think that controlling "deviance" always calls for policies and programmes that increase conformity. This usually involves establishing more rules, making rules more strict and consistent, developing a more comprehensive system of detecting and punishing rule violators, and making everyone more aware of the rules and what happens to those who do not follow them (see figure 6.1). This approach often subverts creativity and change, and it assumes that all conformity, especially extreme conformity, is a cultural ideal. This assumption is questionable, because obsessive and excessive conformity can be dangerous, a possibility discussed in the section on interactionist and critical theories (pp. 151–152).

Despite these problems, many people use a functionalist approach when they discuss "deviance" in sports. When actions do not match their ideals they define them and their perpetrators as "deviant." The solution, they say, is to "get tough," make the punishments more severe, and throw out the "bad apples." The solution is based on the idea that people violate rules because they lack moral character and that "normal" people in normal situations are not "deviant." This approach may be useful when people are unaware of norms, but it ignores the influence of powerful social processes in sports and leads people to label athletes unjustly as moral failures when, in fact, most athletes are "hyper-conformers" whose main fault is that they have not learned to critically assess norms or set limits in what they will

"If they had more rules and better enforcement, all this deviance would stop."

FIGURE 6.1   Many people use a functionalist approach when they think about "deviance" in sports. They call for more rules and better enforcement. This approach has only limited usefulness in sports today.

do to conform to norms in sport. We say more about this throughout the chapter.

Using Conflict Theory: "Deviance" Interferes with the Interests of Wealthy People

According to conflict theory, social order is based on economic interests and the use of economic power by those who own the means of production in society. Therefore, social norms reflect the interests of those people, and any actions, ideas, or people violating those norms are defined as "deviant."

Those who use this approach assume that most people act in their own interests, and that people in power use their position to turn their ideas of right and wrong into the official definitions of conformity and "deviance" in a society.

Those who lack economic power in society have nothing to say about the content and enforcement of rules and they are more likely to be identified as "deviant" than people with wealth and power. Furthermore, legal processes are organized so that people who lack power do not have the resources to resist being labelled as "deviant" when their actions do not conform to the standards of the rule makers.

Conflict theorists assume that rules in sport organizations reflect the interests of owners and sponsors and ignore the interests of athletes and most fans. Therefore, they see "deviance" among athletes as a result of rules that discriminate against them and force them to follow the expectations of those in power, even though their health and well-being may be harmed in the process. Athletes are viewed as victims of a profit-driven system, in which progressive change requires rejecting and remaking the rules.

A problem with conflict theory is that "deviance" in sports is always assumed to be the result of biased norms and law enforcement processes controlled by wealthy owners and sponsors who convince everyone that their rules are the only rules. Conflict theorists cannot explain why "deviance" exists in non–revenue-producing sports in which athletes themselves may be in positions of power and control. Furthermore, many athletes voluntarily use dangerous growth hormones and other substances because they seek acceptance from teammates, not sponsors and team owners.

Therefore it is unlikely that all "deviance" in sports would disappear if athletes were in charge. Athletes should have more control over their sport participation, but without the critical consciousness needed to eliminate the profit motive and transform sports, it is unlikely that shifting more power to athletes would eliminate "deviance" in sports. Explaining all forms of "deviance" in economic terms is difficult. Although the commercialization of sports and financial motives may account for certain forms of "deviance," other factors and dynamics must

be considered to understand why "deviance" occurs in sports that are neither commercialized nor driven by profit motives.

Using Interactionist and Critical Theories: "Deviance" as a Social Construction

Although functionalist and conflict theories call attention to socialization and economic factors, they overlook the possibility that much of the deviance in sports involves overconformity to the norms[3] that athletes use to evaluate themselves and others.

Most people who violate rules in sports can not be classified as morally bankrupt, as functionalists often conclude, or as exploited victims, as conflict theorists often conclude. For example, it is not accurate to say that young people lack moral character when they accept without qualification the notion that athletes are dedicated to the game and willing to do what it takes to become and remain an accepted participant of a sport culture, even if it means going beyond normal limits as they train. Nor is it accurate to define all athletes who engage in "deviance" as passive victims of an exploitative, profit-driven sport system; after all, athletes participate in the creation and maintenance of the norms that guide their decisions and actions in sports. This means that we need an alternative explanation of "deviance" in sports, an explanation that takes into account the experiences of athletes within the actual contexts in which they play sports.

In searching for such an explanation, most sociologists now use a constructionist approach based on interactionist and critical theories. This approach focuses on two issues: (1) the meanings

---

[3]We have referred to norms previously as normal or conformist behaviour at a societal level, but norms can also vary with the different groups and subcultures to which we belong. We are referring here to particular ways of behaving that are normal and acceptable in sport cultures (although these will vary markedly depending if they apply to, for example, skateboarders or lacrosse players).

that people give to actions, traits, and ideas and (2) the ways that people use those meanings to "construct" their definitions of what and who is "deviant." It acknowledges that norms change over time and from situation to situation so that it is possible for something or someone to be considered "deviant" at one time or place and not at other times and places. For example, Arnold Schwarzenegger took steroids to help him win seven Mr. Universe and seven Mr. Olympia titles between the late 1960s and 1980, and then used his reputation and enhanced body to become an action hero in films; but he is not considered "deviant" by most people today because steroids were legal in bodybuilding in the 1960s and 1970s. However, voters in California used a constructionist approach to "deviance" when they elected Schwarzenegger as governor—they decided that it was not appropriate to use today's norms to judge actions in the past as unethical or criminal.

People who assume that social reality contains absolute truths about right and wrong and good and evil reject a constructionist approach to "deviance." They believe that unchanging moral truths are the foundation for all norms. Therefore, every norm represents an ideal, and every action, trait, or idea that departs from that ideal is "deviant," immoral, or evil. When this "absolutist" approach is used, "deviance" becomes increasingly serious as the departure from the ideal increases. For example, if using drugs violates an absolute principle of fairness in sports, any use of drugs at any time or place would be "deviant." People using an absolutist approach do not accept that norms and "deviance" are social constructions. They cling to the notion of absolute moral truths and use it to divide the world into good and evil and to make decisions about "deviance" and social control in everyday life. For example, media commentators who discuss criminal cases or drug use in sports often use an absolutist approach when they say without qualification that athletes today lack moral character to the point that they cannot distinguish right from wrong.

A CONSTRUCTIONIST APPROACH TO "DEVIANCE" IN SPORTS

"Deviance" always involves violating a norm. But sociologists using a constructionist approach say that a definition of "deviance" must take into account the process of *identifying* and *responding to* actions, traits, and ideas. Therefore, they define **"deviance"** as *an action, trait, or idea that falls outside a range of acceptance as determined by people with the power to enforce norms in a social world*. This definition emphasizes the following points about deviance:

1. Norms are socially constructed as people interact with each other and determine a range of accepted actions, traits, or ideas that are consistent with their values; norms *do not* represent absolute ideals against which all actions are evaluated. This point is illustrated in figure 6.2 where line A shows that norms are constructed in ways that permit variations within accepted limits so that everyone is not required to act, look, and think exactly alike to conform to values and avoid being labelled as "deviant." Line B, on the other hand, illustrates an absolutist approach in which every norm is based on an ideal that identifies a specific action, trait, or idea as right, good, and moral; and any departure from the ideal represents a degree of "deviance," immorality, or perversity.

2. "Deviance" is socially constructed as people negotiate the limits of what they will accept and then identify the actions, traits, and ideas that go beyond those limits. This is illustrated in line A by the two "limit lines" that separate socially accepted or "normal" actions, traits, and ideas from those that are unacceptable, or "deviant."

3. Power relations influence the process of negotiating normative limits because limits are seldom meaningful unless they can be enforced. Therefore, people who possess the power to administer sanctions (that is, punishments or rewards) generally have the

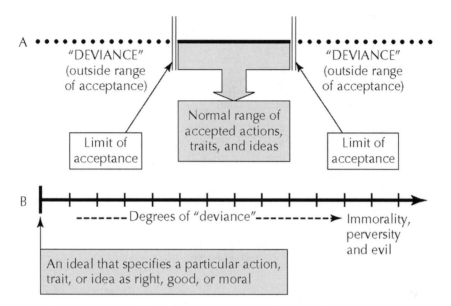

FIGURE 6.2 Norms set limits but permit a range of acceptable actions, traits, or ideas.

most influence in determining normative limits.

4. Most actions, traits, and ideas in a social world fall into a normally accepted range, and those that fall outside this range involve "deviant" underconformity *or* "deviant" overconformity as illustrated in figure 6.3.

Figure 6.3 is useful when trying to understand deviance in sports, especially the use of performance-enhancing substances and other extreme actions that most people in society define as outside the normal range of acceptance because they jeopardize health and well-being. The figure depicts a normal bell-shaped curve. The horizontal line below the curve represents a continuum of actions, traits, and ideas that encompasses cases of extreme underconformity on the left to cases of extreme overconformity on the right.

Actions, traits, and ideas that fall into a normally accepted range are located in the middle of the bell curve to show that they occur with the most frequency. The height of the curve represents the frequency of actions along the continuum. The shaded areas at each end of the continuum represent "deviance"—that is, actions that fall outside the limits of what is normally accepted in society. **"Deviant" underconformity** consists of *actions based on ignoring or rejecting norms*, whereas **"deviant" overconformity** consists of *actions based on uncritically accepting norms and being willing to follow them to extreme degrees*. Both types of "deviance" can be dangerous.[4] For

---

[4]Some social scientists (Heckert and Heckert, 2002, 2004, 2007; Hughes and Coakley, 1991; Irwin, 2003; West, 2003) use the terms *negative "deviance"* and *positive "deviance"* to refer to "deviant" underconformity and "deviant" overconformity, respectively. The term *positive "deviance"* does *not* imply that such "deviance" is good or beneficial to self or others. In fact, positive "deviance" involves extreme actions, traits, and ideas that often are unhealthy and dangerous. Additionally, this discussion focuses on actions only; a more detailed discussion of "deviance" in sports would also focus on traits and ideas.

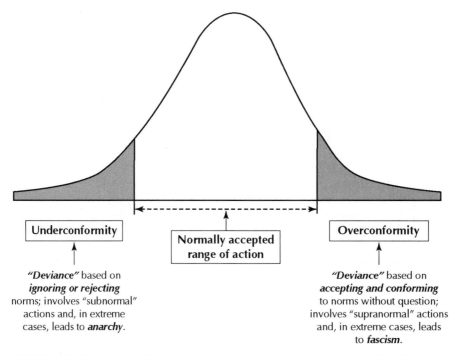

Underconformity

↑

"Deviance" based on
ignoring or rejecting
norms; involves "subnormal"
actions and, in extreme
cases, leads to ***anarchy***.

**Normally accepted
range of action**

Overconformity

↑

"Deviance" based on
accepting and conforming
to norms without question;
involves "supranormal" actions
and, in extreme cases, leads
to ***fascism***.

FIGURE 6.3   Two types of "deviance" in sports. Most actions in sports fall within
a normally accepted range in society as a whole. "Deviance" occurs when actions,
traits, or ideas go beyond normative limits on either side of this range. "Deviance" that
involves underconformity is grounded in different social dynamics than "deviance"
that involves overconformity. Most discussions of "deviance" in sports focus on athletes
or others who engage in "deviant" underconformity by ignoring or rejecting norms.
Generally overlooked or misinterpreted are cases of "deviant" overconformity that occur
when the actions, traits, and ideas of athletes and coaches involve such extreme and
unquestioned normative conformity that they endanger themselves and others.

example, extreme, widespread underconformity
leads to lawlessness or anarchy in a group or society, whereas extreme, widespread overconformity
leads to blind obedience or fascism as people
accept without question a rigid belief system or
the commands of a charismatic leader.

"Deviant" Overconformity in Sports

Research shows that "deviant" overconformity
occurs often in sports. For example when Keith
Ewald and Robert Jiobu (1985) studied men seriously involved in bodybuilding or competitive
distance running, they concluded that some of the

men displayed classic characteristics of "deviance"
in the form of unquestioned overconformity to the
norms related to training and competition. This
occurred when the bodybuilders and distance runners followed these norms to such an extent that
family relationships, work responsibilities, and/or
physical health were affected negatively, yet they
never questioned what they were doing or why
they were doing it.

This is not unique. Many elite athletes prepare so intensely for their sports that they ignore
the needs of family members. Bette McKenzie
(1999), a daughter of an NHL player and a
former wife of an NFL player, notes that her

ex-husband's "deviant" overconformity to the norms of professional football interfered with family relationships so much that it was a key factor in their divorce. Such overconformity may even become normalized for athletes' families. Thompson (1999) notes a time when every spouse and partner of an NHL player that she interviewed, who had a baby during the playing season, had her labour induced. The date was determined by the playing schedule in order to facilitate the father's presence at the birth.

Research has identified other forms of "deviant" overconformity, such as self-injurious overtraining, unhealthy eating behaviours and weight-control strategies among female athletes in elite amateur sports and among men in wrestling or those who work as jockeys,[5] extreme dedication to training among ultra marathon bicyclists (Wasielewski, 1991) and triathletes (Hilliard and Hilliard, 1990), and uncritical commitment to playing sports with pain and injury.[6]

When we use a critical constructionist approach to study "deviance" in sports, we see that it is important to distinguish between actions that show indifference toward norms or a rejection of norms, on the one hand, and actions that show an uncritical acceptance and overconformity to norms on the other hand. This approach also forces us to examine sport cultures and the social dynamics that occur in them. For example, athletes in high-performance sports are often encouraged to overconform to a set of norms or guidelines that they then use to evaluate themselves and others as they train and compete (Donnelly, 1996b; Howe, 2004; Ingham et al., 1999, 2002; Johns, 1997; Waldron and Krane, 2005). Because of this, much of the "deviance" among athletes (and coaches) involves *unquestioned acceptance of and conformity to* the value system embodied in the ethics of contemporary power and performance sports.

The Sport Ethic and "Deviance" in Sports

When Bob Hughes and Jay Coakley studied athletes and coaches in the late 1980s, they found four norms that were especially important in their lives. They referred to them as the **sport ethic**—that is, *a set of norms accepted as the dominant criteria for defining what it means, in their social worlds, to be defined and accepted as an athlete in power and performance sports.* The sport ethic constitutes the normative core of high-performance sport culture and consists of the following four norms:

1. *An athlete is dedicated to "the game" above all other things.* This norm stresses that athletes must love "the game" and prove it by giving it priority over all other interests. This is done by having the proper attitude, demonstrating unwavering commitment, meeting the expectations of fellow athletes, making sacrifices to play the game, and facing the demands of competition without question. Coaches' pep talks and locker room slogans are full of references to this norm.

   A U.S. university football player who had ten knee operations in six years and continued to play the game he loved between each operation explains this norm with these words: "I've told a hundred people that if I got a chance to play in the NFL, I'd play for free. It's never been about money. It's never been about anything but playing the game" (Wieberg, 1994, p. 8C). There are many similar examples of athletes who prove their dedication and love of "the game" by paying a price to play. Retired athletes say that they want to give back to the game because

---

[5]See Beals, 2000; Davis, 1999; Donnelly, 1993b; Franseen and McCann, 1996; Hawes, 2001; Johns, 1992, 1996, 1997; Johns and Johns, 2000; Sundgot-Borgen, 2001; Thompson and Sherman, 1999; also see Wilmore, 1996, for a review of thirty-five studies.

[6]See Curry, 1993; Cotton, 2005a; Curry and Strauss, 1994; Grant, 2002a, 2002b; Haney and Pearson, 1999; Howe, 2004; Ingham et al., 2002; Keown, 2004; P. King, 2004; Lyons, 2002; Nixon, 1993a, 1993b, 1994a, 1994b, 1996a, 1996b; Peretti-Watel et al., 2004a, 2004b; Pike and Maguire, 2003; Schefter, 2003; White and Young, 1997; Wood, 2004; Young and White, 1995; Young, 2004; Young et al., 1994.

they care so much about it, despite having disabilities caused by their playing careers

2. *An athlete strives for distinction.* The Olympic motto "Citius, Altius, Fortius" (swifter, higher, stronger) captures the meaning of this norm. Being an athlete means relentlessly seeking to improve and achieve perfection. Winning symbolizes improvement and establishes distinction; losing is tolerated only because it increases the desire to win and magnifies winning as a sign of distinction. Breaking records is the ultimate achievement because it shows that athletes are a special group dedicated to climbing the pyramid, reaching for the top, pushing limits, excelling, exceeding others, and being the best they can be no matter what it takes.

   This norm is highlighted by a Canadian university student who referred to striving for distinction despite pain and injury as "having an athlete mentality....Even if you know your limits as an athlete, oftentimes you'll push way past that, especially if you have a very short season....And you know if I play this game, I am going to die, and it's gonna hurt so much, but I'll have the whole year to rehab" (cited by Safai, 2001, p. 83).

3. *An athlete accepts risks and plays through pain.* According to this norm, an athlete does not give in to pressure, pain, or fear. Willingly accepting risks is a sign of being a true athlete; and playing under pressure is expected. The norm is that athletes do not back down from challenges; they accept the increasing risk of failure and injury as they ascend the pyramid of competitive sports.

   The language of sports is full of references to this norm (see the quote from Angelo Mosca on the first page of this chapter). Brian Burke, director of operations in the NHL, notes, "The code among our athletes is, if you have a pulse you play. There is no logical explanation for their pain threshold" (*Denver Post*, 1998, p. 7D). He also explains that coaches in hockey and other sports look

for players willing to take risks and play through pain; they like injured players in the lineup because it shows teammates that overconformity to the norms of the sport ethic is valued on their team.

4. *An athlete accepts no obstacles in the pursuit of possibilities.* This norm stresses "the dream" and the obligation to pursue it without question. An athlete does not accept obstacles without trying to overcome them and beat the odds; dreams are always seen as achievable *if* a person gives in to no obstacles when pursuing them.

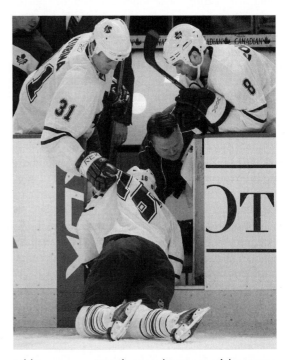

Athletes may overconform to the norms of the sport ethic to demonstrate commitment and courage. This often leads to high rates of injury in certain sports, as during a 2008 NHL game between the Toronto Maple Leafs and the Ottawa Senators, when Darcy Tucker was injured in the third period. Of course, these athletes do not see their overconforming behaviours as "deviant." Coaches and teammates praise their unquestioned acceptance of the norms of the sport ethic. [CP(Sean Kilpatrick)]

Overconformity to this norm is clearly illustrated by a Canada West track and field athlete who, after injuring his shoulder, noted:

> I got up and I jumped again and I actually jumped another six or so times and I recall afterwards basically being doubled over and not being able to do anything because it didn't hurt until I hit the mat. (cited by Young, White, and McTeer, 1994, p. 183)

And a Canadian female athlete stated:

> I never skated or played basketball without constant pain. However, this just made me push harder to beat it…The pain, while playing, was often enough to make me cry once I got home (never at the rink!). I dealt with it through the use of painkillers and denial. (cited by Young and White, 1995, p. 52)

To understand the connection between the sport ethic and "deviance" in sports, three points must be kept in mind. *First,* the norms of the sport ethic are widely accepted in cultures in which people believe that it is important to be dedicated to what you do, strive for improvement, make sacrifices to achieve goals, push yourself even when things are difficult or painful, and pursue dreams despite obstacles. For example, in Canada many parents teach these norms to their children, they are incorporated into academic curricula, emphasized in motivational speeches and self-help books, and portrayed on posters hung on office walls. *Second,* it is expected that those who wish to be accepted as athletes in (high-performance) sport cultures will conform to these norms. *Third,* people with power in sports take great care to control "deviant" underconformity, but they often ignore or encourage overconformity, even though it may lead to injuries and have long-term negative implications for the health and well-being of athletes. Therefore, in the culture of high-performance sports, these norms are usually accepted uncritically, without question or qualification, and often followed without recognizing the limits or thinking about the boundaries that separate normal from "deviant."

Alberto Salazar, the retired marathon runner, discussed the dangerous consequences of "deviant" overconformity when he coached U.S. middle-distance runner Mary Decker Slaney during the mid-1990s. Slaney had undergone nineteen sport-related surgeries and was living in constant pain at the time. Salazar explained that

> [t]he greatest athletes want it so much, they run themselves to death. You've got to have an obsession, but if unchecked, it's destructive. That's what it is with [Slaney]. She'll kill herself unless you pull the reins back. (Longman, 1996, p. B11)

Salazar's warning shows that dangerous forms of "deviance" occur when athletes do not critically assess the sport ethic and the context in which "deviant" overconformity becomes commonplace. The lack of critical assessment allows this type of "deviance" to exist even though it is one of the biggest problems in sports today.

"Deviant" underconformity is also a problem, but when athletes reject norms or refuse to take them seriously, they are immediately reprimanded or dropped from teams. Players who underconform to the norms of the sport ethic are not accepted as athletes by others associated with high-performance sports.

But reactions to "deviant" overconformity are different. When players conform to the norms of the sport ethic, they are praised and hailed as models, even if they risk their safety and well-being in the process. Media commentators glorify these athletes, praising those who play with broken bones and torn ligaments, have surgery after surgery to play the game, and request or submit to injections of huge doses of painkilling drugs to play through pain.

Spectators often express awe when they hear these stories, even though they realize that athletes have surpassed normative boundaries as defined in the society as a whole. Fans like to see deviance when it reaffirms an acceptance of values; they condemn deviance when it is based on a rejection of values. In January 1999, Governor General Roméo LeBlanc even awarded the Meritorious Service Cross to Elvis Stojko for competing at the Nagano Olympics while injured. "'I salute your unbeatable spirit,' Leblanc told Stojko" (Stevens, 1999). (See quoted citation below.) In light of the way that many people respond to the actions and traits of athletes, it is not surprising that many athletes uncritically overconform to the norms of the sport ethic without question or qualification, even when it creates problems, causes pain, disrupts family life, jeopardizes health and safety, or shortens their life expectancy (Safai, 2003; Tracey and Elcombe, 2004). This type of "deviance" raises interesting and important sociological questions.

The following is Mr. Stojko's citation:

Elvis Stojko, M.S.C., M.S.M.
Richmond Hill, Ont.
Meritorious Service Cross (civil division)

Despite a painful injury, Elvis Stojko, a three-time world champion, displayed an extremely high level of professionalism while competing in the Men's Figure Skating Singles at the Nagano Olympic Winter Games in 1998. His tremendous courage under such adversity won him a Silver Medal and demonstrated his indomitable spirit and dedication to the pursuit of excellence. This is the second award of a Meritorious Service Decoration to Mr. Stojko; he was awarded the Meritorious Service Medal in April 1995.

—(Press release, "Governor General to launch Canadian Figure Skating Championships and present Elvis Stojko with Meritorious Service Cross," January 26, 1999. © Office of the Secretary to the Governor General of Canada 1999. Reproduced with the permission of the Minister of Public Works and Government Services Canada, 2008.)

Why Do Athletes Engage in "Deviant" Overconformity?

Many athletes overconform to the norms of the sport ethic, but some do not. The main reasons for overconformity are:

1. Playing is so exciting and exhilarating that athletes will do almost anything to stay involved.

2. Being selected to play high-performance sports often depends on a perceived willingness to overconform to the norms of the sport ethic; coaches praise overconformers and use them as models on their teams.

3. Exceeding normative boundaries infuses drama and excitement into people's lives because it increases the stakes associated with participation, and bonds athletes together in a form of "bunker mentality" that encourages putting one's body on the line for teammates and expecting them to do the same.

For these reasons, athletes often use cases of "deviant" overconformity as standards to define and evaluate their sport experiences. Nike and Gatorade do this in TV commercials by highlighting athletes who throw up, shed blood, collapse from exhaustion, break bones, and morph into superbeings as part of regular training and competition. "Just doing it" is fine, even commendable, but "just overdoing it" until you vomit, bleed, lose consciousness, or need surgery is generally defined as "deviant." However, most athletes do not see overconformity to the sport ethic as "deviance" because it is required to reaffirm their identities as athletes and retain membership in a special group, separated from normal everyday people who live boring lives and never push the edge of the envelope. When Tom Wolfe (1979) studied astronauts and test pilots, he found that pilots who overconformed to norms similar to those of the sport ethic were defined as having "the right stuff" to move up the pyramid and become one of the special few in the world. Dangerous overconformity, according to Wolfe, was a small price to pay for living such an exciting life.

Of course, not all athletes are equally likely to overconform to the sport ethic. Hughes and Coakley hypothesize that those most likely to do so include

1. Athletes who have low self-esteem or are so eager to be accepted as athletes that they will do whatever it takes to be acknowledged by their peers in sport.

2. Athletes who see achievement in sports as their only way to get ahead, gain respect, and become significant in the world.
3. Male athletes who link together their identities as athletes and as men so that being an athlete and being a man become one and the same in their minds.

Therefore, athletes whose identities or future chances for recognition and success depend exclusively on sport participation are most likely to engage in "deviant" overconformity. An athlete's vulnerability to group demands, combined with the desire to gain or reaffirm group membership, is a critical factor underlying "deviant" overconformity.

This is why some coaches create team environments that keep athletes in a perpetual state of adolescence, a time in life characterized by identity insecurities and a strong dependence on acceptance by peers. It encourages a never-ending quest to confirm identity and eliminate self-doubt by going overboard to follow team norms and be accepted by athlete peers. Dependency-based commitment fuels overconformity to the sport ethic, making it common for athletes to willingly sacrifice their bodies and play with reckless abandon. When coaches use this strategy, they promote dangerous forms of "deviance." If coaches were concerned with controlling all forms of "deviance" in sports they would help athletes set limits for conformity to the norms of the sport ethic; they would also encourage athletes to ask why they do what they do and how their lives as athletes are connected with the rest of their lives.

If athletes do not learn to set such normative limits, their participation in sports often subverts the process of building character.

"Deviant" Overconformity and Group Dynamics

Being an athlete is a social as well as a physical experience. At elite levels of competition, special bonds form between athletes as they conform to the norms of the sport ethic. When people join together and collectively dedicate themselves to a goal and willingly make sacrifices and endure pain in the face of significant challenges, they often create a social world in which overconformity to the sport ethic becomes "normalized," even as it remains "deviant" in society as a whole (Albert, 2004; Curry, 1993; Pike, 2004). As athletes in high-performance and high-risk sports collectively overconform to the norms of the sport ethic, the bonds between them become extraordinarily powerful. This is because their overconformity sets them apart and separates them from the rest of the community. It also leads many athletes to assume that people who are not high-performance athletes cannot understand them and their lives. Athletes may appreciate fan approval, but fans cannot reaffirm their identity as an athlete because fans do not really know what it takes to pay the price day after day, face risk and pain, subordinate one's body and total being to the needs of the team, and do anything required to be among a select few who can perform as no others in the world can perform. Only other athletes understand this, and this makes everyone else peripheral to an athlete's life in sports.

The separation between athletes and the rest of the community makes the group dynamics associated with participation in high-performance sports very powerful. However, they are not unique. Other select and exclusive groups, usually groups of men, experience similar dynamics. Examples are found in the military, especially among Special Forces units. Former soldiers sometimes talk about these dynamics and the powerful social bonds formed while they faced danger and death with their teams. Tom Wolfe (1979) explains that trusting your life to fellow pilots when a small mishap or misjudgement means death creates special bonds, along with feelings that you and your peers are special. These bonds may exist in fraternities and sororities, where "pledges" voluntarily submit to systematic hazing processes designed to emphasize that membership in this special group must be earned by paying the price.

In fact, hazing rituals have long been a part of the initiation into groups that see themselves as special and separate from the rest of the community. Sport teams often have preseason hazing rituals, during which rookies are expected to follow the commands of team veterans, no matter how demeaning, sickening, painful, or illegal the "mandated" actions (Alfred University, 1999; Bryshun and Young, 2007; Johnson, 1999; Johnson and Holman, 2004; Hawes, 1999a; Wieberg, 2000a, b). (See the box "Hazing and University Policy," page 162). The bonds in these groups and the need for group acceptance and approval can be so strong that they prevent group members from reporting deviant and criminal forms of hazing to people outside the group.

As high-performance athletes endure the challenges of maintaining their membership in select groups and teams at the highest level of accomplishment in their sports, they develop not only extremely strong feelings of unity with other athletes but also the sense that they are unique and extraordinary people. After all, they are told this day after day by everyone from coaches to autograph seekers. They read it in newspapers and magazines, and they see it on TV and the Internet.

When the sense of being unique and extraordinary becomes extreme, as it does among many high-profile athletes in certain settings, it may be expressed in terms of pride-driven arrogance, an inflated sense of righteousness and power, and a public persona that communicates superiority and even insolence. The Greeks used the word **hubris** to describe this *expression of and the accompanying sense of being separate from and above the rest of the community.* Hubris is so common in some sports that it has become a key dimension of the public personas of many athletes. A few even market it and use it to attract attention and make people remember them, whereas others may be very selective in choosing when to express it.

The point in this section is that the social processes that exist in many sports, especially high-performance and professional (power and performance) sports, may do three things:

1. They bond athletes together in ways that encourage and normalize "deviant" overconformity.
2. They separate athletes from the rest of the community at the same time that they inspire awe and admiration from people in the community.
3. They lead athletes to develop hubris, which simultaneously bonds athletes together, separates them as a group from the rest of the community, and sometimes creates among them a sense of entitlement.

As we understand the impact of these social processes on athletes, we see that much of the "deviance" in sports is less motivated by winning or making money than by a desire to play the game, successfully claim an identity as an athlete, and maintain membership in an elite athletic in-group. This is not to say that winning and money are irrelevant, but they do not explain why "deviant" overconformity often is as high among athletes who know they will never win championships or sign large contracts as it is among athletes who can make a great deal of money and win championships (see figure 6.4). These athletes, just like their more talented and money-making peers, are motivated by the belief that being a "real athlete" means taking risks, making sacrifices, and paying the price to develop skills and stay in the game, and be accepted by other athletes, even if they are not champions.

This means that the roots of "deviant" overconformity in sports go deeper than individual desires to win or make money. In fact, they are grounded in the social organization of sports, processes of identity development, and the failure of people in sports to effectively control "deviant" overconformity. Fines and jail sentences seldom control this form of "deviance." Throwing out the so-called bad apples may help in the short run, but the social processes that operate in the social world of many sports guarantee that next season the crop in the orchard will look the same.

FIGURE 6.4 Winning is important to athletes. But winning and standing on the victory podium is usually secondary to the goal of being defined and accepted as true athletes by their peers in sports.

"Deviant" Overconformity and "Deviant" Underconformity: Is There a Connection?

After identifying "deviant" overconformity in sports, there are additional issues that require investigation:

- If the social bonds created in sports are powerful enough to normalize "deviant" overconformity that jeopardizes health and well-being, are they powerful enough to foster other forms of "deviance"?
- If the actions of athletes separate them from the rest of the community, do athletes come to disdain or disrespect nonathletes to the point that they might be likely to harass or assault them?
- If athletes develop hubris, might they feel entitled to the point of concluding that community standards and rules do not apply to them?
- If people in the community view athletes with awe and fascination because of their displays of "deviant" overconformity, are those people less likely to enforce laws and other community standards when athletes, especially high-profile athletes, violate them?

Research is needed on these questions. Our sense is that long-term overconformity to the sport ethic creates social conditions and group dynamics in sports that encourage notable forms of "deviant" underconformity, such as binge drinking, academic cheating, group theft and property destruction, drunken and careless driving, sexual harassment, physical assault, spousal abuse, and sexual assault. The connection between these two types of "deviance" is identified by an NFL football player who proudly said, "Hey, I have no problem sharing women with my teammates. These guys go to battle with me" (Nelson, 1994: 144).

This player's comment may be shocking, but it is consistent with other cases. For example, there are cases where young male athletes maintain group silence after witnessing teammates gang rape a woman (Curry, 1991, 1996, 1998; Lefkowitz, 1997; Robinson, 1998; Safai, 2002). Groups of athletes have mercilessly taunted and harassed other students, whom they defined as "unworthy" of respect because of how they looked or dressed (ESPN, 1999). Hazing rituals have subjected prospective teammates to demeaning and even criminal treatment—coercing rookies to steal, drink to the point of passing out, harass others, urinate on each other, drink urine, hold each other's genitals, appear nude in public, and endure various forms of sodomy, beatings, and brandings (Bryshun and Young, 2007; Hawes, 1999b; Johnson, 1999; Johnson and Holman, 2004).

The awe and adulation accorded to athletes who entertain as they push and exceed normative limits in sports on the field have in some cases, interfered with the enforcement of laws and community standards off the field. For example, alumni, sponsors, and fans who usually express "get-tough-on-crime" attitudes have threatened women who are alleged assault and rape victims of athletes (Benedict, 1997; Lipsyte, 1998; Robinson, 1998). This occurred to, among others, the victim of an alleged sexual assault by NBA player Kobe Bryant. There are cases where police officers have asked athletes who are being

REFLECT ON SPORTS   Hazing and University Policy

In this chapter, we have referred to the often demeaning, sickening, painful, or illegal nature of hazing activities. Initiation rituals on Canadian university sport teams have been described by Bryshun and Young (2007), Johnson (1999), and Johnson and Holman 2004). The forms of hazing activities vary by sport, by university (depending on traditions), and by gender. However, at the very least, hazing usually involves excessive drinking.

In the late 1990s, following a number of well-publicized incidents of hazing that involved student orientations and athletics teams (e.g., an incident at the University of Guelph in which a coach suspended two players for refusing to participate), many Canadian universities developed anti-hazing/initiation policies. These were zero-tolerance policies imposed under the Code of Student Behaviour to deal with frosh week, fraternity, and sport team initiations, or specifically for athletes by athletics departments. Coaches were no longer permitted to sanction or participate in team hazing ceremonies, and athletes were supposed to be informed of their right to refuse to be coerced into excessive drinking.

The response of many university sports teams was to go underground; ceremonies were taken off campus to student houses, bars, and motels. Jay Johnson (1999) found evidence that the abuse of new team members on some teams escalated as the activities moved off campus. Students reported that this was because the previous limits established by the presence of coaches, and sometimes alumni, no longer existed, and that ceremonies were taking place beyond the reach of campus security. For example, the McGill University football team hazing ceremonies became widely known in Canada in 2005 only when a rookie reported his experiences to the university authorities before leaving McGill. The team was subject to the university's

zero-tolerance policies, with several players and the coach being suspended, and the team forfeiting the remainder of its games.

Jay Johnson felt that universities and athletics departments may have made a bad situation even worse with their zero-tolerance policies, and that they needed to take a little more responsibility for the behaviour of student athletes. With the support of the associate dean for athletics at the University of Toronto, Johnson received a grant from the university administration to develop alternative initiation ceremonies for sports teams. These included outdoor activities such as ropes courses or short stays at a camp where athletes from several teams were involved in canoeing, rock climbing, and so on. They were held before the team's season started; coaches were also involved and sometimes brought their children.

Recent evaluation research indicates that hazing has not been eliminated; there are still some underground initiations, and heavy drinking is still involved. However, some teams have reported that hazing ceremonies are less degrading than in previous years because rookies and veterans had already bonded during the alternative initiations. The key seemed to be the inclusion of activities that are new to all players, both veterans and rookies, giving a sense of equality and cooperation from the start. When these are combined with good communication and clear athletics department policies regarding the rights and responsibilities of athletes, and with an increasing assertiveness on the part of some student-athletes who refuse, for example, to become involved in heavy drinking, it appears that some changes to long-established traditions are possible.

We think that these are valuable policy alternatives. *What do you think?*

arrested to sign autographs for their children, and judges in the U.S. have made favourable decisions involving athletes who play on teams representing their *alma mater* or teams for which the judges have season tickets.

Controlling "Deviant" Overconformity in Sports

"Deviant" overconformity presents special social control problems in sports. Coaches, managers, owners, and sponsors—people who exercise control of sports—often benefit when athletes accept without question and overconform to the sport ethic. These people often see athletes who willingly engage in "deviant" overconformity as a blessing, not a curse. Athletes see their overconformity to the sport ethic as proof of their dedication and commitment rather than a form of "deviance," and people associated with sports often see it as a factor that contributes to wins and high TV ratings. This is why those who control sports are unwilling to discourage this type of "deviance," even though they know it is outside of normative boundaries.

The issue of social control is further complicated by the tendency to promote overconformers into positions of power and influence in sports. Because they have proved they will do anything it takes as players, they are seen as ideal candidates for certain jobs in sports, especially coaching jobs. For example, Bobby Clarke, most recently general manager of the NHL's Philadelphia Flyers, was the player who reportedly deliberately slashed Valery Kharlamov during the famous 1972 series between Canada and the Soviet Union, breaking his ankle. The attack was evidently carried out at the request of coach John Ferguson, and it had no real consequences for Clarke until the issue was raised recently at the thirtieth anniversary ceremonies by series star, Paul Henderson.[7] This creates a situation in which "deviance" and ethical problems among athletes are rooted in the organization of sports and in athletes' relationships with each other and with coaches and managers.

Controlling "deviant" overconformity is difficult. It requires that parents, coaches, and sport administrators teach athletes to set limits as they play sports. (See, for example, the Reflect on Sports box, "Hazing and University Policy.") This, of course, conflicts with accepted practices in sports. Controlling "deviant" underconformity is less difficult because it is quickly identified by authority figures, and everyone understands that it will be punished. "Deviant" overconformity, however, is more subversive because it is widely ignored. For example, when a fourteen-year-old gymnast is late for practice, her coach immediately identifies this as a type of "deviance" and acts to eliminate it. However, when the same gymnast loses weight and becomes dangerously thin as she strives for distinction and pursues her dream, many coaches, parents, and judges do not see possible "deviance" as much as they see the mindset of a champion and the culture of excellence in the gym—that is, until stress fractures interfere with competition and put their athlete daughter in hospital.

The control of "deviant" overconformity requires that people associated with sports raise critical questions about the goals, purpose, and organization of sports, as well as the ways that coaches and others enforce the norms of the sport ethic. In the absence of these questions, dangerous forms of "deviance" will persist, including the use of performance-enhancing substances. Unfortunately, many coaches encourage "deviant" overconformity as they tell athletes that the team is their family and that family members put their bodies on the line for each other when they go to battle. Similarly, fostering the belief on teams that "outsiders are out to get us" and that "we have to stick together because nobody understands us" clearly promotes hubris and further separates athletes from the surrounding community and its laws.

The most effective strategy for controlling "deviant" overconformity is to encourage athletes to set limits that respect their health and use sport participation as a means of connecting more meaningfully with the rest of the community. This also could be an important step in controlling "deviant" underconformity because it would make athletes feel less like outsiders

---

[7]This should be contrasted with the punishment of Roy Keane, the Manchester United soccer player who claimed, in his autobiography, to have deliberately injured an opponent in a game. His fine and suspension is the highest ever handed out by the British Football Association (FA)—a five-game suspension and a fine of £150,000 (over C$300,000).

and help them to identify with the community so that they would not see themselves as above the law. A major barrier to controlling "deviant" overconformity is that sport fans want athletes to exceed normative limits and put their bodies on the line. Fans see this as entertaining. But they cannot have it both ways—if fans want "deviant" overconformity, it will sometimes come in forms that make them uncomfortable

RESEARCH ON "DEVIANCE" AMONG ATHLETES

Headlines and media coverage of "deviance" among athletes are common, but systematic studies are rare. Lists of arrest records and criminal charges filed against athletes attract attention, but they do not tell us if "deviance" is out of control in sports, if there is more "deviance" today than in the past, if "deviance" involves overconformity or underconformity, or what causes "deviance" in sports. Most media reports blame "deviance" on the character weaknesses of athletes and the financial greed of people associated with sports. Generally ignored is the possibility that "deviance" could be related to the culture and organization of sports or the social dynamics that exist in social worlds created around sports.

When we discuss "deviance" among athletes, it is important to distinguish the actions that occur on the field and in sport settings from the actions that occur off the field and away from sports. They are related to different types of norms and rules, and they have different causes and consequences.

"Deviance" on the Field and in the Realm of Sports

This type of "deviance" includes cheating (such as using the spitball or having an excessive curve on the blade of a hockey stick), gambling, shaving points, throwing games or matches, engaging in unsportsman-like conduct, fighting, taking illegal performance-enhancing drugs,

and generally finding ways to avoid the rules of the game. Some people claim that these types of "deviance" have become serious today, because the personal and financial stakes have become so great in sports.

But historical research indicates that cheating, dirty play, fighting, and the use of violence are less common today than in the days before television coverage and high-stakes commercialization (Dunning, 1999; Guttmann, 2004; Maguire, 1988; Scheinin, 1994). This research also shows that sports today are more rule-governed than in the past and that on-the-field "deviance" is more likely to be punished and publicly criticized. Therefore, it is a mistake to blame "deviance" in sports today on money and TV as some people do.

Comparing rates of on-the-field "deviance" among athletes from one time to another is difficult because rules and enforcement standards change over time. Research shows that athletes in most sports interpret rules very loosely during games and that they create informal norms, which stretch or bend official rules (Shields and Bredemeier, 1995). But this is not new. Athletes have done this ever since umpires and referees have enforced rules. In fact, athletes in organized sports traditionally play to the level permitted by umpires and referees—that is, they adjust their actions according to the ways that referees enforce rules (cf., Rains, 1984). However, this does not mean that players ignore rules or that "deviance" is out of hand. Nor does it mean that we ought to ignore "deviance" when it occurs.

The perception that "deviance" on the field and in sport settings is increasing also exists today because there are more rules now than ever before, and sports are more rule-governed than in the past. Rule books in sport organizations show that there are thousands of rules today that did not exist a generation ago in sports, and every year more rules are added. International sport organizations now provide catalogues of banned substances. Today, there are more ways to be "deviant" in sports than at any time in history!

There is no evidence that rates of deviance on the field are higher today than in the past. What is different today is the media coverage and video technology, which enable us to see rule violations in slow motion, stop action, and replay after replay after replay. Actually, many forms of deviance were more prevalent and blatant eighty years ago when the technology of enforcement was limited. [Peter Cosgrove, AP/Wide World Photos]

Furthermore, the forms of surveillance used today and the increased emphasis on rule enforcement means that more rule violators are caught today than ever before.

Finally, evidence shows that athletes in power and performance sports expect and engage in certain forms of on-the-field "deviance" such as "good fouls" and "cheating when you can get away with it" (Anonymous, 1999; Pilz, 1996; Shields et al., 1995). This is most prevalent at higher levels of competition, it increases with the number of years that people play sports, and it is also more common among men than women. These patterns are consistent with other research suggesting that participating in power and performance sports does not generally promote moral development and moral decision making (Stoll and Beller, 1998, 2000). However, no historical studies show that "deviance" on the field and in the realm of sports is more common than in the past.

"Deviance" does exist in sports; *it is a problem.* It ought to be studied, and efforts should be made to control it without violating individual rights and principles of due process. The only form of sport-related "deviance" that is more prevalent today than in the past is the use of banned performance-enhancing substances. This is clearly a serious problem, which is discussed later in the chapter.

"Deviance" off the Field and Away from Sports

Off-the-field "deviance" among athletes receives widespread media attention. When athletes are arrested or linked to criminal activity, they make headlines and become lead stories on the evening news. Media reports of bar fights and assault charges appear regularly (Starr and Samuels, 2000). Research does not tell us if rates of off-the-field "deviance" have gone up or down, or if general crime rates are higher among athletes than among comparable people in the general population. However, there have been studies of (1) delinquency and sport participation, particularly among U.S. high school students, (2) excessive alcohol use, particularly among U.S. high school and university athletes, and (3) particular felony rates among athletes.

Delinquency Rates Research on U.S. high school students shows that delinquency rates among athletes are usually lower than rates for other students from similar backgrounds. With a few exceptions,[8] this general finding seems to hold

for athletes in various sports, athletes in different societies, and both boys and girls from various racial and social class backgrounds (see Miracle and Rees, 1994, for a summary of these studies; McHale et al., 2005; Miller et al., 2002).

The problem with most of these studies is that they do not take into account that students with histories of deviance may not try out for sport teams, that coaches may cut them when they do try out, or that athletes may receive preferential treatment enabling them to avoid being labelled a delinquent. It is also possible that forms of deviance among some athletes are obscured by a façade of conformity—conforming to norms in public and violating them in private where they are rarely publicly detected (Miracle and Rees, 1994).

Even when sport programmes are designed as "interventions" for "at-risk youth," success is difficult to achieve. In a review of this issue, Hartmann (2003b) notes that we lack a clear theory to explain how and why we might expect sport-based intervention programmes to be effective in reducing delinquency or producing other positive effects. Most of these programmes have little effect because they do nothing to change the unemployment, poverty, racism, poor schools, and other delinquency-related factors that exist in most neighbourhoods where sports for at-risk youth are offered (Coakley, 2002; Donnelly and Coakley, 2002, 2004; Pitter, 2004).

We know from Chapter 4 that we cannot make generalizations about athletes because sport experiences vary from programme to programme and sport participation constitutes only a part of a person's experience. Therefore, when someone says "playing sports keeps me out of trouble," we need to investigate what that means and if there are ways to organize sports and sport experiences that provide young people with opportunities to identify positive alternatives for their lives. Until more of this research is done, we must say that sport participation does not create models of virtue, or delinquents, in any systematic way, although both may play sports. (This issue is discussed further in the box, "Is Sport Participation a Cure for

---

[8]For example, Miller et al., (2005) found that U.S. adolescent athletes who identify themselves as "jocks" were more likely to report involvement in delinquent acts than adolescent athletes who do not identify as "jocks."

"Deviant" Behaviour?", which is available on the Online Learning Centre.)

Alcohol Use and Binge Drinking Underage and excessive alcohol consumption in high school and university is not limited to athletes. However, data collected from Canada and the U.S. through the 1990s indicated that male and female interuniversity athletes engaged in more alcohol use, abuse, and binge drinking than other men and women students (Bacon and Russell, 2004; Eccles and Barber, 1999; Naughton, 1996; Spence and Gauvin, 1996; Wechsler et al., 1997; Wechsler and Wuethrich, 2002). The data on high school athletes are more equivocal. One recent U.S. study suggests that rates of alcohol use may be lower among teens under eighteen years old who play on sport teams than among teens who do not play on sport teams (SAMHSA, 2002). However, studies of U.S. high schools by Miller, et al. (2001, 2003) report the following:

- highly involved athletes are more likely to drink excessively than non-athletes
- the association between sports and alcohol consumption is largely a male phenomenon
- those who identify as "jocks" engage in more problem drinking
- alcohol misuse increases the likelihood that an adolescent will become a "jock"
- self-identification as a "jock" increases alcohol misuse

Thus, it seems that male high school athletes who are highly involved in their sport and who identify as "jocks" may be more like both male and female university athletes in terms of drinking behaviour than they are like other U.S. high school athletes.

Research on this topic is important because alcohol use and abuse is related to other forms of "deviance." Studies are needed to see if the group dynamics of alcohol use and binge drinking at the university level are related to the dynamics underlying overconformity to other group norms among athletes. Getting drunk with fellow athletes may not be very different, sociologically speaking, from playing with pain to meet the expectations of teammates: "Have another shot of tequila—it's what we teammates who make sacrifices and take risks together are doing tonight. Are you a part of this special group or not?" Again, research is needed to see if, why, when, and how often this occurs.

Felony Rates In North America, widely publicized cases of assault, hard drug use, and driving under the influence of drugs or alcohol (DUI) in which male athletes are the offenders have created a growing sense of urgency about the need for systematic studies of these forms of "deviance." At this point, research is scarce and the studies that do exist (almost all carried out in the U.S.) report mixed findings (see Crosset, 1999, for a review and critique of research that focuses on sexual assault).

One problem with the studies of felony rates is that the data on arrest rates for athletes are seldom compared with arrest rates in the general population or in populations comparable to the athletes in age and race. For example, when Benedict and Yaeger (1998) reported that 21.4 percent of a sample of NFL players had been arrested at least once for something more serious than minor crimes since the year they started university, many people were horrified. However, a follow-up study by Blumstein and Benedict (1999) showed that 23 percent of the males living in cities of 250,000 or more people are arrested for a serious crime at some point in their lives, usually during young adulthood; the arrest rate for whites is 14 percent, and for blacks it is 51 percent. When they focused on crimes of domestic violence and non-domestic assault, and compared NFL players with young adult males, Blumstein and Benedict found that the annual arrest rate for NFL players was half the arrest rate for males in the general population. This pattern was nearly the same when the rate for white NFL players was compared with the rate for young white men, and the rate for black NFL players was compared with the rate for young black men.

When Blumstein and Benedict compared arrest rates for property crimes, NFL players had distinctively lower rates than the rest of the population, a finding they explained partly in terms of the salaries made by NFL players. However, their overall conclusion was that when NFL players are compared with young men in the general population, their off-the-field "deviance" does not seem to be out of control. Of course, this does not mean that "deviance" among athletes is not a problem or that professional sport leagues and universities should not take actions to control it.

Benedict (2004) also collected data on NBA players during the 2001–2002 season and found that 40 percent of them had a police record involving a serious crime—a lower rate than young black men in the general population. However, after doing over 400 interviews, reviewing police records, and searching court documents, Benedict focused on the issue of sexual assault and concluded that the social world of NBA basketball is organized so that it is "nearly impossible for a rape victim to file a criminal complaint against an NBA player without being labelled a groupie or a gold digger." He suggested that it would take "nothing less than Snow White to obtain a conviction in a sexual assault case against a celebrity athlete and emerge with a reputation still intact" (p. 29). The incidence of assault and sexual assault among male athletes is an especially important topic and is discussed in chapter 7.

Off-the-Field "Deviance": A Final Comment
The point of this section is that off-the-field "deviance" among athletes does not seem to be out of control. Although research is scarce, existing studies contradict the attention-grabbing news headlines that we often see and hear. Research suggests that delinquency and crime rates may not be higher than they are for comparable peers. At the same time, rates for alcohol abuse, binge drinking, and certain forms of assault may be higher among athletes. But until we have better data and good theories to explain these data, we can only speculate why these patterns exist.

Why Focus on "Deviance" Only Among Athletes?

This chapter focuses almost exclusively on "deviance" among athletes. However, athletes are not the only people in sports who violate norms. The following are other examples of sport-related "deviance."

- Coaches who hit players, treat them inhumanely, use male players' insecurities about masculinity to motivate them, sexually harass women in and out of sports, subvert efforts to provide girls and women with equal participation opportunities in sports, and violate organizational rules
- Coaches and sport administrators who ignore or subvert organization regulations about eligibility; and about equity issues related to gender, sexuality, race, language, and disability when they recruit, evaluate, hire, and promote administrative staff and coaches
- Sport team owners and others who violate anti-combines legislation, collude with each other to hold down player salaries, and deliberately mislead city officials and voters in connection with stadium, arena, or major sports event funding issues
- Sport administrators, including those on the International Olympic Committee and related organizations, who take bribes and gifts in return for favours and who violate public trust and organizational principles by making decisions clearly based on their personal interests (Jennings, 1996, 2006; Jennings and Sambrook, 2000); since the 1999 revelations about corruption, the IOC no longer permits its members to visit cities that are bidding for future Olympics —perhaps they do not trust themselves to refuse offered bribes and gifts

When a black NBA player loses his temper, throws a ball in anger, and appears ready to fight, many people "see" deviance and worry about it. When a white coach does similar things—throws towels, chairs, rolled-up programmes, and appears ready to fight—many people "see" him (Bobby Knight, for example) as a legend, as an authority figure who controls subordinate players with tactics that might be defined as criminal if a teacher used them in the classroom. How do people define "deviance" in sports? Are race and roles (authority) related to these definitions? These questions must be answered for a full understanding of deviance in sports. [Jake Schoellkopf; AP/Wide World Photos]

- Judges and other officials in events who take bribes, fail to correct mistakes, or make agreements with others to alter the outcome of sports events such as boxing (Jennings, 1996), gymnastics (e.g., incidents affecting Canadian gymnasts at the 2004 Athens Olympics), and figure skating (e.g., the Jamie Salé/David Pelletier incident at the 2002 Salt Lake City Olympics)
- Media promoters and commentators who deliberately distort and misrepresent sport

events, so that they can generate high television ratings or newspaper/magazine sales
- Agents who mislead athletes, misrepresent themselves, or violate rules as they solicit junior and student-athletes and represent professional athletes
- Parent-spectators who berate, taunt, and fight with each other, referees, and players as they watch their children in youth sports
- Spectators who attack or throw objects at athletes and referees, fight with each other, and destroy property as they mourn a loss or celebrate a victory; and who place illegal bets on sports, and sell forged autographs of athletes

Some of these and other examples of "deviance" are discussed in chapters 5, 7, 8, and 11–14.

PERFORMANCE-ENHANCING SUBSTANCES: A CASE OF "DEVIANT" OVERCONFORMITY IN SPORTS

Stories about athletes using performance-enhancing substances are no longer shocking; they appear regularly in the media. However, many people do not know that drug and substance use in sports has a long history.[9] Athletes have taken a wide variety of everyday and exotic substances over the years, and substance use has never been limited to elite athletes. Data suggest that, if today's drugs had been available in past centuries, athletes would have used them as frequently as athletes use them today (Hoberman, 1992, 2004; Todd, 1987). This makes it difficult to blame all drug use on the profit motive, commercial interests, television, and the erosion of traditional values.

Research also suggests that drug and substance use by athletes generally is not the result of defective socialization or lack of moral

---

[9]See the *Sports in Society* website (www.mcgrawhill.ca/olc/coakley) for a summary of this history.

character because many users and abusers are the most dedicated, committed, and hard working athletes in sports! Nor are all substance users helpless victims of exploitive coaches and trainers, although coaches and trainers who push the sport ethic without question may indirectly encourage the use of performance-enhancing substances. Instead, most substance use and abuse seem to be an expression of uncritical acceptance of the norms of the sport ethic. Therefore, it is grounded in the same type of overconformity that occurs when injured distance runners continue training, even when training may cause serious injuries; when young female gymnasts control weight by cutting their food intake to dangerous levels; and when football players risk their already injured and surgically repaired bodies week after painful week in the CFL.

Apparently, many athletes enjoy playing their sports so much that they will do whatever it takes to stay involved and meet the expectations of their fellow athletes. Of course, they seek on-the-field success, enabling them to avoid being cut or eliminated, but the desire to win is usually secondary to the desire to play and be accepted as an athlete. This means that most high-performance athletes will do whatever it takes to pursue their dreams. As long as some athletes are willing to take performance-enhancing substances to gain the edge they need, others will use similar substances to stay competitive at that level, even if it is against their better judgment.

These dynamics, all connected with overconformity to the sport ethic, operate at various levels of sports—from local gyms, where high school athletes work out, to the locker rooms of professional sport teams—and among women and men across a wide variety of sport events, from the 100-metre sprint to the marathon and from tennis to football.

> If the purpose of sport is personal growth and self-discovery, the athlete loses all in the Faustian pact with steroids.
>
> —Bruce Kidd, *University of Toronto Magazine* (1989)

Defining and Banning Performance-Enhancing Substances

Defining *performance-enhancing substances* is difficult. They can include anything from aspirin to heroin; they may be legal or illegal, harmless or dangerous, natural or synthetic, socially acceptable or unacceptable, commonly used or exotic. Furthermore, they may produce real physical changes, psychological changes, or both (see figure 6.5).

Problems with definitions are faced whenever a sport organization develops an anti-drug or no-doping programme. For example, until 1999, the International Olympic Committee (IOC) defined doping in this way:

> [Doping is] the administration of or use by a competing athlete of any substance *foreign* to the body or any *physiological substance* taken in *abnormal quantity* or taken by an *abnormal route of entry* into the body with the *sole intention* of increasing in an *artificial and unfair* manner his/her performance in competition. When necessity demands *medical treatment* with any substance that, because of its nature, dosage, or application, is able to boost the athlete's performance in competition in an artificial and unfair manner, this too is regarded by the IOC as doping. (USOC, 1992, p. 1; italics added)

This definition may sound good, but the IOC had difficulty defining all the terms in italics. For example, what is a substance "foreign" to the body, and why are the "foreign" substances of aspirin and ibuprofen not banned, while the "natural" hormone testosterone and naturally grown marijuana are banned? What is an "abnormal" quantity or an "abnormal" route of entry? Why are megadoses of vitamins not banned, while small amounts of decongestants are banned? Why can athletes be stripped of medals when they swallow medications without intending to enhance performance, while others keep their medals after having intravenous needles inserted into their veins to be rehydrated during competitions?

SIDELINES

"Is this what those hormones are supposed to do, Carl?"

FIGURE 6.5 The negative side effects of various combinations of substances ("stacking and cycling") are difficult to identify. Controlled studies of banned substances are difficult to do, because it may not be ethical to experiment with the same dosages that athletes use. This means that the side effects of many substances are unknown.

With scientific discoveries being made every day and applied to sports, what is artificial and what is unfair? Why are needles permitted to inject certain painkillers, whereas the same needles are considered dangerous and artificial when used to inject a cyclist's or distance runner's own red blood cells into a vein (blood boosting)? Why is the electronic stimulation of muscles permitted? Isn't it artificial? Is it fair to compete with knees strengthened with surgically inserted synthetic ligaments after "natural" ligaments were torn beyond repair? Why are biofeedback and other psychological technologies defined as "natural" and "fair," while certain naturally grown herbal teas are defined as "unnatural" and "unfair"? Are vitamins natural? Amino acids? Caffeine? Human growth hormone? Gatorade? Protein drinks? Creatine? Eyeglasses? What if an athlete could wear contact lenses that would boost vision acuity from 20-20 to 20-5?

How about so-called natural herbs, chemicals, and compounds now stacked floor to ceiling in stores that sell nutritional supplements with the promise of performance enhancement? Is it natural to deprive yourself of food to make weight or meet the demands of a coach who measures body fat every week and punishes athletes who eat "normal" diets? Should athletes who binge and purge, become anorexic, or exercise in saunas wearing rubber suits to lose weight be considered normal? In fact, what is normal about any of the social, psychological, biomechanical, environmental, and technological methods of manipulating and changing athletes' bodies and minds in today's high-performance sports? Are U.S. university football players "deviant" when saline solutions are dripped into their veins through intravenous needles in a pregame locker room to minimize the threat of dehydration on a hot playing field? Surely this is a performance-enhancing procedure. Is it normal, safe? How about twelve-year-old gymnasts and sixteen-year-old football players who pop a dozen anti-inflammatory pills every day, so that they can train through pain? Are they "deviant"? Are they different from hockey players who pop a dozen Sudafed pills (containing pseudoephedrine) to get "up" for the game or baseball players will use the anti-fatigue drug Modafinil?

How about NFL players who became addicted to painkillers after being regularly injected by team physicians? Why do we call athletes heroes when they use an intravenous procedure to play in extreme heat or take injections of painkilling drugs to keep them training and playing, and then condemn the same athletes when they take drugs to help them build muscles damaged by overtraining or other drugs to help them relax and recover after their bodies and minds have been pushed beyond limits in the pursuit of dreams?

Why do many athletes see the use of drugs as a noble act of commitment and dedication, while many spectators see it as a reprehensible act of "deviance" yet pay a great deal of money to watch athletes do superhuman things requiring extreme training regimes and strategies made possible by drugs or random genetic mutations?

These and hundreds of other questions about what is artificial, natural, foreign, fair, and abnormal show that any definition of *doping* will lead to endless debates about the technical and legal

WADA's World Anti-Doping Code uses the following definitions (www.wada-ama.org):

Article 1: DEFINITION OF DOPING

Doping is defined as the occurrence of one or more of the anti-doping rule violations set forth in Article 2.1 through Article 2.8 of the *Code*.

Article 2: ANTI-DOPING RULE VIOLATIONS

The following constitute anti-doping rule violations:

2.1 The presence of a *Prohibited Substance* or its *Metabolites* or *Markers* in an *Athlete's* bodily *Specimen*.

    2.1.1 It is each *Athlete's* personal duty to ensure that no *Prohibited Substance* enters his or her body. *Athletes* are responsible for any *Prohibited Substance* or its *Metabolites* or *Markers* found to be present in their bodily *Specimens*. Accordingly, it is not necessary that intent, fault, negligence, or knowing *Use* on the *Athlete's* part be demonstrated in order to establish an anti-doping violation under Article 2.1.

    2.1.2 Excepting those substances for which a quantitative reporting threshold is specifically identified in the *Prohibited List*, the detected presence of any quantity of a *prohibited Substance* or its *Metabolites* or *Markers* in an *Athlete's Sample* shall constitute and anti-doping rule violation.

    2.1.3 As an exception to the general rule of Article 2.1, the *Prohibited List* may establish special criteria for the evaluation of *Prohibited Substances* that can also be produced endogenously.

2.2 *Use* or *Attempted Use* of a *Prohibited Substance* or a *Prohibited Method*.

Added to these items are a number of explanatory "Comments."

WADA's Prohibited List, known as *The List,* is 16 pages long, with items grouped into four sections:

- substances and methods prohibited at all times
- substances and methods prohibited in competition
- substances prohibited in particular sports
- specified substances

---

meaning of terms. After the IOC transferred its anti-doping responsibilities to the World Anti-Doping Agency (WADA) in 1999, Montréal-based WADA developed its own definition of doping as part of the *World Anti-Doping Code*. However, even the more simplified definition in the World Anti-Doping Code (v. 3; WADA, 2003) is subject to pages and pages of qualifications (see box, p. 172).

Meanwhile, physicians, pharmacists, chemists, inventors, and athletes continue to develop new and different aids to performance—chemical, "natural," and otherwise. For example, the founders of the supplement producer and distributor, EAS, made many millions of dollars by finding all of the loopholes in the drug policy of every sport and creating substances that fit those loopholes. We now have a seemingly endless game of scientific hide and seek, which persists despite new definitions and drug policies. This game will become more heated and controversial as scientists manipulate the brain and nervous system and use genetic manipulation and engineering to improve athletic performance. With new performance-enhancing technologies, we are approaching a time when defining, identifying, and dealing with doping and drugs will be only one of many strategies for manipulating athletes' bodies and improving performance (Bjerklie and Park, 2004).

Further complicating decisions about which substances to ban is confusion about their effects on athletic performance. Ethical and legal considerations have constrained researchers who study the impact of megadoses and multiple combinations of substances that are "stacked and cycled" by athletes. Athletes learn things in locker rooms faster than scientists learn them in the lab, although the validity of locker room knowledge is frequently suspect. Furthermore, by the time researchers have valid information about a substance, athletes have moved on to others, which are unknown to researchers. This is why many athletes ignore "official statements" about the consequences and dangers of doping—the statements are about two to five years behind the "inventors" who supply new substances.

As the market for substances and the wealth of athletes have grown, so have the labs that are dedicated to "beating the system" with "designer drugs," undetectable substances, and masking agents that hide certain molecules in the testing process. For example, IGF-1 (insulin-like growth factor-1) is a muscle builder that can be injected directly into the bloodstream. It improves strength development and it is undetectable with current tests. The same is true for dozens of other "designer substances" rumoured to be available for the right price (Assael, 2003, 2005; Sokolove, 2004b).

The Internet has made information about and access to substances immediately available to athletes around the world (www.t-nation.com, www.musclemedia.com, www.getbig.com, www.elite-fitness.com, and www.muscleandfitness.com). Magazines such as *Muscle Media* provide dozens of references to these sites. Most athletes know that even though sport organizations have drug policies, the people who control those organizations are not eager to find drug users because too many positive tests may jeopardize the billions of dollars that corporate sponsors and TV networks pay for events that are promoted as "clean and wholesome"—hence the concerns about the 2008 Tour de France (ESPN *The Magazine*, 2005; Jennings and Sambrook, 2000). Certain performance enhancers are now listed as controlled substances in countries such as Canada and the U.S.

However, testing remains a challenge in most sport organizations (Keating, 2005). In fact, if the random testing of all professional athletes across all major sports in North America was required to be carried out by an independent enforcement agency, it would cost over US$10 million per year just for the NFL. It would cost billions of dollars to test all international, university, and high school athletes over the next decade.

Most antidoping policies are at least partially based on the belief that these substances are dangerous to the health of athletes. Although this is true in some cases, it is tough to argue this point to athletes who already make sacrifices, pay the price, and take many health risks as they strive for distinction and pursue dreams in their sports. For example, when athletes who have dedicated between four and fifteen years of their youth to make a national team or play a pro sport are told that taking certain hormones could shorten their lives by a few years or do damage to their livers or hearts, they do not listen very closely. Such messages do not scare many of them; they know that being an athlete means that you take risks

and sometimes suffer in the process. Furthermore, when they are not encouraged to question the extreme commitment that promotes other dangerous forms of overconformity to the sport ethic, how can they be convinced to avoid substances that may negatively affect their health? After all, real athletes know that participation in power and performance sports is itself a threat to their health (Waddington, 2000a)!

Finally, some people ask why drugs should be banned in sports when they are widely accepted in society and used to improve performance or treat conditions that interfere with performance at home, work, or play. Adults in most wealthy, high-tech societies use tranquilizers, pain controllers, mood controllers, antidepressants, decongestants, diet pills, birth control pills, insulin caffeine, nicotine, sleep aids, and alcohol. Doctors readily prescribe prohormone and hormone therapies to improve strength and counteract the negative effects of aging; these include thyroid hormone, testosterone (patches, gels, and pills now taken by over 2 million men in the U.S.A. alone; Hoberman, 2004; Noonan, 2003), anabolic steroids, human growth hormone (HGH), HGH stimulants, androstenedione, DHEA, and creatine.[10] Every six months the list changes and grows longer as new discoveries are made and new supplements manufactured. In fact, if people really did say no to drugs, life in most Western societies would change dramatically. When a fifty-five-year-old man takes HGH to maintain strength so he can outperform others in his highly paid job, why should his twenty-five-year-old son not do the same thing in the CFL?

---

[10]Dehydroepiandrosterone (DHEA) is a hormone widely available over the counter in most countries (although not in Canada). It is a product of the adrenal glands, and it stimulates the production of testosterone. Some athletes and people over age forty take it to maintain lean body mass. DHEA has recently been added to WADA's *List of Prohibited Substances*. Creatine is a compound produced by the liver, kidneys, and pancreas. It may facilitate the renewal of anaerobic energy reserves, delay the onset of fatigue during intense exercise, and cut recovery time between workouts (Kearney, 1999).

These issues lead to an important question. Why control athletes in ways that other people are not controlled? After all, do universities have rules banning caffeine and other drugs that students use so that they can study all night for a test? Do teachers make students sign an oath to avoid drugs that might enable them to perform better in a course? Do employers tell executives not to use hormone therapies to keep them fit for work? Do wives tell their husbands not to take Viagra, Cialis, Levitra, or other substances that elevate sexual performance (and are now reportedly being used increasingly to elevate athletic performance)? Why should athletes be tested and denied access to substances, when others competing or working for valued rewards are often encouraged to take similar substances? As these questions are asked, it remains difficult to define drugs, doping, and substance abuse in sports.

Why Is the Challenge of Substance Control So Great in Sports Today?

In the final analysis, an athlete must make the decision to ingest or inject a performance-enhancing substance, but athletes do not live in a vacuum. They are a part of their particular sport subculture, a part of the larger sport culture, and members of the national and global society. As such, they are subject to a wide range of influences that are likely to affect their decision (Donnelly, 2008). Many factors contribute to the tendency among today's athletes to seek substances for the edge they need to pursue their dreams and stay involved in the sports they love and the jobs for which they are paid. These include the following:

1. *The visibility and resources associated with sports today have fuelled massive research and development efforts devoted to performance-enhancing substances.* Entrepreneurs and corporations have tied the development of performance-enhancing substances to the general realm of "alternative medicine" and now use it to make quick and substantial

profits. These substances are especially profitable because aging baby boomers (the massive population cohorts born between 1946 and 1964) see these substances as health aids. This creates an extremely large market that pushes the supplement industry to make available an ever-expanding array of substances.

2. *People in postindustrial societies are deeply fascinated with technology and how they can use it to push or extend human limits.* Advertising that promotes hyperconsumption as a lifestyle in society encourages this fascination. Athletes, because they live in social worlds characterized by a "culture of excellence," hear those corporate messages loud and clear. Like many of us, they see consumption as a way to pursue their dreams, and because they are willing to overconform with the norms of the sport ethic, they can become hyperconsumers of whatever it takes to stay on the field.

3. *The rationalization of the body has influenced how people conceptualize the relationship between the body and mind.* People in postindustrial societies see the body as a malleable tool serving the interests of the mind. Separating the body from the mind is common in cultures with Judeo-Christian religious beliefs, and it leads people to objectify their own bodies, view them as machines, and use them as tools for doing what the mind has determined. Using substances to improve the performance of the body fits with this orientation. This orientation also leads athletes to use their minds to ignore physical pain and injury (Grant, 2002a, b).

4. *There is a contemporary emphasis on self-medication.* People in wealthy postindustrial societies increasingly seek alternatives to mainstream medicine. They use friends, ads, and the Internet for medical information, and they are open to experimenting with substances that can be purchased online and over the counter without licensed medical advice or approval.

5. *Gender relations are changing in contemporary society*. As traditional ideas about masculinity and femininity have been challenged, the threat of change has fuelled a desire among some men to do whatever it takes to develop a physique that reaffirms an ideology of male strength and power. At the same time, the promise of change has fuelled a desire among many women to revise their notions of femininity and do whatever it takes to achieve strength, power, and physical ability and to lose weight at the same time. Therefore, men and women define performance-enhancing substances as valuable in their quests to preserve or challenge prevailing gender ideology.

6. *The organization of power and performance sports encourages overconformity to the norms of the sport ethic*. Many sports are organized so that continued participation at the level needed to sustain an "athlete identity" requires competitive success—*making the cut*, so to speak. The desire to maintain participation makes winning personally important to athletes and fuels their search for performance-enhancing substances.

7. *Coaches, sponsors, administrators, and fans clearly encourage "deviant" overconformity*. Athletes who make sacrifices and put their bodies on the line for the sake of the team, the university, the community, or the nation are defined as heroes. Athletes realize this, and many willingly take substances to "do their duty."

8. *The performance of athletes is closely monitored within the social structure of high-performance sports*. High-performance sports today emphasize control, especially control over the body; conformity, especially to the demands of a coach; and guilt, especially when one does not meet the expectations of fellow athletes and sponsors, parents, universities, communities, clubs, and corporations. The desire to control one's body, plus the need to meet performance expectations, is a powerful incentive to do whatever it takes to remain a high-performance athlete.

When these eight factors are combined, access to substances and the willingness to use them are high. Such conditions exist today, and this makes it more difficult than ever to control substance use.

Drug Testing as a Deterrent

Drug testing is controversial. There are powerful arguments for and against it. The arguments in favour of testing are these:

1. Drug testing is needed to protect athletes' health and reduce the pressures that they feel to take substances to keep up with competitors. In cycling, the blood-boosting drug EPO was implicated in the deaths of about twenty riders from Europe since 1988 (Zorpette, 2000) (see the box "Blood Boosting," p. 176). In professional wrestling steroids are suspected in forty-five deaths among wrestler-performers under the age of forty between 1997 and mid-2008; ten of those deaths occurred in the first six months of 2002 (Marvez, 2002), and steroids are reportedly implicated in the recent double murder-suicide involving Canadian wrestler, Chris Benoit. Furthermore, the use of steroids and other substances may partially account for the rising injury toll in certain sports in which severe muscle and tendon tears and bone fractures are common (Keating, 2004; Verducci, 2002). Other serious health risks are associated with various substances, including ephedrine; steroid precursors such as androstenedione; diuretics; epogen; and beta-blockers (Meyer, 2002).

2. Drug testing is needed to achieve a level playing field where competitive outcomes reflect skills and training rather than access to substances. Many athletes and spectators believe that some of the most visible and talented athletes today owe part

REFLECT ON SPORTS — Blood Boosting

The complexities of defining and banning performance-enhancing substances and methods are captured in the case of blood boosting—human blood being a most "natural" substance.

Increasing the oxygen-carrying capacity of blood is an aid to sport performance, particularly in endurance sports. There are four generally recognized ways to increase the number of red blood cells/boost the oxygen-carrying capacity of blood—two are considered to be legitimate (*legal*) at this time by WADA, and two are considered to be illegitimate (*illegal*):

Legitimate

a) *Be born, live, and/or train at altitude*: Living and training at altitude can increase an individual's hematocrit—the percentage of blood composed of red blood cells (normally around 40–45 percent) —by several percentage points.

b) *Hypoxia tent/training in a hypoxia/hypobaric chamber*: The effects of altitude may be simulated by re-creating the reduced barometric pressure of altitude, or by reducing the oxygen content of air at normal barometric pressures. Such equipment was originally available at labs and training centres, but is now widely available for home use.

Illegitimate

c) *Blood doping/blood boosting/blood packing*: "[Normally] starts with the removal of blood from the athlete. This blood is then frozen and stored for 6 to 8 weeks. The athlete continues training with a reduced amount of blood [which] rebuilds itself over the next weeks. Just before competition, the stored blood is given back to the athlete. The athlete's blood now contains an above normal number of blood cells" (http://www.uihealthcare.com/topics/sportsmedicine/spor3322.html). Sometimes, blood doping may involve the use of blood or blood products from another person.

4. *Use of drugs such as EPO*: The effects of "blood doping" may be simulated by the use of a synthetic hormone such as erythropoietin (EPO), a protein hormone produced by cells in the kidneys that promotes the production of red blood cells. The use of EPO is less complicated than the use of blood transfusions.

There are a number of things to consider with regard to these methods of increasing an athlete's hematocrit:

1) *The practice is dangerous.* "Negative effects that are associated with blood boosting are that too many blood cells result in "thick blood." As dehydration progresses, the blood becomes even thicker. There have been many cases of reported strokes and deaths from this practice. Although blood boosting can improve athletic performance, it is an extremely dangerous practice" (http://www.uihealthcare.com/topics/sportsmedicine/spor3322.html).

2) *What is available, and to whom?* The principle of "accidents of birth," often cited with regard to those who supposedly benefit from being born at altitude, also applies to individuals who are born in wealthy countries with advanced sport development systems. Often, athletes in those countries are able to take advantage of the scientific performance-enhancing measures available in an advanced and scientific sport development

of their success to drugs (for example, the controversy surrounding Barry Bonds' home run record; see also the quote by Fetisov on the first page of their chapter). This damages the integrity of sports and jeopardizes sponsorships, television rights fees, and the

willingness of spectators to buy tickets and pay cable fees so that they can see games.

3. Requiring people to submit to drug tests is legally justified because the actions of those who take substances affect the lives of other people. While there is no specific

system *and* take time to train at altitude, or use hypoxia tents or hypoxia/hypobaric chambers. In this way, they maintain the advantage over athletes who live in poorer countries, whose only advantage may be to have been born and live at altitude. Blood boosting is expensive in terms of staff, and the procedures involved, but it is often more convenient than altitude training and sleeping in a hypoxia tent; and drugs such as EPO are less expensive, more convenient ways to increase an athlete's hematocrit. In fact, some have argued that the only reason WADA achieved widespread support among wealthy nations was because the use of drugs was a relatively inexpensive way for athletes from poorer nations to match the scientific advantages enjoyed by athletes in wealthy nations.

3) *Contradictions*. Contradictions are raised by the fact that: (a) blood boosting is a dangerous practice and yet, (b) some means of achieving a higher hematocrit are legal and others are not, and (c) there are inequities in the availability of the means to achieve a higher hematocrit. Thus, two of the most outspoken critics of drugs (primarily EPO) are a British distance runner who trained at altitude in Mexico (Paula Radcliffe), and a Canadian cross-country skier who used a hypoxia tent in her training regime (Becky Scott).

4) *Banning hypoxia chambers*. In 2006, WADA considered banning the use of hypoxia chambers. They took into account the dangers of higher hematocrit levels, and the fact that hypoxia chambers were available only to athletes in wealthy countries. In the final analysis,

they deferred any action at this time, primarily because of the impossibility of policing the use of hypoxia chambers.

5) *More sophisticated testing*. Although WADA permits hypoxia chambers for the moment, increasingly sophisticated tests have been developed to determine the use of EPO (for a long time undetectable), and most recently—as evidenced in the 2007 Tour de France—to determine the use of blood products from another person. At the time of writing, there is news that a means will soon be available to determine if an athlete has used his/her own blood for blood boosting.

6) *Harm reduction*. Given the complexity of this issue, the contradictions involved, and the dangers to athletes of engaging in these practices, an alternative "harm reduction" strategy is available. It has been in use in cycling for some time, and was introduced to cross-country skiing at the Torino Olympics (2006). Athletes provide blood samples before competition—if their hematocrit is over 50%, they are not allowed to compete until it has returned to a safer level. Testers are aware that the athlete may have used "legal," or "illegal" but undetectable means to achieve the higher ratio of red blood cells; but they take as their first priority the health of the athlete.

A number of analysts are beginning to advocate a harm reduction strategy for all banned substances and methods (cf., Beamish and Ritchie, 2006), and we believe that WADA should follow the IOC Medical Commission in taking a stronger stand on the health and safety of athletes. *What do you think?*

government legislation in Canada regarding the use of performance-enhancing substances or methods, the policies are quite stringent. The Canadian Anti-Doping Program (CCES, 2004) "is governed by the Canadian Policy Against Doping in Sport (2000).

Sport Organizations and their members and participants who are subject to the Canadian Anti-Doping Program agree to be bound by the provisions and the spirit of the Canadian Policy Against Doping in Sport" (p. 3). Thus, if a Canadian sport organization is to receive government funding, or if an athlete wants to participate in a sport run by a Canadian sport organization, they are bound by the anti-doping policy. For an athlete, "refusal or failure to comply with doping control procedures, without sufficient cause, constitutes a doping-related infraction," and the same sanctions apply as if the athlete tested positive.

4. Drug testing is becoming part of normal law enforcement because drug use is illegal and must be controlled, as other criminal acts are controlled. This means that punishments must be clearly explained, fairly administered, and severe enough to deter future substance use.

5. Drug tests must be expanded to anticipate genetic engineering because genetically altered athletes will change the meaning of sports and athletic achievements. According to one member of the World Anti-Doping Agency's (WADA) special committee on "gene doping," genetic manipulation will lead to "the end of sport as we know it. Sport will be a circus of unbelievable performances" (in Swift and Yaeger, 2001, p. 91). Unless testing is used to discourage genetic manipulation, sports will be replaced by spectacle, and athletes will become pawns in video gamelike contests controlled by genetic engineers competing against each other to produce the best-performing bodies.

The arguments against testing are equally powerful. They emphasize the following points:

1. Testing is ineffective because athletes are one step ahead of rule makers and testers (see figure 6.6). By the time certain substances are banned and tests are developed to detect them, athletes are taking new substances that tests cannot detect or are not calibrated to detect (Assael, 2005; Sokolove, 2004b; Zorpette, 2000). Don Catlin, head of the UCLA lab that does the U.S. tests for WADA says, "You may think testing is wonderful and great, but . . . [athletes] have little trouble beating the test and there are many doctors telling them how to do it" (in Patrick, 2005). The NFL policy, reputedly the toughest in pro sports, was described by the founder of a supplement company as having "numerous loopholes." He noted that "athletes are out there looking for anything to give them an edge. And there are always people out there to fill that need" (in Saunders, 2005).

2. Requiring people to submit to drug tests without cause violates rights to privacy and sets precedents for invasive testing programmes that produce medical and biological information that could be used against a person's interest apart from sports (Malloy and Zakus, 2002). Testing protocols now require blood samples, and future protocols could require muscle biopsies, genetic testing, and DNA analysis. WADA and the International Cycling Union agreed in June, 2008, to carry out a pilot programme in which athletes must carry a "biological passport" indicating the results of all drug tests, their "normal" biochemical levels, and potentially genetic information. Such information could be extremely detrimental to athletes' lives—since confidentiality and privacy are becoming things of the past, the information could be used for everything from stigmatizing certain athletes to denying them medical insurance.

3. Drug tests are expensive and drain resources that could be used to fund health education programmes for athletes. The test administered to athletes in Olympic sports by the Canadian Centre for Ethics in Sport (CCES) and WADA costs well over C$400 per athlete every time it is administered. Testing 100,000 potential Olympic athletes around the world once a year would cost about C$40 million. Furthermore, athletes

taking substances are unlikely to be deterred by a test administered only once a year, especially if it is set up to detect only a limited number of substances. CIS and Canadian universities incur significant costs in order to run a minimal drug testing programme in interuniversity sport. Athletes could still take the substances during the off-season while they train and then stop prior to the season when they would be tested. This would teach athletes nothing about health and how to set health priorities in sports.

4. Drug tests often cannot detect substances that are designed to match substances naturally produced by the body. EPO (erythropoietin), HGH (human growth hormone), IGF-1 (insulin-like growth factor-1), and testosterone are powerful performance enhancers produced by the body, and normal levels of these substances vary from person to person.[11] This makes it difficult to determine an amount of each substance that would be considered illegal for all bodies. And, once legal levels are determined, athletes who test positive frequently use lawsuits to challenge the limits in individual cases (Zorpette, 2000).

5. Drug tests provide an incentive for developing forms of genetic engineering that alters physical characteristics related to performance (Assael, 2005; Longman, 2001; Parrish, 2002; Sokolove, 2004b; Sweeney, 2004; Swift and Yaeger, 2001; Zorpette, 2000). When genetic engineering occurs, it will make steroids and other drugs obsolete.

---

[11]HGH (human growth hormone) is a hormone produced naturally by the pituitary gland, and it stimulates physical growth in children. However, it can be used to increase muscle mass and overall strength in adults, and some adults take it in the belief that it slows the aging process. IGF-1 (insulin-like growth factor-1) is a protein that helps muscles to grow and repair themselves when they are damaged. It can be used to reduce muscle-recovery time after strenuous workouts.

Gene therapies are seen as crucial treatments to deal with the negative effects of aging and to cure or reduce the symptoms of certain diseases. These therapies will make "gene doping" possible for athletes—therapies to enhance muscle size, strength, and resiliency. Gene doping and other forms of genetic manipulation will be difficult if not impossible to detect, and tests will cost at least US$1,000 per athlete (Sweeney, 2004). Chuck Yesalis, a professor at Penn State university who has studied drugs in sports for many years, argues that drug testing will be made irrelevant by "genetic engineering" (in Patrick, 2002, p. 6C).

In the face of arguments for and against drug testing, many athletes have mixed feelings about testing policies and programmes. They realize that political and economic interests can cloud the validity and reliability of testing programmes. They also know that drug testing is an enormously complicated bureaucratic process and that mistakes can occur at many points. This has already provoked legal challenges to test results. These challenges are complicated because they often cross national borders where judicial processes and definitions of individual rights and due process are inconsistent. In the meantime, athletes know that fellow athletes continue to overconform to the sport ethic and seek creative ways to push their bodies to new limits in the pursuit of dreams.

When drug testing is done by the same organizations that promote and profit from sports, athletes have good reason to have mixed feelings. Promoting, profiting, and policing just do not go together. To avoid conflicts of interest, international athletes in Olympic sports are tested by "independent" agencies. WADA conducts random, unannounced tests around the world. The CCES conducts similar tests on Canadian athletes wherever they are training around the world. These two agencies work together. Both agencies have an educational emphasis, which may be more important than the tests they conduct if educational programmes are expanded to emphasize the control of all forms of deviant overconformity in elite sports. But this is unlikely.

"Don't worry, honey. Most of these are legal, some can't be tested for, others mask the ones they can test for, and some are too now for the tests!"

FIGURE 6.6   Some athletes take vast amounts of various substances in many combinations. The industries that produce performance-enhancing substances have stayed ahead of the testers in sports, and they will probably continue to stay ahead.

Controlling Substance Use in Sports: Where to Start

Today's athletes, like their counterparts in the past, seek continued participation and excellence in sports. When they overconform to norms promoting sacrifice and risk in the pursuit of distinction and dreams, they are not likely to define the use of performance-enhancing substances as "deviant." Even Ben Johnson, the Canadian sprinter who lost his gold medal for the 100-metre dash—at the 1988 Seoul Olympics (see box on Ben Johnson in chapter 13), said: "You can never clean it up. People are always gonna

be doing something. They feel good about themselves, and they feel it's right to do it" (Fish, 1993, p. A12). Johnson's point is made in another way by a physician who works with athletes; he observes that "athletes don't use drugs to escape reality—they use them to enforce the reality that surrounds them" (Di Pasquale, 1992, p. 2).

A central point in this chapter is that most athletes use performance-enhancing substances not because they lack character, as might be concluded when using functionalist theory or an absolutist approach to "deviance"; nor do they use them because they are victims of biased and coercive rules, as might be concluded when using conflict theory. The solutions based in these theoretical approaches are unsatisfactory. Tougher rules and increased testing have not been effective, and changing the organization of sports so that athletes made and enforced rules would not necessarily lead to the elimination of dangerous substances.

As long as athletes accept without question or qualification the norms of the sport ethic, they will voluntarily try or take anything to remain in sports. Moral panics over drug use and oversimplified solutions will not stop athletes from using substances they see as essential in maintaining their identities and their exciting experiences as athletes. Because of the health dangers associated with a sport ethic that encourages doping, two Canadian researchers, Rob Beamish at Queen's University and Ian Ritchie at Brock University (2006), believe that athletes themselves, in a genuinely democratic process, should be able to decide, on a sport-by-sport basis, what performance-enhancing practices and substances should be permitted and which, if any, should be banned. In the case of banned practices and substances, athletes in the affected sport(s) should also determine how those banned practices will be monitored.

Drug use and future forms of genetic manipulation can be controlled only when the people associated with sports critically assess the norms of the sport ethic in ways that lead them to set limits on conformity to those norms (Shogan and Ford, 2000). In light of this approach, recommendations for controlling substance use in sport should begin with the following changes:

- *Critically examine the deep hypocrisy involved in elite power and performance sports.* How is it possible to encourage athletes to limit their use of performance-enhancing substances when federations and teams formally or informally approve the use of legal performance-enhancing drugs and procedures? Using creatine, painkillers, massive injections of vitamin B-12, hydration therapies, and pure oxygen, are condoned if not encouraged by coaches and teams. This is also the case for playing with pins in broken bones, with high-tech "casts" to hold broken bones in place during competition, and using special harnesses to restrict the movement of injured joints. These practices are common, and they foster a sport culture in which the use of performance-enhancing substances is defined as logical and courageous.

- *Establish rules indicating clearly that certain risks to health are undesirable and unnecessary in sports.* When fourteen-year-old girls who compete with training-induced stress fractures in high-performance gymnastics are turned into national heroes and poster children for corporate sponsors, we promote "deviant" overconformity in sports. This sets up athletes for permanent injuries and disabilities. It is clearly unnecessary, and sport organizations should not allow this to occur.

- *Establish rules stating that injured athletes are not allowed to play until certified as "well" (not simply "able to compete") by two independent physicians apart from doctors hired by teams and sport organizations.* Too many team physicians and trainers have divided loyalties because they are paid by teams or by medical organizations that have contracted with teams or leagues (ESPN, *The Magazine*, 2005; Pipe, 1998; Polsky, 1998; Safai, 2003). Trainers and physicians also must be able to identify the ways that athletes hide injuries, and be prepared to negotiate strategies for healthy recoveries.

- *Establish education programmes for young athletes.* Young people should be taught to define *courage* in terms of recognizing limits and accepting the discipline necessary to accurately and responsibly acknowledge the consequences of "deviant" overconformity and sports injuries. They should also be taught to distinguish between the "pain of effort" and the "pain of injury." Learning to be in tune with one's body rather than to deny pain and injury is important in controlling the use of potentially dangerous performance-enhancing substances.

- *Establish codes of ethics for sport scientists.* Too many sport scientists assist athletes as they overconform to the norms of the sport ethic, rather than helping them to raise critical questions about how "deviant" overconformity is dangerous to their health and development. When they do this, scientists become part of the problem rather than the solution. For example, sport psychology should be used to help athletes understand the consequences of their choices to play sports and reduce the extent to which guilt, shame, and pathology influence participation and training decisions. This is the alternative to

> Drug testing itself does not address the root problem. We must look beyond testing as the panacea that will cure this sickness in sport. While testing will always be necessary, we must ground the integrity of sport on the firmer base of fair play, ethics, and a sense of what is right.
>
> —Charles Dubin, Ontario Chief Justice (1990)

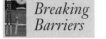

Breaking Barriers

Technology Barriers
That's an Act, Not Sports

Marlon Shirley ran faster and jumped further than any person had ever run or jumped with a below-the-knee amputation. In 2003 after winning a gold medal in the 100-m dash at the 2000 Paralympics in Sydney and setting a world record in the long jump in 2002, he became the first person in the T44 category (below-the-knee amputee) to break eleven seconds in the 100-m dash.

When he was six years old, Shirley lost his left foot and ankle in a lawnmower accident at the children's home where he lived. During high school, he had a second amputation on the same leg after fracturing a bone in his stump as he tried to dunk a basketball (Price, 2005). Not long after that, he was spotted by a coach who had worked with Paralympians. Shirley then began training and running as a pro. Success brought him prize money and an offer to become a spokesperson for Ossur, a company in Iceland that makes racing prostheses (see photos below and on p. 15).

With a carbon-fibre prosthesis designed to match the movements of a human foot, Shirley continued to win medals and set records. In Athens his goal

When Oscar Pistorius edged out Marlon Shirley while setting a world record in the 200 m, both runners were sponsored by Team OSSUR, the company that makes their carbon-fibre Flex-Foot® Cheetah prosthesis. The Flex-Foot replicates the hind leg of the cheetah whose small profile foot extends and reaches out to paw at the ground while the large thigh muscles pull the body forward. These prosthetic legs will return about 95 percent of the energy put into them by the runners' upper legs; a human lower leg can return about 200 percent of the energy put into them. OSSUR researchers want to duplicate the running power of a human leg. [David Biene; Photo courtesy of Ossur, www.ossur.com]

Continued

was to win five gold medals—in the long jump, the 100- and 200-m dashes, and the 4 × 100 and 4 × 400 relays. However, seventeen-year-old Oscar Pistorius from South Africa outran him in the 200-m dash. Pistorius was born without a fibula in both legs, and during infancy had his legs amputated just below his knees.

As Shirley trained for the 2008 Paralympic Games in Beijing, he regularly heard about Pistorius, now known as "the fastest person on no legs." In 2004, Pistorius ran the sixth-fastest 400-m ever by a South African, able-bodied or (dis)abled. In 2005 he competed against able-bodied runners in a Grand Prix event sponsored by the International Association of Athletics Federations (IAAF), the world governing body for track and field.

When Marlon Shirley runs, his prosthetic leg is designed to match the length of his other leg. But when Oscar Pistorius runs, how long should his legs be? Shirley and others, including a former Paralympian and current prosthetist who fit Pistorius for his dual carbon-fibre legs before the 2004 Games in Athens, think that the legs he raced on during the Paralympics were longer than the legs he had earlier in the summer. The prosthetist claims that the original legs made Pistorius 185 cm tall, but his height in Athens was at least 190 cm. Pistorius and his current prosthetist disagree, saying he was actually shorter than he should have been.

This issue raises the question of what counts as "deviance" when technology improves faster than governing bodies can make rules? With lightweight carbon and fibre and rapid changes in prosthetic foot design, we may soon see a race in which a person with prosthetic legs has an advantage over runners with flesh and blood legs. In the meantime, Pistorius is currently attempting to qualify for Beijing in both the Olympics and the Paralympics. The IAAF has attempted to prevent him from competing in the Olympics, but a May, 2008 ruling by the Court of Arbitration for Sport cleared his path. He realistically expects that he will not be able to qualify for the Olympic 400 m, but is hoping to qualify for the 4 × 400-m relay team for South Africa.

There are no rules about the length of prosthetic legs for someone with no legs.

Some say that if Pistorius comes to Beijing at 198 cm tall, he will find himself in court again, rather than on the track. Others want him to run in the hope that he could come close to breaking some long-standing records. Shirley says that if a 198 cm tall Pistorius runs the 200-m in 20 seconds or less, it would be cool, although he quickly adds, "But that's an act, not sports" (in Price, 2005, p. 58). Then again, as sports and technology merge, what will count as sports and how will they be distinguished from "acts"? Will rules create technology barriers for athletes with disabilities in the future? Should they?

• •

the technique of "psycho-doping," which encourages "deviant" overconformity by making athletes more likely to give body and soul to their sports without carefully answering critical questions about *why* they are doing what they are doing and *what* it means in their lives.

• *Make drug education part of larger "deviance" and health education programmes.* Parents, coaches, league administrators, managers, trainers, and athletes should participate in formal educational programmes in which they consider and discuss the norms of the

sport ethic and how to prevent "deviant" overconformity. Unless these people understand their roles in reproducing a culture supportive of substance use and abuse, the problems will continue. Such a programme would involve training to do the following:

• Create norms regulating the use of new and powerful technology and medical knowledge that go beyond the use of drugs.

• Question and critically examine values and norms in sports, as well as set limits on conformity to those values and norms.

- Teach athletes to think critically about sports, so that they understand that they can make choices and changes in sports.
- Provide parents, coaches, and athletes with the best and most recent information available on performance-enhancing technologies, so that they can make informed decisions about it and how they will be used.

We now face a future without clearly defined ideas about the meaning of achievement in sports in light of (1) new financial incentives to set records and win events, (2) the new importance of sport participation in the lives and identities of many young athletes, (3) the new technologies, which clearly enhance performance, and (4) the new forms of corporate sponsorship, which make image as important as ability.

Therefore, we need *new* approaches and guidelines. Old approaches and guidelines combined with coercive methods of control will not work. Trying to make sports into what we believe they were in the past is futile. We cannot go back to an imagined past. We face new issues and challenges, and it will take new approaches to deal with them effectively (Smith, 2005). As described in Breaking Barriers, pages 182–183, this is evident in the Paralympics where new technologies have created a number of challenges related to fairness. New swimsuit technologies are currently helping to rewrite swimming records, leaving former champions wondering how fast they might have been with such technology.

Widespread participation is needed in this process of dealing with new issues and challenges, or powerful entities, such as transnational corporations, will appropriate sport culture and the bodies of athletes as sites for delivering their messages about success, performance, efficiency, winning, and enduring pain for the sake of achieving goals. We are already headed in that direction, and we are travelling at a pace that makes it difficult to put on the brakes or change directions. But change remains possible if we work to create it.

SUMMARY

IS "DEVIANCE" IN SPORTS OUT OF CONTROL?

The study of "deviance" in sports presents interesting challenges due to four factors: (1) the forms and causes of "deviance" in sports are so diverse that no single theory can explain all of them; (2) actions, ideas, and traits accepted in sports may be defined as "deviant" in the rest of society, and what is permitted in society may be defined as "deviant" in sports; (3) "deviance" in sports often involves uncritically accepting norms rather than rejecting them; (4) training in sports has incorporated such new forms of science and technology that people have not had the opportunity to develop norms to guide and evaluate the actions of athletes and others in sports.

Widely used conceptual frameworks in sociology do not offer useful explanations of the full range of "deviance" in sports, nor do they offer much help in devising ways to control it. Problems are encountered when functionalist theory is used. Functionalists define *"deviance"* as failing to conform to ideals and "deviants" are seen as lacking moral character. But ideals are difficult to identify, and athletes often violate norms as they go overboard in their acceptance of them, not because they lack character.

Similarly, problems occur when conflict theory is used. Conflict theorists define *"deviance"* as actions violating the interests of people with money and power, and "deviants" are seen as exploited victims of the quest for profit. But people with power and money do not control all sports, and it is not accurate to define all athletes as victims.

A constructionist approach using interactionist and critical theories seems to be most useful when explaining much of the "deviance" in sports today. Such an approach emphasizes that the dynamics of sport participation are grounded in the social worlds created around sports and that people in sports make choices and can act as agents of change in sports and the culture as a whole. Our use of a constructionist approach in this chapter highlights the distinctions between cases of "deviant" underconformity and overconformity. Such distinctions are important because the most serious forms of "deviance" in sports occur when athletes, coaches, and others overconform to the norms of the sport ethic—a cluster of norms that emphasizes dedication to the game, making sacrifices, striving for distinction, taking risks, playing with pain, and pursuing dreams. When little concern is given to setting limits in the process of conforming to these norms, "deviant" overconformity becomes a problem.

Research supports this explanation. Most on-the-field and sport-related actions fall within an accepted range; when they fall outside this range, they often involve overconformity to the norms of the sport ethic. Rates of off-the-field "deviance" among athletes are generally comparable with rates among peers in the general population; when rates are high, as they are with binge drinking and sexual assault, they often are connected with the dynamics and consequences of overconformity to the sport ethic.

The use of performance-enhancing substances is a form of "deviance" that is reportedly widespread among athletes, despite new rules, testing programmes, educational programmes, and strong punishments for violators. Historical evidence suggests that recent increases in rates of use are due primarily to increases in the supply and range of available substances, rather than to changes in the values and moral characters of athletes or increased exploitation of athletes. Most athletes through history have sought ways to improve their skills, maintain their athlete identity, and continue playing their sports, but today their search is more likely to involve the use of widely available performance-enhancing substances.

Despite new enforcement efforts by sport organizations, athletes using performance-enhancing substances have generally stayed one jump ahead of the rule makers and testers. When one drug is banned, athletes use another, even if it is more dangerous. If a new test is developed, athletes switch to an undetectable drug or use masking drugs to confuse testers. The use of HGH, blood doping, testosterone, and many new substances still escape detection, and testing programmes are often problematic because they are expensive and often violate privacy rights or cultural norms in many societies. However, many people are strongly committed to testing, and new testing procedures have been developed. The prospect of "gene-doping," or performance-enhancing genetic manipulation, will present significant challenges for testing in the future. In the meantime, testers are struggling to stay ahead of athletes who overconform to the norms of the sport ethic.

Controlling "deviant" overconformity requires a critical assessment of norms and social organization of sports. A balance must be struck between accepting and questioning norms and rules; people in sports must critically qualify norms and rules and set limits on conformity, so that athletes who engage in risky and self-destructive actions are not defined and presented as heroes. Everyone in sports should question existing norms and create new norms related to the use of medical science and technology.

An effecive transformation of sports also requires that all participants be involved in a continual process of critical reflection about the goals, purpose, and organization of sports. Controlling "deviance" requires an assessment of the values and norms in sports, as well as a restructuring of the organizations that control and sponsor sports. Critical assessment should involve everyone, from athletes to fans. It is idealistic, but it is worth trying.

Visit *Sports in Society*'s Online Learning Centre at <u>www.mcgrawhill.ca/olc/coakley</u> for additional information, website resources, and study tools for this chapter.

[AP Photo/Tom Olmscheid]

Violence in Sports

How does it affect our lives?

It's all bulls__t that you have to hate your opponent. You can absolutely respect them and be friends with them and then still absolutely die out there on the court, trying to win.

—**Martina Navratilova, pro tennis player (1999)**

Hockey is, by its nature, a physical game....But we've crossed the line on some of the physical play in recent years, putting our players in peril.

—**Mario Lemieux, former NHL player (1999)**

Without violence, there would be no such thing as hockey.

—**Clarence Campbell, former NHL president (1975)**

It's all fun and games until somebody loses an eye; then it's sport.

—**Anon**

How did hockey come to this place? How did the game come to be this way? Truth is, now more, now less, it has *always* been this way. And maybe, just maybe, that's why we like it. Maybe we like a little blood with our beer and our popcorn and our "He shoots! He scores!"

—**Lawrence Scanlan, commenting on the Todd Bertuzzi/Steve Moore case (2004)**

Discussions of violence in sports, like discussions of "deviance," are often connected with people's ideas about the moral conditions of society as a whole. When violence occurs in sports, many people are quick to use it as an indicator that the moral foundation of society is eroding and that people, especially children, are learning a warped sense of morality as they watch athletes and use them as models for their own actions.

Statements about violence in sports are often confusing. Some people say that violence is an inherent part of many games, while others say that it destroys the dynamics of games. Some people say that violence in sports reflects natural tendencies among males in society, while others say that men use violence in sports to promote the idea that physical size and strength is a legitimate basis for maintaining power over others. Some say that violence in sports is worse today than ever before, while others say it is less frequent and less brutal than in the past.

Contradictory statements and conclusions about violence in sports occur for five reasons. *First*, many people fail to define important terms in their discussions. They use words such as *physical, assertive, tough, rough, competitive, intense, intimidating, risky, aggressive, destructive, and violent* interchangeably. *Second*, they may not distinguish players from spectators, even though the dynamics of violence differ in these two groups. *Third*, they categorize all sports together, despite differences in meaning, organization, purpose, and amount of physical contact involved. *Fourth*, they may not distinguish the immediate, short-term effects of experiences or watching violence in sports from the more permanent, long-term effects. *Fifth*, it is possible that we have actually underestimated the amount of violence associated with sports. Sociologist Kevin Young (2000b), of the University of Calgary, has argued that we need to be concerned about all "sport-related violence," which would include not only the issues addressed in this chapter but also forms of violence such as hazing (see chapter 6), terrorism and terrorist threats at sports events (Atkinson

and Young, 2002), and forms of sexual harassment and abuse (see the Reflect on Sports box, "Sexual Harassment and Abuse," on the Online Learning Centre).

The goal of this chapter is to enable you to include information based on research and theories in your discussions of violence in sports. Chapter content focuses on five topics:

1. A practical definition of *violence* and related terms
2. A brief historical overview of violence in sports
3. On-the-field violence among players in various sports
4. Off-the-field violence among players, and the impact of sports violence on their lives apart from sports
5. Violence among spectators who watch media coverage of sports or attend events in person, and play sport video games.

In connection with the last three topics, we make suggestions about how to control violence and limit its consequences on and off the field.

WHAT IS VIOLENCE?

Violence *is the use of excessive physical force, which causes or has the potential to cause harm or destruction.* We often think of violence as actions that are illegal or unsanctioned, but there are situations in which the use of violence is encouraged or approved in many groups or societies. For example, when violence involves "deviant" underconformity based on a rejection of norms in society, it is often classified as illegal and is sanctioned severely. However, when violence occurs in connection with enforcing norms, protecting people and property, or overconforming to widely accepted norms, it may be approved and even lauded as necessary to preserve order, reaffirm important social values, or entertain spectators. Therefore, violence is often, but not always, accepted and defined as legitimate when soldiers, police, and athletes are perceived to be protecting people, reproducing accepted ideologies, or pursuing victories in the name of others.

When violence occurs in connection with the widespread rejection of norms, it is often described as anarchy. When it occurs in connection with extreme methods of social control or extreme overconformity to norms, it often is associated with a sense of moral righteousness even when it produces harmful or destructive consequences. Under certain political conditions, this latter expression of violence is tied to fascism and fascist leaders.

In the case of sports, pushing a referee who penalizes you or a coach who reprimands you is violence based on a rejection of norms. These actions are defined as illegal and punished severely by teams and sport organizations, even if the referee or coach was not seriously injured. However, it is different when a football player delivers a punishing tackle, breaking the ribs or blowing out the knee of an opposing running back after his coach told him to be aggressive and to put his body on the line for the team. Such violence involves conformity to norms and is often defined as appropriate, accepted by fans, highlighted on video replays, and approved by teammates and many other football players. The player might feel righteous in being violent, despite the harmful consequences, and would not hesitate to be violent again. His violence would not be punished because it conforms to norms endorsed in the social world of football. Furthermore, his ability to do violence and to endure it when perpetrated by others would be used to affirm his identity as a football player.

The term **aggression** is used in this chapter to refer to *verbal or physical actions grounded in an intent to dominate, control, or do harm to another person.* Aggression is often involved in violence, but some violence occurs without aggressive intent. This definition allows us to distinguish aggressive actions from other actions that we might describe as assertive, competitive, or achievement-oriented. For example, a very competitive person may use violence during a game without the intent to dominate, control, or harm others. However, there is often a difference between being aggressive and simply being assertive or trying hard to win or achieve other goals. The term **intimidation** is used to refer to *words, gestures, and actions that threaten violence or aggression.* Like aggression, intimidation is used to dominate or control another person. These definitions help to focus our discussion, but they do not eliminate all conceptual problems.

VIOLENCE IN SPORTS THROUGH HISTORY

Violence is certainly not new to physical activities and sports (Dunning, 1999; Guttmann, 1998, 2004). As noted in chapter 3, so-called blood sports were popular among the ancient Greeks and throughout the Roman Empire. Deaths occurred regularly in connection with ritual games among the Mayas and Aztecs. Tournaments during medieval and early modern Europe were designed as training for war and often had warlike consequences. Folk games were only loosely governed by rules, and they produced injuries and deaths at rates that would shock people today. Bearbaiting, cock fighting, dog fighting, and other "sporting" activities during those periods involved the treatment of animals that most people today would define as brutal and violent.

Research indicates that, as part of an overall civilizing process in Europe and North America, modern sports were developed as more rule-governed activities than the physical games in previous eras (see figure 7.1). As sports became formally organized, official rules prohibited certain forms of violence that had been common in many folk games. Bloodshed decreased, and there was a greater emphasis on self-control to restrict physical contact and the expression of aggressive impulses often created in the emotional heat of competition (Dunning, 1999).

SIDELINES

"Now that we've invented violence, we need a sport to use it in."

FIGURE 7.1   Violence in sports is not new. However, this does not mean that it is a natural or inevitable part of sports.

Social historians who study these changes, also explain that rates of sports violence do not automatically decrease over time. In fact, as actions and emotional expression have become more regulated and controlled in modern societies, players and spectators view the "controlled" violence in sports as exciting. Furthermore, the processes of commercialization, professionalization, and globalization have given rise to new forms of instrumental and "dramatic" violence in many sports. This means that goal-oriented and entertainment-oriented violence has increased, at least temporarily, in many Western societies. Dunning (1999) notes that violence remains a crucial social issue in modern sports because their goal is to create tension rather than to relieve or discharge it. Additionally, violent and aggressive sports serve, in patriarchal societies, to reproduce an ideology that naturalizes the power of men over women. Overall, historical research shows that sports are given different meanings by time and place and that we can understand violence in sports only when we analyze it in relation to the social, historical, and cultural contexts in which it occurs.

VIOLENCE ON THE FIELD

Violence in sports comes in many forms, and it is grounded in social and cultural factors related to the sport ethic, commercialization, gender ideology and ideas about masculinity, the dynamics of social class and race, and the strategies used in sports. Violence also has significant consequences for athletes and presents challenges to those who believe that it should be controlled. Each of these topics is addressed in this section.

Types of Violence

The most frequently used typology of on-the-field violence among players is one developed by Mike Smith, a Canadian sociologist, who worked at York University until his untimely death in 1994 (1983; see Young, 2000a; 2002a). Smith identified four categories of violence associated with playing sports:

1. *Brutal body contact.* This includes physical practices that are common in certain sports and accepted by athletes as part of the action and risk in their sport participation. Examples are collisions, hits, tackles, blocks, bodychecks, and other forms of forceful physical contact that can produce injuries. Most people in society define this forceful physical contact as extreme, although they do not classify it as illegal or criminal, nor do they see a need to punish it. Coaches often encourage this form of violence.

2. *Borderline violence.* This includes practices that violate the rules of the game but are accepted by most players and coaches as conforming to the norms of the sport ethic and representing commonly used competitive strategies. Examples are the "brush back" pitch in baseball, the forcefully placed elbow or knee in soccer and basketball, the strategic bump used by distance runners to put another runner off stride, the fist-fight in ice hockey, and the forearm to the ribs of a quarterback in football. Although

these actions are expected, they may provoke retaliation by other players. Official sanctions and fines are not usually severe for borderline violence. However, public pressure to increase the severity of sanctions has grown in recent years, and the severity of punishments has increased in some cases.

3. *Quasi-criminal violence.* This includes practices that violate the formal rules of the game, public laws, and even the informal norms used by players. Examples are cheap shots, late hits, sucker punches, and flagrant fouls that endanger the players' bodies and reject the norm of respecting the game. Fines and suspensions are usually imposed on players who engage in such violence. Most athletes condemn this form of violence and see it as a rejection of the informal norms of the game and what it means to be an athlete.

4. *Criminal violence.* This includes practices that are clearly outside the law to the point that athletes condemn them, usually without question, and law enforcement officials may prosecute them as crimes. Examples are assaults that occur after a game and assaults during a game that appear to be premeditated and serious enough to kill or maim a player. Such violence is relatively rare although there is growing support that criminal charges ought to be filed when it does occur. This support grew in early 2000 when a hockey player intentionally slashed an opponent's head with his stick (see the box, "Cases of Criminal Violence?" on p. 191).

Kevin Young (2002a; 2004b) noted that this is a useful general typology but that the lines separating the four types of violence shift over time as norms change in sports and societies. Furthermore, the typology fails to address the origins of violence and how violent acts are related to the sport ethic, gender ideology, and the commercialization of sports. Despite these weaknesses, this typology enables us to make distinctions between various types of violence discussed in this chapter.

Violence as "Deviant" Overconformity to the Norms of the Sport Ethic

In Pat Conroy's novel *The Prince of Tides* (1986), there is a scene in which the coach uses words that many athletes in heavy contact sports have heard during their careers:

> Now a real hitter is a headhunter who puts his head in the chest of his opponents and ain't happy if his opponent is still breathing after the play. A real hitter doesn't know what fear is except when he sees it in the eyes of a ball carrier he's about to split in half. A real hitter loves pain, loves the screaming and the sweating and the brawling and the hatred of life down in the trenches. He likes to be at the spot where the blood flows and the teeth get kicked out. That's what this sport's about, men. It's war, pure and simple. (p. 384)

Not all coaches use such vivid vocabulary because they know it can inspire dangerous forms of violence. However, there are coaches and team administrators who seek athletes who think this way.

When athletes think this way, violence occurs regularly enough to attract attention. Journalists describe it, sociologists and psychologists try to explain it, and athletes brag or complain about it. When an athlete dies or is paralyzed by on-the-field violence, the media present stories stating that violence is rampant in sports and in society, and then they run multiple replays or photos of violent acts knowing that this will increase their ratings or sales.

Although players may be concerned about brutal body contact and borderline violence in their sports, they generally accept them. Even those players who do not like them may use them to enhance their status on teams and popularity with spectators. Athletes whose violence involves overconformity to the sport ethic become legends on and off the field. Athletes who engage in quasi- and criminal violence often are marginalized in sports, and they may face criminal charges, although prosecuting such charges has been difficult and convictions are almost nonexistent (Young, 2000a, 2002a, 2004b, 2007a).

REFLECT ON SPORTS

Cases of Criminal Violence?

One of the most striking contradictions regarding violence in sports concerns the place of the criminal law in sports. On the one hand, many people believe that the rules of sport do not trump the rule of law. This was first expressed in the U.K., some 130 years ago, by Lord Justice Bramwell in the soccer manslaughter case of *Regina v. Bradshaw* (1878): "No rules or practice of any game can make that lawful which is unlawful by the law of the land; and the law of the land says you shall not do that which is likely to cause the death of another." On the other hand is the view that criminal law has no place in sports. Paul Kelly, the lawyer for Marty McSorley in one of the cases noted below, said: "No legislative body has seen fit to… pass laws that specifically target violence in sports" (cited by Smith, 2002, p. S5).

While there are few cases of criminal assault charges being laid against athletes, two recent Canadian cases raise interesting questions:

- On February 21, 2000, near the end of an NHL game played in Vancouver between the Canucks and the Boston Bruins, Marty McSorley of the Bruins clubbed the Canucks' Donald Brashear on the head with his stick. The attack left Brashear unconscious and bleeding from the nose—he was treated on the ice for ten minutes, and diagnosed with a grade 3 concussion. McSorley was given a match penalty and a game misconduct. On March 7, a Vancouver Crown prosecutor filed charges of assault with a weapon against McSorley. The NHL reviewed the incident, and on March 23, McSorley was suspended for the remainder of the season—23 games, that cost him $100,000 in lost pay. Because this was the longest suspension ever given for a game incident, the NHL believed that the matter was settled and that charges would be dropped. However, six months later McSorley was found guilty, and given a conditional discharge of 18 months.

- On March 8, 2004, near the end of an NHL game played in Vancouver between the Canucks and the Colorado Avalanche, Todd Bertuzzi of the Canucks grabbed the Avalanche's Steve Moore from behind, punched him and drove him to the ice. The attack left Moore with a grade 3

concussion, three fractured vertebrae in his neck, vertebral ligament damage, stretched brachial plexus nerves, and facial cuts; it also effectively ended his career as a professional hockey player. Bertuzzi was suspended for the remainder of the season, costing him some $500,000 in lost pay, and more in endorsements. The Canucks were fined $250,000 by the NHL for fostering an atmosphere in which the attack took place. Again, a Vancouver Crown prosecutor filed charges, and Bertuzzi was sentenced to probation and 80 hours of community service. A civil lawsuit filed by Moore against Bertuzzi and the Canucks is still before the courts.

These events generated enormous North American and international media attention, and a great deal of debate in Canada about whether the courts should have become involved. Although a fellow player said, "[McSorley's] lost the respect of every player in the league, Atkinson's (2004) systematic analysis shows that "players, league administrators, fans, and court officials [in general, framed] the event as both non-criminal and essentially victimless." The sentences given to McSorley and Bertuzzi also appear to indicate that the criminal courts are reluctant to become involved in such cases.

Hilary Findlay, of the Canadian Centre for Sport and the Law, points out that "criminal assault is proved by showing an intent to inflict injury on another. While the Supreme Court of Canada ruled that you cannot consent to a fist fight, the sport arena is an exception. According to the law, players may consent to violent treatment, but the consent is limited" (Cited by Smith, 2002, p. S5).

What are the limits of this consent? Do players consent to being clubbed unconscious, or to being attacked from behind and driven to the ice hard enough to break vertebrae? We think that it is necessary to establish clear limits regarding what is acceptable conduct on any sport playing surface. If sport organizations will not bring charges against players who deliberately attempt to injure an opponent, then the courts must step in. Does someone have to die before we establish limits? *What do you think?*

Violence as "deviant" overconformity is also related to the insecurities among athletes in high-performance sports. Athletes learn that "you're only as good as your last game," and they know that their identities as athletes and status as team members are constantly tested. Therefore, they often take extreme measures to prove themselves, even if it involves violence. Violence becomes a marker of self-worth and leads other athletes to reaffirm their identities. This is why athletes who do not play in pain are defined as failures, whereas those who do are defined as courageous. Playing in pain and with injuries honours the importance of the game, and it expresses dedication to teammates and values in high-performance sport culture.

It is important to understand that violent expressions of overconformity to the sport ethic are not limited to men, although it is more common among male athletes than female athletes. Women also overconform to the norms of the sport ethic (Young and White, 1995) and, when they play contact sports, they face the challenge of drawing the line between physicality and violence. For example, when University of Waterloo sociologist Nancy Theberge (1999) spent two seasons studying the sport experiences of women on an elite ice hockey team in Canada, she discovered that the women loved the physicality of hockey and the body contact that occurred, even though bodychecking was not allowed. As one woman said,

> I like a physical game. You get more fired up. I think when you get hit…like when you're fighting for a puck in the corner, when you're both fighting so you're both working hard and maybe the elbows are flying, that just makes you put more effort into it. (p. 147)

The experience of dealing with the physicality of contact sports and facing its consequences creates drama, excitement, strong emotions, and special interpersonal bonds among women athletes, as it does among men. Despite the risk and reality of pain and injuries, many women in contact sports feel that the physical intensity and body contact in their sports make them feel alive and aware. Although many women are committed to controlling brutal body contact and more severe forms of violence, the love of their sport and the excitement of physicality can lead to violence grounded in overconformity to the norms of the sport ethic.

Commercialization and Violence in Sports

Some athletes in power and performance sports are paid well because of their ability to do violence on the field. However, it is difficult to argue that commercialization and money in sports cause athletes to be violent. Violent athletes in the past were paid very little, and athletes in high schools, universities, and club sports today are paid nothing, yet many of them do violence, despite the pain and injuries associated with it.

Commercialization and money have expanded opportunities to play certain contact sports in some societies, and media coverage makes these sports and the violence they contain more visible than ever before. Children watch this coverage, and they may imitate violent athletes when they play informal games and organized youth sports, but this does not justify the conclusion that commercialization is the cause of violence in sports.

Football players and athletes in other heavy-contact sports engaged in violence on the field long before television coverage and the promise of big salaries. Players at all levels of organized football killed and maimed each other at rates that are higher than the death and injury rates in football today. There are more injuries today because there are more people playing football. This is a serious problem that must be addressed, but to think that it is caused mainly by commercialization and money is a mistake.

This is an important point, because many people who criticize sports today blame violence and other problems in sports on money and greed. They claim that, if athletes were true amateurs and played for love of the game

The fighting that occurs in many men's sports is connected with issues of masculinity. In men's ice hockey, unless you throw down your gloves and fight in certain circumstances, your manhood is questioned. [CP(Jeff McIntosh)]

instead of money, there would be less violence. However, this conclusion contradicts research findings and it distracts attention away from the deep cultural and ideological roots of violence in particular sports and societies. This means that we could take money away from the athletes tomorrow, but violence would be reduced only if there were changes in the culture in which athletes, especially male athletes, learn to value and use violence in sports.

Many people resist the notion that cultural changes are needed to control violence because it places the responsibility for change on all of us. It is easy to say that wealthy and greedy team owners, athletes without moral character, and TV executives seeking high viewer ratings are to blame for violence in sports. But it is more difficult to critically examine our culture and the normative and social organization of the sports that many people watch and enjoy. Similarly, it is difficult for people to critically examine the definitions of *masculinity* and the structure of gender relations that they have long accepted as a part of the "natural" order of things. But these critiques are needed if we wish to understand and control violence in sports.

The point in this section is that commercialization is not the *primary* cause of violence in sports. But money is not irrelevant. Consider, for example, Don Cherry's enormously popular *Rock 'em, Sock 'em* video series, which has been included on the gift lists of many Canadian boys and some girls. The series—and its imitators—glorifies violence in the sport, or makes it humorous, and presents it for our entertainment. And consider the video clips that are very often assembled as a part of sport news broadcasting, often put together with funny music and amusing voiceovers. The clips involve people falling

> Hockey is the only team sport in the world that actually *encourages* fighting. I have no idea why we let it go on. The game itself is so fast, so exciting, so much fun to watch, why do we have to turn ice red so often?
>
> —Wayne Gretzky, hockey player (1990)

off horses, baseball fielders running into each other, gymnasts falling awkwardly, hockey players falling over the boards, and so on. These are real people (not cartoons) experiencing real pain and injury, and they are presented for our amusement. Does this become part of the desensitization-to-violence process that has been hypothesized to be a result of our experience of so much violence on news broadcasts and in the entertainment industry?

When CFL players, for example, tell reporters that they want to hurt one another and rip someone's head off, their violent rhetoric tells us less about the way they *play sports* than it does about how they want us to *think* they play sports. Professional athletes are entertainers, and they now use a promotional and heroic rhetoric that presents images of revenge, retaliation, hate, hostility, intimidation, aggression, violence, domination, and destruction. These images attract attention and serve commercial purposes. The CFL, the NHL, and even the NBA have used these images for many years to promote their games. They sell videos that present image after image of glorified violence in slow-motion close-ups accompanied by the actual sounds of bodies colliding, bones and tendons snapping on impact, and players gasping in agony and pain. In true promotional fashion, the same media companies that sell or promote these videos also publish articles that condemn violence and violent players. Their marketing people know that violence *and* moral outrage about violence attracts audiences and generates profits. Even Canada's national public broadcaster, the Canadian Broadcasting Corporation (CBC) is complicit in this process by making Hockey Night in Canada and NHL play-off images and clips available to Don Cherry for his *Rock 'em, Sock 'em* series (Gillett et al., 1996).

> The Canadians were the inventors of the bodycheck, the penalty bench, and the widespread view of fans that athletes who shirk bodily contact are pansies.
>
> —Karl Adolph Scherer, hockey historian (1988)

Does this commercially inspired discourse represent the real on-the-field orientations of athletes, or does it represent efforts to create personas and attract attention, which have commercial value? Research is needed on this, but our sense is that most athletes do not really want to hurt opponents and make them bleed. At the same time, some athletes have become expert at using violent rhetoric to enhance the entertainment value of what they do and the events in which they participate. It is part of the spectacle dimension of sports, similar to dramatic storylines delivered by paid announcers, sexy cheerleaders, and halftime dancers.

However, it raises this question: How far can the spectacle be emphasized before people conclude that a particular sport has lost its authenticity as a game and has become a planned confrontation devoid of play (for example, WWE)? People may be willing to watch violence in the context of an authentic game, but they may not pay to watch violence week after week apart from the goal-oriented game that legitimizes it.

Violence and Masculinity

Violence in sports is not limited to men. However, research based on critical and feminist theory indicates that, *if we want to understand violence in sports, we must understand gender ideology and issues of masculinity in culture.* Sociologist Mike Messner explains:

> Young males come to sport with identities that lead them to define their athletic experience differently than females do. Despite the fact that few males truly enjoy hitting and being hit, and that one has to be socialized into participating in much of the violence commonplace in sport, males often view aggression, within the rule-bound structure of sport, as legitimate and "natural." (1992, p. 67)

In fact, Messner explains that many male athletes learn to define injurious acts as a necessary part of the game, rather than as violence, as long as they are within the rules of the game and within the informal norms the players use to judge and evaluate each other.

In many societies today, participation in power and performance sports has become an important way to prove masculinity. Boys discover that, if they play these sports and are seen as being able to do violence, they can avoid social labels such as *lady*, *fag*, *wimp*, and *sissy* (Ingham and Dewar, 1999). In a review of the research on this issue, Phil White of McMaster University and Kevin Young of the University of Calgary (1997) note that, if a boy or young man avoids these sports, he risks estrangement from his male peers.

Boys and men who play power and performance sports learn quickly that they are evaluated in terms of their ability to use violence in combination with physical skills (Lance, 2005). This learning begins in youth sports and, by the time young men have become immersed in the social world of most power and performance sports, they accept brutal body contact and borderline violence as part of the game as it is played by "real" men.

Such "real" men are often the same people who reject rules against fighting in hockey. For example, when rules were passed in the early 1990s to partially limit fighting in hockey, Tie Domi, a player with a reputation for doing violence complained:

> If you take out fighting, what comes next? Do we eliminate checking? Pretty soon, we will all be out there in dresses and skirts. (Domi, 1992, p. C3)

Domi's point is that, unless men can do violence in hockey, there will be nothing that makes them different from women—a point endorsed, of course, by Don Cherry who once commented that, "If you don't like the fighting, go into the kitchen and make a cup of tea." Their perception is that nothing is worse for a man than being like a woman—except, perhaps, being gay.

When gender is viewed in these terms, the ability to do violence becomes "one of the cornerstones of masculinity" (White and Young, 1997, p. 9).

A tragic example of the connection between masculinity and violence in sports occurred in 2000 at a Massachusetts hockey arena. As a few boys practised hockey skills during an informal skating session, a father watching the skaters became angry because his son failed to stick up for himself when other boys pushed him around. The father entered the rink and told his son that he had to "be a man" on the ice. The boy turned away and walked to the locker room as his father continued to harass him. Another father passed by and told the boy's father to ease up because it was a minor incident. This further irritated the angry father, and he punched the man who gave him the unwanted advice. He exited the rink, but then came back, found the man he had punched, and beat him to death in the lobby of the rink, in front of a few children (the players), mothers, and a young rink employee.

This case was covered in the media as an extreme example of parental "rink rage," but it was never discussed as an issue related to particular ideas about masculinity in American society.[1] The father, who was later convicted of voluntary manslaughter, first became enraged when his son failed to meet his definition of what a "man" should be on the ice, and then he killed another man who had said that the issue was minor. This case highlights the problems associated with a gender ideology on which people think that masculinity is proved by doing violence in sports.

---

[1] At the time of writing there are no examples of deaths occurring in Canada as a result of "rink rage," but many Canadians have observed incidents like the one described here, and they could easily have gone as badly wrong as the one in Massachusetts.

When women do violence in sports, it may be seen as a sign of commitment or skill, but it is not seen as proof of femininity. Dominant gender ideology in many cultures links manhood with the ability to do violence, but there is no similar link between womanhood and violence. Therefore, female athletes who engage in violence do not receive the same support and rewards as men—unless they wrestle in the WWE or skate on a roller derby team where the sport personas of female athletes are constructed to shock or titillate spectators (Berra, 2005; Blumenthal, 2004). The emergence of women's boxing provides a context in which female athletes are rewarded for doing violence, but most female boxers do not feel that doing violence in the ring makes them more of a woman than the boxers they defeat. Overall, none of us lives outside the influence of ideology. This point is highlighted in connection with a rapidly growing sport that participants call murderball. Officially known as wheelchair rugby, murderball is the focus of Breaking Barriers on pages 197–198.

The Institutionalization of Violence in Sports

Certain forms of violence are built into the structure and culture of particular sports (Guilbert, 2004). Athletes in these sports learn to use violence as a strategy, even though it may cause them pain and injury. Controlling institutionalized violence is difficult because it requires changes in the structure and culture of particular sports—something that most people in governing bodies are hesitant to do (the ongoing debates about fighting in hockey is an obvious example). These topics are discussed in the following sections.

Learning to Use Violence as a Strategy: Noncontact Sports In some noncontact sports, participants may try to intimidate opponents, but violence is rare. For example, tennis players have been fined for slamming a ball to the ground in protest or talking to an official or opponent in a menacing manner. Players in noncontact sports are seldom, if ever, rewarded for violent actions. Therefore, it is doubtful that playing or watching these sports teaches people to use violence as a strategy on the field.

Some athletes may use violent images as they describe competition, but they do not have actual opportunities to convert their words into deeds. For example, U.S. sprint cyclist and 1996 Olympic silver medalist Marty Nothstein used violent images as he described his approach to a race:

> I am really aggressive out there. I pretty much hate the guy I'm racing. It wouldn't matter if it were my brother....I want to destroy the guy. End it quick. Boom. One knockout punch. (Becker, 1996, p. 4E)

Of course, cycling does not allow him to physically destroy or punch a competitor, but the language he used had violence built into it.

Men who play noncontact sports use violent images in their descriptions of competition much more often than women use them. The use of a "language of violence" is clearly linked to masculinity in most cultures. Women may use it on occasion, but men use it more frequently. It may be that many women realize that a language of violence reaffirms a version of gender ideology that privileges men, works against their interests, and subverts the health and well-being of everyone in society.

Learning to Use Violence as a Strategy: Men's Contact Sports Athletes in power and performance sports involving heavy physical contact learn to use intimidation, aggression, and violence as strategies to achieve competitive success on the field. Success in these sports depends on the use of brutal body contact and borderline violence. Research shows that male athletes in contact sports readily accept certain forms of violence, even when they involve rule-violating behaviours, and that, as the amount of physical contact

Breaking Barriers

Ideological Barriers
The Hit Isn't Real Unless It Bends Steel

The Paralympic sport of wheelchair rugby has come to be known as "murderball." It is four-on-four competition with players in wheelchairs customized to function like minichariots: angled wheels, bucket seats, safety harnesses, and protective metal bars that shield legs and feet during crashes. Using a volleyball and a basketball court, the teams engage one another in a contest that resembles a mix of rugby, team handball, and football organized by an X Games promoter.

Many people call it quad rugby because participants have quadriplegia or limited use of three or four limbs.

Each of the twelve members of a team is rated in terms of upper-body muscle function, from 0.5 to 3.5 (least impaired). During games the four players on the court from each team may not exceed a cumulative rating of 8.0 points. Participation is open to men and women, but men only comprise most teams. During the four eight-minute quarters, points are scored when a player possessing the ball crosses the opponents' end line.

Wheelchair rugby was invented in Canada (1981) and first played in the Paralympics in 1996. It immediately became popular among people with

Wheelchair rugby, aka quad rugby and murderball, is played in the Paralympics. These players are on one of the many teams in North America. Some participants use a highly masculinized vocabulary to describe the intimidation and violence that occur in games. Wheelchair rugby challenges stereotypes about people with a disability, but it also reaffirms a gender ideology in which manhood is defined in terms of the ability to do violence. When sports embody contradictory ideological themes making clear sense of them is difficult. [Jason E. Kaplan Photography, Portland, Oregon]

· ·

Continued

increases in a sport, so does this acceptance (Pilz, 1996; Shields and Bredemeier, 1995; Weinstein et al., 1995; White and Young, 1997). These athletes routinely disapprove of quasi-criminal and criminal violence, but they accept brutal body contact and borderline violence as long as it occurs within the rules of the game. They may not intend to hurt, but this does not prevent them from putting the bodies of opponents in jeopardy.

In boxing, football, ice hockey, rugby, and other heavy-contact sports, athletes also use intimidation and violence to promote their careers, increase drama for spectators, and enhance the publicity given to their sports and sponsors (see figure 7.2). These athletes realize that doing violence is expected, even if it causes harm to themselves and others. This was illustrated in 2004 when it was alleged that Todd Bertuzzi was under

Breaking Barriers   **Ideological Barriers**
continued

quadriplegia, especially those who favoured power and performance sports involving heavy contact. Paul Davies, a former player and now manager of the British national team, describes wheelchair rugby as "a real in your face sport [resembling] chess with violence" (BBC Sport Academy, 2005).

Many wheelchair rugby players have impairments caused by accidents in risky activities, including high-risk sports. They like wheelchair rugby because it differs from other sports in the Paralympics. When players and other insiders refer to the sport as murderball, it implies a closer connection to able-bodied heavy-contact sports than there is for other Paralympic sports.

Some athletes say that murderball allows them to express their aggression and therefore gain a sense of control over their bodies. But as one member of the U.S. team said, "Of course, you're gonna have healthy aggression and unhealthy aggression." And then one of his teammates added, "But when you can use your body and your chair just to go knock the shit out of somebody, it helps" (in Anderson, 2005; from the documentary film, *Murderball*).

Although other Paralympic sports, except perhaps sledge hockey, are organized so that violence is inconsistent with the strategy and rhythm of participation, some athletes with disabilities want to play a sport involving violence and use their ability to do violence to reaffirm their identities as athletes and men. For example, when the U.S. team faced Canada in the gold medal game of the 2002 Wheelchair Rugby World Championships, the coach reminded

the players that, "It's not buddy-buddy time anymore, guys." And when a member of the U.S. team was asked about their goal for the 2004 Paralympics in Athens, he quickly replied, "We're not going for a hug, we're going for a f___ing Gold Medal" (in *Murderball*, 2004). "Hugs" are associated with the Special Olympics, which are organized to emphasize play and personal accomplishment among athletes with intellectual disabilities. There is little emphasis on competitive success in the Special Olympics, and none on dominating opponents. Volunteer coaches, in fact, are known for hugging athletes when they complete an event, regardless of the outcome.

Many Paralympians, using the ideology of ableism, want to distance themselves from the Special Olympics because it does not match dominant sport forms in society, and perpetuates the idea that people with disabilities cannot play "real" sports—that is, the sports played by able-bodied athletes. **Ableism** is a *web of ideas and beliefs that people use to classify bodies perceived as unimpaired as normal and superior, and bodies perceived as (dis)abled as subnormal and inferior*. This ideology is widespread in society and many people, including some with disabilities, use it to evaluate themselves and others. Similarly, some murderball athletes use traditional gender ideology to connect power, status, and male identity with the ability to do violence. As expressed through words on a player's tee-shirt: "The hit isn't real unless it bends steel" (Grossfeld, 2005). This is not surprising because none of us lives outside the influence of ideology.

coach's orders when he attacked Steve Moore (see box, "Cases of Criminal Violence?"). The message was clear—when a player uses quasi-criminal or criminal violence, the player may be fined/punished by the NHL and by the courts, but not by the coach.

ENFORCERS AND GOONS: BEING PAID FOR PUSH-ING THE LIMIT AND CROSSING THE LINE Violence is also incorporated into game strategies when

coaches use players as designated agents of intimidation and violence for their teams. In hockey, these players have been called "enforc-ers," "goons," and "hit men."[2] They are expected to protect teammates and strategically assist their teams by intimidating, provoking, fighting with, and injuring opponents.

_____

[2]It is interesting to note that "enforcers" in the NHL sometimes refer to themselves as "policemen."

SIDELINES

"When are you gonna learn when it's necessary to use unnecessary roughness?"

FIGURE 7.2 In men's contact sports, players sometimes learn physical intimidation and violent behaviours as strategies. Both have been used to win games and build reputations.

The violence of these enforcers and goons is well known to other players. For example, one hockey player described such a player this way: "His job is to hurt people. He goes for the knees a lot. He takes runs at you, and really all he's trying to do is hurt you and knock you out of the game" (Scher, 1993). For many years, the violence of enforcers and goons was accepted widely. Many people associated with hockey even claimed that this violence limited other forms of violence that might be even more dangerous. However, this argument was challenged more often in recent years, when highly paid superstars such as Mario Lemieux and Paul Kariya, with entertaining and nonviolent physical skills, were sidelined by injuries caused by attacks by enforcers on opposing teams. Some players continue to act as enforcers and goons; but under new rules in the NHL the paid position has almost disappeared as all players are required to have skating and puck-handling skills. Football, basketball, and baseball have taken actions to control certain forms of institutionalized violence, but hockey has been slow to do so and there are still many who argue that fighting has a place in the game. Once violence has been

built into the culture, structures, and strategies of a sport, controlling or eliminating it is difficult.

Learning to Use Violence as a Strategy: Women's Contact Sports Information on violence among girls and women in contact sports remains scarce even though more women are participating in them (Lawler, 2002). This creates the possibility for cases of violence among female athletes, but there are few studies that tell us if and why this is true.

Women's programmes have undergone many changes over the past thirty years. They have become more competitive with a greater emphasis on power and performance, and higher stakes associated with success. Today, as the level of competition rises, and as women become increasingly immersed in the social world of elite power and performance sports, they become more tolerant of rule violations and aggressive actions on the playing field, but this pattern is less clear among women than men (Nixon, 1996a, b; Shields and Bredemeier, 1995; Shields et al., 1995).

"We know of no biological reason that would prevent women from using intimidation and violence or being as physically aggressive as men" (Dunn, 1994). However, most girls and women become involved in and learn to play sports in ways that differ from the experiences of most boys and men. As women compete at higher and higher levels, they appear to begin to play in the same way as men in the way they embrace the sport ethic and use it to frame their identities as athletes. Like men, women are willing to dedicate themselves to the game, play with pain and injury, and overcome barriers. Perhaps this is because the male "model" of high-performance sport is the only one available at this time, and because so many women and women's teams have male coaches (see chapter 8). However, it is rare for women to link toughness, physicality, and aggression to their gender identities. In other words, women do not tie their ability to do violence to their definitions of what it means to be a woman in society. Similarly, coaches do not try to motivate female athletes by urging them to

Roller derby is a women's sport with plenty of action and contact, as in this inter-league bout in Montréal between "The Eh! Team" (Hammer City Roller Girls, Hamilton, Ontario), and "New Skids on the Block" (Montréal Roller Derby). Both men and women are capable of aggressive behaviours. However, they may not link those behaviours to their identities in the same ways. What vocabulary and discourse do women in contact sports use to explain their involvement and achievements in sports? Do they use references to domination and control to the same extent that men do? [Derek Lang, www.BagelHot.com]

"go out and prove who the better woman is" on the field. Therefore, at this time, women's contact sports are less violent than men's.

With this said, there are many research questions that have not been answered:

1. Do elite female athletes develop the same form of hubris (pride-based arrogance) as many elite male athletes? If so, how is it linked to their identities, and how do they express it in sports?

2. Do female athletes use a rhetoric of violence when they talk about sports? Some studies suggest that they do not (Nelson, 1994, 1998; Theberge, 1999, 2000a; Young and White, 1995), but more information is needed. A good place to start might be with the women now playing heavy-contact sports such as

football, ice hockey, rugby, and boxing or participating in dramatic spectacles such as professional wrestling.

Pain and Injury as the Price of Violence

Many people today think about sports in a paradoxical way: they accept violence in sports but the injuries caused by that violence make them uneasy. They seem to want violence without consequences—like the fictionalized violence they see in the media and video games, in which characters are involved in brutal actions but not really injured. However, sports violence is real, and it does cause real pain, injury, disability, and even death (Dater, 2005; Farber, 2004; Rice, 2005; Smith, 2005b; Young, 2004a).

Research on pain and injury among athletes helps us to understand that violence in sports has real consequences. As noted in chapter 6, studies indicate that professional sports involving brutal body contact and borderline violence are among the most dangerous workplaces in the occupational world (Nixon, 2000; Waddington, 2000a; White, 2004; White and Young, 1997; Young, 1993, 2000a, 2004a).

Nixon's research suggests that over 80 percent of the male and female athletes in top-level inter-university sports in the United States sustain at least one serious injury while playing their sport, and nearly 70 percent are disabled for two or more weeks. Nearly all players, both men and women, say that they play while they are hurt, and many experience chronic pain. Rates of disabling injuries vary by sport, but they are high enough in many sports to constitute serious health issues. The "normal" brutal body contact and borderline violence in contact sports regularly cause arthritis, concussions, bone fractures, torn ligaments, and other injuries. In other words, the violence inherent in power and performance sports takes a definite toll on the health of athletes (Young, 2004a).

Research shows a close connection between dominant ideas about masculinity and the high rates of injury in many sports. Ironically, some power and performance sports are organized so that players feel that their manhood is up for grabs. Men who define *masculinity* in terms of physically dominating others often use violence in sports as an expression of this code of manhood. As long as athletes do not critically examine issues related to gender and the organization of their sports, they will mistakenly define *violence* as action that adds "value" to their lives rather than restricting, limiting, and sometimes threatening their lives.

> Becky Zerlentes took a shot to the head above her left eye, then staggered forward and fell to the canvas. . . . [She] never regained consciousness and died, becoming the first female boxer to die in a sanctioned event.
> —*CBS News*, 5 April 2005

Controlling on-the-Field Violence

The roots of violence on the field are deep. They are grounded in overconformity to the sport ethic, processes of commercialization, and definitions of *masculinity*. Therefore, many of the men who control and play power and performance sports resist efforts to control violence. They have come to think that their identities depend on approving of and doing violence and that competitive success in sports depends on the use of strategic violence.

The most difficult type of violence to control is brutal body contact. It is grounded in the culture of power and performance sports and dominant gender ideology. Unfortunately, about 90 percent of the serious injuries in power and performance sports occur *within the rules* of those sports. This means that many men pay the price for their destructive definitions of *sports* and *masculinity*. As U.S. sociologist Mike Messner (1990) noted, when players use their bodies as weapons, players' bodies are also the targets of those weapons. In this sense, it is possible to see expressed in sports a type of "dangerous masculinity" that, in fact, victimizes many young men (Young and White, 1999).

Efforts to control brutal body contact require changes in the culture and ideology of certain sports.

This requires relentless strategies that call attention to the dangers and absurdity of the actions and language that men and women use to reproduce violent sport cultures and the gender ideology that supports them. People should demand and keep accurate records and publish information on injuries on a team-by-team, league-by-league, and sport-by-sport basis. Parents should be informed of these rates before they enlist their children in the service of reproducing patriarchy and a gender ideology that jeopardizes health and development (see box on Injuries in

REFLECT ON SPORTS   Injuries in Children's Hockey

The issue of bodychecking, and its relationship to injuries, has been controversial in children's hockey in Canada. There is overwhelming evidence indicating that bodychecking causes injuries in children. The Canadian Academy of Sports Medicine, and the American Academy of Pediatrics advocate limiting bodychecking for players 15 years of age and younger. The Canadian Medical Association recommends that bodychecking not be introduced until most physical growth is complete, around 17 years of age.

In contrast, Hockey Canada has argued that the younger boys learn how to bodycheck properly, the safer they will be. Thus, a decision was made in 2002 to reduce the age at which bodychecking was introduced, from peewee to atom. These age categories have changed—at one time peewees were 12 and 13 years old—in 2002 they were 11 and 12 years old.

Hockey Canada also commissioned a research study, by William Montelpare at Lakehead University, which showed that there was no increase in injuries when atom-aged players began bodychecking. The CBC television investigative journalism programme, *Disclosure*, examined the statistics, and found that, in comparison to non-bodychecking leagues, there was a fourfold increase in injuries in the leagues that introduced bodychecking for atom players (Robidoux and Trudel, 2006). In other words, the data had been

miscalculated, and that miscalculation had supported Hockey Canada's position.

Subsequent data (e.g., a study carried out by York University and the Hospital for Sick Children—Macpherson et al., 2006) further confirms the negative effects of bodychecking. A comparison was made of 10–13 year old children who were taken to a hospital emergency department in Ontario (where bodychecking was allowed) and Québec (where it was not allowed). Hockey playing children in Ontario were two times more likely to have a checking related injury, and were also more likely to have a concussion or a fracture than hockey playing children in Québec.

Research by a neurosurgeon suggests that:

> The incidence rates of concussion and other hockey-related injuries increases with increasing age, when more bodychecking is expected, and with higher levels of play, which suggests a dose-response effect. Learning to bodycheck when young does not reduce a players' rate of injury as he or she ages, and it prolongs the risk exposure. (Marchie and Cusimano, 2003, p. 125)

We agree with Robidoux and Trudel (2006) that Hockey Canada appears to be more concerned about producing the next generation of NHL players than it is with the safety of Canadian children. *What do you think?*

....

Children's Hockey). People should also calculate the cost of injuries due to brutal body contact and other types of violence in terms of medical expenses, lost work time and wages, days missed in university classes, disability payments, family problems, and even loss in life expectancy.[3]

---

[3]Canadian data are rare. Using 1995 data, the Institute for Social Research (1996) at York University calculated the annual cost of sport and physical recreation injury in Ontario as C$637 million (health care costs, 42 percent; lost productivity/earnings, 46 percent; costs borne by individual and/or family, 12 percent). See White (2004) for a comprehensive review of data on the prevalence and costs of sport injuries.

This will help us to better understand the connections between sport participation and health.

It is less difficult to control borderline, quasi-criminal, and criminal violence, although many people continue to resist taking necessary actions. Enforcers, and players who act in the role of enforcer, should be completely eliminated. This may be accomplished by suspending them without pay, prohibiting teams from replacing suspended players, and fining coaches and team owners for the violence of their players. Unless these or similar actions are taken, owners will simply replace one "headhunter" with another. When team owners and league officials think that violence boosts their profits, they have little incentive to control it unless they lose money when their players cross the line. Suspensions prevent players from doing what they love to do, and if they cannot be replaced on rosters, the suspensions also hurt coaches and team owners, who have some of the power needed to discourage violence on the field.

Controlling brutal body contact and certain forms of borderline violence is difficult. In basketball, for example, there is a fine line between a "hard foul," as encouraged by many coaches, and a flagrant or intentional foul, as defined by league rules. However, when enforced consistently, rules can limit some forms of violence. [AP Photo/ Jason Babyak]

VIOLENCE OFF THE FIELD

When athletes in contact sports are arrested for violent crimes, many people assume that their violence off the field is related to the violent strategies they have learned and are rewarded for on the field.

Even some athletes are persuaded by this view. For example, John Niland, a former NFL player, stated:

> Any athlete who thinks he can be as violent as you can be playing football, and leave it all on the field is kidding himself. (Falk, 1995, p. 12)

However, research on the issue of whether violence carries over to other areas of life is difficult to do, and good studies are rare. When people refer to statistical correlations that show a relationship between playing certain sports and high rates of off-the-field violence, it does not prove that playing violent sports causes people to be violent outside of sports. There are other issues that must be considered before it is possible to consider causality.

First, the people who choose to play sports that involve violent actions may already be inclined to use violence in their lives, either to establish status or cope with problems. Playing violent sports does not make them violent as much as it attracts them because they already feel comfortable about doing violence. *Second*, off-the-field violence among athletes may be due to unique situational factors encountered by some athletes. For example, athletes with reputations as tough players may be encouraged by others to be tough on the streets. Others may even challenge them to fight because of their reputations in sports. This sometimes occurs when athletes who grew up in neighbourhoods with high crime rates return home and find that they have been identified as "marks" by locals who push drugs or run scams to make money. If athletes hang out in those neighbourhoods, they may also attract locals who define them as "sellouts" to big money and corporate sponsors. Some of these locals would like nothing better than to take the athletes down a notch or two. If trouble occurs and an athlete is arrested for fighting in these circumstances, it is not accurate to say that their actions were caused by what they learned in sports.

Research on male hockey players in Canada suggests that those who have many years of experience in power and performance sports are more likely than recreational players or non-players to approve of off-the-field violence and use violence when they play other sports (Bloom and Smith, 1996). Such evidence is useful, but it does not indicate if violence in hockey is the cause or the effect of violence that occurs in other spheres of the players' lives. (see the Reflect on Sports box, "Sexual Harassment and Abuse," on the Online Learning Centre, for other aspects of sexual violence in sports.)

Assaults and Sexual Assaults by Athletes

Highly publicized cases of assaults, sexual assaults, rapes, gang rapes, and even murders that involve athletes who play power and performance sports have led many people to think that the violence in those sports carries over to personal relationships off the field, especially relationships with women. Athletes are public figures and celebrities, so when they are accused, charged, arrested, or tried, people hear and read about it time and time again—as was the case with sexual assault charges filed against NBA player Kobe Bryant, or the charges of having unprotected sex while HIV positive (aggravated sexual assault), of which CFL player, Trevis Smith (Saskatchewan Roughriders), was found guilty. Although people have studied arrest rates and other aspects of particular reported incidents, there is little information that compares what athletes do to similar groups of young men or women who are not high-profile athletes (Benedict, 1997, 1998; Lefkowitz, 1997; Robinson, 1998). Research on the conversations and biographies of athletes has presented important information suggesting that the social worlds created around men's power and performance sports subvert respect for women

and promote the image of women as "game" to be pursued and conquered (Curry, 1991, 1996, 1998; Lefkowitz, 1997; Loy, 1995; Messner and Stevens, 2002; Nack and Munson, 1995; Reid, 1997; Robinson, 1998). However, data on the arrest records of NFL players do not support the carry-over hypothesis (Blumstein and Benedict, 1999).

How do we make sense of these seemingly contradictory pieces of information? In a critical assessment of the debate about male athletes' violence against women, sport sociologist Todd Crosset (1999) reviewed all the published, primarily U.S. research on the issue. His review indicated that male interuniversity athletes, in particular, seem to be involved in more sexual assaults than other male students, but the differences are not statistically significant in any study, and differences often are related to other factors, which make the data difficult to interpret. Crosset explains that when people conclude that the hypermasculine world of men's power and performance sports causes male athletes to engage in violence against women, they overlook important cultural and ideological issues related to sexual assault and distract attention away from the following important points:

- Violence against women occurs regularly and is a serious problem.
- Some male athletes have perpetrated sexual assault and rape, but nearly all violence directed against women is perpetrated by heterosexual men who are not currently playing competitive sports.
- We must understand the problem of violence against women within the context of North American culture and the forms of gender relations that exist in sports and other spheres of society if we wish to significantly cut the rates of sexual assault and rape.

Building on the framework developed by Crosset, and combining it with other research on patterns of violence in all-male groups, we hypothesize that a combination of the following factors accounts for male athletes' violence against women:

1. Support from teammates and fellow athletes for the use of violence as a strategy for being a "man" and controlling women in their lives
2. Perceived cultural support for using physical domination to establish an identity as a man and an athlete, and enhance one's status among certain male peers
3. Social bonds created among athletes who engage in "deviant" overconformity to the norms of the sport ethic, strong feelings that people outside sports cannot understand athletes or their experiences in sports, and a strong sense of hubris (pride driven arrogance) among some high-performance and professional athletes
4. Collective hubris among team members who believe that people outside the fraternity of elite athletes do not deserve respect, that outsiders should defer to their wishes, and that elite athletes live outside the norms of the general community
5. The taken-for-granted belief among male athletes that women, apart from their own mothers and sisters, are celebrity-obsessed "groupies" who can be exploited for sexual pleasure without consequences
6. Institutional (team, athletic department, club, community) support for elite athletes, regardless of their actions
7. Institutional failure to hold elite athletes accountable when they violate community norms and rules

Research is needed on the relevance of these factors in an overall theory of assault and sexual assault perpetrated by male athletes. It appears that assaults perpetrated by athletes are most commonly directed toward women, gay men, and "cocky straight men" in the community who publicly challenge an athlete's assumed status and privilege. These are people who have characteristics directly opposed to the athletes' definitions of their own worth as athletes and as men. It may be true that rates of certain forms of violence are higher among athletes than others, but we need research to help us to understand violence *in the full social and cultural contexts in which it occurs.*

As noted in chapter 6, the norms and group dynamics in certain all-male sport groups encourage athletes to demean and humiliate those who do not come close to matching what they see as their own unique, elite status. In other words, off-the-field violence is not simply on-the-field violence that carries over to the rest of life. Instead, it is action grounded in complex social processes related to the social worlds in which athletes live, define their identities, and deal with their social relationships. As athletes are increasingly being separated from the rest of the community, these processes become more important, if we wish to explain assault rates among athletes. The fact that high-performance and professional athletes are more separate from the rest of the community (on campus and in town) than ever before is an important issue. Until this separation is institutionally bridged or eliminated, assaults will continue to be a problem.

When discussing this issue it is important to remember that even if studies indicated that male athletes had higher sexual assault rates than other categories of people, this would not change the fact that "nonathletes" perpetrate nearly all violence, including violence against women. Jackson Katz, a violence prevention expert, explains that it would be useful to explain why some male athletes assault women, but this is only part of what we need to know when trying to answer the main question of why "stockbrokers, teachers, priests, auto mechanics, and Ivy League students also commit rape" (Katz, 2003). People from all racial and ethnic groups, social classes, and occupational groups perpetrate violence. But one thing is apparent: Men commit nearly all rapes.

Overall, the issues of assault and sexual assault go far beyond the realm of sport. They are part of a larger issue in many societies, especially in the United States where rates of violence in general and rape in particular are high compared to other nations.

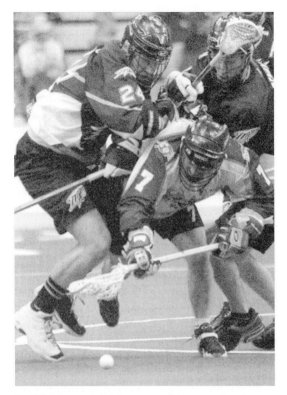

Establishing an identity as an athlete may involve being willing to take risks and to do violence to others. [CP(Ted Jacob); Reprinted with permission of *The Calgary Herald*]

Control versus Carryover

Is it possible that athletes learn things in sports that help them to control violent actions off the field? Does sport participation teach people to control violent responses in the face of adversity, stress, defeat, hardship, and pain?

This possibility was explored in research that found a decrease in aggressive tendencies among male juvenile delinquents who received training in the philosophy and techniques of tae kwon do (Trulson, 1986; summarized in the Reflect on Sports box, "Is Sport Participation a Cure for 'Deviant' Behaviour?", which can be found on the Online Learning Centre). The philosophy emphasized respect for self and others, confidence,

physical fitness, self-control, honour, patience, and responsibility. Similar young men who received training in tae kwon do *without* the philosophy actually measured higher on aggressive tendencies after a training period, and young men who participated in running, basketball, and football with standard adult supervision did not change at all in terms of their aggressive tendencies.

French sociologist Loic Wacquant studied these issues for three years as he trained and "hung out" at a traditional, highly structured, and reputable boxing gym in a Chicago neighbourhood. During that time, he observed, interviewed, and documented the experiences and lives of more than fifty men who trained as professional boxers at the gym. He not only learned the craft of boxing but also became immersed in the social world in which the boxers trained. He found that the social world formed around this gym was one in which the boxers learned to value their craft and to become dedicated to the idea of being a professional boxer; they also learned to respect their fellow boxers and to accept the rules of sportsmanship that governed boxing as a profession. In a low-income neighbourhood where poverty and hopelessness promoted intimidation and violence all around them, these boxers accepted taboos on fighting outside the ring, they avoided street fights, and they internalized the controls necessary to follow a highly disciplined daily training schedule.

Trulson and Wacquant's findings, suggest that participation in sports, even martial arts and boxing, can teach people to control violence. Of course, this depends greatly on the conditions under which sport participation occurs. *If* the social world formed around a sport promotes a mindset and norms emphasizing nonviolence, self-control, respect for self and others, physical fitness, patience, responsibility, and humility (the opposite of hubris), then athletes *may* learn to control violent behaviour off the field. Those most likely to benefit seem to be young men who lack structured challenges and firm guidance as they navigate their way through lives where there are many incentives to engage in violence (see the Reflect on Sports box, "Fair Play Leagues," on the OLC).

Unfortunately, many sports are not organized around these norms. Instead, most sport cultures emphasize hostility, physical domination, and a willingness to use one's body as produce ...munity, ...thers do ...and the ...orts; the ...ons; and ...imilarly, ...identity, ...gical is- ...he inci- ...violence ...ly carry ...gs, nor ...y teach ...looking ...haps we ...between ...gh rates ...er ...n

...tentious statement today. However, many people still believe it, mostly because the hierarchical structure of gender relations in many cultures depends on the extent to which people in a society accept it as true.

Power and performance sports emphasize *difference* in terms of physical strength, they emphasize *control* through domination of others, and they emphasize *status* as dependent on victories over others. This serves to "naturalize" hierarchical differences and reaffirm the belief that power differences are inevitable and that success depends on one's rank compared to others. These beliefs are perpetuated through the stories that people tell about power and performance sports and the way that victories and championships have been won by using strength and strategy to overcome or dominate others, often using violence in the process (Burstyn, 1999).

Power and performance sports celebrate, among other things, the use of strength and violence in a quest for victory over others. At the same time, they reproduce an ideology of masculinity stressing the same factors. The irony in this approach is that, if gender were really based exclusively in biology and nature, there would be no need for sports to reaffirm the importance of gender in people's lives. Gender would be something that "just comes naturally," even without painting our children's bedrooms different colours and spending so much time and effort making sure that they are taught about gender differences. If differences are natural, why is there a need to reinforce them through socialization and laws? The answer is that the actions and orientations of males and females do not come naturally. This is why power and performance sports are favoured by people whose privilege depends on maintaining a gender ideology that emphasizes sex differences. This is the reason some men celebrate sports in which aggression is commonplace. They want to keep alive the notion of difference because it privileges them in the gender order.

What happens to gender ideology when women play power and performance sports and use violence on the field? On the one hand, this contradicts the ideological notion that women are frail and vulnerable. On the other hand, it reaffirms values and experiences that have worked to the disadvantage of many women. This is why many women feel that it is wise for them to avoid the emphasis on physical domination so characteristic in men's sports. Many women have learned that there are ways to be strong and assertive without being aggressive and violent.

"Hey, watch it, pal! You stepped on my foot."

FIGURE 7.3 The language used in association with sports often refers to violence, but it is not known if such language actually incites violent behaviour.

The social impact of the ideology reproduced by sports goes far beyond the actions of athletes. It affects the cultural context in which we all live.

VIOLENCE AMONG SPECTATORS

Do sports incite violence among spectators? This is an important question, because sports capture widespread public attention around the world and spectators number in the billions. To answer this question, it is necessary distinguish between watching sports on television and attending events in person to understand the emotional dynamics of identifying with teams and athletes, and to know how spectators use sports to give meaning to people and places.

Violence Among Television Viewers

Most sport watching occurs in front of the television. Television viewers may be emotionally expressive during games and matches. They may even become angry, but we know little about whether their anger is expressed through violence directed at friends and family members at home.

We also do not know much about violence among those who watch sports in more public settings, such as bars or pubs. Most viewers are supportive of each other and restrict their emotional expressions to verbal comments. When they do express anger, they nearly always direct it at the players, coaches, referees, or commentators or the televised event, rather than at fellow viewers. Even when fellow viewers define outbursts of emotions as too loud or inappropriate, their efforts to settle a fan down are supportive rather than aggressive. When fans from opposing teams are in the same bar, there are usually other sources of mutual identification that keep them from identifying each other as targets of aggression, and they tend to confine expressions of their differences to verbal comments.

Since the mid-1990s, there has been an increase in cases where people, usually men, who have been watching sports in a bar or other public places, gather in crowds after the favoured team wins a big game or championship. Predicting if and when celebratory violence will occur is difficult, but a combination of heavy alcohol consumption and the presence of television cameras are apparent factors that increase its likelihood.

The belief that watching sports is associated with violence has led some people to wonder if watching sports—the Super Bowl, for example—leads to domestic violence in a community or the U.S. as a whole. During the 1990s, a journalist misleadingly reported that women's shelters filled on Super Bowl Sunday because of increased domestic violence on that day. Subsequent statements and research proved this wrong (Cohen, 1994; Sachs and Chu, 2000), but the belief persists. The anger caused by something in a televised sport event *could* be a factor in particular cases of domestic violence. However, violence in the home is a complex phenomenon and to blame it on watching sports overlooks more important factors. Furthermore, we do not know enough about the ways that spectators integrate televised sport content into their lives to say that watching sports does anything in particular (Coakley, 1988; Crawford, 2004).

Violence at Sport Events

Spectators attending noncontact sport events seldom engage in violence. They may be emotionally expressive, but violence directed at fellow fans, players, coaches, referees, ushers, or police is rare. The attack and wounding of tennis player Monica Seles in 1993 stands out as one of the only violent incidents at a noncontact sport event, and that had more to do with celebrity stalking than with sports. Of course, there are occasions when fans use hostile words or engage in minor skirmishes, but such cases of violence are usually controlled effectively by the fans themselves.

Spectators attending contact sports tend to be vocal and emotional, but most of them have not been involved in violent actions. However, crowd violence does occur with enough regularity and seriousness in certain sports to be defined as a problem for law enforcement, and a social issue for which it would be helpful to have an explanation (Briggs, 2004; Upton, 2005; Young, 2002b, 2007b).

Historical Background Media reports of violent actions at sport events around the world, especially at soccer matches in Europe and South America and interuniversity football games in the U.S., have increased our awareness of crowd violence. However, crowd violence is not new. Data documenting the actions of sport spectators through the ages are scarce, but research suggests that spectator violence did occur in the past and that much of it would make crowd violence today seem rare and tame in comparison (Dunning, 1999; Guttmann, 1986, 1998; Scheinin, 1994; Young, 2000a).

Roman events during the first five centuries of the Common Era contained especially brutal examples of crowd violence (Guttmann, 1986, 1998, 2004). Spectators during the medieval period were not much better, although levels of violence decreased in the late medieval period. With the emergence of modern sports, violence among sport spectators decreased further, but it remained common by today's standards. For example, a baseball game in 1900 was described in this way:

> Thousands of gunslinging Chicago Cubs fans turned a Fourth of July doubleheader into a shootout at the OK Corral, endangering the lives of players and fellow spectators. Bullets sang, darted, and whizzed over players' heads as the rambunctious fans fired round after round whenever the Cubs scored against the gun-shy Philadelphia Phillies. The visiting team was so intimidated it lost both games . . . at Chicago's West Side Grounds. (Nash and Zullo, 1986, p. 133)

This newspaper account goes on to report that, when the Cubs scored six runs in the sixth inning of the first game, guns were fired around the stadium to the point that gunsmoke made it difficult to see the field. When the Cubs tied the score in the ninth inning, fans again fired guns, and hundreds of them shot holes in the roof of the grandstand, causing splinters to fly on to their heads. As the game remained tied during three extra innings, fans pounded the seats with the butts of their guns and fired in unison every time the Phillies' pitcher began his wind up to throw a pitch. It rattled him so much that the Cubs scored on a wild pitch. After the score, a vocal and heavily armed Cub fan stood up and shouted, "Load! Load at will! Fire!" Fans around the stadium emptied the rest of their ammunition in a final explosive volley.

Between 1900 and the early 1940s, baseball crowd violence was common in the U.S.: bottles and other objects were thrown at players and umpires (Scheinin, 1994). Players feared being injured by spectators as much as they feared the "bean balls" thrown regularly at their heads by opposing pitchers.

These examples are not meant to minimize the existence or seriousness of crowd violence today. They are mentioned here to counter the argument that violence is a bigger problem today than in the past, that coercive tactics should be used to control unruly fans, and that there is a general decline of civility among fans and in society as a whole (Jayson, 2004; Saporito, 2004). Some spectators do act in obnoxious and violent ways today. They present law enforcement challenges and interfere with the enjoyment of other fans, but there is no systematic evidence to suspect that they are unprecedented threats to the social order or signs of the decline of civilization as we know it.

Celebratory Violence Oddly enough, some of the most serious and destructive crowd violence occurs during the celebrations that follow victories in important games. When these occur inside stadiums, they often are defined as displays of youthful exuberance and loyalty to the team or community. However, in the wake of injuries and mounting property damage associated with these displays, local and university authorities have banned or limited alcohol sales in stadiums and arenas, and they now use police and security officials to prevent fans from rushing onto the playing field when games end. Post-event riots in Canada, usually but not always celebratory, have taken place in Toronto in 1983; Montréal in 1986; Hamilton, Ontario, in 1986; Montréal in 1993; the most violent of all, Vancouver in 1994 (Young, 2002b); and Edmonton in 2006.

Cases of celebratory violence still occur, but new social control methods have been reasonably successful in stopping them from happening *inside* the stadium. Controlling celebratory violence is especially difficult when crowds gather in multiple locations throughout a city. Local police are usually prepared to anticipate celebratory crowds around the stadium, but effective control depends on specialized training, advance planning, and officers who can intervene without creating backlash in the crowd. Breakdowns are relatively common in the face of massive crowds and uncertainty about what might happen.

Unfortunately, there are few sociological studies of this type of violence. Lang (1981) included it in her typology of sport riots, referring to those involved in "victory" riots as "the licentious (or exuberant) crowd." But there has been no systematic data collection or attempts to understand the social dynamics of celebratory violence, and scholars in the sociology of sport usually do not have the resources to study sport-related celebratory violence.

However, if celebratory violence continues to occur at the current rate, there will be resources for law enforcement research. Furthermore, professional sport teams will develop strategies to defuse violence through announcements by highly visible players and respected coaches, bar owners will be asked to control drinking and contain the movement of their customers, and universities will attempt to control the binge drinking that accompanies most celebratory violence. The goal will be to discourage the formation of norms that encourage violence in connection with celebrations.

Research and Theories about Crowd Violence
Researchers in North America have generally ignored violence at sport events. Apparently, this form of violence has not been seen as significant enough, relative to other forms of violence, to attract research attention. The research that does exist has focused primarily on issues of race relations, and little attention has been given to other issues (Young, 2000a).

Kevin Young, of the University of Calgary, has been almost a lone voice in attempting to draw attention to the very real issues of spectator violence at North American sport events. In his analysis, he begins with these scenarios:

> ...officials clear the playing area and delay the game for eight minutes when missiles are thrown at players by irate fans; a riot involving approximately 2,000 fans results in parts of the stadium being vandalized, several fans being seriously injured, and the arena being evacuated; home fans

We need more research on so-called celebratory riots. Research on other forms of collective behaviour suggests that they may not be as spontaneous and unplanned as many people think, as in 2006 on White Avenue in Edmonton. [CP(Tim Smith)]

are threatened with a game forfeit, 15 fans are arrested and 175 ejected for pelting players and officials with missiles; a city council intervenes following stabbings, repeated episodes of assault, and mass fighting involving players and fans; hundreds of police dressed in riot gear use tear gas to disperse 70,000 fans in a downtown area. A man is shot dead by a police officer, hundreds of people are injured, and over 50 arrests are made; vandalism, arson, and fighting provoke police into using rubber bullets and batons as players are detained inside the stadium until the rioting quells. (Young, 2002b, p. 237)

This is not European soccer hooliganism, but actual events that have taken place at North American sport events in recent years. Young then goes on to outline the nature and patterns of spectator violence, which involve seven characteristics all seen at North American sport events—(1) missile throwing (coins, bottles, batteries, etc.), (2) use of firearms and other weapons, (3) field invasions,

(4) property destruction and vandalism, (5) fighting among fans, (6) disorder primarily occurring at the games themselves (unlike soccer hooliganism) with the exception of, (7) post-event riots (following both victories and defeats).

Young raises the troubling question of why spectator violence in North America has not received nearly the same amount of media and police/security attention that soccer hooliganism has in Europe, and outlines some important directions for research.

British and other European scholars have done most of the research on crowd violence, and most of their studies have focused on soccer and "soccer hooliganism." Studies grounded in social psychological theories emphasize that displays of intimidation and aggression at soccer matches involve ritual violence, consisting of fantasy-driven status posturing by young males who want to be defined as tough and manly (Marsh, 1982;

Marsh and Campbell, 1982). These studies are interesting, and they describe classic examples of ritualistic aggression but they have understated the serious and sometimes deadly violence perpetrated by soccer fans, especially during pre- and postgame activities.

Research inspired by various forms of conflict theory emphasizes that violence at soccer matches is an expression of the alienation of disenfranchised working-class men (Taylor, 1982a, 1982b, 1987). In addition to losing control over the conditions of their work lives, these men also feel they have lost control of the now commercialized clubs that sponsor top-level professional soccer in England. This research helps us to understand that violence may be associated with class conflict in society, but it does not explain why violence at soccer matches has not increased proportionately in connection with the declining power of the working class in England.

Research inspired by interactionist and critical theories emphasizes a variety of factors, including the importance of understanding the history and dynamics of the working-class and youth subcultures in British society and how those subcultures have been influenced by the professionalization and commercialization of society as a whole, and soccer in particular (Giulianotti, 1994; Giulianotti, et al., 1994). More work is needed to develop critical analyses of crowd violence across various situations.

Figurational theory has inspired the most research on crowd violence. The work of those using a figurational approach represents a synthesis of approaches grounded in biology, psychology, sociology, and history. Much of this work, summarized by Dunning (1999), Dunning et al. (1988, 2002), and Young (2000a) emphasizes, that soccer hooliganism is grounded in long-term historical changes that have affected working-class men, their relationships with each other and their families, and their definitions of community, violence, and masculinity. Taken together, these changes have created a context, or social figuration, in which soccer represents

the collective turf and identity of people in local communities and the identity of British people as a whole. Soccer then becomes a site for defending and/or asserting community and identity through violence. Figurational research has provided valuable historical data and thoughtful analyses of the complex social processes of which soccer hooliganism is a part. It has also been used as a guide by those who have formulated recent policies of social control related to soccer crowds in England and around Europe.[4]

As the police have become more sophisticated in anticipating violence associated with soccer crowds, young men, some of whom may not be avid soccer fans, take it as a challenge to outsmart the police and create discord and violent confrontations with rival groups. Research indicates that current forms of hooliganism involve semi-organized confrontations that are strategically staged to avoid arrest. At the same time, the police play the role of umpire between groups and attempt to confine confrontations to spaces where they are prepared to deal with them and make arrests before serious injuries and property damage occur (Armstrong, 2007; Brown, 1998; Dunning et al., 2002; Giulianotti and Armstrong, 2002). Cell phones, handheld GPS devices, and other forms of communications technology are used to formulate on-the-spot strategies and escape detection and arrest in this cat-and-mouse scenario. The police use similar technologies combined with surveillance cameras to contain violence. The dynamics associated with this form of violence are not related to sports to the same degree that so-called hooliganism was in the past. Today, soccer matches and tournaments are not the focus of those involved in the violence; instead, men may simply use soccer matches as occasions for seeking excitement through violence.

---

[4]Theories of violence at soccer games in Europe are too complex to explain in this chapter. Those interested in this phenomenon should consult the following: Armstrong, 1998, 2007; Dunning, 1999; Dunning et al., 1988, 2002; Giulianotti and Armstrong, 2002; Weed, 2001.

Two rival fans pretend to fight at a Grey Cup game in Edmonton. Crowd violence has not been a major problem at most sport events, but, when it happens, there is a need for controlled intervention to prevent serious injuries. [CP(Ryan Remiorz)]

General Factors Related to Violence at Sport Events Crowd violence at sport events is a complex social phenomenon related to three factors:

1. The action in the sport event itself
2. The crowd dynamics and the situation in which the spectators watch the event
3. The historical, social, economic, and political contexts in which the event is planned and played

Violence and action in the event If spectators perceive players' actions on the field as violent, they are more likely to engage in violent acts during and after games (Smith, 1983). This point is important, because spectators' perceptions often are influenced by the way that events are promoted. If an event is hyped in terms of violent images, spectators are more likely to perceive violence during the event itself, and then they are more likely to be violent themselves. This leads some people to argue that promoters and the media have a responsibility to advertise events in terms of the action and drama expected, not the blood and violence.

Research by Daniel Wann and his colleagues (1999; 2001a, b; 2002; 2003; 2004) has shown that the perceptions and actions of spectators depend heavily on the extent to which they identify with teams and athletes. Highly identified fans are more likely than others to link their team's performance to their own emotions and identities. Although, by itself, this does not cause violence, it predisposes fans to take action if and when they have the opportunity to do something that they think might help their team. This is important because teams and venues encourage fans to believe that they can motivate home team players and distract visiting team players. Although most fans restrict their "participation" to cheering, stomping, and waving objects, some fans and groups of fans systematically harass and taunt opposing players.

Taunts from fans are not new, but they have become increasingly obscene and personal in recent years. Players are expected to ignore taunts, but there are occasions when they have gone into the stands to attack an obnoxious fan. This has occurred more often in South America and Europe than in North America, but it appears to be increasing in the Canada and the United States. In 2005 there was a highly publicized case in the U.S. when three NBA players on the Indiana Pacers fought with fans during a game in Detroit, with the Pistons, after a fan hit a player with a cup of liquid and ice thrown from the stands. The cup was thrown following an incident of brutal body contact on the court. For a few moments, many people feared a major riot, but players, coaches, security officers, and fans intervened to prevent an escalation of violence.

This incident provoked discussions nation-wide in the United States. In sociological terms, it highlighted the need to manage player–fan relationships more carefully. This is a challenge under current circumstances. Fans pay high prices for tickets, they are encouraged to be emotion-ally involved in the action, they expect players to give them their money's worth, and they often detest what they perceive as arrogance displayed by highly paid players. To complicate matters, in the NBA over 90 percent of the fans are white and over 75 percent of the players are black; this frames the expectations and perceptions of fans and the attitudes of players in potentially vola-tile racial terms, especially in the U.S. From the players' perspective, there is a strong sense of vulnerability when standing amidst 20,000 fans who could kill or maim them in minutes if a mass brawl occurred.

Also important in the sport event are the calls made by officials. Data suggest that when fans believe that a crucial goal or a victory has been "stolen" by an unfair or clearly incompetent deci-sion made by a referee or an umpire, the likeli-hood of violence during and following the event increases (Murphy et al., 1990). This is why it is important to have competent officials at crucial games and matches and why it is important for them to control game events so that actions per-ceived as violent are held to a minimum. The knowl-edge that fan aggression may be precipitated by a crucial call late in a close, important contest puts heavy responsibility on the officials' shoulders.

VIOLENCE, CROWD DYNAMICS, AND SITUATIONAL FACTORS The characteristics of a crowd and the immediate situation associated with a sport event also influence patterns of action among specta-tors. Spectator violence is likely to vary with one or more of the following factors:

- Crowd size and the standing or seating patterns among spectators

- Composition of the crowd in terms of age, sex, social class, and racial/ethnic mix
- Importance and meaning of the event for spectators
- History of the relationship between the teams and among spectators
- Crowd-control strategies used at the event (police, attack dogs, surveillance cameras, or other security measures)
- Alcohol consumption by the spectators
- Location of the event (neutral site or home site of one of the opponents)
- Spectators reasons for attending the event and what they want to happen at the event
- Importance of the team as a source of identity for spectators (class identity, ethnic or national identity, regional or local identity, club or gang identity)

The following comparison of game situations illustrates how many of these factors might be related to spectator violence.

The *location of an event* is important because it influences who attends and how they travel. If the stadium is generally accessed by car, if specta-tors for the visiting team are limited due to travel distance and expense, and if tickets are costly, it is likely that people attending the game have a vested interest in maintaining order and avoiding violence. On the other hand, if large groups of people travel to the game in buses or by train, and if tickets are relatively cheap and many of the spec-tators are young people more interested in creat-ing a memorable experience than simply seeing a game, confrontations between people looking for exciting action increase, as does the possibility of violence. If groups of fans looking for excitement have consumed large amounts of alcohol, the pos-sibility of violence increases greatly.

If spectators are respected and treated as pa-trons rather than as bodies to be controlled, and if stadium norms emphasize service as opposed to social control, people are less likely to engage in defensive and confrontational actions which could lead to violence. If the stadium or arena is crowded and if the crowd itself is comprised mostly of young men rather than couples and families, there is a greater chance for confrontations and violence, especially if the event is seen as a special rivalry whose outcome has status implications for the communities or nations represented by the teams.

Spectator violence, when it does occur, takes many forms. There have been celebratory riots among the fans of the winning team, fights between fans of opposing teams, random property destruction carried out by fans of the losing team as they leave town, panics incited by a perceived threat unrelated to the contest itself, and planned confrontations between groups using the event as a convenient place to face off with each other as they seek to enhance their status and reputations or reaffirm their ethnic, political, class, national, local, or gang identities.

Whenever thousands of people gather together for an occasion intended to generate collective emotions and excitement, it is not surprising that crowd dynamics and circumstances influence the actions of individuals and groups. This is especially true at sport events where collective action is easily fuelled by what social psychologists call *emotional contagion*. Under conditions of emotional contagion, norms are formed rapidly and may be followed in a near spontaneous manner by large numbers of people. Although this does not always lead to violence, it increases the possibility of potentially violent confrontations between groups of fans and between fans and agents of social control, such as the police.

VIOLENCE AND THE OVERALL CONTEXT IN WHICH THE EVENT OCCURS Sport events do not occur in social vacuums. When spectators attend events, they take with them the histories, issues, controversies, and ideologies of the communities and cultures in which they live. They may be racists who want to harass those they identify as targets for discrimination. They may come from ethnic neighbourhoods and want to express and reaffirm their ethnicity, or from a particular nation and want to express their national identity. They may resent negative circumstances in their lives and want to express their bitterness. They may be members of groups or gangs in which status is gained partly through fighting. They may be powerless and alienated and looking for ways to be noticed and defined as socially important. They may be young men who believe that manhood is achieved through violence and domination over others. Or they may be living lives so devoid of significance and excitement that they want to create a memorable occasion they can discuss boastfully with friends for years to come. In other words, when thousands of spectators attend a sport event, their actions are grounded in factors far beyond the event and the stadium.

When tension and conflict are intense and widespread in a community or society, sport events may become sites for confrontations that cannot be considered as sport violence, but as sport-related violence (Young, 2000b). For example, in 1955, francophone Maurice "Rocket" Richard, the star player of the MontréalCanadiens, was suspended by the anglophone NHL president Clarence Campbell. The suspension was the result of a stick-swinging incident, but it jeopardized both Richard's chance of achieving the single-season scoring record and the Canadiens' playoff chances. When Campbell showed up at the next Canadiens game, the resentment of the francophone fans spilled out into the streets of Montréal, resulting in a riot that lasted two days and caused dozens of injuries, thousands of dollars worth of property damage, and one hundred arrests. While the riot was triggered by the suspension of Richard, it came to express resistance to a long period of historical domination of Québec politics and economy by an anglophone elite, and some have interpreted it as an action that anticipated "La Révolution tranquille."

Finally, it must be noted that nearly all crowd violence involves men. This suggests that future research on the topic must consider the role of masculinity in crowd dynamics and the behaviour of particular segments of crowds (Hughson,

REFLECT ON SPORTS

Terrorism: Planned Political Violence at Sport Events

Terrorism is another example of what Kevin Young refers to as "sports-related violence."

The visibility of sport events and the concentration of many people in one place make sport venues a possible target of terrorist attacks. These concerns have increased since the 9/11/2001 attacks on New York and Washington, when those in charge of sport events initiated increased security measures at arenas and stadiums. Spectators often are searched as they enter venues, and rules regulate what they may bring into events. However, most security changes take place behind the scenes in the form of bomb searches, electronic surveillance, and undercover tactics.

As sport teams and venues deal with security issues, their costs have increased between a few thousand dollars at smaller venues to well over US$50,000 per event at larger venues. Furthermore, professional teams and some U.S. university teams face significant increases in the premiums they pay for liability insurance. For example, an NFL stadium that was insured for a US$250,000 annual premium before

9/11 now pays over US$1 million in premiums for the same coverage (Hiestand, 2002). During the Olympic Games in Athens (2004), nearly US$1.5 billion was reportedly spent on security.

Terrorism has occurred in connection with sports in the past. For example, during the early morning hours of September 5, 1972, members of a Palestinian group called Black September entered the Olympic Village in Munich, Germany. They were carrying grenades and automatic weapons in sports bags, and entered the area that housed Israeli athletes and coaches, killing a wrestling coach and a weightlifter and capturing nine other Israeli athletes.

After a twenty-one hour standoff and a poorly planned rescue attempt, seventeen people were dead—ten Israeli athletes and one coach, one West German police officer, and five members of the Black September group. The remainder were sought out and killed by Israeli commandos. The Olympics were suspended for a day, *but events resumed and the closing ceremonies occurred as planned*. About US$2 million had been spent

Continued

2000). Female fans generally do not tip over cars and set them on fire or throw chairs through windows during so-called celebratory riots. They may become involved in fights, but this is relatively rare. Crowd violence may be as much a gender issue as it is a racial/ethnic or social class issue, and controlling it may involve changing notions of masculinity as much as hiring additional police to patrol the sidelines at the next game.

Control of Crowd Violence Effective efforts to control spectator violence are based on an awareness of each of the three factors previously listed. *First*, the fact that perceived violence on the field positively influences crowd violence indicates a need to minimize violence among players during events. If fans do not define the actions of players as violent,

the likelihood of crowd violence decreases. Furthermore, fans' perceptions of violence are likely to decrease if events are not hyped as violent confrontations between hostile opponents. Players and coaches could be used to make public announcements that might defuse hostility and emphasize the skills of the athletes involved in the event.[5] High-profile fans for each team could make similar announcements. The use of competent and professionally trained officials is also important. When officials maintain control of a game and make calls the spectators see as

---

[5]This occurred in 2003, during a tense time in U.S./Canada relations, after the U.S. invasion of Iraq. Following several incidents of booing national anthems at sport events, players made pre-game announcements to ask for respect for the opponents' anthem.

on security at the Munich Olympics—thirty-two years later Athens spent 750 times that amount.

Although the terrorism in Munich has been remembered by those responsible for planning subsequent Olympic Games, it has seldom been mentioned in media coverage of those Games. The reasons for overlooking this event are complex, but it is clear that many people do not want their favourite sport events disrupted or defined in connection with the nasty realities of everyday life, even though sports cannot be separated from the world in which they exist.

It is also important to remember that other forms of terrorism exist in sports. For example, what might be termed "state terrorism" occurred in relation to the 1968 Mexico City Olympics. In an attempt to ensure that the Olympics took place without any dissent, the Mexican government sanctioned the use of troops to break up student protests that were organized to draw attention to the cost of the Games, and the unmet needs of low-income Mexicans. The troops fired on unarmed students, and conservative estimates suggest that some 300 students were killed for protesting the Olympics. This massacre has received even less attention than the Munich massacre.

Death threats received by athletes may also be thought of as a form of terrorism. These may be made for the purposes of gambling, or for political reasons—including issues related to the race and/or gender of athletes. Such concerns also are connected with the celebrity culture of sport, and a number of athletes have been "stalked" by fans.

Because terrorism occurs regularly, it is useful to remember that sports cannot be separated from the policies, events, and material conditions of life that create deeply felt resentment and hatred around the world. This means that it is in everyone's interest to learn more about the world and how peace might be achieved. This takes time and commitment on our part, and it will not be easy to change the conditions that precipitate terrorism. In the meantime, it is difficult to escape the threat of terrorism, not even at the sport events we attend. *What do you think?*

....

fair, they decrease the likelihood of spectator violence grounded in anger and perceived injustice. Referees also could meet with both teams before the event and explain the need to leave hostilities in the locker rooms. Team officials could organize pregame unity rituals involving an exchange of team symbols and displays of respect between opponents. These rituals could be given media coverage, so that fans could see that athletes do not view opponents with hostility. These strategies conflict with media interests in hyping games as wars, so we are faced with a choice: the safety of fans and players versus media profits and gate receipts for team owners. Until now, media profits and gate receipts have been given priority.

Second, an awareness of crowd dynamics and the conditions that can precipitate violence is critical. Preventive measures are important. The needs and rights of spectators must be known and respected. Crowd-control officials must be well trained, so that they know how to intervene in potentially disruptive situations without creating defensive reactions and increasing the chances of violence. Alcohol consumption should be regulated realistically, as has been done in many facilities throughout North America. Facilities should be safe, and organized to enable spectators to move around while also limiting contact between hostile fans of opposing teams. Exits should be accessible and clearly marked, and spectators should not be herded like animals before or after games. Encouraging attendance by families is important in lowering the incidence of violence.

Third, an awareness of the historical, social, economic, and political issues that often underlie crowd violence is also important.

Restrictive law-and-order responses to crowd violence may be temporarily effective, but they will not eliminate the underlying tensions and conflicts that often fuel violence. Policies dealing with oppressive forms of inequality, economic problems, unemployment, a lack of political representation, racism, and distorted definitions of *masculinity* in the community and in society as a whole are needed. These are the factors often at the root of tensions, conflicts, and violence. As noted in the box "Terrorism," dealing with the threat of political terrorism at sports events also requires an awareness of these factors on a global level. It may be that war is another factor that creates the tensions that precipitate sport-related violence.

Also needed are efforts to establish connections between teams and the communities in which they are located. These connections can defuse potentially dangerous feelings or plans among groups of spectators or community residents. This does not mean that teams merely need better public relations. There must be *actual* connections between the teams (players), and the communities in which they exist. Effective forms of community service are helpful, and team owners must be visible supporters of community events and programmes. Teams must develop programmes to assist in the development of local neighbourhoods, especially those around their home stadium or arena.

The goal of these guidelines is to create antiviolence norms among spectators and community residents. This is difficult but more effective than using metal detectors, moving games to remote locations, hiring hundreds of security personnel, patrolling the stands, using surveillance, cameras, and scheduling games at times when crowds will be sparse. Of course, some of these tactics can be effective, but they destroy part of the enjoyment of spectator sports. We see them as last resorts or temporary measures taken only to provide time to develop new spectator norms.

SUMMARY

DOES VIOLENCE IN SPORTS AFFECT OUR LIVES?

Violence is certainly not new to sports. Athletes through history have engaged in actions and used strategies that cause or have the potential to cause injuries to themselves and others. Furthermore, spectators through history have regularly engaged in violent actions before, during, and after sport events. However, as people see violence in sports as something that can be controlled, they deal with it as a problem in need of a solution.

Violence in sports ranges from brutal body contact and borderline violence to quasi-criminal and criminal acts. It is linked with "deviant" overconformity to the sport ethic, commercialization, and cultural definitions of *masculinity*. It has become institutionalized in most contact sports as a strategy for competitive success, even though it causes injuries and permanent physical impairments among athletes. The use of enforcers is an example of institutionalized violence in sports.

Controlling on-the-field violence is difficult, especially in men's contact sports, because it is often tied to players' identities as athletes and men. Male athletes in contact sports learn to use violence and intimidation as strategic tools, but it is not known if the strategies learned in sports are carried over to off-the-field relationships and situations. Among males, learning to use violence as a tool within a sport is frequently tied to the reaffirmation of a form of masculinity that emphasizes a willingness to risk personal safety and a desire to intimidate others. If the boys and men who participate in certain sports learn to perceive this orientation as natural or appropriate, then their participation in sports may contribute to off-the-field violence, including assault and sexual assault. However, such learning is not automatic, and men may, under certain circumstances, even learn to control their expressions of violence as they play sports.

The most important impact of violence in sports may be its reaffirmation of a gender ideology that assumes "the natural superiority of men." This ideology is based in the belief that an ability to engage in violence is part of the essence and reality of being a man.

Female athletes in contact sports also engage in aggressive acts, but little is known about how those acts and the willingness to engage in them are linked to the gender identities of girls and women at different levels of competition. Many women seem to prefer an emphasis on supportive connections between teammates and opponents, and regulation of the power and performance aspects of sports. Therefore, aggression and violence do not occur in women's sports as often or in connection with the same dynamics as they occur in men's sports.

Violence among spectators is influenced by violence on the field of play, crowd dynamics, the situation at the event itself, and the overall historical and cultural contexts in which spectators give meaning to their lives and the world around them. Isolated cases of violence are best controlled by improved crowd management, but chronic violence among spectators usually signals that something needs to be changed in the culture and organization of sports and or the social, economic, and political structures of a community or society.

Terrorism in the form of planned, politically motivated violence at sports events is rare, but the threat of terrorism alters security policies and procedures at sport venues. The terrorist attack at the 1972 Olympic Games reminds us that global issues influence our lives, even when we attend our favourite sport events. Just as violence in sports affects out lives, the social conditions in the rest of our lives affect violence in sports.

Visit *Sports in Society*'s **Online Learning Centre at <u>www.mcgrawhill.ca/olc/coakley</u> for additional information, website resources, and study tools for this chapter.**

[CP(Andrew Vaughan)]

Gender and Sports

Does equity require ideological changes?

What changes when a woman becomes an athlete? Everything.

> —**Mariah Burton Nelson**

[I]t's both demeaning and infantilizing to assign women's sports the chore of cleaning up the industry....[W]omen shouldn't be relegated to the ladies' auxiliary of men's sports—making less money and getting less attention, but proud in the knowledge that their play is uncorrupt.

> —**Rachel Giese, columnist (1998)**

[The] little sister principle: Like the legions of girls who have played in goal for their brothers when an extra player was needed...[f]emale players are still largely looked upon as the little sisters who don't really belong in hockey.

> —**Elizabeth Etue and Megan Williams, authors (1996)**

Gender and gender relations are central topics in the sociology of sport. It is important to explain why most sports around the world have been defined as men's activities, why half the world's population generally has been excluded or discouraged from participating in many sports through history, and why there have been dramatic increases in women's participation since the mid-1970s. To explain these issues we must understand the relationship between sports and widespread beliefs about masculinity and femininity and homosexuality and heterosexuality.

Discussions and research on gender relations and sports usually focus on issues related to fairness and equity, as well as to ideology and power. *Fairness and equity issues* concern topics such as

- Sport participation patterns among girls and women
- Gender inequities in participation opportunities, support for athletes, and jobs in coaching and administration
- Strategies for achieving equal opportunities for girls and women

Ideological and power issues concern topics such as

- The production and reproduction of gender ideology in connection with sports
- The ways in which prevailing gender ideology constrains people's lives and subverts the achievement of gender equity
- The cultural and structural changes required to achieve gender equity and democratic access to participation in sports

The goal of this chapter is to discuss these two sets of issues and to show that, even though many people deal with them separately, they go hand in hand in our lives. We cannot ignore either one if we define sports as important in the lives of human beings.

PARTICIPATION AND EQUITY ISSUES

The single most dramatic change in sports over the past two generations is the increase in participation of girls and women. This has occurred mostly in wealthy postindustrial nations, but there have been increases in some developing nations as well. Despite resistance against change, more girls and women now participate in sports than ever before.

Reasons for Increased Participation

Since the mid-1960s, five interrelated factors account for the dramatic increases in sport participation among girls and women:

1. New opportunities
2. Government equal rights legislation
3. The global women's rights movement
4. The health and fitness movement
5. Increased media coverage of women in sports

New Opportunities New participation opportunities account for most of the increased sport participation among girls and women in the last three decades. Prior to the mid-1970s, many girls and women did not play sports for one simple reason: Teams and programmes did not exist. Young women today may not realize it, but the opportunities they enjoy in their schools and communities were not available to many of their mothers or any of their grandmothers. Teams and programmes developed since the late 1970s have inspired and supported interests ignored in the past. Girls and women still do not receive an equal share of sport resources in most organizations and communities, but increased participation has clearly been fuelled by the development of new opportunities. Many of these opportunities owe their existence to some form of political pressure or government legislation.

Government Equal Rights Legislation Literally millions of girls and women would not be playing sports today if it were not for local and national legislation mandating equal rights. Policies and rules calling for gender equity exist today mainly because of persistent political action focused on raising legal issues and pressuring political representatives. The individuals and groups making these efforts are committed to the struggle to achieve fairness in sports. In Canada, legal concerns about gender equity in sports coincide with the "official" start of the so-called "second wave" of feminism in Canada, the 1970 *Report of the Royal Commission on the Status of Women*. Two recommendations directly addressed the issue:

> **Recommendation 77:** We recommend that the provinces and territories (a) review their policies and practices to ensure that school programmes provide girls with equal opportunities with boys to engage in athletic and sports activities, and (b) establish policies and practices that will motivate and encourage girls to engage in athletic and sports activities.
>
> **Recommendation 78:** We recommend that, pursuant to Section 3(d) of the federal Fitness and Amateur Sport Act, a research project be undertaken to (a) determine why fewer girls than boys participate in sports programmes at the school level and (b) recommend remedial action.

The process of working toward achieving these, and other aspects of gender equity in Canadian sports has been long and slow, and, of course, we still have "fewer girls than boys participat[ing] in sport programmes at the school level," (see chapter 14) although many more than was the case in 1970. In 1980, the Women's Programme of the Fitness and Amateur Sport Branch was formed in Ottawa (Ponic, 2000), showing some level of federal commitment to gender equity. However, the main tools for equity arrived with the repatriation of the Constitution in 1982. Schedule B of the Constitution Act, the Charter of Rights and Freedoms, gave all Canadians equal rights under the law. The 1985 Canadian Human Rights Act (together with various provincial Human Rights Acts) sharpened the tools, and women and men who had been lobbying for gender equity in sports were now in a position to press their claims. As a consequence, in 1986, Sport Canada published their *Policy on Women in Sport*, and steps have been gradually taken to implement that policy of equal opportunity at all levels of the Canadian sport system.

Governments in various countries also have passed laws and formulated policies that support equal rights for girls and women in sports (e.g., Title IX, the 1972 Educational Amendments to the Civil Rights Act, in the United States). Women around the world have formed the International Working Group on Women and Sport (the IWG; see www.iwg-gti.org) to promote the enforcement of these laws and policies and to pressure resistant governments and international groups to pass equal rights legislation of their own. Political power in these nations and organizations rests in the hands of men, and they often see women's sport participation as disrupting their ways of life, and as violating important moral principles grounded in nature and/or their religious beliefs.

The women and men working to produce changes in these settings have had to be persistent and politically creative to achieve even minor improvements. Progress has been made in some nations, but at least half the women in the world today lack regular access to sport participation opportunities.

The Global Women's Rights Movement The global women's movement over the past forty years has emphasized that females are enhanced as human beings when they develop their intellectual *and* physical abilities. This idea has encouraged women of all ages to pursue their interests in sports, and it has inspired new interests among those who, in the past, never would have thought of playing sports (Fasting, 1996).

The women's movement also has initiated and supported changes in the occupational and family roles of women. These changes have, in turn, provided more women with the time and resources they need to play sports. As the goals of the women's movement have become more widely accepted, and as male control over the lives and bodies of women has weakened, more women choose to play sports. More changes are needed, however, especially in low- and middle-income nations and among low-income women in wealthy nations, but the choices now available to women are less restricted than they were a generation ago.

The global women's movement has fuelled both national and international political action. Many politically influential women's sport organizations have emerged in connection with the women's movement. For example, the Canadian Association for the Advancement of Women and Sport and Physical Activity (CAAWS) and similar groups in other nations have become important lobbying groups for change. The IWG emerged from a 1994 conference, which brought women delegates from eighty countries to Brighton, England, to discuss "women, sport, and the challenge of change." After three days of discussion and debate, the delegates unanimously passed a set of global gender equity principles now known as the "Brighton Declaration." This document, updated and reaffirmed at world conferences on women in sport in Windhoek, Namibia (1998), Montréal (2002), and Kumamoto, Japan (2006), continues to be used by people as they pressure governments and sport organizations to create new opportunities for girls and women in sports.

Lobbying efforts by representatives from these and other organizations led to the inclusion of an article (10g) specifically related to women's participation in sports and physical activity in the United Nations' Convention on the Elimination of All Forms of Discrimination against Women (CEDAW; www.unhchr.ch.html/menu3/b/e1cedaw.htm), and to statements related to sports and physical education in the official Platform for Action of the U.N.'s Fourth World Conference on Women, held in Beijing, China, in 1996.

Due to a combination of factors, girls and women today see a wider range of sport participation images than they saw in the past. This has encouraged dramatic increases in sport participation. [AP Photo/Vincent Yu]

These statements called for new efforts to provide sport and physical education opportunities to promote the education, health, and human rights of girls and women in countries around the world. Canadians have been particularly active in these initiatives. What began as inspiration based in the women's movement has become a widely accepted global effort to promote and guarantee sport participation opportunities for girls and women. A Fifth World Conference on Women in Sport has been scheduled for 2010 in Sydney, but the goals of the 1996 conference are far from being achieved in 2008.

The Health and Fitness Movement Since the mid-1970s, research has made people more aware of the health benefits of physical activities (Sabo et al., 2004). This awareness has encouraged women to seek opportunities to exercise and play sports. Although much of the publicity associated with this movement has been influenced by traditional ideas about femininity and tied to the prevailing feminine ideal of being thin and sexually attractive to men, there also has been an emphasis on the *development of physical strength and competence*. Muscles have become increasingly accepted as desirable attributes for women of all ages. Traditional standards for body image remain, as illustrated by the clothing fashions and marketing strategies associated with women's fitness, but many women have moved beyond those standards and have focused on physical competence and the good feelings that go with it rather than trying to look like anorexic models in fashion magazines.

Many companies that produce sporting goods and apparel also have recognized that women can be serious athletes. They continue to sell apparel and equipment, but they now focus on function in their designs and marketing approaches. For example, they have produced ads that appeal to women who see sport participation and achievements as symbols of independence and power. In the process, they have encouraged and supported sport participation among girls and women at the same time that they do the opposite in other ads (Wearden and Creedon, 2002).

Increased Media Coverage of Women in Sports Even though women's sports are not covered as often or in the same detail as men's sports (see chapter 12), girls and women now can see and read about the achievements of female athletes in a wider range of sports than ever before. This encourages girls and women by publicly legitimizing their participation (Heywood and Dworkin, 2003) as was clearly evident in Canada in 2002. The Canadian national women's ice hockey team has won most World Championship competitions that have been held, but won its first gold medal Olympic victory in Salt Lake City in 2002. The media images in the coverage of those events were very powerful and inspirational to girls and women.

As girls grow up, media images help them to envision possibilities for developing athletic skills. This is important because the media present so many other images and messages that emphasize versions of femininity that are inconsistent with playing sports and being identified as a serious athlete. For example, girls' visions of being an athlete can be clouded by powerful images connecting thinness, vulnerability, and nonathletic bodies with sex appeal and heterosexual femininity. Despite mixed messages, the media coverage of everything from professional women's basketball to synchronized swimming helps girls and young women conclude that sports are human activities, not male only activities.

Media companies, like their corporate counterparts that sell sporting goods, now realize that women make up over half the world's population and, therefore, half the world's consumers. In Canada, the CBC has made a conscious effort in recent years to provide equal coverage of men's and women's sports at the Olympics. Production and on-camera staff received media training with regard to equity issues, and one formal analysis of CBC television coverage of the Sydney Olympics (Cluer et al., 2001) indicates that both the quantity and quality of men's and women's coverage was similar. The launch of the digital channel, the Women's Sports Network (WTSN), was an indication that commercial media in Canada were beginning to take women's sports seriously.

However, its short life is also an indication that there are still challenges for women's sport in the media. Women's sports will continue to be covered in the media, and this will influence the images that all of us associate with women's sports and the achievements of female athletes. The most influential coverage occurs when female athletes demonstrate physical skills and present body images and forms of self-presentation that push traditional ideas and beliefs about the characteristics and potential of women on and off the field (Lafferty and McKay, 2004; Thomsen et al., 2004).

Reasons to Be Cautious When Predicting Future Participation Increases

Increases in the sport participation rates of girls and women have not come easily. They are the result of dedicated efforts by many individuals and groups. Progress has been remarkable, but gender equity does not exist yet in many sport programmes in most parts of the world. Furthermore, there are seven reasons to be cautious about the pace and extent of future sport participation increases:

1. Budget cuts and the privatization of sport programmes
2. Resistance to government regulations
3. Backlash among those who resent changes that threaten dominant gender ideology
4. Underrepresentation of women in decision-making positions in sports
5. Continued emphasis on "cosmetic fitness"
6. Trivialization of women's sports
7. Homophobia and the threat of being labelled "lesbian"

Budget Cutbacks and the Privatization of Sport Programmes Gender equity is often subverted by budget cutbacks. Compared with programmes for boys and men, programmes for girls and women are often vulnerable to budget cuts because they are less well established, they have less administrative and community support, and they have less revenue-generating potential.

Because sport programmes for girls and women often are relatively new, they have start-up costs that long-standing and well-established programmes for boys and men do not have. Therefore, equal budget cuts may cause women's programmes to fail at a faster pace than men's programmes because they have not developed institutional support or market presence. Many programmes for boys and men are less vulnerable, because they have had decades to develop legitimacy, value, support, and an audience. It should be pointed out, however, that cuts to, or non-implementation of, programmes for girls and women rarely happens without a fight in Canada. Equity legislation has provided the tools for those with the energy to resist a situation where access to sports and physical activity returns to the bad old days of provision for boys but not girls.

As public, tax-supported programmes are cut, and user fees are introduced or increased, sport programmes often become prioritized. This has a negative impact on sport participation opportunities for girls and women, especially those who live in low-income households. Public programmes are accountable to voters, and they are regulated by government rules related to equal rights and opportunities. Private and non-profit programmes are accountable to the needs of their paying members, and this means that they are influenced by market forces more than commitments to equal rights and opportunities.

When free and affordable public programmes are cut, people must buy sport participation from private or non-profit providers. This is easy for females from well-to-do backgrounds: they just buy what they want and private providers seek their business. "Free enterprise sports" are great things for people with money. But they are not free for people on tight budgets; nor are they "enterprising" in providing opportunities for women with low salaries and little discretionary money. Private programmes serve only people who can buy what they sell. When money talks, poor people are seldom heard, and poor girls and women often are reduced to silence. Therefore, future participation increases may be unevenly distributed among girls and women, and those who lack resources may suffer participation setbacks in the future (Braddock et al., 2005; Sabo et al., 2004). Research also shows that when the quality of sport programmes is poor, as often occurs when there is a lack of public funding, girls lose interest and do not take sport participation seriously (Cooky, 2004).

Resistance to Government Legislation Those who benefit from the *status quo* often resist government legislation that mandates changes. This is certainly true in the case of legislation calling for gender equity in sports. They may claim that there is too much government interference in everyday life. They also say that if girls and women were really interested in sports, there would be opportunities for them and that laws interfere with a more basic and natural order related to gender and sports (Gavora, 2002; Knudson, 2005). Of course, they have operated programmes for boys and men for over a century without ever considering the needs and interests of girls and women, so it is easy to see why they would resist "government interference" demanding that they open their eyes. These people cannot turn back the clock when it comes to changes already made, but they can slow future changes.

Backlash Among People Who Resent Changes That Threaten Dominant Gender Ideology When women play certain sports, they become strong. Strong women challenge the prevailing gender ideology that underlies the norms, legal definitions, and opportunity

structures that frame the conditions under which men and women form identities, live their lives, and relate to each other. Those who are privileged by the prevailing gender ideology in society see strong women as a threat. They do all they can to discredit most women's sports and strong female athletes, and they call for a return to the "good old days," when men played sports and women watched and cheered.

The effects of this backlash on sport participation among girls and women are not completely clear. However, our guess is that it contributes to the mixed messages girls and women receive and even give to one another about sports, and it fuels the trivialization of women's sports and the marginalization of strong women athletes. If this is occurring, future increases in sport participation rates will be slowed.

Underrepresentation of Women in Decision-Making Positions in Sports Despite increased sport participation among girls and women, women have not seen the same increases in the ranks of coaching and sport administration (Acosta and Carpenter, 2004; Carpenter and Acosta, 2005; McKay, 1997).

Many men do a good job of coaching and administering women's sports, but unless girls and young women see women in decision-making positions in their programmes, and perhaps even in men's programmes, they will be reluctant to define sports and sport participation as important in their futures. If women are not visible leaders in sport programmes, some people conclude that women's abilities and contributions in sports are less valued than men's. This conclusion certainly limits progress toward gender equity in sports (Ligutom-Kimura, 1995).

Continued Emphasis on "Cosmetic Fitness" There are competing images of female bodies in many cultures today. Girls and women receive confusing cultural messages that they should be "firm but shapely, fit but sexy, strong but thin" (Markula, 1995; see also, MacNeill, 1998a;

Smith Maguire, 2002). Although they see images of powerful female athletes, they cannot escape the images of fashion models whose reputations depend on a body shape that women can match only by depriving themselves of the nourishment they need to be strong. Girls and women also hear that physical power and competence are important, but they see disproportionate rewards going to women who look young, vulnerable, and nonathletic. They are advised to "get strong but lose weight." They learn that muscles are good, but too many muscles are unfeminine. They are told that athletic women are attractive, but they see men attracted to professional cheerleaders and celebrity models with breast implants and airbrushed publicity photos. They also see conventionally attractive athletes, such as Russian tennis player Maria Sharapova "packaged and sold as the... giggly gal who just wants to have fun: Hillary Duff with a forehand" (Glock, 2005). Therefore, they may conclude that even if you are a good athlete, it is "hot" looks that bring fame. And they know that Anna Kornikova turned her looks, not her success in tennis, into fame, and they see that her fame has lasted far longer than her tennis skills.

Despite cultural messages that promote athletic performance, they are outnumbered and out-hyped by cultural messages promoting appearance and beauty (Hargreaves, 1994; Heywood and Dworkin, 2003). Effective commercial messages for everything from makeup to clothing are based on well-established marketing assumptions that insecurities about appearance promote consumption, whereas positive body image does not. Therefore, even many ads that show women doing sports are carefully staged to make women feel insecure rather than confident about their bodies (MacNeill, 1998a).

In sports, Brandi Chastain's removal of her shirt after the U.S. national women's team won the first Women's World Cup in soccer received a great deal of media attention in many countries. In Canada and internationally, we have the case of women's beach volleyball where, in a stunning attempt to attract media attention to the sport, the international volleyball federation (Fédération Internationale de Volleyball, or FIVB) required women players to wear revealing outfits. Of course, some women were comfortable with such outfits, but others were not. Those who tried to refuse to wear the new uniforms were told that they would not be allowed to participate (Drakich, 2002; Robinson, 2002a).

Messages about feminine and sexy bodies are so powerful that some women avoid sports until they are thin enough to look "right" and to wear the "right" clothes; other girls and women combine participation with pathogenic weight-control strategies to become dangerously thin. Research shows that some female athletes use laxatives, diet pills, diuretics, self-induced vomiting, binges, and starvation diets in conjunction with their training (Beals, 2000; Hawes, 2001; Johns, 1997; Madison and Ruma, 2003; Wilmore, 1996). This increases the probability of injuries, jeopardizes health, and keeps alive the idea that women must conform to the media-based beauty standards or be rejected by men and by women who use those standards to evaluate females of all ages.

Although most female athletes do not develop eating disorders, they may choose sports and/or monitor their appearance and actions in light of the standards of cosmetic fitness. Overall, the tensions between cosmetic fitness and being strong and physically skilled create for many girls and women the challenge of negotiating the meaning that they and others give to their bodies (Dworkin, 2001; Garrett, 2004; Heywood and Dworkin, 2003; Shakib, 2003; Wedgewood, 2004; Young, 1998). This challenge is especially daunting for female athletes with a disability (see the Breaking Barriers box, p. 228).

When the goal of playing sports is cosmetic fitness, women may define their participation as a means of achieving an unrealistic body image, burning calories so they can eat without guilt, or punishing themselves when they have eaten too much (Krane et al., 2001). Additionally, young women seeking cosmetic fitness sometimes drop

Breaking Barriers

Narrative Barriers
I Was Too Ashamed of My Body

Anna was born with underdeveloped arms and feet. Despite encouragement and support from a close friend, she resisted going to the gym and becoming involved in sports. She explained her resistance in the following way:

> I really wanted to go—inside, I was dying to be physical, to have a go at "pumping iron." . . . But at the time I just couldn't say yes. . . . I was too ashamed of my body. . . . It was the same thing with swimming. I just couldn't bear the thought of people looking at me. I felt *really* vulnerable. (in Hargreaves, 2000, p. 187)

Anna's fear of her body being seen and judged is not unique. Negotiating the meanings that we and others give to our bodies is a complex and challenging process. But in contemporary cultures it is more challenging for women than men, and for people with a disability than their able-bodied peers.

In cultures where femininity is tied to physical attractiveness and sexual desirability, the women who accept dominant gender ideology often make choices that interfere with sport participation. For example, a young woman with an amputated leg may choose a prosthesis that is more natural looking, rather than one that is more functional and better suited to sport participation. As one woman explained, "It's one thing to see a man with a Terminator leg. . . . It may inspire people to say, 'Cool.' But body image for women in this country is model thin and long sexy legs" (in Marriott, 2005). In agreement, Nick, a twenty-year-old student who lost his legs after contracting a rare bacterial disease at summer camp when he was fourteen, says, "I love my Terminator legs," and he does not think twice about plugging them into the nearest electrical outlet when they run short on their charge.

Although Nick loves his "Terminator legs," negotiating the meaning given to one's body is more challenging for men with a disability than for most able-bodied men. This is especially true when they accept a gender ideology that ties masculinity to power and the ability to outperform or dominate others. For example, after filling his car with gas and putting his wheelchair in the back, Mark had trouble starting his car. A man who had just driven up behind him laid on his horn and shouted obscenities. Mark said that before the accident that paralyzed his legs "I would have got out of the car and . . . laid him out, but now I'm useless . . . This is why I say my manhood has been shattered" (in Sparkes and Smith, 2002, p. 269).

Although Mark did not use the same words that Anna used, he also felt vulnerable. When men with disabilities feel vulnerable, some may do what Anna did and avoid sport participation, whereas others may view sport as a site for asserting or reaffirming masculinity.

Sociologists Brett Smith and Andrew Sparkes (2002) point out that people create identities, including feminine and masculine identities, through narratives—that is, the stories that they show and tell others about themselves. Their research indicates that playing power and performance sports is a masculinizing narrative—a story in which manhood is constructed through physical accomplishments and dominance over other men. Such narratives are the foundation of dominant gender ideology.

When alternative or oppositional narratives are not available to women with disabilities, they often avoid sports because sports do not contain femininity narratives. Similarly, some men like Mark may avoid sports for fear that they will not be able to overpower other men. Therefore, males and females with disabilities would benefit if they had access to new, counternarratives that construct gender in less constraining terms (Thomas, 1999). When there are multiple ways to be a woman or a man, people with a visible disability have more options for negotiating the meanings that they and others give to their bodies. Maybe this would enable Anna to become more physical and have a go at pumping iron. And maybe it would enable Mark to accept help and still feel like a man.

out of sports if they gain weight while they train, and others drop out after they achieve weight-loss goals. Overall, it appears that cultural messages about cosmetic fitness will interfere with future increases in sport participation.

Trivialization of Women's Sports "Okay, women play sports, but they are not as good as men and people want to see the best." Statements like this assume that "real" sports involve "manly" things—such as intimidation, violence, and physical domination over others—and that women's sports are second-rate. This orientation is widespread enough that it interferes with achieving gender equity in sports (Laurendeau, 2004; Vincent, 2004).

Power and performance sports are historically grounded in the values and experiences of men, and they use evaluative standards that disadvantage women. By these male standards, women play rugby but they do not hit as hard as men do; women play basketball but they do not dunk; women play hockey, but they do not check or fight. They do sports, but they do not do them in the same way as men. Therefore, by this logic, they do not do them well enough to receive equal support.

An extension of this "logic" was used in 2004 by Sepp Blatter, president of FIFA (the world governing body for soccer). He told international women players that more spectators would watch them if they would wear tighter shorts (Christenson and Kelso, 2004). He assumed that the women's game was trivial, compared with the men's game, and using sex appeal would make it more fan friendly.

When enough people trivialize women's sports by dismissing competent and talented female athletes or defining them primarily as sex objects, it is difficult to generate gate receipts and commercial sponsorships to sustain high performance and professional programmes. Even though most people know they should not say that a person

> If I wanted to wear a bikini I would have chosen to play beach volleyball.
>
> —Solveig Gulbrandsen,
> professional soccer player, Norway
> (in Christenson and Kelso, 2004)

"throws like a girl" when he or she does not throw well, many people continue to think that playing like women is, by definition, second-rate. This form of trivializing women's sports and female athletes continue to interfere with achieving gender equity at all levels of sport.

Homophobia and the Threat of Being Labelled "Lesbian" Homophobia *is a generalized fear or intolerance of lesbians, gay men, and bisexual people* (Griffin, 1998). It is based on the notion that homosexuality is "deviant" or immoral, and it supports prejudice, discrimination, harassment, and violence toward those identified or believed to be homosexual or bisexual. Homophobia is a powerful element of culture that has discouraged many girls and women (and "out" gay men) from playing sports or making sports an important part of their lives.

Homophobia causes some parents to steer their daughters away from sports that they believe attract lesbians, and away from teams or programmes where lesbians are believed to play or coach. Homophobia and public expressions of homophobic discourse influence and often limit the sport participation choices available to women (Dworkin, 2003; Howe, 2003; Veri, 1999). When women fear the label of *lesbian*, or fear being associated with lesbians, they may avoid certain sports, limit their commitment to sports, de-emphasize their athletic identities, or emphasize their heterosexuality. Closeted lesbians may fear the loss of secrecy so much that they limit their relationships with others and become lonely and isolated in the process (Bredemeier et al., 1999; Griffin, 1998; Lenskyj, 2003; Swoopes, 2005).

Heterosexual men may use homophobic discourse to tease female athletes, and to control women who are intimidated by it. This occurs in some high schools and universities, and it can cause women to become defensive and give sport participation a lower profile in their lives. Effectively challenging homophobic discourse and forcing others to confront their homophobia

This Barbie doll is a classic example of sport images mixed with the notion of cosmetic fitness. The beauty myth remains strong in popular ideas about femininity. Does Barbie reproduce those myths? [M. MacNeill]

is a daunting task. Some people, gay and straight, are good at this, but most people lack the experience to do it effectively.

In the meantime, many women athletes go out of their way to emphasize traditional feminine attributes and even say in interviews that being an athlete is not nearly as important as eventually getting married, settling down, having children, and becoming a nurturing homemaker.

Like athletes, people who market women's sports often avoid acknowledging lesbians for fear that it will decrease attendance among potential spectators who are homophobic. Players know this and often say that if a woman wants to make a team, she had better grow her hair long and talk about wanting to be married and have children. As one Canadian international player said, it is well known that team officials "don't want a bunch of dykes representing our country" (Hall, 2002, p. 200).

Homophobia affects all women, lesbian and straight alike; it creates fears, it pressures women to conform to traditional gender roles, and it silences and makes invisible the lesbians who manage, coach, and play sports (Griffin, 1998; Hall, 2002; Lenskyj, 1999; Nelson, 1998).

Gender and Fairness Issues in Sports

Sport participation among girls and women will not continue to increase automatically. Without continued efforts to achieve gender equity, there is a tendency in most cultures to give priority to men's sports and male athletes. This is because sport worlds are usually organized to be:

1. *Male dominated* so that the characteristics of men are used as standards for judging qualifications
2. *Male identified* so that the orientations and actions of men are used as standards for defining what is right and normal
3. *Male centred* so that men and men's lives are the expected focus of attention in sport programmes, stories, legends, and media coverage

Therefore, female athletes, coaches, officials, and administrators are considered qualified if they play or do their jobs "like a man." If a woman in sports does not think and act like a man, she is not likely to be defined as right or normal. And when people talk about athletes and sports in such a social world, it is assumed that they are talking about men and men's sports unless they specify otherwise—such as saying that they are talking about women's teams, women's records, the best female athletes, the Women's World Cup, and so on.[1]

The impact of social organization that is male dominated, male identified, and male centred is illustrated through a review of information on sport participation, support for athletes, and jobs for women in sports.

Participation Opportunities: Organized and Mainstream Sports Prior to the early 1970s, most people did not question the male dominated/identified/centred organization of sports. They believed that females were naturally frail and unsuited for most sport participation. When girls and women were encouraged to be physically active, they were steered into figure skating, gymnastics, swimming, tennis, and other sports that people thought were assumed to not require strength, power, and speed—the traits associated with masculinity. Some girls and women ignored these assumptions and played sports involving strength, power, and speed and they lived with the consequences, which often involved some form of social rejection. But overall, there were limited opportunities for girls and women to play sports.

Over the past fifty years, female athletes demonstrated clearly that notions of female frailty were grounded in ideology, rather than nature. They expanded ideas about what girls and women could and should be encouraged to do in sports. Today, most people in North America and many other regions agree that women should have opportunities to play sports. But there continue to be disagreements about girls and women playing certain contact sports, playing certain sports with men, and having access to the same resources as men (see box on "Equality versus Equity," p. 236).

These disagreements have perpetuated inequities in participation opportunities in many international sports. For example, there are still fewer sports for women than for men in the Olympics and other international events. Although important changes have occurred since the early 1980s, female athletes remain underrepresented in international competitions. The data in figure 8.1 and table 8.1 illustrate that women in the modern Summer Olympic Games always have had fewer events than men, and there always have been fewer women participants than men. The International Olympic Committee (IOC), which from 1894 to 1981 had no women members, did not approve a women's 1,500-metre race until the 1972 Games in Munich. It was not until the 1984 Games in Los Angeles that women had the opportunity to run the marathon. Women waited until 1988 to run the Olympic 10,000-metre race and until 1996 to run the 5,000-metre race.

Interestingly, because of specific circumstances, Canada has achieved gender equity in athlete representation at three recent Summer Olympics. Despite the fact that there are still more events for men, Canada sent 153 men and 154 women to Atlanta, 155 men and 156 women to Sydney, and 132 men and 134 women to Athens. Although this is, in part, a result of Sport Canada's gender equity policies, the equal numbers were assisted by the failure of a number of men's team sports to qualify for the Games. That changed in Beijing (2008) when Canada sent 189 men and 132 women.

However, despite the introduction of women's hockey in 1998 (Nagano), Canada has not achieved similar results at the Winter Olympics—the country was represented by 89 men and 65 women in Nagano, 91 men and 66 women in Salt Lake City, and 110 men and

---

[1]This is known as "gender marking" in sport media studies; see chapter 12.

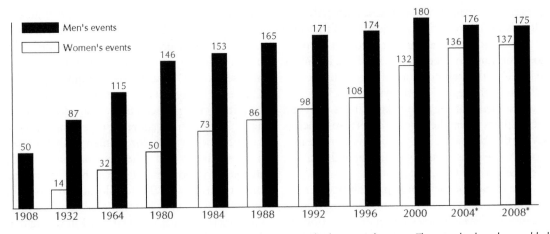

*Twelve events in 2004 and ten events in 2008 were mixed, or open to both men and women. These twelve have been added to both totals for men and women. This procedure of adding mixed events to the total events for women and men was also used for each of the other Olympics in this graph.

FIGURE 8.1   Number of Summer Olympic events open to women and to men, 1908–2008

86 women in Torino. But despite these changes, in 2000, the French Minister of Sports noted that, "Women's involvement in sports [around the world] is characterized by deep inequalities."

Equity sometimes is difficult to achieve because of fundamentalist religious beliefs in certain nations. For example, a strict interpretation of Islamic beliefs forbids women from publicly exposing any surface of their bodies to the sight of men. Women in traditionally Catholic nations have not faced moral restrictions, but they have often lacked power and resources to play sports traditionally played by men only. Women in traditional and poor societies often face barriers that preclude or discourage sport participation, as well as limit the extent to which any woman could take sport seriously enough to train at an elite level. These barriers are both ideological and structural. In other words, they are related to (1) *webs of ideas and beliefs* about what is and is not appropriate for girls and women to do (*gender ideology*), and (2) the organization of *opportunities*, and the distribution of *resources* to take advantage of opportunities (*social structure*).

Opportunities to play professional sports always have been scarce for women. Until recently, many people did not believe that spectators would pay to watch women play anything but "ladylike" sports, in which they competed alone (figure skating, golf) or with nets separating the opponents and preventing physical contact (tennis, volleyball). Norms in some countries began to change in the 1980s, but many people still doubted that spectators would pay to watch women play sports that went beyond the limits of dominant definitions of *femininity*. Although these limits have been pushed and broken, there remains "cultural encouragement" to highlight traditional notions of femininity. Therefore, many female athletes are still referred to as "ladies," and any recognition of the participation of lesbians is usually carefully erased in the media profiles of teams and leagues. The media emphasis is on heterosexual habits, lifestyles, and "looks"; children and husbands are made visible and discussed often. Homophobia continues to shape the public image of women's sports, and lesbians have been made invisible, despite their strong presence in many sports. Opportunities for women at the professional level will continue to be limited until ideas and beliefs about femininity expand to embrace multiple notions of womanhood.

Participation Opportunities: Informal and Alternative Sports Gender and fairness issues are not limited to formally organized, mainstream sports. Informal games often have gender dynamics that present girls and women with special challenges for gaining access to participation and claiming identities as athletes. Similar challenges exist in alternative sports, both informal and formal. This is because boys and men generally control who plays and who is defined as a "fellow" athlete.

Regardless of where informal sport participation occurs—backyards, driveways, local parks, school playgrounds, gyms and playing fields at high schools and universities, or on the streets—the contexts are male dominated/identified/centred. This often discourages the

Girls and women are eager participants in alternative sports such as climbing. However, in many "action sports," boys and men control who plays and who is defined as an athlete, and girls and women are seldom treated seriously in those sports unless they use boys and men as models in their approach to sport. [CP(Aaron Harris)]

participation of girls and women, and it creates a situation in which they must be exceptionally good athletes and have clever inclusion strategies to be given the chance to play and be accepted as an athlete by male peers. In many cases, the best inclusion strategy is to be "sponsored" by an influential boy or man who vouches for a girl's or a woman's "right" to demonstrate what she can do as an athlete. Gender equity laws do not apply to these settings. Therefore, changes come more slowly than they do in formal sport settings such as school and university sports.

Forms of excluding or restricting the participation of girls and women in informal sports have received little attention in the sociology of sport. However, we do know that girls and women face unique participation and identity challenges in both informal and alternative sports and that there are equity and fairness issues related to who plays under what conditions (Wheaton and Beal, 2003). The most important consequence of these issues is that many girls and women feel that they are not welcome to develop and display their skills. This leads many boys and men to say that they should receive priority when using sports facilities or resources because girls and women are not interested in sports. It's a "Catch-22" situation for girls and women: they have fewer opportunities than men to develop interests and skills, and then they are denied opportunities to play because they have fewer interests and skills!

Research on alternative sports shows that they are clearly organized around the values and experiences of boys and young men (Anderson, 1999; Honea, 2007; Rinehart and Syndor, 2003). Observations at nearly any open, noncommercial skateboard park will reaffirm this point. Girls and young women are usually spectators, "skate Bettys" (perceived as "groupies" with boards), or they are cautious participants earning the right to be taken seriously (Beal and Weidman, 2003)—and a disproportionate number of girls are in-line skaters, which puts them lower in the skateboard park status hierarchy. The few girls who do claim space for themselves in bowls or ramp areas have earned the "right" to participate, but they have done so on terms set by the boys. As one hard-core mountain biker noted as he described expert women riders: "Testosterone is contagious" (in Bridges, 2003, p. 181). In sociological terms, this means that to be accepted as an authentic athlete in alternative sports, a female must perform "like a guy."

Alternative sports have emerged in connection with the lifestyles of boys and young men who value, among other things, facing one's fears, taking risks, and pushing normative limits. The boys and young men in these sports say that inclusion is based on skill, guts, and aggressiveness, not gender. But when pressed on this point, one skater said with a swagger,

Table 8.1   Male and female athletes in the modern Summer Olympic Games, 1896–2008

Year	Place	Countries represented	Male athletes	Female athletes	Percent female
1896	Athens	14	241	0	0.0
1900	Paris	24	975	22	2.2
1904	St. Louis	12	645	6	0.9
1908	London	22	1,971	7	1.8
1912	Stockholm	28	2,359	48	2.0
1916	Olympics scheduled for Berlin cancelled (World War I)				
1920	Antwerp	29	2,561	65	2.5
1924	Paris	44	2,954	135	4.4
1928	Amsterdam	46	2,606	277	9.6
1932	Los Angeles	37	1,206	126	9.5
1936	Berlin	49	3,632	331	8.4
1940	Olympics scheduled for Tokyo cancelled (World War II)				
1944	Olympics cancelled (World War II)				
1948	London	59	3,714	90	9.5
1952	Helsinki	69	4,436	519	10.5
1956	Melbourne	72	2,938	376	11.3
1960	Rome	83	4,727	611	11.4
1964	Tokyo	93	4,473	678	13.2
1968	Mexico City	112	4,735	781	14.2
1972	Munich	122	6,075	1,059	14.8
1976	Montréal	92	4,824	1,260	20.7
1980	Moscow	81	4,064	1,115	21.5
1984	Los Angeles	140	5,263	1,566	22.9
1988	Seoul	159	6,197	2,194	26.1
1992	Barcelona	169	6,652	2,704	28.9
1996	Atlanta	197	6,806	3,512	34.0*
2000	Sydney	199	6,582	4,069	38.2
2004	Athens	201	6,452	4,412	40.6
2008	Beijing	205	6,449	4,747	42.4

Source: www.olympic.org/uk/games/index_uk.asp
*Twenty-six countries sent only male athletes to the 1996 Summer Games.
Note: These data show 112 years of gradual progress toward gender equity. At this rate, the 2016 or 2020 Summer Games may have equal numbers of men and women. The number of athletes participating in 1976, 1980, and 1984 was lower than expected, due to boycotts.

"It takes too much coordination for a girl, and it's too aggressive" (in Beal and Weidman, 2003, p. 345). Therefore, the girls who are identified as athletes in the "extreme" versions of alternative sports are those who demonstrate "Kodak Courage"—that is, enough skill and guts to attempt and occasionally accomplish creative and dangerous unique tricks that others want to see in person or on film (Kay and Laberge, 2003).

The consequences of the male-dominated/ identified/centred culture and organization of alternative sports are seen in media-created, corporate-sponsored versions such as the X Games, Gravity Games, and Dew Action Sport Tour (Kilvert, 2002). For example, there were fifty-six female athletes in the 1995 X Games but only twenty-six in 2003; in 2005 only four of the fifty-four *invited* participants were females. Patterns vary from one alternative sport to another, but gender inclusion is relatively rare in the case of participation opportunities.

Support for Athletes Female athletes in most North American high schools and universities seldom receive the same support enjoyed by the boys and men. This is also the case in sport-sponsoring organizations around the world. Historically, there have been serious inequities in the following areas:

- Access to facilities
- Quality of facilities (playing surfaces, locker rooms, showers, etc.)
- Availability of scholarships
- Programme operating expenses
- Provision and maintenance of equipment and supplies
- Recruiting budgets
- Scheduling of games and practice times
- Travel and *per diem* expenses
- Numbers of coaches assigned to teams
- Salaries for administrators, coaches, trainers, and other staff

- Provision of medical and training services and facilities
- Publicity for individuals, teams, and events

Inequities in some of these areas remain a problem at all levels of education, but they also are a problem in many community programmes.

When they exist in community programmes, they often go undetected unless someone digs through data from public, nonprofit, and private programmes. Access to facilities, the number of programmes available, and the staff assigned to programmes are the most likely areas of inequity in community-based sports in North America and around the world.

Most people today realize that a lack of support for female athletes subverts sport participation among girls and women. For well over a century, men have built their programmes, shaped them to fit their interests and values, generated interest in participation, sold them to sponsors, and marketed them to potential spectators. During this time, public funds and facilities and student fees have been used to start and maintain programmes for boys and men. As CAAWS noted:

> Many fitness, recreation and sport organizations across Canada do not allocate their resources, programs and decision-making fairly to both females and males without bias. As a result, the demographic profile of the people who use the organization's facilities does not match the demographic profile of the community. (2002, p. 6)

Girls and women want only the same treatment. Mary Jo Kane, director of the University of Minnesota's Tucker Center for Research on Girls and Women, says,

> Women are not asking for a handout, we're just asking for an investment. Just put the same investment in us that you put into men. Then we'll see what happens. (Lamb, 2000, p. 57)

For those who believe in fairness, it is difficult to argue with this point.

REFLECT ON SPORTS

Equality versus Equity

We have used the term *equity* throughout this chapter, but there is still a great deal of confusion about the difference between *equity* and *equality*, and the term *equity* is often used when what is actually being referred to is *equality*. For example, in 2005 CIS surveyed Canadian university athletics departments with an Equity Practices Questionnaire. However, almost all of the issues dealt with in the report (www.universitysport.ca) concern equality between men's and women's athletics. Legal definitions of *equity* vary from one nation and community to another. In Canada, the Charter of Rights and Freedoms provides useful definitions of both equality and equity. Under Equality Rights, Subsection 15(1) defines equality:

> Every individual is equal before and under the law and has the right to the equal protection and equal benefit of the law without discrimination based on race, national or ethnic origin, colour, religion, sex, age or mental or physical disability.

Subsection 15(2) deals with *equity*:

> Subsection (1) does not preclude any law, program, or activity that has as its object the amelioration of conditions of disadvantaged individuals or groups including those that are disadvantaged because of race, national or ethnic origin, colour, religion, sex, age or mental or physical disability.

The difference between equality and equity has frequently been expressed in the form of a sporting analogy regarding *fairness* in a footrace. U.S. President Lyndon Johnson first used it with regard to race relations in the United States, but it was refined with reference to social class by then Federal Minister for Health and Welfare in Canada, John Munro, in his 1970, *A Proposed Sport Policy for Canadians:*

> We must face the fact that the opportunity for involvement in sports and recreation is extremely unequal between the socio-economic classes within our population....It's only fair, just as a dash [sprint] in a track meet is only fair, that everyone has the same starting line, and the same distance to run. Unfortunately, in terms of facilities, coaching,

promotion and programming, the sports scene today resembles a track on which some people have twenty-five yards to run, some fifty, some one-hundred, and some as much as a mile or more. (pp. 4–5)

Providing everyone with an equal starting line (i.e., an opportunity) is now considered to be *equality*. However, not everyone comes to that starting line with the same experiences and having had the same opportunities—so equality is not very meaningful if you announce that the recreational swim programme is open to everyone, or that everyone may try out for the swim team. People come to that opportunity having had a pool at home, having had public or private swimming lessons, or never having had the opportunity to swim or to learn to swim. Access to the opportunity is open and equal, but the opportunity

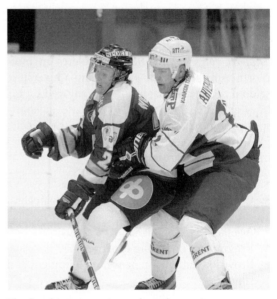

The legal interpretations of gender equity generally have supported girls who have wanted to play in sports traditionally reserved only for boys. But there is still resistance from some sport organizations, which is why Hayley Wickenheiser (above, left) played in Finland rather than Italy. [CP/Lehtikuva(Jussi Nukari)AP]

itself is not the same for everyone. Bruce Kidd proposes that, "Equality focuses on creating the same starting line for everyone; equity has the goal of providing everyone with the opportunity to reach the finish line." A more programme-specific example of gender equity notes that: "An athletics program is gender equitable when the men's program would be pleased to accept as its own the overall participation, opportunities and resources currently allocated to the women's program and vice versa" (*Athletics Administration*, 1993, p. 22).

Both equality and equity are important, and the following examples show how each has been addressed (see also the Reflect on Sports box, "Girls Playing on Boys' Teams: The Justine Blainey Case," p. 238). In Coquitlam, B.C. in 1999, David Morrison won a sex discrimination case at the B.C. Human Rights Commission on behalf of his daughter Katie, a gymnast. He argued that the municipality did not give boys and girls equal access to sport and recreation facilities in that it subsidized male-only sports, especially hockey, but not his daughter's nonprofit gymnastics club. As a result of losing the case, the city introduced what they called a Gender Equity Fund ($50,000 a year for at least five years) and a Gender Equity Programme. In the initial monitoring steps introduced by the programme, Coquitlam found, for example, that at one arena, of the 207 hours of available ice time, 200 hours went to boys. Although these solutions were called an "equity" fund and programme, they were really about taking some steps towards equality in provision—about helping girls to reach the starting line.

Equity involves additional steps to make up for the years of underfunding and underservicing experienced by girls' and women's sports. Following the implementation of gender equity policies in athletics and recreation at the University of Toronto in 1994, a number of steps were taken to introduce both equality and equity. In terms of equality, men's and women's interuniversity sports teams were provided with equal (total) funding. This was only achieved by removing the *most* expensive sport, men's football, from the calculation—a step made possible only when alumni agreed to fund football.

Steps to achieve equity involved the introduction of some women-only hours for a pool and a weight room. These met the requirements of some religions that require women's exercise to take place out of the sight of men, but also create a level of comfort for many women who are not experienced at swimming or weight training, or who have had negative experiences exercising in male-dominated facilities. For example, a member of a women's national team who had been weight training for years began to use the women-only hours in the weight room. She reported that it was rare, in the co-ed weight room, for her to complete an exercise session without a male (often less experienced at weight training) coming over to offer to show her how to carry out the exercise properly.

The department also introduced the START instruction programmes, providing an introduction to a number of activities such as swimming and skating to people who have not previously had the opportunity to learn these skills. The courses were originally designed with gender equity in mind, but the department quickly realized that, in a multicultural city with so many immigrants from so many parts of the world, there were broader equity issues—and the courses were open to men and women.

With the women-only hours, the university is practising what has been critically referred to as "reverse discrimination"—it is offering services to women that are not currently available to men.[1] In this way, it is attempting to meet the requirements of Subsection 15(2) of the Charter of Rights and Freedoms: "the amelioration of conditions of disadvantaged individuals or groups." The university recognizes that services and opportunities to participate in physical activity have not been available to all men, but that such opportunities have, historically, been far more available to men than to women.

Equity is difficult and controversial, but it is an important step towards equality. *What do you think?*

---

[1]The university recognizes that separate facilities for women, such as those available at many fitness clubs, would be a better solution than closing the facilities to men for several hours a day. However, this would require both space and funding, neither of which are currently available.

REFLECT ON SPORTS   Girls Playing on Boys' Teams: The Justine Blainey Case

One of the key gender equity issues involves girls and women playing on a team that is appropriate to their talents. When there are fewer opportunities for female athletes, one of the only solutions may involve playing on a boys'/men's team. The Justine Blainey case was a landmark in terms of gender equity.

In 1984, twelve-year-old Justine Blainey and her brother David (to the relief of their mother who was driving them to practices and games) both made the Toronto Olympics peewee hockey team. When the Metro Toronto Hockey League discovered that a girl was playing on a boys' team, they immediately barred her from play (Robinson, 2002).

Blainey decided to challenge the ruling, and the case had important legal and human rights implications. The Ontario Court, in 1985, ruled that, although it violated the Canadian Charter of Rights and Freedoms, the Ontario Human Rights Code (OHRC) supported the right of the Ontario Hockey Association to prevent a girl from playing on a boys' team. In 1986, the Ontario Court of Appeal changed the OHRC on a majority decision. Justice Charles Dubin (who was later to lead the Inquiry on doping in sport; see chapter 6) pointed out that, in its present form, the OHRC "permits the posting of a 'no females allowed' sign by every athletic organization in this province" (cited by Hall, 2002, p. 181).

The cases produced a number of bizarre arguments for the Ontario Hockey Association, from the view that integrated hockey would damage girls both physiologically and morally, to the view that losing to a girl would damage a boy psychologically. With

appeals, the case was not resolved finally until 1988, and effectively prevented Blainey from playing top-level hockey for a number of years (she eventually played university hockey at the University of Toronto). Perhaps even more damaging were the death threats, hate mail, and accusations (from men) that she was "that girl who wanted to destroy hockey" (cited by Robinson, 2002, p. 196).

The Blainey case also caused a split in women's sports, with some supporting her right to play on the best team available, and others arguing that it was a precedent that would damage women's sports by taking away all the best players.

In a strange case of history repeating itself, Canadian national team captain Hayley Wickenheiser was, in early 2003, denied by the Italian Ice Hockey Federation an opportunity to play professional hockey on a men's team in the Italian league. The ban was supported by the president of the International Ice Hockey Federation. Despite this, she eventually found a place on a men's professional team in Finland.

Should girls be allowed to play on boys' teams if they have the talent and there is no comparable opportunity for girls? As CAAWS recently pointed out, "There have been court challenges, usually under provincial Human Rights legislation, but the legal opinion has largely been that females have the right to compete for a position on a male team on the same basis as males, as long as they demonstrate sufficient skills and ability to meet the requirements of the team" (www.caaws.ca/e/advocacy). *What do you think?*

Jobs for Women in Coaching and Administration Most sport programmes are controlled by men. Although women's programmes have increased in number and importance around the globe, women often have lost power over them. Data at all levels of competition show that women do not have equal opportunities when it comes to jobs in coaching and administration. Women are especially under-represented at the highest levels of power in

sports. For example, in Canada, only 17 percent of the national team coaches are women, while 47 percent of national team athletes are women (CAAWS, 2002).

The situation is hardly better in interuniversity sports in Canada. In a 2005 survey of CIS sports, only 20 percent of the coaches were women (see table 8.2). While no university had more female than male coaches in CIS sports, Canadian universities differed significantly in terms of their representation of women coaches. For example, St. Mary's (7M, 5F), UQAM (2M, 2F), Toronto (10M, 7F), and Alberta (8M, 6F) were among the most equitable; St. FX (10M, 0F), McGill (13M, 1F), Waterloo (12M, 0F), and UBC (10M, 1F) were among the least equitable. The university athletic departments are aware of this. The 2005 CIS Equity Practices Survey found few inequities in coaching salaries between men and women, but a number of universities recognized "the challenge... in attracting and hiring qualified females" and the problem of "balanc[ing] the desire to hire more female coaches against the demands of the female athletes to have the best coach for their team regardless of the gender of the coach" (www.universitysport.ca). However, it is possible to imagine that, if the situation was reversed, what men would say if 70 percent of the coaches in men's programmes were women, while men held only 4 percent of the coaching jobs in women's programmes.[2] They would be outraged! They would file lawsuits and demand affirmative action programmes to achieve fairness—and they would be justified in doing so.

The coaching situation is much the same on a global level (McKay, 1997). Systematic data on coaches are not easy to collect from nation to nation, but over 80 percent of all national team coaches are men. The IOC was encouraged to recognize the situation for women in other national and international leadership positions in sport in the mid-1990s, and published their Women and Sport Policy in 1997. The policy called for targets for the IOC and National Olympic Committees (NOCs)—international sport federations (IFs) were encouraged to apply the same targets—of 10 percent of their membership (IOC) or Executive Committees (NOCs and IFs) to be women by December, 2001, and 20 percent by December, 2005.

There were *no* women on the IOC from 1896 until the 1980s. Between 1990 and 1996, forty of forty-two new appointments went to men. Since 1997, the IOC added enough women to meet its goal of 10 percent by 2001, but the majority of these were elected athlete representatives who only serve a four-year term. By 2006, there were fourteen women and ninety-nine men on the IOC—the 12.4 percent representation means that the IOC has yet to meet its own 2005 target.[3] A study of NOCs' efforts (White and Henry, 2004) to achieve the IOC's targets found that, of 184 NOCs who reported by 31 December, 2004, 29 percent had achieved the 20 percent target, 68 percent had achieved the 10 percent target, and over 98 percent had at least one woman on the Executive Board. By June, 2005, of the 34 Olympic IFs, 29 percent had already achieved the 20 percent target, 68 percent had met the 10 percent target, and 91 percent had at least one woman on their Executive Board (Report on Women's Representation at the IOC, 3 October, 2005—www.olympic.org).

Thus, the goal of having women in 20 percent of the top decision-making positions in sport organizations around the world by 2005 has not been achieved. At the current rate of progress, it is possible that job equality in most sport organizations will not be achieved until today's twenty-year-olds are grandparents. However, as White and Henry (2004) point out,

> the introduction of minimum targets has had a clear and positive impact on the proportion of women in NOC Executive Committees. The rapid growth of the numbers of women in such positions, from a very low base, immediately following the announcement of the minimum targets is clear.... (p. 7)

Other data collected by White and Henry suggest that the women recruited to meet the targets are also proving to be a major asset to the NOCs.

---

[2] The situation may be even worse internationally. For example, at the 2002 Salt Lake City Olympics, only the Canadian women's team in the hockey tournament had a female coach.

[3] In a calculation error that is somewhat self-serving, the IOC reported (www.olympic.org, 2006) that 14 women and 99 men represented a 14.1 percent proportion of women.

Table 8.2   Male and female coaches in CIS sports, 2005

Men's sports	Coaches		Women's sports	Coaches	
	M	F		M	F
Basketball	40	1**	Basketball	21	20
Cross country	27	2	Cross country	27	4
Football	27	0	Field hockey	4	10
Hockey	31	0	Hockey	19	6
			Rugby***	12	11
Soccer	40	0	Soccer	31	12
Swimming	29	1	Swimming	27	3
Track & field	17	5	Track & field	16	6
Volleyball	26	1**	Volleyball	22	14
Wrestling	16	0	Wrestling	16	0
TOTAL*	253	10		195	86

*These totals are misleading because, at some universities, men's and women's teams have the same coach; also track and field and cross-country teams often have the same coach. Thus, the actual numbers of coaches for CIS sports are 348 men (80%) and 86 women (20%).

**It is striking that there were two women who were head coaches of men's team sports at Canadian universities—in basketball at UQAM, and in volleyball at Queen's.

***In an attempt to achieve some semblance of gender equality, CIS sanctions 10 women's sports and 9 men's sports at the national level; thus, there is no men's rugby as a national championship sport (although it is at the provincial levels).

Source: Adapted from Analysis of Male and Female Coaches in CIS Sports, January 2005. Available online: http://www.cisport.ca/e/research/documents/analysisofmensandwomenscoachesinCIS_000.pdf

The reasons for the underrepresentation of women in coaching and administrative positions in women's sports have been widely debated and studied (McKay, 1997, 1999; Pastore et al., 1996; Theberge, 1988, 1992; Wilkerson, 1996). The major reasons appear to include the following:

- Men have used well-established connections with other men in sport organizations to help them during the job search and hiring process.
- Compared with men, most female applicants for coaching and administrative jobs do not have the strategic professional connections and networks that they need to compete with male candidates.
- Job search committees often use ideologically-based evaluative criteria, making it more likely that female applicants for coaching and administrative jobs will be seen as less qualified than male applicants.
- Support systems and professional development opportunities are scarce

for women who want to be coaches or administrators, and for women already in coaching and administrative jobs.[4]

- Many women know that it is difficult to work in athletic departments and sport organizations that have corporate cultures organized around the values and experiences of men.
- Sport organizations are seldom organized in family-friendly ways.
- Sexual harassment is more often experienced by women, and female coaches and administrators often feel that they are judged by more demanding standards than men.

---

[4]The Coaching Association of Canada (CAC) sponsors a National Team Coaching Apprenticeship Program for women, providing a three-year national team experience for eighteen women in fourteen sports (www.coach.ca/women/). Also, since 2001, the CAC has partnered with other agencies to sponsor a Canada Games Coaching Apprenticeship Program for women (www.coach.ca).

These factors affect aspirations and opportunities. They influence who applies for jobs, how applicants fare during the hiring process, how coaches and administrators are evaluated, who enjoys his or her job, and who is promoted into higher-paying jobs with more responsibility and power.

People on job search committees seek, interview, evaluate, and hire candidates who they think will be successful in sport programmes that are male dominated/identified/centred. After looking at the objective qualifications, such as years of experience and win–loss records, search committee members subjectively assess such things as a candidate's abilities to recruit and motivate players, raise money, command respect in the community (among sponsors, fans, sport reporters), build toughness and character among players, maintain team discipline, and "fit" in the athletic department or sport organization.

None of these subjective assessments occur in a vacuum and some are influenced by gender ideology in addition to the facts. Although people on search committees do not agree on all things, many think in terms that favour men over women (Hovden, 2000; McKay, 1997). This is because coaching and other forms of leadership in sports often are seen to be consistent with traditional ideas about masculinity: If you "coach like a girl," you are doing it wrong; if you "coach like a man," you are doing it right. In a male-dominated and identified organizational culture, this is taken for granted.

Under these conditions, women are hired only when they present compelling evidence that they can do things as men have done them in the past. In sport programmes and athletic departments where men have routinely been hired and women have been ignored, there may be pressure to recruit and hire women so that charges of discrimination can be deflected. When a woman is hired in such circumstances, it is often said that, "*We had to hire a woman*." But a more accurate statement is this: "*We've favoured men for so long that people were going to rightfully accuse us of gender discrimination if we didn't hire a woman or two*."

When women are hired, they are less likely than men to feel welcome and fully included in sport organizations. Therefore, they often have lower levels of job satisfaction and higher rates of job turnover (Pastore et al., 1996). When turnover occurs, some people accuse women of not having what it takes to survive in the "real" world of sports. But this ignores the fact that the expectations for coaches and administrators were developed over the years by men who often had wives who raised their children, provided them and their teams with emotional support, hosted social events for teams and sponsors, coordinated their social schedules, handled household finances and maintenance, made sure they were not distracted by family and household issues, and faithfully attended games season after season.[5] If female coaches and administrators had the opportunity to build programmes and coach teams under similar circumstances, job satisfaction would be high and turnover would be low, and there would certainly be child care provided for the children of coaches and administrators (McKay, 1999).

Finally, some sport organizations have records of being negligent in controlling sexual harassment and responding to complaints from women coaches and administrators who wish to be taken seriously in the structure and culture of sport organizations and programmes. This means that people in the programmes must critically assess the impact of male dominated/identified/centred forms of social organization on both males and females. Unless this is done and changes are made, gender equity will never exist in the ranks of coaching and administration.

---

[5] Of course, such times are coming to an end, as evident in the story of a Southern Ontario high school basketball coach who returned home from a road game very late on a Saturday evening to find a photograph of his wife and children placed strategically in the bathroom, with a Post-It note attached reading, "Remember us?"

Strategies to Achieve Equity and Fairness

Most men support the idea of gender equity, but few of them are willing to give up anything to achieve it. This resistance has forced equity proponents to ask governments for assistance or to file lawsuits or human rights actions. Governments have been helpful, but they often are slow to respond. Legal actions have been effective, but lawsuits involve costs and/or long-term commitments (see the Reflect on Sports box, "Girls Playing on Boys' Teams: The Justine Blainey Case," p. 238).

Therefore, Donna Lopiano, former executive director of the Women's Sport Foundation (WSF), identified strategic political organization and pressure as the key to achieving gender equity. This involves the development of grass-roots organizations to systematically support and publicize sport programmes for girls and women. As these organizations publicly recognize the achievements of female athletes and their sponsors, more people will see the value of women's sports and join their efforts to achieve equity. The WSF and other organizations have facilitated this process with their resources, and they have been effective in bringing about progressive changes.

Lopiano (1991) also has urged people in sport organizations to use the following strategies to promote gender equity:

- Confront discriminatory practices in your organization and become an advocate for women athletes and female coaches and administrators.
- Insist on fair and open employment practices in your organization.
- Keep track of equity data and have an independent group issue a public "gender equity report card" every three or four years to your organization or programme.
- Learn and educate others about the history of discrimination in sports and how to recognize the subtle forms of discrimination that operate in sports worlds that are male

dominated, male identified, and male centred.
- Object to practices and policies that decrease opportunities for women in sports and inform the media of them.
- When possible, package and promote women's sports as revenue producers, so there will be financial incentives to increase participation opportunities for women.
- Recruit female athletes into coaching by establishing internships and training programmes (see footnote 4).
- Use women's hiring networks when seeking coaches and administrators in sport programmes.
- Create a supportive work climate for women in your organization and establish policies to eliminate sexual harassment.

These are useful suggestions. They emphasize a combination of public relations, political lobbying, pressure, education, and advocacy. They are based on the assumption that increased participation and opportunities for women will not come without struggle and that favourable outcomes depend on organization and persistence. More important, they have already produced varying degrees of change in many organizations. CAAWS is the leading lobbying agency for equity in sports for girls and women in Canada. In their last major campaign, they actively lobbied the federal government to ensure that gender equity was an important part of the new sport policy (2001) and sport legislation (2002; see chapter 13).

Those who use critical and critical feminist theories to study sports in society have argued that gender equity cannot be achieved in contexts that are organized by men who are unwilling to critically assess dominant gender ideology. Therefore, real equity requires cultural and structural changes in existing sports and sport programmes combined with the development of new models of sport participation and sport organizations that acknowledge the values and experiences of women (Birrell, 2000; Nelson,

1998; Theberge, 2000a). This is discussed in the section, "Ideological and Power Issues."

Girls and Women as Agents of Change Some people assume that women are empowered when they play sports and that empowered women become effective agents of gender equity in sports and in society as a whole. Research supports this claim, but only to a point (Eitle and Eitle, 2002; Stoelting, 2004).

Sport participation does provide girls and women with opportunities to connect with the power of their bodies. This is important, because social life sometimes is organized to encourage girls and women to see themselves as weak, dependent, and powerless. Additionally, many images of women in society present the female body as an object to be viewed, evaluated, and consumed, and girls and women learn to objectify their bodies as they view and assess themselves through the eyes of others (Fredrickson and Harrison, 2005; Young, 1990). Because identity and a personal sense of power are partly grounded in one's body and body image, sport participation can help women overcome the feeling that their bodies are objects. Furthermore, the physical skills and strength often gained through sport participation go beyond simply helping a woman to feel fit. They also can make her feel less vulnerable, more competent and independent, and more in control of her physical safety and psychological well-being (see Blinde et al., 1994; Chastain, 2004; Ference and Muth, 2004; Frederickson and Harrison, 2005; Pelak, 2002, 2005; Roth and Basow, 2004; Theberge, 2000a; Wedgewood, 2004).

Empowerment does not occur automatically when a girl or woman plays sports, nor is a sense of empowerment always associated with a desire or an ability to actively promote fairness and equity issues in sports and other spheres of life. Feeling competence as an athlete does not guarantee that women will critically assess gender ideology and gender relations or work for fairness and equity in sports or society at large.

For example, some female athletes express negative attitudes toward the idea of feminism, and they distance themselves from social activism related to women's issues. In other words, those who play elite-level sports are not likely to be "boat rockers" critical of the gender order (McClung and Blinde, 1998; Young and White, 1995). There are four possible reasons for this:

1. Female athletes may feel that they have much to lose if they are associated with civil and human rights issues for women, because others might identify them as ungrateful or marginalize them by tagging them with labels such as *radical*, *feminist*, or *lesbian* (Crosset, 1995).
2. The corporation-driven "celebrity feminism" promoted through media sports today focuses on individualism and consumption rather than everyday struggles faced by ordinary girls and women who want to play sports but are also concerned with obtaining child care, health care, and a decent job (Cole, 2000b).
3. The "empowerment discourses" associated with fitness and sports often emphasize self-empowerment through physical changes that enhance feminine beauty (Eskes et al., 1998; MacNeill, 1999; Smith, 2002); they do not emphasize social or cultural changes.
4. Female athletes, even those with high media profiles and powerful bodies, have little control over their own sport participation and little political voice in sports or society as a whole (Lowe, 1998).

Similarly, women hired and promoted into leadership positions in major sport organizations are expected to promote power and performance sports in society. The men who control many sport organizations are usually not eager to hire women who put *women's issues* on the same level as *sport issues*. Of course, not all female leaders become uncritical cheerleaders for power and performance approaches to sports, and society.

However, it takes effort and courage to critically analyze sports and use one's power to actually change the culture and structure of sports. But, without this effort and courage, gender inequities tend to persist.

Boys and Men as Agents of Change Gender equity is not just a women's issue. Equity also involves creating options for boys and men to play sports that are not based exclusively on a power and performance model. Sports that emphasize aggression and domination often encourage orientations and actions that lead to chronic injuries, an inability to relate to women, fears of intimacy with other men, homophobia, and a compulsive concern with comparing oneself with other men in terms of what might be called "life success scores" (Burstyn, 1999; White and Young, 1997).

Sports privilege men over women, but they also privilege some men over others. When men realize that some sports constitute cultural contexts that constrain and distort their relationships with one another and with women, they are more inclined to view sports critically. Bruce Kidd (1987), a former Olympic runner and now a physical educator and social scientist at the University of Toronto, used his experience to suggest that:

> Through sports, men learn to cooperate with,
> care for, and love other men, in [many] ways, but
> they rarely learn to be intimate with each other or
> emotionally honest. On the contrary, the only way
> many of us express fondness for other men is by
> teasing or mock fighting. (p. 259)

Men who want to move beyond an expression of fondness based on teasing and mock fighting have good reason to join with those women concerned with critically assessing dominant sport forms in their society (Anderson, 2005; Pronger, 1999).

IDEOLOGICAL AND POWER ISSUES

Ideology often is so deeply rooted in our social worlds that we seldom think about it and almost never raise questions about it. We take it for granted and use it as a form of "cultural logic" to make sense of the world. This is especially the case with gender ideology.

Gender is a central organizing principle of social life, and gender ideology influences how we think of ourselves and others, how we relate to others, and how social life is organized at all levels, from families to societies. It influences what we wear, how we walk, how we present ourselves to others, and how we think about and plan for our future. Most people take gender ideology as a "given" in their lives; they do not question it because it is so deeply rooted in their psyches and the way they live their lives.

The tendency to ignore ideology is a serious problem when we deal with gender equity in sports. The achievement of equity requires changes in the gender ideology that has been used to organize, play, and make sense of sports. The following sections critically examine the prevailing gender ideology in society, its effects on our lives, its connection with sports, and some strategies for changing it as well as how power is distributed in sports.

Gender Ideology in Society

Gender ideology varies from culture to culture. In most societies where men have been privileged in terms of legal status, formal authority, political and economic power, and access to resources, gender ideology is based on a *simple binary classification model*. According to this model, all people are classified into one of two **sex categories**: *male* or *female* (see figure 8.2). These categories are defined in biological terms, and they are conceptualized to highlight difference and opposition; they are commonly defined as "opposite sexes." All people in the male category are believed to be naturally different from all people in the female category, and they are held to different normative expectations when it comes to feelings, thoughts, and actions. These expectations outline the basis for how

SIDELINES

©1982 M.T.F.-T.W.S.-Lakewood. CO

FIGURE 8.2 Women traditionally have been expected to play support roles for men in sports, as well as in society at large. This is changing, but these roles are still present in the gendered social structure of many societies.

people define and identify **gender**—that is, *what is considered masculine and what is considered feminine in a group or society*. This classification and interpretation model is so central to the way many people see the world that they resist thinking about gender in new ways and they often feel uncomfortable when people do not fit neatly into one sex category or the other.

It takes dedication and hard work to maintain a simple binary classification system, because it is inconsistent with biological evidence showing that anatomy, hormones, chromosomes, and secondary sex characteristics vary in complex ways and cannot simply be divided neatly into two sex categories, one male and one female. As biologist Anne Fausto-Sterling (2000) explains, "A body's sex is simply too complex. There is no either/or. Rather, there are shades of difference" (p. 3). Real bodies have physiological and biological traits, which are distributed along continua related to these dimensions of biochemistry and appearance.

This natural sexual variation does not fit with a binary classification system. Therefore, when people are born with physical traits that do not

fit our definitions of *male* and *female*, genitals and reproductive organs usually are surgically "fixed" to make them fit (Fausto-Sterling, 2000).

Hormones vary from one person to the next, and both men and women have testosterone and estrogen in their bodies. However, testosterone is identified as a "male hormone" and estrogen as a "female hormone." This way of thinking about and referring to hormones is misleading, but it enables people to maintain their two-category gender classification model without asking critical questions about it.

Even chromosomal patterns do not always fit neatly into two distinct categories. Nor do secondary sex characteristics, which vary greatly. But we do our best to cover variations with sex-appropriate clothes and forms of body management that highlight characteristics that identify us as male or female. Most people spend considerable time, energy, and money to ensure that their physical characteristics and appearance fit general expectations based on the two-category gender classification model. Those who ignore these expectations risk being marginalized or treated as if they are "out of gender bounds" (Fenstermaker and West, 2002). A woman who does not remove natural hair growth above her upper lip or on other parts of her body, or a slender man with "fine" features who does not avoid wearing clothes defined as effeminate, risks ridicule in many situations.

Physical variation is real, and to say that all variation can be reduced to two separate and "opposite" categories forces biology to fit socially constructed definitions of what males and females are supposed to be in physical terms (Butter, 2004).

Being "Out of Bounds": A Problem for Gays and Lesbians

Another problem created by a binary classification model is that the model comes with relatively fixed ideas and expectations about how men and women are each supposed to think, feel,

Developing physical skills often improves health and provides girls and women with a sense of empowerment. This is true for Reshma, a seven-year-old in Dhaka, Bangladesh. But if the culture and social structure in Bangladesh do not provide Reshma with opportunities to express her sense of empowerment as a woman, beating all the boys in this race will not enable her to participate in society as they will when they become adults. [Photo courtesy of The Hunger Project; www.thp.org/]

and act. These ideas and expectations emphasize *difference*, and they are the foundation for gender. A binary gender classification model is based on the assumption that heterosexuality is natural and normal and that those who express feelings, thoughts, and actions that do not fit neatly into the two socially constructed categories of masculine and feminine are "out of bounds" when it comes to gender (review figure 8.3).

When gender ideology is based on this classification model, many people, including gay men, lesbians, bisexuals, and transsexuals do not fit into either of the two categories, so they usually are defined as "deviant." A two-category model

provides no legitimate social space or recognition for those who are neither heterosexual males nor heterosexual females. This, in turn, serves as a foundation for **homophobia,** *a general fear and/ or intolerance felt for those who are "out of bounds" in the classification model.*

Power in Society: Gender Ideology in Action

Another important aspect of a binary classification model is that the two categories are seldom equal. As represented in figure 8.3, males have access to higher levels of privilege, power, and influence than females, and men occupy the highest levels of power and influence in greater numbers than women. However, there is a social and personal cost that comes with access to and possession of power.

When a two-category gender classification model exists in cultures that emphasize equal rights and freedom of expression, the accepted range of feelings, thoughts, and behaviours for men often is more restricted than it is for women. This means that the normative boundaries associated with masculinity are more restrictive and more closely regulated than the normative boundaries associated with femininity. Masculine characteristics are believed to be consistent with positions of power and influence; therefore, men have more to lose collectively if they do not conform to gender expectations. This is why men strictly police their gender boundaries and sanction those who push or move outside them. Women, on the other hand, have less to lose and more to gain if they push boundaries, although they must do so carefully.

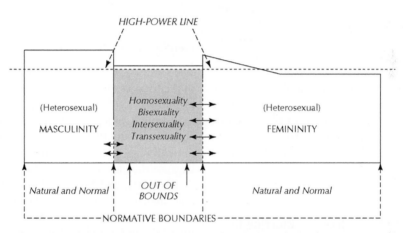

Note: Heterosexual masculinity and heterosexual femininity are depicted as separate, nonoverlapping categories. Each has clearly marked normative boundaries that limit what is defined as normal. The "FEMININITY" category is wider than the "MASCULINITY" category because girls and women have more latitude in what they can do without being out of bounds. Other forms of sexuality are in a grey area that many people define as being outside the normative boundaries of the two gender categories widely perceived as "natural." People in this grey area include lesbians, gay men, bisexuals, the intersexed, and transsexuals.

The short double arrows (↔) indicate two processes: (1) movement into and out of the categories of heterosexual male and female and (2) efforts to push normative boundaries to make space for different expressions of masculinity and femininity, create new sexual categories, or to transcend sexual categories by making them socially irrelevant.

The "high-power line" indicates that heterosexual men are more likely to occupy high-power and influential positions, such as heads of state, Members of Parliament, CEOs, and top-level leaders and decision makers in religious organizations, education, media, and sports. The high-power line can also be viewed as a representation of the "glass ceiling" for women, although a few women have cracked through it in certain spheres of social life.

FIGURE 8.3   The two-category gender classification model: a representation of gender construction in Canadian culture.

What this means in everyday life is that men have less social permission to express the feelings, thoughts, and actions associated with femininity than women have to express the feelings, thoughts, and actions associated with masculinity. This is why boys are teased for being "sissies," while girls are often praised for being "tomboys"; it is also why male ballet dancers and interior designers are less likely to be socially accepted in society than are women wrestlers and women in Parliament (Laberge and Albert, 1999).

To demonstrate this point, ask the women in a gender-mixed group how many of them have bought clothing for themselves in a men's store or the men's section of a department store; most will say they have done so. Then ask the men how many of them have bought clothing for themselves in a women's store or the women's section of a department store, and listen to the laughter caused by the tension of even thinking about the question! The responses illustrate that men face more restrictive normative boundaries related to gender. However, the payoff for men is that they have more access to power, although some men have more access than others.

Challenging Gender Ideology: Blurring the Old Boundaries

A binary classification model has socially constructed normative boundaries. However, not everyone accepts or conforms to them. The double arrows in figure 8.3 represent efforts by men and women to push, erase, pass through, and revise normative boundaries. Of course, women do more pushing and passing through than men, although there are potential costs associated with challenging gender boundaries (i.e., "gender bending"). However, as boundary pushers and crossers raise issues that promote revised definitions of *masculinity* and *femininity*, the normative boundaries for women and men change. Change comes slowly though because most people have vested interests in the two-category gender classification model. After all,

they have learned to use the model as a guide for perceiving and making sense of themselves, their relationships, and the world around them.

For example, when Annika Sorenstam became the first woman to compete on the traditionally male-only PGA Tour, a PGA golfer felt threatened and declared, "I'll do what men do, and she should do what women do" (*Newsweek*, 2004, p. 122). After Sorenstam beat him by three strokes, his assumptions about sex differences and male superiority were shown to be wrong (although he could use football to maintain his ideas about gender and male superiority) (Caudwell, 2003; Messner, 1992).

Gender Ideology in Sports

Ideas and beliefs about gender are a crucial part of the foundation on which sports are organized, promoted, and played. Sports are sites for reaffirming beliefs about male–female *difference* and valourizing masculine characteristics. At the same time, women's sports are often marginalized because they are not seen as "real" or as good as men's sports, and female athletes sometimes are marginalized or seen as "deviant" because they violate femininity norms. Sports are also sites for challenging and revising gender ideology, a fact that makes gender interesting to study when trying to understand sports in society.

Celebrating Masculinity Gender is not fixed in nature. Therefore, gender logic grounded in a binary classification model can be preserved only if people work hard to police gender boundaries and maintain them through myths, rituals, and everyday cultural practices. People must "do" gender to keep the model viable, and the model is most effectively maintained when gender categories become embodied dimensions of people's lives—that is, they are built into the way people move and experience the world with and through their bodies (Fenstermaker and West, 2002). This is how and why sports become important in connection with gender (Messner, 2002).

Sports have been important sites and activities for preserving gender ideology in most cultures. The meaning of gender and its application in people's lives have been symbolized and powerfully presented in the bodily performances that occur in sports. Men's achievements in power and performance sports have been used as evidence of men's aggressive nature, their superiority over women, and their rights to claim social and physical space as their own. Sociologist Doug Hartmann explains the issue:

> [Sport] makes male advantages and masculine values appear so normal and "natural" that they can hardly be questioned. Therein may lie the key to the puzzle connecting men and the seemingly innocent world of sports: they fit together so tightly, so seamlessly that they achieve their effects—learning to be a man, male bonding, male authority, and the like—without seeming to be doing anything more than tossing the ball or watching a Sunday afternoon game. (2003a, p. 20)

Hartmann's words help us understand why Bruce Kidd (1987) describes sports stadiums, particularly the Sky-Dome, (now the Rogers Centre) as "men's cultural centres." These facilities, often built with public funds, host events that present manhood based on aggression, physical power, and the ability to intimidate and dominate others. A major league baseball coach emphasized this when he was asked about the orientations of male professional athletes. He stated that "the bottom line is… you're dealing with the male ego. It's not just about winning… It's about dominating" (Armstrong, 2000, p. 3D). In this way, sports reproduce a gender ideology that privileges the interests of men and favours a particular form of manhood.

Canadian political scientist Varda Burstyn (1999) explains that the major men's sports in most societies provide people with a vocabulary

> I shudder to think what would have happened to the Canadian World War II effort if we had depended on track and swimming participants instead of mannish hockey players.
>
> —Stan Obodiac, in *Toronto Telegram*, June 7, 1970

and a set of stories that erase diverse and contradictory masculinities and present a homogenized manhood in which the heroic warrior is the model of a real man. For example, when television sports announcers give special recognition to a male athlete, they often refer to him as "a warrior."

Girls and Women as Invaders When girls and women play certain sports, they are seen to be invaders of male turf. This is why they have been excluded from some sports (Theberge, 2002), at the same time they have been encouraged to play sports that emphasize grace, beauty, and coordination. Through most of the twentieth century, this exclusion was rationalized by physicians and educators, who told women that, if they played strenuous sports they would damage their uteruses and breasts and experience other physical problems endangering their abilities to give birth and nurture their children (Coakley, 1990). Today's students laugh at these myths from the past, because they have information that refutes them. However, it has taken many years to refute the myths and challenge traditional gender ideology. Unfortunately, myths continue to be widely believed in cultures where literacy rates are low and men control the production and distribution of knowledge.

The legacy of traditional gender ideology has not disappeared, even in postindustrial societies (McGarry, 2005). U.S. journalist Joan Ryan (1995) writes about this in women's gymnastics and figure skating:

> Talent counts, but so do beauty, class, weight, clothes and politics. The anachronistic lack of ambivalence about femininity in both sports is part of their attraction, harkening back to a simpler time when girls were girls, when women were girls for that matter: coquettish, malleable, eager to please. In figure skating especially, we want our athletes

thin, graceful, deferential and cover-girl pretty. We want eyeliner, lipstick and hair ribbons. (p. 5)

Living with this gender ideology is not easy. When U.S. women's figure skating champion Tara Lipinski was fifteen years old and training for the 1998 Nagano Olympics, she said that her most difficult challenge was maintaining the strength and power needed to do seven triple jumps in a routine while still looking cute, soft, and feminine. Trying to meet that challenge has forced many female athletes to play by rules that lead to serious injuries. Lipinski, for example, suffered a serious hip injury that forced her to retire before she was twenty years old—but she looked cute when she went down with the injury.

Many girls and women have challenged traditional gender ideology, and gender boundaries for females have been revised as a result. However, remnants of old boundaries continue to exist. For example, as girls enter their teens and their bodies are sexualized in terms of traditional gender ideology, they still hear powerful cultural messages that being a tomboy may interfere with meeting expectations for heterosexual attractiveness, lifestyles, and self-presentation. Playing most sports is widely accepted today, but the cuteness of being a tomboy still begins to fade during adolescence. If young female athletes do not conform to dominant definitions of *femininity*, they may experience certain forms of social rejection, or less credit than they deserve.

Traditional gender ideology is reproduced in many men's sports. Some of those sports inspire fantasies and symbols of a heroic manhood, in which playing the role of warrior becomes the substance of being a man. Do these fantasies and symbols influence how boys define *masculinity*? [CP(Jacques Boissinot)]

FOREVER "LADIES"?

Female athletes deal with the consequences of traditional gender ideology in various ways (Cox and Thompson, 2000; Harris, 2005; Krane et al., 2004). For example, those who play contact and power sports sometimes discover that, unless they are seen as "ladylike" (sometimes referred to as "emphasized femininity," cf., Theberge, 2000a), the *tomboy* label may change to *lesbian*. Therefore, they sometimes try to be more feminine by wearing hair ribbons, ponytails, makeup, dresses, tights, heels, or engagement or wedding rings; by saying how they like to party with heterosexuals in heterosexual clubs; and by making statements about boyfriends or husbands and their desire to eventually settle down and have children (Mennesson, 2000). In the absence of these heterosexualized "femininity insignias," some people define women in contact and power sports as threats to their ideas about "nature" and morality. This illustrates how the two-category gender classification model fuels homophobia in sports and the lives of female athletes (Griffin, 1998).

The pressure to be "forever ladies" was intensified in the mid-1960s through the late 1990s when many international sport events, including the Olympics, demanded that female competitors take "gender tests" to prove that they were women (see www.pponline.co.uk/encyc/0082.htm). The assumption was that, if they were really good at sports, they might not be real women! At first, the female athletes were required to present themselves, naked, to a panel of doctors. But the all-male IOC decided that for the 1968 Olympics in Mexico City they would use a Barr-body chromosome test to establish the gender of female athletes. Each competitor had cells scraped from the inside of her cheek so that a testing lab could determine of she had a female (XX) chromosome profile. Chromosome profiles do not always match the socially constructed two-gender classification model used by IOC officials. For example, some people with only one X chromosome grow up as females, others have two X chromosomes and one Y and grow up as men, and there are "XX males and XY females whose sex doesn't match their chromosomes" (Lehrman, 1997). This meant that some athletes who had lived their lives as women failed the Barr-body test and were disqualified from the Olympics. This surprised the parents and friends of the athletes who knew that they were women.

Most female athletes objected to gender testing, and the tests were eliminated by most international sport organizations in the 1990s. However, all 3,500 female athletes at the Olympic Games in Atlanta were required to take the Barr-body test or show their "fem card" from a previous test certifying that they were "real" women. The IOC continued testing through 1999, but dropped it before the 2000 Sydney Games in response to the protests and research that challenged the test's

> Gender is much more than a biochemical construct. It's bizarre to think you can determine whether someone is male or female based on [lab] tests.
>
> —Andrew Pipe, former president of the Canadian Academy of Sports Medicine and chair of the Canadian Centre for Ethics in Sport (in Lehrman, 1997)

validity (although the IOC maintains the right to impose "random" tests).

SPORTS AS SITES FOR CHANGE

Although female athletes still live with the consequences of traditional gender ideology and homophobia, their achievements have challenged certain ideas and beliefs and encouraged many people to think in new ways about masculinity, femininity, and gender relations (Theberge, 2000a). When this occurs, women's sports are important sites for pushing the normative boundaries of *femininity*. For example, author Leah Cohen points out that "any girl who boxes challenges, unwittingly or not, the idea of what it means to be a girl in our culture" (2005, p. xiii). In some cases, female athletes even encourage people to raise questions about the validity of the two-category gender classification model and rethink the meaning of gender in society. For example, in 2004, IOC executive board members revised their thinking about gender when they approved a proposal to allow athletes who have undergone sex change operations to participate in the Olympics (Hui, 2004). The athletes must have had their new gender legally recognized and had post-operative hormone therapy for at least two years. Although this decision assumes a two-gender classification model, it recognizes that gender is changeable. This is a significant change that now applies worldwide in international sports.

Gender Ideology: The Challenge of Being Gay or Lesbian in Sports

When a two-category gender classification system is used to define *gender*, the identities and actions of gay men, lesbians, bisexuals, and transsexuals (GLBTs) are outside of normative boundaries (refer to figure 8.3, p. 247). Therefore, GLBTs are sometimes feared, marginalized, or seen as oddities or sinners.

Discussions about the identities and lives of those who live outside boundaries established in connection with a two-gender classification model sometimes evoke strong emotions, defensive reactions, and moral judgments. Exceptions to this exist when people do not accept such a model or define *gender* in normative terms that reflect the reality of people's lives (see figure 8.4).

The same is true in sports. GLBTs play sports but they are seldom recognized. When discussions do occur, many people express ambivalence, mixed feelings, and inconsistencies. For example, a 2005 survey in the United States indicated that 78 percent of the respondents in a nationally representative sample agreed that, "It is OK for gay athletes to participate in sports, even if they are open about their sexuality" (NBC/USA Network, 2005). But about one in four said that openly gay athletes would hurt their teams and sport and would cause them as

fans to enjoy the sport less and care less about the athletes. Additionally, about 40 percent of youth sport coaches and 20 percent of university and professional coaches thought it is inappropriate for homosexuals to work in sports.

Acceptance of GLBTs has increased in society as a whole *and* in sports (Anderson, 2000, 2002, 2005). Today, there are teams and sport programmes in which GLBTs are accepted and supported by heterosexual athletes and coaches, and there are more teams and programmes exclusively for those with sexualities that are not heterosexual (Elling et al., 2003). But significant challenges remain for both lesbian and gay athletes, and even when acceptance occurs, it is defined in terms set by heterosexual athletes, not terms preferred by gay and lesbian athletes (Anderson, 2002). Therefore, many GLBT athletes remain closeted, pass as heterosexual, cover their identity, or selectively reveal identity to trusted others and in situations where their sexuality is accepted (Griffin, 1998). Because of different levels of acceptance, identity management strategies often differ between athletes in women's and men's sports.

FIGURE 8.4   Gender ideology is changing. However, when men or women become seriously involved in sports that challenge the two-category gender classification model, some people may tease or discourage them.

Lesbians in sports Acceptance of homosexual, bisexual, and transsexual athletes is greater in women's than men's sports. When the first high-profile female athletes came out as lesbians in the 1980s, they were the focus of praise, hostility, and endless media discussions. When tennis star Martina Navratilova came out, it is estimated that she lost over US$10 million in endorsement contracts—a major price to pay in the 1980s. Today, she receives endorsement offers *because* of her sexuality. As other top-level female athletes come out today, they face short-term media attention, some negative reactions from fans and other athletes, and the personal challenges that most women face when they come out to friends and family (Griffin, 1998). But they are also likely to find people who will support them, even if most corporations are hesitant to sign them to endorsements (Swoopes, 2005). Pat Griffin's groundbreaking book *Strong Women, Deep Closets: Lesbians and Homophobia in Sports* (1998), provides clear evidence that "sports and lesbians have always gone together" (p. ix). She notes that this evidence has been ignored in popular conciousness largely because of cultural myths about lesbians. Although most myths have been challenged and discredited, some remain. For example, some people think that lesbians are predatory and want to "convert" others to their "way of life," which is imagined to be strange, immoral, or downright evil. To the extent that lesbian athletes fear such people, they may turn inward and experience isolation and loneliness. When heterosexual athletes believe these myths or even wonder about their veracity, they avoid lesbian athletes and coaches; when coaches and administrators believe them, they are less likely to hire and promote lesbians in coaching and sport management. For example, there were rumours in the Canadian media before the Nagano Winter Olympics in 1998 of friction on the women's hockey team between coaches and players of different sexualities. After the team won a silver medal, these same rumours were sometimes used to account for why the team had not won gold.

Some women's sports and teams are characterized by a "don't ask, don't tell" atmosphere in which lesbians work to hide their identity so that they may play the sports they love without being marginalized or harassed. However, such a strategy has costs, and it does not encourage changes that might defuse and even eliminate homophobia in women's sports. Ethics educator Pat Griffin (1998) makes a strong case for being open and truthful about sexual identity, but she also notes that open lesbians must be prepared to handle everything from hostility to cautious acceptance when they come out. She notes that handling challenges is easier when friends, teammates, and coaches provide support; when there are local organizations that challenge homophobia and advocate tolerance; and when there is institutionalized legal protection for gays and lesbians in organizations, communities, and society. In Theberge's study of an elite hockey team, both heterosexual and lesbian players agreed that "in the dressing room, we're all hockey players" (2000b, p. 93).

Gay men in sports In men's sports, changes are not as visible as in women's sports. The culture of many sports continues to support a vocabulary of exclusion, marginalization, and homophobia, but this vocabulary does not always predict the response of heterosexual athletes when a teammate comes out (Anderson, 2005; Bull, 2004). Men's sports have always been key sites for reproducing dominant ideas about masculinity. Playing sports has been a rite of passage for boys to become men, and many people define male athletes in contact and power sports as the epitome of what it means to be a heterosexual man in society. Therefore, there is much at stake in maintaining the silence about gay men in sports and in discouraging gay male athletes from revealing their identities. This is necessary to maintain the integrity of existing normative gender boundaries and the privilege that is available to some men as long as the two-gender classification model is widely accepted (Pronger,

1999, 2002). Therefore, men in locker rooms use a vocabulary that reaffirms the norms of heterosexual masculinity. Policing gender boundaries preserves the glorified status of male athletes and men's access to power and influence in society as a whole.

It is due to these issues that the message to boys and men is loud and clear: "Don't be a fag," and "don't play like a girl." The message to gay males of all ages is also clear: "Don't challenge the two-category gender classification model because it works for us men and has given some of us privilege and power in sports and in society." These messages create a combination of commitment to the cult of masculinity and deep fears of homosexuality in men's sports (Anderson, 2005; Tuaolo, 2002).

These messages also create a context in which boys and men feel ashamed about feelings of affection toward other men and feel compelled to mimic violent caricatures of masculinity to avoid being labelled "fags" (Messner, 1996). This maintains (reproduces) the norm that "real" men play with pain and injuries, never confide affectionately in other men, even—or especially—when they care deeply for another man. Instead, connections between male athletes are expressed through bell-ringing head-butts, belly bashes, arm punches, forearm crosses, fist touching, and other ritualistic actions that disguise and belie intimacy. Although, in a challenge to these traditions, it is clear that male hugging is becoming more common.

Stories about gay male athletes are nearly nonexistent; Canadian gay athletes such as Mark Tewksbury (Olympic gold medalist in swimming) and Mark Leduc (Olympic silver medalist in boxing) waited until their competitive careers were over before they "came out." (Tewksbury, 2007). Heterosexual men have kept quiet, even when male coaches have sexually abused them (Donnelly and Sparks, 1997; Nack and Yaeger, 1999; Robinson, 1998); and most men will sacrifice their bodies to maintain the myth that real men are tough, no matter what the consequences (White and Young, 1997).

The power of gender ideology among male athletes is illustrated with a simple example: The first man to come out as gay in a major men's team sport will be guaranteed a place in history. He will be seen as a hero by closeted and openly gay men of all ages. He will be on every talk show on television and radio. His website will receive millions of hits. Corporations that market to the gay demographic will knock his door down with endorsement deals. He will be an overnight celebrity and eventually defined as a hero in the company of Jackie Robinson, Mohammed Ali, and others who stood up for a principle that would later be taken for granted in the culture as a whole.

So why are dozens, even hundreds, of high-profile athletes taking a pass on this status and fame? Research by sociologist Eric Anderson (2005), who in 1993 became the first openly gay male high school coach in the United States, indicates that all male athletes, including gays, have learned to see themselves in strict ideological terms and they conform to the norms of hegemonic masculinity in cultlike ways, even when they would benefit by leaving the cult. This explanation makes sense, and it highlights the point that problems for gay athletes are ultimately grounded in a sport culture organized around a two-category gender classification model. Therefore, solutions rest in finding strategies to change gender ideology in the ways we do sports.

> Being a gay icon is a great honour for me. I'm quite sure of my feminine side.
>
> —David Beckham (in Wahl, 2003)

Strategies for Changing Ideology and Culture

Gender equity in sports ultimately depends on transforming gender ideology, including ideas and beliefs about *masculinity* and *femininity*, and changing the ways we do sports in society. These are complex and challenging tasks.

Alternative Definitions of Masculinity

Dominant gender ideology today normalizes and naturalizes the idea that masculinity involves aggressiveness and a desire to physically dominate others. Men with the power and willingness to do whatever it takes to dominate others are lionized and defined as heroes in sports, business, and politics. Men seen as nurturing and supportive of others are often defined as weak and emasculated.

As boys and men apply this ideology to their lives, they learn to view manhood in terms of things that jeopardize the safety and well-being of themselves and others. They may ride the tops of elevators, drive cars at breakneck speeds, play various forms of "chicken," drink each other under the table, get into fights, use violence in sports as indicators of manhood, use dangerous substances to build muscles, avoid interacting with women as equals, keep sexual scores in heterosexual relationships, and physically control girlfriends and wives. Some men learn that size and toughness allow them to violate norms and control others through fear and physical coercion.

Despite the dangers and socioemotional isolation caused by this ideology, male athletes are seldom criticized for using it to guide their words and actions in sports. Coaches do not make athletes run laps for hitting someone too hard, or showing no feeling when they have blown out someone's knee, knocked someone unconscious, or paralyzed—even killed—an opponent (as in boxing). Instead, coaches want athletes who can hurt others without hesitation or remorse and simply see it "as part of the game." But in the larger social and cultural context, does this ideology destroy men's ability to empathize with others and feel their pain, even the pain of opponents? Does it discourage the development of intimate and supportive relationships with other men or with women? Does it lead to high assault and sexual assault rates in society?

The frightening record of men's violence (e.g., Robinson, 1998) suggests that it would

The legacy of the two-category gender classification system remains strong in many cultures. Pairs figure skating is one example that emphasizes the differences in strength and appearance between men and women. But which athlete in this photo is taking the risks? [CP(Frank Gunn)]

be useful to answer these questions and create new cultural space for alternative definitions of *masculinity*. The dual notion that hormones irrationally drive boys and that "boys will be boys" continues to be closely associated with seriously dangerous actions in many societies around the world (Loy, 1995). If dominant forms of sport in today's society prevent people from questioning and transforming this gender ideology, it is important to critically examine sports in society. However, the dominant forms of sports seem to prevent people from raising questions about gender ideology. The study of sports in society has an important role to play in raising these questions.

***Alternative Definitions of* Femininity** The experiences of many female athletes also suggest a need to develop additional definitions of *femininity*. This process has already begun but requires commitment to maintain. For example, how are girls socialized to avoid objectifying their bodies to the point that they refrain from becoming physically skilled in a wide range of sports? We know that parents and others monitor the bodies and actions of girls more closely than they do for boys, even during infancy. Does this pattern of protectiveness continue through the entire life course and, in the process, limit physical skill development and participation in sports? Research suggests that it does (Fredrickson and Harrison, 2005; Young, 1990). Therefore, alternative definitions of *femininity* are needed. This does not mean that girls and women should become like men as much as they should explore and connect with the power of their bodies across many activities, including competitive sports. In the past, large and/or strong girls and women without conventionally feminine characteristics and mannerisms have challenged the two-gender classification model, and sport seems to be a context for extending this challenge to the point of transforming gender ideology. If this occurs, there will be new femininities that recognize and support more women than are now supported by traditional notions of femininity.

Changing the Way We Do Sports Gender equity involves more than socially constructing new ways to define and perform masculinity and femininity. It also depends on changes in how sports are defined, organized, and played. New and creative sport programmes, new vocabularies to describe those programmes, new images that people can associate with sports, and new ways to evaluate success and enjoyment in sports are the foundation of such changes (Burstyn, 1999; Hargreaves, 2000). When women and men who participate in sports as athletes, coaches, and administrators can critically assess sports and

sport organizations from the inside, changes are more likely to occur (see chapter 15).

One strategy for achieving gender equity is to develop new programmes that change how we do sports. Possibilities include the following:

1. Programmes that promote lifetime sport participation and emphasize combinations of competition and partnership, individual expression and teamwork, and health and skill development
2. Programmes that embody an ethic of care and connection between teammates and opponents (Duquin, 1993)
3. Programmes that provide coaching and administrative opportunities for lesbians, heterosexual women, and gay men, thereby adding new voices in decision-making processes, expanding ideas about the organization and purpose of sports, and opening sports to a wider range of participants
4. Programmes bringing boys and girls, men and women, and heterosexuals and GLBTs together in shared sport experiences that promote new ideas about gender and sports in society

New programmes are useful, but strategies to effect change require that people realize that there may be political challenges associated with them. These include the following:

1. When women's sport programmes are structured differently from men's programmes, it is difficult to determine if there are equal opportunities for girls and women.
2. New sport programmes for girls and women run the risk of being perceived as "second class," thereby perpetuating notions of female inferiority.
3. New sport programmes are difficult to promote, and it is easier to apply pressure for equal resources in schools, universities, and other organizations when asking for

comparable programmes rather than new ones.

4. Sports that do not reproduce dominant gender ideology often are devalued and defined as "not real" and are (under) funded accordingly.

In the long run, gender equity depends on maintaining both approaches simultaneously. This means that changes will occur if those who participate in existing sports can envision and work toward creating alternatives for the future. Likewise, those who envision and favour new sport forms will contribute to changes if they establish credibility and gain access to the power and resources needed to develop new programmes.

All of us participate in ideological and cultural change when we critically assess how we talk about and do sports. This occurs when we do the following:

- Eliminate the language of difference and domination associated with sports and sport participation.
- Refrain from using labels such as *sissy*, *tomboy*, *fag*, and *wimp* in conversations and relationships.
- Object to coaches who motivate young men by telling them to go out and prove their masculinity on the playing field.
- Speak out against language that bashes gays and demeans women.
- Discourage the use of military metaphors that masculinize descriptions of sports (e.g., "throwing long bombs," "he/she is a warrior," "putting in the big guns," and "punishing opponents").

Rule changes in sports are useful strategies to achieve gender equity. For example, rules to restrict violence in hockey, football, rugby, and soccer create contexts where female athletes are more likely to be taken seriously. Men will object to this, saying that such rules make sports into "girls' games," but these comments only reaffirm

that the rules are necessary. Similarly, rules that support rituals that bring opponents together in ways that emphasize partnership rather than hostility and rivalry can provide images that change ideas about the goals and purposes of sports.

As one of the ads in the IOC's Celebrate Humanity series states:

> You are my adversary, but you are not my enemy.
> For your resistance gives me strength, your will
> gives me courage, your
> Spirit ennobles me.
> And though I aim to defeat you, should I succeed
> I will not humiliate you.
> Instead, I will honour you, for without you I am a
> lesser man (sic).

Gender equity depends on seeing and doing sports that reflect the values and experiences of everyone including women and of men who do not identify themselves in terms of the dominant definition of *masculinity*. Therefore, gender equity does not automatically mean that the goal is to have girls and women play sports just as men have played them. Full equity means that people have a wide range of choices when it comes to organizing, playing, and giving meaning to sports.

SUMMARY

DOES EQUITY REQUIRE IDEOLOGICAL CHANGES?

Sport participation among females has increased dramatically since the late 1970s. This is the result of new opportunities, equal rights legislation, the women's movement, the health and fitness movement, and increased publicity given to female athletes.

Despite this trend of increased participation, gender equity is far from being achieved, and future increases in sport participation among girls and women will not be automatic. In fact, there are reasons to be cautious when anticipating changes for the future. These reasons include budget cuts and privatization of sports, resistance to government policies and legislation, backlash in response to changes favouring strong women, a relative lack of female coaches and administrators, a cultural emphasis on cosmetic fitness among women, the trivialization of women's sports, and the existence of homophobia.

More women than ever are playing sports and working in sport organizations, but gender inequities continue to exist in participation opportunities, support for athletes, jobs for women in coaching and administration, and informal and alternative sports. This is because sports have traditionally been organized to be male dominated, male identified, and male centred.

Even when sport participation creates feelings of personal empowerment among women, the achievement of full gender equity is impossible without a critical analysis of the gender ideology used in sports and society as a whole. Critical analysis is important because it gives direction to efforts to achieve equity and it shows that there are reasons for men to join women in trying to achieve equity.

The major point of this chapter is that gender equity in sports is integrally tied to ideology and power issues. Gender equity will never be complete or permanent without changes in how people think about masculinity and femininity and in how sports are organized and played.

Dominant sport forms in society are currently based on a two-category gender classification model, which leads to the conclusion that girls and women are, by definition, inferior to boys and men. The gender ideology based on this classification system includes beliefs about male–female differences that "naturalize" the superiority of men over women and erase the existence of gay men, lesbians, bisexuals, and transsexuals from cultural images about sports and athletes. Therefore, sports celebrate a form of masculinity that marginalizes women and many men. As this form of masculinity is celebrated through sports, sexism and homophobia are built right into the structure of sports and sport organizations.

When gender ideology and sports are organized around the values and experiences of heterosexual men, real and lasting gender equity depends on changing dominant definitions of masculinity and femininity and the way we do sports. Useful strategies include developing new sports and sport organizations, and changing existing sports from the inside and through outside actions and pressure.

Changes also depend on strategies such as these: using new ways to talk about sports, developing new rules to control violence and injuries and foster safety for all players, and creating new rituals and orientations based on the pleasure and participation approach to sports rather than the power and performance approach. Unless gender ideology and sports change, gender equity will never be completely and permanently achieved. This is why those interested in gender equity in sports should be interested also in gender and gender-relations outside of sports.

Visit *Sports in Society*'s **Online Learning Centre at www.mcgrawhill.ca/olc/coakley for additional information, website resources, and study tools for this chapter.**

[Arthur Tilley/Taxi/Getty Images]

Race and Ethnicity

Are they important in sports?

The challenge in sports in the 21st century is going to be diversity.

—**Harry Edwards, sociologist/activist (2000)**

What if Wayne Gretzky's grandfather had decided not to emigrate from Russia?

—**Paul Quarrington, author (1988)**

Canadian Wins Gold Medal.
Jamaican-Canadian Accused of Steroid Use.
Jamaican Stripped of Gold Medal.

—**Frank Edwards, cartoonist, captioning Ben Johnson controversy (1988)**

It's a vast country, so that inspires you. It's also the greatest hotel on earth: It welcomes people from everywhere. It's a good country to write from because in many ways Canada is the world.

—**Yann Martel, author (2002)**

Canada is today the most successful pluralist society on the face of the globe, without any doubt in my mind. . . . That is something unique to Canada. It is an amazing global asset.

—**Aga Khan IV, Imam of the Shia Ismaili Muslims (2002)**

Sports involve complex issues related to race and ethnicity. These issues have increasing social relevance as global migration and political changes bring together people from different racial and ethnic backgrounds and create new challenges for living, working, and playing together. The challenges created by racial and ethnic diversity are among the most important ones we will face in the twenty-first century (Edwards, 2000).

Ideas and beliefs about race and ethnicity influence self-perception, social relationships, and the organization of social life. Sports reflect this influence and are sites where people challenge or reproduce racial ideologies and existing patterns of racial and ethnic relations in society. As people make sense of sports and give meaning to their experiences as athletes and spectators, and the experiences of others, they often take into account skin colour and ethnicity.

Not surprisingly, the social meanings and the experiences associated with skin colour and ethnic background influence access to sport participation, decisions about playing sports, and the way that people integrate sports into their lives. People in some racial and ethnic groups use sport participation to express their cultural identity and evaluate their potential as athletes. In some cases, people are identified and evaluated as athletes because of the meanings given to their skin colour or ethnic background.

Sports are also cultural sites where people formulate or change their ideas and beliefs about skin colour and ethnic heritage and then use them as they think about and live other parts of their lives. This means that sports are more than mere reflections of racial and ethnic relations in society and why it is important to study them if we want to understand the dynamics of racial and ethnic relations in society.

This chapter focuses on the following topics:

1. Definitions of *race, ethnicity,* and *minority group,* as well as the origins of ideas about race in contemporary cultures

2. Racial classification systems and the influence of racial ideology in sports
3. Racial and ethnic relations in Canada
4. The dynamics of racial and ethnic relations[1] in Canadian sports
5. The challenges of racial and ethnic relations in Canadian sports

DEFINING *RACE, ETHNICITY,* AND *MINORITY*

Discussions about race and ethnicity are confusing when people do not define their terms. In this chapter, **race** refers to *a population of people who are believed to be naturally or biologically distinct from other populations.* When people identify a racial population, they use or infer a classification system that divides all human beings into distinct categories, which are believed to share genetically based physical traits passed from one generation to the next. Therefore, race involves a reference to physical traits, but it is ultimately based on a socially constructed classification system that people develop around the meanings that they give to particular traits (see the section "The Origins of Race and Racial Ideologies" for further explanation).

Ethnicity is different from race in that it refers to *a particular cultural heritage that is used to identify a category of people.* Ethnicity is *not* based on biology or genetically determined traits; instead, it is based on cultural traditions and history. This means that an **ethnic population** *is a category of people regarded as socially distinct because they share a way of life, a collective history, and a sense of themselves as a people.* In an immigrant society such as Canada, ethnicity is also related to a person's national origin such that people may

[1]The term "relations" is not used here in the organizational sense of promoting good relations between groups, but in the sociological sense of exploring the ways in which groups stand in relation to one another, especially in terms of power.

be seen as, for example, "Italians," ignoring both their diversity and the fact that they may have been born in Canada.

Confusion sometimes occurs when people use the term *minority* as they talk about racial and ethnic populations. In sociological terms, a **minority** is *a socially identified population that suffers disadvantages due to systematic discrimination and has a strong sense of social togetherness based on shared experiences of past and current discrimination.* Therefore, all minorities are *not* racial or ethnic populations, and all racial and ethnic populations are *not* minorities. For example, whites in Canada often are identified as a race, but they would not be a minority unless another racial or ethnic population had the power to subject them to systematic discrimination, which would put the population as a whole at a collective disadvantage in Canadian society. Similarly, people of Ukranian heritage in Alberta are considered an ethnic population, but they are not a minority. An additional complication in Canada is the use of the term **visible minority** to refer to *racial minority groups who are identifiably different, often by skin colour, from the majority group.*[2]

Chinese Canadians often are referred to as a race because of the special meanings that people have given to skin colour in Canada; additionally, Chinese Canadians are referred to as an ethnic group because of their shared cultural heritage. This has led many people to use *race* and *ethnicity* interchangeably without acknowledging that one is based on a classification of physical traits and the other on the existence of a shared culture. Many sociologists avoid this confusion because

they realize that "race" has always been based on the social meanings that people have given to physical traits. These meanings, they say, have been so influential in society that shared ways of life have developed around them. Therefore, the focus in sociology today is on ethnicity rather than race, except when sociologists study the social consequences of the ideologies that have been organized around the idea of race.

This information about race is confusing to many people in Canada because they have been socialized to take for granted that race is a biological reality. To be told that race is based on social meanings rather than biological facts is difficult to understand. This issue is clarified in the next section.

THE ORIGINS OF RACE AND RACIAL IDEOLOGIES

Human diversity is a fact of life, and people throughout history have always categorized one another, often using physical appearance and cultural characteristics to do so. However, the idea that there are distinct, identifiable races is a recent invention. Europeans developed it during the seventeenth century as they explored the world and encountered people who looked and lived unlike anyone they had ever known. As they colonized regions on nearly every continent, Europeans developed classification systems to distinguish the populations that they encountered. They used the term *race* very loosely to refer to people with particular religious beliefs (Hindus), language or ethnic traditions (the Basque people in Spain), histories (indigenous peoples such as New World "Indians" and "Aborigines"), national origins (Chinese), and social status (chronically poor people such as Rroma in Europe or Dalits in India).

Ideas about race emerged from religious beliefs, scientific theories, and a combination of political and economic goals (Omi and Winant, 1994).

---

[2]As noted subsequently, Native Canadians are not considered to be "visible minorities" in Canadian law. Of course, even the designation "Native Canadian" is full of complications because, even in the simplest of terms, this designation refers to status and non-status "Indians" from various tribal populations, and Inuit and Métis peoples. The term "First Nations" is used to correspond with the constitutional terminology regarding "two founding peoples."

However, people have gradually come to use the term *race* to identify populations that they believe are naturally or biologically distinct from other populations. This shift to a biology-based notion of race occurred as light-skinned people from northern Europe sought justification for colonizing and exercising power over people of colour around the world. Intellectuals and early scientists facilitated this shift by developing "objective" racial classification frameworks that enabled them to "discover" dozens of races, sub-races, collateral races, and collateral sub-races—terms they used as they analyzed the physical variations of people in colonized territories and other regions of the world.

"Scientific" analyses combined with the observations and anecdotes told by explorers led to the development of racial ideologies. As noted in chapter 1, **racial ideology** consists of *a web of ideas and beliefs that people use to give meaning to specific physical traits such as skin colour and to evaluate people in terms of how they are classified by race.* The racial classification models developed in Europe were based on the assumption that the appearance and actions of white Europeans were normal and that deviations from normal were strange, primitive, or immoral. In this way, "whiteness" became the standard against which the appearance and actions of *others* ("those people") were measured and evaluated.

Between the seventeenth and early twentieth centuries, whites used this racial ideology to conclude that people of colour around the world were primitive beings driven by brawn rather than brains, instincts rather than moral codes, and impulse rather than rationality. This in turn enabled whites to colonize and subsequently exploit, subjugate, enslave, and even murder dark-skinned peoples without guilt or the sense that they had sinned (Hoberman, 1992; Smedley, 1997, 1999; Winant, 2001). Racial ideology also led some whites to view people of colour as pagans in need of spiritual salvation. They worked to "civilize" and save souls, and in the process dark-skinned people came to be known as "the white man's burden." Over time, these racial ideologies were widely accepted, and whites used them to connect skin colour with other traits including intelligence, character, and physical characteristics and skills.

Research since the 1950s has produced increasing evidence that the concept of race is not biologically valid (Omi and Winant, 1994). This point has received powerful support from the Human Genome Project, which demonstrates that external traits such as skin colour, hair texture, and eye shape are not genetically linked with patterns of internal differences among human beings. We now know that there is more biological diversity within any one human population than there is, on average, between any two populations, no matter how different they seem on the surface (AAA, 1998; Williams, 2005). Noted anthropologist Audrey Smedley (2003) explains that the idea of race has had a powerful impact on history and society, but it has little to do with real biological diversity among human beings. This is because it is based on categories and classifications that people have developed for social and political reasons. Therefore, race is a myth based on socially created ideas about variations in human potential and abilities that are assumed to be biological.

This conclusion is surprising to most people in Canada because they have learned to "see" race as a fact of life and use it to sort people into what they believe to be biology-based racial categories. They have also used ideas and beliefs about race to make sense of the world and their experiences. This is because racial ideology is so rooted in Canadian culture that many people see race as an unchangeable fact of nature that cannot be ignored when it comes to understanding human beings, forming social relationships, and organizing social worlds.

When racial ideology is put aside, we see that definitions of race and approaches to racial classification vary widely across cultures and over time. Thus, a person classified as black in Canada would not be considered to be "black" in Brazil, Haiti, Egypt, or South Africa where approaches to racial classification are different. For example, Yannick Noah, a French pop singer and former professional tennis player, is classified as white in Cameroon because his mother is a light-skinned woman from France, but he is classified as black in France because his father is a dark-skinned man from Cameroon. Brazilians use over one hundred different terms when asked to identify their race. Less than 5 percent of Brazilians classify themselves as black, even though people in Canada would say that half of all Brazilians are black according to the way they define race. These cultural and historical variations indicate that race is a social construction instead of an objective, unchanging biological fact.

Another trouble with race is that racial classification models involve making racial distinctions related to *continuous traits* such as skin colour and other physical traits that exist in all people. Height is a good example of a continuous physical trait: Everyone has some height, and height varies along a continuum from the shortest person in the world to the tallest. But if we wanted to classify all human beings into particular height categories, we would have to decide where and how many lines we should draw along the height continuum. To do this, we would have to form social agreements about the meanings we wanted to give to various heights. Therefore, in some societies a 180-cm tall man would be classified as tall, whereas "tall" in other societies might mean 200 centimetres or more. To make classification matters more complicated, people in particular societies sometimes change over time their ideas about what they consider to be short or tall, as Canadians did through the twentieth century. Additionally, evidence clearly shows that the average height of people in different societies changes over time as diets, lifestyles, and height preferences change, even though height is a physical, genetically based trait for individuals (Bilger, 2004). This is why the Japanese now have an average height nearly the same as Canadians, and northern Europeans have surpassed Canadians in average height.

Skin colour also is a continuous physical trait. It varies from *snow white* at one end of the skin colour continuum to *midnight black* on the other, with an infinite array of colour shades in between. When skin colour is used to identify racial categories, the lines drawn between races are based on the meanings that are given to skin colour by the people who are doing the classifying. Therefore, the identification of races is based on social agreements about where and how many racial dividing lines to draw; it is not based on objective biological division points. For example, racial classification in the United States was traditionally based on the "one-drop rule." This meant that a person with any black ancestor was classified as "Negro" (black) and could not be considered white in legal terms even if he or she appeared to be white. The trouble with using legal definitions such as the "one-drop rule," or other socially constructed racial categories, is that they hide diversity and also hide the various heritages of "mixed-race" people. For example, when golfer Tiger Woods was identified as "black," he said he was "Cablinasian"—a term he invented to explain that he is one-fourth Thai, one-fourth Chinese, one-fourth African American, one-eighth Native American, and one-eighth white European (*Ca*ucasian + *Bl*ack + *In*dian + *Asi*an). Mixed-race persons in sports are constantly described as black even though a parent or multiple grandparents are not of African heritage. Similarly, describing a person as "Asian," for example, also loses sight of enormous diversity—even if we use qualifiers such a "East" Asian or "South" Asian. Thus, the enormous diversity of Japan, Korea, all of the various regions of China, Southeast Asia, the Indian subcontinent, and Western parts of Asia are lost when a person is referred to as "Asian."

To say that race is a social construction does not deny the existence of physical variations between human populations. This is obvious to all of us. However, when scientists have identified biologically meaningful variations, such as those related to disease or responses to drugs, they do not fit into the skin colour–based

Tiger Woods is only one-fourth African American, yet he is often identified as black because of the way race has been defined by most people in the United States. Annika Sorenstam, a highly talented Swedish golfer, is defined as white, even though her physical characteristics are quite different from those of Italians, Greeks, and others commonly described as whites according to the racial classification system used by many people in North America. [Mark J. Terrill, AP/Wide World Photos]

racial classification models used in Canada and some other cultures. Additionally, scientists now realize that physiological traits, including genetic patterns, are also related to the experiences of particular individuals as well as the long-term experiences of particular populations.

Even though race is not a valid biological concept, its social significance has profoundly influenced the lives of millions of people for three centuries. This has occurred as people have developed webs of ideas and beliefs around race. In the process, racial ideologies have become deeply embedded in many cultures. These ideologies change over time, but at any point in time they influence people's lives.

The primary trouble with racial ideologies is that their main purpose over the last three centuries has been to justify the oppression and exploitation of one population by another (Smedley, 1997, 1999). Therefore, they have led to and supported **racism**, or *attitudes, actions, and policies based on the belief that people in one racial category are inherently superior to people in one or more other categories.* In extreme cases, racial ideology has been used to support racist beliefs that people in certain populations are (1) childlike beings in need of external control, (2) subhuman beings who may be exploited without guilt, (3) forms of property that can be bought and sold, or (4) evil beings who should be exterminated through **genocide**, or *the systematic destruction of an identifiable population.*

Another trouble with racial ideologies is that they foster the use of **racial stereotypes**, or *generalizations used to define and judge all individuals in a particular racial category.* Because stereotypes provide ready-made evaluative frameworks for making quick judgments and conclusions about others, they are widely used. They are used most often by people who do not have the opportunity or are not willing to learn about and interact with those who have different race-related experiences. Knowledge undermines racial stereotypes and gradually subverts the ideologies that support them and the racism that accompanies them.

Race, Racial Ideology, and Sports

None of us is born with racial ideology. We acquire it over time as we interact with others and learn to give meanings to physical characteristics such as skin colour, eye shape, the colour and texture of hair, or even specific bodily movements. These meanings become the basis for classifying people into racial categories and associating categories with particular psychological and emotional characteristics, intellectual and physical abilities, and even patterns of action and lifestyles. This process of making race and racial meanings is built into the cultural fabric of many societies, including Canada. It occurs as we interact with family members, friends, neighbours, peers, teachers, and people we meet in our everyday lives. General cultural perspectives as well as images and stories in children's books, textbooks, popular films, television programmes, video games, song lyrics, and other media content influence it. We incorporate these perspectives, images, and stories into our lives to the extent that they fit with our experiences. Therefore, when eight blacks line up in the Olympic finals of the 100-metre dash or play in an NBA All-Star game, many people talk about "natural speed and jumping abilities," and some scientists want to study bodies wrapped with dark skin to discover what underlying physical traits allow them to perform well—that is, *better than whites*.

> Science has a long and disreputable history of making false extrapolations from inconclusive hard data—extrapolations that merely parrot the prejudices of the age.
>
> —Gary Kamiya, executive editor, *Salon* (2000, online)

On the other hand, when white athletes do extraordinary physical things, dominant racial ideology leads people to conclude that it is either expected or a result of fortitude, intelligence, moral character, strategic preparation, coachability, and good organization. Therefore, few people want to study bodies wrapped in white skin when all the finalists in multiple Olympic Nordic (cross-country skiing) events are "white." When white skiers from Austria and Switzerland—countries that together are a little smaller than New Brunswick and Nova Scotia, with populations that together are about half the size of the Canadian population—win nearly all World Cup championships year after year, people do not say that the genetic traits of the white population explain their success. Everyone already knows why the Austrians and Swiss are such good skiers: They live in the Alps, they learn to ski before they go to preschool, they grow up in a culture in which skiing is highly valued, they have many opportunities to ski, all their friends ski and talk about skiing, they see fellow Austrian and Swiss skiers winning races and making money in highly publicized (in Europe) World Cup competitions, and their cultural heroes are skiers.

Racial ideology focuses attention on *social* and *cultural* factors when the athletes are white. This is why people do not do studies to find genes that give Canadian hockey players strong ankles, instinctive eye-hand-foot coordination, and the ability to endure cold climates. Racial ideology prevents people from seeing whiteness as an issue in these cases because, in a white-dominated culture, whiteness is the taken-for-granted standard against which everything else is viewed.

When dominant racial ideology serves as the cultural foundation of a white-dominated, white-identified, and white-centred society, the success of white athletes is seen as "normal."

At the same time, the success of black athletes is a "problem" in need of an explanation focused on dark-skinned bodies. This was the approach taken in 1997 when the white editors of *Sports Illustrated* titled a feature-length cover story, "What Happened to the White Athlete?" (Price, 1997). The story was based on their sense that blacks had taken over sports and white athletes were fast disappearing. However, data ignored by the story indicated that black athletes played only a limited number of the most visible and best revenue-producing sports (for white owners and media companies), whereas white athletes made up all or nearly all participants in dozens of other sports from the youth to professional levels. This illustrates that when racial ideology influences how topics are chosen and stories are told in the media, race-related ideas and beliefs become self-perpetuating, even when they portray reality in distorted and inaccurate terms.

Like the rest of us, scientists do not live or do their research outside the influence of ideology. For example, when people study human performance, it is important for them to understand how racial ideology influences the research questions that they ask, the people who they study, the data that they collect, and the analysis and interpretation of the data. This is because scientific "truth" depends on the facts that we choose to examine, the way that we classify those facts, and the theories that we use to analyze and interpret facts. Therefore, racial ideology can exert significant influence on knowledge about racial difference as well as the processes through which people give meanings to physical traits and use those meanings to organize their lives. This issue is discussed further in the box "'Jumping Genes' in Black Bodies" (on the Online Learning Centre).

Of course, racial ideology does not only affect white people. This is a controversial issue, but we suspect that many young black men and women in Canada and the United States grow up believing that the black body is special and superior when it comes to physical abilities in certain sports. If life chances are perceived to be limited, this could lead to a single-minded focus on becoming a professional athlete (see the Reflect on Sports box, "The Odds of Becoming a Professional Athlete," in chapter 10), to the detriment of pursuing education and other career possibilities. While this ambition may be more prevalent in the U.S., the evidence suggests that similar ambitions are encouraged among young African-Canadian males, particularly given the pervasiveness of U.S. media and popular culture icons, and access to U.S. athletic scholarships and professional leagues (cf., James, 2005; Joyce, 1997; Spence, 1999; Wilson, 1999).

The Challenge of Escaping Racial Ideology in Sports The most effective way to defuse racial ideology is to bring people from different ethnic backgrounds together under conditions that enable them to deal with one another as individuals, and discover that ideologies obscure important aspects of people and the realities of their lives. For example, in the U.S. there is evidence that black males tend to be labelled as *athletes* rather than *honours students*, even when they excel at academic work and are placed in honours classes. Asian and white athletes in those classes are clearly identified as honours students rather than athletes. Research on African-Canadian students both supports and contradicts these U.S. findings. Christopher Spence, a former CFL player, and a middle-school principal in Toronto at the time he wrote *The Skin I'm In* (1999), described the experiences of young African-Canadian males in terms of pressure and encouragement to focus on sports. However, research by Carl James (2005), a professor at York University, illustrates that among some African-Canadian high school students, high school sport participation can provide exactly the experiences that are usually claimed for all students: opportunities to extend one's circle of friends and interact with teachers in non-classroom settings, and increased desire and confidence to achieve academically.

Racial Ideology and Sport Choices Among Whites Young people watch sports on television and listen to people discuss the abilities of athletes. In the process, they may develop ideas about race, physical abilities, and their chances for success in various sports. For young white people, their whiteness is a taken-for-granted characteristic in the rest of their lives, but it may influence (and limit) their decisions about their athletic futures. This may be why the times of white runners in certain sprints and long-distance road races have actually become slower over the years; their genes have not changed, but their choices and motivation have changed (Bloom, 1998; George, 1994; Merron, 1999; Weir, 2000). Informal observations at several Ontario Federation of School Athletic Associations (OFSAA) track and field championships and basketball playoff games reveal similar characteristics in white Ontario high school students. White sprinters on 4 × 100 relay teams often assumed that they were going to lose when competing against relay teams with black sprinters. This assumption was reinforced by coaches who, in pre-race talks, sometimes tried to prepare the students for the fact that they may not win. Similar conversations were heard at basketball tournaments when predominantly white teams were about to face predominantly black teams. This reinforced racial ideology, and any beliefs that the black students may have had that they were superior athletes.

Research in the U.S. suggests that racial ideology and the resulting stereotypes influence sports participation choices and how people perform in sports (Harrison and Lawrence, 2004; Harrison et al., 1999; Stone et al., 1997, 1999), but this is a complex issue to study. Racial ideology exerts subtle and indirect influence that often is difficult to detect. Therefore, researchers must use subtle and creative methods to examine how it affects people's lives and the organization of the social worlds in which people make choices.

Racial Ideology, Gender, and Social Class

There are complex interconnections between racial and gender ideologies in the social world of sports. However, the vast majority of research in the area of race and ethnicity concerns African-American males; there is far less research on African-American females, and none that we are aware of on African-Canadian females. Again, to the extent that views of African-American males have a cross-border influence in Canada[3]—an influence that has been detected by, among others, Brian Wilson at the University of British Columbia and Gamal Abdel-Shehid at York University—we conclude this section by examining the ways in which race, masculinity, and social class have come together in both Canada and the United States.

Richard Majors (1998) suggests that as African-American males from low-income families faced limited life chances, they experienced a combination of frustration, self-doubt, anger, and emotional withdrawal from schools, families, and the mainstream economy. They cope "by channeling their creative energies into the construction of unique, expressive, and conspicuous styles of demeanor, speech, gesture, clothing, hairstyle, walk, stance, and handshake" (Majors, 1998, p. 17). Majors calls this strategy "cool pose." It has become part of the public personas of many black males in the U.S., and an integral part of some sports, especially basketball and football.

Brian Wilson (Wilson and Sparks, 1996) and Patrick Solomon of York University have both discovered evidence of "cool pose" in Canada (specifically in Toronto). However, as Wilson (1999) points out, while their "findings cannot be directly paralleled to the 'cool pose' of inner-city America because of Canada's distinct racial context, there is still a symbolic resistance against

---

[3]Because of travel, education, and widespread exposure to, and enjoyment of, U.S. media and sports, Canadians enjoy a great deal of knowledge of the U.S.—a level of knowledge that is not generally reciprocated. This is a result primarily of the relative power of the two countries.

Race logic operates in many ways. In some case it influence white athletes to avoid the sports in which black athletes have a record of excellence. This race logic did not influence Nicholas Macrozanaris on the Canadian 4 x 100m relay team. [CP(Paul Chiasson)]

systemic and structural racism" (p. 242). This distinct racial, and ethnic, context is discussed in the next section.

RACIAL AND ETHNIC RELATIONS IN CANADA

Canada is such an unlikely country. Unlike most other countries, the population does not share an ethnicity, or even have a common language. It is complicated in terms of climate, size, geography, population, and the distribution of that population. It has two or three founding nations (depending on who is counting); two official languages; a complex sharing of governmental power between the federal government, ten provinces, and three territories; and more spiritual, ethnic, and racial diversity, as well as a higher rate of immigration, than any country in the world. When Toronto was bidding to host the 1996

Olympics, one of the slogans was: "Everyone in the world has a relative in Toronto." With more than 190 recognizable racial/ethnic groups in the city, the statement has a reasonable degree of accuracy.

The "elephant in the room" for Canada is the United States—continually there just south of the border, the world's most prolific manufacturer and exporter of cultural products (films, television programmes, magazines, books, music, sports, etc.) that are readily available to Canadians. Even before the signing of the 1988 Free Trade Agreement, and the subsequent (1994) signing of NAFTA, Canada's politics and economy were often developed in relation to the U.S. Since the late 1980s, that relationship has intensified, and it has had an ongoing effect on Canadian political and economic decisions. The proximity of the U.S. is so pervasive that Canadians love to celebrate their differences—delighting, for example, in Joe, from the "I Am Canadian" Molson beer commercials, and Rick

Mercer's "Talking to Americans." The Canadian team hockey victories in the 2002 Winter Olympic Games had a special significance because both teams beat U.S. teams in the gold medal games—in the United States.

For the purposes of this chapter, the most striking characterization of "difference" between the two countries is the widely held belief that, with regard to immigration, the United States is a "melting pot," while Canada is a "cultural mosaic." This belief is grounded in two theories of the way colonial and immigrant societies are, or ought to be, organized.

Assimilation, or the "melting pot" view, sees a society constructed of different ethnicities and races; a society in which immigrants (and colonized native peoples) are to abandon their traditional identities and cultures and become "American." The process(es) by which assimilation occurred were widely explored by U.S. sociologists in the middle of the last century. Park (1950) proposed four stages of assimilation: initial contact between immigrants (or natives) and members of the core society (or colonizers); a period of *competition* between their respective cultures; a period of *accommodation* in which immigrants (or natives) learned to adapt to the new culture while the members of the new culture perhaps accommodated or even incorporated some aspects of the traditional cultures; followed finally by *assimilation* of the immigrants (or natives) into the new culture. Gordon (1964) developed a rather more complicated model, involving seven stages of assimilation.

The theories were based primarily in the idea that immigrants were Europeans rather than from other parts of the world, and did not really take account of their different cultures or religions or reasons for coming to North America. These ranged from the voluntary "seeking a better life" to the involuntary fleeing from war or persecution. The circumstances of immigration and the culture of origin both influence the inclination to assimilate, and

attempts to preserve aspects of traditional culture. Canada (until the 1970s) and the United States both practised assimilation, but in neither country was it official policy. Adult immigrants were frequently left to their own devices, with assimilation occurring to differing degrees. Both countries had forms of cultural pluralism, with communities and populations readily identifying themselves, for example, as Italian-Canadians or Irish-Americans.

The real focus of assimilation was the children of immigrants, and schools and sports and recreation became significant mechanisms by which people were incorporated into Canadian and U.S. society (Loy and Booth, 2001). Children are often the first to learn the language of their new society, and they often become the language bridge for contact between their parents and the new society. School curricula directly and indirectly teach children how to be Canadian or American, and their exposure to media and cultural practices such as sports and games also involves assimilation. LaFlamme's (1977) study of cricket in Buffalo, New York, provides an ideal example of this process. A significant number of West Indian immigrants settled in Buffalo in the 1950s and 1960s, and developed an active cricket league. However, despite encouragement from their parents to play cricket, the children of these immigrants were exposed to North American games and U.S. "black" culture, both in school and in their social lives—they began to play the games of their new society (football, baseball, and basketball). As their parents grew older and no longer played, cricket died out in the community.

Multiculturalism (cultural plurality), or the "cultural mosaic" view, began to emerge in Canada in the 1960s. Following on the heels of the Royal Commission on Bilingualism and Biculturalism (1963–69), Canada began to formally recognize two official languages and two distinct cultures deriving from the original French and English immigrants to Canada. It was a short step to recognize that if a country, whose primary source of population growth was immigration, was enriched by having two cultures it would be even more enriched by recognizing and supporting the distinct cultures of the immigrant communities. In 1971, Prime Minister Pierre Trudeau stated:

> Every ethnic group has the right to preserve and develop its own culture and values within the Canadian context. To say that we have two official languages is not to say that we have two official cultures and no particular culture is more "official" than another. A policy of multiculturalism must be a policy for all Canadians. (*House of Commons Debates*, October 8, 1971; cited by Hall et al., 1991, p. 174)

Assimilation and multiculturalism are not, in practice, opposite or conflicting theories or policies, and "melting pot" and "cultural mosaic" are not strictly accurate characterizations of the United States or Canada respectively. A number of jurisdictions in the United States, usually in large cities, practise multiculturalism policies and even bilingualism (English and Spanish). However, in many places, there is little attempt to accommodate immigrants, an observation outlined clearly by Mark Grey (1999) in his study of sports in Garden City (Kansas) High School.

It is important to recognize that no immigrants are permitted to incorporate their entire culture of origin into the multicultural society. For example, all immigrants are assimilated with regard to the laws and political system of Canada, and many embrace assimilation—wanting to become Canadian and wanting their children to be Canadian. The multicultural society in Canada offers the possibility of multiple identities—it is possible to be Canadian *and* also to be Korean, Serbian, or Chilean. Under Canadian policies, it is not necessary to deny or abandon one's, or one's parents', culture of origin. In fact, that culture is considered to enrich Canadian culture, and is celebrated with festivals, religious and cultural celebrations, dances, cuisines, sports,

and the opportunity to maintain and pass on language. However, it is precisely these aspects of multiculturalism that have led some to criticize the way the policies are implemented as being superficial and apolitical.

The sporting manifestations of multiculturalism are fascinating and sometimes unexpected. Peter Donnelly's students at the University of Toronto are encouraged in one assignment to seek an aspect of physical culture (sports, exercise system, or dance) associated with particular ethnocultural communities in Ontario, and to examine them in terms of multiculturalism and assimilation. They have found that, in general, there is a rather slow assimilation of sports and games, with increased evidence of traditional physical cultural practices among more recent immigrant communities than among more established communities. For example, people actively involved in kabbadi (Indian), cricket (various Commonwealth countries), capoeira (Brazil), tinikling (Philippine dance), and the raffia ball games (e.g., sepak takraw) of Southeast Asia can all be found in the Toronto region. However, Gaelic football and hurling (Irish), eisstock (Austrian, German, Swiss), and pesapallo (Finnish) have far fewer participants than in the past, though they are still in evidence.

Soccer provided some unexpected results with regard to multiculturalism and assimilation. In an early study, John Pooley (1981), who taught for many years at Dalhousie University, studied ethnic soccer clubs in Milwaukee. He had expected to find that, in the melting pot society, soccer would be one of the ways in which assimilation was encouraged. He found precisely the opposite. All of the players on teams run by, for example, the German, Polish, and Hungarian clubs were from those ethnic groups, and they spoke their language rather than English. Donnelly and Day (Day, 1981) replicated Pooley's study in London, Ontario, expecting to find similar results precisely because of multiculturalism policies. However, in the various soccer and social clubs they studied (e.g., Portuguese, German, Polish, Italian, etc.), soccer seemed to be promoting assimilation! The club officials explained it in this way: Through the 1960s, when immigration to Canada from Europe was quite easy, the clubs only had players from their country of origin, and they spoke their original language on the field and at social events at the clubs. If a club needed a new striker, they would recruit one from the "old country." ("We'd just get on the phone to Portugal and say, 'We need a striker,' and he'd be there in a couple of weeks.") As immigration policies changed, the clubs began to recruit players from other communities, with, for example, Scottish players on the Italian team and even Serbian players on the Croatian team. With the new multi-ethnic teams, a common language was needed on the field of play and in the social club, and that language was invariably English. Jim McKay, a Canadian sport sociologist now working at Durham University, carried out a similar study among Italian soccer clubs in metro Toronto. He also found that "the necessity of recruiting from outside the Italian community promoted assimilation and inter-ethnic contact rather than the preservation of ethnic identity and solidarity" (Hall et al., 1991, p. 178).

In a sense, this blending of assimilation and multiculturalism produces many of the better features of multiculturalism. Rather than a distinct "mosaic" of ethnic communities, the communities come together socially and through intermarriage, not as something that is homogenized as "Canadian," but as new and distinct possibilities. Sports have an interesting place in these processes, sometimes becoming a part of the process of assimilation, and sometimes a part of the process of resisting assimilation and reproducing a cultural community (e.g., Dallaire, 2000; Dallaire and Denis, 2000; Dyck, 2001). Research is needed to better understand the contexts in which these processes occur (cf., Donnelly and Nakamura, 2006).

The possibility of assimilation, both to the degree necessary and to the degree preferred, together with the option of retaining some aspects of a traditional culture, has many interesting manifestations. For example, the Toronto Parks and Recreation department was approached by a group of Muslim women who had emigrated from Somalia. They had decided that, in order to become Canadian, they had to become involved in sports—they had recognized sports as a distinct feature of Canadian life. With the support of the Toronto Maple Leafs, Toronto Parks and Recreation established a ball hockey programme under the conditions necessary for practising Muslims (Berck, 2003). Involvement in ball hockey is a step in assimilation, but it does not mean that other aspects of Somali culture and identity, including games, have to be abandoned. Immigrants to Canada seem to be quite capable, to varying degrees, of maintaining multiple aspects of identities. They are Somali, for example, and are able to pass on aspects of being Somali to their children, while at the same time becoming Canadian. It is the success of these policies that attracts researchers and policymakers from immigrant countries in Europe, the U.S., and Australia and New Zealand to study Canadian multiculturalism with a view to developing and fine-tuning their own policies. This does not mean that there are *no* tensions between ethnic and racial groups, or that there are *no* inequalities in access to power, but there seem to be fewer than in other diverse societies.

A Snapshot of the Canadian Population, 2006

Data from the 2006 Census released by Statistics Canada (www.statcan.ca)[4] provide a thorough picture of the racial and ethnic structure of Canada. This structure has important implications for the distribution and meaning of sports and physical activity in the country. The population of Canada today is a little over 33 million. Definitions of "visible minority" and "ethnicity," which have been operationalized in order to determine measurement are, as a consequence, somewhat

[4]All data in this section are from the 2006 Census, and can be found at this web site.

different from those given at the beginning of the chapter, and the definitions show the complexity of such measurements. The definition of visible minority is taken from the Employment Equity Act: "persons, other than Aboriginal peoples, who are non-Caucasian in race or non-white in colour." Ethnic origin, which is also self-reported in the census, is defined as "the ethnic or cultural group(s) to which an individual's ancestors belonged." Statistics Canada (2003, p. 16) noted that:

> The reporting of ethnic origin, and subsequent in-terpretation of the results, has become increasingly complex due to a number of factors. The concept of ethnicity is fluid and is probably the *most complex concept measured in the census*. Respondents' understanding or views about ethnicity, awareness of their family background, number of generations in Canada, and the length of time since immigration can affect the reporting of ethnicity from one census to another. Increasing intermarriage among various groups has led to an increase in the report-ing of multiple origins, which has added to the complexity of the ethnic data (emphasis added).

The following provides some highlights of the ethnic and racial structure of Canada in 2006:

- Respondents listed more than 200 ethnic origins.
- 6.2 million people (19.8 percent) were born outside Canada, the highest proportion in 75 years. (Only Australia has a higher proportion of its population born outside the country.)

- Immigration continues at a rate of less than 1 percent of the population each year, and has recently been averaging approximately 200,000/year (0.6–0.7 percent of the population). There were 1.1 million immigrants between 2001 and 2006: Asia (including the Middle East)—58.3 percent; Europe (primarily Eastern Europe)—16.1 percent; Central and South America and the Caribbean—10.8 percent; Africa—10.6 percent; and the U.S.—3 percent.
- Before 1961, 90 percent of all immigrants came from Europe.
- Between 1991 and 2006, almost 70 percent of all immigrants settled in three major cities: Toronto (43 percent), Vancouver (18 percent), and Montréal (12 percent).
- Over 5 million (non-Aboriginal) Canadians identified themselves as visible minorities (16.2 percent), an increase from 4.7 percent in 1981; these include those shown in table 9.1 (as a proportion of the total visible minority population and, for the first four, a proportion of the national population).
- There are almost 1.2 million Aboriginal people (this is the first census in which the number has exceeded 1 million): Inuit—4.3 percent; Métis—33.2 percent; and First Nations—59.5 percent.
- Intermarriage (primarily) resulted in over 12.9 million (41.4 percent) reporting multiple ethnicities in 2006 (an increase from 7.8 million in 1991).

Table 9.1   Canadians self-identifying as visible minorities, 2006 Census

Visible minority group	Population	Percentage of visible minority population	Percentage of Canadian population
South Asian	1.26 million	25%	4%
Chinese	1.22 million	24%	3.9%
Black	.78 million	15.4%	2.5%
Filipino	.41 million	8.1%	1.3%
Latin American	.30 million	6.0%	
Southeast Asian	.24 million	4.7%	
Other	.86 million	17%	

Source: Data from Statistics Canada "Ethnocultural Portrait of Canada" (2006 Census). Accessed online at: http://www12.statcan.ca/english/census06/data/highlights/ethnic/index.cfm?Lang=E.

Table 9.2 shows the most frequently reported ethnic origins (the total exceeds 100 percent because of the reporting of multiple ethnicities).

In table 9.2, the fact that over 32 percent of the population identified their ethnicity as "Canadian" is intriguing, and it causes complexity for Statistics Canada. Some 18 percent (5.75 million people) claim Canadian as their only ethnic origin; 14 percent (about 4.3 million people) claim Canadian in addition to other ethnic origins (e.g., Chilean and Canadian; Sri Lankan and Canadian; French, Irish, and Canadian). Most non-Aboriginal Canadians are aware that their ancestors came from another country sometime in the last 400 years. As Statistics Canada notes, a combination of political views (in an immigrant society, to identify one's ancestry is a political act), a person's awareness of his or her ancestors, and the number of generations one's ancestors have been in Canada, all have an effect on this claim of ethnicity. Thus, all Canadians have one or more ethnicities, but some of that record is being lost as Canada becomes more secure in its identity.

Related to the ethnic and racial structure of Canada is its language structure. As noted above, the country is officially multicultural and bilingual, and government resources are sometimes available to assist in the maintenance of heritage languages and Aboriginal languages in addition to the two official languages. In the 2006 census, 98 percent of the population is able to speak one or both official languages. However, only 80 percent of the population reports English (58 percent) or French (22 percent) as their mother tongue, and over 17 percent of the population are bilingual in English and French. Over 200 languages, including Aboriginal languages, were reported by Canadians as their mother tongue. After English and French, Chinese languages are reported most frequently by 3 percent of the population (the census counts seven major Chinese languages). The 20 percent of the population whose mother tongue is not English of French are referred to in the census as "Allophones."

Canadian and U.S. Differences in Racial Ideology

The racial and ethnic structure of Canada outlined above is quite different from that of the United States. German is now the most frequently cited ethnic heritage in the U.S., and a dominant European-heritage, English-speaking majority ranks ahead of Latin American and African-American minorities. As in Canada, there are growing South Asian and East Asian populations. In Canada, the most frequently cited ethnic heritage (after Canadian) is English; the dominant European-heritage majority

Table 9.2 Most frequently reported ethnic origins, 2006 Census

Reported ethnic origin	Population	Percentage of Canadian population
Canadian	10.07 million	32.2%
English	6.57 million	21.0%
French	4.94 million	15.8%
Scottish	4.72 million	15.1%
Irish	4.35 million	13.9%
German	3.18 million	10.2%
Italian	1.45 million	4.6%
Chinese	1.35 million	4.3%
Aboriginal	1.25 million	4.0%
Ukrainian	1.21 million	3.9%

Source: Data from Statistics Canada "Ethnocultural Portrait of Canada" (2006 Census). Accessed online at: http://www12.statcan.ca/english/census06/data/highlights/ethnic/index.cfm?Lang=E.

is divided linguistically, and ranks ahead of Aboriginal, Chinese, and South Asian minorities. Visible minorities in Canada, although a rapidly increasing segment of the population, constitute some 16.2 percent of the total population—a smaller proportion than in the United States.[5] Thus, while both populations are characterized by diversity, Canada's population is rather more diverse and, because of a higher rate of immigration, is growing increasingly diverse. Many urban and suburban Canadians regularly negotiate a set of racial, ethnic, and language relations, in their neighbourhoods and workplaces. Racism is considered to be a U.S. problem, and the commitment to multiculturalism often results in an incorrect assumption that racism does not exist in Canada.

The primary focus of race/ethnicity issues and research in the United States concerns "black" and "white" relations and, more recently, Latino and white relations. The long history of slavery, which, in part, resulted in a Civil War; the re-victimization of African Americans through the "Jim Crow laws" following the abolition of slavery; and the Civil Rights movement of the 1960s, have made these relations a central focus of U.S. consciousness. The Canadian experience of this particular axis of racial relations is rather different. While slavery was practised in Canada from the seventeenth to the nineteenth centuries, it began to decline after 1793 when John Graves Simcoe, the Lieutenant Governor of Upper Canada, sponsored "a bill...passed by the Legislature of Upper Canada making it illegal to bring a person into the colony to be enslaved" (see "The Anti-Slavery Movement in Canada" Exhibition on the National Archives of Canada website, www.archives.ca). This preceded the end of the trans-Atlantic slave trade in Britain (1807) and, following William Wilberforce's successful campaign in Britain, the practice of slavery formally ended in Canada in 1834.

The end of slavery in Canada, and its continuing practice in the southern U.S., led to the formation of a number of anti-slavery societies, the last and most successful of which was the Anti-Slavery Society of Canada founded in 1851 by the Hon. George Brown, owner of *The Globe* newspaper and a Father of Confederation, and Rev. Dr. Michael Willis, Principal of Knox College at the University of Toronto (www.archives.ca). The Anti-Slavery Society of Canada was active in the "Underground Railroad" that brought many escaped slaves to Canada.

These differences do not mean that African Canadians were exempt from discrimination in Canada, or that Canada was immune to continuing U.S. influences with regard to racial ideology. The segregation of U.S. professional baseball as a result of the "Jim Crow laws" in the 1890s had its counterpart in Canada with the removal of African-Canadian players from teams (Fosty and Fosty, 2004; Humber, 1983), and there were even some African-Canadian hockey teams formed after hockey began to practise segregation.[6] African Canadians were not the only group to suffer from intolerance, as the following examples indicate:

- The use of Chinese immigrants to construct railroads was followed by the imposition of a Head Tax to discourage further immigration from China.
- The anti-Semitic, "one is too many" policy, which denied access to Jewish immigrants trying to escape Nazi Germany before World War II, ended too late to save many from the concentration camps.
- Relations with Aboriginal peoples resulted in many children suffering in the residential school system, and in the traumatic forced resettlement of some Inuit peoples.

---

[5]This figure is expected to increase to approximately 20 percent in Canada by 2017—one out of five Canadians.

[6]Morton (1983) notes that, in the 1920s, "nothing could hide the raw racial intolerance that had flourished since the [First World] war" (p. 170), and the Ku Klux Klan even made an appearance in western Canada in 1928.

- The imprisonment of German immigrants in internment camps during World War I was repeated during World War II with German-, Italian-, and Japanese-Canadians.

After World War II, racial and ethnic relations slowly began to settle in Canada. The Brooklyn Dodgers signed African-American baseball player Jackie Robinson to their Montréal farm team, the Montréal Royals, in 1946 before bringing him to Brooklyn to break the U.S. colour barrier in baseball in 1947. And Willie O'Ree became the first African Canadian to play in the NHL (with the Boston Bruins) in 1958. However, as noted in the following section, African Canadians constitute only a little over 2 percent of the Canadian population, and while "black" and "white" relations in Canada demonstrate some ongoing problems (related, in part, to Canadian consciousness about this set of racial relations in the United States), other axes of racial and ethnic relations figure rather more prominently in Canada.

THE DYNAMICS OF ETHNIC AND RACIAL RELATIONS IN CANADIAN SPORTS

Sports have been significant sites of cultural, political, linguistic, and nationalistic struggles in Canada since 1970, when Pierre Trudeau began to see sports as one of the vehicles for the development of pan-Canadian unity. These struggles were first played out when, in an assertion of Canadian sovereignty, federal funding suddenly became available for the proposed Arctic Games (for Inuit and Dene peoples) after a U.S. oil-tanker (the *Manhattan*), accompanied by a U.S. icebreaker sailed, without Canadian permission, through territorial waters in the Northwest Passage in 1969. They continued in the lead-up to and during the Montréal Olympics in 1976 (Kidd, 1992), and leaped onto the front pages during the 1984 Sarajevo Winter Olympics when, following Gaétan Boucher's gold medals in two

speed-skating events, Québec Premier René Lévesque was reported to have said, "Québec 2, Canada 0." They were still evident in 1994 when the then leader of the Parti Québécois, Jacques Parizeau, pointed out that athletes from Québec had won nine of the thirteen Canadian medals at the Lillehammer Winter Olympics (Laberge, 1995); in 1995, when Québec City was bidding for the 2002 Winter Olympics (Rail et al., 1995); in 1998, when the Bloc Québécois published a Dissenting Report on the Mills Report (Mills, 1998); and in 2002, when Swim Canada head coach Dave Johnson made some unfortunate remarks concerning Québec swimmers.[7]

It is evident that the major axis of racial/ethnic relations in Canadian sports concerns francophone and anglophone relations. However, Hall et al. (1991, p. 179), pointed out that there are two other important axes: relations between natives and non-natives, and relations between the two principal colonizing groups (French and English) and other immigrants and their descendants. In the following sections, we draw on these three axes, while also extending the latter category to consider relations between whites and visible minorities in Canada.

Francophone and Anglophone Relations

Under federal jurisdiction, Canada is officially a bilingual country. Francophones live in every province and territory of Canada; however, New Brunswick is the only officially bilingual province, and Québec is the only French-language province and has the largest francophone population. Bilingual federal services and schools are often available across the country, but provincial and

---

[7]The remarks followed an incident when a Québec swimmer had been reprimanded for carrying her provincial flag to a medal ceremony at the 2002 Commonwealth Games. The incident led to an outcry in Québec media and in Parliament, with commentators pointing out, for example, that Catriona LeMay Doan had not received a similar reprimand for carrying the Saskatchewan flag to a medal ceremony.

territorial bilingual services vary significantly, with Québec usually making many more accommodations for anglophones living in the province than are made for francophones living in the predominantly anglophone provinces.

After 1759, with the defeat of French forces at Québec City, there was a long period of colonial rule and discrimination—economic, political, and cultural/linguistic—against francophone Canadians that is well-documented in Canadian history. In many ways, the twentieth century was characterized by a long slow struggle against this discrimination, culminating in *la révolution tranquille* of the 1960s and early 1970s. Shifts in Canadian federal policy towards official bilingualism, bi- and multiculturalism, and asymmetrical federalism have modified, but not ended, discrimination; and the formation of the Parti Québécois, and its electoral successes in Québec, have maintained the possibility of Québec changing the terms of its relationship with Canada.

The Montréal anglophone community figures prominently in Canadian sport history (see chapter 3), and anglophones dominated the development of sports and sport organizations in Québec.[8] While sports remained a major interest of francophones in larger communities, where there was a significant level of participation in organized sports, several researchers have pointed out that the major influence of the Catholic Church (especially in smaller communities) resulted in a different pattern of sport development in francophone Québec (Bellefleur, 1986, 1997; Harvey, 1988). For the francophone Catholic hierarchy in the first half of the twentieth century in Québec, sports under the control of anglophones (including professional hockey) posed a danger of assimilation. Unable to prevent the growing interest of francophones in sports, the clergy took the initiative to create a separate

sport system with a less competitive set of values (Meisel and Lemieux, 1972). For example, in hockey, the Confédération des Loisirs du Québec established a *"section hockey"* separate from the anglophone-dominated Québec Amateur Hockey Association. The hockey section had the aim of opposing the commercialization and professionalization of amateur hockey, with the following goal: *"replacer le hockey dans sa perspective d'activité physique salutaire, hygiénique et éducative."*[9] Less explicit goals involved the maintenance of Québec culture and language under clerical influence, and the maintenance of nationalist sentiments.

The long period of discrimination had certain characteristics that led some, by the 1960s, to equate the anti-discrimination struggles of francophones with those of African Americans (and the Civil Rights movement) in the United States. The two situations were so different that the analogy is a stretch—the primary similarity being that both were self-assertive movements against a long history of discrimination. However, in terms of the sociology of sport, the type of research that was initially carried out on the francophone/anglophone situation in Canada was quite similar to that carried out on the "black" and "white" situation in the United States. This was "distributive" research, designed to determine and explain the ways that sports were distributed in the population—the proportions of "blacks" and "whites," anglophones and francophones in different sports. These distributions were then compared to the proportion of "blacks" and francophones in the population in order to determine if the population was fairly represented, underrepresented, or overrepresented in the sport.

Distributive Research Just a few weeks after the publication of John Munro's *A Proposed Sport Policy for Canadians* (1970), the document

---

[8]Parts of the following discussions of francophone/anglophone relations in sports are drawn from Donnelly et al. (2001).

[9]Translation: "return hockey to its place as beneficial, healthy and educational physical activity."

that proved to be the real turning point in the transformation of Canada's sport system, it was announced that Montréal had been awarded the 1976 Summer Olympic Games. Bruce Kidd (1992) outlined the way in which francophone/anglophone politics were played out in the context of hosting the Olympics in Québec. These politics were fuelled, in part, by a series of studies outlining the underrepresentation of francophone athletes on Canadian national teams and in the NHL (e.g., Boileau et al., 1976; Landry et al., 1966, 1972; Marple, 1975). For example, Roger Boileau, Fernand Landry, and Yves Trempe (1976) studied francophone representation on Canadian national teams for the years 1908 to 1974. During this period of time, when the proportion of francophones in Canada varied between 25 and 30 percent, francophone representation on Canadian national teams at Summer Olympics, Winter Olympics, Pan-Am Games, and Commonwealth Games rarely exceeded 10 percent. In only one sport (*haltérophilie*/weightlifting) were francophones overrepresented (43 percent).

Following this earlier work, Marc Lavoie of the University of Ottawa carried out a series of studies that showed under representation of francophone athletes in the NHL. However, in another parallel to research on African Americans in the United States, Lavoie (1989) showed that francophones were also "stacked"[10] in certain playing positions—goalies mostly, followed by forwards, and very few defencemen. Lavoie and Grenier (1992) also showed that while anglophone and francophone goalies and forwards had similar levels of pay in the NHL, francophone defenders were paid 10 to 15 percent less than anglophones (see also Lavoie, 1998).

In its planning and athlete development programmes for the 1976 Olympics, the Québec government set a target of 30 percent francophones on the Canadian team, and funded the

development of Québécois athletes. The goal was almost achieved, and the percentage of francophones on the Canadian team (28 percent) was just about exactly representative of the francophone proportion of the Canadian population (although there were no francophones in a number of sports). The national team studies continued after the 1976 Olympics (e.g., Haut Commissariat à la Jeunesse, aux Loisirs et aux Sports, 1978), and showed a decline in the proportion of francophone athletes. In the most striking parallel between U.S. and Canadian research, Kjeldsen (1984) compared francophone representation on Canadian Olympic teams and African-American representation on U.S. Olympic teams. Although Canada followed the U.S. boycott and did not send athletes to the Moscow Olympics in 1980, a team was announced, and Kjeldsen found that less than 15 percent of the athletes and almost 8 percent of the coaches were francophone. For the 1980 Winter Olympics in Lake Placid, francophone representation on the Canadian team was 17.6 percent for athletes and 3.6 percent for coaches. Research by Hall et al. (1991), on Canadian teams at the 1984 Los Angeles Olympics (12 percent of the athletes) and the 1988 Seoul Olympics (12.7 percent of the athletes) showed that the decline continued. There was similar underrepresentation at the executive level of sport organizations. Hall et al., pointed out that "in 1955, 8.6 percent of the executive positions were filled by francophones; 7.8 percent in 1975; and approximately 10 percent in 1980" (1991, p. 177).

Recently, the proportion of francophone athletes on national teams has increased. There are some clear specialties—short track speed skating, freestyle skiing, diving, women's water polo, synchronized swimming, etc.—although there are still a number of teams with no francophone athletes. Sport development has maintained a high priority in Québec, and the situation for francophone athletes on national teams has improved since the 1980s. However,

---

[10]"Stacking" is discussed in detail in a feature on the Online Learning Centre.

although the proportions of athletes may be more representative, there are still problems of concern—for example, the number of coaching and executive positions occupied by francophones, and language issues (see the next section). The history of distributive issues outlined above is important because of the sociological issues it highlights. How do we account for these differences in the distribution of francophone and anglophone athletes on Canadian national teams and in the NHL?

Two clear approaches emerged as sociologists attempted to explain their data—*cultural* explanations and *structural* explanations. Gruneau and Albinson describe the *cultural interpretation* of national team data given by Boileau et al. (1976):

> They note that Québec was largely a rural and "traditional" society until the early 1960s. Intensely competitive urges and a need for achievement in sport were not a part of the dominant value system. At the same time, Boileau et al. argue that the lack of involvement in sports was also contingent upon a rejection of the personal values of anglophones—many of which were thought to be reflected in the structure and organization of sport. (1976, p. 104)

In other words, sports were not important in francophone culture in Québec, and maintaining a francophone culture in Québec was associated with rejecting the type of power and performance sports associated with anglophones. Lavoie (1989) reviewed (and rejected) similar cultural explanations for the underrepresentation of francophones in the NHL: the francophone style of play (characterized by anglophone coaches as too much offence and too little aggression and work ethic), the belief that it was necessary to pay francophone players more to induce them to leave Québec, and the language problems associated with having a non-English-speaking player on the team. Thus, Québec culture and the (anglophone) culture of the NHL clashed to the disadvantage of nonstar francophone players.

Structural explanations take into account the differences in power (political, economic, etc.) between anglophones and francophones, and argue that underrepresentation was a result of discrimination. Talented francophone athletes often were not selected for national teams because of discrimination on the part of the anglophone sport executives making the selections. Coulombe and Lavoie (1985) argue that francophone players reached the NHL primarily in those positions where there were objective measures of performance—the statistics indicate clearly that one goalie is better than another and, almost with the same degree of clarity, that one forward is better than another. Assessing the play of defencemen is more subjective. Where a francophone player was objectively the better player, he would be selected; more subjective assessments opened the door to stereotypes and discrimination.

The clash between *cultural* and *structural* explanations came to a head in an academic debate in the *Sociology of Sport Journal* in 1992. The debate was sparked by the publication of two articles, by Phil White of McMaster University and Jim Curtis of the University of Waterloo (White and Curtis, 1990a; 1990b), which proposed a cultural explanation of francophone/ anglophone differences in sport participation. The articles reviewed 1976 national survey data in Canada showing that francophones had a lower rate of participation in competitive sports (and a higher rate of participation in recreational sports) than anglophones. Both articles indicate that the data support a "values-differences" interpretation—that there are differences in the orientation to achievement between anglophones and francophones (with anglophones being more achievement-oriented), which explain the differences in involvement in competitive sports. White and Curtis (1990b) also focused on the differences in school socialization for francophones and anglophones in Canada to account, in part, for the values differences (i.e., that before the Quiet Revolution it was not common for francophone schools to be involved in interschool sports). Critical commentaries on the articles by researchers from the Université de Montréal (Laberge and Girardin, 1992; McAll, 1992) advocated a structural interpretation, pointing to a long history of structural inequality between francophones and anglophones in Québec that was reflected in discrimination in many aspects of life including sports. Curtis and White (1992) replied by re-advocating their cultural explanation and providing additional data.

Academic debates such as this are often presented as an either/or situation—you must accept either a *cultural* explanation or a *structural* explanation of the differences in sport participation, and the underrepresentation of francophones on national teams and in the NHL. However, explanations of social life are often far more complex and nuanced. There is clear evidence of cultural differences between anglophones and francophones in Canada; and there is clear evidence of a long history of structural inequality and discrimination. The question that remains, and is suggested by Laberge and Girardin (1992), is to what extent are cultural differences a result of structural inequality—of being subject to, and resisting, discrimination?

By 1986, research in Québec was shifting from a singular focus on underrepresentation to what was now being termed, *le fait français ("si le fait d'être francophone pouvait nuire aux athlètes québécois dans la réalisation de leur performance sportive"*[11]). Suzanne Laberge (1986) of the Université de Montréal pointed to both the underrepresentation of, and subtle discrimination against, francophone high-performance athletes, and she produced a short statement of the ongoing problems in 1988. The most recent analysis, the report of the Comité sur la place du Québec dans le système sportif Canadien (2001) also shows ongoing problems, the most significant of which is the issue of language.

---

[11]Translation: "if the fact of being francophone could be a disadvantage to Québécois athletes in realizing their goals in sport."

Gold medal-winning biathlete, Myriam Bédard, signalled the struggles over language in Canadian sports when she refused to accept the unilingual (English) services, including coaching, provided by Biathlon Canada. [CP(Frank Gunn)]

Language Issues in Canadian Sports Language issues in Canadian sports have received a great deal of attention in recent years. Three events in particular sparked this interest. The first was the case of Myriam Bédard, "which made it possible to publicly denounce the kind of discrimination experienced by a number of athletes. Ms. Bédard won medals in the most prestigious international competitions after refusing to accept the unilingual English services provided to her by Biathlon Canada" (Sports Québec, 1998, p. 22). In the second, the Canadian Olympic Association (COA/AOC) was accused of making little provision for the use of French at an athletes' reception before the 1998 Nagano

Olympics. A representative of the COA/AOC was called before the parliamentary committee on official languages to explain and apologize (Feschuk, 1998). Just six months later, at a ceremony held at the CBC in Toronto to announce the Canadian flag-bearer at the forthcoming Commonwealth Games in Kuala Lumpur, it quickly became apparent to the media present that Jeux du Commonwealth Games Canada had made no provision for statements/announcements or interviews in French. The proceedings were saved when the flag-bearer, New Brunswick swimmer Marianne Limpert, stepped forward to translate and answer questions in both English and French (Christie, 1998). Sport Canada increased its efforts to address the issue of bilingualism in Canadian sports, and, in November, 1999, the newly appointed Secretary of State for Amateur Sport, Denis Coderre, following a letter of complaint from Bloc Québécois MP Caroline St-Hilaire, initiated a study by the Commissioner for Official Languages (Office of the Commissioner of Official Languages [OCOL], 2000).

Sports became a distinct part of Canadian language politics in 1982 when the issue of official languages was first added to the issue of underrepresentation. Max Yalden, then Commissioner of Official Languages, presented a report to the Ministry of Fitness and Amateur Sport that noted: "In our opinion, it is unacceptable that [federal] taxpayers' money be used to support such national bodies [sport organizations] if adequate services are not provided in both official languages." Federal and provincial study groups were formed, and while the federal study group acknowledged a "real determination" on the part of the Ministry and Sport Canada to encourage national sport organizations (NSOs) to offer their services in both French and English, the Québec inquiry press release noted:

...97.5 percent of the respondents estimate they have some trouble to obtain information in French from the Canadian Sport Associations. The

problems they face are numerous and vary from one federation to another. Officer training, clinics, meetings and general information are all scarcely available in French. (Regroupement. . ., 1983)

Following the upheaval associated with the Ben Johnson affair at the 1988 Seoul Olympics, Sport Canada set about transforming national sport policy, including the poor state of language relations reported by the Federal-Provincial Advisory Committee on Equal Linguistic Access to Services in Sport.

Despite these policy initiatives, very little changed, and embarrassing incidents continued. For example, the case of Myriam Bédard refusing to work with Biathlon Canada (noted above), and the accusations of discrimination voiced by Bloc Québécois members of parliament in the House of Commons when it became apparent that the hockey team Canada sent to the 1994 Lillehammer Olympics included only one francophone player (Canadian Press, 1994). However, since federal funding has been linked to requirements to establish services in both official languages, through the 1995–96 Sport Funding and Accountability Framework (SFAF; see chapter 13), and as sports organizations are showing greater sensitivity to equity issues, there are real signs of change.

The Official Languages Act applies to Sport Canada (now part of the Department of Canadian Heritage), rather than the NSOs. However, the Sport Canada website includes the Treasury Board Policy on Official Languages, indicating that French and English have equal status in Canada and that the policy applies to NSOs receiving federal funds:

...federal institutions providing grants or contributions to voluntary non-governmental organizations for activities, projects or programmes involving service to a public composed of members of both official language communities must take the necessary measures to ensure that the recipients of public funds respect the spirit and intent of the Official Languages Act when serving the public. (www.pch.gc.ca/progs/sc/pol/ lang/index_e.cfm)

This commitment from Sport Canada was specified most recently in the SFAF (see the Reflect on Sports box, "Sports and Bilingualism," pp. 283–284).

Native and Non-Native Relations

With a population of over one million—some 3.8 percent of Canada's population—Aboriginal Canadians represent one of the most rapidly growing segments of the population. Although officially classified as one minority group in Canada, First Nations peoples comprise many dozens of diverse cultural groups—the usual Canadian designation of "Indian and Inuit" does not capture this diversity. Furthermore, Native Canadian lifestyles and sport participation patterns are diverse and vary depending on social class and whether people reside on or off reserves. The diverse cultures are also characterized by diversity in physical culture, with many different sports and games, for men and women, a part of native cultures. Many sports in traditional Native Canadian cultures have combined physical activities with ritual and ceremony.

For example, in perhaps the most intriguing tradition, "Running is said to bring myths to life, and to create a link between runners and the universe" (Unwin, 2001, p. 21). Native lore in North and Central America is full of stories about feats of speed and endurance in running, and a number of well-known runners (in the European sport tradition) have emerged from Aboriginal cultures. Lacrosse (tewaarathon, to the Iroquois) is perhaps the best known of the originally native sports in Canada, and is now officially designated Canada's national summer sport (see chapter 3).

Although there is research on anglophone/francophone relations in sports in Canada, quite the reverse is the case with regard to native and non-native relations. There is a substantial body of descriptive historical research on Aboriginal sports and physical activities, but few researchers have carried out systematic social scientific research on the issue: Janice Forsyth at the University of Manitoba; Audrey Giles and Michael Robidoux, both at the University of Ottawa; Michael Heine, now at the University of Western Ontario; and Vicky Paraschak at the University of Windsor. Forsyth shows how the Indian Act served to structure and limit Aboriginal sport participation in Canada, "and legitimized Euro-Canadian ways of playing as the most appropriate forms of play" (2007, p. 95). And Paraschak's (1989) review of the history of native sports in Canada indicates that relations between non-natives and natives were characterized by *exploitation*, *racism*, and *ethnocentric distortion*. To these, we can add *assimilation* and *resistance* as characteristics of the relationship.

Exploitation Exploitation is evident in numerous examples of the use of native athletes and their sports. For example, when George Beers, a Montréal dentist, "Europeanized" the game of lacrosse and formed the Lacrosse Club of Montréal in 1860, he effectively ended traditional ways of playing the game and made continued native participation in their own game problematic. Natives were used, because of the novelty value of their "Indianness," on international tours to promote the game, but were often excluded from play in Canada because of the strict amateur rules and the inability of native players to afford travel and membership fees without compensation. In fact, some amateur rules (e.g., the Montréal Pedestrian Club) specifically precluded native athletes from participation (Kidd, 1988). As the sport began to professionalize by the end of the nineteenth century, clubs again turned to native players because of their skills at the game, and paid them to play.

Similar examples of exploitation are evident in distance running, which was an extremely important, often professional, sport in the early years of the twentieth century. Bruce Kidd (1980), of the University of Toronto, has painstakingly detailed the exploitation of one of the best-known native runners, Tom Longboat, an Onondagan from the Six Nations reserve in

Ontario. As noted below, such examples of overt exploitation would nowadays meet with a great deal more *resistance*.

Racism In partnership with *exploitation*, native athletes also met with a great deal of racism in the nineteenth and twentieth centuries. For example, native athletes were often excluded from participation in organized sports, especially those in which they had skill and experience (e.g., lacrosse, running, snowshoeing). As noted above, this was sometimes a result of the enforcement of strict amateur rules, which were associated with a European distaste at possibly being defeated by individuals who they considered to be socially inferior and of a lower social class (similar motives were evident in the segregation of black athletes from participation at this time). Eddington (2000) points out that, "Not until twenty years after it became Canada's national game were the Iroquois Nationals allowed to join the International Lacrosse Federation" (p. 14), as the first native team in the league in 1887.

Racism also had vicious personal effects, with racist slurs aimed at native athletes by spectators; slurs were even considered legitimate expression in the media. For example, Lou Marsh, a sportswriter for the *Toronto Star*, and the individual after whom the Canadian Athlete of the Year trophy is named, "carried on a bizarre campaign against [Tom] Longboat...describ[ing] him as 'the original dummy....Wily...unreliable...as hard to train as a leopard'" (Unwin, 2001, p. 23). Bruce Kidd's research effectively challenged the traditional characterizations of Longboat as "unmanageable" and "obstinate." While this type of casual racism is no longer unchallenged, native athletes still report negative experiences with non-native athletes and spectators. For example, in major junior and NHL hockey, there are reports of incidents between players and with spectators, and Mann Cup and Minto Cup games between native and non-native lacrosse teams are sometimes characterized by brutality (Campbell, 1995).

Other recent incidents give pause because, while they may seem to be racist, no evidence is available. For example, Ted Nolan, a former NHL player who became the first Native Canadian head coach of an NHL team, was fired by the Buffalo Sabres shortly after he was named as NHL Coach of the Year in 1997. There was no explanation, and, unlike most head coaches who lose their jobs, he did not work in the NHL again until 2006 (as coach of the New York Islanders) where he was the lowest paid coach in the NHL ($600,000) He was fired in 2008 with one year left on his contract. Brenda Zeman's (1988) book on native athletes, and a series of articles by Laura Robinson (e.g., 1995, 1997, 2000b, 2002b) dramatically outline continuing difficulties and discrimination experienced by Native Canadian athletes.

Ethnocentric Distortion Paraschak (1989) points out that most of our knowledge about Native Canadians is distorted because the experience is presented from a Euro-Canadian perspective rather than from the standpoint of native peoples. This has resulted in certain native practices (e.g., gambling) being condemned; in athletic ability being defined as "natural" rather than as a result of training and skill development (cf., black athletes; Heine, 1991); and in ethnocentric assumptions about the character of native peoples (e.g., they are "less civilized"). And it also resulted in the assumption, only recently questioned by Robidoux (2006) who took a Native Canadian perspective, that the use of native imagery (e.g., the logos of the Chicago Blackhawks or the Cleveland Indians) can only be considered as disrespectful. Robidoux showed the widespread use of such imagery by Native Canadian hockey teams, and provides a persuasive explanation of why their use can be considered as more ironic than disrespectful.

In a subtle and complex analysis, Paraschak (2007) brings together race and gender to explore the differences between the meaning of gendered action in Native Canadian sports

Sports and Bilingualism

The Sport Funding and Accountability Framework (1995–96) introduced a series of five-year funding plans to support thirty-eight of the approximately sixty Canadian national sport organizations (NSOs). Funding was linked to government social and sport policy objectives, including "minimum expectations in five areas of social policy: official languages, athlete-centredness, women in sport, harassment and abuse in sport, and athletes with a disability" (OCOL, 2000, p. 19). The agreement between Sport Canada and the NSOs stated: "The Recipient agrees... to take into account official languages considerations when providing services to the public or members" (OCOL, 2000, p. 18).

A series of steps were outlined for the NSOs, as well as for the national sport centres and multi-sport organizations (e.g., the Canadian Olympic Committee and Canadian Interuniversity Sport) that receive federal funding. The steps required that written materials (rules, policies, etc.), websites, and services to athletes and the public be available in both official languages by March, 1999. Very few of those receiving federal funds met the expectations, and ongoing funding was not tied to meeting the minimum expectations. OCOL reports on Official Languages in the Canadian Sport System in 2000, and 2003, showed that Sport Canada was not meeting its obligations under the Official Languages Act (1985).

What difference does it make if we have a primarily unilingual sport system in a bilingual society? In her review of the high-performance sport system (2000), Official Languages Commissioner Dyanne Adam stated:

[T]he Canadian sport system does not meet the needs of francophone [high performance] athletes, and does not provide them equal access... In a system that boasts that it is centred around the athlete, francophone athletes should not have to overcome the double challenge of mastering English in addition to their sport in order to succeed at a high level. (Clark, 2000, p. S2)

In addition to having to learn a second language, OCOL (2000) found many examples of unequal treatment of francophone national team athletes. For example, at one national team selection camp, all the coaches were unilingual (English); a bilingual francophone athlete who had been selected to the team had to accompany a coach to translate as the coach informed a francophone athlete that he had not made the team.

Of course, anglophones in the sport community, as the linguistic majority, also view bilingualism as a burden. They complain about translation costs and delays—"why should we have to wait for documents to be translated so that everyone may receive them at the same time?" They also point out that they are in a "no win" situation—"even when we spend money on translation, we get into trouble because it's not accurate." However, in a study of language relations in CIS and Hockey Canada (Donnelly et al., 2001), the real consequences of translation problems were evident. For example, there was a difference in the interpretation of the Canadian Interuniversity Athletic Union (now CIS) eligibility rule, which was not quite the same in English and French. Because the regulations state that the English version stands in case of a dispute, there was a possibility that francophone athletes and teams could be disadvantaged. In other examples, Hockey Québec had numerous translation problems with Hockey Canada materials. For example:

- Delays in the receipt of translated documents were sometimes so long that when the French text arrived it was outdated. Staff received translated invitations to events that had already occurred. One staff member said, "Often, the French version of the administrative regulations was received months after they had been distributed in English. When the updated rule book is not in the hands of the coaches and referees by August or September, it is too late. They already are in the arenas working with the kids; they have to know about the rule changes and the new

Continued

REFLECT ON	**Sports and Bilingualism**
SPORTS	continued

rules...." Hockey Canada programmes that were supposed to be implemented immediately, were also delayed.

- Translations carried out by Hockey Canada were full of errors, sometimes to the point of being unintelligible. All translated materials sent from the CHA had to be carefully proofread, and thousands of books or documents had to be destroyed because of translation errors.
- The potentially serious consequences of translation errors were evident when an English document on concussion stated that, following a violent blow to the head, a player should be prevented from playing for the rest of the *game*; the French version provided by the CHA stated that a player should be prevented from playing for the rest of the *period*.

All of the above examples, and even some of the solutions proposed by anglophones, involve extra time and work for francophones. For example, in an attempt to avoid the financial cost of providing bilingual services, some anglophone sport executives suggested that francophone and bilingual volunteers should do translation and interpretation work.

The Office of the Commissioner of Official Languages (OCOL) regularly heard arguments about the cost of translation and interpretation services and demands that the federal government meet these costs because they were incurred as a result of federal regulations. They responded: "We do not believe that the federal government alone should bear the

cost of enabling national organizations to function in both languages: providing services to members in both English and French represents a benefit to the organization and should be considered a normal cost of doing business in Canada" (2000, p. 26). One benefit is that the existence of bilingual services attracts francophones and builds membership. In turn, this creates a larger selection pool for representation on national teams. Some of the predominantly anglophone NSOs have followed precisely this pattern, either to increase their francophone representation or because a large pool of talented francophone athletes already existed (e.g., Skate Canada).[1] An additional benefit lies in the legitimacy achieved by an organization that is seen to be bilingual. However, while some level of bilingualism is necessary for funding, for membership and representation, and perhaps for legitimacy, these factors are also associated with a quite widespread belief that Canada is a better place because of bilingualism and multiculturalism. *What do you think?*

---

[1]Following the two critical reports from OCOL (2000, 2003), there has been quite a strong shift towards bilingualism. CIS, Hockey Canada, and a number of other NSOs have made major efforts to become more bilingual in the last few years. However, Svoboda and Donnelly (2005) found that the double burden for francophone high-performance athletes still existed—the need to become skilled enough to make the national team and the need to learn English. Services at the National Sport Centres, and coaching were still primarily in English.

....

and physical activities from the standpoint of Native Canadians and Euro-Canadians. Take, for example, the different views of masculinity evident in native (Inuit) and non-native styles of play in hockey, which has resulted in non-native complaints about the Inuit style of play:

> [The] Inuit style of play fits with traditional Native methods of violence expression, which rarely involve face-to-face confrontation [in hockey,

for example, taking the form of hitting people from behind and skating away]. Non-Inuit players, however, adhere to different norms [dropping gloves and fighting face-to-face] which is perceived to be more manly....Inuit athletes construct different norms of masculinity...in which Native male athletes see themselves as being more athletically talented [skating faster, shooting harder] than White athletes. (Paraschak, 2007, p. 142)

These differences can only be resolved with greater knowledge and understanding of each other's perspectives. At the present time, Native Canadian athletes have far more knowledge of the non-native sport perspective than vice versa.

Assimilation and Resistance Among the civil and equal rights movements that started in the 1960s was a native rights movement in North America that began to challenge (resist) discrimination and attempts to assimilate (annihilate) native cultures. A part of this movement involved, first, a self-conscious attempt to maintain and restore traditional native sports and physical activities, such as pow-wows, snow-snake competitions, the Northern Games, and Dene Games; and second, to establish native-only sporting events in which native solidarity and self-determination could be developed during participation in non-native sports, such as the North American Indigenous Games, and native hockey tournaments (Paraschak, 1996; Robidoux, 2006). These became necessary because of legal actions by colonists banning traditional native activities (e.g., Potlatch, Sun Dance), because of the activities of Christian missionaries that also led to the loss of traditional cultures, and because of government action in mandating education in residential schools. These various actions had the effect of assimilation and the loss of native languages and cultures. Cultural loss meant that many natives were more familiar with hockey, baseball, and other Euro-Canadian sports than they were with traditional sports. The establishment of two forms of games (traditional and native-only) recognized this reality.

Assimilation also takes more subtle forms. Paraschak (1982) pointed out that the only television available in the Arctic was from southern Canada and the United States, showing only mainstream sports; young physical education teachers from southern Canada, usually spending only one or two years in the Arctic, tended to teach Euro-Canadian sports and physical activities rather than learning native activities. The combined effect of these is additional loss of traditional sporting cultures. The forms of resistance outlined above—organizing traditional and native-only events—create an additional problem. As Hall, et al., note, the actual organization of such activities "seems so removed from the spontaneous play and games of a traditional culture" (1991, p. 181). And, despite attempts to re-create "bush consciousness" (Heine, 1995), "Native time" (Paraschak, 1996), and traditional ways of organizing activities (e.g., choosing judges at the last minute who then determine the rules for that event), as Mrozek (1987) pointed out, "the consciousness of having to preserve the culture fundamentally alters what is preserved—turning it into a museum piece" (p. 38).

Perhaps the most striking symbolic piece of Native Canadian resistance occurred at the 1984 Los Angeles Olympics when Alwyn Morris, a gold medalist in canoeing, held up an eagle feather on the podium during the medal ceremony (see the photo in chapter 2). The action was carried out with the permission of the IOC (who have rules against political protests or statements at the Games), since it was presented to them as a spiritual and traditional aboriginal action. However, the action combined the traditional with the modern—a Native Canadian medalist in a traditional Canadian activity that had been Europeanized and modernized for the Olympics, holding aloft an eagle feather. It sent a powerful symbolic and political message to Native Canadians. Morris has since helped to found the North American Indigenous Games and the Aboriginal Sport Circle in Canada.

Colonizing Nations and Immigrant Relations

While there is little research on native and non-native relations in Canada, there is even less on the final axis of racial and ethnic relations. The

Lacrosse has an interesting history: the traditional native game was Europeanized, native players were then excluded from play, and now, native players are actively involved in the Europeanized version of their game. Here, the Six Nations Arrows celebrate their Ontario Lacrosse Association major junior A championship in 1998. [CP(Brian Thompson) *Brantford Expositor*]

editor of a special ethnic sports issue of *Polyphony* (Harney, 1985, p. 10) noted:

> [The] study of sports organizations and their sponsors could enrich our understanding of the problems of immigrant integration in Canadian society and of the constant encounter of immigrants and their values with the host society and its ways....In fact the formation of any sports team, or the events and rituals surrounding any organized game, contain those elements of a cultural artifact...which show ethnicity to be a complex process and a negotiation, not just a hard fact acquired from the census or from looking at someone's surname.

In the three examples that follow, we consider Canadians and Americans as national groups in Canadian sports, and examine European-Canadian relations with Asian- and African-Canadian visible minorities.

Canadian/American Relations Major U.S. professional sports leagues have plans to expand internationally. Part of the process of preparing for such expansion has been the introduction of NBA basketball players and NHL hockey players into Olympic competition, and all four major sport leagues playing international exhibition games and even some regular season games. However, three of the leagues (baseball, basketball, and hockey) already have international teams—in Canada, the fourth enjoys a reciprocal relationship with a Canadian league (NFL/CFL), and some of the Buffalo Bills regular season games will be played in Toronto in 2008; all the leagues have U.S. and Canadian players playing in both countries. These relationships produce different tensions that require an analysis of Canadians and Americans as national groups. This has been the case particularly with the CFL.

The ongoing reliance of the CFL on U.S. players was formalized in 1965 when players were first designated as "imports" (usually Americans) and nonimports (usually Canadians).[12] In 1970, the controversial "designated import" rule was introduced, allowing two U.S. quarterbacks on each team, ensuring that Russ Jackson was the last Canadian to regularly play quarterback in the CFL. Currently, the game roster has been set at 39 players, 19 nonimports, 17 imports, and three quarterbacks (essentially 20 American players, two of whom are "designated imports," and 19 Canadians—the highest proportion of Canadians for some years).

Imports include both black and white players (as did the nonimports), and some elements of Canadian and U.S. race relations were played out in the CFL. Smith and Grindstaff (1972) found

---

[12]The rule is rather more complicated than place of birth since it defines imports as those who played football outside Canada before their seventeenth birthday. The nonimports (sometimes referred to by those analyzing the CFL as "nonimportant") did not play outside Canada as youngsters, but the age designation permits those Canadians whose university football careers were in the U.S. to be counted as nonimports, even if they became naturalized Americans.

Canadians know a great deal about the U.S.—and U.S. sports—but that knowledge is not reciprocated. We wonder what the response might have been if an R.C.M.P. honour guard had flown the U.S. flag upside-down in Toronto during the 1992 Blue Jays–Braves World Series. [CP(Hans Deryk)].

that, although the status of black athletes in the league improved during the 1950s and 1960s, black players were, in general, not treated equally. During the early 1970s, U.S. research began to show that African Americans in the NFL and in MLB were "stacked" in noncentral positions (see the Online Learning Centre feature on "Stacking"), and Donald Ball (1973), a sociologist at the University of Victoria, carried out a study to determine if the stacking of black players was also evident in the CFL.

When Ball adjusted the centrality model slightly to designate "primary" and "supporting" positions in the game, he found that it was not African-American players but white Canadian players who were "stacked" in the supporting positions. They were unlikely to play in the central and primary positions, and they earned lower salaries than the Americans. Cantelon's (2001) update on this research suggests that little has changed in the last 30 years. It was common in the early 1970s (as it is even more so today) to criticize Canadian dependency on U.S. corporations by referring to Canada as a "branch plant" (of the U.S.) economy. Ball (1973) concluded his study by pointing out that the "lack of expectations about Canadian players" could be taken to mean that the CFL "is just one more tile in the mosaic of the branch plant economy" (p. 110).

The "designated import" rule, which virtually rules out a career in professional football for Canadian university quarterbacks (as quarterbacks), has received only one serious challenge.[13] In 1979, Jamie Bone, who had been a star quarterback with the University of Western Ontario Mustangs, was cut from the Hamilton Tiger-Cats tryout camp. Hall et al. (1991), describe his response, and the result:

> [Bone] complained to the Canadian Human Rights Commission that the CFL's designated import rule discriminated against him on the grounds of national or ethnic origin because it prevented Canadians from being hired to play quarterback. The Commission…concluded that it was always in a team's best interest to select the most talented quarterback regardless of his national origin, and that although a particular CFL coach may mistakenly perceive the designated import rule to favour hiring imports to play that position, the rule itself does not. (p. 178)

---

[13]The last Canadian to start as quarterback in a CFL regular season game was Larry Jusdanis in 1995 (for the Hamilton Ti-Cats); others, such as Queen's Tom Denison (2004) and Laval's Mathieu Bertrand (2004) were drafted; Bertrand switched to running back.

Since the majority of coaches and general managers in the CFL are Americans, or have U.S. football experience, it is generally assumed that they will look first to the United States for their key (skill, primary, and central) players, and fill up the remainder of their roster with the required 19 Canadians. In both the Ball study and the Bone case, Canadians appear to have become a minority group in their own country, a group that seems to be subject to unequal treatment. However, the treatment of black players has improved markedly in the last 30 years, to a point where several African Americans have served in leadership positions in the CFL.

More recently, nationalistic tensions have taken a different form that sometimes leaves Canadians shaking their heads, or smiling wryly at international misunderstanding. For example, the issue of booing national anthems at NHL games became the basis for tension. Some people in the crowd booed the U.S. national anthem before a game in Montréal in March, 2003, an action that was interpreted as a protest against the U.S. invasion of Iraq and was given widespread negative publicity in both the United States and Canada (where it became the subject of a Don Cherry anti-francophone rant). However, U.S. fans booing the Canadian national anthem before a 2002 Stanley Cup playoff game on Long Island, just a few days after four Canadians were killed and eight were injured when they were victims of U.S. "friendly fire" during the invasion of Afghanistan, only generated a small amount of negative publicity in Canada, and very little in the U.S. Major League Baseball has been particularly insensitive about national differences, with incidents ranging from the flying of the Canadian flag upside down at a World Series game in Atlanta (against Toronto) in 1992, to a directive from the Commissioner's office that "God Bless America" be played during the seventh inning stretch at all home openers, and Sunday and holiday games, to honour U.S. military involved in the invasion of Iraq. The Commissioner's office clearly did not give any

thought about how this was to be carried out, or received, in Montréal (at that time) and Toronto; or to the fact that the Canadian government determined that, without United Nations sanction, the invasion of Iraq was an illegal action and that Canada would not participate. If the four U.S. major professional sport leagues show similar insensitivity to national feelings in countries other than Canada, it does not bode well for international expansion.

Americans are not the only "imports" to play in Canada. Canadian sport teams also have, for example, Latino baseball players and European hockey players. The experiences of sporting migrants in the new global economy of sports is only now beginning to be explored. Alan Klein (1991, 1999) focused on the experiences of Dominican baseball players in Canada and the United States, and Joe Maguire (1995) studied Canadian hockey players in the U.K. But hockey has the largest number of imports in Canada, and research on the experiences of European players is only just beginning (Allain, 2004; Cantelon, 2006).

Asian-Canadian/European-Canadian Relations
A small amount of research focuses on European-Canadian relations with Asian visible minorities in Canada. British and Australian research shows lower participation levels in sports and physical activities among Muslim girls and women (immigrants and children of immigrants from South and West Asia), and interpretations suggest that such girls are constrained by parental rules about activities outside the home and that their time is devoted to domestic and familial duties. These interpretations suggest that sports and physical activity are not valued in the various ethnocultural groups that practise Islam, especially for girls.

However, Canadian research, while showing some similar results, reached a different interpretation because it involved interviews directly with Muslims and South Asians. This research suggests that it is not sports and physical activity itself, but sports and physical activity structured in Western ways that has less value. For example, Nakamura (2002) found that some Muslim women prefer to participate under specific conditions, such as with a modest and flexible dress code and/or in segregated spaces. Islam is not monolithic. The religion can be expressed in varying ways that do not preclude physical activity for men or women. Many of Nakamura's subjects were interested in participating in sports and physical activity, and some had been active in their country of birth. However, they had specific needs related to Islam that affected when and how they could participate, needs that illustrate how activities themselves can have religious connotations. For some, the needs are simple—young women played basketball or soccer in high school while wearing track pants and/or the *hijab*. High schools and interschool leagues that were flexible permitted this, and it was only at the higher levels—when international rules were enforced—that participation was considered to be impossible (e.g., international soccer federation [FIFA] rules require that shorts be worn). For others, the needs are more complex and involve segregated spaces that cannot be observed by men. Some schools and universities have taped windows, and have scheduled women-only hours to accommodate such needs. However, when such accommodations in rules or scheduling are not available, the young women interviewed preferred not to participate.[14]

Studies of South Asians in Canada, carried out by Susan Tirone at Memorial University of Newfoundland, found that the South Asian teens and young adults they interviewed were

In Canada, there have been few studies of Asian Canadians in sports. Like other young people who seek alternatives to organized competitive sports, this young Asian Canadian has taken up snowboarding. [John Terence Turner/Taxi/Getty Images]

more likely to participate in leisure activities with family and with members of their ethnic group (Tirone and Pedlar, 2000). Such activities are less likely to register in surveys of physical activity. Tirone (1999–2000) also found that some South Asian teens experienced racism and indifference towards their culture when they participated in community recreation programmes and competitive sports. As a way of coping with such experiences, they would either withdraw from participation altogether, or overcompensate, feeling the need to excel precisely because they were visible minorities. Tirone found that many of the South Asian young adults felt hurt at the indifference "Canadians" showed toward their culture; they felt that the people around them had little interest in learning more about their country of origin or their traditions, despite Canada's policy of multiculturalism. This feeling of disenchantment with multiculturalism could lead to isolation—to the sense that one's ethnic identity and community are a haven where one feels welcome.

[14]There are some differences between Québec—where the issue of *accommodation raissonable* is currently being debated—and other parts of Canada. In Québec recently there have been several incidents (in soccer and tae kwan do) where strict interpretation of rules by officials has resulted in Muslim girls wearing the *hijab* being removed from competitions.

Canadian research has only scratched the surface of analysis of these complex racial and ethnic relations, and we have found no research on the largest visible minority groups in Canada: East Asians.

African-Canadian/European-Canadian Relations
Giller Prize–winning author Austin Clarke wrote:

> For years, television did not show the faces of black hockey players—even though there were a few. And I remember that during an international tournament of junior world hockey played in some European country, that the Canadian television media went to Herculean lengths not to show the face of a black player! (2003, p. 10)

The vast majority of research on race and ethnicity, and on race and ethnicity in sports, has been carried out in the United States. By far the majority of that research concerns one particular set of racial relations—that between people of sub-Saharan African heritage and people of European heritage. As noted previously, this particular set of relations has a history in the United States that is rather different from the overall development of racial and ethnic relations in Canada, and different issues must be discussed in Canada. However, because of the complex, interdependent, and often dependent relations between Canada and the United States—for example, economic ties; the widespread exposure of Canadians to U.S. media; and, in sports, the interconnection of players between the two countries in all major team sports—many Canadians have absorbed U.S. ideas about the "black and white" issue of race relations. Wilson (1997, 1999), Wilson and Sparks (1996, 2001), and Abdel-Shehid (2000, 2002, 2005) have pointed to the ways in which American "blackness" has been appropriated into understanding Canadian "blackness" in sports.

And while this has often been the case, there are other connections to explore than that between African Americans and African Canadians. For example, there is a long history of African-Canadian participation in hockey and, despite the cruelty of racism, the long-delayed entry of African-Canadian players into the NHL. Also, there is a strong connection between African Canadians and the Caribbean (particularly Jamaican) rather than the African-American sprinting tradition. However, this paved the way for what Henry and Tator (2002) term "the discourse of Canada's national identity," which they characterize as being "marked by erasures, omissions, and silences" (p. 232). For example, Jackson (1998) examined the celebration of Ben Johnson as a Canadian hero at the 1988 Olympics. That Canadian identity was withdrawn by the media after the positive steroid test, and Johnson was then referred to as an immigrant, or Jamaican, rather than "Canadian." In terms of Henry and Tator's *Discourses of Domination*, this overlaps with the discourse of otherness, in that it created a distance between "us" ("white" Canadians) and "them" (Jamaicans), despite the fact that Johnson was a Canadian citizen. Jackson (1998) cites a 1988 newspaper article that captures ironically the patronizing tone of the discourses: "But then why would anyone expect an immigrant boy from rural Jamaica to be able to handle the pressure and temptations of such success."

A great deal of research remains to be done on African-Canadian experiences and relations with European-Canadians in sports. Several researchers have made a valuable start: Carl James of York University on the experiences of black high school athletes, and Gamal Abdel-Shehid (University of Alberta) and Brian Wilson (University of British Columbia) on black youth, sports, and identity. As with all other aspects of racial and ethnic relations in Canadian sports, we need a great deal more information. All kinds of other relations are possible in addition to the ones discussed here, and, in a country as diverse as Canada, it will become increasingly important to understand these sets of relations. For example, Margaret MacNeill's (University of Toronto) exploration of the meaning of, and positive reaction to, Daniel Igali's wrestling gold medal on the final day of the 2000 Sydney Olympics (2004). His Nigerian background, Canadian citizenship, and embrace of the Canadian flag following his victory raise all kinds of questions about skin colour, immigration, and identity; and his more recent participation in *kabaddi* with South Asian Canadians highlights the complexity and diversity of racial and ethnic relations in Canada.

THE CHALLENGES OF RACIAL AND ETHNIC RELATIONS IN CANADIAN SPORTS

Racial and ethnic relations in most sport settings are better today than in the past, but many changes are needed before sports are a model of intergroup fairness. The challenges faced today are different from the ones faced twenty years ago, and experience shows that they will always be a part of social life. When one set of challenges are met, a new social situation is created, and it presents its own challenges. For example, once racial and ethnic segregation is eliminated and people come together, there is the challenge of living, working, and playing with people who have diverse experiences and cultures. Meeting this challenge requires a commitment to equal treatment, *plus* learning about the perspectives of others, understanding how they define and give meaning to the world around them, and then determining how to form and maintain relationships while respecting differences, making compromises, and supporting one another in the pursuit of goals that may not always be shared. None of this is easy, and challenges are never met once and for all.

Many people think in fairy-tale terms when it comes to racial and ethnic relations: they believe that opening a door so that others may enter a social world is all that is needed to achieve racial and ethnic harmony. However, coming together is just the first step in a never-ending process of building relationships,

producing a representative culture, and sharing power with others. Racial and ethnic diversity brings potential vitality and creativity to a team, organization or society, but this potential does not automatically become reality. It requires constant awareness, commitment, and work to achieve and maintain it.

The following sections deal with three major challenges related to racial and ethnic relations in sports today: (1) eliminating racial and ethnic exclusion in sport participation, (2) dealing with and managing racial and ethnic diversity by creating an inclusive culture on sport teams and in sport organizations, and (3) integrating positions of power in sport organizations.

Eliminating Racial and Ethnic Exclusion in Sport Participation

Why are some sports characterized by disproportionately high rates of participation by racial and ethnic minorities, while others have little or no racial or ethnic diversity? When sociologist Harry Edwards (1973) answered this question in the early 1970s, he said that certain sports had built-in incentives for eliminating racial segregation. These included:

1. The people who control teams that make money when they win games benefit financially when they do not exclude players who can help them win games.
2. The individual performances of athletes can be measured in concrete, objective terms that are less likely to be influenced by racial ideology than is the case in other occupations.
3. Sport teams are organized so that all players benefit when a teammate performs well regardless of the teammate's skin colour or ethnicity.
4. When athletes play well on a sport team there is no expectation that they will be promoted into leadership positions where they have control over other players.

5. The success of most sport teams does not depend on friendships and off-the-field social relationships between teammates from racial or ethnic backgrounds different from their own.
6. When ethnic minority athletes are signed to a contract, they remain under the control of (white) coaches, managers, administrators, and owners in the organizational structure of a sport or sport team.

These six incentives offset the threats that whites often perceive when they consider racial and ethnic desegregation in non-sport situations and organizations. When the people who controlled professional sports realized that they could benefit financially from recruiting ethnic minority players without giving up power and control or upsetting the existing structure and relationships in their sports, they began to do so.

Desegregation has come more slowly in sports lacking these incentives. This is why golf, tennis, swimming, and other sports played in private clubs where social interaction is personal and often involves relationships between males and females have been slow to welcome racial and ethnic diversity. As the degree of social closeness increases in any setting, including sports, people are more likely to enforce various forms of exclusion. When others define exclusion as unfair and challenge it, racial and ethnic conflict often occurs. The history of this conflict is well documented, and it shows that policies of racial and ethnic exclusion in many sports are changed only when government legislation makes them illegal or when civil rights lawsuits threaten the financial assets of people and organizations that have proven histories of discrimination.

The forms of racial and ethnic exclusion that are most important today occur at the community level, where they are hidden behind policies that tie participation to fees and access to transportation. Some communities claim to have open sport and recreation programmes, when there are few or no facilities in areas where racial

and ethnic minorities live and when fees and ready access to transportation are required for participation. (This is one of the points made in Breaking Barriers on p. 293.) This is exacerbated in isolated Northern communities where there may be no facilities and where transportation may mean expensive air fares. Furthermore, as sports are organized by nonprofit and private organizations, there is a tendency for class-based patterns of exclusion to have an impact on some racial and ethnic groups more than others. Even though this form of exclusion is not grounded directly in racial and ethnic discrimination, its effects are much the same as those of past forms of exclusion, and they are more difficult to attack on the grounds that they violate charter rights. Eliminating these forms of exclusion will be one of the most difficult racial and ethnic challenges of this century (Donnelly and Coakley, 2002).

Dealing With and Managing Racial and Ethnic Diversity in Sports

As sports become more global, as teams recruit players from around the world, and as global migration creates pressures to develop racially and ethnically sensitive policies related to all aspects of sports, there will be many new racial and ethnic challenges faced by players, coaches, team administrators, and even spectators. It is naïve to think that the racial and ethnic issues that exist around the world today have no impact on sports or that sports can deal with these issues in ways that eliminate them once and for all time. Sport history in Canada and the United States shows that a host of new challenges were encountered when Jackie Robinson signed with the Brooklyn Dodgers in 1946 and Willie O'Ree signed with the Boston Bruins in 1958.[15] As the

---

[15]In the late 1940s, Conn Smythe, owner of the Toronto Maple Leafs, epitomized the casual racism and explicit barriers to black athletes when he was reported to have said, "I would give $10,000 to anyone who could turn Herb Carnegie white." The highly talented Carnegie never had a chance to play in the NHL (Carnegie, 1997).

Breaking Barriers

Point-of-Entry Barriers
We Are Out There

Toni Davis was training for the 2004 Paralympics in Athens. As a swimmer, she had heard about Martiza Correia, a new member of the Athens-bound U.S. Olympic team. Correia had broken U.S. swimming records held by the highly touted Amy Van Dyken and Jenny Thompson in the 50- and 100-metre freestyle. When Davis looked online for information about the new record-setting swimmer, she discovered that Correia was also an African American. Davis was heartened and said to herself, "*We are out there.*"

When Davis referred to "we," she meant *black swimmers*. As a former interuniversity athlete, she knew that a black person on a swim team caused many people to do a double take. She also knew that when people saw her—a black swimmer with only one arm—they often did a triple take.

Davis says that she gets more looks for having one arm than for being black, but she knows that race influences choices and opportunities in sports. "I'm not afraid to speak out and get black swimmers more attention, more participation," she says, but "I also want to get more notice for the Paralympics" because many people do not know it exists. "What we need to do for minority kids," Davis explains, is to have a programme that is "low-cost but gets them into the water, [and] gets them the instruction they need...to find out if they have the ability" (quotes in Schaller, 2005).

Davis knows that sport participation always has a point of entry—a point at which a person is hooked up with an opportunity. In the case of people with a disability, the point of entry is often connected with rehabilitation or occupational therapy programmes, medical care and treatment, or a local network of friends and family.

Taking advantage of an entry opportunity is most likely when people from ethnic minority backgrounds see others in a programme who will understand them and with whom they can identify. If everyone in a programme, including administrators and coaches, is white, most ethnic minority people, especially those with a disability, will think twice before taking the first step toward participation. "Fitting in" is always an issue when it comes to joining up and trying out.

This means that point-of-entry issues have complex dynamics related to race, ethnicity, health care, medical insurance, trusting medical providers, transportation, and the "look and feel" of disability sport programmes. Policy and legislation are also involved. Sport Canada's Sport Funding and Accountability Framework involves disability inclusion but, surprisingly, there are no policies for ethnic diversity at this time. If ethnic diversity and a sense of inclusiveness are not apparent, people of colour may conclude that they will be seen as "different." Playing sports is fun, but it becomes tedious when forced to deal with people doing triple takes when they see you.

Eliminating point-of-entry barriers related to race and ethnicity is a major challenge in sports for people with a disability. As in most sport organizations, there is a need to open coaching and administrative positions to men and women from traditionally underrepresented ethnic minorities. Inclusiveness must be apparent so that prospective participants can see people who look like them. Additionally, there is a need to create new entry points that are part of the structure of everyday life in neighbourhoods and communities where ethnic minorities live and work. Churches, schools, hospitals, medical clinics, and veteran's organizations are sites at which institutionalized entry points can be created. Once they exist, more people from ethnic minority backgrounds will know that "we are out there."

• •

first black players in their respective leagues, they faced enormous challenges, but so did their teammates, other players in the leagues, coaches, and fans. Both Robinson and O'Ree had to endure incident after incident of unspeakable racism by opponents, spectators, and racists in the general population. Teammates had to make decisions about if and how they would support their new teammate. Coaches had to manage a new set of racial dynamics that they had not previously experienced, such as who would be the black players' roommates on road trips and how to deal with players who made racist remarks that could destroy team morale. Fans who had never socialized across racial lines had to deal with supporting an integrated team, and perhaps sitting next to someone from a different race—something they had never done before. Announcers and reporters had to decide how they would report on the black players' experiences— whether they would report on the racism of other players who were fan favourites, or whether they would pretend that race was not a major issue, even though it was.

The outcomes in MLB and the NHL were quite different. Baseball with 29 percent of the players not born in the U.S. continued to integrate; black (9 percent), Latino (26 percent), and Japanese and Korean (2 percent) players are now well represented in the league (Lapchick, 2005), and while racism has not disappeared (e.g., in terms of management opportunities), there has been clear progress. In the NHL, progress has been much slower (Harris, 2005). Willie O'Ree played in only two games for the Bruins in 1958, and 43 more during the 1960–61 season. In 1977, Tony McKegney was cut by the Birmingham Bulls of the World Hockey Association after season ticket holders complained about having a black player on the team. And in 2003, former NHL goalie John Vanbiesbrouck resigned in disgrace from his position as coach and general manager of the Sault Ste. Marie Greyhounds of the Ontario Hockey League after using the "N" word to refer to the nineteen-year-old team captain, Trevor Daley. Black and native players report racist comments at all levels of hockey, and even francophone and European players find that they are subject to ethnic abuse. But there are some signs of progress. Although the NHL is still 98 percent white, there are now 13 active black players (blackvoices.com), and several of East Asian heritage; Jarome Iginla was a star at the 2002 men's Olympic hockey tournament; and Anson Carter scored the gold medal winning goal at the 2003 World Hockey Championships. Perhaps Willie O'Ree's current position as

"I love it when they line dance after they score a touchdown!"

FIGURE 9.1   Experiences and traditions vary from one racial or ethnic group to another. What happens when people from various groups bring their experiences and traditions to sports and use them to guide how they play or how they celebrate on-the-field success? If white players from the University of Calgary did a line dance after scoring a touchdown, would the CIS make a rule prohibiting it?

Director of Youth Development on the NHL's Diversity Task Force is beginning to have an impact.

This example of just two professional sports is intended to illustrate how racial and ethnic issues are never settled permanently. Issues faced today present new challenges. For example, some NHL hockey coaches have players on their teams from six different national and cultural backgrounds. These players sometimes hold negative racial and ethnic stereotypes at the same time that they have customs that other players and staff may define as strange (see figure 9.1).

Translators are used on hockey and baseball teams, cultural diversity training is needed, coaches must learn new ways to communicate effectively, and the marketing departments for teams must learn how to promote an ethnically diverse team to predominantly white fans. Ethnic and cultural issues enter into sponsorship considerations and the products sold at games. Cultural and ethnic awareness is now an important qualification for employees who handle team advertising and sponsorship deals.

These and related issues are central to the success of Major League Soccer in Canada and the United States because some teams have a strong base of European or Latino spectators. The commercial success of soccer in Canada and the U.S. depends on attracting ethnic spectators to games and television broadcasts. Sport teams in western Europe increasingly face the challenge of coping with new racial and ethnic tensions created by high rates of migration from Africa, Asia, and eastern Europe. The challenges are related to matters of national identity, labour migration, and citizenship status. Populist leaders in some nations have raised questions about allowing immigrants to play on national teams; and some fans use players with African or Asian backgrounds as scapegoats for social and economic problems in their lives. These issues will not go away anytime soon in Europe, North America, or other parts of the world. Challenges related to managing racial and ethnic relations are here to stay, and they will change over time.

Integrating Positions of Power in Sport Organizations

Despite progressive changes in many sports, the major positions of power and control are held primarily by white men. There are exceptions to this, but they do not eliminate pervasive and persistent racial and ethnic inequalities related to power and control in sports. Data regarding who holds positions of power change every year, and it is difficult to obtain consistent information from sport teams and organizations.

Richard Lapchick (2005), at the Institute for Diversity and Ethics in Sport at the University of Central Florida, publishes regularly a *Racial and Gender Report Card* for sport organizations. It contains data on the racial and ethnic composition of players in major professional team sports, and provides an analysis of the number and types

of jobs held by women and people of colour in major professional sports organizations. Unfortunately, no racial report card is available specifically for Canada, so there are no CFL data and other data must be extrapolated from the reports. Also, since 2002, Lapchick's report cards have not included any NHL data.

However, among the major men's professional team sports in North America, it is clear that hockey is the "whitest." In addition to having over 98 percent of white players (in comparison to MLB—63 percent; MLS—64 percent; NBA—22 percent; and NFL—29 percent), there has only ever been one non-white coach in the 92-year history of the NHL—Ted Nolan, who coached the Buffalo Sabres from 1995–97, and the New York Islanders from 2006–08. Interestingly, the Islanders is the only team in the NHL owned by non-whites: Charles B. Wang of China and Sanjay Kumar of Sri Lanka (also, Rual Fernandez was listed as a limited partner of the Washington Capitals (Lapchick, 2004)).

Other U.S. leagues have sometimes found leadership positions for visible minorities in their Canadian branch plants. For example, Cito Gaston managed the Toronto Blue Jays to consecutive World Series wins in the 1990s, and the Montréal Expos had a long-term, and highly respected, Latino manager with Felipe Alou. The short-lived Vancouver Grizzlies of the NBA had African Americans as coach (Sidney Lowe) and President/General Manager (Stu Jackson). The Toronto Raptors also had African Americans in leadership positions—Isiah Thomas was Vice President and General Manager, and Sam Mitchell is currently the team's coach. In the CFL, African Americans coached the Toronto Argonauts (Mike "Pinball" Clemons) and the Saskatchewan Roughriders (Danny Barrett), and another visible minority, Joe Paopao (Samoan heritage), coached the Ottawa Renegades.

We have noted the ongoing underre-presentation of francophone Canadians in leadership positions in Canadian sports, but there are signs of change in, for example, the NHL, where a number of coaching positions have been taken by francophones in recent years. Of course, francophone Danielle Sauvageau held the highest profile women's leadership position in Canada when she coached the national hockey team to Olympic gold in 2002. While opportunities have increased, there are still barriers to be overcome.

Prospects for Change

People do not give up racial and ethnic beliefs easily, especially when they come in the form of well-established ideologies rooted deeply in their cultures. Those who have benefited from those ideologies will resist changes in the relationships and social structures that reproduce their beliefs. This is why certain expressions of racism and ethnic bigotry have remained a part of sports in Canada and other societies.

Sports may bring people together, but they do not automatically lead them to adopt tolerant attitudes or change long-standing policies of exclusion. White team owners, general managers, and athletic directors in the United States worked with black athletes for many years before they ever hired black coaches. It often requires social and legal pressures to force people in power positions to act more affirmatively in their hiring practices. In the meantime, ethnic minorities remain underrepresented in coaching and administration.

Although there is resistance to certain types of changes in sports, many sport organizations are more progressive than other organizations when it comes to some aspects of racial and ethnic relations. However, these good things do not happen automatically or as often as many think; nor do changes in people's attitudes automatically translate into changes in the overall organization of sports. Challenging the negative beliefs and attitudes of individuals is one thing; changing the relationships and social structures that have been built on those beliefs and attitudes is another. Both changes are needed, but neither occurs automatically just because sports bring people together in the same locker rooms and stadiums.

Racial and ethnic relations will improve in sports only when those who have power work to bring people together in ways that confront and challenge racial and ethnic issues. This means that changes must be initiated and supported by all racial and ethnic groups, or else they will fail (Oglesby and Schrader, 2000). It has never been easy for people to deal with racial and ethnic issues, but if it can be done in sports, it would attract public attention and possibly inspire changes in other spheres of life.

Change also requires a new vocabulary to deal with racial and ethnic diversity in social life and to promote inclusive practices and policies. A vocabulary organized around the belief that skin colour or ethnicity signifies a unique biological essence only perpetuates racial and ethnic discrimination. In connection with sports, there is a need for research to go beyond documenting racial and ethnic performance differences and begin to explain how social and cultural factors, including racial ideologies, create and perpetuate differences. Simply documenting differences without explaining them too often reproduces the very racial ideologies that have caused hatred, turmoil, and confusion in much of the world for nearly 300 years. This is why many scholars in the sociology of sport now ask research questions about the meanings that people give to physical and cultural characteristics and how those meanings influence actions, relationships, and social organization.

The racial and ethnic diversity training sessions used over the past two decades have produced some changes, but promoting positive changes in intergroup relations today requires training leaders to create more inclusive cultures and power structures in sport organizations. This means that training sessions should go beyond athletes and include everyone from team owners and athletic directors to the people in middle management, coaching, marketing, and public information. One of the problems with diversity training sessions in the past is that they were directed at low-level employees who often did

The Irish Football Association began in 2000 to use soccer as a site for eradicating the Protestant-versus-Catholic sectarianism that led to decades of violence and terrorism in Northern Ireland. Aaron Hughes, captain of Northern Ireland's National Soccer Team, and his teammates work with young people to promote equality and diversity. The team motto is "Sectarianism and racism in Northern Ireland Football is not welcome and will not be tolerated." [Mike Collins, Irish Football Association, Northern Ireland]

not take them seriously because they did not see their supervisors taking them seriously.

Even people who are sensitive to diversity issues require opportunities to learn new things about the perspectives of those whose experiences and cultures are different from our own. This means that effective training sessions are organized, in part, around the perspectives of racial and ethnic minorities—an essential strategy if positive changes are to occur. When making things better means doing them to fit the interests of those currently in power, real change is unlikely.

SUMMARY

ARE RACE AND ETHNICITY IMPORTANT IN SPORTS?

Racial and ethnic issues exist in sports, just as they exist in most other spheres of social life. As people watch, play, and talk about sports, they often take into account ideas about skin colour and ethnicity. The meanings that are given to skin colour and ethnic background influence access to sport participation and the decisions that people make about sports in their lives.

Race refers to a category of people identified through a classification system based on meanings given to physical traits among humans; *ethnicity* refers to collections of people identified in terms of their shared cultural heritage. Racial and ethnic minorities are populations that have endured systematic forms of discrimination in a society.

The idea of race has a complex history, but it has served as the foundation for racial ideology, which people use to identify and make sense of racial differences. Racial ideology, like other social constructions, changes over time as ideas and relationships change. However, over the past century, racial ideology has led many people to assume that there are important biological and even cognitive differences between the races and that these differences explain the success, or lack of success, of non-whites in sports.

Racial ideology has influenced the ways that many people connect skin colour with athletic performance. At the same time it has influenced the ways that some whites and Asians make sport participation decisions and the ways that many people explain the performance of black males or Asians who excel in certain sports. Race, gender, and class relations in North American society have combined to create a context in which black males emphasize a personal presentation of self that has been described as "cool pose," a stylized persona that has added to the commodity value of the black male body in sports and enabled some black athletes to use widely accepted ideas about race to intimidate opponents, especially white opponents, in sports.

The sport participation patterns among francophones, Native Canadians, and other ethnic and visible minority peoples have their own histories. Combinations of historical, economic, cultural, social, and political factors have influenced those histories. However, sport participation in minority populations usually occurs under terms set by the dominant ethnic population in a community or society. Minority populations are seldom able to use sports to challenge the power and privilege of the dominant group, even though individual minority-group members may experience great personal success in sports.

The fact that some sports have histories of racially and ethnically mixed participation does not mean that problems have been eliminated. Harmonious racial and ethnic relations never occur automatically, and ethnic harmony is never established once and for all time. As current problems are solved, new relationships and new challenges are created. This means that racial and ethnic issues require regular attention if challenges are to be successfully anticipated and met. Success also depends largely on whether members of the dominant ethnic population see value in racial and ethnic diversity and commit themselves to dealing with diversity issues alongside those who have different ethnic backgrounds.

Sports continue to be sites for racial and ethnic problems. However, it is important to acknowledge that, despite problems, sports can also be sites for challenging racial ideology and transforming racial and ethnic relations. This happens only when people in sports plan strategies to encourage critical awareness of ethnic prejudices, racist ideas, and forms of discrimination built into the cultures and structures of sport organizations. This awareness is required to eliminate ethnic exclusion in sports, deal with and manage ethnic diversity, and integrate ethnic minorities into the power structure of sport organizations. Without this awareness, ethnic relations can become volatile and lead to overt forms of hostility.

Visit *Sports in Society*'s Online Learning Centre at www.mcgrawhill.ca/olc/coakley for additional information, website resources, and study tools for this chapter.

chapter 10

[Laura Robinson]

Social Class

Do money and power matter in sports?

Cost restricts access to recreational activities for low-income families. Less than half of low-income families with children spend money on user fees for recreational activities, compared to 72% of high-income families.

—**The Progress of Canada's Children,** *Canadian Council on Social Development (1998)*

High performance sport is a demanding undertaking in a ruthlessly competitive international environment....It involves...a more than full-time commitment without ever guaranteeing a payoff in the end. It is not a job that just anyone can do; there are few jobs that are more demanding.

—**Rob Beamish and Jan Borowy, authors (1988)**

I've never been in a place where someone's mom is a doctor, and someone's dad is a lawyer, or whatever.

—**Andre Wilkin (2007), an athlete from a low-income neighbourhood in Toronto, about to go to Cornell University on a basketball scholarship**

People like to think that sports transcend issues of money, power, and economic inequalities. They see sports as open to everyone, watch many sports on "free" television, and often define success on the field in terms of ability and hard work. However, all organized sports depend on material resources, and those resources must come from somewhere. Therefore, playing, watching, and excelling in sports depend on resources supplied by individuals, families, governments, or corporations.

More than ever before, it takes money to play sports and receive the coaching needed to develop sport skills. Tickets are expensive, and spectators often are segregated by social class in the stadium: The wealthy and well-connected sit in club seats and luxury suites, whereas fans who are less well off sit in other sections, depending on their ability to pay for premium tickets or buy season tickets.[1] It even takes money to watch sports on television when events air on subscriber cable (the way most Canadians receive their TV signals), digital, satellite, or pay-per-view formats. This means that sports and sport participation are connected with the distribution of economic, political, and social resources in society. Money and power do matter in sports.

Many people also believe that sports are avenues for economic success for people from all social classes. Rags-to-riches stories are common when people talk about athletes. However, these beliefs and stories distract attention from how sports often reflect and perpetuate existing economic inequalities in society.

This chapter deals with matters of money and wealth, as well as larger issues related to social class and socioeconomic mobility. Our discussion focuses on the following questions:

1. What is meant by *social class* and *class relations*?
2. How do social class and class relations influence sports and sport participation?
3. Are sports open and democratic in the provision of economic and career opportunities?
4. Does playing sports contribute to occupational success and social mobility among former athletes?

SOCIAL CLASS AND CLASS RELATIONS

Social class and the related concepts of social stratification, socioeconomic status, and life chances are important concepts when studying social worlds. This is because economic resources are related to power in society, and economic inequalities influence nearly all aspects of people's lives. In fact, in many ways social class is "the elephant in the room"—usually given less research attention in North American sociology of sport than gender and race/ethnicity—and yet social class has profound effects on sport participation, and must also be considered in terms of the ways that it intersects with other forms of social inequality.

Social class refers to *categories of people who share an economic position in society based on a combination of their income (earnings), wealth (possessions), education, occupation, and social connections.* People in a particular social class also share similar **life chances**—that is, they share *similar odds for achieving economic success and gaining economic power* (and other forms of power that those chances confer) *in society*. Social classes exist in all industrial societies because life chances are not equally distributed across all populations.

Social stratification is the concept that sociologists use when referring to *structured forms of economic inequalities that are part of the organization of everyday social life*. In other words, when compared with people from upper social classes,

---

[1]In fact, seating in a stadium or arena may be seen as a metaphor for the class stratification system. The wealthy sit close to the action, or in exclusive seating areas; other seats are graded—in terms of wealth—up to the "nosebleed" seats farthest away from the action. Those even lower down the social ladder are unable to afford access at all. See figure 10.1.

people from lower-class backgrounds have fewer opportunities to achieve economic success and gain economic power. Children born into wealthy, powerful, and well-connected families are in far better positions to become wealthy, powerful, and well-connected adults than children born into poor families that lack influence and social networks connecting them with educational and career opportunities.

Most of us are aware of economic inequalities in society, but there are few public discussions about the ways that social class influences our views of ourselves and others, our social relationships, and our everyday lives (Perrucci and Wysong, 2003). In other words, we do not often discuss **class relations**—that is, *the social relations and interactions between people of different social classes that result from the power differences between different classes of persons.* In schools and the media, we hear about the importance of equal opportunities that are supposed to exist in a *meritocracy*—a society where achievement and success are supposed to be based on a person's skills and abilities; but we rarely hear about *social reproduction*—how people in upper socioeconomic classes use their income, wealth, and power to maintain privileged positions in society and pass that privilege from one generation to the next. We hear about those who have moved up and out of the lower socioeconomic classes through hard work and strong character, and about "millionaires next door" and "regular guys" who are CEOs making tens of millions of dollars a year. But we learn little about the oppressive effects of poverty and the limited opportunities available to those who lack economic resources, access to good education, and well-placed social connections. However, social class differences are real, they have real consequences for life chances, they affect nearly every facet of people's lives, and all of this is clearly documented by valid and reliable data (Clement, 1975; Domhoff, 2002; Kozol, 1991; Lareau, 2000; Perrucci and Wysong, 2003; Sernau, 2005).

People in many postindustrial societies are often uncomfortable with critical discussions of social class and class relations (hooks, 2000; Sage, 1998). The myth of equality in many democratic societies (the idea that "we are all middle class now") discourages such discussions, even though we are aware of class and class relations in our lives. This is especially true when it comes to sports and sport participation in which we like to think that money and class-based privilege do not matter.

The discussion of social class and class relations in this chapter is grounded in critical theories. The focus is on economic inequality, the processes through which it is reproduced, the ways that it serves the interests of those with wealth and economic power, and how it affects what happens in sports and the lives of people associated with sports.

SPORTS AND ECONOMIC INEQUALITY

Money and economic power exert significant influence on the goals, purpose, and organization, of sports in society (Gruneau, 1999; Sugden and Tomlinson, 2000; Tomlinson, 2007). Many people believe that sports and sport participation are open to all people and that inequalities related to money, position, and influence do not spill over into the organized games we play and watch. However, formally organized sports could not be developed, scheduled, or maintained without economic resources. Those who control money and economic power use their financial clout to organize and sponsor sports. As they do so, they give preference to sport forms that reflect and maintain their own values and interests.

The wealthy aristocrats who organized the Olympic Movement and sponsored the modern Olympic Games even used their power to establish a definition of *amateur* that privileged athletes from wealthy backgrounds around the world. This definition excluded athletes from working-class

An ideology of achievement through competitive success infers that being wealthy and powerful (winning) is proof of individual abilities, moral worth, and character. Exclusive sports clubs such as this one highlight this ideology. Therefore, they promote the interests of powerful and wealthy people and, at the same time, provide them with luxurious places to play sports. [Jay Coakley]

backgrounds,[2] who could afford to train only if they used their sport skills to help them to earn a living. The definition of *amateur* has been revised over the years, so that more people are able to participate in sports. However, money and economic power now operate in different ways as powerful corporations use the Olympics to expand profits by linking their logos and products to particular athletes and global sport images that express their interests.

Elite and powerful groups in society always have had considerable influence over "what counts as sport" and how sports will be organized and played. Even when grassroots games and physical activities become formally organized as sports, they are not widely sponsored or promoted unless they can be used to promote the interests and ideologies of those with money and economic power in society. For example, ESPN organized and televised the X Games to fit their corporate interests and orientations rather than those of the athletes, although the athletes have

struggled to have their concerns taken into account. Similarly, the informal games played by people of all ages often depend on the availability of facilities, equipment, and safe play spaces. These are more plentiful in the everyday lives of people from upper- and upper-middle-income families and neighbourhoods. Low-income families and neighbourhoods often lack the resources and well-maintained public spaces needed to initiate and sustain informal activities; they do not have large lawns at their homes, cul-de-sacs without traffic, or well-maintained parks where they can play. This is why it is important to understand the dynamics of class relations when we study sports.

The Dynamics of Class Relations

One way to understand the dynamics of class relations is to think about how age relations operate in sports. Consider this: even though children are capable of creating their own games, adults intervene and develop youth sport programmes. These programmes are organized around the ideas and orientations that adults think are best for their

---

[2]In Canada, the definition extended to Native Canadians when, in the late nineteenth century, native lacrosse players were arbitrarily designated as professionals.

children. As noted in chapter 5, adults possess the *resources* to develop, schedule, and maintain organized youth programmes that reflect their ideas of what children should be doing and learning as they play. Children often enjoy adult-controlled, organized sports, but their enjoyment occurs in a framework that is determined by adults and serves to legitimize and reproduces the power that adults have over the lives of children.

When children's behaviour in organized sports deviates from adult expectations, adults use their power to force compliance or convince children that it is in their best interest to play "the right way." When children comply and meet adult expectations, the adults say they possess "character" and reward them accordingly. This is why many adults like coaches who are autocratic and controlling. Such coaches reaffirm the cultural belief that the world is a better place when adults have full and strict control over young people and when young people consent to that control. In this way, sports reproduce a hierarchical form of age relations, in which adult power and privilege are defined as natural and necessary aspects of social life.

Class relations work in similar ways. People in the upper social classes have the resources to organize and promote sports that support their ideas about "good character" and how social life should be organized. One of the first things that people do when they obtain power in a social world is to make sure that "character" is defined in terms that fit their interests and match the characteristics that they possess. For example, if wealthy and powerful people play sports in exclusive clubs it is important that everyone believe that this is the way that society and sports should be organized and that wealthy and powerful people deserve their privilege to play sports as they do. In addition to playing on their terms, people with resources also are able to create and sponsor forms of organized sports that reinforce ideologies that support and legitimize existing economic relationships and the class structure of society. This is, in part, why popular spectator sports around the world are presented in ways that emphasize

competition, individualism, highly specialized skills, the use of technology, and dominance over opponents. The people who benefit from an emphasis on these values and cultural practices have usually been successful in convincing most people in society to believe that this is how sports should be organized and presented. Visions of sports that emphasize partnership, sharing, open participation, nurturance, and mutual support are outside of popular consciousness because most people have accepted that sports are sports only when they stress individual achievement through competition and the consumption of technology and equipment to outscore and dominate others.

Class Ideology in Canada

Sociologists define **class ideology** as a *web of ideas and beliefs that people use to understand economic inequalities, identify themselves in terms of their class position, and evaluate the manner in which economic inequalities are and should be integrated into the organization of social worlds.* The dominant class ideology in Canada has long been organized around a belief that Canada is a meritocracy.

A **meritocracy** is *a form of social organization in which rewards and positions of leadership and power are earned when people prove that their characteristics and abilities are superior to those of others.* The idea that Canada is a meritocracy legitimizes the economic inequalities that are inevitably created in a capitalist economy. In a meritocracy, it is assumed that power and success are associated with strong character and smart choices, whereas failure is associated with weak character and poor choices. Class ideology in Canada emphasizes that economic success (winning) is proof of individual ability, worth, and character. People who uncritically accept this ideology and use it to give meaning to their lives often engage in an endless quest for victories and status. They measure success in terms of how many "things" they can acquire and how they rank relative to their peers when it comes to "life scores." A locker-room slogan born of this class ideology is, "When you're satisfied with your performance, you're finished."

This and similar ideas drive market economies and enable people with wealth and power to preserve and extend their resources.

When people in a society adopt an ideology that links competitive success with moral worth, they assume that "you get what you deserve, and you deserve what you get." This advantages those who have more wealth and economic power than others, and it promotes the idea that economic inequality in society is necessary if society is to operate efficiently. This ideology is usually reproduced through the sports sponsored by corporations that are financially profitable. These corporations favour sports that promote competition as a "natural" way to allocate rewards, and define winners as those who deserve valued rewards. This, of course, is how sports come to be connected with class relations.

Class Relations and Who Has Power in Sports

Sport decisions are made at many levels, from neighbourhood youth sport programmes to the International Olympic Committee. Although scholars who study sports in society identify those who exercise power in various settings, they usually do not develop lists that rank powerful people in sports. But such lists do exist. For example, the *Globe and Mail*, often considered to be Canada's national newspaper, has published an annual list of Canada's sports leaders for several years. The list appears at the end of the calendar year, and is based on several sportswriters' assessments of which people during the year have been the leading figures in Canadian sports (based on factors such as influence and newsworthiness). Non-Canadians are sometimes included (e.g., NHL Commissioner Gary Bettman), but they are included because of their influence on Canadian sports.

Table 10.1 identifies the 25 for 2007, along with their ranking in 2006. Because the list usually includes people who have been in the news for various reasons, it varies quite a lot from year to year; in 2007, only 11 were also ranked in 2006.

(Those from the 2006 list not ranked in 2007 are footnoted in the table.) Of the 24 people on the list[3] there are two women (four in 2006), one person of colour (one in 2006), one francophone Canadian (one in 2006) and 21 white men (20 in 2006). There are fewer athletes than in previous years—four of the men on the list, including the person of colour, are active athletes. Of the 20 remaining: nine white males are owners or executive board members of professional sport franchises, two are NHL executives (including the Commissioner), three are media executives and one female runs the revamped Canada Sports Hall of Fame, four are Olympic, anti-doping, or national sport organization executives, and one female is General Manager of the women's national hockey team.

The list is most striking for who is absent—who is not considered to be newsworthy, or is not considered to have power and influence in Canadian sports. For example, it is interesting to compare this list with table 10.2, the CAAWS list of the twenty most influential women in Canadian sport in 2007. The two women on the *Globe and Mail* list are also on the CAAWS list; there are three athletes, one politician, one broadcaster, and one Olympic media executive. The remaining women are all in important ancillary and service positions—Olympic executives, consultants, coaches, and organizers. These women have improved sport, and they have made it happen, but they are not considered to be "powerful," or "influential" enough to have made the *Globe and Mail* list. Both lists are also striking for the limited presence of francophones and people of colour.

If this list is compared with the annual *Sporting News* list, in the U.S., of the 100 most powerful people in sports (www.sportingnews.com), there are also some important differences. The U.S. list focuses more on power than on influence and

---

[3]First place on the 2007 list is awarded to the loonie! While unusual for a list of influential people, this is a clear indication of the interdependency of professional sports in Canada and the United States; a Canadian dollar close to par with the U.S. dollar has changed the economies of professional sports teams in Canada in striking ways, because many of their costs (including players' salaries) are paid in U.S. dollars.

Table 10.1 The *Globe and Mail's* 25 most influential figures in Canadian sports, 2007

Rank/Name	Position/Organization	2006 Rank[a]
1. The Canadian dollar		NR
2. Sidney Crosby	NHL player, Pittsburgh Penguins	13
3. Bryan Colangelo	President & General Manager, Toronto Raptors	NR
4. Ken Read	CEO, Alpine Canada Alpin	6
5. Gary Bettman	Commissioner, National Hockey League	2
6. Larry Tanenbaum	Chair, Maple Leaf Sport & Entertainment (MLSE)	5
7. Richard Stursberg	Head of CBC Television	NR
8. Chris Chelios	NHL player and NHLPA activist	NR
9. Keith Pelley	President, Toronto Argonauts, CFL	16
10. George Gillett Jr.	Owner, Montréal Canadiens & Liverpool FC	NR
11. Jim Balsillie	Owner, RIM; seeking Ontario NHL team	NR
12. Ted Rogers	President & CEO, Rogers Communications / Jays	11
13. Scott Moore	Head of CBC Sports	NR
14. Steve Nash	NBA player, Phoenix Suns	1
15. Colin Campbell	Senior VP, Operations for the NHL	8
16. Russell Martin	MLB player, Los Angeles Dodgers	NR
17. Pierre Lafontaine	CEO and coach, Swimming / Natation Canada	NR
18. Mark Cohon	Commissioner, Canadian Football League	NR
19. Rick Brace	President, Business Planning, Revenue & Sports, CTV	NR
20. Richard Pound	(outgoing) President, World Anti-Doping Agency	18
21. Eugene Melnyk	Owner, Ottawa Senators	25
22. Brian Cooper	President & CEO, Sports and Entertainment LP	NR
23. Melody Davidson	General Manager, women's national hockey team	NR
24. John Furlong	CEO, Vancouver Olympics Organizing Committee	24
25. Sheryn Posen	COO, Canadian Sports Hall of Fame	NR

[a] Rank in 2006 list, NR=not ranked in 2007

Athletes (rank)	Organization/sport	Owners/Execs. (rank)	Organization
Cindy Klassen (3)	speed skater	R. Wetenhall (4)	CFL Alouettes
Clara Hughes (9)	speed skater	Ivan Fecan (7)	Bell Globemedia
Justin Morneau (20)	Minnesota Twins	David Braley (10)	CFL Lions
Jonathan Cheechoo (21)	San Jose Sharks	Pierre Boivin (12)	NHL Canadiens
Media (rank)	**Organization**	R. Peddie (24)	MLSE
Nancy Lee (14)	Olympic Broadcasting	S. Allaster (17)	WTA Tour
Pierre Maguire (22)	TSN & NBC	Tim Finchem (19)	PGA Tour
John Levy (25)	Score Media	Mark Lowry (23)	Canadian Olympic Cttee.

Source: Houston, William. "Power players of 2007." The *Globe and Mail*, 18 December, 2007, p. S1. Reprinted with permission from the *Globe and Mail*.

newsworthiness, so fewer athletes are in the top 25. The U.S. list is also a sobering reminder of the power of U.S. and international corporations on the world of sports. However, there are also some striking similarities between the U.S. and Canadian lists (see the Online Learning Centre

Table 10.2   The CAAWS list of 20 most influential women in sport and physical activity, 2007[a] (alphabetical order)

Name	Position/Organization
Cassie Campbell	Broadcaster; Calgary, AB
Polly Craik	Chair, Women's World Hockey Championships; Winnipeg, MN
Charmaine Crooks	VANOC Board member; Vancouver, BC
Sheilagh Croxon	Consultant, CAC's Women in Coaching Programme; Toronto, ON
Melody Davidson	General Manager, national Ice Hockey team; Calgary, AB
Guylaine Demers	Academic, Laval University; NCCP adviser; Québec City, QC
Hon. Helena Guergis	Secretary of State (Sport); Angus, ON
Silken Laumann	Author and children's advocate; Victoria, BC
Nancy Lee	COO, Olympic Broadcast Services Vancouver; Toronto, ON
Pat Messner	Water ski coach for athletes with a disability; Carleton Place, ON
Margo Mountjoy	FINA Executive and IOC Medical Commission; Guelph, ON
Kelly Murumets	President & CEO, ParticipACTION; Toronto, ON
Carla Qualtrough	President, Canadian Paralympic Committee; Vancouver, BC
Sheryn Posen	COO, Canada's Sports Hall of Fame; Toronto. ON
Cathy Priestner Allinger	Executive VP, Sport, VANOC; Vancouver, BC
Sara Renner	Cross country skier; climate change activist; Canmore, AB
Jane Roos	Fundraiser for national team athletes; Toronto, ON
Teresa Schlachter	High Performance Advisor, Own the Podium 2010; Calgary, AB
Beckie Scott	Cross Country skier; drug free sport activist; Panorama, BC
Hayley Wickenheiser	Hockey player; Right to Play; Calgary, AB

[a]Many of the women named to the CAAWS list were nominated by colleagues and the general public. The final list was compiled by the CAAWS selection panel from both public nominations, and contributions from knowledgeable sport and physical activity leaders. The panel reviewed the submissions and based its decision on the scope of activities in the 2007 calendar year.

Source: CAAWS Press Release, 17 Jan 2008; retrieved from www.caaws.ca/influentialwomen/e/index.htm

for the *Sporting News* list and Jay Coakley's analysis). It is clear that, in addition to wealth and control of the resources of major corporations, leagues, and franchises, dominant forms of gender ideology and race ideology also have an effect on who has power in sports.

Those who control economic resources in Canada and around the world make decisions that influence the visibility of sports, the ways in which they are organized, and the images and meanings associated with them. Although these decisions do not ignore the interests of people in Canada and around the world, their main purpose is to expand the power and profitability of the organizations represented by the decision makers. Therefore, sports tend to revolve around the meanings and orientations valued by those with economic resources and power while providing enjoyable and entertaining experiences for people like you and us.

This is why some critical theorists have described sports as cultural vehicles for developing "ideological outposts" in the minds of people around the world: When transnational corporations become the primary providers of popular pleasure and entertainment, they are able to use the very things that give people joy and excitement to deliver messages about what should be important in people's lives. This is a clear manifestation of class relations and the process of hegemony at work.

Sports as a Vehicle for Transferring Public Money to Wealthy Individuals and Private Corporations

The dynamics of class relations sometimes have ironic twists. This is certainly true in connection with the ways that sports have been used as vehicles for transferring public monies collected through taxes into the hands of wealthy individuals and corporations in the private sector. For example, Andrew Zimbalist, a sports economist, points out that, since 1990, the four major sport leagues in North America have built seventy-two new stadiums and arenas costing US$19.4 billion. He also notes that 66 percent of this cost was paid from public funds (cited by McGregor, 2003). Most of this construction has taken place in the United States, although there is evidence that U.S. cities are beginning to learn the lesson that Canada learned in the 1970s and 1980s. The enormous cost overruns associated with construction of the Montréal Olympic Stadium and Toronto SkyDome led to the end of significant corporate welfare for professional sport arena and stadium construction. While governments have shown an inclination to use public funds to support professional sports, public opinion has been dead set against it, as then Industry Minister John Manley discovered in 2000. He first acceded to Canadian NHL teams' requests for public subsidies, and then withdrew the offer within a few days because of the public outcry. The majority of the professional sport arenas built in Canada since 1990 (e.g., Scotiabank place in Ottawa, GM Place in Vancouver, the Air Canada Centre in Toronto) were, for the most part, financed privately.

However, in Canada, there are a number of other ways of transferring public money into private hands in professional sports, including the following:

- *National unity subsidies:* After the nearly successful separation referendum in Québec in 1995, the federal government established a national unity programme in 1997 that involved, in part, displaying the Canada wordmark and the Maple Leaf flag in as many public places as possible. Events that received federal funding were required to display the Canada wordmark, and subsidies were offered to events for patriotic displays. Among the beneficiaries of this C$40 million per year programme, run by the Ministry of Public Works, were the Canadian NHL teams, which received approximately C$1 million a year to show the Canada wordmark at games, and the CFL which received C$1 million to have Maple Leaf flags displayed on football players' helmets. Funds were also paid to auto races, such as the Formula 1 Grand Prix in Montréal. The terms of the programme were changed in December 2002, following evidence of misuse of funds.
- *Tax breaks:* The federal and provincial governments have devised various ways to benefit professional sports through tax breaks. For example, in the last days of Mike Harris's premiership in Ontario, he secretly signed a C$10 million tax break for each of the two NHL teams in the province. Rod Bryden's attempt to create a tax relief form of ownership for the NHL Ottawa Senators in 2002, which received approval from the Canada Customs and Revenue Agency, would have meant the withdrawal of C$100 million from federal income (which means either cuts to federal programmes, or an increase in other forms of taxes). Fortunately, the deal fell through at the last minute. Professional sports also benefit from the much abused entertainment tax write-off—businesses and corporations may write off 50 percent of the cost of season tickets and luxury boxes, which means that they are more likely to lease luxury boxes and pay the ticket prices being charged by

the leagues and events.[4] Alberta's plan to use provincial lottery funds to support the province's two NHL teams, while not a tax break, removes money from public revenue to support wealthy owners and well-paid players.

• *Hosting major events:* Perhaps the most significant public subsidy to professional sports occurs as a result of hosting major events such as the Olympics, Commonwealth Games, Pan American Games, Jeux de la Francophonie, the World Track and Field Championships, the World Junior Hockey Championships, other world championships, FISU Games, and even Canada Games. It is now widely recognized that hosting a Summer or Winter Olympics is very popular with the construction and development industries in the city and country where the Games are held. For example, when Atlanta hosted the Olympics in 1996, the major payoffs associated with the new construction and increased property values went directly to a small group of real estate developers and major corporations, which were in a position to use the millions of dollars of public money invested in the Atlanta area to their benefit. At the conclusion of the Games, major new facilities were turned over to the owners of professional sport franchises in Atlanta (see figure 10.1). The lesson of Atlanta was, perhaps, first learned in North America at the Montréal Olympics in 1976, when an enormously expensive Olympic Stadium came to be used by the Expos of MLB and the Alouettes of the CFL—the owners only responsible for rent, not construction costs. Two years later, the Commonwealth Games in Edmonton resulted in the construction of Commonwealth Stadium (to be used subsequently by the Eskimos of the CFL) and the arena now known as Rexall Place, where the NHL Oilers play (it is not clear why a hockey arena was built for the Commonwealth Games other than to take advantage of public funds available for a Commonwealth Games to support an NHL team). The Calgary Saddledome (now called the Pengrowth Centre), built for Olympic ice hockey, was used by the Calgary Flames of the NHL even before the 1988 Olympics. Stadium and arena upgrades are also publicly funded for hosting events, but provide a long-term, low-cost benefit to professional sports. For example, Winnipeg hosted the Pan Am Games in 1999, and Edmonton hosted the World Championships in Athletics (track and field) in 2001. In both cases, the stadia primarily used by the local CFL teams—the Blue Bombers and the Eskimos respectively—were upgraded at public cost.[5] The upgrades included construction of a Jumbotron in each stadium which, in the case of Edmonton, was one of the first major expenditures of the World Championship organizing committee, and was being used by the Eskimos two years before the event. Vancouver/Whistler will host the Winter Olympic Games in 2010 and receive over C$600 million in federal and provincial funds—an amount that is certain to increase, and some of which is likely to be used to support the upgrading of Vancouver's professional sport facilities (McCloy, 2002; 2006).

---

[4]Tax write-offs for entertainment are a frequent site of tax fraud. Tickets are provided to friends, family members, or even scalpers and the deduction for "entertainment" for business purposes is still claimed.

[5]In the case of Edmonton, the federal (C$40 million), provincial (Alberta, C$40 million), and municipal (Edmonton, C$6 million) governments contributed C$86 million toward the cost of hosting the World Championships in Athletics. The annual budget for Sport Canada, supporting all "amateur" high-performance sports in Canada, was, at the time, some C$77 million.

"Oh sure, they told us that 'sports unite ALL the classes,' when they wanted us to PAY for this place!"

FIGURE 10.1 As they sit in the distant bleachers and spot wealthy people in luxury boxes and club seats, these fans discover that the dynamics of social class operate in ways that privilege some people more than others. To say that "sports unite the social classes" is to ignore these dynamics that often separate people from different social class backgrounds.

Studies indicate that middle- and lower-income individuals pay disproportionately more to support these various subsidies and, for the last decade, this corporate welfare has been occurring at a time when there have been numerous cuts to health care, education, and the social services relied on by low-income and unemployed individuals. Of course, there is a small trickle-down benefit to the community in terms of jobs (often part-time and/or low-paying; see the Online Learning Centre for a feature on jobs created by sports) and trade for local businesses. But the average taxpayers who help to fund the Olympics and other events will never see the benefits enjoyed by those whose power and wealth gave them the ability to take advantage of public investments. Even the facilities that are constructed are

of much more benefit to professional and high-performance sports than they are to the community in terms of public access. For example, while admission to the highly touted Canada Olympic Park in Calgary is free, there are fees for using the facilities for active recreation (e.g., $12 for cross-country skiing, and $15 for cross- country ski rental); and Calgary Olympic Oval, while open for public recreation, is not easily accessible to low-income people. However, the recently constructed BMO Field, home of Toronto FC soccer team, was built primarily using public (federal, provincial, municipal) funds, and is readily available to the public at a reasonable cost.

As journalist Andrew Jennings has noted, the emerging pattern in connection with hosting the Olympics is that "the IOC will take its profits, the sponsors and television networks will make theirs and the local taxpayers will foot the bill" (1996, p. 293). Helen Lenskyj (2000, 2002), of the Ontario Institute for Studies in Education, has addressed these issues specifically with regard to the Sydney Olympics and the two Toronto Olympic bids. And the 2010 Watch web site (www.2010 watch.com) is providing a critical monitoring of the costs, and environmental and social implications of hosting the Winter Olympics in Vancouver/ Whistler. This method of transferring public money to powerful individuals and corporations in the private sector is another clear manifestation of class relations at work in connection with sports.

SOCIAL CLASS AND SPORT PARTICIPATION PATTERNS

In all societies, social class and class relations influence who plays, who watches, who consumes information about sports, and what information is available in the mainstream media. Involvement with sports goes hand in hand with money, power, and privilege. Organized sports are a luxury item in the economies of many nations, and they are most prevalent in wealthy nations where people have discretionary money and time (see chapter 11).

In all societies, it is people in high-income, high-education, and high-status occupational groups who have the highest rates of active sport participation, attendance at sport events, and even watching of sports on television (Booth and Loy, 1999; Donnelly and Harvey, 2007; Scheerder et al., 2002; Stempel, 2005; White and Wilson, 1999; T. Wilson, 2002). This also has an effect on who becomes a high-performance athlete. Bruce Kidd (1995) notes that Olympic athletes and officials have always come from the most privileged groups in society (see also Collins and Buller, 2003).

The social class limitations on sport involvement were recognized early in the direct involvement of the federal government in Canadian sports. John Munro's *A Proposed Sport Policy for Canadians* (1970) introduced the Athlete Assistance Programme, and the construction of sports facilities in underserviced areas. A study of 1971 Canada Winter Games athletes carried out at that time (Gruneau and Albinson, 1976) found that 42 percent of the athletes' fathers came from the highest occupational levels in Canada (which represented 17 percent of the Canadian population).

By 1986, Rob Beamish of Queen's University found that 68 percent of the fathers of national team athletes came from the highest occupational categories. This pattern also exists in high-performance sports in countries around the world, except for those where there is direct state support of national team athletes (e.g., China and Cuba).

Even the health and fitness movement, which often has been described as a grassroots phenomenon in Canada and the U.S., is confined primarily to people who have higher-than-average incomes and educations and work in professional or managerial occupations (Stempel, 2005). People in lower-income groups may do physical labour, but they do not run, bicycle, or swim as often as their high-income counterparts. Nor do they play as many organized sports on their lunch hours, after work, on weekends, or during vacations. This pattern holds true throughout the life course, for younger and older age groups, among men and women, among various racial and ethnic groups, and among people with disabilities. Social class is related strongly to participation, regardless of the category of people in question (see Donnelly and Harvey, 2007).

The Canadian evidence in support of this is overwhelming. For example, table 10.3 shows the Canadian Council on Social Development's (2006) analyses of the Statistics Canada National Longitudinal Survey of Children and Youth (NLSCY for 2000), which reported the relationship between children's recreation participation and family income.

When the data are analyzed by family income quartiles (separating families into four equal groups from the lowest 25 percent family income to the highest 25 percent), in all cases the relationships are linear: the more a family earns, the more likely its children are to participate in sports and physical activity. The 1998 NLSCY (Statistics Canada, 2001; see also, Trussell and McTeer, 2007) provided additional information about, and showed the consistency of these findings:

- Children who were least likely to participate in organized activities were those in lower-income families, those with very young parents, those whose primary caregiver had less than a high school education, and those in single-parent families.
- Younger children in the lowest-income quartile were three times more likely to have never participated in organized activities (sports, music, art, or clubs) than children in the highest quartile.
- Younger children whose parents had less than a high school education were more than twice as likely to have never participated in organized activities than those children whose parents had higher education.

Recent data from Québec also indicate that, "Children from low-income families were significantly less likely to participate in physical activity or organized sports outside of school hours" (Desrosiers and Eid, 2007, p. 2), and these

Table 10.3   Weekly recreation participation for children aged 10–13 by family income[a]

Participation	Above $40,000	Below $40,000
Participation in sports with a coach one or more times a week	61%	51%
Participation in dance/gymnastics one or more times a week	36%	32%
Participation in community clubs (e.g., Guides/Scouts, Boys and Girls, 4H)	24%	19%
Participation in arts/drama/music	29%	23%
Attendance at day camp	34%	22%

[a] NLSCY data indicate that weekly participation figures are even lower for children aged 4–9 from families earning less than $40,000

Source: Statistics Canada. *The Daily*. National Longitudinal Survey of Children and Youth: Participation in activities (1998/99), May 30, 2001. http://www.statcan.ca/Daily/English/010530/d010530a.htm (accessed May 4, 2008) and adapted from *The Progress of Canada's Children and Youth 2006*, published by the Canadian Council on Social Development. Supplementary web data (www.ccsd.ca). Reprinted with permission.

general survey findings are confirmed by more focused community studies (e.g., Hughes and Griffiths, 1992; Offord, Lipman, and Duku, 1998).

Participation patterns also may be explained in terms of class relations. The long-term impact of economic inequality on people's lives has led to connections between certain sports and the lifestyles of people with differing amounts of wealth and power (Bourdieu, 1986; Laberge and Sankoff, 1988; Stempel, 2005). For the most part, these connections reflect patterns of sponsorship and access to opportunities for involvement. For example, wealthy people have lifestyles that routinely include participation in golf, tennis, skiing, sailing, and other sports that are self-funded and played at exclusive clubs and resorts. These sports often involve the use of expensive facilities, equipment, and/or clothing, and they have come to be associated with "class" as people with money and power define it. The people who engage in these sports usually have considerable control over their work, so they have the freedom to take the time needed to participate, or they can combine participation with their work, such as going to the club, gym, game (luxury box), and tournament with business associates. They may even use the company credit card to pay for these things, and the company then uses 50 percent of the expenses as a tax deduction, thereby decreasing the federal and provincial tax receipts that

could be used to fund sport programmes for people who do not own gold club memberships.

The lifestyles of middle-income and working-class people, on the other hand, tend to include sports that by tradition are free and open to the public, sponsored by public funds, or available through public schools. When these sports involve the use of expensive equipment or clothing, participation occurs in connection with some form of financial sacrifice. For instance, buying a motocross bike means not taking a vacation this year and working overtime for six months.

The lifestyles of low-income people and those living in poverty seldom involve regular forms of sport participation. This is exacerbated by the fact that the majority of people living below the poverty line are women, who have not had the same level of access to sports as men. Life chances vary by social class, and when people spend much of their time and energy coping with the challenges of everyday life, they have few resources left to develop sport participation as part of their lifestyles. Spending money to play or watch sports is a luxury few can afford. At the same time, those who are successful in the economy like sports because they reaffirm a class ideology that works to their advantage.

This is partly why they are willing to spend thousands of dollars each year to buy club memberships, season tickets, and luxury suites—or have their companies buy them. It should come

Children in suburban areas often have safe streets on which they can play. The boys in this cul-de-sac have access to many portable basketball nets, and they often recruit friends to play full court games in the street. Of course, they also play roller hockey, soccer, baseball, and football, and they water ski behind one of the boats owned by families in the neighbourhood. They grow up with opportunities to play many different sports. [Jay Coakley]

as no surprise, given these relationships between social class and participation in sports and physical activity, that there is also a striking relationship between social class and population health:

> Working class people have on average lower birth weight and higher rates of infant mortality, are smaller at maturity, less healthy, and die at a younger age than those in higher class categories. Major types of mental disorder and physical illness including heart disease, cancer, diabetes, pneumonia and bronchitis are all more common at lower levels of the class structure….(Giddens, 1989, p. 215)

It is often assumed that these findings are a result of lower levels of physical activity among people in a lower social class, but there is no evidence to support this assumption. Surveys of population physical activity are usually based on

middle-class assumptions about white-collar sedentary jobs, and are likely to presume that individuals who do not go to the gym, jog, or take other forms of recreational exercise are "inactive." However, "housework, child care, manual labour, work that involves being on your feet, and [other activities] . . . account for the majority of energy expenditure of Canadians [and] remain unrecorded in most surveys" (Donnelly and Harvey, 1996). Since lower-income people are more likely to be occupied in manual work, to take public transport, and to have limited access to services for child care and house cleaning, it would be inaccurate to assume "inactivity" because of a lack of involvement in recreational activity.

Despite this, "top people live longer" (Evans et al., 1994), and they do so despite various statistical controls for smoking and physical inactivity (i.e., if you smoke twenty cigarettes a day and you are rich, you are likely to live longer than someone who smokes twenty cigarettes a day and is poor). Canada's National Forum on Health attributes these differences not to "lifestyle choices," or to more participation in fitness activities, better knowledge of health among the better educated, or greater ability to purchase health care among the wealthy, but to the sense of being in control of one's life (National Forum on Health, 1997). As noted above, higher-income people have considerable control over their work lives, so they have the freedom to take time to participate in healthy recreational activities, or even combine such activity with their work.

Homemaking, Child Rearing, and Earning a Living: Class and Gender Relations in Women's Lives

The impact of social class on everyday lives often varies by age, gender, race and ethnicity, and geographic location. For example, women in family situations have been less likely than men to be in positions enabling them to negotiate the time and resources needed to play sports (Thompson, 1999a, b). For example, when a married woman with children joins a soccer team that schedules practices late in the afternoon, she may wonder if it is okay with her family because she is the family chef, chauffeur, and tutor. "Time off for good behaviour" is not a principle that applies to married women with children.

On the other hand, married men with children have more freedom to make such decisions. When they play softball or soccer after work, their wives may delay family dinners, keep dinners warm until they arrive home, or even go to the games and watch them play. Women in middle- and lower-income families most often feel the constraints of homemaking and child rearing. Women sociologists in Canada began to focus on these issues in the 1980s, combining gender and social class (socialist feminism) in order to examine the implications for the lives and leisure of working-class women (e.g., Armstrong, 1984; Bray, 1984; Luxton, 1980). Without money to pay for child care, domestic help, and sport participation expenses, these women have few opportunities to play sports. They also lack time, a car to take them to where sports are played, access to gyms and playing fields in their neighbourhoods, and the sense of physical safety that they need to leave home and travel to where they can play sports. Because many sports require multiple participants, the lack of resources among some women affects others. This is also true for men, but women from middle- and lower-income families are more likely than their male counterparts to lack the network of relationships out of which sport interests and participation emerge and come to be supported.

In a striking "made in Canada" solution, Wendy Frisby of the University of British Columbia started a fitness programme called Women Organizing Activities for Women for low-income single mothers in several communities in British Columbia (Frisby et al., 1997, 2007). The targeted population was involved in the planning process, which resulted in the provision of child care—something that the

professionals involved in the process had not anticipated. Without involvement of the "clients" in the planning, they would not have been able to participate ("Who would look after our children?"), the programme would have failed, and the targeted population would have been blamed for lack of interest. "[T]he women felt ownership for the programs because they had the freedom to choose whether to get involved and their voices were taken into account during the project" (Frisby et al., 1997, p. 20).

Women from upper-income families often face a different situation. They have the resources to pay for child care, domestic help, carryout dinners, and sport participation fees. They participate in sports activities by themselves and with friends and family members. Their social networks include other women who also have resources to play sports. Women who grow up in these families play sports during their childhoods and attend schools with good sport programmes. They seldom experience the same constraints as their lower-income counterparts, even though their opportunities may not equal those of upper-income men.

The sport participation of girls and young women also may be limited when they are asked to shoulder adult responsibilities at home. For example, in low-income families, especially single-parent and immigrant families, teenage daughters often are expected to care for younger siblings after school until after dinner, when their mothers get home from work. According to one girls' team coach in a New York City high school, "It's not at all unusual that on a given day there may be two or three girls who aren't [at practice] because of responsibilities at home" (Dobie, 1987). The coach also explained that child-care duties keep many girls from coming out for teams. His solution was to coordinate a cooperative child-care programme at practices and games, so that girls from low-income families could meet family expectations *and* play sports. However, when coaches are not so creative or accommodating, some girls drop out of sports to meet responsibilities at home.

Boys and girls from higher-income families seldom have household responsibilities that force them to drop out of sports. Instead, their parents drive them to practices, lessons, and games; make sure they have all the equipment they need to play well; and then give them cars, so they can drive themselves to practices and games.

The implications of class dynamics become very serious when health and obesity issues are considered. Limited opportunities to exercise safely and play sports are part of a series of factors contributing to a rise in obesity, diabetes, and heart disease, especially among girls and women from low-income backgrounds (NHANES, 2002). The availability of facilities, safe spaces, transportation, and sports programmes all vary by social class, and the girls and women in low-income households experience the effects of social class in different and more profound ways when it comes to involvement in physical activities and sports.

Being Respected and Becoming a Man: Class and Gender Relations in Men's Lives

Boys and young men learn to use sports to establish a masculine identity, but the dynamics of this process vary by social class. For example, in a qualitative analysis of essays written about sports by fifteen- to sixteen-year-old francophone boys in the Montréal area, Suzanne Laberge, of the Université de Montréal and Mathieu Albert (1999) discovered that ideas about sports and masculinity varied among upper-class, middle-class, and working-class boys. The upper-class boys connected sport participation to masculinity because they saw sports as an arena in which they could learn to be leaders, and leadership was important to their definition of masculinity. The middle-class boys connected sport participation to masculinity because they saw sports as an arena for sociability and opportunities to gain acceptance in male groups, thereby confirming their manhood. The working-class boys connected sport participation to

masculinity because they saw sports as an arena for displaying tough, hypermasculine actions and personas, which represented their conception of manhood.

Sociologist Mike Messner has noted that, in U.S. culture, "the more limited a boy's options appear to be, and the more insecure his family situation, the more likely he is to make an early commitment to an athletic career" (1992, p. 40). In other words, the personal stakes associated with playing sports are different and greater for boys from low-income backgrounds than they are for boys from high-income backgrounds. Messner found that former elite male athletes from low-income backgrounds often saw sport participation as a way to obtain "respect." However, this was not as important among males from middle-class backgrounds. One former athlete who became a junior high school coach explained,

> For...the poorer kids, [sports are] their major measuring stick....They constantly remind each other what they can't do in the sports arena. It's definitely peer-acceptable if they are good at sports—although they maybe can't read, you know—if they are good at sports, they're one of the boys. Now I know the middle- and upper-class boys, they do sports and they do their books.... But as a whole, [they put] less effort into [sports]. (quoted in Messner, 1992, pp. 57–58)

This coach suggested that social class factors create social conditions under which young men from lower-income backgrounds often have more at stake when it comes to sport participation. What he did not mention is that the development of sport skills often requires material resources that do not exist in low-income families. Thus, unless equipment and training are provided in school sport programmes, young men from low-income groups stand little chance of competing against upper-income peers, who are able to buy equipment and training if they want to develop skills—except in the few sports that are provided in high schools in lower-income neighbourhoods.

Professional boxing has long been a sport for men from low-income groups in Canada and the United States, one of the few avenues of achievement and success available. vWhile most professional boxers start as amateurs, amateur boxing is a sport in its own right, drawing from both middle- and low-income populations. Alex Bear of Saskatchewan and George Kalunga of Newfoundland are participating in the 64 kg event at the 2007 Canada Winter Games in Whitehorse, YT. [CP(Chuck Stoody)]

In fact, young people from upper-income backgrounds often have so many opportunities to do different things that they may not focus attention on one sport to the exclusion of other sports and other activities. For someone who has a car, nice clothes, money for university education, and good career contacts for the future, playing sports may be good for enhancing popularity, but it is not perceived as a necessary foundation for an entire identity (Messner, 1992). Therefore, young men from middle- and upper-income backgrounds often choose to disengage gradually from exclusive commitments to becoming professional or high-performance athletes. When these young men move through adolescence and into adulthood, opportunities may take them in a variety of directions. Playing sports may be important to them, but not in the same ways that it is for young men from working-class and low-income families. (See, for example, the feature, "Fighting to Survive," on the Online Learning Centre.)

Class Relations in Action: The Decline of School Sports and Physical Education, and the Increase of User Fees

In a 2003 speech, Chris Rudge, CEO of the Canadian Olympic Committee, criticized Ontario (while praising Alberta, British Columbia, and Québec) for its lack of commitment to athlete development at both the high-performance and grassroots levels. By 2006, Ontario's contribution was still in decline: "In 1984, Ontario provided 52 percent of Canada's Olympic team members for both the Summer and Winter

Games. By 2004, it was down to 38 percent for the Athens Summer team and in 2006, at the Torino Winter Games, it had fallen to just 18 percent" (Campbell, 2007, p. A12). Rudge blamed cuts in public sector funding and the tax reduction policies of the Harris government, noting that there had been a 42 percent decline in funding for provincial sport organizations.

Cuts in public sector financial support for sport programmes and facilities intersect in various ways with the cuts in funding to education and municipal recreation in Ontario. There is a cumulative effect on who is able to participate:

- Cuts to education, combined with a new academic curriculum, meant that there were fewer physical education specialist teachers, and fewer physical education classes being taught. When combined with teacher burnout and alienated teachers, fewer extracurricular activities/interschool sports were available; and cutbacks meant user fees for almost all activities (Donnelly et al., 2001). [The subsequent government in Ontario began to restore some of the funding to education, and has increased the number of specialist physical education teachers being hired.]

- Cuts and downloading to municipal budgets mean that all Parks and Recreation Departments now have user fees, and that, in many cases, they provide fewer services for more money. As noted in chapter 5, municipal Parks and Recreation Departments in Canada stopped organizing youth sport leagues in the mid-1970s, in part as a cost-saving measure. The remaining programmes of physical activity and instruction (e.g., skating and swimming) were increasingly subject to user fees, and there is now evidence of a resulting decline in participation. Following the 1998 amalgamation of Toronto into a mega-city, the former City of Toronto, which had no user fees, joined with five other municipalities that all had different user fees. This was harmonized into a single fee-structure—introducing user fees into the former City of Toronto and reducing user fees in the five suburban municipalities. In the initial harmonization model, fees were introduced for all adult programmes, but removed for all children's and seniors' programmes. The subsequent assessment of the effects showed a significant increase in the number of participants in the suburban municipalities (e.g., an increase of 45 percent in Scarborough) where fees were reduced, and a significant reduction (33 percent) in participation in the former City of Toronto where fees were introduced (Clutterbuck and Howarth, 2002; Sewell, 2000; Slack, 2003). These data appear to provide clear evidence that user fees are a barrier to participation.

- Sports and recreation organizations often relied on low-cost rental of school facilities. In order to make up for budget cuts, schools increased rental fees, increasing the financial difficulties for those organizations. For example, a basketball club in Collingwood which used to charge $50 per player increased its fees to $400 per player. Increasing costs of up to 2,000 percent have been recorded (Campbell, 2003; Picard, 2003).

- Many swimming pools in Toronto are located in schools, but are available for joint school and community use with the costs shared by the municipality and the Board of Education. Cutbacks created a crisis whereby many pools are threatened with closure.

In every case, public sector cutbacks increased the costs of participation in sports, and reduced the numbers of participants at the grassroots level. With fewer athletes to draw from, those cuts are now being felt at the high-performance level. When high-performance sport programmes are only able to draw from that sector of the population that can afford private lessons and coaching, because publicly supported community and school programmes are in trouble, they are likely to experience

Breaking Barriers

Resource Barriers
I'm Trying to Make Do

Stories about space-age materials like Kevlar and carbon fibre are heartening. These and other high-tech materials are used to make light, fast racing chairs, running prostheses shaped like a cheetah's leg, and racing mono-skis that can be maneuvered down steep slopes.

This technology is seductive for those who see it for the first time. So seductive, that they often overlook the person and focus on the device (Belson, 2002). However, as most athletes know, technologies are only as good as the people who use them. And as many people with a disability know, adaptive technologies for sports often are prohibitively expensive.

In the United States, Diane Cabrera discovered the cost of adaptive technology when she lost her leg to cancer in 2001. The bill for her prosthesis was $11,000, and her medical coverage paid only $4,000 per year. She spread payments over two years and struggled to find $2,200 for co-payments related to diagnostics, fitting, tuning, and maintenance. When she needed a new leg socket a few years later, she put it off because her original prosthesis no longer fit correctly and she could not afford a new one. When asked about her situation, Diane said with resignation, "I'm trying to make do right now."

"Making do right now"—that's a common strategy for many people who need prostheses. This is because most below-the-knee prosthetics cost $6,000 to $8,000. An arm or an above-the-knee prosthetic leg costs $10,000 to $15,000 (Sweeney, 2005). Health-care subsidies for prosthetics in Canada are quite generous compared with the U.S. For example, Alberta Aids to Daily Living (AADL) pays 75 percent of the cost of a prosthesis to people registered with Alberta Health Care; individuals are responsible for the remaining 25 percent up to $500 per year. Similar programmes are available in other provinces, and these are subsidized by other agencies such as the War Amps, employee health plans, and Blue Cross. However, all of these agencies specifically preclude funding for "recreational" or "very high-tech" prostheses (only the War Amps Child Amputee Programme (CHAMPS) will fund a prosthesis for recreational use), and prosthetic limbs and adaptive devices for sports involve additional costs. Sport prosthetics require replacement every year or two, and other prosthetic limbs should be replaced every four to six years. Racing wheelchairs cost about $4,000, and Kevlar wheels push the cost up to $6,000.

The cost of equipment is a real barrier to sport participation among many people with a disability. Accentuating resource barriers in Canada are the following facts (www.mcss.gov.on):

- The unemployment rate among 3.6 million people with a disability in Canada (12.4 percent of the population) is five times higher (26 percent) than the unemployment rate for people without a disability (5 percent).
- People with a disability in Ontario have an average income that is less than a third (33 percent) of the average income of people without a disability.
- Some 46 percent of adults with a disability in the labour force make less than $15,000 a year compared to 32 percent of people without a disability.
- People with a disability are less likely to have regular access to transportation and more likely to go without needed medical care than people without a disability.

These are the realities of social class and disability in Canada. Government assistance for people with a disability has been cut in recent years, charity is spotty and uneven, and community programmes are scarce, even if people have transportation to play sports regularly.

For young elite athletes, there are a few sponsorships available from companies that develop and manufacture prostheses and other adaptive technologies. This is one way for a select few to bypass resource barriers. But for others who do not have wealthy and connected advocates the barriers are formidable. Their goal is simply "to make do right now."

more limited success. These concerns about fewer opportunities are also being related to increasing childhood obesity, a condition that is likely to lead to significantly higher costs to the public sector (medical care) in the future than investment in sports and physical activity would cost today.

When it comes to sport participation, the socioeconomic status of the family you were born into has never been more important—participation is a family affair and is driven by family resources. This often is the case for people with a disability, as explained in the Breaking Barriers box, page 317.

Class Relations in Action: The Cost of Attending Sport Events

It is still possible to attend recreational, high school, and university sports for free or at little cost, and, in some communities, the tickets for minor league sports are reasonably priced. But tickets to most professional events are now beyond the means of many people, even those whose taxes may be being used to pay for the facilities in which the events are played. The cost of attending these events has increased far beyond the rate of inflation over the past fifteen years.

The average ticket price for attending games at the four major sport leagues in North America increased significantly between 1991 and 2004: MLB, 129 percent; NFL, 117percent; NBA, 142 percent; and NHL, 99 percent. These increases are more than five times the rate of inflation in Canada (28 percent, as measured by the Consumer Price Index) for that period. Table 10.4 shows the league average Fan Cost Index (Team Marketing Report, 2007; www.teammarketing. com) and the Fan Cost Index for Canadian teams in those leagues.[6]

Stadiums and arenas are now built or refurbished to attract wealthier spectators. Team owners want to "capture" the people who have money to spend. Therefore, these new facilities are shopping malls built around a playing surface. They house expensive luxury boxes and sections of club seating where upper-income spectators have special services available to them: wait staff, special food menus, private restrooms, televisions, telephones, refrigerators, lounge chairs, temperature controls, private entrances with no waiting lines or turnstiles, special parking areas, and other things to make attendance at a game resemble going to a private club.

As ticket prices increase and as spectators are increasingly segregated by their ability to pay, social class and class relations become more evident in the stands. Spectators may cheer at the same times and experience similar emotions, but social class differences in society are seldom transcended at the events; in fact, they are reaffirmed and are becoming more apparent.

For middle- and working-class fans wanting to resist rising prices, class relations often subvert their efforts. This is because people in luxury boxes, club seats, and other exclusive seats are not eager to be identified with fans who cannot afford the high-priced tickets or concessions. Wealthy spectators use expensive tickets as status symbols with their friends and business associates. They *want* class distinctions to be preserved in connection with attending games, and they are willing to pay, for example, over US$1,500 per ticket for NBA courtside seats in New York and Los Angeles to conspicuously display their status and experience the game without mixing with average fans. Attendance and seating at many events, from the opening ceremonies at the Olympics to the Stanley Cup Finals, also are tied to conspicuous displays of wealth, status, and influence. As long as this is the case, efforts to make games affordable to the people whose taxes build or subsidize the facilities will fail.

GLOBAL INEQUALITIES AND SPORTS

When we discuss social class and sports, it is essential to think beyond our own society. Inequalities exist at all levels of social organization—in

---

[6]The Fan Cost Index has not been applied to teams in Canadian leagues. However, data from the CFL for 2007 indicate that the average ticket price is approximately C$45.

Table 10.4   Fan cost index for Canadian teams in North American leagues

League/Team	Increase/Decrease from previous season	Fan cost index[a] (US$)
MLB average (2007–08)	+3.8%	$176.55
Toronto Blue Jays	-0.1%	$182.51
NFL average (2007–08)	+5.7%	$367.31[b]
NBA average (2007–08)	+2.6%	$281.90
Toronto Raptors	+8.5%	$320.47
NHL average (2007–08)	+5.2%	$282.95[c]
Toronto Maple Leafs	+4.8%	$476.02
Vancouver Canucks	+6.5%	$384.78
Ottawa Senators	+3.2%	$303.63
Montréal Canadiens	+5.1%	$388.24
Calgary Flames	+9.6%	$344.56
Edmonton Oilers	+5.2%	$331.95

[a]The Team Marketing Report's Fan Cost Index is based on the cost for two adults and two children to attend a game (average price tickets, parking, drinks and hot dogs, 2 hats)

[b]The NFL average is included for comparative purposes; there are no Canadian NFL teams at this time although, at the time of writing, a number of Buffalo Bills games are scheduled to be held in Toronto

[c]All Canadian teams cost more than the league average

Source: Team Marketing Report Inc., 2007 (www.teammarketing.com)

families, groups, organizations, communities, societies, and the world. Global inequalities related to *per capita* income, living standards, and access to developmental resources are the source of the most serious problems that we face today. Research clearly shows that the gap between the richest and poorest nations is growing wider.

The World Bank classifies countries based on a measurement of Gross Nation Income (GNI)/ *per capita* (in US$): in Low Income countries the average is less than $906/year; Middle Income countries range from $906–$3,595; Upper Middle Income countries range from $3,596–$11,115; and in High Income countries the *per capita* GNI is more than $11,115. Canada, which ranks sixth in the most recent UN Human Development Index, has a per capita GNI of US$36,170 (2006)— almost US$100 per day. Niger, which ranked 177th in the recent Human Development Index, is typical of Low Income countries, having a per capita GNI of US$260—far less than US$1 per day.

Another way to look at social class in global terms is to determine how many of the world's 6.6 billion people (2006) live on less than US$1

a day, or US$2 a day—figures used by the World Bank as indicators of extreme poverty. These figures are clearly below basic subsistence levels in any country, regardless of the cost of living. In 2004, approximately 1.2 billion people lived on less than US$1 per day, and a further 2 billion people lived on less than US$2 per day. As a point of comparison, the *median* income in Canadian households containing two or more people was C$54,100 per annum after taxes in 2004.

The meanings given to this global gap between the wealthy and the poor differ depending on the ideologies that people use to guide their understanding of world affairs. But apart from ideological interpretations, it is clear that half the people in the world have few resources to use on anything but basic survival. Those who are not sick or disabled may engage in physical play or games, but they do not have resources for organizing and playing sports as we know them. Therefore, half the people in the world see the sports played in Canada and other postindustrial nations as "dreamlands." They cannot understand why some professional athletes can make

REFLECT ON SPORTS   The Odds of Becoming a Professional Athlete

In the United States, the athlete development system to most professional team sports is relatively straightforward—high school team to university team to professional team. Therefore, it is relatively straightforward to calculate the chances of high school and university players making it to the professional level (see the Online Learning Centre feature, "Career Opportunities are Limited"). These odds are not good in the U.S., ranging from 3,333:1, for a male high school basketball player ever being drafted by the NBA, to 5,000:1, for a female high school basketball player ever playing in the WNBA.

In Canada, the development system is not nearly so straightforward. Student-athletes play basketball in high school and university in Canada, but that is not usually considered to be a track to a top-level professional career—some of the better players may play professional basketball in a men's or women's league in Europe. A scholarship to a U.S. university provides one of the only routes to the NBA or WNBA. Football provides similar opportunities for Canadian students, with chances to play at Canadian universities, win a scholarship to a U.S. university, and play in the CFL or occasionally the NFL. However, there is a parallel junior football system that also makes tracking from high school to university to professional football problematic. In the case of baseball, while many high schools and some universities have teams in Canada, serious young players are usually involved in youth baseball leagues. The case is similar for hockey, with few considering high school or even university hockey as a potential route to the NHL.

Given these various routes—high school, youth leagues, junior leagues, Canadian university, U.S. university—is it possible to calculate the odds of Canadian players becoming professional athletes? There are no academic studies of this topic, but two Canadians have collected data that are comparable, and which give a sense of the odds of becoming a professional player in hockey and golf:

- Jim Parcels (2000), who worked for the Ontario Minor Hockey Association, wrote a research paper entitled, "The chances of making it in pro hockey for Ontario minor hockey players." Since the competitive structure of minor hockey is based on a player's age, Parcels used players born in 1975 as his sample. Of all the boys born in Ontario in 1975, 30,000 played minor hockey at one time or another. By 1991, 22,000 were still registered as players. Here's what happened to them:
  - 22,000 were eligible for the Ontario Hockey League Junior draft in 1991 (underage Bantam) and 1992 (open Midget)
  - 232 were drafted by (then) sixteen major junior teams (only 105 played at least one game in the OHL)
  - 90 completed three to four years of OHL eligibility
  - 41 opted to play NCAA Division I hockey[1]
  - 48 were drafted from OHL and NCAA to NHL
  - 4 signed NHL free agent contracts
  - 35 signed contracts with NHL teams
  - 26 played at least one NHL game by April 2000[2]
  - 16 were active in the NHL in April 2000

  Thus, of the 30,000 original players from the 1975 cohort, sixteen remained active in 2000, giving odds of 1,875:1; if only those 22,000 who participated in minor hockey long enough to be eligible for the junior draft are counted, the odds are 1,375:1. The odds are also becoming longer as each of the major leagues further globalizes its search for players—the proportion of Canadian players in the NHL is down to a little over 50 percent.

- Henry Brunton, the national coach for the Royal Canadian Golf Association, tracked Canadian male golfers who accept scholarships at U.S. universities (considered to be one of the main routes to the PGA Tour). In 2002, he calculated

Continued

that there were 3,000 varsity golfers at U.S. universities, and 227 of them were Canadian. Assuming that 750 (25 percent) of those players were in their fourth year of university and were eligible, "only three made it to the finals of the PGA Tour's qualifying school. Not one got his tour card" (Brunton, cited by Rubenstein, 2003, p. S5). Brunton argues that U.S. golf scholarships are not a good idea for most talented young golfers in Canada (see next section for problems with scholarships for Canadian student-athletes in the U.S.).

We admire the ambition and drive of talented young athletes who dream of becoming professionals, but we

are also concerned that they may not leave themselves alternatives if their dream does not work out. Given these odds, we think that young players, and their parents, should always give themselves alternatives (e.g., in terms of education and other interests). *What do you think?*

---

[1]Very few completed a degree; meanwhile, 60 of the former major junior players went on to play CIS hockey at Canadian universities, and data indicate that 50 percent to 60 percent graduate.

[2]1975 was the best draft year ever in Ontario; for the 1971 cohort, only 11 played at least one NHL game, and for 1976, only 9 had played by April 2000.

annual incomes that are the equivalent of the combined incomes of many thousands of the poor people in their country. Neither would it be understood by people in other countries who make less than $1 an hour producing the balls, shoes, and other equipment and clothing used by most Canadians who play sports, including professional athletes.

When there is a dirt soccer pitch or basketball surface in a community in a Low or Middle Income country, it often attracts young people who have seen a televised soccer or basketball game. This has not escaped the people who scout for new talent for U.S. universities or professional soccer and basketball teams in wealthy nations (Darby, et al., 2007; Donnelly and Petherick, 2004; see chapter 5). When they find a prospect, they know that he will not have an agent and will sign a contract for little money in "Western" terms, and also will appreciate a chance to experience "dreamland." Only a few of these prospects have made it to the NBA or to top-level professional teams in European soccer. And the irony is that some have found themselves nearly penniless after using most of their incomes to keep the

people in their home village from starving. But the owners of the teams they played for usually made money from their labour as players. This is one of the ways that class relations operate on a global scale.

ECONOMIC AND CAREER OPPORTUNITIES IN SPORTS

Do sports and sport organizations provide opportunities for upward social class mobility in society? **Social mobility** is a term used by sociologists to refer to *changes in wealth, education, and occupation over a person's lifetime or from one generation to the next in families.* Social mobility can occur in downward or upward directions. On a general level, career and mobility opportunities exist in sports and sport organizations. However, as we consider the impact of sports mobility in Canada, it is useful to know the following things about sport-related opportunities:

1. The number of career opportunities in sports is limited, and playing careers for athletes are short term.

"Ah, the glamorous life of a spoiled, overpaid professional athlete!"

FIGURE 10.2   Only a few professional athletes achieve fame and fortune. Thousands of them play in minor and semipro leagues, where salaries are low and working conditions are poor.

2. Opportunities for women are growing but remain limited on and off the field.
3. Opportunities for blacks, Aboriginals, and other minorities are growing but remain limited on and off the field.

These points are discussed in the following sections.

Career Opportunities Are Limited

Young athletes often have visions of becoming professional athletes or going to the Olympics; their parents may have similar visions for them. But the chances of turning these visions into reality are very low regardless of social class. (See the box, "The Odds of Becoming a Professional Athlete," pp. 320–321, and figure 10.2.)

Most professional sport opportunities are short term, averaging three to seven years in team sports and three to twelve years in individual sports. This means that, after a playing career ends, there are about *forty additional years* in a person's work life. Unfortunately, many people, including athletes, coaches, and parents, ignore this fact.

Ideas about careers in professional sports often are distorted by misinterpretations in media

coverage. The media focus on the best athletes in the most popular sports. The best athletes tend to have longer playing careers than others in their sports. Little coverage is given to those who play for one or two seasons before being cut or forced to quit for other reasons, especially injuries. We hear about the long football careers of popular quarterbacks, but little or no coverage is given to the numerous players whose one-year contracts are not renewed after their first season. The average age of players on the *oldest* NFL team in 2004 was less than twenty-eight years old. This means that few players older than thirty are still in the league. Much more typical than thirty-year-olds contemplating another season are twenty-three-year-olds trying to deal with the end of their professional playing careers.

Finally, many professional athletes make less than their peers in nonsport occupations. For example, Robidoux (2001) pointed out that the average salary in the American Hockey League was US$55,000, which means that many players were earning far less than that. In Major League Soccer (MLS) 86 of the 331 players made less than US$20,000 per year in 2005 (Bell, 2005).[7] Another 57 players made less than US$30,000, and many others had salaries less than US$50,000. Elementary school teachers who have trained in their occupations for as many years as these soccer players make more money, have more security and stability, and usually have a pension plan. But the teachers have less fame.

Opportunities for Women Are Growing but Limited

Career opportunities for female athletes are limited relative to opportunities for men. Tennis and golf provide opportunities for women; however,

---

[7]Of course, David Beckham's multimillion dollar contract with the Los Angeles Galaxy MLS team will distort the team, and league, average salaries without changing the fact that the majority of players are not well paid (see chapter 11 for the problems of using averages when presenting salary data).

Given the millions of dollars that Lance Armstrong's cycling team spent on technology to prepare for the 2005 Tour de France, people in wealthy societies generally forget that sports are a luxury item. At least half the people in the world do not have regular access to the time, resources, equipment, or spaces enabling them to play sports. This little boy lives in Nairobi, Kenya, and this is his sport. [Karel Prinsloo, AP/Wide World Photos]

the professional tours for these sports draw athletes from around the world, rather than from North America, Australia, and a few European nations. This means that the competition to make a living in these sports is greater than it has ever been. There are expanding opportunities in professional figure skating, volleyball, basketball, soccer, curling, show jumping, bowling, skiing, cycling, track and field, and rodeo, but the number of professional female athletes remains very

low, and only a few women make large amounts of money.

Professional leagues for women now exist in ice hockey, soccer, beach volleyball, and basketball, but they provide opportunities for fewer than 400 athletes at any given point in recent years. For example, in the WNBA, the pay is a fraction of what men in the NBA make. The minimum salary for players with one to three years experience is US$30,600; for players with four or more years of experience, it is US$43,700. No WNBA player has a salary more than US$89,000, the amount Shaquille O'Neill makes in about thirteen minutes of one game. In fact, the total payroll for all WNBA players in 2004 was about US$8.8 million, the amount that Shaquille O'Neill made in the first twenty-six games of the 2005 NBA season. For every dollar that a player in the NBA makes, a player in the WNBA makes about one cent. Opportunities exist to play in Europe, but, again, they are limited and salaries are low. Overall, the advice for women who aspire to make a living as professional athletes is have a backup plan and be ready to use it.

What about other careers in sports? There are jobs for women in coaching, training, officiating, sport medicine, sports information, public relations, marketing, personal training, and administration. As noted in chapter 8, most of the jobs in women's sports continue to be held by men, and women seldom are hired for jobs in men's programmes, except in support positions. Women in most postindustrial nations have challenged the legacy of traditional gender ideology, and some progress has been made in various administrative positions in some sport organizations (Lapchick, 2005) In recent years in Canada, for example, there have been a small, but growing, number of women athletic directors, with overall responsibility for both men's and women's sports.[8]

---

[8]It is interesting to note that there have been a few significant administrative opportunities in Canada for women including: the first Minister of Sport, Iona Campagnolo; the first Director General of Sport Canada, Abbie Hoffman; a General Manager of the former Ottawa Rough Riders, Susan Pollack; and the CEO of CIS, Marg McGregor.

However, there is a need for systematic data in Canada on positions held by men and women, and some comparative data on salaries. A heavily gendered division of labour continues to exist in nearly all organizations (McKay, 1997, 1999). In traditional and developing nations, the record of progress is negligible, and very few women hold positions of power in any sport organizations (Rintala and Bischoff, 1997; White and Henry, 2004).

For a number of reasons, including the persistence of traditional gender ideology, job opportunities for women have not increased as rapidly as women's programmes have grown. This pattern exists in nearly all job categories and nearly all sport organizations.

Opportunities for women in sports will continue to shift toward equity, but people continue to resist the ideological changes that would open the door to full equity. In the meantime, there will be gradual increases in the number of women coaches, sports broadcasters, athletic trainers, administrators, and referees. Changes will occur more rapidly in community-based recreation and fitness programmes and in high school and university programmes where financial rewards are relatively low, and in certain sport industries that target women as consumers and need women employees to increase their sales and profit. But the gender ideology used by influential decision makers *inside* many sport organizations will continue to privilege those perceived as tough, strong, competitive, and aggressive—and men are more likely to be perceived in such terms.

Many women who work in sport organizations continue to face the burden of dealing with organizational cultures that are primarily based on the values and experiences of men. This contributes to high turnover among women. Professional development programmes, workshops, and coaching clinics have not been widely sponsored for women employees, although some organizations, such as the Canadian Association for the Advancement of Women and Sport (CAAWS and the Coaching Association of Canada [CAC]), have stepped in to provide assistance and guidance for women working in sports. These have been developed since the 1990s to assist women as they live in and try to change these cultures in ways that will make them more inclusive. However, equity requires that many men in sports and sport organizations change their ideas about gender and its connection with sports and leadership.

As we noted in chapter 9, there has been only one non-white coach in the NHL. Ted Nolan, an Ojibway from Northern Ontario, coached the Buffalo Sabres, and was named NHL Coach of the Year for the 1996–97 season. He was fired before the following season, without any public explanation, and did not coach in the NHL again until 2006 (New York Islanders). [CP(Bill Sikes)/AP]

Opportunities for Racial and Ethnic Minorities Are Growing but Remain Limited

The dynamics of racial and ethnic relations in any culture are unique, and they vary from one group to another (see chapter 9). Making generalizations about racial and ethnic relations and how they are related to opportunities in sports is difficult. However, dominant sport forms in any culture tend to reproduce dominant cultural values and the social structures supported by those values. This means three things: (1) members of the dominant social class in a society may exclude or define as unqualified those who have characteristics and cultural backgrounds different from their own, (2) racial and ethnic minorities often must adopt the values and orientations of the people in the dominant social class if they want to be hired and promoted in sport organizations, and (3) the voices of ethnic minorities are seldom represented in the stories that people tell one another about themselves. In any case, visible minorities are likely to perceive that they have fewer career opportunities than their white counterparts, and they may have higher levels of job dissatisfaction (Cunningham and Sagas, 2005).

Of course, some members of the dominant culture have valued cultural diversity and have made cultural spaces for racial and ethnic minorities in sport organizations. For example, this has occurred in baseball and soccer in the U.S. as Latinos have been hired for management and administrative jobs. Also, some members of ethnic groups assimilate and willingly accept the "cultural terms" on which dominant sports are based. However, those who give priority to their culture in their identities may not be willing to assign secondary importance to their own cultural values and orientations to play sports or work in sport organizations in which their culture is not valued or even acknowledged by other employees, or respected within organizational rules and practices.

As we noted in chapter 9, racial and ethnic relations are significantly different in Canada than in the U.S. There are intersections between visible minorities and social class, as in the U.S., but these have not been examined systematically in sports in Canada, except in the case of francophones and anglophones. Thus, we have no data at this time with which to explore careers in sports for visible minorities, either as athletes or in management and administrative positions. It is probably safe to speculate that, in Canada, visible minorities are underrepresented in many sports and sport organizations. There are various reasons for this, but at least part of this underrepresentation is related to racism, as well as to fears of diversity and a lack of understanding of how diversity can contribute in a positive way to the operation and overall culture of an organization. However, given the policies of multiculturalism, and recognition of equity issues and ethnic diversity, there has been some sensitivity in Canada to identifying and responding to issues of diversity in sports. Given that the best evidence available at this time is anecdotal, to what extent this has been successful we cannot say until relevant research is available.

SPORT PARTICIPATION AND OCCUPATIONAL CAREERS AMONG FORMER ATHLETES

What happens in the occupational careers of former athletes? Do they have career patterns that are different from the patterns of those who have never played competitive sports? Is sport participation a stepping stone to future occupational success and upward social mobility? Does playing sports have economic payoffs after active participation is over?

These are difficult questions, and there are only a few studies that have compared former athletes with others on issues related to social class and social mobility. These studies usually suggest that, as a group, the young people who had played sports on high school, community, and university teams experienced no more or less occupational success than others from comparable backgrounds. However, two Canadian studies carried out twenty years apart suggest that there may be some career or social mobility advantages to early sport participation. Norman Okihiro (1984), of Mount Saint Vincent University, found that involvement in extracurricular activities did not lead to more prestigious jobs, but it was associated with a "facility for dealing with people" that could have a long-term career benefit in the new economy. Curtis et al. (2003), found that those who participated in organized youth sports tend to have higher incomes as adults (a finding that was stronger for males than females). Interestingly, both studies suggest similar explanations for their results— youth sport participation produces net gains in social, cultural, and physical capital, which are assets in the job market. The meaning and cultural significance of sport participation changes over time, and those changes may be related to career processes in some way.

Research done a decade ago may not tell us what is happening today because the meanings and cultural significance of sport participation changes over time, and those changes may be related to career processes in some way. However, past research suggests that, *if* playing sports is connected to processes of career success, it may operate in one or more of the following ways (see Coakley, 1983; and 1998, p. 317, for references to thirty of these studies):

- Playing sports, under certain circumstances (see list below), may teach young people *interpersonal skills*, which carry over into various jobs and enable them to be successful in jobs that require those skills.
- Some people with power and influence may define former athletes as good job prospects and give them opportunities to develop and demonstrate work-related abilities, which serve as the basis for career success.
- Individuals who were very high-profile athletes may be able to use their reputations to obtain certain jobs and be successful in them.
- Playing sports, under certain circumstances (see list below), may connect athletes with others who can help them to obtain good jobs after they retire from sports.

After reviewing the research on this topic, our view is that playing sports is positively related to occupational success and upward mobility when it does the following things:

1. Increases opportunities to complete academic degrees, develop job-related skills, and/or extend knowledge about the organization and operation of the world outside of sports
2. Increases support from significant others for *overall* growth and development, not just sport development
3. Provides opportunities to make friends and develop social contacts with people outside of sports and sport organizations
4. Provides material resources and the guidance needed to use those resources to create or nurture career opportunities
5. Expands experiences in ways that foster the development of identities and abilities unrelated to sports
6. Minimizes risks of serious injuries that restrict physical movement or require extensive and expensive medical treatment

This is not a surprising list of conditions and tends to affirm why Okihiro (1984) and Curtis et al. (2003) found positive career results for Canadian university and high school athletes— athletes from sport programmes where more of these conditions are likely to be found. It emphasizes that playing sports can either constrict or expand a person's overall development (see chapter 4). When expansion occurs, athletes often develop work-related abilities and connections that lead to career opportunities and success. When constriction occurs, the development of work-related abilities and career opportunities are likely to be limited.

Highly Paid Professional Athletes and Career Success after Playing Sports

Conclusions about *the connections among* sport participation, career success, and social mobility must be qualified in light of the dramatic increases in the salaries of *some* professional athletes over the past twenty to thirty years (see chapter 11). Before the late 1970s, few athletes made enough money in sports to pave their ways into other careers after they retired. However, some top athletes today make enough money in a few years to finance any one of a range of career alternatives after they retire from sports—if they do not throw their money away or hire irresponsible agents to manage their money.

Of course, many professional athletes have short careers or play at levels at which they do not make much money (see figure 10.3). When they retire, they must deal with the challenge of entering another career and making a living. Many experience patterns of success and failure similar to the patterns experienced by comparable others, who did not play sports. Their post-sport careers may not enable them to drive new cars, travel to exciting places, or read their names in newspapers every week, but this does not mean they are failures or victims of sports.

As noted in chapter 4, retirement from sports is best described as a process rather than a single event, and most athletes do not retire from sports on a moment's notice—they gradually disengage from sports and shift their priorities over time. Although many athletes disengage smoothly from sports, develop other interests, and move into relatively satisfying occupational careers, some do encounter adjustment problems that interfere with occupational success and overall life satisfaction.

When sociologist Mike Messner interviewed former elite athletes, he found that those who had been heavily involved in sports since childhood encountered serious adjustment problems as they tried to make the transition out of sports. A former NFL player explained:

You miss the camaraderie of the fellas. There's an empty feeling....The one thing that has been the major part of your life is gone....You don't know how people are going to react to you....You wonder and question. (Messner, 1992, p. 121)

Anecdotal evidence from other team sports suggests that these feelings are common to many athletes. Bette McKenzie (1999) makes this point with regard to both her father (former NHL player) and her husband (former NFL player).

The two challenges that face many retired athletes are (1) reconstructing identities in terms of activities, abilities, and relationships that are not directly related to sport participation and (2) renegotiating relationships with family members and friends so that new identities can be established and reaffirmed. Messner's study also indicated that young men from low-income families were more likely to have problems when retiring from sports because they had fewer material resources to use in the transition process and they were more likely to have identities deeply rooted in sports. The men from middle-class backgrounds, on the other hand, had greater material resources and support that enabled them to take advantage of opportunities and social connections; and they were less likely to have identities exclusively rooted in sports.

Studies also have shown that adjustment problems are more likely when an injury forces retirement from sports (Coakley, 1983; Swain, 1999; Weisman, 2004). Injuries complicate retirement and tie it to larger issues of self-esteem and health. Injuries also disrupt life plans by throwing off the timing of retirement and forcing a person into life-changing transitions before they are expected. This is not surprising, and athletes often need career-related assistance when it occurs.

When athletes have problems making the transition out of sports into careers and other activities, it would be helpful if they received support from the sport organizations that benefited from their labour, especially when athletes

SIDELINES

FIGURE 10.3   Only a few former athletes are able to cash in on their athletic reputations. The rest must seek opportunities and work just like the rest of us. Those opportunities vary, depending on qualifications, experience, contacts and connections, and a bit of luck.

never made enough money to make the transition less problematic (Dacyshyn, 1999). Some sport organizations, including Sport Canada and AthletesCAN, are beginning to do this through career transition programmes that involve workshops focusing on career self-assessments, life skills training, career planning, résumé writing, job search strategies, interviewing skills, career placement contacts, and psychological counselling. In many cases it is helpful just to have guidance in identifying the skills learned in sports and the ways that they are transferable to other settings or jobs.

Athletic Scholarships and Occupational Success

Discussions about sport participation and social mobility in the United States, and increasingly in Canada, often include references to athletic scholarships. Most people believe that these scholarships are valuable mobility vehicles for many young people. This belief raises many questions: How many students receive athletic scholarships as opposed to other forms of financial assistance? How much are athletic scholarships worth to those who receive them? Who receives them, and how many recipients would not attend university without them?

Answering these questions has been possible in the U.S. since 1994 when Congress passed the Equity in Athletics Disclosure Act. This forced most universities to inform people about what was going on in their athletic departments. The data that are reported annually indicate that the actual number of *full* athletic scholarships is often exaggerated. This occurs for the following reasons:

1. High school students who receive standard recruiting letters from university coaches often tell people they are anticipating *full* scholarships when in fact they may receive only partial aid or no aid at all
2. Students receiving tuition waivers or other forms of partial aid sometimes lead people to believe that they have full scholarships
3. Athletic scholarships are awarded one year at a time and may not be renewed for certain athletes, who may continue their education while people believe they have scholarships
4. Many people assume that student-athletes, especially at major U.S. universities, all have scholarships when this is not true

These factors cause people to think that sport participation has more relevance for upward mobility than it actually does.

According to NCAA data, there were 5.75 million undergraduate students in NCAA institutions in 2003. Of these, 377,651 (6.6 percent) students were on interuniversity teams. Division I and II universities had 70,244 scholarships to award either as full scholarships or partial athletic aid. Of 232,473 Division I and II athletes, 132,758 athletes, or about 58 percent of them, received some amount of athletic aid, but most received only partial scholarships. According to NCAA sources, an estimated 17,561 athletes—4.7

percent of all NCAA athletes—received full scholarships (tuition, room, and food). The remaining 52,683 scholarships were split in various ways between 115,197 athletes—30.5 percent of all university team members. The fact that surprises most people is that about 65 percent of all interuniversity athletes receive no athletic aid.

Another way of making sense of the data is to say that among all undergraduate students in NCAA universities, only 0.3 percent of them have full athletic scholarships, and only 2.3 percent of all undergraduates receive some form of athletic aid. Clearly, far fewer students receive full athletic scholarships than is commonly believed. In fact, in Canada and the U.S., academic scholarships are many times more plentiful than athletic scholarships, even though many high school students and their parents think otherwise.

This information is especially relevant for Canadian students who often see (as do their parents) particular status associated with achieving an athletic scholarship to a U.S. university. Some Canadian athletes have extremely rewarding experiences. A few gain the opportunity for a university education that may not have been available to them in Canada because of somewhat lower and more flexible admission standards at many U.S. universities (James, 2005). Some Canadian athletes enjoy sport training opportunities that may not have been available to them in Canada—high-level coaching, opportunities that result from the climate in the southern U.S. (e.g., year-round outdoor track season, year-round swimming training and competitions in outdoor pools), and the opportunity to be drafted into professional sports. For example, Canadian track athletes Kevin Sullivan and Perdita Felican both had successful scholarship experiences in the U.S.

But many Canadian students are disappointed by their U.S. university athletic scholarship experiences. They may find themselves involved in a much more intense level of competition and training than they have previously experienced, often resulting in burnout and overuse injuries. To many, it is made clear that a scholarship puts them in the employ of the Athletics Department, and that the requirements of their sport participation must be given priority over any other aspects of their lives as students if they wish to keep their scholarship (Wells, 2008). Many do not achieve the education that they expected, are unable to take the degree programme or courses of their choice, and may not graduate (e.g., because the scholarship ends before they have enough courses to complete their degree). And the majority of Canadian athletes find that the financial costs of attending a U.S. university are significant, despite the scholarship.

Parcels (2000) and Brunton (Rubenstein, 2003), whose work on tracking Canadian athletes to professional careers was noted in the Reflect on Sports box, "The Odds of Becoming a Professional Athlete," pages 320–321, have reservations about U.S. scholarships. For example, many NCAA hockey teams carry a roster of thirty players, but only have seventeen scholarships available. Parcels notes that the number of Ontario players receiving a *full* scholarship declined 63 percent between 1990 and 2000. Because coaches are likely to spread scholarships among the team, most Canadians find they receive 40 to 60 percent of a full scholarship. Given that they are classed as "out of state" for the purposes of tuition, and that they may incur greater travel expenses than a U.S. player, Canadians are likely to end up paying a great deal more than they may have at a Canadian university (Parcels estimates that students could end up with US$50,000–$75,000 of debt). NCAA Division I golf teams carry ten to twelve players, but are only allocated four or five scholarships. A highly ranked Canadian player may receive 50 to 75 percent of a scholarship, but is also likely to end up incurring more costs than expected, and therefore debt or significant expenses for parents. Golfers on a U.S. university team may miss five weeks of classes each year because of travel and competition obligations, and also find it difficult to graduate in four years.

Many Canadian students who receive a U.S. athletic scholarship claim that they have received a *full* scholarship, thus increasing the motivation of others to aspire to the athletic scholarship route. In reality, they are likely to be incurring a great deal of unexpected expenses and debt, and possibly earning a less-than-complete education. [It should be noted that, although athletic scholarships are increasingly available at Canadian universities, these are limited to the cost of tuition and fees, and the stipulations regarding requisite grade point average and eligibility vary between the Regional Associations.]

Athletes in nonrevenue sports at U.S. universities often come from wealthier backgrounds than those in revenue-producing sports. Ironically, football and basketball players may be more isolated from campus and community life than athletes in swimming, tennis, soccer, volleyball, rowing, lacrosse, field hockey, and other sports in which white students predominate. If isolation subverts the opportunities that expand experiences and contacts, then playing sports is more likely to contribute to career success for students who already come from successful backgrounds, thereby reproducing existing forms of economic inequality in society. Of course, the few football and basketball players who sign big contracts distract attention away from this more important aspect of class relations.

When athletic aid goes to financially needy young people who focus on learning and earning their degrees, sport participation certainly increases their chances for career success. But how many of those athletic scholarships, full and partial, go to young people who could not or would not attend university without them? A portion of scholarship recipients would attend university without them. This does not mean that scholarships are unjustified, but it does mean that they contribute little to upward social mobility in society.

SUMMARY

DO MONEY AND POWER MATTER IN SPORTS?

Social class and class relations are integrally involved in sports. Organized sports depend on resources. Those who provide the resources do so in ways that fit their interests and foster ideas supportive of economic arrangements that work to their advantage. This is why the dominant sport forms in North America, and other nations with market economies, promote an ideology based on the idea that "you always get what you deserve, and you always deserve what you get" (meritocracy).

This ideology constitutes a class logic that drives a combination of individual achievement and consumption, along with corporate expansion, in society. Using it leads to favourable conclusions about the character and qualifications of thosewho are wealthy and powerful, but it disadvantages the poor and powerless. Furthermore, using it leads to the conclusion that economic inequality in society is natural and beneficial.

Class relations also are connected with the ways in which wealthy and powerful people around the world have become involved in sport team ownership, event sponsorship and organization, and the media coverage of sports. Sport events are one of the vehicles these people can use to transfer public money into their own hands. As public funds support major forms of sport entertainment in their cities and regions, those with wealth and power receive subsidies and income, which they use to maintain their privilege. At the same time, class relations have ideological implications in the sense that large segments of the population continue to see sports as enjoyable forms of entertainment brought to them by corporate sponsors. Although fans do not automatically see sports in the way that sponsors would like them to, most fans raise no critical questions about the ideology of success emphasized in media coverage of sports.

Sport participation patterns in society and around the world reflect the impact of material resources and social class on the ways in which people live their lives. Organized sports are a luxury that many people around the world cannot afford. Even in wealthy societies, sport participation is most common among those in the middle and upper classes. Patterns of sport participation throughout a society reflect class-based lifestyles, which emerge as people make decisions about how they will use the resources they do have.

Sport participation patterns also reflect the combination of class and gender relations. We see this in the case of lower-income girls and women who have low participation rates, and lower-income men who see sports as a means of obtaining respect. Public sector cutbacks are having an increasing impact, limiting sport participation for those from low-income families. That impact is now beginning to be felt at the high-performance level as the pool of talented athletes declines.

Patterns of watching sports also are connected with social class and class relations. This is demonstrated by the increased segregation of fans in stadiums and arenas. Luxury boxes, club seating, and patterns of season ticket allocations separate people by a combination of wealth and power, so that social class often is reaffirmed when people attend sport events.

Opportunities for careers that hold the hope of upward social mobility exist for some people in sports. For athletes, these opportunities often are scarce and short-lived, and they reflect patterns of gender and ethnic relations in society. The patterns take various forms in the case of careers in sport organizations. Although opportunities in these jobs have become increasingly open over the past decade, white men still hold most of the top positions in sport organizations. This will change only when the organizational cultures of sport teams and athletic departments become more inclusive and provide new ways for women and visible minorities to participate fully in shaping the policies and norms used to determine qualifications in sports and to organize social relations at the workplace.

Research generally indicates that people who use sport participation to expand their social worlds and personal experiences often have an advantage when seeking occupational careers. However, when sport participation constricts social worlds and personal experiences, it is likely to have a negative effect on later career success. The existence of these patterns varies by sport and by the resources that athletes can accumulate during their playing careers.

Retirement from athletic careers often creates stress and personal challenges, but most athletes move through the retirement process without experiencing *excessive* trauma or difficulty. Those who do experience difficulties are usually those whose identities and relationships have been built exclusively on and around sports. These people may need outside assistance as they move into the rest of their lives and face the challenge of seeking jobs, maintaining satisfying careers, and nurturing mutually supportive and intimate social relationships.

Athletic scholarships help some young people further their educations and possibly achieve career success, but athletic aid is relatively scarce compared with other scholarships and forms of financial aid. Furthermore, athletic scholarships do not always change the future career patterns of young people, because many recipients would attend university without sport-related financial assistance.

In conclusion, sports clearly are tied to patterns of class, class relations, and social inequality in society. Money and economic power do matter, and they matter in ways that often reproduce existing patterns of social class and life chances.

Visit *Sports in Society*'s Online Learning Centre at <u>www.mcgrawhill.ca/olc/coakley</u> for additional information, website resources, and study tools for this chapter.

[Alison Derry]

chapter

11

Sports and the Economy

What are the characteristics of commercial sports?

The National Hockey League is a business. Its business is entertainment. The entertainment it presents is sport.

—**John Ziegler, former NHL Commissioner (1978)**

When I started in track and field, there was no confusion about goals, no lure of money. I didn't think of money, because nobody did then. You did track and field because it was wonderful to do. It was something very deep inside you, something very personal. It was not something to barter.

—**Debbie Brill, Canadian high jumper (1986)**

We played hockey because we loved it. Anything we got paid was a bonus.

—**Maurice "Rocket" Richard (n.d.)**

I don't see myself as a hockey team owner. I see myself as a sports/entertainment/media brand manager.

—**Ted Leonsis, owner, Washington Capitals (2000)**

You've got to get these kids [who excel on the court] in your product. You've got to get these kids walking around being a Reebok kid…. They will be your messengers.

—**Sonny Vaccaro, Reebok representative (in Alesia, 2004)**

Sports have been used as public entertainment through history. However, sports have never been so thoroughly commercialized as they are today. Never before have economic factors so totally dominated decisions about sports, and never before have economic organizations and large corporate interests had so much power and control over the meaning, organization, and purpose of sports.

The economic stakes for athletes and sponsors have never been higher than they are today. The bottom line has replaced the goal line. As an editor at *Financial World* magazine notes, "Sports is not simply another big business. It is one of the fastest growing industries… and it is intertwined with virtually every aspect of the economy…. [Sports are] everywhere, accompanied by the sound of a cash register ringing incessantly" (Ozanian, 1995, p. 30).

Sports today are evaluated in terms of gate receipts, concessions, and merchandise sales, licensing fees, media rights contracts, and website hits. Games and events are evaluated in terms of media criteria such as market shares, ratings points, and advertising potential. Athletes are evaluated in terms of their entertainment value as well as their physical skills. Stadiums, teams, and events are named after corporations and are associated with corporate logos instead of people and places that have local meaning.

Corporate interests influence team colours, uniform designs, event schedules, media coverage, and the comments of announcers during games and matches. Media companies plan events, and they own a growing number of teams. Many sports are corporate enterprises, tied to marketing concerns and processes of global capitalist expansion. The mergers of major corporate conglomerates that began in the 1990s and now continue into the twenty-first century have connected sports teams, and events with media and entertainment companies. The names of transnational corporations are now synonymous with the athletes, events, and sports that provide pleasure in the lives of millions of people.

Because economic factors are so important in sports, this chapter focuses on these questions:

1. Under what conditions do commercial sports emerge and prosper in a society?
2. What changes occur in the meaning, organization, and purpose of sports when they become commercial activities?
3. Who owns, sponsors, and promotes sports, and what are their interests?
4. What is the legal and financial status of athletes in commercial sports?

Because of the overwhelming presence of male professional team sports, and the availability of economic data, this chapter tends to focus on those forms of sports. Also, because of the globalized nature of economies and sports, it is difficult to take a particularly Canadian approach to this chapter on sports and the economy. Many of Canada's sports are shared with the U.S., or even more internationally in the case of, for example, golf and hockey. Canada's economy is integrated with the U.S. to a very great extent, and some of our major sport teams and leagues are "branch plants" of U.S. leagues.[1] Players and coaches are mobile, crossing borders with little difficulty, and Canada has seen three major teams (Vancouver Grizzlies of the NBA and the Québec Nordiques and Winnipeg Jets of the NHL) move to the United States in recent years. Even those most Canadian of sports, curling and lacrosse, are influenced—the National Lacrosse League is a cross-border league, and curling is not only international, it is also produced and mediated as a part of the international sportainment industry. These interconnections are reflected in this chapter.

---

[1]Cantelon (2001) has argued that even the CFL is Americanized to a disturbing extent. *Note:* The term North American is used in this chapter to refer only to Canada and the United States, and excludes Mexico.

THE EMERGENCE AND GROWTH OF COMMERCIAL SPORTS

Commercial sports are organized and played to make money as entertainment events. They depend on a combination of gate receipts, concessions, sponsorships, the sale of media broadcasting rights, and other revenue streams associated with sport images and personalities. Therefore, commercial sports grow and prosper best under six social and economic conditions.

First, they are most prevalent in market economies, where material rewards are highly valued by athletes, team owners, event sponsors, and spectators.

Second, commercial sports usually exist in societies with large, densely populated cities, because they require large concentrations of potential spectators. Although some forms of commercial sports can be maintained in rural, agricultural societies, revenues would not support full-time professional athletes or sport promoters. Thus, only four provinces in Canada have NHL teams, and only six provinces have CFL teams.

Third, commercial sports are a luxury, and they prosper only when the standard of living is high enough that people have time and resources they are able to use to play and watch events that have no tangible products required for survival. Transportation and communications technologies must exist for sponsors to make money. Therefore, they are most often found in relatively wealthy, urban, and industrial or postindustrial societies; they are found less often in labour-intensive, poor societies where people must use all their resources to survive.

Fourth, commercial sports require *large amounts of capital* (money or collateral) to build and maintain stadiums and arenas in which events can be played and watched. Capital can be accumulated in the public or private sector but, in either case, the willingness to invest in sports depends on anticipated payoffs in the form of publicity, profits, or power. *Private* investment in sports occurs when investors expect financial profits; *public* investment occurs when political leaders believe that commercial sports serve their interests, the interests of "the public," or a combination of both (see chapter 13).

Fifth, commercial cross-border sports depend, to a certain extent, on a favourable exchange rate. The artificially low Canadian dollar of the 1990s and early 2000s created difficulties for some Canadian teams competing in leagues where they are obliged to make payments in U.S. dollars. Those teams became increasingly profitable with the increasing strength of the Canadian dollar against the U.S. dollar.

Sixth, commercial sports are most likely to flourish in cultures where lifestyles involve high rates of consumption and emphasize material status symbols. This enables everything associated with sports to be marketed and sold: athletes (including their names, autographs, and images), merchandise, team names, and logos. When people express their identities through clothing, other possessions, and their associations with status symbols and celebrities, they will spend money on sports that are popular in their sphere of social life. Commercial sports depend on selling symbols and emotional experiences to audiences, and then selling audiences to sponsors and the media (Burstyn, 1999).

Class Relations and Commercial Sports

Which sports become commercialized in a society? As noted in chapter 10, priority is usually given to the sports that are watched or played by people who control economic resources in society. For example, golf is a major commercial sport, even though it does not lend itself to commercial presentation. It is inconvenient to stage a golf event for a live audience, or to televise it. Camera placements and media commentary are difficult to arrange, and live spectators see only a small portion of the action. Golf does not involve vigorous action or head-to-head competition, except in rare cases of match play. If you do not play golf, usually you have little or no reason to watch it.

Sports are played in all cultures, but professional sports seldom exist in labour-intensive, poor nations around the world. The Afghan horsemen here are playing *buzkashi*, a popular sport in their country, but Afghanistan lacks the general conditions needed to sustain buzkashi as a professional sport with paid athletes and paying fans. [Efren Lukatsky, AP/Wide World Photos]

But a high proportion of those who *do* play golf are relatively wealthy and powerful people. They are important to sponsors and advertisers because they make consumption decisions for themselves, their families, their businesses, and thousands of employees. They buy luxury cars and other high-end products for themselves; more important to advertisers, however, is that they buy thousands of company cars and computers for employees, and make investment decisions relating to pensions and company capital.

Golfers as a group have economic clout that goes far beyond their personal and family lives.

This makes golf an attractive sport for corporations with images and products that appeal to consumers with money and influence. Thus, auto companies with high-priced cars sponsor and advertise on the PGA, LPGA, and Senior PGA tours; and major television networks cover golf tournaments: they can sell commercial time at a high rate per minute because those watching golf have money to spend—their money *and* the money of the companies, large and small, that they control. The converse of this is also true: sports attracting low- and middle-income audiences often are ignored by television or covered only under special circumstances. If wealthy executives bowled, we would see more bowling on television and more bowling facilities on prime real estate in cities.

Market economies always privilege the interests of those who have the power and resources to influence which sports are selected for promotion and coverage. Unless people with power and resources play, sponsor, or watch a sport, it will not be commercialized on a large scale, nor will it be given cultural significance in society. A sport will not come to be known as a "national pastime" or become associated with ideal personal character, community spirit, civic unity, and political loyalty unless it is favoured by people with resources.

This is one reason hockey has become "Canada's game." Hockey celebrates and privileges the values and experiences of the men who control and benefit from corporate wealth and power in North America. This explains why men pay thousands of dollars to buy expensive season tickets to professional hockey games, why male executives use corporate credit cards to buy blocks of "company tickets" to hockey games, and why corporation presidents write hundred-thousand-dollar cheques to pay for luxury boxes and club seats for themselves, friends, and clients. Hockey is entertaining for them, but more important, it reproduces an ideology that fosters their interests.

Women who want to be a part of the power structure often find that they must learn to talk sport. If women executives do not play golf, or go to the next big game, and take clients with them, they may be cut out of the "masculinity loop" that is the core of corporate culture.

The Creation of Spectator Interest in Sports

What leads people to become sport spectators? Why do they look to sports for entertainment? These questions have multiple answers. However, spectator interest is related to four factors in modern and post-industrial societies: a general

quest for excitement, a cultural emphasis on material success, early life experiences in sports, and easy access to sports through the media.

The Quest for Excitement When social life becomes highly controlled and organized people may become stuck in everyday routines to the point that we become emotionally constrained. This leads to a search for activities that offer tension-excitement and emotional arousal? According to figurational sociologists Eric Dunning and Norbert Elias, historical evidence suggests that this occurs in modern societies. Sports, they argue, provide activities in which rules and norms can be shaped to foster emotional arousal and exciting actions, thereby eliminating boredom without disrupting social order in society as a whole (Dunning, 1999; Elias and Dunning, 1986).

Sports generally are characterized by a tension between order and disruption. Managing this tension involves a challenge: norms and rules in sports must be loose enough to break boredom, but not so loose that they permit violence or other forms of destructive "deviance." When norms and rules are too controlling, sports are boring and people lose interest; when they are too loose, sports become sites for reckless and dangerous behaviours, which can jeopardize health and social order. The challenge is to find and maintain a balance. This explanation of spectator interest raises the question, Why do so many people give priority to sports over other activities in their quest for excitement? Critical theorists suggest that answers can be found by looking at the connection between ideology and cultural practices. This leads us to consider three other factors.

Success Ideology and Spectator Interest Many people watch games or follow them in the media, but spectator involvement is highest among those who are committed to the ideas that success is always based on hard work and hard work always leads to success. Such ideas are part of class ideology in societies with capitalist economies (see chapter 10). The people who hold this ideology often use sports as a model for how the social world *should* operate. When sports promote the idea that success is achieved only through hard work and dedication to efficiency, these people have their beliefs and expectations reaffirmed, and they are willing to pay for that reaffirmation. This is why sport media commentators emphasize that athletes and teams make their own breaks and that luck comes to those who work hard. This is why corporations use the bodies of elite athletes to represent their public relations and marketing images; the finely tuned bodies of athletes are concrete examples of efficiency, power, the use of technology, and the achievement of success (Hoberman, 1994). Under such ideological conditions, some high-profile, celebrity athletes make large amounts of money. Their very existence reaffirms a class ideology that reproduces privilege among powerful people around the world.

Youth Sport Programmes and Spectator Interest Spectator interest often is created and nurtured during childhood sport participation. When organized youth sport programmes are publicized and made available to many young people in a society, commercial sports have a good chance to grow and prosper. With some exceptions, sport participation during childhood leads to spectator interests during adulthood. Children who learn to value sport skills, competition, and competitive success in their personal experiences generally grow up wanting to watch "experts" compete with one another. For those who continue to participate actively in sports, watching the experts provides models for improving skills and motives for playing and improving skills. For those who no longer play sports, watching the experts maintains connections with the images and experiences of success learned in organized competitive youth and interschool sports.

Media Coverage and Spectator Interest Media promote the commercialization of sports (see chapter 12). They provide publicity and sustain spectator interest among many people. In the past, newspapers and radio did this, but television today has the greatest effect on spectator involvement. Tomorrow it is likely to be the Internet.

Television increases spectator access to events and athletes worldwide, and it provides a unique "re-presentation" of sports. It lets viewers see close-up camera shots of the action on the field/court/ice, and the athletes and coaches on the sidelines/benches/dugouts. It replays selected action and shows it in slow motion, helping viewers become further immersed in the action.

On-air commentators serve as fellow spectators for the media audience, including those "interactive" spectators watching television while they are online with sports websites. Commentators dramatize and embellish the action and heighten identification with athletes. They provide inside stories, analyze strategies, describe athletes as personalities, and present the event in ways that magnify its significance.

Television recruits new spectators by providing a means of learning the rules and strategies of a sport without purchasing tickets. Furthermore, newcomers to a sport can do their learning at home with family and friends. Overall, television provides a painless way to become a spectator, and it increases the number of people who will buy tickets, regularly watch televised games, pay for cable and satellite programming, and even become pay-per-view customers in the future.

Economic Motives and the Globalization of Commercial Sports

Commercial sports have become global in scope for two reasons. *First*, those who control, sponsor, and promote them seek new ways to expand markets and maximize profits. *Second*, transnational corporations with production and distribution operations in many countries can use sports as vehicles for introducing their products and services all around the world.

Sport Organizations Look for Global Markets Sport organizations, like other businesses, wish to expand their operations into as many markets as possible. For example, profits for the U.S.–based NFL and the North American–based NBA, NHL, and Major League Baseball (MLB) could expand significantly if the leagues were able to sell broadcasting rights to television companies in countries worldwide and licensed merchandise (hats, shirts, jackets, etc.) to people in countries outside North America. This already occurs to some extent but the continued commercial success of major sport organizations requires that they create spectators worldwide. Success also depends on using the media to export a combination of game knowledge and athlete-identification. In this way, sport organizations become exporters of culture as well as products to be consumed. The complex export–import processes that occur in connection with sports are new topics studied by scholars in the sociology of sport (Donnelly, 1996a; Klein, 1991, 1997; Maguire, 1999).

The desire for global expansion was the main reason why the NBA allowed its players to represent their national teams in the Olympics starting in 1992, even though the players risked injury and fatigue, which could have jeopardized their participation in the following NBA season (and did, in a few cases). The global media attention provided the NBA with publicity worth many millions of dollars. This helped market NBA broadcasting rights and official NBA products worldwide. Today the NBA finals and All-Star games are televised in nearly 200 countries every year, about one in four players in the league was born outside the United States, and there are NBA fans in over forty nations.

NHL hockey followed the NBA's lead in 1998, entering national "dream teams" in the Olympics. And, although baseball was recently dropped from the Olympic schedule, and MLB never considered including its professional players in the Olympics because of the disruption to the baseball schedule, even professional baseball, has now developed a truly international competition (the "World" Series never included a non-U.S.-based team until the Blue Jays in 1992) (Klein, 2006). The first World Baseball Classic was held in 2006, and the international strength of baseball was evident in that Canada beat Team USA, and Japan beat Cuba in the final. The Classic will be held again in 2009, with Toronto as one of the host cities.

The recruitment of international players also has an impact on expanding markets. Interest in the NHL has grown significantly in Europe with the increase in the number of European players. Star players can also have a surprising impact. Ichiro Suzuki and several other Japanese players have not only increased interest in MLB in Japan (Nakamura, 2005), but also attracted Japanese tourists and Japanese-Canadian and Japanese-American fans to baseball games. Similarly, Yao Ming's success with the Houston Rockets of the NBA has greatly increased interest in the NBA in China, and attracted Chinese-Canadian fans to games when Houston plays in Toronto. International interest also expands the market for league products.

The spirit of global expansion has led NFL, NBA, NHL, and MLB teams to play games in Mexico, Japan, England, France, Germany, Spain, Italy, and Australia and to subsidize leagues and outreach programmes for marketing purposes.

This spirit is not new, nor is it limited to North American sport organizations. The International Olympic Committee (IOC) gradually has incorporated National Olympic Committees (NOCs) from over two hundred nations and has turned the Olympic Games into the most successful and financially lucrative media sport events in history. Furthermore, the IOC, like some other

Breaking Barriers	**Brand Barriers**	
	There Was Nothing We Could Do	

When is a flag not a flag? Dr. Jens Bromann discovered in 1983 that this is not a trick question. As a representative of athletes with a disability, he sat in a meeting called by Juan Antonio Samaranch, the newly elected president of the International Olympic Committee (IOC). Samaranch told Bromann and others from disability sport organizations that they could no longer use "Olympics" in any way and that the IOC would never include events for athletes with a disability in the Olympic Games.

Samaranch also declared that the Paralympics could no longer use Olympic symbols because the IOC was establishing the Olympics as a brand with commercial interests and goals. Then came the answer to the question: A flag is not a flag when it is a licensed logo to be used *only* by those who pay for the right to do so. As Bromann left the meeting, he told reporters that the Olympics had been branded and "there was nothing we could do" (Jennings, 1996).

Upset, but not wanting to cut ties with the IOC, Bromann and his peers turned their attention to the Games that they planned to have in Los Angeles, after the 1984 Olympic Games. But neither the Los Angeles Olympic Organizing Committee nor the United States Olympic Committee (USOC) would support them. So they held competitions in two locations: New York and Stoke Mandeville, England. They also formed the International Coordinating Committee of World Organizations for the Disabled (ICC) and made it the governing body for the Paralympic Games.

As ICC president, Bromann focused on organizing the 1988 Paralympic Games in Seoul, Korea. With support from Korean Olympic officials, the games were a huge success, bringing together over 3,000 athletes from sixty-one nations. At the opening ceremonies, Bromann, who had once competed in sports for blind athletes, was presented with a flag that the Korean organizers designed for the Games. It was white and had five *tae-geuks*, or traditional Korean line symbols, that resembled teardrops in the same positions and colours as the five interlocking rings on the Olympic flag. This was meant to show that the Paralympics were related to the Olympic movement and that Paralympians endured hardships to train and compete (Sheil, 2000).

The ICC reorganized in 1989 and would become the International Paralympic Committee (IPC) after the 1992 Paralympic Games in Barcelona, Spain, with Robert Steadward, a professor at the University of Alberta, serving as president until 2001. In the meantime, it used the five *tae-geuks* as its symbol, but this infuriated the IOC. The symbol, they declared, was too similar to their brand logo. In 1991 the IOC told the ICC to change the flag or face sanctions. This prompted noted author and journalist Andrew Jennings to ask sarcastically, "Sanctions against the disabled? What would they do? Shoot some guide dogs? Smash up a few wheelchairs?" (1996, p. 228). But the ICC knew exactly what sanctions meant: *No more funding from the IOC.*

To appease the IOC, a new symbol with three *tae geuks* was officially launched at the 1994 World Championships in IPC sports. The *tae-geuks* again appeared as three teardrops representing the Paralympic motto: "Mind, Body, and Spirit." It was used by the IPC through the 2004 Games in Athens. But in 2003, after years of failed attempts to gain full IOC recognition and support, the IPC decided to set itself apart from the IOC. It adopted a new symbol and flag to represent the unique purpose and identity of the Paralympic Games. It consisted of three elements in red, blue, and green—the colours most often used in national flags. The elements are known as *Agitos* (a Latin word meaning "I move"), and they appear to be in motion around a central point, representing a dynamic, global "Spirit in Motion," the new motto of the Paralympics. It emphasizes that the goal of the IPC is to bring athletes from all regions of the globe to compete. The Spirit in Motion flag was flown at the 2008 Paralympics in Beijing.

Continued

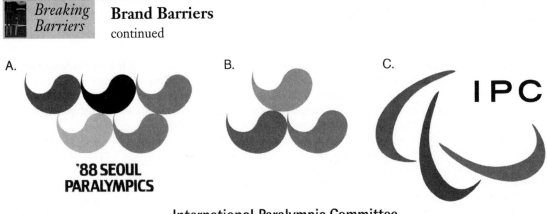

Breaking Barriers

Brand Barriers

continued

A.

'88 SEOUL
PARALYMPICS

B.

C.

IPC

International Paralympic Committee

These are the flags that have been used by the Paralympics. Because of brand confusion that might discourage sponsors, the IOC demanded that the five-teardrop flag (A) be changed. The three-teardrop flag (B) was used between 1994 and 2004, and the new Spirit in Motion flag (C) was flown at the Beijing Paralympic Games in 2008. [Flag images © 1988 SPOC. All rights reserved. Courtesy of the International Paralympic Committee.]

With these changes, the IPC embraced a commercial model of sport as a survival strategy. Today, its flag is a licensed logo, like the five rings logo that is licensed by the IOC. This raises the question, Who will benefit from and who will be hurt by commercialization? Athletes who can attract an audience will certainly benefit, but will this inspire sport participation among those who cannot attract an audience or will it relegate them to the sidelines? Will there be resources for people who are not elite athletes. or will they see most resources going to top Paralympic athletes and say, "There's nothing we can do"? Hopefully not.

••

powerful sport organizations, has turned itself and the Olympics into a global brand. This has had serious implications for the Paralympic Games, as explained in the Breaking Barriers box.

Soccer's FIFA (Fédération Internationale de Football Association) has a long history of global expansion, which predates the global expansion of any North American sports (Sugden and Tomlinson, 1998, 1999). Soccer/football teams such as Manchester United in England and Real Madrid in Spain have clearly used strategies to expand their global marketing reach. They have been so successful that they are valued at a half billion dollars (U.S.) more than many North American sport team franchise (as of 2005). Concern is now being expressed in England that Premier League teams are increasingly being bought by multimillionaires and billionaires from the U.S. and Russia.

Corporations Use Sports as Vehicles for Global Expansion Because certain sports capture the attention and emotions of so many people worldwide, corporations have been eager to sponsor them. Corporations need symbols of success, excellence, and productivity that they can use to create "marketing hooks" for their products and services and to create public goodwill for their policies and practices.

For example, people around the world still associate Michael Jordan with the "Air Jordan" trademark copyrighted by Nike, and many people associate the Olympics with Coca-Cola. In Canada and the United States, the crowning

Olympic achievement is to have your image associated with a product or brand. Status among many children depends on wearing expensive shoes and clothing with official logos and other sport images on them. The Canadian-based athletic clothing company, Roots, which first came to international attention when it outfitted the Canadian team at the Nagano Olympics in 1998, achieved a marketing coup when it won the rights to clothe both the Canadian and U.S. (and several other) teams at the Salt Lake City Olympics in 2002—enjoying huge sales of replica items in both Canada and the U.S.

Companies whose profits depend on the sales of alcohol, tobacco, fast food, soft drinks, and candy are especially eager to have their products associated with the healthy image of athletes and sports (Dewhirst and Sparks, 2003). This enables them to counter negative publicity related to the nutritional value of their products. They want people to think that "if beer, cigarettes, sugar-based soft drinks, beef burgers, deep-fried foods, and candy bars bring us the sports we love, they can't be bad for our health."

Scholars and sportswriters have identified Michael Jordan as a key figure in the process of corporations' using sports to boost bottom lines (Andrews, 2001; Andrews and Jackson, 2001). Jordan "commercialized his sport and himself, turning both into brands for an emerging legion of sports marketers....In his own way, Jordan did spread an ideology. It was that sports are not just games but tools for advertisers. It was that basketball isn't a playground thing, but a corporate thing" (in Weiner, 1999, p. 77).

We now live in an era of the transnational corporation. About half of the world's 100 largest economies (in terms of revenues) are corporations, not nations (Anderson and Cavanagh, 2000). General Motors, Exxon, Mobil, Mitsubishi, Mitsui, and General Electric each has more economic power than over 60 percent of the nations. The 200 largest corporations in the world control over one-third of the economic activity around the globe. The executives in these corporations make decisions that influence the economies of entire nations and even regions of the world. They affect who has jobs, the kinds of work they do, their salaries, working conditions, the products that they can buy, where they can buy them, and what they will cost.

When corporations enter the world of sports, they negotiate deals that promote their interests and increase their power, which has grown largely unchecked over the last few decades. Free trade agreements now enable many companies to move capital at will and operate largely outside the laws of any single nation. As corporations and the extremely wealthy people who own or control them continue to do business around the world, they need to create global images of themselves as both citizens and leaders. Sport serves as a site through which they can do this.

This is partly why corporations pay billions of dollars every year to sponsor sports and why, in the U.S., for example, they spend three times as much sponsoring sports as they do sponsoring the arts, festivals and fairs, and attractions. For example, General Motors and Coca-Cola together spent nearly US$2 billion to sponsor Olympic sports between 1998 and 2008. Like other transnational corporations, they want to promote the belief that enjoyment and pleasure in people's everyday lives depend on corporations and their products. Their goal is to use this belief as the foundation for *ideological outposts* in the minds of people around the world (see chapter 4). Corporate executives realize that they can use such outposts to defuse opposition to corporate policies, and deliver ideological messages about what is and should be happening in the world. This is a useful strategy for global corporations that want to defuse resistance to products that may not be compatible with local attitudes and cultural practices. For example, when Coca-Cola and Kentucky Fried Chicken face anti-American attitudes in Islamic Pakistan, they can associate their products with international sports rather than U.S. culture and foreign policy.

When a Coca-Cola executive gave a presentation to IOC officials before the 1996 Olympics in Atlanta he assumed that, after nearly eighty years of sponsoring the Olympics, the officials owed loyalty to Coke. So he told the officials the following:

> Just as sponsors have the responsibility to preserve the integrity of the sport, enhance its image, help grow its prestige and its attendance, so too, do you [in sports] have responsibility and accountability to the sponsor. (Reid, 1996, p. 4BB)

The IOC officials knew that drinking cola was not consistent with the nutritional needs of elite athletes or the health goals of the Olympic movement. But after taking millions of sponsorship dollars from Coca-Cola they did not resist the soft drink executive's message. Coca-Cola had colonized their minds—the outposts were firmly established in most of their heads.

Outposts in Action: Branding Sports Ranchers sear their logos (brands) onto the hide of animals, so there is no doubt about ownership or control. Corporations have done the same things with sports.

At the time of writing in Canada some 34 stadiums and arenas have sold naming rights to various corporations. These include airlines (Air Canada Centre in Toronto; Centre Air Creebec in Val-d'Or), banks (Scotiabank Place in Ottawa; BMO Field in Toronto; Colisée Desjardins in Victoriaville; Credit Union Centre in Saskatoon; TD Waterhouse Stadium in London; Interior Savings Centre in Kamloops; Prospera Centre in Chilliwack; Prospera Place in Kelowna), brewers (John Labbat Centre in London; Molson Centre in Barrie; Steelback Centre in Sault Ste. Marie), and companies selling cars (GM Place in Vancouver; General Motors Centre in Oshawa) energy (Pengrowth Saddledone in Calgary; ENMAX Centre in Lethbridge; ENMAX Centrium in Red Deer), soft drinks (Colisée Pepsi in Québec City; Powerade Centre in Brampton), and communications services and products (Bell Centre in Montréal; Rogers Centre in Toronto; CanWest Global Park

in Winnipeg; CN Centre in Prince George; Telus Field in Edmonton; MTS Centre in Winnipeg; Ricoh Coliseum in Toronto). Candy (Hershey Centre in Mississauga), pharmacies (Rexall Centre in Toronto; Rexall Place in Edmonton), hotels (CanadInns Stadium in Winnipeg), auto parts (Magna Centre in Newmarket), and supermarkets (Save-on-Foods Memorial Centre in Victoria) are also included.

The branding of sport also exists inside the stadiums and arenas where every available surface is sold to corporate sponsors. Surfaces without corporate messages are now defined as wasted space, even in publicly owned facilities. Corporations have also started to make their presence felt in schools where they have a captive audience. One Alberta business executive argues:

> Canadian "tweens" influence $20 billion in household purchases…. Access "tweens," and ultimately their parents:
>
> - Affiliate your business with a sports program or team…;
> - Sponsor programs at school like Student of the Week, Athlete of the Year, Honour Roll;
> - What can you learn from the fast food industry? Think incentives, playgrounds, contests, clubs, games. (cited by Canadian Teachers' Federation et al. 2006, p. 17)

Thus, McDonald's (with the support of the Canadian Olympic Committee) sponsors the "Go Active! Olympic Fitness Challenge" in 445 schools in Canada (50,000 students) by providing $200 credits for buying gym equipment. As Robertson (2004) points out, "fast and junk food companies are quick to blame inactivity for poor fitness and rising obesity levels among children rather than an unhealthy diet" (Canadian Teachers' Federation et al., 2006, p. 22).

As corporations brand public spaces, community identities are transformed into brand identities, and the physical embodiments of local traditions and histories are transformed into corporate advertisements that promote consumption and identify corporations as sources of pleasure and excitement in our lives.

This is Ford McDonald at Bombardier Field where the Roots Raiders will battle the Zeller's Titans. Team captains, Nike Bauer and Labbatt Williams, prepare for the Royal Canadian Mint coin toss, right after this message from our sponsor, Tim Horton's, who are rrready to "rrroll up the rrrim" on this game.

FIGURE 11.1 Televised versions of commercial sports have become inseparable from the logos and products of corporate sponsors. It is not too far fetched to imagine this scene in the near future.

Sport events have been branded. The public good is replaced by the corporate good, even in spaces owned by citizen-taxpayers, as illustrated in figure 11.1. For example, tennis has the Rogers Cup for women and men (alternating between Montréal and Toronto); golf has the RBC Canadian Open, the Telus Skins Game, and the CN Canadian Women's Open; curling has the Tim Horton's Brier, the Scotties Tournament of Hearts, and the Ford World Curling Championships; alpine skiing has the Coupe Pontiac GMC Cup races, and the Pontiac GMC Canadian Championships; and skating has the HomeSense Skate Canada International, and the BMO Canadian Championships. Mountain, road, and track cycling national championships in Canada are all sponsored by Tim Hortons. And equestrian events at Spruce Meadows have such illustrious sponsors as the BMO Financial Group (again), Shell, BP, Chrysler, and Direct Energy.

Corporations brand teams worldwide in cycling, soccer, rugby, and many other sports. Professional baseball teams in Japan are named

after corporations, not cities. Players and even referees in most sports wear the corporate logos of sponsors on their uniforms. Because European soccer was televised for many years by public TV networks that had no commercials, corporations put their logos on the players themselves and all around the pitches (playing fields) so that spectators would see them constantly. For example, in 2000, Vodaphone, the world's largest telecommunications company, paid US$48 million to have their names on the uniforms of Manchester United—the most recognized and followed sport team in the world; in 2003 they paid US$58 million to extend the deal another four years. Manchester United, with over 50 million fans worldwide, also has sponsorship deals with Nike (US$450 million for thirteen years, 2002–2015), Fuji, Lycos, Anheuser Busch, and Pepsi.

Corporate branders now give priority to sports that appeal to younger demographics. So there is the ESPN X Games, Dew Action Sport Tour, Van's Triple Crown, and McDonald's All-American High School Basketball Game.

Agents today tell celebrity athletes that they are brands in themselves and that their goal is to merge with other commercial entities rather than simply endorse another company's products. Michael Jordan was the first to do this. He initially endorsed Nike products, gradually became a brand in his own right, and now has his own line of products in addition to "Air Jordan." Tony Hawk has done this with his own line of skateboards and other products. However, this strategy is possible only for those athletes whose celebrity is so great that it can be converted into a brand name.

In other cases, it is corporations who choose who and what they wish to brand. For example, some athletes, as young as twelve years old, may be known as Nike, Adidas, or Reebok athletes. Corporate executives know that it is best to brand athletes as early as possible so that they can influence the athletes' lives and careers to promote corporate interests. This is why Reebok signed Sidney Crosby in 2005 for a reported US$2.5 million, five-year contract, and Nike gave seventeen-year-old LeBron James a US$90 million contract before he was drafted by Cleveland's NBA team. Gillette recently proclaimed the global reach of sport, and its products, by bringing together Thierry Henry, Roger Federer, and Tiger Woods in its commercials.

The Super Bowl, too expensive for even a large corporation to brand on its own, is known as much for its television commercials as for the game itself. The game generates much interest in Canada, though Canadians rarely see the ads that cost so much money—US$2.7 million for 30 seconds in 2007.

Future forms of corporate branding are difficult to predict because it is hard to say where people will draw the line to stop corporations from colonizing their lives. Ads during television coverage are now inserted digitally on the field, court, and other surfaces of arenas and stadiums so that viewers cannot escape them even when they record events and delete commercials. Corporations now spend more of their advertising money to purchase brand placement rights, so their names, logos, and products appear directly in the content of sports. This means that we will see more branding of playing fields/spaces, uniforms, and athletes' bodies. For example, boxers go into the ring with henna tattoos of corporations on their backs. English soccer player Robbie Savage had an Armani logo tattooed on his arm. Action sport star Shaun Palmer has Cadillac tattoos because he likes old Cadillacs. However, what would happen if Cadillac used a photo of his body in one of their ads? Who owns Shaun Palmer's body and the images on its surface? Does he, the artist who created the tattoos, or Cadillac who owns copyrights on Cadillac images? There are already lawsuits filed in cases like this, and we will see more in the future.

The Limits of Corporate Branding

Can corporations go too far in their branding of sports? Schools struggling to provide health and nutrition education and physical education in the curriculum find that a small grant from McDonald's may be the only way to obtain new equipment, and that the school board's contract with a soft drinks company obliges them to have vending machines in the lobby. Olympic officials, dedicated to health and fitness, did not turn down US$65 million from McDonald's in a deal naming it the Official Restaurant of the 2004 (Athens) and 2006 (Torino) Olympics. However, people did object when the CBS journalists wore Nike logos on their jackets as they covered the 1998 (Nagano) Winter Olympics. Similarly, baseball fans were so upset in 2004 that Major League Baseball cancelled a US$3 million contract with Columbia Pictures that called for decorating bases, pitching mounds, and on-deck circles with spider-web patterns at fifteen home fields of teams playing games on the weekend before the release of *Spider Man 2*. But despite a few cases of resistance, sports generally are for sale, and corporations are willing buyers when deals boost their power and profits and promote consumption as a lifestyle.

Corporate executives realize that sports produce enjoyable and emotional identifications with athletes, teams, events, and places. Therefore, they think it makes economic sense to brand sports so that people will recognize corporate names and products and associate them with the things that provide excitement and pleasure in their lives (Pennington, 2004). In less than a generation, sports have been so thoroughly branded that many people, especially those under thirty years old, see it as "normal"—as the way it is and should be. Does this mean that corporations have established ideological outposts in people's heads to the point that they accept corporate power as inevitable and even desirable? If so, corporate hegemony is being maintained successfully, even if a few people say it is unwise to turn sports over to entities accountable only to market forces.

COMMERCIALIZATION AND CHANGES IN SPORTS

What happens to sports when they shift from activities being organized for players to being activities organized for paying spectators and sponsors? Do they change, and, if so, in what ways?

When a sport is converted into commercial entertainment, its success depends on spectator appeal. Although spectators have many reasons for watching sports, their interest usually is tied to a combination of four factors:

- Attachment to those involved ("Do I know or like the players and/or teams?")
- The uncertainty of an event's outcome ("Will it be a close contest?")
- The risk or financial rewards associated with participating in an event ("How much money, ego, or personal safety and well-being is at stake in the contest?")
- The anticipated display of excellence, heroics, or dramatic expression by the athletes ("How entertaining are the players and/or teams?")

The goal of branding is to establish outposts in people's heads by connecting pleasure and excitement with corporations and their products. Corporations sponsor sports because many people are emotionally tied to athletes and teams. This man's emotional connections with the soccer club Manchester United is inscribed permanently on his body. Vodafone, the club's primary corporate sponsor, uses such connections to their advantage.
[Luca Bruno, AP/Wide World Photos]

When spectators say they saw a "good game," they usually are talking about one in which (1) they were attached personally or emotionally to people involved, (2) the outcome was in doubt until the last minutes or seconds, (3) the stakes were so high that the players were totally committed to and engrossed in the action, or (4) there were skilled, heroic, or dramatic performances. Events containing all four of these factors are remembered and discussed for many years.

Because attachment, uncertainty, high stakes, and performance attract spectators, successful commercial sports are organized to maximize the probability of all four factors. To understand how this affects sports, it is necessary to consider the impact of commercialization on the following:

1. The internal structure and goals of sports
2. The orientations of athletes, coaches, and sponsors
3. The people and organizations that control sports

Internal Structure and Goals of Sports

Commercialization influences the internal structure and goals of newly developed sports, but it has less influence on long-established sports. Among new sports developed explicitly for commercial purposes, it is clear that rules are designed to promote on-the-field action that will be defined as entertaining by a targeted audience.

Entertainment is *not* the only issue that influences the internal structure and goals of new sports, but it is the *primary* issue. This is apparent in the case of indoor soccer, arena football, beach volleyball, roller hockey, and commercial action sports. For example, rules in the X Games are designed to maximize "big air," dangerous and spectacular moves, and the technical aspects of equipment, often manufactured by event sponsors.

The rules in established sports also undergo changes to make the action more exciting and understandable for spectators, but the changes seldom alter the basic internal organization and goals of the sports. For example, the

commercialization of the Olympic Games has led to minor rule changes in certain events, such as the introduction of rally scoring in volleyball and the cutting of compulsory routines from gymnastics and figure skating, but the basic structure of the typical event has remained much as it was before the days of corporate endorsements and the sale of television rights. Of course, there is ongoing talk about some events with little spectator appeal being dropped from the Olympics (e.g., fencing, modern pentathlon, and baseball/softball have recently been cut). The Olympic Programme Commission, which develops and presents recommendations on sports and Olympic events to the IOC Executive Board, has media interest as a primary mandate for admitting or retaining a sport in the Games. Thus, new sports have been added to attract new viewers (e.g., beach volleyball, snowboarding), especially younger viewers from wealthy countries where people have money to spend on sponsors' products.

Changes in all commercialized spectator sports usually do one or more of six things: (1) speed up the action, (2) increase scoring, (3) balance competition, (4) maximize drama, (5) heighten attachment to players and teams, and (6) provide strategic breaks in the form of "commercial time outs." A review of rule changes in many sports shows the importance of these six factors. For example, the designated hitter position in baseball's American League was added to increase scoring opportunities and heighten the dramatic action. Soccer and hockey rules were changed to prevent matches from ending in ties. Tennis scoring was changed to meet the time requirements of television schedules. The four-rock rule was introduced to encourage more offensive play in curling. Golf tournaments now involve total stroke counts, rather than match play, so that big-name players will not be eliminated in the early rounds of televised events. Free throws were minimized in basketball to speed up action.

Although these changes are grounded in commercialization, they have not altered the internal structure and goals of long-established sports: teams are still the same size with similar positions, and teams win when they score more runs, goals, or points than their opponents. Furthermore, some of these changes also reflect the concerns of athletes, who have more fun when there is more action, more scoring, and a closer contest. Players may object to TV time outs, but they and their coaches anticipate them and now use them in game strategies. This is new, but the structures of their games have not changed.

Because sports are social constructions, they change in connection with shifts in social conditions and power relations in the society as a whole. This means that *people* establish rules for sports. And those people are always influenced by social and cultural conditions at the time that *they* make or revise rules. However, commercial issues are carefully considered today when changes are suggested, discussed, and made.

Another change that has come with commercialization is that many events today are organized intentionally as *total entertainment experiences*. There is loud music, attractive and rapidly changing video displays, cheerleaders and mascots who plan entertaining performances, light displays, and announcers who heighten drama with excited verbal descriptions of the action. As dedicated long-time sports fans view these things, they may complain that the game has changed when it is actually the content surrounding the game that has changed.

Orientations of the Athletes, Coaches, and Sponsors

Commercialized sports are characterized by a "promotional culture" (Gruneau and Whitson, 1993). Like other entertainment industries, they are geared to selling public performances to audiences and selling audiences to sponsors. Commercial sports are promoted through marketing hype based on stories, myths, and images created around players and teams. Athletes become entertainers and the orientations of nearly everyone in sports shifts towards an emphasis on heroic actions and away from aesthetic actions.

The shift towards heroic orientations is necessary to attract a mass audience to buy tickets or watch televised events. Entertaining a *mass* audience is difficult because it contains many people who lack technical knowledge about the complex physical skills and strategies involved in sport. Without technical knowledge, hype and drama become primary sources of entertainment for the audience. Hype and drama are easily understood, and spectators are entertained when athletes take risks and face clear physical danger. Spectators are also impressed by the dramatic expressions of athletes; and they are impressed by athletes dedicated to the game and to victory, regardless of personal cost.

When spectators lack technical knowledge about football, they are entertained more by a running back's end-zone dance after a touchdown than by the lineman's block that enabled the running back to score the touchdown. Those who know little about the technical aspects of ice skating are more entertained by triple and quadruple jumps than by routines carefully choreographed and practised until they are smooth and flawless. Without dangerous jumps, naïve spectators become bored because they are not aware of subtle differences in the skills of skaters. Those who lack technical knowledge about basketball are more likely to talk about a single slam dunk than about the well-coordinated defence that enabled the team to win a game. Players know this, and realize that their dunks will be shown on news replays regardless of who plays a technically good game. Thus, dunkmania rules, and fans are disappointed when they do not see "big jams" during games; they want to see the heroic rather than the aesthetic aspects of sports.

Spectators without technical knowledge about a sport tend to enjoy watching athletes project exciting or controversial personas, and they often rate performances in terms of a player's style as much as his or her technical proficiency. They are thrilled by long touchdown passes, not 7-minute touchdown drives made up of 4- to

6-yard runs. They want to see home runs, not sacrifice flies. They are more impressed by athletes who collapse as they surpass physical limits than by athletes who know their limits so well that they can play for years without going beyond them.

After observing many athletes in all the major sports in the United States, commentator Bob Costas noted the following:

> The players have caught on to what the cameras want. They know what postures and noises will get them on air. [NBA players] know that cameras are under the basket. So a guy dunks the ball, looks right at the camera and screams. (Pluto, 1995, p. 275)

Costas understands that orientations change when players become entertainers. Players today even look at the replay screens and become spectators watching themselves.

Figure 11.2 illustrates that when a sport depends on entertaining mass audiences, the athletes, coaches, and team administrators often revise their ideas about what is important in athletic performances. The danger of movement becomes important *in addition to* the beauty of movement; style and dramatic expression become important *in addition to* fundamental skills; pushing beyond personal limits becomes important *in addition to* exploring limits; and commitment to victory for the team and sponsor becomes important *in addition to* participation. When sports become commercialized, most people associated with them develop *heroic orientations* in addition to *aesthetic orientations*, they even describe games and matches as "showtime."

This does *not* mean that aesthetic orientations cease to be important or that people are no longer impressed by beauty and skills in sports, but it does mean that heroic orientations enter into the mix of what constitutes a good sport performance. Heroic actions are what attracts a mass audience.

Some athletes realize the dangers associated with heroic orientations, and some even try to limit the emphasis on heroic actions in their sports. For example, some figure skaters want restrictions on the number of triple and quadruple jumps required in skating programmes. They worry that the quest for commercial success is putting their bodies on the line. Other skaters, however, adopt heroic orientations to please audiences and conform to shifts in the orientations of judges, coaches, and other skaters (Mihoces, 2005). Thus, it is not surprising that figure skaters train to hit a long succession of triple jumps and hope to perform occasional quad jumps without breaking bones or destroying the continuity of their skating programmes. Aesthetic orientations still exist, but heroic orientations are becoming more central in defining the "quality" of a figure skater.

What happens to a sport when heroic orientations are pushed to extremes? Are spectators willing to have aesthetic orientations abandoned in favour of the heroic? What would events be like if this happened? One way to answer this is to study professional wrestling—a sport turned into spectacle in a quest to be entertaining. This is discussed in the box "Raw Entertainment," which can be found on the Online Learning Centre.

The People and Organizations That Control Sports

Commercialization changes the ways that sports are controlled. When sports depend on the revenues they generate, the control centre in sport organizations usually shifts away from the athletes and toward those who have the resources to produce and promote sports. Athletes in heavily commercialized sports generally lose effective control over the conditions of their own sport participation. These conditions are controlled by a combination of general managers, team owners, corporate sponsors, advertisers, media personnel, marketing and publicity staff, professional management staff, accountants, and agents.

The organizations that control commercial sports are designed to coordinate these people,

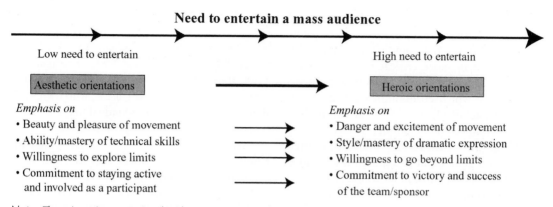

Need to entertain a mass audience

Low need to entertain   High need to entertain

Aesthetic orientations   Heroic orientations

Emphasis on   *Emphasis on*
• Beauty and pleasure of movement   • Danger and excitement of movement
• Ability/mastery of technical skills   • Style/mastery of dramatic expression
• Willingness to explore limits   • Willingness to go beyond limits
• Commitment to staying active   • Commitment to victory and success
  and involved as a participant   of the team/sponsor

Note: The orientations associated with many commercial spectator sports today have shifted from the aesthetic to the heroic. Many people in a mass audience do not have the technical knowledge about a sport to be entertained by aesthetic action; instead, they seek and focus on heroic action. Therefore, athletes and others associated with the game emphasize heroic orientations in their performances. "Heroic" as it is used in this chapter and figure refers to "villains" and others who emphasize dramatic expression in their sport performances. This is exemplified in professional wrestling where both the stereotypical "good character" and "bad character" engage in heroic rather than aesthetic performances in the ring.

FIGURE 11.2   Shifting orientations: what happens when there is a need to entertain a mass audience?

so that their profits are maximized. This means that decision making in commercial sports reflect economic interests and have only incidental connections with the athletes involved. The power to affect these decisions is grounded in resources that may not be connected with sports. Therefore, athletes in many commercial sports find themselves cut out of decision-making processes, even when the decisions affect their health and the rewards they receive for playing.

As decision making in sport organizations moves further away from athletes, there is a need for athletes to develop strategies to represent their interests, financial and otherwise. As corporate interests come to dominate sports, athletes often discover that they must defer to the decisions of team owners, agents, advertising executives, media people, and corporate sponsors.

This has occurred repeatedly in ESPN's X Games as athletes discovered that it is nearly impossible to maintain the spirit and norms of the sport culture they created when they participate under conditions controlled by a media company and corporate sponsors. This is evident as a 33-year-old former pro skateboarder described what one of his friends did after he won an event at the X Games:

> He had this shirt on... that said ESPN down the side. For the "E" it said "Extreme," for the "P" it said "Profits"—the "S" was a dollar sign—and for the "N" it said "Network:" Extreme Profit$ Network. And he wore that [to the awards ceremony].... got his little trophy, flipped the camera off, threw [the trophy] into the audience, walked away and said, "I'll never ride in the X Games again." So, you've got certain guys that will really stay true to the roots of skateboarding... and then you've got others... that are pros competing [because] they've got kids and a family, so they've kind of gotta do that. (in Honea, 2005, p. 162)

Like many athletes before them, athletes in action sports are becoming resigned to the power of the media and corporate sponsors in their lives. They learn that to play commercialized sports, you must answer to the sponsors first.

Commercialization has brought with it a structure in which sponsors define the conditions of sport participation (Rinehart and Grenfell, 2002).

Most North Americans do not define this as an issue today because they accept the corporate branding of sports. But some people view commercialization in more critical terms, assessing more carefully the pros and cons of a commercial model in which corporations set the terms and conditions of playing sports at the highest levels of competition. Commercialization may not change the structure and goals inside their activities and games, but it dramatically changes the cultural and organizational contexts in which they are played.

OWNERS, SPONSORS, AND PROMOTERS IN COMMERCIAL SPORTS

Commercial sports are organized in different ways from one society to the next, but in all cases, owners, sponsors, and promoters control the conditions under which professional athletes perform. In this section, we focus on the overall control structure that exists in the most visible professional sports in North America.

Professional Sports in North America

Professional sports are privately owned. The owners of many teams and franchises, from the smallest minor league teams to the top franchises in the NFL, NBA, NHL, and MLB, are individuals or small partnerships. Large corporations, especially entertainment and real estate companies, own a growing proportion of the top teams and franchises (Harvey et al., 2001), including a growing number of teams in other countries (e.g., British soccer). Similarly, sponsors and event promoters range from individuals to large transnational corporations, depending on the size of the event.

The ownership model established in North American professional team sports is by no means normal, or natural, or universal. The private ownership model is one choice out of

several possible forms of ownership, one of which is the more public form of ownership uniquely exemplified in North America by the Green Bay Packers of the NFL. The team has 1,800 shareholders (90 percent of whom live in the Green Bay, Wisconsin, area), who own 4,700 shares in the team—no individual may own more than 200 shares.[2] In Europe and Australia, there are examples of teams owned by membership-based clubs. Club members democratically elect a board, which employs professional managers and coaches to run the team. These models allow shareholders and members to have some control on major decisions, and ensure accountability on the part of board members and employees. In a very real sense, it permits a community to share in, and enjoy a sense of ownership of, the team that claims to represent that community. Corporate laws also ensure that there is some transparency with regard to the team's accounts.

Recently, a new model of ownership has emerged, taking advantage of the democratizing and community building opportunities presented by the Internet. In England, a group called MyFC (myfootballclub.co.uk) created an online community of 28,000 soccer fans from around the world—they paid approximately $70 each to collectively purchase a 75 percent stake in a soccer club (Ebbsfleet United). "It's the first community website takeover of a football club in the world and, I think, of any business…" (Will Fleet, spokesperson for MyFC, speaking to Agence France-Presse, 2008). The new owners will manage the team democratically—"voting online to choose match lineups and buying new players… [T]he [owner/] fans will be able to view all of the matches online and, after the game, receive statistics on how each player performed… and weekly updates from the head coach on how

---

[2]The Green Bay Packers are an anomaly that reportedly makes the NFL and other major leagues quite uncomfortable. The NFL would much prefer that the team be sold to private owners; public ownership keeps alive the idea that other teams could be owned in this way.

each player is performing in practice" (Colchester, 2008, p. B5). Similar initiatives are occurring in Denmark (mitsuperligahold.dk) and the U.S. (mysoccerclubusa.com).

In contrast, the private ownership model ensures that each of the major leagues functions as a private men's club for the owners (the vast majority of the owners are male), who are able to control the terms of their business in private, away from the eyes of the communities they supposedly represent and the fans of the teams. When funds are needed, these owners seek help from the taxpayer (through government subsidies or local government assistance in stadium rent relief or construction), rather than offering local people an opportunity to own part of "their" team through a sale of shares. The private ownership model benefits team owners far more than fans.

Most people who own the hundreds of minor league teams around North America do not make much money. In fact, most are happy to break even and avoid the losses that are commonplace at this level of professional sports ownership. Also, many teams, leagues, and events have been financial disasters over the past forty years. Four football leagues, a hockey league, a few soccer leagues, a volleyball league, four men's and five women's basketball leagues, a team tennis league, and a number of basketball and soccer teams have all gone out of business, leaving many owners, sponsors, and promoters in debt. This list does not include all those who have lost money on tournaments and special events.

Ownership of the top professional franchises in North America is very different from ownership at other levels of professional sports. Franchise values at the end of 2007 ranged from about US$143 million (Nashville Predators) to over US$1.5 billion (Dallas Cowboys). Owners are large corporations, partnerships, and wealthy individuals whose assets range from hundreds of millions to many billions of dollars. Leagues are organized as monopolies, teams often play in publicly subsidized facilities, owners make good to excellent returns on their investments, and support from media companies and corporate sponsors almost guarantees continued financial success at this level of ownership.

Similarly, the large corporations that sponsor particular events, from major golf and tennis tournaments to Grand Prix races, know the costs and benefits that are involved. Their association with top events not only provides them with advertising platforms but also connects them with clearly identified categories of consumers (see figure 11.3). Television companies sponsor events, so that they can control their own programming.

Entertainment companies own teams and sponsor events, so that they can control multiple aspects of the entertainment marketplace and link them together in mutually supportive ways—in the U.S., for example, from Disneyland to ABC television to ESPN to the Anaheim Angels and Mighty Ducks to nationwide promotions at fast-food restaurants, where action figures of sport celebrities are sold with meals for children.

Sport sponsorship enables companies that sell tobacco, alcohol, and foods with questionable nutritional value to link their products and logos to popular activities. Because people associate sports with healthy and strong bodies instead of cancer, heart disease, obesity, tooth decay, and other forms of poor health related to their products, these companies are eager to be sponsors. It increases their legitimacy in society and defuses resistance to corporate policies and practices. However, government concerns about the costs of health care resulting from the ongoing use of tobacco products led, in Canada and other countries, to regulations against tobacco sponsorship and advertising. Bill C-71, the Tobacco Act, was passed in 1997. The bill specified a "phasing out" period, to be completed in 2003, for tobacco sponsorship of sports and cultural events. Event organizers had to seek replacement sponsors for events ranging from tennis and golf to auto

"Winning at sports is easy when you own them and can prevent others from playing."

FIGURE 11.3 The growth and profitability of commercial sports around the world have little to do with athletes. Owners, sponsors, and media executives control sports today, and they make money when governments allow them to operate as cartels and keep competitors out of the game.

racing and equestrian. Grand Prix auto racing, which relied heavily on tobacco sponsorship, threatened to withdraw races from countries (including Canada) that no longer permitted tobacco companies to advertise or sponsor events—hence the new races in the Middle East, Southeast Asia, and China.

Investments in sports and sport events are motivated by many factors. In some cases, investors are sports fans with money; they invest to satisfy life-long fantasies, to build their egos, or to socialize with celebrity athletes. Owning or sponsoring sports gain them more enjoyment and prestige than other business ventures, often making them instant celebrities in their cities; they are famous all over town, from the mayor's office and the Chamber of Commerce to neighbourhood bars and local elementary schools. Commercial sports enable these wealthy people to combine business and power seeking with fun.

However, those who invest in sports seldom get so carried away with fun and fantasy that they forget business or capitalist expansion. They do not enjoy losing money or sharing power. They

may look at their athletes as heroes, but they want to control them and maximize returns on their investments. They may be civic boosters and supporters of public projects, but they define the "public good" in terms that emphasize capitalist expansion and their business interests (Ingham and McDonald, 2003; Schimmel et al., 1993). Their goals are to generate revenues and to establish a firm basis for continued financial success. They may not agree with fellow owners and sponsors on all issues, but they do agree on the need to protect their investments and maximize profits.

Team Owners and Sport Leagues as Cartels
The tendency to think alike has been especially strong among the team owners in the major North American sport leagues. Unity among these owners has led to the formation of some of the most effective cartels in North America. A **cartel** *is a centralized organizing group that coordinates the actions of a collection of people or businesses.* Therefore, even though each sport franchise in each league is usually a separate business, the team owners in each sport have come together to form a cartel representing their collective interests (Downward and Danson, 2000). The cartel is used by these organizations to limit the extent to which teams compete against one another for players, fans, media revenues, and sales of licensed merchandise. It is also used to eliminate competition from other people who might form additional teams and leagues in their sports. When they succeed, as they usually have, the cartel becomes a **monopoly**, or *the one and only provider of a particular product or service.*

Each league (the NBA, the NFL, the NHL, and MLB) is also a **monopsony** because they have organized themselves to be *the single buyer of athletic labour in a particular sport.* This means that if a junior hockey player wants to play professional hockey in North America, he has one choice: the NHL. And the NHL, like other leagues, has developed a system to force new players to negotiate contracts only with the team that drafts them. This enables owners to sign new players to contracts without bidding against other teams, which might be willing to pay the players more money.[3]

As a cartel, the owners prevent new leagues from being established and competing with them for players, and they also prevent new teams from being added to their leagues without their collective permission. When permission is given, it involves conditions set by the cartel. For example, the new team owner is charged an entry fee to become a part of the league and must give back to the cartel some of the team's profits for a certain number of years. Since the 1960s, when these fees were first assessed, they have escalated from the US$600,000 paid by the Dallas Cowboys to join the NFL in 1960 to the US$700 million paid by the Houston Texans in 2002. Between 1991 and 1994, four teams (including the Ottawa Senators) were added to the NHL, each paying expansion fees of US$50 million; between 1998 and 2001, four more teams were added, each paying expansion fees of US$80 million. These are just *entry fees*, divided among the existing owners. They do not include other start-up expenses, player salaries, or operating costs. Nor do these fees include "infringement payments" made to existing teams in the same TV markets or the forfeiture of TV revenues during the first year(s) of operation (causing a US$5–US$20 million annual loss, depending on the sport). Furthermore, a new owner can locate only in a city approved by the cartel, and no current owner can move a team to an other city without cartel approval.

Acting as a cartel, the owners in each sport league also collectively sell the broadcasting rights to their games and then share the revenues from media contracts. This maintains the cartel's control over the conditions under which fans can see televised games. This is why games are not televised in the home team's region when games are not sold out, and why cable and satellite fees are so high when fans wish to purchase access to more than the primary games telecast by media companies. Such a strategy enables team owners to make huge sums of money in their media contracts while forcing people to buy tickets to games.[4] The Canadian and U.S. governments have approved this monopolistic method of doing business, which guarantees relatively predictable revenues for team owners and gives them the power to influence television companies and the commentators working for those companies. This is why announcers often sound like cheerleaders for the sports their companies pay to broadcast.

Furthermore, team owners have also negotiated exclusive-use clauses in their contracts with the stadiums or arenas they use, a strategy that effectively prevents new leagues and teams from using the stadiums and arenas that they need to make a profit. Potential competing leagues in each sport have been driven out of business, because existing leagues are being allowed to operate as cartels.

Being a part of a legal cartel enabled most team owners to make impressive sums of money over the past four decades. For example, in the mid-1960s, NFL teams were bought and sold for about US$10 million. in 2006, the average franchise value was US$957 million. That amounts to an average *annual* return of US$24 million on an original investment of US$10 million (before including any actual profits made). This is what a cartel does: it limits the supply of teams and

---

[3]This system has been successfully challenged only once, by Eric Lindros, who refused his draft by the Québec Nordiques of the NHL, successfully arguing that he could only realize his economic potential by playing in a larger media market where more sponsorships and endorsements would be available (he went on to play for the Philadelphia Flyers). The challenge was also complicated by language and regional politics in Canada, with some distasteful remarks being made about playing in Québec. Ironically, the Nordiques were shortly thereafter sold to Denver (to become the Colorado Avalanche), where they went on to win several Stanley Cups.

[4]It should be noted that the media revenue bonanza has not been as readily available to the NHL as it has to the other three major leagues. Also, the CFL has been criticized severely by the Canadian public in recent years for its local media blackout.

drives up the value of existing teams. Of course, team owners do not count capital gains in their discussions of expenses and revenues, and they usually argue that they must constantly raise ticket prices to meet expenses. When you are part of a cartel, you can get away with this.

Even though the NBA, the NFL, the NHL, and MLB are grouped together in this section, these leagues differ in many ways. These differences are complicated, and they change from year to year as each league encounters new economic challenges and opportunities. For example, contracts with networks and major cable television companies vary from one league to another. The NHL has been the least successful in negotiating major contracts due to the low viewer/spectator value of ice hockey in most of the U.S., while the NBA and the NFL have been the most successful in recent years.

Each league also has its own internal agreements regulating how teams can negotiate the sale of *local*

broadcasting rights to their games. The NFL does not allow teams to sign independent television contracts for local broadcasts of their games, but MLB does. This creates significant disparities in the incomes of baseball teams. For example, in 2002 the New York Yankees sold their local rights for about US$60 million, while the Montréal Expos (since moved to Washington) sold theirs for about US$500,000. Today, the media landscape is changing as leagues negotiate deals with satellite radio and begin online streaming of audio and video for games. This is why cable and satellite companies that own and broadcast sports are buying Internet companies with high-hit websites (Siklos, 2005); they want to guarantee that they will always have a piece of the sport media action.

The biggest differences between major men's sports leagues are related to their contractual agreements with players' associations in each league. Although each league traditionally has tried to give athletes as few rights and as little

What defines a world-class city? Powerful local businesspeople and their political allies often believe that sports and sport facilities are needed to stimulate the economy and attract people to their cities. Therefore, they lobby for new stadiums and other sport-related facilities. [CP(Frank Gunn)]

money as possible, athletes have fought for over forty years to gain control over their careers and to increase their salaries. This is discussed later in the section, "The Legal Status and Incomes of Athletes in Commercial Sports."

Team Owners and Forms of Public Assistance The belief that cities must have professional sport teams and big sport events to be "world-class" has led to public support for sport owners and sport organizations. Most common is the use of public funds to construct, maintain, and do business in arenas and stadiums. As noted in chapter 10, this type of "stadium socialism" enables wealthy and powerful capitalists to use public money for their personal gain. Of course, capitalists are not opposed to welfare when it comes to them, and they call this "economic development," not welfare. The New Democratic Party in Canada has regularly referred to public subsidies to wealthy corporations as "corporate welfare."

Owners justify stadium subsidies and other public support for professional sport teams using five major arguments (Lavoie, 2000):

1. A stadium and pro team create jobs; those who hold the jobs spend money and pay taxes in the city.
2. Stadium construction infuses money into the local economy; this money is spent over and over as it circulates, generating tax revenues in the process.
3. The team attracts businesses to the city and brings in visitors who spend money.
4. The team attracts regional and national media attention, which boosts tourism, and contributes to economic development.
5. The team creates positive psychic and social benefits, boosting social unity and feelings of pride and well-being in the local population.

These arguments are often supported by studies commissioned by team owners and promoters.

However, *independent* studies by both social democratic *and* conservative researchers, do *not* support them.[5] The social democratic economists tend to argue that there are far more important things (health, education, housing, etc.) on which taxpayers' money should be spent; the conservative economists often point to what they consider to be inappropriate spending of taxpayers' money, in this case on corporate welfare that is not likely to produce any major returns. Independent studies generally conclude the following:

1. Teams and stadiums create jobs, but apart from highly paid athletes and team executives, these jobs are low-paying and seasonal. Football stadiums may be used less than three weeks per year, and the ushers, parking lot attendants, ticket agents, and concessions workers do not make full-time living wages. Additionally, many athletes do not live in the city or spend their money there.
2. The companies that design and build stadiums are seldom local, and construction materials and workers on major projects often come from outside the region; they spend most of what they earn in other places.
3. Stadiums attract other businesses, but these are restaurant and entertainment franchises with headquarters in other cities. These franchised businesses often drive out locally owned businesses. Spectators come from out of town, but most live close enough to make day trips to games, so they do not spend much money outside the stadium and the immediate area outside the stadium.
4. Stadiums and teams generate public relations for the city, but this has mixed results for tourism because some people stay away

---

[5]Studies of this issue are numerous: see Bandow, 2003; Bast, 1998; Brown et al., 2004; Cagan and deMause, 1998; Chapin, 2002; Curry et al., 2004; Delaney and Eckstein, 2003; Eckstein and Delaney, 2002; Friedman et al., 2004; Hudson, 2001; Noll and Zimbalist, 1997; Palmer, 2000, 2002; Rosentraub, 1997; Silk, 2004; Smith and Ingham, 2003; Spirou and Bennett, 2003; Troutman, 2004; Weiner, 2000.

from cities on game days. Most important, *regional* economic development often is limited by a new facility because fans who spend money at and around the stadium have fewer dollars to spend in their neighbourhoods. A stadium helps nearby businesses, but it often hurts outlying businesses (Hudson, 2001). Spending $9,000 on four NBA season tickets each year means that a family will spend less money on dinners and entertainment close to home.

5. A pro sport team makes some people feel better and may enhance general perceptions of a city, but this feeling is difficult to measure. Additionally, feelings often vary with the success of teams, and some people are unimpressed by the male-oriented, heroic orientations that are glorified in some men's sports.

These counterarguments are supported by research, but independent researchers make one qualification: *whenever* a city spends $300–$800 million on a public project, there are bound to be some positive benefits. However, the issue is whether the public good could be better served if the money were spent on other things (see the Reflect on Sports box, "Stadium Construction: A Tale of Two Cities," pp. 357–358).

The stories in the box have been repeated many times in cities, particularly in the United States (Eitzen, 2000; Howell, 2005; Schimmel, 2006; Smith and Ingham, 2003; Whitson and Macintosh, 1996). Team owners enlist the services of large architectural firms, which provide them with lobbyists, political advisors, and public relations people, who make sure the local media cover the campaign for a new stadium from a positive angle. The lobbyists focus on gaining support from politicians and members of committees formed to study the feasibility of building a stadium. Public relations people devise ads that subtly threaten that teams will move unless public money is used in their interest. This tactic of threatening to move teams unless

facilities are built is a form of blackmail used by sport team owners to "encourage" public support. Team owners and advisors in the U.S. try to have votes on bond issues held in political off years, so that voter turnout will be light. They recommend the formation of stadium taxing districts that encompass white suburbs, where they can count on support at the polls, even if voters in the inner city are opposed to subsidizing the wealthy. They set up "public" support groups, to which they donate large amounts of money, usually one hundred times more than opponents can raise, to fund massive advertising campaigns. Meanwhile, sportswriters run supportive stories in major newspapers, sports anchors on the local news talk about the benefits of the new team or new stadium, and sports radio talk show hosts hype the subsidies, even though they are usually supporters of right-wing politics (after all, their jobs often depend on the vote).

Once a stadium is built, franchises increase in value about 25 percent, and team owners are in a powerful negotiating position to get what they want when it comes to using the stadium for their own benefit. Their success has been so complete that *Financial World* magazine noted that "virtually every stadium [in the U.S.] is a money pit for taxpayers by any normal measure of return on investment" (Osterland, 1995, p. 107). Of course, the final irony is that many taxpayers cannot afford to buy tickets to see games in the stadiums their money has built.

The enormous public costs associated with Olympic Stadium in Montréal and the SkyDome in Toronto eventually became a lesson for Canada, and no major stadiums have been constructed since the SkyDome; new arenas that are used for professional sports (e.g., the Air Canada Centre in Toronto, Scotiabank Place in Ottawa, and the Bell Centre in Montréal) have been built by the owners of the teams that use them. Some public concessions have been made in terms of taxes, planning and zoning permission, and other rights, but these have not been cases of public investment for private profit in the way

REFLECT ON SPORTS

Stadium Construction: A Tale of Two Cities

Two cities, one on the north shore of Lake Ontario, the other on the south shore of Lake Erie, each built new stadiums in the last twenty years. Toronto built the SkyDome; (now the Rogers Centre) for baseball and football; the Air Canada Centre for hockey and basketball; and BMO Field for soccer. Cleveland built Cleveland Browns Stadium (football), Progressive Field (baseball), and Quicken Loans Arena (basketball). They all cost taxpayers a great deal of money.

TORONTO

When Toronto decided to build a downtown, multi-sport, domed stadium, city planners decided that they had learned the lesson from Montréal's Olympic Stadium—the stadium would have a roof that worked, and a financial plan that worked. The prime tenant was to be the Toronto Blue Jays, which played in the not-very-glamorous Exhibition Stadium. A public–private partnership was developed in which twenty-eight companies each paid C$5 million (totalling C$140 million). Ontario Premier David Peterson guaranteed the remainder of the costs from Ontario taxpayers. The SkyDome was supposed to cost C$180million, and it was supposed to make a profit.

During construction, the scope of the project mysteriously expanded—a major hotel and a health club added C$112 million to the stadium's cost. Restaurants, Skyboxes (luxury boxes), and the Jumbotron were also added, although no one is able to say who approved these expenditures. With "rush charges" imposed in an attempt to meet "opening day" (two months later than MLB's official opening day of the 1989 season), the final cost of the SkyDome was C$600 million.

For their $5 million investment, the twenty-eight companies received a Skybox, and those who sold applicable products received vending rights. Thus, McDonald's became famous for its $7 hot dogs, and Labatt which, at the time, owned the main tenant, the Blue Jays, saw the team increase in value to about C$180 million while winning back-to-back World Series in 1992 and 1993. In the meantime, the province and its taxpayers became responsible for the debt.

[CP(Scott MacDonald)]

The SkyDome declared C$17 million profit (before debt payments) in its first year and owed C$40 million for the year in debt payments, so the debt continually increased. By 1993, that debt had risen to C$400 million, and the government decided to cut its losses, paid off the debt, and sold the SkyDome to a group of private investors (including Labatt) for C$151 million in 1994.

The Blue Jays were transferred to Interbrew (makers of Stella Artois) when Labatt was sold, and are now owned by Rogers (the cable and tele-communications company). The Toronto Raptors played in the SkyDome while they waited for the Air Canada Centre to be built, and the Toronto Argonauts still play in the stadium. Ownership of the SkyDome has also changed hands several times. In 1998, Sportsco International paid $85 million, rescuing the stadium from bankruptcy; and Rogers Communications bought the SkyDome from Sportsco in 2004 for $25 million (about four percent of the cost of construction) and renamed it the Rogers Centre. In 1999, fearful of losing its only major tenant, the SkyDome signed a new ten-year lease with the Blue Jays that is estimated to be $72 million less that its first lease. At least the roof works.

Continued

Stadium Construction: A Tale of Two Cities
continued

CLEVELAND

During the 1990s, about US$1 billion of mostly public money was spent to build three sport facilities and related infrastructure in Cleveland. Inner-city residents during the same time had to fight the city to fund a drinking fountain in a park in a working-class area of the city, and teachers were holding classes in renovated shower rooms in the public schools. The owners of the sport teams enjoyed profits, because they received a fifty-year exemption on taxes related to their teams and facilities, as well as the equivalent of US$120 million in tax abatements on other real estate development in the areas around the stadiums (Bartimole, 1999). This meant that, in 1998, the city lost nearly US$50 million in city and county tax revenues.

Cleveland decided to publicly fund a football stadium to attract a team to replace the Cleveland Browns, which had moved to Baltimore in 1995 because Maryland provided a rent-free US$200 million stadium, all its revenue-generating potential, and a US$50 million bonus for moving. Maryland spent this money because, in 1984, the Baltimore Colts moved to Indianapolis because the city offered better facilities and more money. When many people in Maryland complained about such a large public subsidy to a wealthy team owner while schools in Baltimore were rationing toilet paper and chalk and students were wearing coats to class because the schools could not pay their heating bills, the owner of the Browns responded to the critics as follows:

> I feel for the schools. I feel for welfare. But look at the positive effects of pro football on a community,

the emotional investment of people at large. You can't equate that with fixing up the schools. (Brady, 1996, p. 19C)

Meanwhile, back in Cleveland, Richard Jacobs, who had bought the Cleveland Indians for US$45 million in late 1986, saw the value of his team skyrocket, and he sold it for US$323 million to Larry Dolan, whose two brothers control the massive media company Cablevision. This gave Jacobs capital gains amounting to US$21.4 million per year for the time he owned the team. The new stadium built by the taxpayers certainly contributed greatly to this gain.

Of course, there are people who object to this form of public stadium subsidy, but they do not have the resources needed to oppose well-financed, professionally packaged plans developed by political advisors hired by team owners. Furthermore, most of the social activists who might lead the opposition are already busy dealing full-time with problems related to drugs, education, homelessness, poor schools, and the overall shortage of social services in cities. They cannot take leave from these urgent tasks to lobby full-time against the use of public money to benefit millionaire team owners and millionaire celebrity athletes.

We think that cities need to hold referenda on construction projects such as these; and that municipal governments should be obliged to fund social and economic impact studies (carried out by independent agencies) and citizens' information meetings before committing to such projects. *What do you think?*

....

that has been so evident in the U.S. However, as we pointed out in chapter 10, both Canada and the U.S. take advantage of hosting major international sports events to construct and upgrade sports facilities that are often then made available to professional sports teams. Most recently in Canada this was the case with BMO Field in Toronto. The stadium was constructed for the

under-19 World Cup of soccer in 2006, and is now used by Toronto FC, the MLS team owned by Maple Leaf Sports and Entertainment (owners of the Maple Leafs and the Raptors).

In addition to facility subsidies, team owners receive other forms of public support. The federal governments in Canada and the U.S. allow businesses to deduct 50 percent of the cost of game tickets and luxury box leases as business expenses. This is why businesses buy about 75 percent of all season tickets sold by top sport teams. Not only do companies save on taxes while their executives and clients use company tickets to attend games, but they also help teams sell out their seats. This in turn drives up ticket prices for the average fan whose taxes are, in some cases, paying off the debt for the stadium. Meanwhile, wealthy people sit in luxury suites and club seats that may have been built with public money, and deduct the leases as business expenses for their corporations. This lowers tax revenues, which could be used for needed public programmes. At the same time, sportswriters publish stories about the great public service of athletes who visit classes in dilapidated schools in the city.

It has regularly been pointed out in Canada that such use of business-expense tax deductions constitutes an important site of tax fraud, since many of the users of season tickets or luxury boxes are not business clients but family members and friends or other employees in the business. Atkinson (2000) points out that many of the unused tickets, for which a tax reduction has been received, are sold to scalpers.

When thinking about public subsidies to sport teams, it is useful to consider alternative uses of public funds. Which of these two alternatives would improve the overall quality of life in a city more? Youth facilities that would be open seven days a week to everyone in the community for nominal fees; or a new stadium built at great public cost that will host a large number of people at a high cost for however many home games are played.

According to urban politics professor Charles Euchner, "Cities have two choices. Forget about major league sports. Or feed the monster" (Brady and Howlett, 1996, p. 13C). Unfortunately, people in the media and local politics often support feeding the monster, because they benefit from the monster's existence. Do sport reporters make their reputations covering youth sports? Do politicians raise money and attract votes by taking big campaign donors to a local soccer field to watch a pickup game? In the last major campaign to use public money to support a professional team in Canada, the failed 1995 "Save the [Winnipeg] Jets" campaign, there were some disturbing examples of the ways in which local people could be encouraged to feed the monster—more donations were received in one week than the Winnipeg United Way received in a year. Also, the provincial and municipal governments were prepared to make major donations of taxpayers' money towards the construction of a new arena at a time when the provincial government was laying off teachers and nurses, and the city was closing libraries and swimming pools (Scherer, 2001; Silver, 1996; Smith, 1997). Feeding the monster raises serious public policy questions about who should receive public subsidies, and what activities and facilities should be supported by public funds.

Sources of Income for Team Owners The owners of top pro teams in the major men's sports make money from the following sources: (1) ticket sales; (2) media revenues (radio, Internet, and national, local, and pay-per-view television); (3) league expansion and mergers (share of expansion fees); (4) tax shelters; (5) increase in franchise value (difference between the price paid for a team and its current worth); (6) revenue through sale of stocks (as in the Toronto Maple Leafs in the 1970s and early 1980s and the proposed stock sale of the Ottawa Senators in 2002—such sales rarely offer any ownership or control) (Beamish, 1988, pp. 144–48); (7) stadium revenue, including leases on club seats and luxury suites, concessions and parking, and the sale of stadium advertising and naming rights; and (8) licensing fees and merchandise sales. The amounts and proportions of each of these sources of revenue vary from league to league, and they are difficult to track because team owners try to shelter them, so they will not be counted as part of "league revenues" and included in the total amounts to compute salary caps and player salaries. The majority of revenue for NFL owners comes from television—over 60 percent of all their revenues—while TV revenues for NHL owners are less than 20 percent of their total revenues. Stadium revenues have become increasingly important in all leagues, and it should be noted that naming rights in Canada for some of the newer stadiums and arenas reportedly sold for as much as $64 million for 20 years (Bell Centre in Montréal).

The recent wave of new stadiums in the U.S. is the result of owners who demand venues that can generate new revenue streams. This is why new stadiums in both Canada and the U.S. resemble shopping malls with a playing field, ice, or court in the middle. Sociologist George Ritzer describes them as "cathedrals of consumption" designed so that consumption is seamlessly included in spectator experience (see figure 11.4; see also Hannigan, 1998). In fact, most stadia will not permit fans to bring their own refreshments to a game—they are captive consumers who must purchase anything they want to eat or drink on site. Owners see this as important because it enables them to capture a greater share of the entertainment dollar in a highly competitive urban market. The stadium now is considered to have so much revenue-generating potential that the value of a franchise with a new stadium increases about 25 percent.

Of course, owners realize that many people may not feel comfortable with the idea of putting public money into the pockets of the wealthy, so they make sure that when their teams take the field, court, or ice announcers describe them as "your" B.C. Lions, Calgary Stampeders, or Toronto Rock (Sage, 1996). The owners are happy to have people feel as if the teams belong to the local community, as long as they collect all the revenues and keep all the capital gains when they sell the teams.

FIGURE 11.4   Recently built stadiums resemble shopping malls, and some fans define their attendance as a shopping opportunity. They are a captive audience, and team owners want to capture as many of their entertainment dollars as possible. This fan has fallen for the lure of consumption to the point that he is less interested in the game than he is in buying products to prove he was at the game.

Amateur Sports in North America

Amateur sports do not have owners, but they do have commercial sponsors and governing bodies, that control events and athletes. Generally, the sponsors are large corporations interested in using amateur sports for publicity and advertising purposes. The governing bodies of amateur sports operate on a nonprofit basis, although they do use revenues from events to maintain their organizations and their power over amateur sports.

Centralized sport authorities administer amateur sports in most countries. They work with the national sport organizations (NSOs) of individual sports, and together they control events, athletes, and revenues. Sport Canada, C.I.S., and the Canadian Olympic Committee are examples of such centralized authorities; they develop the policies that govern the various national sport organizations in Canada.

All amateur sport organizations share an interest in controlling two things: (1) *the athletes* in their sports and (2) the *money* generated through sponsorships and competitive events. Sponsorship patterns in amateur sports also take many forms. Interuniversity sport programmes seek various forms of corporate support. Some universities have, in effect, sold their athletic departments, consisting of all athletic teams and the bodies of athletes, to corporate sponsors in exchange for money, scholarships, equipment, and apparel. Corporations and universities usually enter these agreements outside of any democratic processes involving votes by students, athletes, or the taxpayers whose money funds the universities.

Universities in Canada are seeking various alternative sources of funding for their athletics teams, ranging from the private sector funding of football teams at Laval University and the University of Regina, to the attempt by various universities to raise an endowment fund to support each interuniversity teams. A growing number of university athletic departments have contracts with sports apparel and/or soft drink corporations. Contracts may require athletes and other students to drink only certain soft drinks or eat certain candy bars on campus or in the locker room at halftime. Of course, this form of sponsorship is a clever way for private corporations to use tax-supported institutions as vehicles for their own profit making, while being hailed on campus as the saviours of sport teams. Corporations and universities enter these agreements outside of any democratic processes, which might involve votes on the part of students, athletes, or the taxpayers whose money funds the universities. The only significant democratic intervention so far by students at major Canadian and U.S.

universities has been protests against Coca-Cola, and ensuring that items carrying the university logo sold at campus stores (e.g., sweat shirts) are made by companies that are subject to fair labour agreements.

Although Sport Canada provides some base funding to fifty-one NSOs and another thirty multi-sport/service organizations, the NSOs of amateur sports long have depended on corporate sponsorship money, and they continue to seek those sponsorships to pay for athlete training, operating expenses, and the staging of events. Corporate logos now appear on the clothing and equipment of amateur athletes. In some cases, athletes sign deals as individuals, but they cannot do so when the deals might conflict with the interests of the NSO sponsors (Beamish and Borowy, 1988). Nowadays NSO's may require personal appearances at events involving the NSO's major sponsors. Athletes may gain more money with their own sponsors, but they rarely gain more control of their lives because their personal sponsors also require appearances by the athletes. Some athletes find it difficult to maintain an appropriate training regimen because of these obligations. Many NSOs now hold media training sessions for their athletes, who are told that they must thank the NSO's sponsors during any press conference or interview.

As this model of corporate sponsorship is used more and more around the world, the economics of sports increasingly becomes tied to the fortunes and fluctuations of market economies and large corporations. Corporations sponsor only those sports and athletes that foster their interests, and economic conditions influence their ability and willingness to maintain sponsorships. Agreements increasingly require athletes and coaches to be spokespersons and cheerleaders for the interests of international corporate capitalism in the world.

THE LEGAL STATUS AND INCOMES OF ATHLETES IN COMMERCIAL SPORTS

When sports are commercialized, athletes are entertainers. This is obvious at the professional level, but it is true in other commercial sports, such as junior hockey and highly sponsored sports such as figure skating and equestrian. Professional athletes are paid for their efforts, while amateur athletes receive rewards within limits set by the organizations that govern their lives. This raises three questions: (1) what is the legal status of the athlete-entertainers who work in "amateur" sports? (2) how are athlete-entertainers rewarded for their work? and (3) how might underage elite athletes (in sports ranging from hockey to tennis) in this system be protected from exploitation?

Many people do not think of athletes as workers, and they hesitate to consider owner–player relations in professional sports as a form of labour relations. This is because people associate sports with play in their own lives, and they see sports as fun rather than work. However, when sports are organized to make money, players are workers, even though they may have fun on the job (Beamish and Borowy, 1988; Zimmer and Zimmer, 2001). This is not unique; many workers enjoy their jobs. But regardless of enjoyment, issues of legal status and fair rewards for work are important.

This section focuses on commercial sports in North America. We do not consider the sports that may collect gate receipts but never make enough money to pay for anything beyond basic expenses for the events (i.e., high school sports, nonrevenue-producing university sports, or other nonprofit local sports where teams sell tickets to events).

Professional Athletes

Legal Status: Team Sports The legal status of athletes always has been the most controversial issue in professional team sports in North America. Until the mid-1970s, professional athletes in the major sport leagues had little or no legal power to control their own careers. They could play only for the team that drafted and owned them. They could not control when and to whom they might be traded during their careers, even when their contracts expired. Furthermore, they were obliged to sign standard contracts forcing them to agree to forfeit to their owners all rights over their careers. Basically, they were bought and sold like property and were seldom consulted about their own wishes. They were at the mercy of team owners, managers, and coaches.

In all sports, this system of employee restriction has been called the **reserve system** because it was *a set of practices that enabled team owners to reserve the labour of athletes for themselves and control the movement of athletes from team to team.*

As long as the reserve system was legal, owners could maintain low salaries and near total control over the condition under which athletes played their sports. Parts of the reserve system continue to exist in professional sports, but players' associations in each of the major professional sports leagues for men have challenged the system in court and forced significant changes that increased their rights as workers.

In any other business, a reserve system of this sort would violate anti-combines legislation. For example, it is illegal for the owners of all computer software firms to form relationships and decide among themselves whom they want to hire next year among all people with degrees in information systems. It also would be illegal for them to agree not to hire graduates who were "reserved" by another company. This use of employee restrictions would destroy the freedom of professionals in information systems to choose where, and with whom, they wanted to work. Furthermore, if these workers could not take jobs with other companies without permission from their current employers, even after their employment contracts had expired, their salaries would be kept low, because companies would not have to compete with each other to hire the people with the best skills. And, if these workers could be sold or traded to other companies without being consulted, they would have no real control over their own careers.

But this type of reserve system was defined as legal in sports, and owners used it for many years with minimal interference from any government agency. Team owners justify the reserve system by saying it is needed to maintain competitive balance between teams in their leagues. They argue that, if athletes could play with any team, the wealthiest owners in the biggest cities and TV markets would buy all the good athletes and prevent teams in smaller cities and TV markets from being winners. The irony of this argument has been that team owners are capitalists who praise the free market, but say it would destroy the business of sports. They embrace regulation and "sport socialism" to protect their power and wealth, and they form cartels to restrict athletes' rights and salaries, but they praise deregulation and capitalism whenever they have a chance.

Professional athletes always objected to the reserve system, but it was not until 1976 that U.S. courts ruled that professional athletes had the right to become *free agents* under certain conditions. This right allowed some players whose contracts had expired to seek contracts with other teams that could bid for their services. This change had a dramatic effect on the salaries of NBA and MLB players beginning in the late 1970s through today (see table 11.1).

Between 1976 and about 1991, team owners in the NFL and the NHL avoided much of the effect of this legal change by negotiating restrictions on free agency with players' associations. But, in 1992, after players in both leagues mounted challenges, these restrictions were partially lifted. Hockey players went on a ten-day strike during the Stanley Cup playoffs and forced owners to sign a short-term contract, in which the players obtained slightly more control over their careers. Football players, after challenging the NFL for about five years in a series of court cases, won an antitrust suit, which forced team owners to agree to let NFL players become free agents after being in the league for five years.

Players' unions have consistently mounted challenges to lift restrictions; therefore, owner–athlete relations change every time a new case is resolved or a new collective bargaining agreement (CBA) is signed. Although team owners, league officials, and some fans dislike the players' unions /associations, they have enabled players to gain more control over their salaries and working conditions. Labour negotiations and players' strikes in professional team sports have focused primarily on issues of freedom and control over careers (although the media often focus on money as the only issue). As a result, free agency now exists for all players after they have been under contract for a certain number of years. Definitions of who qualifies as a free agent, and what it means, differ slightly from league to league, but owners no longer have absolute control over players' careers.

Although it has been a struggle for professional team athletes to maintain their unions, they realize that there are crucial labour issues that must be negotiated every time they renew their CBA with the league (i.e., team owners). At this time, the main issues negotiated in CBAs include the following:

1. The percentage of league revenues that are dedicated to "player costs" (salaries and benefits), and what counts as "league revenues"
2. The extent to which teams will share revenues with one another
3. Salary limits for rookies signing their first pro contract, salary restrictions for veteran players, and minimum salary levels for all players
4. The conditions under which players become free agents and the rights of athletes who are free agents
5. A salary cap that sets maximum player payroll for teams and a formula for determining the fines that an owner must pay if the payroll exceeds the cap
6. A salary floor that sets the minimum payroll that a team owner must pay players
7. The conditions under which an individual player or team can request an outside

arbitrator to determine the fairness of an existing or proposed contract
8. Changes in the rules of the game

To illustrate the importance of these eight factors, consider the contract signed in 2005 between the NHL and the NHL Players' Association after the owners had locked out the players for 301 days, cancelling the entire 2004–05 season. The contract was nearly 600 pages long, but these eight issues were central negotiating points, and they were resolved in the following way:

1. Player costs cannot exceed 54 percent of hockey-related revenue collected by all teams, and if contracted salaries are greater than 54 percent, salaries are cut proportionately to meet the limit.
2. The ten teams that earn the most income must share some of their income with the ten teams that earn the least money (this is important to players because when teams share revenues, they have fewer incentives to pay salaries high enough to build winning teams).
3. Rookies cannot be paid more than US$850,000; a veteran player may not make over 20 percent of the team's payroll (US$7.8 million in 2005–06); and the minimum salary is US$450,000, an important issue because 15 to 25 percent of all players in pro leagues receive the minimum salary during any given year.
4. A player had to be thirty-one years old to become an unrestricted free agent in 2005–06. This age decreased by one year each season until the 2008–09 season when a player has to be twenty-seven years old or have a minimum of seven years experience in the league to become a free agent.
5. The maximum payroll for teams during the 2007–08 season was US$50.3 million (this is a "hard cap," which means that there are *no* exceptions for any team; a "soft cap" means that teams may exceed the maximum under certain conditions and subject to certain fines that are shared by "poorer" teams). This was the first salary cap in the NHL.

6. The minimum payroll for teams during the 2007–08 season was US$34.3 million.
7. Players and teams may request salary or contract arbitration (in other leagues, only players may request arbitration).
8. Hockey rules were changed to increase scoring and decrease the number of games ending in a tie score.

Hockey players were at a serious disadvantage when negotiating this contract because many NHL teams declared that they were losing money before they locked out the players when no CBA was reached in 2004. The players knew changes were needed, especially to salvage small-market teams in Nashville, Columbus, Raleigh, and San Jose, and the six teams in Canada that had to pay player salaries in U.S. dollars even though most of their revenue was in Canadian dollars (valued at US$0.65 in 2003, and US$0.82 in 2005). Furthermore, ESPN had dropped the NHL media contract. These issues led the players to offer to cut all salaries by 24 percent in addition to the other points they negotiated—but the owners maintained the lockout until players agreed to a salary cap.

Players in the other top leagues generally negotiate their contracts under more favourable conditions. Therefore, they face less restrictive salary limits and are able to negotiate better terms on other issues. Owners and players are more agreeable when money is plentiful, but there always is a question about fairness when it comes to labour: What proportion of revenues should go to workers versus management/owners?

Athletes in most minor leagues and lower-revenue producing sports have few rights and little control over their careers. For the players at this level, who far outnumber players at the top levels of professional sports, the pay is low, careers are uncertain, rights are few, and owners have the last word (cf., Robidoux, 2001). Parcels (2000) reports that minor pro hockey players are traded, on average, three-and-a-half times during a five-year career, and notes that one player was traded

Table 11.1 Average salaries in major North American professional leagues, compared with median family income, 1950–2002[a]

| Year | Sport league | | | | | | Median U.S. family income[c] | Median Canadian family income[d] |
	NFL	NBA	WNBA	NHL	MLB	CFL		
1950	15,000	5,100		5,000	13,300	NA	4,000	NA
1960	17,100	13,000		14,100	19,000	NA	5,620	NA
1970	23,000	40,000		25,000	29,300	NA	9,867	NA
1980	79,000	190,000		110,000	143,000	NA	21,023	C51,698
1990	395,400	824,000		247,000	598,000	NA	35,353	C54,560
2000	1,116,100	3,600,000	60,000	1,050,000	1,988,034	C45,900[b]	50,732	C55,161
2008	1,540,000	5,360,000	50,000	1,900,000	3,150,000	C57,000(est.)	50,000	C56,000

All figures are in US$, except where noted.

[a]Data on players' salaries come from many sources. Average salaries before the mid-1970s are estimates, because players' associations did not exist, and teams were notorious for their inconsistent and creative bookkeeping practices. Average salaries often differ from one source to another, because some are based on rosters at the beginning of the season, whereas others are based on rosters at the end of the season. Differences also reflect whether signing bonuses, prorated portions of those bonuses, and salary deferrals are included with or without interest adjustments.

[b]Although CFL teams have a C$4.05 million salary cap, it is widely believed that the cap was not enforced in the past. CFL salaries have varied widely over time and are also secret. The 2000 figure is based on a player salary survey carried out by the CFL Players' Association in April 2001; the 2008 figure is a more recent estimate.

[c]This represents total family income—parents and children in the same household. Half the families fall above the median, and half fall below. Data are from the U.S. Census; figures for 1950 and 2008 are estimates.

[d]Data are from Canadian census figures. They are not easily comparable with the U.S. figures because (1) Statistics Canada reports figures that are controlled for inflation, so these are in constant 2000 C$, and (2) the exchange rate varied during this time.

Note: Players' salaries increased slowly from after World War II through the mid-1970s. During those years, pro athletes made from two to four times the median family income in the United States. After free agency was put in place in the 1970s, salaries began to skyrocket. As teams made more revenues from gate receipts and television rights and were forced to compete for players, and as players' unions provided support for players' rights, salaries increased dramatically. Although caution should always be used in comparing average (mean) incomes with median incomes (which, as we note on p. 367 are usually lower), in 2008, the ratios between salaries in the major men's professional sports and the median family income were completely disproportionate. No wonder people identify with the women in the WNBA, and why people have so little sympathy for male athletes in labour disputes with team owners, even though many of the owners are billionaires or multibillion-dollar corporations.

twenty-six times in five years. In fact, the average high school teacher in Canada has a higher salary and more rights as a worker than nearly all the pro athletes in the minor leagues.

Legal Status: Individual Sports The legal status of professional athletes in individual sports varies greatly from sport to sport and even from one athlete to another. Although there are important differences among boxing, bowling, golf, tennis, auto racing, rodeo, horse racing, track and field, skiing, cycling, and a number of recently professionalized alternative and action sports, a few generalizations are possible.

The legal status of athletes in individual sports largely depends on what athletes must do to train and qualify for competition in their sports. For example, few athletes can afford to pay for all the training needed to develop professional-level skills in a sport. Furthermore, they may not have the knowledge or connections to meet the formal requirements to become an official competitor in their sport, which may include having a recognized agent or manager (as in boxing), being formally recognized by other participants (as in most auto racing), obtaining membership in a professional organization (as in most bowling, golf, and tennis tournaments), or gaining a special invitation through an official selection group (as in track and field meets).

Whenever athletes need sponsors to pay for their training or have others help them meet participation requirements, their legal status is shaped by the contracts they sign with sponsors, agents, and the groups that sanction participation. This is why the legal status of athletes in individual sports varies so much.

Take boxing as an example. Because many boxers come from low-income backgrounds, they do not have the resources to develop high-level skills or arrange official bouts with other boxers. Therefore, they need trainers, managers, and sponsors. The support of these people always comes with conditions that are written in formal contracts or based on informal agreements. In either case, they require the boxers to forfeit control over much of their lives and a portion of the rewards they may earn in future bouts. This means that few boxers, even those who win large amounts of money, have much control over their careers. They are forced to trade control over their bodies and careers for the opportunity to continue boxing. This is an example of how class relations operate in sports: when people lack resources, they cannot negotiate the conditions under which their sport career occurs.[6]

The legal status of athletes in individual sports is usually defined in the bylaws of professional organizations, such as the Professional Golf

---

[6]This also applies to team sports, where only Eric Lindros—who comes from a well-off middle-class family—was able to negotiate the conditions of his draft.

Association (PGA), the Ladies' Professional Golf Association (LPGA), the Association of Tennis Professionals (ATP), and the Professional Rodeo Cowboys Association (PRCA). Because athletes control many of these organizations, their policies support athletes' rights and enable athletes to control some of the conditions under which they compete. Without such organizations, athletes in these sports would have few rights as workers.

Income: Team Sports Despite the publicity given to the super-contracts of some athletes in the NBA, the NFL, the NHL, MLB, and premier soccer leagues in Europe, salaries vary widely across the levels and divisions in professional team sports. For example, there are about 3,500 Minor League Baseball players on 176 teams in North America, and they make from US$150 a game at the lowest levels to a high of about US$70,00 per year at the top minor league level. The same is true in minor league hockey where there are at least 2,000 players. The average salary for a rookie running back in the eight-team Canadian Football League is about $40,000 for an eighteen-game season. Pre-Beckham, the *median* salary of a player in Major League Soccer is US$38,000; the average is about US$115,000 because one player is paid US$900,000, and a few others make about US$500,000 (David Beckham's US$5.5 million annual salary with the Los Angeles Galaxy is so high that it distorts the average even more). WNBA players earn an average of about US$50,000 per season, and those in the Women's National basketball League average less than US$5,000 for a twenty-four game regular season. Additionally, these are seasonal jobs with few benefits. Clearly commercialization is not as good for most athletes as it is for the special few (see figure 11.5). To understand the range of income in pro sports, consider that, during the 2005 Major League Baseball season, the total salaries of 15 percent of MLB players is about the same as the total salaries of the other 85 percent. This is why the average (that is, *mean*) salary in MLB is about US$3.15

million per year, whereas the *median* salary is less than one-third that amount at about US $900,000 per year. Similarly, in the NHL, average salary for 1999–2000 was US$1,136,375, but the median salary was US$700,000 (Robidoux, 2001). The following shows the salary distribution of the 900 players in the NHL at that time:

- Twenty players (2 percent) earned US$5.4– US$10.3 million.
- One hundred sixty players (18 percent) earned US$1.5–US$5.4 million.
- Three hundred twenty-nine players (37 percent) earned US$600,000–US$1.5 million.
- Three hundred ninety-one players (43 percent) earned US$150,000–US$600,000.

The big salaries for a few players drive up the averages for entire leagues. For example, when Peyton Manning, quarterback for the Indianapolis Colts, made US$35,037,700 (including his signing bonus) in 2004, his salary was about the same as the combined salaries of 61 of his 65 teammates; the team's *average* salary was US$1,397,109, but the *median* salary was only US$384,400, meaning that 33 of the 66 players on the team had salaries less that US$384,400 and that 17 players made less than US$300,000 (as is the case with nearly 25 percent of all NFL players). In team terms, there are also disparities. For example, the New York Yankees' payroll in 2005 was US$12 million higher than the combined payrolls of five teams: Tampa Bay, Kansas City, Pittsburgh, Milwaukee, and Cleveland; and the salary of Yankees' Alex Rodriguez was only US$4.2 million less than the entire Tampa Bay Marlins team. This is true in all the men's major professional leagues: about 15 percent of the players make enormous amounts of money, and 30 percent make close to minimum salary in their respective leagues.

As top stars' salaries are increasing at rapid rates, most of the hockey and baseball players on more than 300 minor league teams across North America would love to make US$20,000

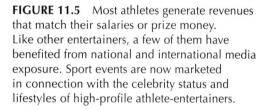

"I make $20 million a year, and I don't feel guilty!"

FIGURE 11.5   Most athletes generate revenues that match their salaries or prize money. Like other entertainers, a few of them have benefited from national and international media exposure. Sport events are now marketed in connection with the celebrity status and lifestyles of high-profile athlete-entertainers.

per season, and they only dream of making the US$475,000 minimum salary in the NHL or the US$390,000 minimum in MLB. So would CFL players who have not kept pace at all with rising salaries in other leagues: "25 years ago, the average CFL salary was about half of that in the [NFL]. Today's average salary (C$50,000) is less than 2 percent" (Naylor, 2002). On the 2000 Players' Association survey, annual salaries ranged from C$28,000 to C$150,000, although, in 2002, Joe Montford of the Toronto Argonauts was believed to be earning C$200,000 a season. The median salary in the CFL is probably much lower than C$45,900.

The data in table 11.1 indicate that players' average salaries have grown far beyond median family income in the United States and in Canada. For example, players in 1950 made average salaries that were not much different than median family income. In 2008, players' salaries were up to eighty times greater than median family income.

This disparity between players' salaries and general family income is why so many fans no longer see the players as "workers" and why they may not side with the players during strikes and lockouts. Of course, siding with owners is also difficult, because most of them make more than even the highest-paid players when you add their salaries and capital gains on franchise values. As of 2005, the percentage of league revenues that went to players was 57 percent in the NBA and MLB, 53 percent in the NHL, and 66 percent in the NFL. The owners used the rest of the annual revenue to cover other expenses and pay themselves. Each league has a team salary cap, and owners pay athletes only what they must to sign them to contracts. Contract amounts are shaped by the economics of the league and the CBAs that players' association have with leagues.

The dramatic increase in salaries at the top level of pro sports since 1980 is due to two factors: (1) changes in the legal status and rights of players, which have led to free agency and the use of a salary arbitration process, and (2) increased revenues flowing to leagues and owners. Salaries in each major men's team sport since 1970 show that increases in salary levels correspond closely with court decisions and labour agreements that changed the legal status of athletes and gave them bargaining power in contract negotiations with team owners. Unions and lawsuits have worked for some athletes, as they have for many workers in other industries.

Income: Individual Sports As with team sports, publicity is given to the highest-paid athletes in individual sports. However, not all players of these sports make enough money from tournament winnings to support themselves comfortably. Many golfers, tennis players, bowlers, curlers, track and field athletes, auto and motorcycle racers, rodeo riders, figure skaters, and others must carefully manage their money so they do not spend more than they win as they travel from event to event. When tournament winnings are listed in the newspaper, nothing is said about the expenses for airfares, hotels, food, and transportation or about other expenses for coaches, agents, managers, and other support people. The top money winners do not worry about these expenses, but most athletes in individual sports are not big money winners.

The disparity between the top-money winners and others has increased considerably on the men's and women's golf and tennis tours. In 2007, Tiger Woods made US$10.8 million in prize money and more than US$90 million in endorsements. The top woman golfer in 2007, Lorena Ochoa, made US$4.4 million in prize money and US$5.6 million in endorsements, less than 10 percent of Woods' annual earnings. No women were included in the top fifty highest-paid athletes in 2007. The top tennis player, Maria Sharapova, earned US$3.8 million in prize money, and about US$20 million in endorsements. But these are unique cases. Many people are surprised to learn that the top 15 to 20 players on the Women's Tennis Association (WTA) Tour make as much prize money as the other 1,800 registered WTA players during the tour year.

The vast majority of men and women playing professional tennis, golf, and other individual sports do not make enough money to pay their competition expenses each year, although some have sponsors who pay for training and travel expenses. Some athletes with sponsors may be under contract to share their winnings with them. The sponsors/investors cover expenses during the lean years but then take a percentage of prize money when the athletes win matches or tournaments. This often occurs with boxers, most of whom never make enough money to live comfortably. Additionally, boxers have no unions, pensions, or (in the U.S.) health insurance. For every big-name boxer who becomes rich "there are 1,000 you never hear of who end up with slurred speech, failing memory and an empty bank account" (Newfield, 2001, p. 14).

Sponsorship agreements cause problems for professional athletes in many individual sports. Being contractually tied, for example, to an equipment manufacturer or another sponsor often puts athletes in a state of dependency. They may not have the freedom to choose when or how often they will compete, and sponsors may require them to attend social functions, at which they talk with fan-consumers, sign autographs, and promote products. For example, when Kim Clijsters was the world's number 2 ranked tennis player in 2004, she discovered that she would not be able to wear her sponsor-logo'd clothing during the Athens Olympics, and she withdrew from the Games.

Overall, a few athletes in individual sports make good money, while most others struggle to cover expenses. Only when sport events are broadcast on television can athletes expect to compete for major prize money and earn large incomes, unless they are amateurs.

Amateur Athletes in Commercial Sports

The status of amateur athletes in commercial sports is often confusing and contradictory. Understanding their situation requires knowledge of their legal status and the restrictions they face when it comes to income related to their sports.

Legal Status of Amateur Athletes The primary goal of amateur athletes is simple: to train and to compete. However, achieving this goal has not always been easy because amateur athletes have little control over the conditions of their sport participation. Instead, control rests in the hands of amateur sport organizations, each setting rules that specify the conditions under which training and competition may occur. Although many rules ensure fairness in competition, others simply protect the power and interests of governing organizations and their leaders.

The rights of amateur athletes in Canada were first given voice by Bruce Kidd and Mary Eberts (1982), and were taken over by athletes themselves with the formation of AthletesCAN in 1994. AthletesCAN was not a union (although many have felt the rights of amateur athletes are so routinely violated that a union would be

beneficial, e.g., Beamish and Borowy, 1988), or even a professional association, but it did provide a forum for athletes to exchange information, and a voice for athletes. However, careers are so short and ephemeral for amateur athletes, and so full of training and competitions, that athletes usually have no time for, and give no thought to, political action. Their NSOs are also likely to discourage such thoughts and actions. AthletesCAN still provides a forum for the exchange of information, but that information is more likely to involve sponsorship and self-marketing opportunities than it is with protecting the rights of athletes. The introduction of the Sport Funding and Accountability Framework by Sport Canada in 1995 linked NSO funding to the introduction of certain equity issues—gender, language, disability—but enforcement has been limited. The Alternative Dispute Resolution (ADR) mechanism introduced in Bill C-12 (see chapter 13) provides another forum for the insurance of athletes' rights in certain disputes with their NSOs, but a clear statement of, and policy to ensure, athletes' rights is still absent in Canadian amateur sports.

The continued lack of power among U.S., Canadian, and international amateur athletes is especially evident in U.S. interuniversity sports. Even in revenue-producing sports, athletes have few rights and no formal means of filing complaints when they have been treated unfairly or denied the right to play their sports. The athletes are not allowed to share the revenues they generate and have no control over how their skills, names, and images can be used by the university or the NCAA. For example, when university athletes become local or national celebrities, they have no way to benefit from the status they have earned. They cannot endorse products or be paid when universities use their identities and images to promote events or sell merchandise.

Many amateur athletes recognize that they lack rights, but it has been difficult for them to lobby for changes. Challenging NSOs and the COC in court is expensive, and would take years of a young person's life. Forming an athletes' organization, as noted above, would make it possible to bargain for rights, but bringing together athletes from various sports would require many resources; and convincing athletes, many of whom have adjusted to their dependency and powerlessness, to take assertive and progressive action would be a major challenge. The prospect of amateur athletes engaging in collective bargaining to gain rights and benefits would be seen as a serious threat to the whole structure of amateur sports. Athletes are often treated as employees by coaches and NSOs, but if they were legally defined as employees, they would be eligible for the same considerations granted to other workers in Canada. This makes everyone from coaches to NSOs nervous (Beamish and Borowy, 1988).

Although recent changes have called for the appointment of athletes to NSO boards, the likelihood of significantly increasing athletes' rights is not great. There are no formal structures for effectively gaining more control over the conditions of training and competition. In the meantime, athlete advocacy groups outside sports are needed, particularly when we remember that some of these athletic workers are children (see chapter 5). Athletes need support in gaining at least some control over their sport lives and the revenues created by their skills.

Amateur athletes in Olympic sports have made some strides to gain control over their training and competition, but as sports become more commercialized, the centres of power in sports move further and further away from athletes. Although athletes are included on the boards of NSOs, sponsors and media people who operate outside the NSOs are making many of the decisions about training and competition. The paradox for athletes is that, as they gain more resources to train and compete, the control of their training and competition moves further away from them. The exceptions are those athletes with national visibility and the individual power to negotiate support that meets their interests.

Income of Amateur Athletes Amateur athletes in commercial sports face another paradox. They generate money through their performances, but they cannot directly benefit from participating in sports. Although Canadian and U.S. national team athletes may receive small stipends for living expenses while they train, many amateur athletes receive no compensation at all for their involvement in events generating gate receipts and media rights payments.

Interuniversity athletes playing big-time university football and basketball in the U.S., including some Canadian students on scholarships, who must also pay significant travel expenses, may generate hundreds of thousands of dollars for their universities, but NCAA rules prohibit them from receiving anything more than renewable one-year scholarships, and those scholarships may not cover anything more than tuition, room, meals, and books. This means that a basketball player from a low-income family, such as Toronto's Jamaal Magloire (who has played for several NBA teams, and is currently with the Dallas Mavericks) can bring fame and fortune to a university for three or four years and never legally receive a penny for expenses outside the classroom—no money for clothes, a personal computer, academic photocopying, school supplies, laundry, transportation around town, dates, travel home for vacations, nonsport-related medical or dental bills, phone calls home, and so on.

The unfairness of this situation for certain athletes promoted under-the-table forms of compensation. This has become so commonplace in the U.S. that some people say that the NCAA should revise its policies on compensation for athletes. However, developing a fair method of compensation is a challenge that has been beyond the NCAA's capabilities so far. Therefore, some top-level athletes leave university long before graduation in the hope of playing professional sports.

Other amateur athletes in both university and Olympic sports face similar difficulties in capitalizing on their commercial value. Changes in eligibility rules now permit some athletes to earn money without jeopardizing their participation status in amateur sports. Rules are less restrictive than they have been in the past. However, they cannot make money *beyond* an approved basic cost-of-living stipend and travel expenses related to training and competition. Therefore, if a sixteen-year-old gymnast on the Canadian national team takes money to be a part of an exhibition tour after the Olympics, she is not eligible to participate in NCAA university gymnastics. This also means she may not receive an athletic grant to attend a U.S. university. Furthermore, if an Olympic figure skater participates in a professional skating competition, her amateur status may be revoked even if she accepted no money (although there is now a re-application process). This would make her ineligible for future Olympic competitions; which makes it difficult for many athletes from lower-income backgrounds to maintain amateur status and continue doing the sports they love (Sokolove, 2004c).

Even though some of the restrictions of amateurism have been lifted in Olympic sports, many athletes do not share in the revenues generated by the events in which they participate. For example, the Olympic Games generate hundreds of millions of dollars in gate receipts and sponsorships, but the athletes who make the games possible receive none of that money, apart from training support through the sport organizations they are affiliated with and the cash awards medal winners *sometimes* receive from those organizations (e.g., the recently introduced awards by the COC) or their governments.

Questions about the fairness of this situation have been raised by an increasing number of athletes. University of Ottawa economist Mark Lavoie (2000) has noted that "the day cannot be too far off when the so-called amateur athletes will threaten to go on strike in order to get their share of the huge revenues generated by worldwide mega-events such as the Olympic Games" (p. 167).

SUMMARY

WHAT ARE THE CHARACTERISTICS OF COMMERCIAL SPORTS?

Commercial sports are visible parts of many contemporary societies. They grow and prosper best in urban, industrial societies with relatively efficient transportation and communications systems, a standard of living that allows people the time and money to play and watch sports, and a culture that emphasizes consumption and material status symbols. Spectator interest in commercial sports is based on a combination of a quest for excitement, ideologies emphasizing success, the existence of youth sport programmes, and media coverage that introduces people to the rules of sports and the athletes who play them.

The recent worldwide growth of commercial sports has been fuelled by sport organizations seeking global markets and corporations using sports as vehicles for global capitalist expansion. This growth will continue as long as it serves the interests of transnational corporations. As it does, sports, sport facilities, sport events, and athletes are branded with corporate logos and ideological messages promoting consumption and dependence on corporations for excitement and pleasure.

Commercialization leads to changes in the internal structure and goals of certain sports, the orientations of people involved in sports, and the people and organizations that control sports. Rules are changed to make events more fan friendly. People in sports, especially athletes, emphasize heroic orientations over aesthetic orientations and use style and dramatic expression to impress mass audiences. Overall, commercial sports have been packaged as total entertainment experiences for spectators, mostly for the benefit of spectators who know little about the games or events they are watching.

Commercial sports are unique businesses. At the minor league level, most of them do not generate substantial revenues for owners and sponsors; in fact, they are risky businesses. However, team owners at the top levels of professional sports have formed cartels to make their leagues into consistently effective sources of income.

Along with event sponsors and promoters, team owners are involved with commercial sports to make money while having fun and establishing good public images for themselves or their corporations and corporate products, policies, and practices. Their cartels enable them to control costs, stifle competition, and increase revenues, especially those coming from the sale of broadcasting rights to media companies. Profits are also enhanced by public support and subsidies, often associated with the construction and operation of stadiums and arenas.

It is ironic that North American professional sports often are used as models of competition, democracy and free enterprise when, in fact, they have been built through carefully planned autocratic control and monopolistic business practices. As one NFL team owner once said about himself and other owners, "We're twenty-eight Republicans who vote socialist." What he meant was that NFL owners are conservative individuals and corporations that have eliminated free market competition in their sport businesses and used public money and facilities to increase their wealth and power.

The administration and control of amateur commercial sports rest in the hands of numerous sport organizations. Although these organizations exist to support the training and competition of amateur athletes, their primary goal is to maintain power over athletes and control revenue. Those with the most money and influence usually win the power struggles in amateur sports, and athletes seldom have had the resources to promote their own interests in these struggles. Corporate sponsors are now a major force in amateur sports, and their interests strongly influence what happens in these sports.

Commercialization makes athletes entertainers. Because athletes generate revenues through their performances, issues related to players' rights and receiving revenues generated by their performances have become very important. As rights and revenues have increased, so have players' incomes. Media money has been key in this process.

Most athletes in professional sports do not make vast sums of money. Players outside the top men's sports, and golf and tennis for women, have incomes that are surprisingly low. Income among amateur athletes is limited by rules of governing bodies in particular sports. In amateur sports, athletes may receive direct cash payments for performances and endorsements, and some receive support from the organizations to which they belong, but relatively few make large amounts of money.

The structure and dynamics of commercial sports vary from nation to nation. Commercial sports in most of the world have not generated the massive revenues associated with a few high-profile, heavily televised sports in North America, Japan, Australia, western Europe and parts of Latin America. Profits for owners and promoters around the world depend on supportive relationships with the media, large corporations, and governments. These relationships have shaped the character of all commercial sports, professional and amateur.

The commercial model of sports is not the only one that might provide athletes and spectators with enjoyable and satisfying experiences. However, because most people are unaware of alternative models, they continue to express a desire for what they already receive, and their desires are based on limited information influenced by people with commercial and corporate interests (Sewart, 1987). Therefore, changes will occur only when spectators and people in sports develop visions for what sports could and should look like if they were not shaped by economic factors.

Visit *Sports in Society*'s Online Learning Centre at www.mcgrawhill.ca/olc/coakley for additional information, website resources, and study tools for this chapter.

[Photographs by M. MacNeill]

Sports and the Media

Could they survive without each other?

We see precious little in the sports pages that corporate entertainment does not want us to see.

> —**Geoffrey Smith, professor, Queen's University (1999)**

Of the millions [of dollars] that circulate in the media sport industry, only a small proportion of it is ever used to nurture grassroots sport…. [Elite] sport is now, more than ever, the playground of corporate capitalism.

> —**Gary Whannel, media scholar (2002)**

I'll tell you what Canadians do better than anyone else in the world—that's produce hockey games. *Hockey Night in Canada* does a hockey game better than ABC, NBC or CBS ever could.

> —**Dan Matheson, TV announcer (1993)**

Hockey has been the source of community pride and national unity; if the CPR held the country together during the early years of Confederation, certainly *Hockey Night in Canada* has done so in recent years.

> —**Bruce Kidd, author (1969)**

The media, including newspapers, magazines, books, films, radio, television, video games, and the Internet, pervade culture. Although each of us incorporates the media into our lives in different ways, the things we read, hear, and see in the media are important parts of our experience. They frame and influence many of our thoughts and conversations.

We use media images as we evaluate ourselves, form ideas, and envision the future. This does *not* mean that we are slaves to the media or passive dupes of those who control media content and the ways it is re-presented to us. The media do not tell us what to think, but they greatly influence *what we think about*, and therefore what we talk about in our relationships. Our experiences and our social worlds are clearly informed by media content, and, if the media did not exist, our lives would be different.

Sports and the media are interconnected parts of our lives. Sport programming is an important segment of media content, and many sports depend on the media for publicity and revenues. In light of these interconnections, five questions are considered in this chapter:

1. What are the characteristics of the media?
2. How are sports and the media interconnected?
3. What images and messages are emphasized in the media coverage of sports in Canada and the U.S.?
4. Do the media influence sport-related choices and actions?
5. What are the characteristics of sports journalism?

CHARACTERISTICS OF THE MEDIA

Revolutionary changes are occurring in the media. The personal computer and the emergence of the Internet have propelled us into a transition from an era of sponsored and programmed media for mass consumption into an era of multifaceted media content and experiences. The pace and implications of this transition are significant, and university students are on the cutting edge of this media revolution. Although it is important to discuss new trends and explain what may occur in the future, our discussion should be based on a general understanding of the traditional media and their connections with sports.

In this chapter, we distinguish between print media and electronic media. **Print media** include *newspapers, magazines, fanzines, books, catalogues, event programmes, and even trading cards*: words and images printed on paper. **Electronic media** include *radio, television, film, video games, the Internet, and online publications and representations*. A variety of new handheld devices take advantage of digital media, and permit a great deal of both one-way and two-way connectivity—these include the new generations of mobile phones and PDAs, and MP3 players of various kinds that make available both the receipt and production of "podcasts." Communications technology has given rise to multimedia publications that blur lines separating print media from electronic media, but it is still useful to make the distinction.

Taken together, the media provide *information, interpretation*, and *entertainment*. Sometimes they provide two or three of these things simultaneously. However, entertainment goals are given higher priority than information and interpretation in commercial media as opposed to "public" media that do not depend exclusively on advertisers. The media connect us with parts of the world and enable us to construct a version of that world. They bring us information, experiences, people, images, and ideas that would not otherwise be part of our everyday lives. However, media content is edited and "re-presented" by others: the producers, editors, programme directors, technicians, programmers, camerapersons, writers, commentators, sponsors, and Internet site providers. These people provide information, interpretation, and entertainment based on their interest in one or more of five goals: (1) making profits, (2) shaping values, (3) providing a public service, (4) building their own reputations, and (5) expressing themselves in technical, artistic, or personal ways.

In nations where most of the media are privately owned and operated, the dominant interest is making profits. This is not the only interest, but often it is the most influential. For example, media expert Michael Real of Royal Roads University explains that there has been no greater force in the construction of media sport reality than "commercial television and its institutionalized value system [emphasi-zing] profit making, sponsorship, expanded markets, commodification, and competition" (1998, p. 17). Because the Internet will be a major force influencing media reality in the future, people with commercial interests are currently using their resources to control online access and content.

In nations where the popular media are controlled and operated by the state, the dominant interests are shaping values, providing a public service, and, to a lesser extent, providing entertainment. However, state control of the media has steadily declined as television companies and newspapers have become privatized and as more people seek online access to information, interpretation, and entertainment.

The particular nature of electronic media available to Canadians is distinct from the U.S., combining both private/commercial forms with a modified form of state-funded media, and providing ready access to U.S. commercial and public television through cable, satellite, and digital access. Because of Canadian geography and population distribution, the first electronic linking of the country coast-to-coast by radio (in the 1930s) and television (in the 1950s) were considered to be as significant as the completion of the CN and CP railroad links across the country in the latter part of the nineteenth century. They provided the possibility of common communication across the country and were significant in developing a sense of national identity.

Canadians now have several French and English private networks on television and radio, and CBC (Canadian Broadcasting Corporation)/SRC (Société Radio Canada) as state-supported networks that are also partially privatized, showing commercials on television and producing some programmes. (CBC/SRC radio is not commercial.) Because of misinformation about the "government owning the CBC," it is important to understand the control of media in Canada. All media, private and public, are regulated by a government agency, the Canadian Radio-television and Telecommunications Commission (CRTC), which grants and renews licences, and sets standards for (and monitors) Canadian content. The CBC/SRC is a Crown Corporation (cf., Canada Post, etc.) that receives partial support for its budget from Parliament through the Ministry of Canadian Heritage. The remainder of its budget is derived from selling commercial time on television, as well as from other sources such as selling productions internationally. Thus, the CBC is not completely private but has to compete with private media corporations for the sale of commercial time; nor is it completely public- or state-owned because, as a Crown Corporation, it has an arms-length relationship with the government and is often critical of the government.[1]

Since most Canadians receive their television signals via cable, their basic cable packages usually also provide the four major U.S. networks and U.S. public television. With increasing digitalization, and the fragmentation of the

---

[1]Public broadcasting in other countries may take other forms: in countries where total funding is received directly from the government (e.g., the People's Republic of China), the government often enjoys a great deal of control and is never criticized by the public broadcaster; other countries fund their public broadcasters by charging viewers a licence fee (e.g., the BBC in the U.K.).

media away from major networks, Canadians also have access to an increasing number of what are termed, in Canada, "specialty channels"— channels where programming is focused on a single theme, or aimed at a specific population segment. Table 12.1 provides a list of specialty sports channels currently available to Canadians. Sports are, of course, also available on the major networks, and on channels such as Country Canada. Multicultural channels also broadcast sports—it is possible to see French league soccer on TV5, and Italian Serie A on Telelatino.

Given that three of the four major leagues in North America have teams in both Canada and the U.S., and the fourth (the NFL) enjoys a relationship with and trades players with the CFL; and given that all four major professional sports (except the CFL) are covered by both Canadian and U.S. commercial network television, often with the Canadian network showing the U.S. coverage, we often refer to "North American" media in this chapter to indicate Canadian and U.S. (but not Mexican) media. Differences between Canada and the U.S. begin to emerge in the coverage of sports that may be shown in one country but not in the other (e.g., curling), occasionally in the quality of coverage (e.g., Canadian expertise at hockey coverage, U.S. expertise at basketball coverage), and regularly in the coverage of events such as the Olympics.

As a consequence of this broad range of coverage, many Canadians enjoy the possibility of comparing coverage. In the case of the Olympics, for example, Canadians have been able to follow recent Olympics (Sydney, Salt Lake City, Athens, Torino) by comparing and contrasting CBC and NBC English-language coverage of the Games, and they have been able to supplement their viewing with SRC French language broadcasts, TSN/RDS commercial supplementary coverage, and CBC/SRC radio hourly updates. However, the flow of U.S. media into Canada, together with the various ideologies discussed later in this chapter, is often considered to be overpowering, and some have argued that we may, as a result, be losing a distinctively Canadian culture (including sports). The relationship is not completely one way though, and many in the U.S. (and other countries) follow CBC radio through the Internet. Also, during the Olympics, many Americans

Table 12.1   Specialty sports channels currently available in Canada[a]

ATN Cricket Plus	RIS Reseau Info-Sports
ESPN Classic	Setanta Sports
Fox Sports World Canada	The Fight Network
GolTV	The Score
	- TSN
	- TSN2
HPItv (horse racing)	Wild TV
- HPItv Odds	World Fishing Network
- HPItv Canada	X-Treme Sports
- HPItv International	
- HPItv West	Regional sports networks:
Leafs TV	- Rogers Sportsnet
NHL Network	- Rogers Sportsnet East
Outdoor Life Network	- Rogers Sportsnet Ontario
Raptors NBA TV	- Rogers Sportsnet West
RDS Réseau des sports	- Rogers Sportsnet Pacific

[a]Both the CBC and the Canadian Olympic Committee have recently proposed amateur sports specialty channels

in border states have taken to watching live Canadian coverage rather than pre-packaged, prime-time coverage from NBC.

Returning to the five goals that drive media content, power relations in society influence the priority that is given to them. Those who make decisions about content act as filters as they select and create the images and messages that they represent in the media. In the filtering and representation process, these people usually emphasize images and narratives consistent with dominant ideologies in the society as a whole. Thus, the media often serve the interests of those who have power and wealth in society. As corporate control of commercial media has increased and media have become hypercommercialized, media content has emphasized consumerism, individualism, competition, and class inequality as natural and necessary in society. Seldom included in the content of commercial media is an emphasis on civic values, anticommercial activities, and political activity (McChesney, 1999; Walker, 2005).

There are exceptions to this pattern, but when people use media to challenge dominant ideologies, they can expect some form of backlash. This discourages counterhegemonic programming and leads people to censor media content in ways that defer to the interests of those with power. Even when there is legal protection for freedom of speech, those who work in the media often think carefully before presenting images and messages that challenge the interests of those who have power and influence in society, especially when those people own the media or sponsor programmes for commercial purposes.

This does not mean that those who control the media ignore what consumers think or that media audiences are forced to read, hear, and see things unrelated to their interests. But it does mean that, apart from email and the websites we create, we seldom have direct control over the content of what we read, listen to, and see in the media. The media re-present to us edited versions of information, interpretation, and entertainment. These versions are constructed primarily to boost media profits and maintain a culture and society in which commercial media can thrive. In the process, people who control the media are concerned with what attracts readers, listeners, and viewers within the legal limits set by government agencies and the preference parameters of individuals and corporations that buy advertising time. As they make programming decisions, they see audiences as collections of consumers to whom they sell advertising (see figure 12.1).

In the case of sports, those who control the media not only select which sports and events are covered but also decide what kinds of images and commentary are emphasized in the coverage (Andrews and Jackson, 2001; Bernstein and Blain, 2003; Brookes, 2002; Martzke and Cherner, 2004; Rowe, 2004a, 2004b; Whannel, 2002). When they do this, they play an important role in constructing the overall frameworks that we in media audiences use to define and incorporate sports in our lives.

Most people do not think critically about media content. For example, when we watch sports on television, we do not often notice that the images and messages we see and hear have been carefully designed to heighten the dramatic content of the event and emphasize dominant ideologies in the society as a whole. The pregame analysis, the camera coverage, the camera angles, the close-ups, the slow-motion shots, the attention given to particular athletes, the announcer's play-by-play descriptions, the colour commentary, the quotes from athletes, and the postgame summary and analysis are all presented to entertain the media audience and keep sponsors happy.

Television commentaries, narratives, and images in North America, for example, highlight action, competition, aggression, hard work, heroism and achievement, playing with pain, teamwork, and competitive outcomes. Television coverage has become so seamless in its representations of sports that we often define televised games as "real" games, more real even than the game seen in person at the stadium. Magazine editor Kerry Temple explains:

> It's not just games you're watching. It's soap operas, complete with storylines and plots and plot twists. And good guys and villains, heroes and underdogs. And all this gets scripted into cliffhanger morality plays....And you get all caught up in this until you begin to believe it really matters. (1992, p. 29)

Temple's point is more relevant today than in 1992. The focus on profits has accentuated an emphasis on soap opera storytelling as a means of developing and maintaining audience interest in both print and electronic media sports coverage. Media expert James Wittebols explains that sports programming has become a "never-ending series of episodes—the results of one game create implications for the next one (or the next week's) to be broadcast" (2004, p. 4). Sports rivalries are hyped and used as a basis for serializing stories through and even across seasons; conflict and chaos are highlighted in connection with an ever-changing cast of "good guys," "bad guys," and "redemption" or "comeback" stories; and the storylines are designed to reproduce ideologies favoured by upper-middle-class media consumers—the ones that corporate sponsors want to reach.

> Sport and the media must surely be the most potent combination of forces amongst the key factors in the globalization game. They have a unique synergy.
>
> —Robert Davies, chief executive, International Business Leaders Forum (2002b)

Even though the media coverage of sports is carefully edited and re-presented in total entertainment packages, most of us believe that, when we see a sport event on television, we are seeing it "the way it is." We also think that, when we hear the commentary or read the report on the event, the commentators and journalists are "telling it like it is." We do not usually think that what we are seeing, hearing, and reading is a series of narratives and images selected for particular reasons and grounded in the social worlds and interests of those producing the event, controlling the images, and delivering the commentary (Crawford, 2004; McCullagh, 2002). Television coverage provides only *one* of *many* possible sets of images and narratives related to a sport event, and there are many images and messages that audiences do *not* receive (Knoppers and Elling, 2004). For example, if we went to an event in person, we would see something quite different from the images that are selected and re-presented on television, and we would develop our own descriptions and interpretations, which would be very different from those carefully presented by media commentators.

This point was clearly illustrated in a comparison of CBC and NBC coverage of the Atlanta and Sydney Olympics. The CBC has a policy of extensive live coverage (regardless of the time of day in the six different time zones across Canada), focusing on all events that include Canadian competitors, and other major competitions. The live coverage is mixed with highlight packages, magazine pieces, and studio and on-site interviews. In contrast, NBC strategically created entertaining drama by re-presenting what media analysts have described as "plausible reality" in their broadcasts. To do this, they deliberately withheld information so they could frame events in their terms, even though they knew those terms to be contrary to what was expressed by the athletes and others involved. They gave priority to entertainment over news and information. Former U.S. Olympic swimmer Diana Nyad, who was in Atlanta, observed, "Compared to the TV audience, the people in Atlanta have seen a completely different Olympics" (NPR, 1996, 6 August broadcast). She also noted that television and other media coverage revolves around a focus on gold medals, which distorts the actual experiences and priorities of most of the athletes and spectators. Both CBC and NBC re-presented the events to their viewers, and both

Quick! Bring the camera—this crash will boost our ratings!

FIGURE 12.1 Media representations of sports highlight "the thrill of victory and the agony of defeat." They contain an abundance of spectacular plays and crashes. However, these are minor parts of the totality of experience in sport events.

had particular stories to tell, but the strategy of packaging events in U.S. prime time was quite distinct from the Canadian representation. In other words, television constructs sports and viewer experiences in important ways. And it happens so smoothly that most people think that when they watch a game on television they are experiencing sports in a natural form.

To illustrate the point, think about this question: What if all prime-time television programmes were sponsored by environmental organizations, women's organizations, or labour organizations? Would programme content be different than it is now? Would the political biases built into the images and commentary be the same as they are now? It is unlikely that they would be the same, and we would be quick to identify all the ways that the interests and political agendas of the environmentalists, feminists, or labour organizers influenced images, narratives, and overall programme content.

Now think about this: Capitalist corporations sponsor nearly 100 percent of all sports programming in the media, and their goals are to create consumers loyal to capitalism and generate profits for corporations and their shareholders. However, we seldom question how this influences *what* we see in sports coverage, *what* we hear in commentaries, and *what* we do *not* read, see, and hear as we consume media sports.

Whether we know it or not, our experiences as spectators are heavily influenced—that is, "mediated"—by the decisions of those who control the media. Those decisions are influenced by social, political, and economic factors—including dominant ideologies related to gender, race, and class (see chapters 8 through 10). We explore this issue in the section, "What Ideological Themes Underlie Media Images and Narratives?"

Characteristics of the Internet

The Internet extends and radically changes our media connections with the rest of the world, because it gives us virtual access to potentially unlimited and individually created and chosen information, interpretation, and entertainment. Being online is partly like having open voice, video, and text connections with everyone in the world also online. Some of these connections allow real-time interaction, and others provide posted text and images, which we can access on our own terms and in our own time frame.

In the case of sports, the Internet extends our access to sport content. We can interact with fellow fans in chat rooms, ask questions of players and coaches, identify scores and statistics, and we can play online games that either simulate sports or are associated with real-time sport events around the world. We can even *create* media content to match our interests and the interests of others worldwide. This gives us a form of control that radically alters media experiences and mediated realities (Crawford, 2004).

Most people interested in sports use the Internet as an extension of the existing media. They visit team sites, listen to live-game audio, and most recently, pay for game video streaming from television feeds. Although subscriber fees are charged for video coverage, the Internet may soon provide access to all televised games in the world. This concerns the five media companies that control most media content worldwide; they want to control access to this content and be able to sell Internet audiences to other corporations who wish to advertise products and services. At the same time, sport leagues plan to stream games on their own sites, bypassing media companies and collecting subscription fees without a "middleman." Scott Moore, head of CBC Sports says, "online streaming is literally moments away from producing the highest quality HD picture" (cited by Houston, 2008, p. S5).

The major sociological question related to the Internet is this: Will it democratize social life by enabling people to freely share information and ideas, or will it become a tool for corporations to expand capital, increase consumption, reproduce ideologies that drive market economies, and maintain the belief that they are the major source of pleasure and excitement in our lives? The answer to this question will emerge as we struggle over issues of Internet access and how Internet use will be funded and incorporated into our lives. For example, giant cable and satellite companies have already convinced state legislatures to pass laws making it illegal for communities in some U.S. states to establish wireless connectivity as a public service for all citizens. These companies want the Internet to be forever a toll road on which they charge and collect the tolls rather than a publicly maintained information highway attached to a local street system.

Other sociological questions deal with the dramatic growth in Internet-based "Fantasy Leagues" and sport gambling. Fantasy Leagues are often referred to as "rotisserie" leagues and, in the case of hockey, as "hockey pools" or (often for the play-offs) "hockey drafts." The first fantasy sport league was invented in 1980 by a baseball fan. It did not require the Internet, but most fantasy sport participants today use Internet sites to play. If we use the CFL as an example, playing fantasy football makes every participant an owner who constructs his or her own pro football team by taking turns with other owners and choosing real CFL players for the positions on their fantasy team. The weekly performance statistics of the players on an owner's team roster are converted into points so that each owner can compete against one or more owners of other teams. Websites are designed to accumulate relevant statistics for all CFL players each week and compute scores for owners' teams in particular leagues.

In the U.S., the average fantasy team owner is a white male (93 percent) about forty years old with a university degree, and an annual household income of about US$80,000. Collectively, owners spend over US$2 billion annually to obtain data about players and compete in online leagues. Individually, each owner devotes about three hours per week to managing his or her team, and a portion of this occurs during work hours (Ballard, 2004; Petrecca, 2005; Wendel, 2004).

Fantasy football, baseball, NASCAR, basketball, hockey, and other sports completely change the way these men and a few women consume sports (Levy, 2005; Wendel, 2004). They care little about teams or team records because they focus on the performances of their players who are on many different teams in a sport. Therefore, many "owners" also subscribe to expensive cable and satellite television "sport packages" that give them access to broadcasts of every game played in the league in which they own fantasy teams. They watch their players, add up their points, scout other players, compare statistics, consider trades with other owners, and decide who they should put in their starting lineups. Fantasy sports combine the Internet and other media and turn many sport fans into avid media sport consumers. Being a fantasy owner provides the white men who constitute over 90 percent of all participants with a sense of power and control, and it connects them with others who share their interests and backgrounds (Levy, 2005).

The Internet also is connected with gambling on sports. Most bets related to sports are made informally with family members, friends, and coworkers. Formal gambling on sports goes back centuries (Cashmore, 2007) and continues today at horse and dog tracks and in Las Vegas–based "sport books" in which people may place legal bets on nearly every possible outcome in sport events—number of points, who scores first, points in first half or second half, who beats the point spread, and so on. The Internet has increased access to both legal and illegal sport gambling opportunities. It does not cause people to gamble, but it makes it very easy to do so twenty-four hours a day, seven days a week. This is partly because there are many offshore websites that now take bets from people in Canada, using software from Canadian companies like Cryptologic. Online gambling is something of a legal grey area in Canada, although it is illegal in many countries such as the U.S. and Australia. Provinces have jurisdiction over gambling, and only online betting on horse racing is clearly legal. However, a credit card is all that is needed to bet online, and there are concerns that the only thing preventing children from making such bets is the lack of a credit card.

Online sport gambling is especially popular in the U.S. among male university students who have access to the Internet and feel that they know more about sports than other people (Brown, 2000; Crist, 1998; Jenkins, 2000; Layden, 1995a, 1995b, 1995c). Gambling changes the way people consume media sports because their bets often involve point spreads. Point spreads are determined by bookies, who want to make sure that they do not take too many bets on a particular outcome in a sport event and find themselves unable to cover the money that must be paid to winners. This means that when a person bets on the BC Lions who are favoured by 21 points in a football game with the Hamilton Ti-Cats, BC must win by more than 21 points for the person to win the bet. This makes the game exciting even if

it is one sided because all the betters are concerned with the final score rather than who wins or loses.

Despite gambling debts that have destructive consequences for a growing number of people, betting on sports is not generally seen as an important moral or legal issue. Many people are accustomed to buying lottery tickets and participating in state-sponsored gambling activities, so they do not take seriously restrictions that limit or ban betting on sports.

Overall, issues related to access will cause the Internet to be contested terrain well into the future as people struggle over the rights of users to share information and ideas. Sports leagues and teams will use the Internet more widely in the future, but they will charge fees for access to events for which they have also sold media rights to television and radio. Furthermore, sponsors of the TV and radio broadcasts will oppose Internet coverage that interferes with selling products and services to sport audiences.

As technology improves over the next decade, it may be possible for a grandparent to see a grandchild playing in a high school basketball game simply by paying a fee to the high school website. High school students could film the game, do the commentary, and produce their own coverage for small audiences of distant friends and relatives. Such a possibility could lead to many creative forms of sport media coverage and income for high schools and their instructional technology curriculum. Furthermore, being a spectator could become a more active and creative experience for online fans who may have opportunities to participate directly in the construction of media reality. How this will change the reality of mediated sports and our experience of them remains to be seen.

The future is difficult to predict. Will people choose 500-channel, high-definition digital television over the medium of the Internet? Will Internet TV become widespread so that people can have both? Will the economics of technology and the "digital divide" between technology haves and have-nots segregate spectators even further by social class? Will the culture of the Internet favour some people over others, or will it enable all spectators to create realities that fit their interests and preferences?

Answers to these questions depend on the social, political, and economic forces shaping the future of the Internet. Economic forces guarantee that the first people to enjoy new spectator experiences and realities will be those who can buy the hardware, software, and bandwidth to move around the Internet at will. Social class will influence Internet access to spectator experiences because broadband providers often overlook lower-income neighbourhoods; they say it does not pay to invest there. But progressive public policies and programmes could mandate the provision of access in these neighbourhoods or provide wireless access as a pubic service, thereby blurring class differences in future access to the Internet.[2] This, however, depends on the public good being given priority over the corporate good when it comes to online access.

Characteristics of Video Games and Virtual Sports

Sports also come into our lives through video games and virtual experiences. Sport video games are popular in wealthy nations, and some people have even participated in virtual sports of various types, although most virtual sports are experimental and not available for general participation.

The images in digital games have become increasingly lifelike, and those who play the games have uniquely active spectator experiences even when they occur in solitude. Social science research has focused mostly on violence and

gender issues, and there is little information about the actual experiences of people who play video games modelled after "real" sports.

It is clear that people who play sport video games have different experiences than those who watch televised sport events. For example golf fans may match their video golf skills with the physical skills of pro golfers by going online and golfing on the same course as Tiger Woods or other high-profile players whose shots have been represented and archived through digitized images. This is a new media experience, and research has not been done to show how people integrate such experiences into their lives.

Those who play video sports games are usually regular customers of standard sport media events. Their interest in and enjoyment of the video games are tied to their knowledge about a sport, sport teams, and athletes. However, the experience of digital gaming will change as more people play one another on the Internet in organized tournaments, while others watch.

Sport teams and individual athletes will sell interactive video games to fans who want to pretend that they are managing the Montréal Canadiens in simulated NHL games, controlling David Beckham's body as he plays for the LA Galaxy, or skating in a digital skateboarding halfpipe with PLG (Pierre-Luc Gagnon). It is unknown whether such interactive sport video games will actually replace or simply extend other forms of sports media consumption (Crawford, 2004).

Game players have choices, but those choices are not unlimited, nor are they ideologically neutral. The experiences of video game players are influenced by the ethos that underlies the programmed images and actions in the games. The games clearly highlight traditional masculinity and other values associated with most major media sports today. It is important that we increase our understanding of how people integrate video game experiences into their lives.

The idea of virtual sports is so new that it has not been discussed in the sociology of sport. As

---

[2]As a result of federal government policy, in 1999 Canada became the first country to have all schools and libraries connected to the Internet. Industry Canada's Community Access and the former Connecting Canadians programme have provided broadband access to remote and northern communities, attempting to ensure more democratic access to the Internet.

the technology of virtual reality evolves, people will become immersed in physical activities in new ways, as evidenced by the instant popularity of, and increasing variety of games that can be played with Nintendo's Wii. Although we do not know exactly what this means, it is possible that many people in the future will prefer virtual sports to what we define as sports today. Instead of going to a gym or fitness centre, people may go to virtual sports complexes where they can put on lightweight headsets that present images allowing them to physically experience sport challenges that transcend time and space. This futuristic arcade will allow cyclists in the year 2050 to race with Oscar Pereiro's granddaughter as they pedal and sweat their way along the virtual roads of the Tour de France on bikes and in environments where they experience feelings of speed, wind, and rain in their faces, and the excitement of developing and carrying out strategies with virtual teammates in the Tour de France. Other sports will merge virtual and real spaces in other ways, changing the meaning of reality when it comes to sports (Marriot, 2004).

In the meantime, it is important to understand the relationship between sports and the media in the early twenty-first century, and to know how each has influenced the other.

SPORTS AND THE MEDIA: A TWO-WAY RELATIONSHIP

The media and the commercialization of sports are closely related topics in the sociology of sport. The media intensify and extend the process and consequences of commercialization. For this reason, much attention has been given to the interdependence between the media and commercialized forms of sports. Each of these spheres of life has influenced the other, and each depends on the other for its popularity and commercial success. In fact, when Sut Jhally, the well-known popular media analyst at the University of Massachusetts, was a Ph.D. student

Commercial sports depend heavily on the media. All media hype events, and television pays rights fees, which have become increasingly important to the overall success of commercial sports. The payoff for corporations is that their logos are continually on camera and in newspaper photographs such as this one. The logo placement costs far less than television commercials and print advertisements. [CP(Chuck Stoody)]

at Simon Fraser University, he coined the term "sport-media complex" to characterize the symbiotic relationship between the two (Jhally, 1984).

Sports Depend on the Media

People played sports long before the media covered and represented sport events. When sports exist just for the participants, there is no urgent need to advertise games, report the action, publish results, and interpret what happened. The players already know these things, and they are the only ones who matter. It is only when sports become forms of commercial entertainment that they depend on the media to represent them.

Commercial sports are unique in that they require the media to provide a combination of coverage *and* news. For example, when a stage play is over, it is over—except for a review after opening night and the conversations of those who attended the play. When a sport event is over, many people wish to know about and discuss statistics; important plays, records, standings, the overall performances of the players and teams; upcoming games or matches; the importance of the outcomes in terms of the season as a whole, and the postseason, and the next season; and so on. The media provide this knowledge and facilitate these discussions, which in turn generate interest that can be converted into revenues from the sale of tickets, luxury suites, club seats, concessions, parking, team logo merchandise, and licensing rights. After games or matches are played, the scores become news, and interpretations of the action become entertainment for fans, regardless of whether they saw an event or not. This is the case worldwide—for bullfights in Mexico, cricket matches in South Africa, soccer matches in Brazil, and sumo bashos in Japan. Reporting often takes a different tone in international competitions or multisport events such as the Commonwealth Games. In these cases, information and inter-pretation of the action are supplemented with national comparisons and evaluations of national sport development systems.

Sports promoters and team owners know the value of media coverage, and they often go out of their way to accommodate reporters, commentators, and photographers. Credentialed media personnel are given comfortable seats in press boxes, access to the playing field and locker rooms, and summaries of statistics and player information. Providing these services promotes supportive and sympathetic media coverage

Although commercial spectator sports depend on the media, some have a special dependence on television because television companies pay fees for the rights to broadcast games and other events. Tables 12.2 and 12.3 indicate that rights fees generally provide sports with predictable sources of income. Once contracts are signed, television revenues are guaranteed regardless of bad weather, injuries to key players, and the other factors that interfere with ticket sales and on-site revenue streams. Without television contracts, commercial success is limited or unlikely for spectator sports, which is why the NHL has been so anxious to negotiate a full-coverage U.S. network contract.

Television revenues also have much greater growth potential than revenues from gate receipts. The number of seats in a stadium limits ticket sales, and ticket costs are limited by demand. But television audiences can include literally billions of viewers, now that satellite technology transmits signals to most locations around the globe. For example, in 2004 it is estimated that a record cumulative audience of 3.9 billion viewers in some 220 countries watched television coverage of the Athens Olympics. The audience was attracted by more than 4,000 hours of coverage supplied by 180 broadcasting organizations that paid about US$1.5 billion in rights fees to the International Olympic Committee (IOC). These organizations covered 300 events with over 12,000 personnel, 1,000 cameras, 450 videotape machines, and nearly 60 trailers of equipment. In 2006, it was estimated that over 715 million people watched Italy beat France in the men's World Cup soccer final, and that the cumulative audience for the tournament was 26 billion in 214 countries.

The goal of the IOC and other sport mega-events organizers is to turn the entire world into an audience that can be sold to sponsors. The size of the potential TV audience and the deregulation of the television industry are the reasons that television rights have increased in value at phenomenal rates since the early 1970s. For example, the IOC received US$225 million from the company that televised the 1984 Los Angeles Summer Olympics—the most commercialized Olympics in history at that time.

In 2012, the IOC will receive US$1.2 billion from NBC and US$700 million from other television companies worldwide to broadcast the London Olympics.

David Whitson (1998), of the University of Alberta, points out that the growth in television rights fees makes commercial sports more profitable for promoters and team owners, and increases the attractiveness of sports as sites for national and global advertising. This allows professional athletes to demand higher salaries and turns some of them into national and international celebrities, who then use their celebrity status to endorse products sold around the world. For example, the global celebrity and endorsement value of Tiger Woods is primarily due to the invention of satellite television.

As video streaming becomes more realistic, and it becomes possible to broadcast more games and events on the Internet, there will be interesting changes in how and with whom media rights are negotiated. The global reach of the Internet creates new possibilities for large corporations wanting to "teach the world" to consume. However, it also creates challenges because webcasts may compete with television—the medium that has traditionally paid rights fees to sport organizations. This challenge has, for example, prevented the International Olympic Committee (IOC) in the past from selling Internet rights for Olympics coverage. Long-term Olympic broadcasting rights for Canada have already been sold to CTV, and CTV does not want people to have the choice of its coverage or InternetTV coverage. However, after several years of disputes and negotiations, in April, 2008, the IOC announced new Internet access regulations. Websites belonging to media organizations can, for normal news and editorial use, now carry unlimited written and photographic coverage of future Olympics. They will also be able to broadcast the daily news conferences with a 30-minute delay. In a separate deal with Australia, websites without an Olympic licensing agreement will be able to show video of three minutes of

Olympic events each day in 60-second clips. However, they must agree to "geoblock" their sites so that they cannot be seen outside Australia (Holton, 2008).

These new arrangements are an indication of the current struggles around new media. The IOC sells "exclusive" access to specific media corporations for vast amounts of money, and tries desperately to protect that exclusivity; but such is the nature of new technology that anyone at the Games with a cell phone camera and Internet access can upload video of Olympic sports events. Will YouTube become a major source for viewing Olympic sports events without paying a licensing fee? Rupert Murdoch, and his global News Corporation, is recognizing the new media realities by buying websites that attract people worldwide; he wants to combine the immediacy and interactivity of the web with the traditional allure of television, and he will use sports programming to attract InternetTV subscribers (Hansell, 2005). Eventually, television as we now think of it will become obsolete.

Have Commercial Sports Sold Out to the Media? There is no question that most commercial sports depend on television for revenues and publicity. For example, about 65 percent of NFL revenues comes from TV rights fees.

However, television money comes with strings attached. Accommodating the interests of commercial television has required many changes in the ways that sports are organized, scheduled, and re-presented. Some of these changes include the following:

- The schedules and starting times for many sport events have been altered to fit television's programming needs.
- Halftime periods in certain sports have been shortened, to keep television viewers tuned to events.
- Prearranged schedules of time-outs have been added to games and matches to make time for as many commercials as possible.

• Teams, leagues, and tournaments have been formed or realigned to take advantage of regional media markets and to build national and international fan support for sports, leagues, and teams.

Many other changes associated with television coverage are not entirely due to the influence of television. For example, professional teams extended their seasons and the number of games played, a change that would have occurred even without television.[3] Commercial sports would have added extra games simply to increase gate receipts and venue revenues. Extra games do make television contracts more lucrative, but the economic reasons for adding games include more than just the sale of television rights. The same is true for the additions of sudden death overtime periods in some sports, the tiebreaker scoring method in tennis, rally scoring in volleyball, the addition of stroke play in golf, the 3-point shot in basketball and the shootout in soccer and hockey. These changes are grounded in general commercial interests, but *television expands and intensifies* the financial stakes associated with producing more marketable entertainment for all spectators and a more attractive commercial package for sponsors and advertisers.

Most changes associated with television coverage have been made willingly by sport organizations. The trade-offs usually are attractive for both players and sponsors. In fact, many sports and athletes not currently receiving coverage gladly would make changes if they could gain the attention and or money associated with television contracts. Are there limits to what they would change for television coverage? Yes, but limits are always negotiated around the issue of sharing control over the conditions of sports

---

Television and Hockey Rule Changes

The enormous television audiences in North America for Olympic ice hockey at the 2002 Salt Lake City Olympics—in Canada, over 10 million for the men's final and some seven million for the women's final—caused the NHL to look more seriously at the international rules for the game. It is clear that the audiences found the large ice surfaces (leading to a more open passing game and less obstruction), the restrictions against fighting, and the hurry-up face-off rule extremely attractive in leading to a faster-paced, more exciting game. Given the NHL Governors' reluctance to tamper with any of the rules of the game lest some parts of the relatively small North American audience become displeased (e.g., the slow change and inconsistent enforcement of the obstruction rule, reluctance to outlaw fighting), and their outright refusal to adopt a larger ice surface because it would mean removal of some of the highest priced seats at their arenas, they adopted the hurry-up face-off with surprising speed. The result was faster games during the 2002–03 season, often lasting only two-and-a-half hours instead of the usual three hours. An unintended consequence was the need for television broadcasters to review their schedule for commercials since there are fewer game breaks in which to show them. The change also produced more time between the first and second games on *Hockey Night in Canada*, which broadcasters learned how to fill.

Following the year long lock-out of players by owners in 2004–05, players were among the first to realize that further rule changes were needed to encourage the television (and ticket buying) audience to return to the game. Thus, further rule changes were initiated to keep the game more open and free-flowing, including changes to the off-side and icing rules, and the introduction of a shoot-out to give every game a winner.

---

participation. For example, surfers have turned down television contracts because they would not allow television companies to dictate the conditions under which they would compete. The companies did not care if waves were too dangerous because they wanted to stay on schedule and provide live coverage. But surfers up until now have decided that selling control over their sport participation and being forced to risk their lives in competitions was not worth television coverage.

Have the Media Corrupted Sports? Some people complain that dependence on the media, especially television, corrupts the true nature of

---

[3]At the time of writing, the NHL and the NHLPA are negotiating to extend the regular season from 82 to 84 games beginning in the 2009–10 season.

sports. However, these people fail to take into account two factors:

1. *Sports are not shaped primarily by the media in general, or by television in particular.* The idea that television by itself has somehow transformed the essential nature of sports does not hold up under careful examination. Sports are social constructions, and commercial sports are created over time through interactions among athletes, facility directors, sport team owners, event promoters, media representatives, sponsors, advertisers, agents, and spectators—all of whom have diverse interests. The dynamics of these interactions are grounded in power relations and shaped by the resources held by different people at different times. It is unrealistic to think that those who control the media determine sports to fit their interests alone, but it is equally unrealistic to ignore their power.

2. *The media, including television, do not operate in a political and economic vacuum.* People who control the media are influenced by the social, political, and economic contexts in which they do business. Government agencies, policies, and laws regulate the media in most countries. Although government regulations have been loosened or lifted in recent years, the media must negotiate contracts with teams and leagues under certain legal constraints. Economic factors also constrain the media by setting limits on the value of sponsorships and advertising time and by shaping the climate in which certain types of programming, such as pay-per-view sports and cable and satellite subscriptions, might be profitable. Finally, the media are constrained by social factors, which influence people's decisions to consume sports through the media.

Connections between the media and sport are grounded in complex sets of social, economic, and political relationships, which change over time

and vary from culture to culture. These relationships influence the media's impact on sports. In other words, the conclusion that the media corrupt sports is based on an incomplete understanding of how the social world works and how sports are connected with social relations in society.

With that said, it is also important to remember that nearly all of the most powerful people in sports around the world are CEOs or owners of major, global corporations. Nearly all of them are white men from English-speaking nations, and each wants to offer programming that people around the globe will watch, and that corporations will sponsor and use as advertising vehicles. The sports selected for national and global coverage depend on the media for their commercial success, and the salaries and endorsement income of top athletes also depend on the media. However, there are two sides to this process.

The Media Depend on Sports

Most media do not depend on sports coverage. This is especially true for magazines, books, radio, movies, and the Internet, although it is less true for newspapers and television. The Internet does not depend on sports, but certain online services may make money when sports fans use the Internet to obtain up-to-the-minute scores, obtain insider information about particular events, place bets with offshore bookies, or enter exclusive online discussions about athletes, teams, and events.

Neither the book publishing nor the film industry depends on sports. Until recently, there were few successful books or films about sports. The urgency and uncertainty that are so compelling in live sports are difficult to capture in these media. However, since the late 1980s, both publishers and film studios have produced projects with tragic, inspiring, and outrageous stories about sports figures.

Many radio stations give coverage to sports only in their news segments, although local football, baseball, hockey, and basketball games often are broadcast live on local radio stations. Some communities have talk radio stations featuring sports talk programmes that attract listeners from a demographic that is attractive to certain advertisers—that is, young men with higher than average incomes.

Most magazines devote little or no attention to sports coverage, although the number of special interest sport magazines and "fanzines" in Canada and other countries is increasing.[4] A visit to a local magazine rack shows that magazines are devoted to information about skiing, skateboarding, snowboarding, biking, moto-cross, car racing, and dozens of other sports.

The media most dependent on sports for commercial success are newspapers and television. This is especially true in the United States.

Newspapers North Amercian newspapers at the beginning of the twentieth century had a sports page that consisted of a few notices about upcoming activities, a short story or two about races or university games, and possibly some scores of local games. Today, there are daily and weekly sports newspapers devoted exclusively to sports, and nearly all daily newspapers have sport sections making up about 25 percent of their content.

Major North American newspapers give more daily coverage to sports than any other single topic of interest, including business or politics. The sports section is the most widely read section of the paper. It accounts for at least one-third of the total circulation and a significant amount of the advertising revenues for big-city newspapers. It attracts advertisers who want to reach young to middle-aged males with ads for tires, automobile supplies, new cars, car leases, airline tickets for business travellers, alcoholic beverages, power tools, building supplies, sporting goods, hair growth products,

Viagra, testosterone, hormone therapies, and even escort services. Additionally, there are ads for bars or clubs providing naked or near-naked female models and dancers, all-night massage parlours, and organizations offering gambling advice and opportunities (see a sample of major-city newspapers to confirm this). Ads for all these products and services are unique to the (men's) sport section, and they generate considerable revenues for newspapers.

It is difficult to predict the future of newspapers' dependence on sports. As the Internet becomes a primary source of information about major sports nationally and worldwide, newspapers may focus mostly on local sports, including high school teams, university teams, and youth sports. This can already be seen as more major-city newspapers publish sections on a weekly basis that highlight local athletes. They know that if people in Regina use the Internet to read about the Roughriders, they will still have to buy the local newspaper to read about Campbell Collegiate's football team.

Television Some television companies in North America also have developed a dependence on sports for programming content and advertising revenues. For example, sport events are a major part of the programming schedules of national networks in Canada, and many cable and satellite-based channels. Some television companies even sponsor events or buy teams, which they then promote and televise (e.g., Rogers and the Blue Jays).

Sports account for a growing proportion of income made on the sales of commercial time by television companies. Many cable and satellite companies have used sport programmes to attract subscribers from particular segments of the viewing public, and then sell the audiences to advertisers for a profit. For example, when TSN first started selling commercial time to businesses, it sent out a flyer stating, "We Deliver the Male" (Sparks, 1992). People in Canada and some other parts of the world can watch sport

---

[4]Interestingly, in English-speaking countries, only the U.S. has been able to produce a long-term, successful, general-interest sports magazine: *Sports Illustrated.*

programmes nearly 24 hours a day, if they have the time, interest, cable/satellite hook-ups, and digital boxes.

Available in Canada via satellite hook-up, and through its partnership with TSN, is Disney-owned ESPN and its multiple networks. In 2005, ESPN showed 5,100 hours of live sports and 2,300 live or taped sport events watched by about 95 million people each week. Between ESPN, ESPN2, ESPNews, ESPN Classic, ESPN Deportes, ESPN HD, ESPN2 HD, ESPN Today, ESPNU, and ESPN International, people in 192 countries received sport information and event broadcasts in twelve languages. These networks provide content for ESPN.com, ESPN Radio, ESPN Deportes Radio, ESPN broadband, ESPN Mobile, ESPNDeportes. com, ESPNRadio.com, ESPNSoccernet.com, EXPN.com, *ESPN The Magazine*, *Bassmaster Magazine*, BASS Times, ESPN Books, ESPN Interactive, ESPN On Demand, and ESPN 360. All of these create consumer demand for products available at ESPN Zone, TeamStore@ ESPN, and Fishing Tackle and Retailer.

Both ESPN and Fox became major networks after they took a risk and spent massive amounts of money to buy the rights to cover NFL games in 1987 and 1993, respectively. Covering NFL games helped to put the networks on the map of major media companies. Today, Fox and other Fox networks (e.g., Sky Sports in Europe, Star TV in Asia) also televise a range of sports coverage around the world (Andrews, 2003). Canadian scholars, Alan Law, Jean Harvey, and Stuart Kemp, pointed out that, through a process of *convergence*, six major media-entertainment conglomerates own the rights to televise most of the world's sport events (since the merger of Disney and AOL Time Warner that is now reduced to five). Additionally, there are dozens of multimedia companies that broadcast sports (see table 12.1).

The convergence of media corporations—a series of vertical and horizontal mergers and acquisitions in the entertainment, news, sports, television, and Internet industries—means that approximately half a dozen media corporations control most of what we do and do not read, see, and hear in the media (McChesney, 1999). Of course, this has serious implications for the types of sports programmes we see and do not see, what we hear and do not hear in commentary, the sites we visit on the Internet, and the corporate messages that are presented in connection with athletes, teams, and sport places. More important, it has serious implications for the viability of democracy around the world.

An attractive feature of sport programmes for the major Canadian networks (CBC/SRC, CTV, TVA, and CanWest Global) is that events are often scheduled on Saturdays and Sundays—the slowest days of the week for general television viewing. Sport events are the most popular weekend television programmes, especially among male viewers who may not watch much television at other times. Therefore, networks are able to sell advertising time at relatively high rates during what normally would be dead time for programming.

Major networks regard sports as attractive programming because they can schedule them on weekend afternoons, usually a slow time for television viewing. Coverage of sports also attracts male viewers, and male viewers attract corporate advertisers for many products. [M. MacNeill]

Media corporations also use sport programmes to attract commercial sponsors that might take their advertising dollars elsewhere if television stations did not cover certain sports. For example, games in the major men's team sports are ideal for promoting the sales of beer, life insurance, trucks and cars, computers, investment services, credit cards, and air travel. The people in the advertising departments of major corporations realize that sports attract male viewers. They also realize that most business travellers are men and that many men make family decisions on the purchases of beer, cars, computers, investments, and life insurance. Finally, advertisers also may be interested in associating their product or service with the culturally positive image of sports. This is especially important for a product such as beer, which may be a target for groups such as MADD, or those with concerns about alcoholism or tobacco use, which are a frequent target of health advocates, among others.[5]

Golf and tennis are special cases for television programming. These sports attract few viewers, and the ratings are usually low. However, the audience for these sports is attractive to certain advertisers. It is made up of people from the highest income groups, including many professionals and business executives. This is why television coverage of golf and tennis is sponsored by companies selling luxury cars and high-priced sports cars, business and personal computers, imported beers, investment opportunities with brokers and consultants, and trips to exclusive vacation areas. This is also why the networks continue to carry these programmes despite low ratings. Advertisers are willing to pay high fees to reach high-income consumers and corporate executives who make decisions to buy thousands of "company cars" and computers at the same time that they invest millions of dollars for employee pension plans. With such valued viewers, these programmes do not need high ratings to stay on the air.

In the mid-1990s, television executives "discovered" women viewers of sports and women's sports. Data indicate that women have made up more than half the viewing audiences for both Winter and Summer Olympic Games since 1988. This led NBC to hype women's sports, appeal to female viewers during subsequent telecasts of the games, and led CBC to emphasize gender equity in all aspects of Olympic coverage.

Other women's sports also attract television coverage, although their coverage pales in comparison with the coverage of men's sports. Women's events do not receive more coverage partly because women viewers of women's games have not been identified as a target demographic by advertisers. Furthermore, men make up over half of the viewing audience for women's sports, and they also watch men's sports, so sponsors have already bought access to them when they advertise during men's events.

Specialty television channels attract advertising money by covering sports that appeal to other clearly identified segments of consumers. For example, the X Games attract young males between twelve and thirty years old, and this attracts corporate sponsors that sell soft drinks, beer, telecommunications products, and sport equipment such as helmets, shoes, skateboards, and dozens of other sport-specific products.

Over the past two decades, television companies have paid rapidly increasing amounts of money for the rights to televise certain sports. This is shown in the data in tables 12.2 and 12.3. The contracts for these rights are negotiated every few years. In the case of the major men's spectator sports in the United States and around the world, contracts may involve hundreds of millions of dollars, and more than a billion dollars for the Olympics, the NFL, the NBA, soccer's World Cup, and Premier League soccer in England.

---

[5]Although tobacco advertising is officially banned on Canadian television, and tobacco companies are no longer permitted to sponsor sports events, tobacco company logos still appear regularly on Canadian screens, especially in coverage of international auto races.

PROFESSIONAL SPORTS Table 12.2 shows the increase in fees paid by major media companies for the rights to broadcast major North American professional leagues. The leagues have recently signed new agreements, and the fees paid are a striking indication of the importance of covering these sports, and attracting the type of audiences they attract, for the financial health of the media corporations. For example, the NBA has negotiated an eight-year agreement with ESPN/ABC and TNT. From 2008–09 to 2015–16 the NBA will receive approximately US$930 million each year, a 20 percent increase over the previous contract despite declining TV ratings. Thus, the Toronto Raptors receive US$31 million each year as their share of this deal, before they sell any tickets or their Canadian media rights. As with many of the new agreements, the arrangement with the NBA includes extensive digital rights, including broadcasting games on the Web and mobile televisions (and including digital media that have not been invented yet). The NFL has the most lucrative media rights arrangements: contracts with Fox, CBS, NBC, ESPN, and DirecTV in the United States produce revenues of over US$3.7 billion each year.[6] This does not include foreign rights—for example, the agreement reached in 2007 with CTVglobemedia and Rogers is estimated to involve fees of C$10–15 million each year. And, unlike the other leagues, the NFL retains digital rights, having relaunched NFL.com in 2007. In comparison, MLB's media arrangements with ESPN, Fox, and TBS currently stand at US$670 million each year, although baseball teams also enjoy local media agreements for radio and television. In the case of the Toronto Blue Jays, Rogers Media owns both the team and the home stadium, and is able to sell broadcast rights to itself and to other media outlets across Canada, as well as enjoying its US$22.3 million share of the U.S. media rights each year.

[6]The current contracts for NFL media rights total more than the combined total of nine previous contracts dating back to 1962.

The two leagues of more interest to Canadians, the CFL[7] and the NHL, are in a rather different category when it comes to media rights. The cost of media rights are not usually announced in Canada, so the following figures are estimates. In 2007, TSN/RDS signed a five-year agreement with the CFL that is believed to be worth C$15 million each year. The deal includes new/digital media rights such as live Internet games, mobile phone, and video-on-demand; however, unlike the previous CBC contract, more than 10 percent of Canadians will not be able to see CFL games on television because of the more limited availability of TSN.

Unlike any of the other North American based leagues, the NHL is far more firmly established in, and dependent on Canadian media; and because of the declining popularity of hockey on U.S. television, the Canadian television deals keeps the league alive. A new six-year agreement with CBC, beginning in 2008–09, is believed to be worth $100 million each year—this includes Internet, video-on-demand, and mobile phone rights. TSN/RDS, which does not have as much access to games played by Canadian teams (other than the Montréal Canadiens), has also signed a six-year agreement beginning in 2008–09 for an estimated $30–40 million each year. Although the NHL Commissioner, Gary Bettman, has been desperate to maintain a U.S. network television deal, that has only been possible by entering a revenue- and expense-sharing agreement with NBC for 2006–08—that is, NBC and NHL share the expenses of broadcasting hockey, and NBC agrees to pay only a share of any profits that are made by televising NHL games. There is also a

[7]Despite a number of claims recently that Canadians are more interested in the NFL than the CFL, the evidence shows that they are incorrect. Reginald Bibby (2006), at the University of Lethbridge, has been polling Canadians about their interests for many years. In a 2006 poll, 19 percent of Canadians said they were fans of the CFL, compared to 13 percent who said they were fans of the NFL (the same as for MLB). This compares to 30 percent who are fans of the NHL.

Table 12.2 Escalating annual media rights fees for major commercial sports in North America (US$millions)[a]

Sport	1986	1991	1996	2001	2005	2008
NFL	400	900	1,100	2,200	2,200	3,735
MLB[b]	183	365	420	420	558	670
NBA	30	219	275	660	767	930
NHL[c]	22	38	77	120	120	210(est.)
CFL[d]	n/a	n/a	n/a	n/a	9(est.)	15(est.)

[a]These amounts are not inflation adjusted; past data are from *USA Today* and the *Globe and Mail*
[b]Amounts for baseball do not include local television or radio rights fees negotiated by individual teams, or national radio rights fees; amount for 1996 includes national radio rights, and amount for 2001 is an estimate
[c]Add C$60 million CBC rights fees for 2001 and 2005, and any revenue shared with NBC for 2008–09; Canadian rights only for 2008–09
[d]Canadian rights only

contract with Versus (formerly OLN) for 2005–08 that was worth approximately US$70 million each year. That agreement has been renewed for three years at approximately US$75 million per year; and NBC has just renewed its agreement for one year. The outdoor game played at Buffalo's Rich Stadium on New Year's Day, 2008, was one of the more successful recent hockey events on U.S. television; renewing the contract gives NBC a chance to show the 2009 outdoor game which, at this time, is scheduled to be the final event played at Yankee Stadium in New York before it is demolished. Renewal for a second year (2009–10) would also give NBC a chance to promote its Vancouver Olympics coverage.

OLYMPICS Table 12.3 illustrates the astonishing increase in media rights fees paid for the Olympics by Canadian broadcasters (CBC and/or CTV), the European Broadcasting Union, U.S. networks, and the total rights fees revenue received by the IOC. It is evident that U.S. media corporations pay far more than the rest of the world put together, a clear indication of the value of Olympic broadcasting in the U.S. market, not only in advertising, but also in the opportunity provided by the Summer Olympics to promote a network's Fall television schedule. Under the guidance of Canadian IOC member, Richard Pound, the IOC began to "bundle" its auctions for Olympic Games, beginning with NBC's extraordinary agreement to pay US$3.55 billion to broadcast five Olympic Games between 2000 and 2008. Media companies in other parts of the world had to bid on the 2006 Torino and the 2008 Beijing Olympics as a package.

All media corporations had to bid on the 2010 Vancouver and the 2012 London Olympics as a package even before London was announced as the site for 2012. The European Broadcasting Union (EBU), which is the umbrella organization for European radio and television corporations (both public and private, and both eastern and western Europe since 1993), negotiates Olympic rights fees for European countries with the IOC. Despite representing a significantly higher population than the U.S., the EBU has traditionally paid much lower rights fees—in part because many of the national broadcasters are public, but it has also been suggested that the EBU receives favourable consideration because so many of the IOC members are European. Despite this, the EBU fees have increased 6,800 percent in the last 32 years of Summer Olympics, compared to 3,600 percent for the U.S. fees and 2,500 percent for the Canadian fees. IOC revenue from media rights has also increased some 3,400 percent over the same period.

Table 12.3 Escalating media rights fees for the Olympics (in US$millions)[a]

Summer Olympics	Canada (CBC/CTV)	EBU[b]	U.S. network	IOC total
1976 Montréal	1.8	6.55	25.0	34.9
1980 Moscow	1.044	7.15	87.0	88.0
1984 Los Angeles	3.0	22.0	225.0	286.9
1988 Seoul	4.17	30.24	300.0	402.6
1992 Barcelona	16.5	94.5	401.0	636.1
1996 Atlanta	22.0	247.0	456.0	898.3
2000 Sydney	28.0	350.0	705.0	1,331.6
2004 Athens	37.0	394.0	793.0	1,494.0
2008 Beijing	45.0	443.4	894.0	1,737.0
2012 London	63.0	577.5[c](est.)	1,002.0	3,500.0 (est.)

Winter Olympics	Canada (CBC/CTV)	EBU	U.S. network	IOC total
1976 Innsbruck	0.36	1.2	10.0	11.6
1980 Lake Placid	0.907	3.855	15.5	20.7
1984 Sarajevo	1.8	5.6	91.5	102.7
1988 Calgary	3.4	6.9	309.0	324.9
1992 Albertville	10.1	20.3	243.0	291.9
1994 Lillehammer	12.0	26.3	300.0	352.9
1998 Nagano	17.0	72.0	375.0	513.5
2002 Salt Lake City	22.0	120.0	545.0	738.0
2006 Turin	28.0	135.0	613.0	831.0
2010 Vancouver	90.0	172.5[c](est.)	998.0	1,127.0 (est.)
2014 Sochi	n/a	n/a	n/a	n/a

[a]All but the most recent data are from the 2008 *Olympic Marketing Fact File*
[b]Combines EBU and eastern European broadcasters (OIRT); the two merged in 1993
[c]Because of bundling, separate EBU figures are not yet available for the Vancouver and London Olympics; these estimates are based on a total of US$750 million—the Summer and Winter estimates use the same ratio as 2006–08

A consortium of CTVglobemedia and Rogers outbid the CBC for the Vancouver and London Olympics by offering what is estimated to be almost three times more than the CBC bid for Vancouver. For the first time, a media group has paid more for the Winter Olympics than the Summer Olympics—a clear indication of the profits that are expected from broadcasting a domestic Olympics. Content will be spread over a large range of CTV and Rogers holdings: CTV, TQS, TSN, RDS, RIS, Rogers Sportsnet, OMNI Television, OLN, CTV Newsnet, Rogers radio stations, and third-party broadcasters APTN and ATN. Olympic related material may be on Discovery Channel, BNN, and The Biography Channel. CTV has recently bought CHUM, and Rogers has taken over CityTV, so even more broadcast sites are possible; although no arrangements have yet been made for French language broadcasts outside Québec.

The Olympics, and the men's World Cup of soccer are the biggest television events in human history; media corporations realize that, which is why the cost of advertising is generally much higher for *top* events than for other types of programmes. Sports involve minimal production costs in comparison to news and comedy/drama, and they have relatively predictable ratings. Thus, even though there have been cases where television companies have lost money on sports, profits are generally good and, as noted, sports programming can be used as a basis for promoting other programmes and for attracting hard-to-reach viewers.

Another trend is that, as televised sport events have increased, the ratings for many particular events have gone down. As people have more choices, the viewing audience becomes fragmented. More people are watching television sports, but there are more choices than ever before. This means that rights fees for the very large events will continue to increase, but fees for other events, including some "special interest" events (such as bowling, in-line skating championships, and international skiing races) will be limited. When interest among particular viewers is especially strong, pay-per-view (PPV) sports programming will push rights fees to high levels. Television companies know that PPV sports can generate massive revenues, but they also know that pay-per-view events must be introduced cautiously and selectively. Many viewers are not willing to pay up front to see an event on television; nor are they accustomed to doing so. In the meantime, pay-TV has become an accepted part of people's lives in the form of subscription fees for cable and satellite channels.

The fragmentation of television sports audiences seems likely to continue. New technology brings hundreds of channels into people's homes, many of which are sports specialty channels. As new digital television technology is sold to consumers around the world, television companies are using sport events strategically to encourage consumers to invest in the switch from their old analogue televisions to digital sets.

Regular sports programming provides opportunities for major television companies to promote their other programmes and boost ratings during the rest of the week. It also serves a public relations function, by enhancing the image and legitimacy of television among people who may watch very few programmes other than sports.

Sports and the Media: A Relationship Fuelled by Economics and Ideology

Commercial spectator sports depend heavily on the media, although noncommercial sports continue to exist and often thrive without media coverage. Similarly, some media companies that publish daily newspapers and produce television programmes in Canada depend on sports to generate circulation and viewer ratings.

When large corporations control the media, the interdependence of sports and the media revolves around revenue streams and profits. Sports generate identifiable audiences that can be sold to capitalists seeking consumers for products and services. In turn, the media generate revenues for sport organizations and create sport-related images, which can be sold in connection with everything from coffee mugs and credit cards to shoes and soccer balls.

Since the 1970s, global economic factors have intensified the interdependency between commercial sports and the media. Major transnational corporations needed vehicles to develop global name recognition, cultural legitimacy, and product familiarity. They also want to promote ideologies that support a way of life based on consumption, competition, and individual achievement. Media sports offer global corporations a means of meeting these needs. Certain sport events attract worldwide attention; satellite technology takes television signals around the world; sport images are associated with recognizable symbols and pleasurable experiences by billions of people; sports and athletes can be presented in politically safe ways by linking them with local identities and then using them to market products, values, and lifestyles that are related to local cultures or popular forms of global culture. Therefore, powerful transnational corporations now spend billions of dollars annually to sponsor the media coverage of sports, especially on television (it will be the Internet in the future). This in turn gives global media companies significant power over sports worldwide (see figure 12.2).

FIGURE 12.2 A few powerful global media companies control most of the media representations of sports worldwide. This has serious implications for what sports we see or do not see, especially in developing nations. Some people wonder what this will mean in the long run, whereas others do not give it much thought as they watch what the media re-present.

An important source of corporate sponsorship money for sports comes from the alcohol and tobacco industries. For them, the sports media are key vehicles for presenting and promoting their products in connection with activities defined as healthy by most people around the world. This enables them to present positive corporate and brand images which they hope will counteract negative images about their products. We find these images most frequently in print media and stadium signage. They regularly appear in the prime advertising space of sports magazines and on the surfaces of stadiums and other facilities that host car and horse races. Following the ban on tobacco advertising on television in Canada, tobacco companies turned their efforts to sponsoring tennis, golf, show jumping, and auto racing events. Data from Physicians for a Smoke-Free Canada indicate the success of this strategy: the tobacco logo often appeared on-screen for far more time than the total of paid advertising time; for example, during the du Maurier men's tennis finals in 1998, the paid advertising time was over 27 minutes, and the du Maurier logo was on-screen for a total of 34 minutes (www.smoke-free.ca/filtertips02/Television.htm). Bill C-71, the Tobacco Act passed in 1997, has generally phased out this type of sponsorship.

It is clear that the marriage of sports and the media has been held together and strengthened by the vast amounts of money coming from corporations whose executives see sports as tools for promoting profits and ideologies consistent with their interests. When profits are low, their shared interest in promoting ideologies supportive of general capitalist expansion keeps the partners together.

IMAGES AND NARRATIVES IN MEDIA SPORTS

To say that sports are "mediated" is to say that they are re-presented to readers, listeners, and viewers through selected images and/or narratives. A growing number of people who study sports in society do research that involves digging into these selected images and narratives to identify the ideas or themes on which they are based. They assume that media sports are symbolic constructions, much like action films, television soap operas, and cartoons (Andrews and Jackson, 2001; Crawford, 2004; McCullagh, 2002; Rowe, 2004a, 2004b; Wenner, 1998; Whannel, 2002).

To say that a telecast of a Canadian football game is a symbolic construction means that it represents the ideas that certain people have about football, values, social life, and their relationships with the viewing audience. Although each of us interprets media images and narratives in different ways, many people use mediated sports as reference points as they form, revise, and extend their ideas about sports, social life, and social relations.

Because media sports are part of everyday experience in today's societies, it is important to consider the following questions:

1. How are sports constructed in and through the media?
2. What ideological themes underlie the images and narratives represented in media sports?
3. Do reading about, listening to, and viewing sports have an effect on our choies and actions in our everyday lines.

How Do the Media Construct Sports?

When media are privately owned and organized to make financial profits, sports are selected for coverage on the basis of their entertainment value and revenue-generating potential. Media images and narratives are presented to provide as much of the event as possible and to fit the perceived interests of the audience and the sponsors. Sports that are difficult to cover profitably usually are ignored by the media, or they are covered only with selected highlights emphasizing spectacular and heroic injuries or achievements.

Sports magazines and the sports sections of newspapers provide scores, statistics, accounts of big plays and individual heroics, and behind-the-scenes stories; they use photos to depict action. Television coverage focuses on the ball (puck, etc.) and individual athletes, especially those who are currently winning the game, match, meet, or race. Television announcers provide narratives designed to entertain a mass audience. The major differences in how print and broadcast media construct sports are summarized in table 12.4.

Sports media generally present images and narratives that "hype" sports by exaggerating the spectacular, inventing and focusing on rivalries, and manufacturing reasons that events are important. Furthermore, they strive to create and maintain the celebrity status of athletes and teams. Cultural studies scholar Garry Crawford explains the strategy used in this process:

> The mass media construction of celebrity often lacks depth of character, as figures are frequently painted in one-dimensional terms…. Much of the language used to describe sports stars…draws on the narrative of melodrama. Heroes rise and fall,

Table 12.4 Differences between newspaper/magazine and radio/television coverage of sports

Newspaper/Magazine coverage	Commercial Radio/Television coverage
• Emphasizes information and interpretation	• Emphasizes entertainment
• Offers previews and summaries of past events	• Offers play-by-play images and narratives
• Provides written representations of events	• Provides real-time representations of events
• Success depends of credibility	• Success depends on hype and visual action
• Highlights facts and dominant ideology	• Highlights heroic plays and dominant ideology
• Most likely to provide criticism of sports and sport personalities	• Most likely to provide support for sports and sport personalities

Source: Based on material in Koppett, 1994.

Breaking Barriers

Image and Narrative Barriers
From a Special Interest Story to a Sports Story

Athletes with a disability receive little or no media coverage. The Paralympics, for example, are televised or covered in newspapers in Canada in limited ways. But the Paralympics occur only once every four years. World Championships and other major events receive no mainstream-media coverage. Most people who make decisions about media coverage do not take disability sports seriously because the events would receive low audience ratings and therefore, would not attract sponsors. The traditional belief is that covering athletes with a disability is a poor commercial risk. Additionally, most media people have never interacted or played sports with people who have disabilities, so they lack the words and experiences that would enable them to provide the kind of coverage that might build a media audience.

Research shows that when coverage does occur in the mainstream media, athletes with a disability often are portrayed in one of two ways: as "poster people" deserving pity for their impairments or as "supercrips" who have heroically overcome disabilities (Brittain, 2004). A closer look at media images and narratives indicates that representations often fall into one of the following categories:

Patronizing: *"Aren't they marvellous!"*
Curiosity: *"Do you think she can really do that?"*
Tragedy: *"On that fateful day, his life was changed forever."*
Inspiration: *"She's a true hero and a model for all of us."*

Mystification: *"I can't believe he just did that!"*
Pity: *"Give her a hand for trying so hard."*
Surprise: *"Stay tuned to see physical feats you've never imagined!"*

Images and narratives organized around these themes construct disability in terms of a medical model—focused on personal deficiencies that must be overcome by individuals [see Breaking Barriers, pp. 44–45, chapter 2]. This ignores issues about why particular social meanings are given to disabilities and how those meanings cause many of the problems faced by people with particular impairments (Brittain, 2004; Smith and Thomas, 2005). Consequently, the coverage does little to challenge the widespread belief that disabilities are abnormalities and that people with disabilities have one-dimensional identities.

Despite misguided representations in the media, most athletes with a disability would choose distorted coverage rather than no coverage at all. They want to be acknowledged and reaffirmed for their athletic competence and hope that becoming visible through the media will weaken and break down stereotypes. Visibility gives them an opportunity to challenge traditional medical discourse about disability and make people aware of the need for maximizing access and inclusion in all spheres of society.

Developing a media audience, says Jil Gravink, begins at the local, recreational level. Gravink is the founder and director of Northeast Passage, an organization that develops community-based programmes to increase the relevance of disability

Continued

villains are defeated, and women play out their roles as supporting cast members to men's central dramatic roles. (2004, p. 133)

Even the villains can be redeemed when they demonstrate that they are heroic warriors and commentators reframe them as "loyal blue collar players"—"willing to take figurative bullets for their teammates"—and "always being there when the chips are down."

Mark Lowes (1999), of the University of Ottawa, points out that they also emphasize elite sport competition. For example, Canadian newspapers and commercial television (since the 1950s) have increased their coverage of professional sports and decreased coverage of amateur sports. This shift has been accompanied by a growing emphasis on the importance of winning and heroic actions instead of

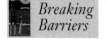

Breaking Barriers

Image and Narrative Barriers
continued

This wheelchair basketball programme is similar to many local sports programs for people with a disability. It brings together people with particular disabilities. This is important for developing skills, self-confidence, and establishing relationships with others. When programmes also foster the full inclusion of people with disabilities into the general community, they break down stereotypes and disability sports "move from a special interest story to a sport story." [Rodolfo Gonzalez, *Rocky Mountain News*]

sports among people with disabilities and among the general population. The programmes provide opportunities for people with a disability and able-bodied people to interact, play sports, and identify one another in terms of multiple characteristics and abilities.

Gravink explains that only when average people with disabilities play sports and become fully integrated into the community can disability sports "move from a special interest story to a sport story" (in Joukowsky and Rothstein, 2002a, p. 98). Then poster people and supercrips will be exposed for the myths they are.

• •

other factors associated with sports and sport participation. The result is that media audiences consume carefully selected and edited versions of sports. These versions represent what corporate sponsors will fund with their advertising money and what media people think audiences want to consume. Representations are constructed to gain the support of corporate sponsors and people in a mass audience.

There is very little research on this process, and what is available was carried out mainly by Canadian researchers. The type of research is known as **production ethnographies**— researchers carry out *detailed observations of the actual production process of sport broadcasts, at production meetings, control centres, editing suites, and commentary positions, taking detailed notes and conducting informal interviews during quiet moments.*

The first of these was carried out by Rick Gruneau, who is now in the Department of Communications at Simon Fraser University. He studied the production, by CBC television, of a World Cup ski competition at Whistler (Gruneau, 1989), discovering in particular how broadcasters establish the "storyline" even before the event takes place. This was followed by Margaret MacNeill's (University of Toronto) research on the CTV host broadcaster production of (men's) hockey at the 1988 Calgary Olympics (MacNeill, 1996), which focused on the ways in which the broadcaster produced different ideas of nationality for the various teams competing in the tournament. MacNeill is continuing this type of research in an extensive study (along with Graham Knight of McMaster University and Peter Donnelly) of the ways in which the CBC/SRC produced ideas of Canadian identity at the 2000 Sydney Olympics. Outside Canada, Silk and Amis (2000) conducted a production ethnography of coverage of the 1998 Common-wealth Games in Kuala Lumpur.

It is important to study this "production process" because popular ideas about sports are heavily informed by the images and narratives represented in media sports. Furthermore, the themes underlying these images and messages influence our ideas about social relations and social life in general. This is discussed in the Breaking Barriers box on pages 397–398.

What Ideological Themes Underlie Media Images and Narratives?

Reality is so complex that it cannot be represented in the media without selecting particular images and narratives from a vast array of possibilities (Knoppers and Elling, 2004). The traditional media are somewhat like windows through which we view what others choose to put in our range of sight and hear what others choose to say to us. Therefore, the only way that we can avoid being duped is to be critical media consumers. In most cases, this means learning to identify the ideologies that guide others as they construct media representations for us. In the case of sports, the most central ideologies that influence what we see and hear are those related to success, gender, race and ethnicity, nationalism, individualism, teamwork, aggression, and consumption.

Success Ideology Media coverage of sports in Canada and the U.S. emphasizes success through competition, hard work, assertiveness, domination over others, obedience to authority, and big plays such as home runs, long touchdown passes, and single-handed goals. The idea that success can be based on empathy, support for others, sharing of resources, autonomy, intrinsic satisfaction, personal growth, compromise, incremental changes, or the achievement of equality is not usually incorporated into narratives or images selected for commentary.

Media representations of sports usually exaggerate the importance of competitive rivalries as well as winning and losing in athletes' lives. For example, media coverage of a sport such as snowboarding is organized around the competitive quest for medals when, in fact, many of the athletes and the spectators at the events are not very concerned about competition or medals (Florey, 1998; Honea, 2005).

The athletes enjoy the external rewards that come with winning and they certainly want to demonstrate their competence, but they also emphasize expression and creativity as more important than scores and competitive outcomes. Furthermore, their friendships with other competitors are more important than media-hyped rivalries. However, media coverage highlights competitive success because it is valued in the culture as a whole, and it is easy to use to attract sponsors and consumers.

The success ideology underlying images and narratives in U.S. media sports is more apparent than in media sports in other cultures (see the Reflect on Sports box, "Sydney 2000: The Disappointment Games," pp. 404–405). Narratives in the United States focus on winners, losers, and final scores. Even silver and bronze medals are inferred to be consolation prizes at best; and games for third place in tournaments are now often not played much less covered by the media.

Sportswriters and announcers focus on "shoot-outs" and sudden death play-offs instead of ties, they define *success* in terms of dominating others, and they praise those who make big plays or big hits. Rare are references to learning, enjoyment, and competing *with* others, even when players see their participation in these terms, and many do. Thus, the media do not "tell it like it is" as much as they tell it like people interested in productivity in the form of competitive success want to see and hear it.

This ideological bias does not mean that most people do not enjoy media sports. Enjoyment is central, and it drives media sport consumption. However, there are many ways to enjoy sports, and the media highlight the ways that fit popular and corporate interests simultaneously. Discovering other ways to enjoy sports is left to individuals and groups, who are curious enough to seek alternatives to commercialized media sports.

Gender Ideology During the first round of the 2008 Stanley Cup play-offs, Montréal Canadiens centre Tomas Plekanec had a couple of bad games. He told the media, "The last two games, I played like a girl out there." Such blatant dismissals of female athletes are commonly heard, but they rarely make it to the media these days. However, relegating girls' and women's sports to second- or third-rate status is still common in the media. The sports reporter for Canada's national newspaper not only failed to comment critically on the derogatory similie, he also gave Plekanec credit for knowing that "the problem with his play has been that he has been soft against the hard-checking Bruins" (Wharnsby, 2008, p. S3).

Masculinity dominates media sports. Men's sports typically receive about 90 percent of the coverage in all media, and the images and narratives tend to reproduce traditional ideas and beliefs about gender (Duncan and Messner, 2005). For example, after buying the rights to broadcast NHL games in the U.S. (2005–08), the vice-president of programming for Versus claimed that they were a "very male-oriented network" and they wanted to emphasize competition by showing sports that involved "man versus man, man versus nature, man versus beast" (in Bechtel and Cannella, 2005, p. 17). Coverage of female sports is characterized quantitatively by its *underrepresentation* and *marginalization*, and qualitatively by its *sexualization* and *trivialization*.

UNDERREPRESENTATION AND MARGINALIZATION
Coverage of women's sports is not a priority in the media, except for the Olympics, figure skating events, major golf and tennis tournaments, and sometimes hockey and soccer world championships. Overall, the coverage of women's sports in major newspapers has increased since the mid-1990s, but it remains significantly *underrepresented* at less than 15 percent of the sports section. Women's sport and female athletes are *marginalized* in that coverage is rarely given prominence in the media. Women's sports are often presented at less popular times in broadcast media or less prominent locations in print media, and they receive less coverage than men's sports—less time, less space, fewer reporters, lower staff and production budgets, and so on.

This pattern of underrepresentation of women's sports in the media exists around the world. For example, the current *Global Women in Sports Media Project*, led by Toni Bruce (New Zealand), Jorid Hovden (Norway), and Pirkko Markula (University of Alberta), is carrying out a comparison in 28 countries of newspapers and their representations of gender; the preliminary findings confirm the pattern of underrepresentation and marginalization. Another example indicates the remarkable persistence of these findings. The Canadian Association for the Advancement of Women in Sport and Physical Activity (CAAWS, 1997), expected that there would be an increase in coverage of women's sports during the 1994 men's professional baseball strike and ice hockey lock-out (when newspapers would presumably be seeking additional sources of sports content); they found that coverage of women's sports actually declined in 13 of 20 Canadian newspapers surveyed in comparison to the same period in the previous year. And projects carried out annually by students at Acadia University and the University of Toronto, find consistent (although slowly improving) underrepresentation and trivialization of female athletes and women's sports in Canadian print and electronic media.

Women's sports are televised more than they were in the early 1990s, especially on certain specialty channels. But the proportion of coverage given to women's sports remains at about 15 percent of all television sports programming. The women's sports covered regularly are tennis, gymnastics, figure skating, golf, and curling. These are traditionally seen as sports emphasizing grace, balance, and aesthetic attributes, all of which are consistent with traditional images of femininity. Individual sports are usually given priority over team sports in television coverage (Tuggle and Owen, 1999), and women's figure skating and tennis are the most frequently televised women's sports events. In contrast, the men's sports most often covered emphasize bulk, height, physical strength, and the use of physical force to dominate opponents—all qualities consistent with traditional images of masculinity. Thus, hockey is the most popular televised sport in Canada, and coverage usually emphasizes traditional notions of masculinity.

SEXUALIZATION AND TRIVIALIZATION Using qualitative methodologies, researchers have consistently shown that media coverage of women's sports differs qualitatively from that of men's sports: women athletes are frequently *sexualized*, and their participation and the sports themselves are frequently *trivialized*. Coverage of women's sports through the 1980s and most of the 1990s contained commentaries that often highlighted the personal characteristics of the athletes such as their attractiveness, their spouses and children, their domestic interests and skills, and their vulnerabilities and weaknesses.

Television commentators for women's sports have in the past referred to female athletes by their first names, and as "girls" or "ladies." Commentators for men's sports seldom refer to male athletes by their first names, unless they are black, and almost never call them "boys" or "gentlemen." It is apparently assumed that playing sports turns boys into men (but not "gentlemen"), while it may turn girls into "ladies." Similarly, references to physical strength have been much more common in commentaries about male athletes although women clearly demonstrate strength and power, even in sports such as figure skating, golf, and tennis (commentaries on the Williams' sisters in tennis represent one of the few exceptions to this finding). And men's sports often are promoted or described as if they had special historical importance, while women's sports events usually are promoted in a less dramatic manner. Men's events usually are unmarked by references to gender and represented as *the* events, while women's events almost always are referred to as *women's* events. A summary of these consistent findings on the sexualization and trivialization of female athletes and women's sports is presented in table 12.5.

MAKING CHANGES There is a clear relationship between the quantity and quality of coverage—less coverage of women's sports can be taken to mean that those sports are less important which, in a circular logic, legitimizes less coverage; but sadly, and in a rather crude way, it may also legitimize in the minds of some men and women the sexualization and trivialization of female athletes and women's sports. However, there are important reasons for keeping them separate in ongoing strategies to change the quantity and the quality of coverage of female athletes and women's sports. Following a sustained period of research and criticism by sociologists of sport and media studies scholars, and by women's sports organizations such as CAAWS and the International Working Group on Women and Sport, there are evident changes since the mid-1990s in the quantity of coverage of certain sports, and even moreso in the quality of coverage of female athletes and women's sports.

However, it is still possible to find many of the characteristics of coverage outlined in table 12.5, and Wensing and Bruce (2003) (following Duncan and Hasbrook, 1988) characterize the recent quality of coverage as ambivalence—"positive images and descriptions of women athletes are juxtaposed with descriptions and images that undermine and trivialize women's efforts and successes" (p. 388). The quality of coverage is far more vulnerable to challenge than the quantity of coverage. Sports media departments have already demonstrated the capacity to change the culture/quality of their coverage with regard to issues of race and ethnicity, and they are aware of critiques of the quality of their coverage. They may not take it very seriously, but there is evidence of increased production quality in coverage of women's sports, and a (slight) decline in the sexualization/trivialization of women athletes and women's sports. The introduction of gender equity policies, and training for CBC television staff at the 2000 Sydney Olympics shows that quality of coverage is not an overwhelmingly difficult issue to resolve (Donnelly, 2004).

The quantity of coverage is a far more difficult issue to resolve. Calls for equal space/time, or even proportional space/time, devoted to coverage of women's sports and female athletes in the media are unrealistic given the preponderance of male professional team sports and their entrenched and profitable relationship with mass media. Media corporations are unlikely to jeopardize this lucrative relationship by cutting men's sport coverage to increase women's sport coverage, and they see little profit in adding additional pages or time to cover women's sports.

However, the effects of critical research and advocacy have been quite dramatic at some levels of sport, increasing the coverage of women's sports and female athletes particularly at the Olympics. When these successes are combined with the growing recognition that Olympic medals and world championships have no gender, it makes sense to strategically target levels of sport and forms of sport (like-with-like—where the events and the rewards are similar) where inequitable coverage is clearly inappropriate. Coverage of interschool sports, campus media, and television contracts for university sports coverage entered into by organizations such as Canadian Interuniversity Sport (CIS) are all potential targets for equity challenges regarding the quantity of coverage.

ERASING HOMOSEXUALITY Homosexuality is ignored in nearly all media coverage, while heterosexuality is regularly acknowledged directly and indirectly among men and women in sports. Heterosexual female athletes are constantly shown with husbands, children, fiancés, boyfriends, and dates; heterosexual men are shown with wives in various media features. Their heterosexuality is so widely taken for granted (sometimes referred to as *compulsory heterosexuality*) that it is mentioned only in passing. Gay athletes are not erased as much as they are assumed not to exist. Lesbian images, however, are carefully erased from coverage, even though the partners of players and coaches are known and visible to many spectators (Collins, 2004). Lesbian relationships are ignored for fear of offending media audiences.

Lesbian athletes in golf, tennis, and basketball are rarely profiled in ways that acknowledge partners or certain aspects of their lifestyles—those parts of their personal stories are not told. In media-constructed sport reality, lesbians and

Table 12.5 Research findings indicating the ways in which media coverage has sexualized female athletes and trivialized women's sports[a]

Gender marking:	Asymmetrical references to the gender of female athletes and women's sports—for example, referring to males as "athletes," and to men's events without reference to gender (e.g., the World Cup) while using the qualifier "*women* athletes," and *Women's* World Cup
Compulsory heterosexuality:	Sports coverage based in the assumption that female (and male) athletes are heterosexual, that portrays them as objects of (heterosexual) attraction, and that shows them in presumably heterosexual roles such as "mother" or "girlfriend"
Emphasizing appropriate femininity:	Sports coverage that focuses on stereotypically "feminine physical and emotional characteristics or behaviours"
Infantilization of women:	Asymmetrical references to female athletes as *girls*, or use of their first name—when similar age male athletes are not referred to as *boys*, and are referred to by their last name or whole name
Non-sport related aspects:	Asymmetrical sports coverage that focuses on female athletes' hobbies and interests, "appearance, family relationships, personal life, and personality"
Comparisons with men's performances:	Coverage of women's sports that includes comparisons (sometimes unfavourable) to men's performances in those sports, or more patronizing references to women's *style of play* (e.g., basketball, and ice hockey)
Photographic representations:	The *active portrayal* of male athletes vs. the *passive portrayal* of female athletes in sports photographs; and the sexual portrayal of female athletes (e.g., low angle shots in tennis or figure skating) or in "model" poses
Attribution of error:	Asymmetrical attributions of female error to *emotional difficulty* or *nervousness*, while male errors are more likely to be attributed to injury, or unfortunate circumstances

[a]The first five are drawn from a summary by Wensing and Bruce (2003, pp. 387–8); the remainder are summarized from the research literature

gay men in sports generally are invisible unless they publicly come "out" as gay. Even then, they are marginalized in coverage. As media studies scholar Pam Creedon notes, "Homosexuality doesn't sell" (1998, p. 96). Meanwhile, heterosexual athletes and their partners are discussed and pictured regularly, and nobody accuses these heterosexual athletes of pushing their values and agendas on others. Living in a heterosexual-dominated culture is especially difficult for female coaches and players who would like to acknowledge the support that they have received from long-time partners. Their partners, instead of sharing the moment in public like heterosexual spouses often do, sit in the stands or at home wondering if their very existence could jeopardize their partners' careers. Completely unknown are the men who discreetly watch their male partners win Stanley Cups and Grey Cups.

MEDIA ORGANIZATIONS ARE GENDERED The patterns associated with gender have been slow to change partly because sports media organizations in all societies are "gendered institutions" (Creedon, 1998). They have been structured and scheduled around men's sports. The work routines and assignments of sport reporters have been established around the coverage of men's events to such an extent that covering women's sports requires changes in institutionalized patterns of sports media work. Furthermore, the *vast* majority of sports media personnel are men, and the highest-status assignments in sports media are those that deal with men's sports.

REFLECT ON SPORTS

Sydney 2000: The Disappointment Games?

The 2000 Summer Olympics are quickly becoming the Disappointment Games for Canada.

—*Ottawa Citizen*, September 20, 2000

The *success* theme is evident to a lesser extent in Canada, where it also has its corollary—the *disappointment* theme (Knight et al., 2005). This theme is produced in the media when the performances of Canadian athletes at international events do not meet the predicted and hyped expectations. After only six days of Olympic competition, and despite an unexpected gold medal in the men's triathlon, the Canadian media began to characterize the Sydney Games as a failure for both Canada and Canadian athletes. Disappointment emerged in a relatively uniform and decisive way as the dominant theme in media coverage, and it persisted long after the Games ended. The theme emerged primarily in response to losses by four athletes—two swimmers, a kayaker, and a track cyclist—who had all been identified as medal prospects.

Predicting which athletes will win medals is standard media practice. However, it sets up expectations not only for athletes but also for the media themselves, whose credibility is put at stake. As a result, the media often interpret specific individual losses as a broader and more abstract issue or problem; in this case, disappointing results by the Canadian team and for Canada as a whole.

As opposed to failure, which is relatively objective (you win or you lose), disappointment is related emotionally to more subjective expectations and aspirations. Disappointment reflects the way that an event such as the Olympics joins individual athletic identities with collective national identities. So when an athlete who was expected to win fails to win, that is a problem for the athlete; but when we (and the media) have invested our emotions in success, disappointment extends to us, and increases the scope for allocating responsibility and blame.

The "Disappointment Games" story developed along a chain of blame and responsibility. This began with the athletes whose losses defined the theme's emergence. In media interviews, three of the four athletes assumed responsibility for their poor results. This allowed the media to absolve them personally, and to extend the chain of blame elsewhere. They had played their part by accepting personal responsibility for failure, and the media was free to seek other causes for its, and our, disappointment.

Continued

Even female reporters and announcers know that their upward mobility in the sports media industry demands that they cover men's events in much the same ways that men cover them. If they insist on covering only women's events, or if they are assigned only to women's events, they will not advance up the corporate ladder in media organizations (Coventry, 2004). Advancement also may be limited if they insist on covering men's sports in new ways that do not reaffirm the "correctness" of the coverage patterns and styles developed by men. Although women in the print media regularly cover men's sports, few women ever have provided regular commentary for men's sports in the electronic media.

Female reporters who cover men's sports are more readily accepted in the locker rooms of men's teams than they were in the past, although male athletes and coaches have been very protective of this "masculinized space." Changes have occurred partly because men have discovered ways to maintain privacy, such as wearing a robe, and having designated interview

Several possible explanations were examined including coaching and cycles of sport success and failure. However, what emerged as the principal explanation—initiated by voices in the sport community—was the lack of administrative support and the lack of sufficient government funding to win medals in the increasingly competitive world of international sports. Comparisons were continually made with Australia, which had made a major financial investment in achieving Olympic success. Analysts estimated that each of Australia's 16 gold medals cost C\$20 million just on spending in the year before the Olympics—approximately five times Sport Canada's budget for that time.

In a striking parallel, New Zealand media also developed a disappointment theme, with exactly the opposite interpretation. New Zealand had also invested heavily in athlete development, and failure was interpreted in terms of a "sporting nation" that had gone soft from losing sight of its traditional values; the athletes had been spoiled by too much economic support!

Given the size of its population, and the fact that it sends full teams to both Summer and Winter Olympic Games, Canada is quite a successful Olympic nation.

Polls of the Canadian public showed that they were satisfied with athlete performances in Sydney, and that they believed more money should be invested in grassroots sports rather than high-performance sports. Many Canadian high-performance athletes are financially distressed, and many of them believe the high-performance sport system in Canada is seriously underfunded. We think that the *disappointment* theme is another version of the success theme; individuals take the blame for their performances, they promise to work harder, and we are encouraged to invest more in their training.[1] In fact, major new high-performance funding programmes have now been introduced: "Own the Podium" in the lead up to the 2010 Vancouver Olympics; and "Road to Excellence" leading to the 2012 London Olympics. We also think that funding decisions should consider all aspects of sports. They should not be made in the light of media-generated stories of disappointment. *What do you think?*

---

[1]It is interesting to note that many of the media sources advocating greater public investment in Canada's high-performance athletes had spent the previous decade calling for more and more cuts to taxes and government expenditures.

....

times—just as female athletes have always done when male reporters cover their events. However, it took the men nearly two decades to think of wearing a robe, because deeply rooted gender ideology often impedes the ability to think creatively.

When it comes to issues of masculinity, most sports coverage uses images and narratives that reproduce dominant ideas about manhood. Most television sports are presented as soap operas for men. The vocabularies and storylines construct a symbolic male community that draws meaning from the culture of big-time men's spectator

sports and allows men to apply those meanings to themselves in ways that women spectators cannot do, even if they are dedicated fans.

The sports coverage most often consumed by boys in the United States depicts aggression and violence as normal and exciting, portrays athletes who play in pain as heroes, uses military metaphors and terminology, and highlights conflict between individuals and teams (Messner et al., 1999). Women are seldom seen except when portrayed as sex objects, cheerleaders, spectators, and supportive spouses and mothers on the sidelines.

Hockey is the most popular televised sport in Canada. The coverage of hockey tends to reflect the traditional gender values that are important to many people in the culture. On the "Coach's Corner" segment of the CBC's *Hockey Night in Canada*, Don Cherry (right) presents a stereotypical form of masculinity. [CP(Phil Snell), *Maclean's*]

Overall, gender ideology informs media representations of sports. However, it is important to note that few of us accept media representations at face value. We make sense of representations in our own terms. When we have special knowledge or personal connections with a sport or the athletes involved, we often give our own meanings to media representations, even if we are not critical in our assessments of them (Bruce, 2007; van Sterkenburg and Knoppers, 2004).

Racial and Ethnic Ideology Just as gender ideology influences media coverage, so does racial and ethnic ideology and the stereotypes associated with it (Davis and Harris, 1998; van Sterkenburg and Knoppers, 2004). For example, Lou Marsh—the well-known *Toronto Star* sportswriter who gave his name to the Canadian Athlete of the Year Award—once showed the generic banality of racism by describing the Six Nations long-distance runner Tom Longboat

as "smiling like a coon in a watermelon patch." Ideology and stereotypes changed during the second half of the twentieth century, and white announcers commonly described black athletes as having natural abilities, good instincts, unique physical attributes, and tendencies to be undisciplined players. At the same time they described white athletes as hard-working, intelligent, highly disciplined, and driven by character rather than instincts (Davis and Harris, 1998).

Research in the 1970s and 1980s discredited the assumed factual basis of racial and ethnic stereotypes at the same time that media studies identified the ways that ideology influenced sport stories and commentaries, particularly in reference to black athletes. This made journalists and commentators increasingly aware of the need to avoid words, phrases, and inferences based on stereotypical ideas and beliefs (Sabo et al., 1998). People in the print media chose their words more carefully, and broadcasters doing live commentary on talk radio and during games became sensitive to the racial implications of what they said. But making these changes was difficult for media people who accepted dominant racial ideology and never viewed it critically or from the perspectives of blacks, Latinos, Asian Canadians, and Native Canadians. Therefore, some made mistakes and a few were fired for them in the U.S., or sanctioned for them in Canada (e.g., Don Cherry's anti-francophone and anti-European comments).

Avoiding stereotypes and covering racial and ethnic relations in an informed way are two different things. Sports coverage today pretends that race and ethnicity do not exist; it is assumed that everyone in sport faces the same challenges and odds for success. But in actuality, race and ethnicity influence experiences and perspectives to such an extent that people cannot talk about them without discovering real, meaningful, and socially important racial and ethnic differences in what they think and feel. Ignoring this story about real differences allows whites in the media and media audience to be comfortably colour-blind and deny the legacy and continuing relevance of skin colour and cultural heritage in Canadian society and in sports. At the same time, blacks, Latinos, Asian Canadians, and Native Canadians are reminded that acceptance in the dominant culture requires them to "be like whites" in how they think, talk, and act. They understand that to be embraced by the media and white fans they should smile in accommodating ways on camera and during interviews (Davis and Harris, 1998). But they also admire athletes who express their racial or ethnic identities and "don't forget where they came from." This creates tension for ethnic minority athletes and coaches, and unique social dynamics in sports where players are racially and ethnically mixed. This is a newsworthy story, but it would make many people, especially white sports fans, uncomfortable, and it would be difficult for most journalists to tell. But as long as it remains untold, white privilege in sports will persist without being recognized, and anyone who does talk about it will be accused of "playing the race card."

IDEOLOGY AND OVERLOOKING WHITENESS Media coverage unwittingly reaffirms dominant racial ideology when whiteness is overlooked. This is best illustrated with an example unrelated to sports. When two young men killed twelve students and a teacher at Columbine High School in the U.S. in 1999, people in the media overlooked the whiteness of the killers, even though shooters in vast the majority of U.S. and Canadian schools, colleges, and universities in the last 20 years were white males. The exceptions (e.g., Dawson College, and Virginia Tech University) prove the rule since the ethnic minority status of the perpetrators did become an issue. Whiteness was never an issue in the coverage of white perpetrators because it is overlooked in a white-centred culture to the point that people do not even "see" it. Therefore, people did not make generalizations about the problem of violence among white male teens, and nobody talked about crossing the street to avoid a white male teen on the sidewalk. However, if the two killers at Columbine had been ethnic minority individuals, the coverage and audience responses would have made race or ethnicity *the* issue, and all other factors would have been given lower priority. This is how ideology influences coverage and stifles critical questions about the accuracy of media representations of reality.

When media ignore the dynamics of living in a white-dominated, white-identified, and white-centred culture, they unwittingly reproduce racial and ethnic stereotypes. Pretending to be colour-blind in a culture where a skin colour-based racial ideology exists is a sure way to guarantee that white privilege is seamlessly incorporated into the media coverage of sports. It allows the sports media to avoid asking why nearly all sports at the high school, university, and professional level are exclusively white, even when they live in communities where there are numerous high school and university teams in swimming, volleyball, softball, tennis, golf, soccer, lacrosse, rowing, gymnastics, wrestling, and many other sports that are predominantly white. And when a journalist does have the temerity to raise the issue—as Geoff Baker did in the *Toronto Star* in the summer of 2003[9]—he was met with controversy, reader outrage, and more negative correspondence than the *Star* had ever received on any issue. Therefore, journalists rarely ask questions about issues of residential segregation, and issues of income and wealth inequality that deeply influence who plays what sports in North America today. When they play golf at their clubs they may not wonder why, eleven years after Tiger Woods won his first major tournament, there are fewer African-, Asian-, Native-, and Latino-North American golfers than there were fifteen years before Woods played his first PGA tournament. Whiteness is ignored because to acknowledge it would make too many people uncomfortable.

Ethnic studies scholars refer to the insistence that we should ignore skin colour as racism, racism based on completely denying the existence of history and the relevance of skin colour and ethnicity in societies where they influence everything from the distribution of income and wealth to where and how people live (Bonilla-Silva, 2001, 2003; Brown et al., 2005; Doane and Bonilla-Silva, 2003). Colour-blind coverage in sports misses a significant dimension of sport reality and reproduces the racial and ethnic *status quo*. But it allows people to use sports as forms of social escapism, as whitewashed worlds devoid of the complex, messy issues that characterize real everyday life. In this way, the sports media do not "tell it like it is" as much as they tell it like many people want to hear it.

ETHNICITY AND NATIONALITY Themes related to ethnicity and nationality also exist in sports media coverage. Although some sports reporters and broadcasters around the world are careful to avoid using ethnic and national stereotypes in their representations of athletes and teams, evidence suggests that subtle stereotypes regularly influence sports coverage (Mayeda, 1999; McCarthy et al., 2003; Sabo and Jensen, 1998; van Sterkenburg and Knoppers, 2004).

For example, the most frequent issue of stereotyping and ethnic misunderstanding in Canada concerns relationships between francophones and anglophones. While language and flag issues concerning French and English, Canada and Québec, are most likely to be reported in both French and English media, ethnic stereotypes also occasionally appear in coverage. In international sports coverage Asian athletes have been portrayed as methodical, mechanical, machinelike, mysterious, industrious, self-disciplined, and intelligent. Their achievements are more often attributed to cognitive rather than physical abilities, and stereotypes about height and other physiological characteristics are sometimes used to explain success or failure in sports (cf., Nakamura, 2005). Latinos, on the other hand, have been described as flamboyant, exotic, emotional, passionate, moody, and hot-blooded (Blain et al., 1993). Margaret MacNeill's production ethno-graphy of the 1988 Calgary Olympics hockey coverage showed that ethnic stereotypes were prevalent in the Canadian broadcasts (1996). The sports journalists most likely to avoid such stereotypes are those who understand the history, culture, and experiences of athletes. But this is a journalist's job, even if it is not taught in journalism courses or in professional development programmes sponsored by newspaper and television companies. For example, when NHL players come from up to 19 different countries,[10] it would be responsible for media companies to hire sports reporters who can speak another language besides English and/or French so that they can talk meaningfully with players whose lives on and off the ice are not understood by most hockey fans.

---

[9]Baker's front-page article, headlined "White Jays," pointed out that the Toronto Blue Jays were fielding "the whitest team in baseball," with only one African American player and only six visible minority players on Opening Day.

[10]Over half of the players are from Canada, and 20 percent are from the United States; another 20 percent of the players are from just four countries—Russia, the Czech Republic, Sweden, and Finland.

MAKING CHANGES The most effective way to reduce subtle forms of racial and ethnic bias in the media is to hire ethnic minority reporters, editors, photographers, writers, producers, directors, camerapersons, commentators, and statisticians (Rowe, 2004a, 2004b). Lip service is paid to this goal, and progress has been made in certain media. For example, for the first time some hockey games are being broadcast in ways that recognize that not all hockey fans in Canada are fluent in English or French. In the 2006–07 season, a regular season game was broadcast in Italian on Telelatino; in February, 2008, the CBC website presented games during *Hockey Day in Canada* in Cantonese, Mandarin, and Hindi; and the Montréal–Boston games during the 2008 Stanley Cup play-offs were broadcast in Mandarin.

But members of racial and ethnic minorities are clearly underrepresented in most sports newsrooms, press boxes, broadcast booths, and media executive offices. This is unfortunate because ethnic diversity among people who represent sports through the media would enrich stories and provide multiple perspectives for understanding sports and the people who play and coach them. When ethnic diversity has existed, and equity training has been done (e.g., CBC Olympic coverage), it has resulted in more accurate and insightful coverage (Thomas, 1996).

Many editors and producers are fond of saying that skin colour is irrelevant to the quality of journalists, and most people agree with them. But if there are fewer than a half dozen Latino beat reporters in MLB—with some 26 percent of Latino players, and only a few black reporters covering the NBA—with black players making up over 70 percent of the league, the *definition of quality* becomes an issue. Are experiences that enable a reporter to understand the backgrounds, orientations, and actions of players included in the definition of quality? Is it important for a player to feel that a reporter understands who he is and how he views the world when he is interviewed? Is it important for the media to provide coverage from different vantage points, angles, and perspectives? If so, reporters and broadcasters defined as qualified should bring diverse ethnic perspectives to sports coverage.

In addition to critically examining the definition of quality used to hire people in sports media, current reporters and broadcasters must do their racial and ethnic homework if they wish to keep their jobs. This involves learning what it means to work in a white-dominated / identified / centred organization and cover sports organized around the values and experiences of white men. It involves learning to view the world through the eyes of the people you write and talk about. For whites, this means learning as much as possible about the history and heritage of everyone from athletes to owners and even reading classic books written by ethnic minority authors and recent research on race and ethnicity. Neither skin colour not gender precludes knowledge about sports or the people involved in them, but knowledge is based on a combination of experience and the richness of the perspective one has to make sense of the ethnically and racially diverse social worlds that are covered by the media.

Other Ideological Themes in Media Sports
Research using critical theories has identified other ideological themes around which images and narratives in media sport have been constructed. In addition to the three themes we have already discussed (success, gender and sexuality, and race and ethnicity), others include nationalism, individualism, teamwork, aggression, and consumerism (Andrews and Jackson, 2001; Kinkema and Harris, 1998; MacNeill, 1996; Real, 1998; Rowe et al., 1998).

These themes should not surprise anyone who has read about, listened to, and viewed media sports in Canada. Images and narratives clearly emphasize *nationalism and national unity*. In fact, the sports that we consider to be "Canadian"—hockey, our version of football, curling, and lacrosse—are, with the exception of lacrosse, the most widely televised sports in the country. When teams and athletes from Canada are competing against teams and athletes from other countries, events are usually framed in an "us versus them" format. In ideological terms, at the height of the Cold War, the 1972 hockey series against the Soviet Union was the most dramatic event. However, it would have been difficult to imagine a more ideologically fitting and dramatic end to the 2002 Olympic men's and women's hockey tournaments. Both Canadian teams faced the host United States teams, and did so at a time when Canada was feeling particularly "dissed" by U.S. foreign, trade, and security policies. The huge television audiences for the two games highlight the nationalist feelings that were involved. Despite CBC media training that explicitly frames commentators as "objective" reporters, and precludes such statements, commentators are still heard to declare that "we won" (see chapter 13).

Media images and narratives also emphasize *individual efforts* to achieve competitive victories, even in the coverage of team sports. Games are promoted with announcements such as this: "It's Jarome Iginla versus Sidney Crosby as the Flames face the Penguins." These promos emphasize the idea that individuals must take responsibility for what happens in their lives and that team failures can be traced to the failures and flaws of one or more individuals. This idea is central to the ideology of individualism, a key element of neo-liberalism, which influences everything from the structure of our welfare systems to the ways employees are evaluated and rewarded in the economy: you are expected to make it on your own, and it is assumed that giving people support creates dependence and stifles initiative.

Images and narratives in sports coverage also stress *teamwork*, which usually means following a game plan developed by a coach/leader, being loyal to the team, and being willing to make sacrifices for the good of the team (Kinkema and Harris, 1998). Media coverage clearly identifies coaches as the organizers and controllers of teams. Commentators praise athletes as "team players" when they follow the game plan; similarly, they praise coaches for their ability to fit players into team roles that lead to victories. This ideological approach to teamwork matches the ideology underlying the market economy and most business organizations: Teamwork means loyalty to the organization and productivity under the direction of a leader-coach. These are also traditional, perhaps even old-fashioned corporate values now. New economy companies are more likely to emphasize democratized workplaces, flexibility, and creativity, but these values have not yet found their way into the ideology of sport coverage.

The importance of *mental and physical aggression* is another ideological theme around which sports images and narratives are constructed in media sports. Rough, aggressive play is assumed to be a sign of commitment and skill, and aggressive players are praised as "warriors" (Messner et al., 1999). Checks in hockey may be described as bone-crushing hits, and hard fouls in basketball are described as warnings to the opposition.

Scores on the late-night news are full of violent images: the Raptors *annihilated* the Knicks, the Alouettes *destroyed* the Blue Bombers, the Flames *scorched* the Canucks, Williams *crushed* Jeyaseelan, and on and on. The scores sound like the results of military operations during a war. In fact, much of the language used in media to represent sports in North America is taken from the realm of violence and warfare (see figure 12.3). Aggression is celebrated while kindness and sensitivity are seen as weakness.

In the U.S., this vocabulary clearly fits with the ideology that many Americans use to determine strategies in interpersonal, business, and international relations, especially in the highly charged and militarily aggressive early years of the twenty-first century. "Kicking ass" is a celebrated goal, and failing to "take out" and "punish" the opposition is a sign of weakness. Presenting games as personal confrontations and mean-spirited turf wars has long been a theme

"Yes I KNOW you watch CSI and Alias, but this hockey game contains real violence, so off to your room now!"

FIGURE 12.3 This father distinguishes between fictional violence and real-life violence on television. Does watching real-life violence in certain sports have an impact on viewers? If video games are rated for violent content, should sports also be rated?

in sports media. When this reaffirms dominant ideology in the culture as a whole, people accept this type of sports coverage.

Finally, the emphasis on *consumerism* is clear in the media coverage of sports: about 20 percent of televised sports consists of commercial time, ads fill newspapers and magazines, and Internet sites use multiple strategies to present ads mixed with scores, commentary, and links. "TV time-outs" are a standard feature in football, hockey, and basketball games, and announcers remind media spectators, "This game is being brought to you by [fill in the corporate name]." The audiences for media sports are encouraged to express their connections to teams and athletes by purchasing shirts, shoes, jackets, official hats, official sweatpants, and team-branded coffee cups, among literally thousands of other branded products. This is clearly consistent with consumer ideology in North American society.

"You are what you buy" is one of the tenets of a market economy.

Overall, the images and narratives in the media coverage of sports in North America stress themes representing dominant ideologies and widespread ideas about how the world does and should work: order, control, and tough discipline are essential; gender differences are grounded in nature, not culture; the primacy of the nation must be preserved, unless capital expansion requires a blurring of national boundaries; individuals must be accountable, work in teams, and outproduce others; and consumption is essential to happiness and is the basis for identity.[11] These themes run through sports media, and are the reason media coverage of sports is heavily sponsored by people and corporations with power and influence in society—they favour these themes, and they sponsor images and narratives that infuse them into public consciousness.

Media Impact on Sports-Related Behaviours

We know that media images and narratives influence people, but we do not know much about who is influenced or in what ways people are influenced. Media coverage is part of our experience, and experiences influence who we are and what we think, feel, and do. However, in this section, we focus only on the connections between consuming sport media and either playing sports or attending events.

Active Participation in Sports Do the media cause people to be more active sport participants, or turn people into couch potatoes? This is an important issue given the high rates of obesity, diabetes, and heart disease in Canada. More people watch sports on television than ever before, and the rates of obesity and diabetes are the

---

[11]These dominant ideological themes are hegemonic, that is, they have, in general, become consensual; but they are never completely consensual and they are continually subject to critical interpretation and re-analysis.

highest in Canadian history. This is not to say that watching sports on television causes obesity and the health problems associated with it, but it suggests issues that should be studied.

When children watch sports on television, some copy what they see if they have or can make opportunities to do so. Children are great imitators with active imaginations, so when they see and identify with athletes, they may create informal activities or seek to join youth sport programmes to pursue television-inspired dreams. Participation grounded in these dreams does not last long, especially after children discover that it takes years of tedious, repetitious, and boring practice to compete successfully and make those glorious trips to the podium. However, other motives may develop in the process and inspire healthy sport participation patterns. But we do not know how many children decide to avoid or quit sports because they cannot meet the performance expectations formed as they watched highly skilled athletes in the media.

Many adults who watch sports on television do not play anything that they watch, while others are active participants in one or more sports (Wenner and Gantz, 1998). As the television coverage of sports increased since the early 1970s in North America, so, too, have levels of inactivity. It is important to be careful about these types of statistical relationships, and while some have speculated that the growth of television sports and the Internet have led to inactivity, there is no evidence that one caused the other. In fact, some have argued that the growth of sports on television may encourage participation. There is little direct evidence of this. In Australia, where the 2000 Olympics received continuous coverage in almost all media outlets, passive involvement in sport and physical activity (spectating, and watching sports on television) was identified as "the most substantial participation-related impact of the Sydney Olympics/Paralympics" (Houlihan, 2005, p. 16; see also Toohey, 2004; Toohey and Veal, 2007).

Media coverage reveals possibilities, and the rapid increases in girls' participation in gymnastics, soccer, and hockey have all been attributed to media exposure of these sports. MacNeill (in press) has also identified what she terms "active viewing"—not in sports, but in early teens who she found engaged in the vigorous physical activity of dancing along with music videos. There is a need to study cultural changes as they are related to the use of the media in people's lives. At this point, the safest conclusion is that consuming sports through the media is connected with each outcome in different situations and with different people.

Attendance at Sport Events Game attendance is related to many factors, and its relationship to the media is complex. On the one hand, the owners of many professional teams enforce a local television blackout rule based on the belief that television coverage hurts game attendance and ticket sales. In support of this belief, many people say that they would rather watch certain sport events on television than attend them in person. On the other hand, the media publicize sports, promote interest, and provide the information people need to identify with athletes and teams and become potential ticket buyers for events (Wann et al., 2001b; Weiss, 1996; Zhang et al., 1997c).

The most logical conclusion is that the people who watch more games on TV also attend more games in person (Zhang and Smith, 1997). However, this conclusion has two qualifications. First, as ticket prices increase, and the numbers of elite "live" games increase across various sports, people may limit attendance when there is the option of watching a local game on television. Second, because the media focus attention on elite sports such as NHL hockey, they may undermine attendance at less elite events such as local junior games. Thus, the media may be positively related to attendance at the top levels of competition but negatively related to attendance at lower levels of competition (Zhang et al., 1997c). Research is needed to explore this issue in more depth.

AUDIENCE EXPERIENCES WITH MEDIA SPORTS

Media sports provide topics of conversation, sources of identity, feelings of success when favourite teams win, opportunities to express emotions, occasions for getting together with others, and a focus for those who are passing time alone (Wenner and Gantz, 1998). A summary of audience research done by media studies experts Lawrence Wenner and Walter Gantz (1998) indicates that, in the U.S., adults integrate sports media into their lives in a variety of ways. Although studies have identified some adults, more men than women, who focus considerable attention on watching sports, overall patterns indicate that watching television sports is not a major activity in the lives of most adults. Furthermore, those studies do not tell us much about the ways that people include consumption of media sports in their lives (Crawford, 2004; Wann et al., 2001b).

Research summarized by Wenner and Gantz shows that men and women who live together often watch televised sports together, and that this usually is a positive activity in their relationships. In other words, "stay-at-home armchair quarterbacks" and "football widows" are not as common as many people believe. Men watch sports more than women do and are more likely to be committed fans. However, when women are highly committed fans, they watch and respond to sports on television in ways that are similar to patterns among men. Research suggests that being a fan is more important than gender or any other factor when it comes to people's viewing experiences. Some couples experience conflicts related to viewing sports, but most couples resolve them successfully. Partners usually learn to accommodate each other's viewing habits over time, and when differences are associated with problems, it usually is in relationships that have other problems unrelated to their patterns of watching sports on television.

Future studies will tell us more about how media sport experiences are integrated into people's lives and when media sports become important sites at which social relationships occur. While there are no major reasons to expect that Canadian results regarding viewing sports on television would differ from those in the U.S., it would be useful to obtain comparative data. The use of the Internet and video games should be included in these studies.

THE PROFESSION OF SPORT JOURNALISM

Some people trivialize sport journalism by saying that it provides "entertaining material about people and events that don't *really* matter too much" (Koppett, 1994). However, sports *do matter*—not because they produce a tangible product or make essential contributions to our survival but because they represent ideas about how the world works and what is important in life. Therefore, sport journalists do things that matter when it comes to ideology and public consciousness.

Sport Journalists on the Job: Relationships with Athletes

As televised sports have increased, sportswriters have had to create stories that go beyond the action and scores in sports. This leads them to seek information about the personal lives of the athletes, and this in turn has influenced relationships between journalists and athletes. For example, athletes today realize that they cannot trust writers to hold information in confidence, even if it was disclosed in the privacy of the locker room. Furthermore, the stakes associated with "bad press" are so great for athletes and teams that everyone in sports organizations is on guard when talking with journalists. Clinton Doaks, a long-time sportswriter explains that, "today's sports world is so driven by public relations that there are very few stories to report. Every player, coach, and team is so image conscious... that they all offer the same homogeneous quotes week in and week out, game after game" (Doaks, 2004).

As journalists seek stories that athletes do not want to tell, it creates tensions in their relationships with athletes. One of the outcomes of this situation is that professional teams and even NSOs (since this has now extended even to national team athletes) have found it necessary to offer players training sessions on how to handle interviews without saying things that sound bad or can be misinterpreted. Research carried out on Canadian Olympic athletes by Margaret MacNeill (1998b) in the 1990s showed that they were in a very difficult situation with the media. On the one hand, they were denied by their NSO the right to comment on their organization or coach to the media. On the other hand, they were not aware of their media rights. For example: "Athletes wrongly assume that communicating 'off-the-record' statements to the sports media will protect either their anonymity and/or the privacy of the person or organization they are commenting about" (MacNeill, 1998b, p. 111). Resulting in part from this research, CAAWS and the Coaching Association of Canada produced *A Media Guide for Athletes and their Coaches* (1998), and the Canadian Olympic Committee (COC) holds media training workshops and has a booklet available to athletes. In fact, in the lead up to the 2008 Beijing Olympics, the COC offered training sessions to athletes to inform them about the political situation in China, so that they would be in a better position to make informed comments to the media. However, media training by sports organizations may just serve as a reminder to athletes to "thank your corporate sponsors" or not to comment on their coaches or NSO; or, as media training does in professional sports, to provide clichéd and non-informative answers to media questions (MacNeill et al., 2001).

Tensions also call attention to ethical issues in sports journalism. Responsible journalists, including writers and announcers, are now sensitive to the fact that they should not jeopardize people's reputations simply for the sake of entertainment. This does not mean that they avoid criticism that might hurt someone, but they are less likely to hurt someone unintentionally or without good reason. Dan Le Batard, a regular columnist for *ESPN The Magazine*, explains that he tries to be "nonjudgmental" when he covers athletes because all people have flaws and exposing them because someone disappoints you with their actions smacks of self-righteousness and raises the ethical issue of invasion of privacy (2005b, p. 14). Unfortunately, journalists constantly face grey areas in which ethical guidelines are not clear, and the need to present attractive stories often encourages them to push ethical limits.

Sportswriters and Sports Announcers: A Comparison

Different media have slightly different goals and strategies. The print media focus on entertaining people with information and in-depth analysis, while radio and television announcers entertain people with action and commentary that create on-the-spot urgency. The implications of these differences are summarized in table 12.6.

Although differences between sportswriters and announcers/commentators are often difficult to identify the print media usually hire writers who can tell reliable and thorough stories, while broadcast companies hire announcers who can excite and entertain an audience with rapid commentary (see figure 12.4). This is why newspaper and magazine writers (especially the latter) usually do more thorough investigative reporting, whereas announcers talk with a sense of urgency to entertain viewing or listening audiences. This does not mean that there are no examples of investigative journalism in electronic media. *Sports Journal*, on CBC Newsworld for a number of years, and the *Inside Track*, on CBC radio, regularly carry investigative pieces; and mainstream investigative journalists from programmes such as *the fifth estate*, *Disclosure*

Table 12.6 Sportswriters and sports announcers: a comparison of roles

Role characteristics	Sportswriters[a]	Sports announcers[b]
• Job security	High	Low
• Salary	Low	High
• Popularity/public recognition	Low	High
• Freedom of expression in job	Moderately restricted	Heavily restricted
• Purpose of role	Entertain and provide information	Entertain and "sell" sport events
• Role expectations	Be trustworthy investigators	Be knowledgeable entertainers
• Management expectations	Do not offend advertisers	Do not offend sponsors
• Opportunities to do investigative reporting	Occasionally	Rarely
• On-the-job contacts	Copy desk editors and subeditors	Broadcast executives, team management, sponsors/advertisers
• Relationships with players	Sometimes tense and antagonistic	Often friendly and supportive
• Attachment with public	Based on style and writing skills	Based on credibility and personality

Source: Adapted from Koppett (1994).

[a]The primary focus here is on newspaper reporters; magazine writers have similar jobs, but they are different in that they often cover issues and topics in greater depth

[b]The primary focus here is on television announcers; radio announcers have similar jobs, but they are different in that they must focus more on description in their commentary and less on interpretation

(both CBC), and *W5* (CTV) occasionally pay attention to sports, with pieces on such issues as sexual harassment in sports, violence and injury in sports, or the influence of the Russian "mafia" on the NHL.

While considering these differences and reviewing table 12.6, remember that there are exceptions to these role descriptions. Some writers go beyond information and analysis and write strictly to entertain, and some television personalities work on investigative stories in which information and analysis are as important as entertainment; and there is some cross-over, with sportswriters appearing regularly on sport discussion items on TSN/RDS and other networks.

The efforts of television companies to provide a combination of play-by-play commentary and entertainment lead them to hire popular retired athletes and coaches to be announcers. Media companies cover sports as "infotainment" rather than news, and those who announce the games must be entertainers. But they must be credible entertainers who can provide insider interpretations

"I used to do sports, so I know the rule at CanTV: If it bleeds, it leads."

FIGURE 12.4 Media coverage of sports news is much like other news in that it contains representations of violence and drama. Such representations are not accurate indicators of what generally happens in sports or our communities.

and stories. This is why announ-cers and commentators may be former athletes and coaches who fans perceive to be credible. However, all radio and television announcers are expected to self-censor their commentary so that they stay within the limits set by teams and television companies. U.S. radio and television announcer Chip Caray, who has worked on broadcasts for the Atlanta Braves, the Seattle Mariners, and the Chicago Cubs, explains, "Our bosses expect us to broadcast a certain way. No one has ever told me how to broadcast. But I draw my paycheck from the same place as the players" (in Russo, 1999, p. 7D). Consequently, announcers seldom stray from a fairly standard entertainment approach, and they provide no critical comments about sports as social phenomena as we watch them on television. For people who consume sports primarily through the popular media, critical discussions of sports, such as the ones in this book, may create defensiveness or discomfort.

SUMMARY

COULD SPORTS AND THE MEDIA SURVIVE WITHOUT EACH OTHER?

To understand social life, we must give serious attention to the media and media experiences. This is why we study the relationship between sports and the media. There are some differences between Canada and the U.S. in this relationship, but also a number of distinct similarities.

Media sports, like other parts of culture, are social constructions. They are created, organized, and controlled by human beings whose ideas are grounded in their social worlds, experiences and ideologies. The media do not *reflect* reality as much as they provide *re-presentations* of selected versions of reality. Power relations in society influence these representations. Therefore, the images and narratives that comprise the media

often reaffirm dominant ideologies and promote the interests of those who benefit most from them. The possible exception to this is the Internet and related digital devices; media that offer revolutionary potential in that they enable people to create their own media content.

Sports and the media have grown to depend on each other as both have become more important parts of culture in many societies. They could survive without each other, but they would be different than they are now. Commercial sports have grown and prospered because of media coverage and the rights fees paid to sport organizations by media companies. Without the publicity and money provided by the meida, commercial sports would be local business operations with much less scope than they have today, and less emphasis would be given to elite forms of competitive sports. Without exposure to sports through the media, people would probably give lower priority to organized power and performance sports in their everyday lives, and they might give higher priority to pleasure and participation sports.

The media also could survive without sports. But they, too, especially newspapers and television, would be different and they might give higher priority to pleasure and participation sports. Newspaper circulation probably would decrease, and television programming on weekends and holidays would be different if they did not have sports to make their programming attractive to young male audiences and the sponsors who wish to buy access to them.

The symbiotic relationship between sports and the media suggests that we will continue to see many commercialized sports covered by the media and the major media presenting regular coverage of sports. However, history also shows that this relationship in North America has developed within a larger cultural context, one in which priority is given to commercial profits and the creation of mega media events. Furthermore, the relationship between sports and the media has been created in connection with the ever-changing interactions among athletes, agents, coaches, administrators, sport team owners, sponsors, advertisers, media representatives, and a diverse collection of spectators. The power dynamics of these interactions have an important impact on the sports–media relationship.

Sports covered by the electronic media are represented to audiences with dramatic, exciting, and stylized images and narratives designed to be entertaining for audiences and attractive to sponsors. The influence of these media sports in our lives depends on how we integrate them into our relationships and routines. Direct experiences with sports influence how we interpret and use what we read, listen to, and view in the media. If we have little direct experience with and in sports, the media play a more central role in creating our sport realities and influencing how those realities are integrated into the rest of our lives.

Research suggests that dominant ideologies related to success, gender, race and ethnicity, nationalism, individualism, teamwork, violence, and consumption are perpetuated through the images and narratives represented in the media coverage of sports in North America. These ideologies support the interests of corporate sponsors, males, and white people, and they are presented seamlessly in sports coverage so that the current distribution of power and privilege seems to be normal and natural. Future research will tell us more about how people use media content as they form ideas about sports, their social relationships, and the social world.

Especially important in the future will be research on how people use the Internet and video games as sites for constructing their experiences in and with sports. Some thirteen-year-olds would much rather play sport video games than watch games on television. In the future, some of them will do both at the same time. And some twenty-five-year-olds enjoy the sport-related interactive experiences that they have on the Internet more than the games themselves. Mediasports and the experiences associated with them are changing rapidly, and it is important to study them in ways that promote critical media literacy rather than the uncritical celebration of media technology and culture (Kellner, 2003a, 2003b, 2004).

Visit *Sports in Society*'s **Online Learning Centre at <u>www.mcgrawhill.ca/olc/coakley</u> for additional information, website resources, and study tools for this chapter.**

chapter 13

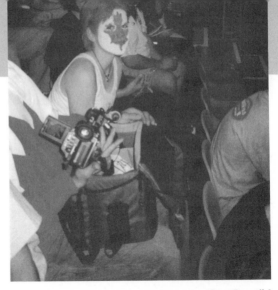

[Peter Donnelly]

Sports and Politics

How do governments and global processes influence sports?

Throughout Latin America, stadiums play a double role: in peacetime they are sports venues; in war they turn into concentration camps.

—R. Kapuscinski, *The Soccer War* (1986), p. 167

I don't see how closing the world's highest mountain to everyone but yourself is in the spirit of the Games.

—Mountaineer Kenton Cool, commenting on China's closure of Mount Everest to ensure that the Olympic torch reaches the summit (on the Tibetan border) without any public political protest (2008)

I don't think sportsmen can use "sports and politics don't mix" as an excuse. I didn't want to represent 50 million English people touring a country where the regime was abhorrent.

—Stuart Barnes, British rugby player, on his refusal to tour South Africa in 1974 (1994)

The Montréal Olympics can no more have a deficit than a man can have a baby.

—Jean Drapeau, then Mayor of Montréal (1976)

No person shall play or take part in any game or sport upon a highway.

—City of Burlington, Uniform Traffic By-Law 1984-1

Organized competitive sports long have been connected with politics, government, and global processes. **Politics** refers to *the processes and procedures of making decisions that affect collections of people, from small groups to societies and even multiple societies that are unified for certain purposes*, such as the European Union consisting of 27 nations, with shared policies, and many sharing a common currency.[1] In a sociological sense, politics involves processes through which power is gained and used in social life. Therefore, people in the sociology of sport study politics in families, communities, local and national sport organizations, societies, and nongovernment organizations (NGOs) such as the International Olympic Committee (IOC) and the Fédération Internationale de Football Association (FIFA), the international federation (IF) or governing body for soccer.

Governments are *formal organizations with the power to make and enforce rules in a particular territory or collection of people*. Because governments make decisions affecting people's lives, they are political organizations by definition. Governments operate on various levels from small communities and large cities to nation-states, and they influence sports whether they occur in a local park, or privately owned stadiums that host international competitions.

Politics involve the actions and interactions of governments, but rule making in sports today often transcends the boundaries of nation-states and occurs in connection with global processes. For example, soccer became a global sport as British workers, students, and teachers brought the game to South America, and British soldiers brought it to Africa, Asia, the West Indies, and other colonized areas of the nineteenth-century British Empire. Therefore, soccer was introduced to people around the world through the global processes of migration, capitalist expansion, British imperialism, and colonization. These processes clearly involve politics. Governments usually are involved, but the processes often transcend particular governments as people, products, ideas, technologies, and money move so rapidly across national borders that time and space become compressed—a phenomenon often referred to as *globalization*.

This chapter deals with sports and politics. The goal is to explain the ways that sports are connected with politics, governments, and global processes. Chapter content focuses on four major questions:

1. Why are governments involved in sponsoring and controlling sports?
2. How are sports are connected with global politics that involve nation-states, transnational corporations, and nongovernment organizations?
3. What is the role of the Olympic Games in global politics and processes?
4. What are the ways that political processes occur in sports and sport organizations?

When reading this chapter, remember that *power* is the key concept in politics. **Power** refers to *an ability to influence people and achieve goals, even in the face of opposition from others* (Weber, 1968/1922). **Authority** is *a form of power that comes with a recognized and legitimate status or office in a government, an organization, or an established set of relationships*. For example, a large corporation has *power* if it can influence how people think about and play sports and if it can use sports to achieve its goals. Sport organizations such as the IOC, FIFA, the CIS, and local parks and recreation departments have *authority* over the sports that they administer, as long as people associated with those sports accept the organizations as legitimate sources of control. Most organized sports are controlled by at least three levels of authority (table 13.2 on p. 449 shows the levels of sport organizations in the Canadian amateur sport community):

---

[1]In fact, the recent European White Paper on Sport represents an attempt to harmonize certain aspects of sport policy across those 27 nations (ec.europa.eu/sport/whitepaper/wp_on_sport_en.pdf).

- The various levels of government who have an interest in, and control of (through legislation and funding), sports and physical activity—in the Canadian confederation these include the municipal and regional levels, the provincial[2] and territorial levels, and the federal level (discussed in the first part of this chapter);
- Businesses and corporations who sponsor sports and athletes, ranging from a local real estate company who sponsors house league soccer to transnational corporations who are the major sponsors of the Olympic Games (referred to in the second part of this chapter); and
- The various sport organizations that run sports at local, regional, provincial, national, and international levels (discussed in the last part of this chapter).

Thus, in this chapter, *politics* refers to the power to make decisions that affect sports and sport participation at all levels of involvement.

THE SPORTS–GOVERNMENT CONNECTION

When sports become popular community activities, government involvement often increases. Many sports require sponsorship, organization, and facilities—all of which depend on resources that few individuals possess on their own. Sport facilities may be so expensive that regional and national governments are the only community entities with the power and money to build and maintain them. Therefore, government involvement in sports often is a necessity. Government

involvement also occurs when there is a need for a third party to regulate and control sports and sport organizations in ways that promote the overall good of people in a community or society.

The nature and extent of government involvement in sports is diverse and it occurs for one or more of the following seven reasons (Houlihan, 2000):

1. To safeguard the public order
2. To maintain health and fitness among citizens
3. To promote the prestige and power of a group, community, or nation
4. To promote a sense of identity, belonging, and unity among citizens
5. To reproduce values consistent with the dominant ideology in a community or society
6. To increase support for political leaders and government
7. To promote economic development in the community or society

Safeguarding the Public Order

Governments often make rules about the legality of sports, where they may and may not be played, the safety equipment that must be used, who must have opportunities to play, and who can use public sport facilities at certain times. Ideally, these rules promote safety and reduce conflict between multiple users of particular spaces. For example, a government might ban bullfighting, bare-fisted boxing, or bungee jumping off public bridges. In the case of commercial sports, governments may regulate the rights and duties of team owners, sponsors, promoters, and athletes. Local governments may regulate sport participation by requiring permits to use public facilities and playing fields. They may pass rules prohibiting potentially dangerous sport activities in public places. For example, skateboarding, street hockey, and bicycling may be banned on city sidewalks or in certain public parks, or they may be confined to certain areas, so that pedestrians will feel safe. These examples remind us that politics is about power:

---

[2]Although the provincial level is extremely important in terms of sport participation and athlete development in Canada, there are very few studies of the provincial level of sport organization; see, for example, Harvey and Proulx (1988) on Québec, and Rob Pitter (1996), of Acadia University, on Alberta. Therefore, the primary focus of this chapter is on the federal level.

several years ago street hockey became a major issue for Hamilton City Council when complaints led to a ban in a neighbourhood where games had traditionally been played; and skirmishes between skateboarders and law enforcement are common in many cities. Local officials may also close streets or parks to the general public, so that sport events can be held under controlled and safe conditions. For example, marathons in Halifax, Nova Scotia, or bicycle races in London, Ontario, require the involvement of the government and government agencies, such as the city police.

Governments may pass laws or establish policies that safeguard the public order by protecting the participation rights of citizens. The Canadian Charter of Rights and Freedoms (see chapter 8) is the constitutional tool of federal government regulation intended to promote fairness in access to all walks of life, including sports and physical activity. Sport Canada, the government agency that oversees sports, has established nationwide policies on women in sports (1986), Aboriginal participation (2005), and sport participation for persons with a disability (2006). Through the 1995 Sport Funding and Accountability Framework, government funding to NSOs may be tied to implementation of gender-, language-, and disability-equity programmes. Governments around the world are

Local governments often regulate where and when certain sports may be played, and these regulations often target street hockey and skateboarding. However, they are frequently ignored, and enforcement usually only follows a complaint. [Louise Donnelly]

enacting or considering similar laws to establish fairness in sport participation opportunities for men and women, and for persons with a disability.

Safeguarding the public order also involves policing sport events. Local police or even military forces may be called on to control crowds and individuals who threaten the safety of others. During the Olympics, for example, the host city and nation provide thousands of military and law enforcement officials to safeguard the public order. In the face of possible terrorist actions, the governments of Athens and Greece spent US$1.5 billion on security at the 2004 Olympic Games (Waterford, 2004). They employed over 100,000 police, military personnel, firefighters, and private security contractors and used a high-tech surveillance system with 1,000 cameras and links to ships, fighter planes, the coast guard, minesweepers along the coast of Greece, bomb squads, and a NATO special forces battalion. Fortunately, less than a dozen incidents occurred during the 17 days of the Games. Security costs for the 2010 Vancouver Olympics, originally budgeted at $175 million, have increased significantly. Current estimates suggest that the cost could be $500 million, and that figure is likely to increase.

Some governments attempt to safeguard the public order by sponsoring sport events and programmes for at-risk youth, such as the Night-Hoops programme in several Canadian cities and programmes offered by various police departments. Sports, they believe, keep youth off the streets, thereby lowering crime rates, vandalism, loneliness, and alienation. However, these programmes generally fail, because they do not deal with the deprivation, racism, poverty, dislocation, unemployment, community disintegration, and political powerlessness that often create "at-risk youth" and social problems in communities and societies (cf., Coakley, 2002; Donnelly and Coakley, 2004; Hartmann, 2001, 2003b).

Finally, sports are used in military and police training, so that the soldiers and police will be more effective protectors of the public order (Mangan, 2003). Military academies in many countries traditionally sponsor numerous sports for their cadets—at the Royal Military College (RMC) in Kingston, some 20 percent of the students participate in interuniversity sports, and many more are involved in intramurals. The World Police and Fire Games are held every two years because people believe that sport participation keeps law enforcement officials and firefighters prepared to safeguard the public order.

Maintaining Health and Fitness

Governments also become involved in sports to promote health and fitness among citizens. Nations with government-funded health insurance programmes often promote and sponsor sports to improve physical health in the general population and thereby reduce the cost of health services. This was one of the major reasons the Canadian government promoted and funded fitness and sport programmes during the mid-1970s. The government was facing serious financial crises, and officials believed that sport participation among Canadians ultimately would increase fitness and cut health-care costs (Harvey and Proulx, 1988).

However, the Canadian government, and most provincial/territorial governments, seem to have an ambivalent attitude towards fitness issues. While ParticipACTION enjoyed a significant period of support from the Ministry of State for Fitness and Amateur Sport, the ministry was closed in 1993, and the responsibilities of Fitness Canada were transferred to Health Canada.[3] Since then, ParticipACTION experienced a period of decline, closed down in 2001, and was not re-established until 2007. Federal government ambivalence about sport

---

[3]While ParticipACTION had some success in drawing the attention of Canadians to the importance of physical activity, Margaret MacNeill (1999), of the University of Toronto, has pointed out that the public service announcements were not without problems. They were aimed at white, middle-class Canadians, not reflecting the diversity of the population, and were full of gender stereotypes.

and physical activity is perhaps best indicated in a comparison with anti-smoking initiatives. For just one anti-smoking initiative, the Federal Tobacco Control Strategy, Health Canada is spending $480 million—substantially more than the annual budget for Sport Canada, and far more than is spent on any physical activity and fitness initiatives.

In response to growing concerns about obesity, especially among Canadian children, the Minister of Health introduced *Canada's Physical Activity Guide* in 2002; but there has been no corresponding campaign of public service announcements to publicize them, or any investment in creating new opportunities for physical activity. The Romanow Report (2002) on health care in Canada drew attention to the need to "[i]ntegrate prevention and promotion initiatives as a central focus of primary health care targeted initially at reducing tobacco use and obesity, and increasing physical activity in Canada." Similarly, Bill C-12, the *Act to Promote Physical Activity and Sport* (2003), identifies physical activity as a determinant of health: "The government's policy on physical activity seeks to promote physical activity as a fundamental element of health and well-being of Canadians…and to help them reduce the barriers that prevent them from being active." However, knowledge of the benefits of physical activity and concerns about the detrimental effects of lack of physical activity, especially among young people, has not yet been translated into any tangible policies and actions. Public funding has been more focused on anti-obesity research, although nonprofit organizations such as Active Healthy Kids Canada are making efforts to fill this public policy gap.

Similar motives have led to government sponsorship and organization of fitness and sport programmes in other nations. Many people believe that sport participation improves fitness, fitness improves health, and good health reduces medical costs. This belief persists in the face of the following factors (Waddington, 2000a, 2007):

- Many of the illnesses that increase health-care costs are caused by environmental factors and living conditions that cannot be changed through sport or fitness programmes.
- Certain forms of sport participation do not produce physical fitness or identifiable health benefits.
- The win-at-all-costs orientation in certain competitive sports often contributes to injuries and increased health-care costs (for example, about 40,000 high school and university athletes in the U.S. have serious and costly knee injuries each year).
- The demand for health care often increases when people train for competitions because they seek specialized medical care to treat and rehabilitate sport injuries.

These factors lead governments to be cautious and selective when they sponsor sports for health purposes. Most governments now emphasize noncompetitive physical activities and exercise with clear aerobic benefits instead of competitive sports. The relationship between sport participation and overall health and fitness is a complex one. Although research clearly shows that physical exercise has health benefits, competitive sports involve more than mere exercise.

Competitive sports may promote overall health when athletes value physical well-being over performance and competitive success. Playing sports is beneficial when it helps us to understand our bodies and maintain physical well-being; it is not beneficial when it involves overtraining, the use of bodies as weapons, and overconformity to the norms of the sport ethic (as explained in chapter 6). This is why health professionals sometimes disagree when it comes to recommending government involvement in sports to promote health and fitness.

Promoting the Prestige and Power of a Group, Community, or Nation

Government involvement in sports frequently is motivated by a quest for recognition and prestige (Allison, 2004; Bairner, 2005). This occurs on local, national, and even global levels. For example, a spokesperson for the South Korean government said that its sponsorship of the 1988 Summer Olympic Games was an announcement to the world of its emergence as a developed nation with a strong economy. Co-sponsorship of the 2002 World Cup of soccer (with Japan) was intended to reinforce the image of South Korea on the world's stage. Sydney, the host of the 2000 Summer Games, was presented to the world as a city with clean air in a country with a pleasant climate and vital business connections with emerging nations in Asia. Salt Lake City used the 2002 Winter Olympics to present itself as an economically progressive area and an attractive tourist destination. Athens used the 2004 Olympics to declare its status as the founding nation of the Olympics, to show the world that Greece was part of the new Europe, and that it was a nation that had more than monuments of a past era. China spent over US$40 billion to present itself during the 2008 Beijing Olympics as a new world power and a dynamic nation that is ideal for business investments and tourism.

This quest for recognition and prestige also underlies government subsidies for national teams across a wide range of sports, usually those designated as Olympic sports. Government officials use international sports to establish their nation's legitimacy in the international sphere, and they often believe that winning medals enhances their image around the world. This belief is so strong that many governments now offer their athletes financial rewards for winning medals in the Olympics. The importance of national success in sports is matched by a belief that a nation's failures in international sport events cause a loss

> Sports have been revered by fascists and communists, by free-marketers and filibusters. They have also been, paradoxically, reviled by all those political factions. Sports may be among the most powerful human expressions in all history.
>
> —Gerald Early, professor of modern letters, Washington University, St. Louis (1998)

of prestige in the global cultural arena. For example, when national teams from England lost in major international competitions to teams from countries that had learned to play sports invented in England, some people in England worried that the losses were symptoms of their nation's general decline in world affairs (Maguire, 1994, 1999).

The declining fortunes of Canadian teams in international hockey, especially the Olympics and World Championships, starting in the 1950s was, in part, responsible for federal government involvement in sports. The lack of hockey success was interpreted as a loss of international prestige by Prime Minister John Diefenbaker, who proposed government involvement to "assure hereafter that Canada's representation in the field of international competition, particularly in amateur sport, shall be of the very best" (cited by Macintosh, Bedecki, and Franks, 1987, p. 35). While Canadian performances in international sports improved, Canada did not win an Olympic gold medal in ice hockey for 50 years (1952–2002). The success of Canadian women at consecutive World Championships throughout the 1990s did nothing to enhance assessments of national strength, and strongly attests to the lack of status of women's sports.

Attempts to gain recognition and prestige also underlie local government involvement in sports. Cities may fund sport clubs and teams and then use them to promote themselves as good places to live, work, locate a business, or spend a vacation. Many people in North America feel that, if their city does not have one or more major professional sport team franchises, it cannot claim world-class status (Delaney and Eckstein, 2003; Sille, 2004; Whitson, 2004; Whitson and Macintosh, 1996). Because of the success of the Oilers in the 1980s, and the frequent success of the Eskimos, Edmonton still declares itself to be the "City of Champions," much to the chagrin of people in Calgary.

During the "Save the [Winnipeg] Jets" campaign in 1995, when Winnipeg-born, Toronto-raised actor Keanu Reeves was booked to play Hamlet in a Winnipeg theatre, he noted that one of the only things he knew about Winnipeg was the Jets (Smith, 1997). The statement was used by those supporting the campaign to indicate that, without the Jets, the city would cease to be known (presumably in U.S. newspapers). In an insult to their prairie neighbour, some Winnipegers started to say that, if the Jets left, they would be just like Regina (see Nauright and White, 1996; Scherer, 2001; Silver, 1996). Of course, the city survived the loss and has experienced an economic boom in recent years. However, the strength of the campaign is a clear indication of how strong an outpost the NHL and other major league sports have in people's minds.

Promoting Identity and Unity

Groups, organizations, towns, cities, and nations use sports to express collective sentiments about themselves (Allison, 2000, 2004; Bairner, 2001; Houlihan, 2000; Jutel, 2002; Maguire and Poulton, 1999; Poulton, 2004; Sam, 2003; Sato, 2005). An athlete or team representing a larger collection of people has the potential to bring individuals together and to create emotional unity among them. When a nation's soccer team plays in the World Cup, people across the nation can be united, regardless of differences in race, religion, language, education, occupation, and income. Even occupied and divided Iraq experienced such a moment of national unity in July 2007 when, against all odds, the national soccer team composed of Shi'ite, Sunni, and Kurdish players defeated Saudi Arabia by a score of 1–0 in the final of the Asian Cup. This unity may be connected with their feelings of attachment to the nation as a whole and their convictions about

the nation's history and traditions, even about its destiny in the world order.[4]

However, it is important to ask critical questions about the short-term nature or the long-term consequences of this emotional unity and about whose interests are served by the images, traditions, and memories around which identities are expressed.

When government involvement in sport is intended to promote identity, it usually benefits some people more than others. For example, when men's sports are sponsored and women's sports are ignored, the sense of national identity and unity among men may be strong, but women may feel alienated. (cf., Robinson, 2000a). When sports involve participants from only one ethnic or language group, or a particular social class, there are similar divisions in the "imagined community" and "invented traditions" constructed around sports. Identity is political in that it can be constructed around many different ideas about what is important in a group or society. Furthermore, neither identity nor the emotional unity created by sports changes the social, political, and economic realities of life in a city or society. When games end, people go their separate ways. Old social distinctions become relevant again, and the people who were disadvantaged before the game remain disadvantaged after it (Smith and Ingham, 2003). However, they may feel justified in making their disadvantage a political issue because, after all, everyone—even the rich and powerful—is part of the big "we" celebrated at the game.

The emotional unity that sports create feels good to many people and it may generate a sense of possibility and hope, but it often glosses over the need for social transformations that might make society more fair and just.

---

[4]The massive television audiences in Canada for the men's and women's hockey finals at the Salt Lake City (2002) Olympics—over 10 million for the men's game and some 7 million for the women's game—included many individuals who would not normally consider themselves to be "hockey fans."

Canadian prime ministers use sports for political advantage. They seldom miss an opportunity to be seen or to be connected with championship teams and successful athletes. However, we should also recognize that athletes often appreciate recognition by the country's leading politician. Here, Stephen Harper celebrates with Canadian Paralympians prior to the 2006 Torino Games. [CP(Fred Chartrand)]

Local government involvement in sports is also motivated by concerns to promote and express particular forms of identity. Club soccer teams in Europe often receive support from local governments, because the teams are major focal points for community attention and involvement. The teams reaffirm community identity among local citizens, and games often are social occasions at which people renew old acquaintances and maintain social networks. In this way, sports are *invented traditions* that people use to reaffirm social relationships.

When the population of a community or society is very diverse, or when social change is rapid and widespread, governments are even more likely to intervene in sports for the purpose of promoting a sense of identity and unity (Maguire and Stead, 2005). For example, as national boundaries have become less and less visible and relevant in the lives of some people, national governments occasionally use sports to promote and reaffirm national identity (Houlihan, 2000; Maguire, 1999, 2005). The long-term effectiveness of this strategy is difficult to assess, but many government officials are convinced that sports create more than temporary good feelings of national "we-ness." Interestingly, nearly all of these officials are men, and the sports that they support are tied to traditions that have privileged men in the past. This shows that there are several layers to the politics associated with sports.

Reproducing Values Consistent with Dominant Ideology

Governments also become involved in sports to promote certain political values and ideas among citizens. This is especially true when there is a need to maintain the idea that success is based on discipline, loyalty, determination, and hard work even in the face of hardship and bad times. Sports are useful platforms to promote these values and to foster a particular ideology that contains taken-for-granted assumptions about the way that social life is organized and how it should operate.

It is difficult to determine the extent to which people are influenced by sports presented in specific ideological terms, but we do know that, in capitalist societies such as Canada, sports provide people with a vocabulary and real-life examples that are consistent with dominant ideology. The images, narratives, and the often-repeated stories that accompany sports in market economies emphasize that competition is clearly the best and most natural way to achieve personal success and allocate rewards to people, whereas alternative approaches to success and allocating rewards (such as democratic socialism, socialism, communism, and the like) are ineffective, unnatural, and even immoral.

Today, the use of sport competitions to make claims about the superiority of political and economic ideologies are less likely than they were during the Nazi era and the Cold War; although it is quite clear that China used the 2008 Beijing Olympics to showcase its political and economic power. With the commercialization of sport,

and the fact that some corporations are now more powerful than many nations, it is often corporations that are likely to use the Olympics and other major international events to make claims about the superiority of their products and services, and the "naturalness" of capitalist, free-market economic principles and lifestyles based on consumption.

Increasing Support for Political Leaders and Government

Government authority rests ultimately in legitimacy: if people do not perceive political leaders and the government as legitimate, it is difficult to maintain social order. In the quest to maintain legitimacy, political officials may use their connections with athletes, teams, and particular sports to boost their acceptance in the minds of citizens.[5] They assume, as Antonio Gramsci predicted they would, that if they support the sports that people value and enjoy, they can increase their *legitimacy* as leaders. This is why so many political leaders present themselves as friends of sport, even as faithful fans. They attend highly publicized sport events and associate themselves with high-profile athletes or teams that win major competitions. For example, Canada's prime ministers often are photographed when attending Grey Cup games have associated themselves with successful athletes and teams, and invited champions to Ottawa for photo opportunities. Of course, Canadian politicians are not the only ones to do this; there are similar examples from other countries. When taken together, these

---

[5]In historical terms, this is a very old idea. The later Roman emperors instituted a policy of *panem et circensem* (bread and circuses—food and entertainment for the potentially rebellious Roman population) in order to maintain their popularity (see chapter 3). The group opposing Toronto's 1996 and 2008 Olympic bids called itself "Bread not Circuses" in a parody of the Roman policy, and to emphasize the need for social spending rather than mega-event spending.

examples provide strong support for the idea that governments and government officials use sports to establish legitimacy and win support.

Promoting Economic Development

Since the early 1980s, government involvement in sports often is based on the hope of promoting economic development (Delaney and Eckstein, 2003; Schimmel, 2000, 2002). Cities spend millions of dollars in their bids to host the Olympic Games, World Cup tournaments, world or national championships, Grey Cups, All-Star Games, high-profile auto races, golf tournaments, and track and field meets. Although some of these events create economic development, the pattern is that events often provide only a temporary boost to the economy and too often leave local citizens with a public debt and facilities that require annual subsidies to keep the doors open.

Governments are also interested in the long-term economic benefits of hosting events. Officials even may use the events as occasions for making contacts with corporations looking for new sites to locate their operations. Or officials may use the events to highlight and promote products made by local businesses. The governments of Japan (1964, 1998), Mexico (1968), and South Korea (1988) invested in hosting the Olympics and in their own national Olympic teams for clear economic development purposes. For Calgary, Vancouver/Whistler, and other hosts of Winter Games, sport events are occasions for promoting tourism and recreational opportunities. In many cases, the hosting of a sport event now combines the interests of civic boosters and government officials in a general effort to enhance the local economy (Huey, 1996). In fact, the policy that guides federal government support for major sport events (*Sport Canada Policy for Hosting International Sport Events*, 2008) stipulates that, in order to receive federal funding, an event must be able to generate sport development and economic, social, and cultural benefits:

"Economic benefits include job creation, particularly in the small- and medium-sized business sector, regional development, increased tourism, increased exports, enhanced infrastructure and increased tax benefit." The federal government monitors the economic outcome of events whenever public money is invested in hosting sports events, even domestic events. For example, the recently published "2007 Canada Winter Games Economic Impact Assessment" (2008; www.canadiansporttourism.com) indicated that the government's investment in the Whitehorse Winter Games was a great success in terms of economic development.

Critical Issues and Government Involvement in Sports

Government involvement in sports is justified because it serves the "public good." It would be ideal if governments promoted equally the interests of all citizens, but differences between individuals and groups make this impossible. Therefore, public investments in sports often benefit some people more than others. Those who benefit most are capable of influencing policymakers. This does not mean that government policies reflect only the interests of wealthy and powerful people, but it does mean that policies are often contentious and create power struggles among various segments of the population in a city or society.

Government involvement in sports occurs in many ways, from funding local parks for recreation and sport participation to supporting high-performance athletes for national teams. When there are debates over policies and priorities, those who represent high-performance and professional sports often are organized, generally have strong backing from other organized groups, and are able to base their requests for support on visible accomplishments achieved in the name of the entire country or community. Those who represent masses of recreational and general-ability sport participants are less likely to be politically organized and supported by powerful organizations, and they are less able to give precise statements of their goals and the political significance of their programmes.

In fact, in recent years those seeking funding for high-performance sports have often used the "participation" argument, claiming that success (usually in the form of Olympic medals) will have a "trickle-down effect" and will *cause* an increase in mass participation. There is absolutely no evidence to support this claim and, in the only actual test so far of the consequences of winning Olympic medals, Australia found that the main outcome of hosting and winning a large number of medals at the Sydney Olympics in 2000 was an increase in spectating and watching sports on television (Houlihan, 2005; Toohey, 2004). The influence of those lobbying for high-performance sport does not mean that government decision makers ignore mass participation, but it does mean that "sport for all" usually has lower priority for funding and support (Green, 2004; Green and Houlihan, 2004; Sam, 2003).

Those who believe the myth that there is no connection between sports and politics are most likely to be ignored when government involvement does occur. Those who realize that sports have political implications, and that governments are not politically neutral arbitrators of differences, are most likely to benefit when government involvement occurs. Sports are connected with power relations in society as a whole; therefore, sports and politics cannot be separated.

Sport and Canadian Governments

Canadian governments at the federal level, and to a lesser extent at the provincial/territorial and municipal levels, have been involved in sports and physical activity for all of these reasons and more. In fact, the 1943 National Fitness Act was motivated by the need for military preparedness, to recruit fit and healthy males into the Canadian military during the Second World War. However, most analysts trace the first formal involvement of the federal government in sports to the passage in 1961 of Bill C-131, the Fitness and Amateur Sports Act.

The reasons for government involvement in sport and physical activity in Canada vary over time. The initial (1961) involvement was associated with ongoing concerns about population health (*to maintain health and fitness*), and with the declining fortunes of Canadian national hockey teams at the Olympics and World Championships (*to promote the prestige and power of a nation*). After 1968, during Prime Minister Pierre Trudeau's first term of office, federal government concerns about national identity and national unity in Canada—Québec separatism, western alienation, northern isolation—became more prominent (*to promote a sense of identity, belonging, and unity among citizens*).

After Canada failed to win any gold medals at the 1976 Montréal Olympics, there was a renewed emphasis on *national prestige* and high performance to the point where, by the end of the 1980s, a U.S. academic was referring to the federally funded Canadian high-performance system as "the Big Red Machine" (MacAloon, 1990).[6] This ended quite abruptly with the Ben Johnson doping scandal in 1988, and the subsequent Dubin Commission (see "Ben Johnson, the Dubin Commission, and Drug Testing in Canada," on the Online Learning Centre), to be followed by an extended attempt to introduce more equity and inclusion into a new "athlete-centred" sport system (to reproduce values consistent with the dominant ideology).

In parallel with, and sometimes in contradiction to the equity and inclusion initiatives, a focused high-performance system has re-emerged

---

[6] This was intended as a comparison with the East German sport system—"Red" being a reference to both communism and the colour of the Maple Leaf —and a contrast to the U.S. sport system where there is very little federal government funding.

(both *national prestige* and *values consistent with dominant ideology*); there have been increasing concerns about health and obesity; and an increasing emphasis on hosting sport events for community and regional economic development (*promote economic development*) that is reflected in two Toronto Olympic bids, and Vancouver-Whistler hosting the 2010 Olympics.

One of the major struggles over this entire period has been, as it is in many countries except perhaps those in Scandinavia, the competing demands of high-performance sport and grassroots participation. These were combined in the original government departments (e.g., the Fitness and Amateur Sport Directorate in the 1970s) but had divided by 1980 with Fitness Canada housed in Health Canada and Sport Canada housed in (what is now termed) Canadian Heritage. In ideal terms, a broad base of participation will build the foundations for the high-performance system. In reality, in most countries there is little support for a broad base of participation—potential high-performance athletes are identified at an early age and their talents are developed in a distinct and relatively exclusive high-performance system. Sport Canada's focus was always high-performance sport, and Health Canada was not interested in grassroots sport (and not very interested in fitness). Despite continually stated concerns about the health and fitness of citizens, federal governments have usually been content to download responsibility for grassroots sport to the provinces (health usually being highlighted as a provincial responsibility) and municipalities, while funding and enjoying the reflected prestige associated with success at high-performance sport. However, with the adoption of the new Canadian Sport Policy in 2001, Sport Canada has now been given responsibilities for both *participation* and *excellence*—the grassroots and the high-performance systems. While the vast majority of government funding still goes to high-performance sport, Sport Canada is beginning to make strides towards increasing general participation in sport.

Mick Green's useful chart (table 13.1) outlines this development in far more detail, pointing to key political moments since 1961; what was involved in terms of organization, administration and funding; and the implications for high-performance sport.

SPORTS AND GLOBAL POLITICAL PROCESSES

Most people have lofty expectations about the impact of sports on global relations. It has long been hoped that sports would serve diplomatic functions contributing to cultural understanding and world peace. Unfortunately, the realities of sports have not matched the ideals. Nations and transnational corporations regularly use sports to promote ideologies favouring their interests, and global political realities have changed so that now a few dozen corporations have assets and budgets surpassing those of most nations worldwide. Smaller scale efforts to use sport to encourage development and peace through the international aid movement, now often referred to as "Sport for Development and Peace" (SDP), have also encountered problems. Furthermore, sports themselves have become much more global with teams recruiting athletes from outside their national borders, and sports equipment being manufactured in low- and middle-income countries where labour is often exploited.

International Sports: Ideals versus Realities

Achieving peace and friendship among nations was emphasized by Baron Pierre de Coubertin, the founder of the modern Olympic Games in 1896, and by many others since then. For more than 100 years people have hoped that international sports would do the following things:

- Create communication lines between people and leaders from different nations
- Highlight shared interests among people from different cultures and nations

Table 13.1 The development of federal policy for Canadian sports, 1961–2003

Key political policy	Organization and administration	Funding	Effect on high-performance sports
1961: Bill C-131, *Fitness and Amateur Sport Act*	Fitness and Amateur Sport Directorate (FASD) established	C$5 million per annum allocated for national programme of fitness and amateur sports	First recognition of support for high-performance sport programmes
1967: Inaugural Canada Games	Major facilities programme; invoked "Unity through Sport" theme	Federal government shares costs with provinces and municipalities	All levels of government involved with facilities for high-performance sports
1969: *Report of the Task Force on Sport for Canadians*	Proposed independent body for elite sports (not realized); highlights inadequate coach training; elite focus led to Ross Report on mass participation programmes	Recommends public/private sector cooperation in creating a structure for sports	Legitimation of federal involvement; first indications of a rational approach to sport planning; "National Unity" theme again linked to high performance
1970: White Paper, *A Proposed Sports Policy for Canadians*	Sport Canada (elite) and Recreation Canada (mass) established Sports and Recreation Centre founded	Budget grows from approx. C$6 million in 1971 to C$25 million in 1976; COA's Game Plan '76 established in 1972; Athlete Assistance Programme (AAP) established in 1973	Mass participation rhetoric, but programmes focused on high-performance sports—key actors[a] played prominent role; "National Unity" theme prominent
1976: Iona Campagnolo, first Minister of State for Sport and Fitness; Montréal Olympics	Construction of elite facilities for Montréal Olympics	Further support promised for amateur sport and fitness programme	Campagnolo states elite sports are priority; 11 medals won but no gold
1977: Green Paper, *Toward a National Policy on Amateur Sport*	Recreation Canada redesignated Fitness and Recreation Canada	Period of economic austerity in Canada; pressure on funding allocations for sports	Focus on elite sports and poor performances in international competitions
1978: Edmonton Commonwealth Games	Facilities constructed for Edmonton Games	Federal funding of C$21 million for Edmonton Games	Federal policy bears fruit, first in unofficial rankings
1979: White Paper, *Partners in Pursuit of Excellence: A National Policy on Amateur Sport*	Renewed calls for autonomous Sport Canada rejected; Fitness and Recreation Canada divided	NSO grants tied to specific goals to be achieved in elite sports; reliance on sport lottery monies	"National Unity" theme; key actors[b] crucial in technical and bureaucratic approach to high-performance sports
1981: White Paper, *A Challenge to the Nation: Fitness and Amateur Sport in the '80s*	Fitness and Recreation Canada amalgamated under Fitness Canada; recommends elite national training centres	Priority funding for sports committed to excellence; AAP consolidated	Elite sports remain in hands of federal government; funding for social-equity issues noted
1982: Approval of "Best Ever" programme for 1988 Calgary Winter Olympics	Four-year plans required from sports involved—the QPP	C$25 million budget for "Best Ever" programme	Confirmation of support for elite sports; strengthening of bureaucratic approach
1988: Calgary Winter Olympics; Ben Johnson drugs scandal at Seoul Summer Olympics	Major facilities constructed for Calgary but later criticized for high-performance focus	Approx. C$300 million overall federal commitment for Calgary, and "Best Ever" funding for both Games	Calgary a success; only ten medals from Seoul; calls for re-evaluation of elite sports after drug scandal

Continued

Table 13.1   continued

Key political policy	Organization and administration	Funding	Effect on high-performance sports
1988: Task Force Report, *Toward 2000: Building Canada's Sport System*	Need "coherent Canadian Sport System"; addressed elite *and* social-equity goals; skepticism regarding link between elite goals and education	Reiterated earlier goal for NSOs to contribute 50 percent of funding; goal, and threats to reduce funding, not realized	Further focus on elite sports; critiques regarding ignoring drugs/ethical issues; reaffirms professionalization at high-performance level
1990: Dubin Inquiry	Recommends a re-evaluation of sporting structures and processes, and anti-doping policy	Critical of federal funding controlling "the entire sports system"	Perceives a "moral crisis" in high-performance sports; critiques federal focus on high-performance sports
1992: Task Force Report on Federal Sport Policy– *Sport: The Way Ahead* (Best Report)	Broad recommendations (many ignored) relating to objectives in respect of wider social goals	Recommends reduction in sports funded; financial constraint in Canada; cut in NSO funding (~25 percent)	Recommends less focus on elite sports; medal targets should not be primary criterion of success
1993: Ministry of State for Fitness and Amateur Sport abolished by Progressive Conservatives	Fitness Canada moved to Health Canada, and Sport Canada to newly created Canadian Heritage	Sports fall victim to general cutbacks in government spending	Seen by some as decrease in importance of amateur sports; by others as less direct government involvement
1995: Sport Funding and Accountability Framework (SFAF) introduced	Attempt to encompass wider social goals in funding process to NSOs	Dependence on government direction reduced to dependency on federal funds	Rhetoric suggests move from QPP, Sport Recognition System, and elite focus
1998: Mills Sub-Committee Report, *Sport in Canada: Everybody's Business*	Examination of the "sport industry" in Canada; creation of Secretary of State (Amateur Sport) position	Recommends federal government continue policy and funding support for amateur sports generally	Recommends increase in number of NSOs to be funded; more funding for coach training; and "carded" athletes
2000: Response to the *Mills Report* (news release from Canadian Heritage)	Commitment to create "national policy on sport"; plans regional conferences	Additional C$7.5 million in funding for amateur sports	Beneficiaries: AAP, National Sports Centres, and agencies involved in fight against doping
2001: *Towards a Canadian Sport Policy: Report on the National Summit on Sport*	Three "priority actions"— Participation, Excellence, Building Capacity (the "3 Pillars")	Recommends additional C$650 million from 2001–08 for sports generally	Recommends funding excellence ("spending by result"); and public-private partnerships
2003: Bill C-12, *An Act to Promote Physical Activity & Sport*	Federal focus moves from high performance to integration of sport system under the "3 Pillars"	No specific policy guidelines with regard to future funding allocations	No initial extra funding for high-performance sports; focus at NSO level remains mainly on high performance
2006–07: *Own the Podium* and *Road to Excellence* funding introduced for high-performance sport	Reassertion of focus on high performance	COC and federal funding	Medal targets announced for Vancouver Olympics, and funding targeted to potential medal winners

[a]John Munro, Minister of Health and Welfare, and Lou Lefaive, at this time Director of the Fitness and Amateur Sport Directorate (Macintosh et al., 1987, p. 57)

[b]Roger Jackson, former Director of Sport Canada; Lou Lefaive, Director of Sport Canada; Geoff Gowan, technical director of the Coaching Association of Canada; Marion Lay, a former Olympic swimmer and, at this time, a consultant with Sport Canada; and Dan Pugliese at the National Sport and Recreation Centre

Source: Adapted from Green, 2003.

- Demonstrate that friendly international relationships are possible
- Foster cultural understanding and eliminate the use of national stereotypes
- Create a model for cultural, economic, and political relationships across national boundaries
- Establish working relationships that develop leaders in emerging nations and close the resource gap between wealthy nations and poorer nations

During the past century, it has become clear that international sports can be useful in the realm of **public diplomacy** because they create *public expressions of togetherness in the form of cultural exchanges and general communication among officials from various nations*. However, international sports have very little impact in the realm of **serious diplomacy**, which involves *discussions and decisions about political issues of vital national and international interest*. In other words, international sports provide political leaders from different nations with opportunities to meet and talk, but sports have little influence on their discussions or decisions. International sports bring together athletes, who may learn from and about one another, but athletes make no political decisions, and their relationships with one another have no serious political significance. These points were illustrated clearly in 1999, when the Cuban National Baseball Team played the Baltimore Orioles in Cuba and then again in Baltimore. Media coverage and public conversations were affected temporarily, but the games had no discernible impact on political relations between the U.S. and Cuba (Pettavino and Brenner, 1999).

Recent history shows that most nations have used sports and sport events, especially the Olympic Games, to pursue self-interests rather than international understanding, friendship, and peace. Nationalist themes going beyond respectful expressions of patriotism have been clearly evident in many events, and most nations have used sport events regularly to promote their own military, economic, political, and cultural

goals. This was particularly apparent during the Cold War era following World War II and extending into the early 1990s. During these years, the Olympics were extensions of "superpower politics" between the U.S. and its allies and the former Soviet Union and its allies.

The connection between international sports and politics was so blatant in the early 1980s that Peter Ueberroth, president of the Los Angeles Olympic Organizing Committee, said that "we now have to face the reality that the Olympics constitute not only an athletic event but a political event" (*U.S. News and World Report*, 1983). Ueberroth was not being prophetic; he was simply summarizing his observations of events leading up to the 1984 Los Angeles Olympics. He saw that nations were more interested in self-interest than global friendship and peace. The demonstration of national superiority through sport was a major focus of world powers.

Wealthy and powerful nations are not the only ones to use international sports to promote political self-interest. Many nations lacking international political and economic power have used sports in a quest for international recognition and legitimacy. For them, the Olympics and other international sports have been stages for showing that their athletes and teams can stand up to and sometimes defeat athletes and teams from wealthy and powerful nations. For example, when cricket teams from the West Indies and India play teams from England, the athletes and other people from the West Indies and India see the matches as opportunities to show the world that they are now equals to the nation that once colonized their land and controlled their people. When their teams win, it is cause for political affirmation and great celebration.

National leaders know that hosting the Olympics is a special opportunity to generate international recognition, display national power and resources to a global audience, and invite investments into their economies. This is why bid committees from prospective host cities and nations have regularly used gifts, bribes, and financial incentives to encourage IOC members to vote for them in the bid selection process. Illegal and illicit strategies reached their peak during the bidding for the 2002 Salt Lake City Winter Olympics when officials from Salt Lake City offered to IOC members and their families money, scholarships, lavish gifts, vacations, and the sexual services of "escorts" as they successfully secured the votes needed to host the games (Jennings, 1996a; Jennings and Sambrook, 2000).

The political goals of the nations hosting major international events are especially clear when nations boycott the Olympics and other international events. For example, the 1980 Moscow Games were boycotted by Canada, the United States, and some of their political allies to protest the Soviet Union's invasion of Afghanistan (possibly at the invitation of the Afghan government to support its fight against Islamic rebels). The Soviet Union and its allies then boycotted the 1984 Los Angeles Olympics to protest the commercialization of the Games. However, each of these Olympic Games was held despite the boycotts, and each host nation unashamedly displayed its power and resources to other participant nations. Furthermore, the boycotts had no major effect on national policies in any of the countries involved. However, there is one example where boycotts appear to have been particularly effective: when they were used to bring about the end of apartheid in South Africa in the early 1990s (see the Reflect on Sports box, "Sport Boycotts and the End of Apartheid," on the Online Learning Centre).

Increased global media coverage has intensified and added new dimensions to the connection between sports and politics. For example,

The sports of wealthy and powerful nations in the Western Hemisphere form the foundation of the Olympic Games. This photo of the 1936 Berlin Olympics shows the U.S. team saluting, in contrast to the straight arm gesture of the Germans that was employed by many other nations including Canada (although Canadian team members argued that they were giving the Olympic salute). The Nazi flag (far right) is prominently displayed by the host nation, and Adolf Hitler used the Olympics to promote Nazi ideology. [USOC Archives]

television companies, especially the U.S. networks, have attracted viewers to their Olympic coverage by stressing political controversies along with national interests and symbols. The theme of their coverage between 1960 and 1988 was less focused on international friendship than on "us versus them" and "this nation versus that nation." The networks justified this approach by claiming that U.S. viewers preferred to see an Olympics that extolled U.S. values and asserted U.S. global political and economic superiority. Canada has not been immune to this type of coverage, which was especially evident during the various Canada Cup hockey tournaments, and which is increasingly evident during Olympic coverage.

Although media coverage of the Olympics and other international sports has traditionally encouraged ethnocentrism and nationalism, more recent coverage reflects the end of the Cold War and the growth of global capitalism. Nationalist themes remain in the media coverage, but they are now accompanied and sometimes obscured by images and narratives promoting capitalist expansion and the products and services of transnational corporations. These issues are discussed in the box, "Olympism and the Olympic Games" (p. 436).

Nation-States, Sports, and Cultural Ideology

Sports often are used to promote ideas and orientations that foster the interests of powerful and wealthy nations. Participating in major international sport events often means that less powerful nations must look to powerful ones for guidance and resources. This encourages people in relatively poor nations to deemphasize their traditional folk games and to focus on sports developed around the values and experiences of powerful others. Furthermore, it leads them to be involved in events over which they have little control. If they wish to play, they must accept the conditions determined by people in powerful

nations. As Vicky Paraschak (1995) has pointed out, federal funding has been available for the Arctic Games, which include mainstream North American sports, but not for the Northern Games, where there is more emphasis on traditional native activities.

When people in traditional cultures want to preserve their native games, they resist the ideological influence associated with this type of "cultural imperialism," but resistance is difficult when popular international sports have rules and customs grounded in the ideologies of powerful nations (Ben-Porat and Ben-Porat, 2004; Mills and Dimeo, 2003). For example, when a U.S. sport such as football is introduced to another country, it comes with an emphasis on ideas about individual achievement, competition, winning, hierarchical authority structures, physical power and domination, the body, and the use of technology to shape bodies into efficient machines (Maguire, 1990). These ideas may not be completely accepted by those learning to play and watch football, but they do encourage orientations that privilege U.S. values and give low priority to the cooperative values more common in traditional cultures.

In more developed nations, the influence of Americanization is less clear. For example, Finland has a popular version of baseball known as *pesapallo*. In some ways, the game is quite different from the U.S. version—different equipment and rules—while in other ways, it is quite similar in terms of the uniforms, colour, and "glitz" associated with the higher levels of the game. Finns are quite adamant that the game is different from the U.S. version and that it is representative of Finnish culture; the fact that the game has not become more like baseball attests to that. In Australia, soccer is considered to be a sport of recent immigrants, a second-class sport in comparison to cricket, rugby, and Australian Rules football. Because of that status, the sport has struggled to maintain interest in the rich sporting culture of Australia, and one way that it has been successful is to take on the trappings of

REFLECT ON SPORTS

Olympism and the Olympic Games
Are They Special?

Are the Olympics just another international sport event, or are they special? The Olympic Charter claims that the Olympic Games express and promote a special philosophy:

> Olympism is a philosophy of life, exalting and combining in a balanced whole the qualities of body, will and mind. Blending sport with culture and education, Olympism seeks to create a way of life based on the joy found in effort, the educational value of good example and respect for universal fundamental ethical principles.

The fundamental principles of the Olympic Charter are simple and straightforward. They emphasize that the Olympics should provide opportunities for people worldwide to learn about and connect with one another. This is important because our future and the future of the earth itself depends on global cooperation.

The goal of Olympism is to establish processes through which we learn to understand and appreciate our differences and work together to sustain healthy and safe lifestyles for people worldwide. If the Olympic Games can be organized and played to promote these goals, they are special. However, at present, they fall short of meeting these ideals. Nationalism and commercialism exert so much influence on how the Olympic Games are planned, promoted, played, and represented by the global media that the goal of global understanding and togetherness receives only token attention (Carrington, 2004). More important has been promoting national and corporate interests.

The current method of selling media broadcasting rights for the Olympic Games subverts Olympic ideals (Andrews, 2007; Real, 1996). Television companies buy the rights to take the video images they want from the Olympics and combine them with their own narratives to appeal to audiences in their countries. Thus, instead of bringing the world together around a single experience, the coverage presents heavily nationalized and commercialized versions of the Olympic Games. Viewers and readers may impose their own meanings on this coverage, but the coverage itself serves as a starting point for most people as they think about and make sense of the Olympics.

Audiences who wish to use the Olympics to visualize a global community constructed around cultural differences can do so, but current TV coverage provides little assistance in this quest. Most coverage highlights the association between human achievement, selected cultural values, and corporate sponsors. In the processes, many people come to believe that corporations really do make the Olympics possible. As they watch the events, about 20 percent of the television time presents messages from these corporations—the companies that, in the words of the announcers, "bring you the Olympics."

People do not accept media images and narratives in literal terms, but corporate sponsors bet hundreds of millions of dollars every two years in the belief that connecting their logos with the Olympic Rings discourages criticism of their products, encourages people to consume those products regularly, and fosters audience acceptance of consumption as a lifestyle. Kevin Walmsley, director of the International Centre for Olympic Studies at the University of Western Ontario, supports these observations and the need to change the Olympic Games: he notes that the Olympic Ideal "is an empty vessel filled up by the ideas of the day" (in Price, 2004).

The IOC issues regular press releases full of rhetoric about friendship and peace, but it has made no concerted effort to develop programmes and processes making it clear to athletes and spectators that the Games are about cultural understanding and working together in socially responsible ways. Bruce Kidd (1996a), a former Olympian, argues that if the Olympic Games are to be special, they must be used to highlight global injustice, and to promote social responsibility worldwide.

Kidd suggests that athletes be selected to participate in the Olympics on the basis of their actions as global citizens, as well as their athletic accomplishments. There also should be a curriculum enabling athletes to learn about fellow competitors and their cultures. The Games should involve formal, televised opportunities for intercultural exchanges, and athletes should be

Continued

ready to discuss their ideas about world peace and social responsibility during media interviews. The IOC should sponsor projects enabling citizen-athletes to build on their Olympic experiences through service to others around the world. A proportion of windfall profits from rapidly escalating TV rights fees could fund such projects, thereby giving IOC members opportunities to talk about real examples of social responsibility connected with the Olympics. The personal stories that media corporations present during coverage of the Games could then highlight the ways that athletes are socially responsible rather than focusing on soap opera-like personal tragedies and triumphs. TV viewers may find such coverage more entertaining and hopeful than tabloid-like stories focusing on training and trauma.

Additionally, the IOC could control both nationalism and commercialism more carefully as it organizes the games and sells broadcasting rights. We offer the following suggestions:

- *Do away with national uniforms for athletes.* Let athletes choose from uniforms created by selected designers to express cultural themes from various regions of the world. This would minimize nationalism and inspire forms of expression that promote cultural understanding. Designs could be trademarked and sold, with profits going to projects to improve the working conditions for people who make clothes for less than a living wage.
- *Revise the opening ceremonies, so that athletes enter the arena by event instead of by nation.* This would emphasize unity and fellowship rather than the political and economic systems into which the athletes were born through no choice of their own. Artists from around the world would be commissioned to design flags for various sports. National flags would be displayed collectively in the middle of the field to emphasize unity amid difference.
- *Eliminate national anthems and flags during the award ceremonies.* Present medals in the stadium at the end of each day of competition in such a way that awards ceremonies emphasize athletes first

as representatives of all humanity, and second as representatives of their nations. Most people are nationalistic enough without encouragement during an event that claims to highlight global unity, not the superiority of some nations over others.
- *Eliminate medal counts for nations.* National medal counts are contrary to the spirit of the Olympic Movement. They foster chauvinism, intensify existing political conflicts, and distract attention from the achievements of athletes as representatives of humankind.
- *Eliminate or revise team sports.* Organizing team sports by nation encourages players and spectators to perceive the Games in us-versus-them terms. Therefore, eliminate all team sports or develop methods of choosing teams so that athletes from different countries play on the same teams and athletes from the same nation play on different teams (cf., intercrosse—Harvey and Houle, 1994). Then "dream teams" would emphasize international unity, rather than nationalist and commercial interests. And athletes might make more friends worldwide and learn about other cultures.
- *Add to each Games "demonstration sports" native to the cultural regions where the Games are held.* The IOC should specify that all media companies purchasing broadcasting rights and receiving press credentials must devote five percent of their coverage to these native games. Because the media influence the ways that people imagine, create, and play sports around the world, this would provide expanded images of physical activities, and facilitate creative approaches to sport participation worldwide. At present, all but two Olympic sports (judo and tae kwan do) are simply a legacy of colonial and economic powers that had the power to export their games around the world (Bale and Christensen, 2004).
- *Use multiple sites for each Olympic Games.* The cost of hosting the summer Olympic Games was US$14.6 billion in Athens (Waterford, 2004), and is estimated to be over US$30 billion in Beijing

Continued

REFLECT ON SPORTS

Olympism and the Olympic Games
continued

(2008). Such costs privilege wealthy nations and prevent less wealthy nations from being hosts and having the opportunity to highlight their cultures and reap some of the profits now associated with presenting the Games. If poorer nations could host a portion of the events, they would benefit culturally and economically, and media spectators would see a wider range of cultural settings as they viewed events over the 18 days of coverage. At present, when nations host the entire Games, they build massive and highly specialized facilities that may never be regularly used or filled to capacity in the future. This form of waste is ecologically irresponsible and often leaves citizens in cities or smaller nations smothered in massive debt created when public money was used to build useless or under-used facilities.

- *Emphasize global responsibility in media coverage and commercials.* Television contracts should mandate an emphasis on global responsibility. Athlete committees—working with committees from the Olympic Academy, which includes scholars committed to the spirit of Olympism—could develop expressions of this theme. This would link corporate sponsors to the special meaning of the Olympics and provide support for athletes as global citizens.

- *Provide television time for public service announcements from nonprofit human rights groups that work with athletes and sport organizations to promote social justice and sustainable forms of development.* This would give viewers of the Olympics an opportunity to hear messages that are not created or censored by corporations and market forces. The commercial media may not like "donating" time for noncommercial purposes, but it should be a condition of receiving the rights to cover the Games. The nonprofit groups receiving the time would be identified and selected by athletes who are involved in human rights and social justice work.

- *Integrate the Olympics and Paralympics.* Eli Wolff, director of Disability Sport at the Center for the Study of Sport in Society, proposes that just as the Olympic Movement has supported efforts to achieve gender equality and end racial apartheid in sports, "it should promote inclusion and equality of persons with disabilities within the Olympic Movement" (2005). This could be done by having common Opening and Closing ceremonies, awarding the same Olympic medals to athletes in both events, and referring to each as "Olympics." This would be in the spirit of Olympism, and it would be a powerful signal to the world that the inclusion of people with a disability is an achievable goal in all spheres of life.

Many people, especially from wealthy and powerful nations, feel that these suggestions are idealistic and do not match their view of the Olympics. However, the Olympic Movement was founded on idealism and intended to inspire visions of what the world could and should be. Just because many of us have learned to define the Olympic Games in terms of national and corporate interests does not mean that we cannot think of changing them to achieve in more direct ways the ideals on which they were founded.

Because the Olympic Games capture the attention of 30 to 60 percent of the world's population every two years, it would be encouraging if they could be used as something other than global marketing opportunities for transnational corporations and political platforms for wealthy nations that produce nearly all the medal-winning athletes. Now is a good time for the ideals of the Olympic Charter to shape the reality of the Olympics. Drop the motto *"Citius, Altius, Fortius"* ("Faster, Higher, Stronger") and replace it with "Achieving Excellence for Peace and Humanity." *What do you think?*

North American "showbiz" sports (Rowe et al., 1994). Thus, in an interesting local paradox, the global process of Americanization has been used to maintain interest in a sport not associated with North American culture.

Ideally, sports facilitate cultural exchanges through which people from different nations *share* information and develop *mutual* cultural understanding. But true 50-50 sharing and mutual understanding are rare when nations have unequal power and resources. Therefore, sports often become cultural exports from wealthy nations incorporated into the everyday lives of people in other nations. These imported sports may be rejected, but they are usually revised and reinterpreted to fit with local values and lifestyles (Ben-Porat and Ben-Porat, 2004; Denham, 2004; Maguire, 2005). However, even when revisions occur, people in traditional cultures become increasingly open to the possibility of importing and consuming additional goods, services, and ideas from the wealthy nations (Jackson and Andrews, 2004). Unless political power and economic resources are developed in connection with this process, poorer nations become increasingly dependent on wealthy nations, and it becomes difficult not to adopt many of their values and ideologies. This is a complex process, involving many issues in addition to those related to sports.

New Political Realities in an Era of Transnational Corporations

Global politics have changed dramatically since the 1970s. Nation-states have been joined by powerful transnational corporations in global power relations. As noted in chapter 11, about half of the largest economies in the world are corporations, *not* nation-states. As nation-states promote capitalist expansion by lifting trade restrictions, lowering tariffs, and loosening regulations, major transnational corporations become increasingly powerful players in global politics; many of them are more economically and politically

powerful than the nations in which their products are manufactured.

Therefore, the differences between national and corporate interests and identities are becoming increasingly blurred. This was highlighted by Phil Knight, the CEO of the U.S.–based Nike Corporation, as he explained his fan loyalties during the 1994 Men's World Cup of soccer:

> We see a natural evolution…dividing the world into their athletes and ours. And we glory ours. When the U.S. played Brazil in the World Cup, I rooted for Brazil because it was a Nike team. America was Adidas. (Lipsyte, 1996a, p. 9)

Knight identified teams and athletes in terms of corporate logos, not nationalities. When Nike paid US$200 million to sponsor Brazil's national team and used its popular players to market Nike products worldwide, Knight gave priority to his corporate logo and consumption as the most important global values. He sees international sports as sites for Nike and other corporate sponsors to deliver advertising messages promoting their products, the ideologies of consumer culture, and the structural foundation for global capitalist expansion. Knight and other executives from powerful corporations see this as good for the world and everyone in it. For them functionalist theory is their guide: sport contributes to the operation of the global social system, and this is good for everyone in the world. Other theories explain global capitalist expansion in ways that view the world from vantage points other than the CEO's top-floor office windows, from which things down on the ground are difficult to see except in terms of general patterns devoid of subjective human experiences (Lenskyj, 2004; Miller et al., 2003).

However, to the extent that corporate sponsors influence sport events and media coverage, international sports televised around the world present images and narratives directed at spectator-consumers, not spectator-citizens (see figure 13.1). Sports that do not enable corporations to deliver messages to consumers with purchasing

"NBC Sports have worked very hard to discourage nationalism during our coverage of the Olympics."

FIGURE 13.1 Nationalism is built into the very structure of the Olympics, and transnational corporations have been successful in combining global sport and national identities with an ideology that promotes consumption, competition, and individualism. Corporate logos now are as visible as national flags at most international sport events.

power are not sponsored. If spectators and potential media audiences are not potential consumers, corporations see little reason to sponsor events, and commercial media have no reasons or resources to cover them.

The global power of transnational corporations is neither unlimited nor uncontested. There are documented cases where local populations have used their own cultural perspectives to make sense of the images and narratives that come with global sports and global advertising and give them meanings that fit their lives. (Donnelly, 1996a; Foer, 2004; Maguire, 1999, 2005). However, those who use critical theory note that global media sports and the commercial messages that accompany them often cleverly fuse the global and the local through thoughtfully and carefully edited images that combine local traditions, sport action, and consumer products in seamless and technically brilliant media representations (Andrews and Silk, 1999;

Carrington and Sugden, 1999; Jackson and Andrews, 2004; Jackson and Hokowhitu, 2002; Jackson and Scherer, 2002; Miller et al., 2001, 2003; Silk, 1999). They argue that these fused images tend to "detraditionalize" local cultures by representing local symbols and lifestyles in connection with consumer products.

The observations of critical theories have not been explored sufficiently in research, but it is clear that, as corporations join or replace nation-states as sponsors of athletes and teams around the world, sports are framed in new political terms. According to John Horan, the publisher of *Sporting Goods Intelligence*, "It's not the Free World versus Communism anymore. Now you take sides with sneaker companies. Now everybody looks at the Olympics as Nike versus Reebok" (in Reid, 1996, p. 4BB). Horan's conclusion is distorted by his hope that global sports are perceived in this way, but it certainly captures the intent of transnational corporations as they spend billions to sponsor sports around the world.

Representatives from many major corporations see sports as vehicles for expanding markets and promoting an ideology that connects status and identity with consumption.

Coca-Cola may sponsor the Olympics because it wants to "teach the world to chill," but its real goal is to sell as many Cokes as possible to the world's 6.8 billion people. This is also why the MARS candy company pays millions to be the official snack food of the Olympics, and why McDonald's does the same because they are the Official Restaurant of the Olympic Games from 1996 through 2012. During the 2004 Athens Olympics, McDonald's not only served two million hamburgers to the athletes and guests in their three venues in the Olympic Village, but they also used the nearly fat-free bodies of athletes to improve their corporate image, so that they are able to more effectively sell hamburgers and fries worldwide and make everyone part of their McFamily (www.mcdonalds.com/usa/sports/olympic.html).

McDonald's and other corporations that sponsor global sports and use them as advertising platforms know that sooner or later the images and narratives associated with sources of pleasure and entertainment in people's lives will in some form enter the imaginations and conversations of those who see and hear them. Commercial messages and images do not dictate what people think, but they certainly influence what people think about, and in this way they become a part of the overall discourse that occurs in cultures around the globe.

This description of new global political realities does not mean that sports have fallen victim to a worldwide conspiracy hatched by transnational corporations. It means only that transnational organizations have joined nation-states in the global political context in which sports are defined, organized, promoted, played, presented, and given meaning around the world (Jackson and Scherer, 2002; Silk, 1999).

Sport for Development and Peace

One form of diplomacy involves international aid from wealthy nations to poorer nations. In the mid-1990s this form of aid began to include sport initiatives, a movement that has come to be known as "sport for development and peace" (SDP). SDP received a boost after the United Nations announced the Millennium Development Goals (MGDs) in 2000, and in 2005, the International Year for Sport and Physical Education, SDP initiatives were combined more specifically with the MDGs. These initiatives are so new that there are no systematic studies at this time, and researchers in the sociology of sport are only now beginning to examine this new global process. (See chapter 15 for more on SDP.)

Other Global Political Issues

As sports have become increasingly commercialized and as national boundaries have become less relevant in sports, more athletes become global migrant workers. They go where their sports are played, where they can be supported or earn money while they play, or where they can have the cultural experiences they seek. This global migration of athletes has raised new political issues in connection with sports.

Another global political issue is related to the production of sporting goods. As the demand for sports equipment and clothing has increased in wealthy nations, transnational corporations cut costs for those products by manufacturing in labour-intensive, poor countries where wages are extremely low. The result is a clear split between the world's haves and have-nots when it comes to sports. Those born into privilege in wealthy nations consume the products made by those born into disadvantaged circumstances in poor nations. This is not a new phenomenon, but it shows that sports are integrally linked with global processes and politics in yet another way.

Athletes as Global Migrant Workers Human history is full of examples of labour migration, both forced and voluntary. Industrial societies, in particular, have depended on mobile labour forces responsive to the needs of production. Now that economies are more global, the pervasiveness and diversity of labour migration patterns have increased. This is true in sports and many other occupational categories (Maguire, 2004, 2005; Maguire et al., 2002; Stead and Maguire, 2000).

Athletes frequently move from their hometowns when they are recruited to play elite sports, and then they may move many times after that, as they are traded from team to team or seek continuing opportunities to play their sports.

This migration occurs from province to province and region to region within nations, as well as from nation to nation within and between continents (Bale and Maguire, 1994; Maguire, 2004; Maguire and Stead, 2005). Each of these moves raises issues related to (1) personal adjustments by migrating athletes, (2) the rights of athletes as workers, (3) the impact of talent migration on the nations from and to which athletes migrate, and (4) the impact of athlete migration on the identities of athletes and fans.

Some migration patterns are seasonal, involving temporary moves as athletes travel from one climate area to another to play their sports. Patterns may follow annual tour schedules as athletes travel from tournament to tournament around a region or the world, or they may involve long-term or permanent moves from one region or nation to another. For example, cricket players and skiers may travel alternately to the northern and southern hemispheres to play or ski year-round.

The range of personal experiences among migrating athletes is great. They vary from major forms of culture shock and chronic loneliness to minor homesickness and lifestyle adjustment. Some athletes are exploited by teams or clubs, while others make great amounts of money and receive a hero's welcome when they return home in the off-season. Some encounter prejudice against foreigners or various forms of racial and ethnic bigotry, while others are socially accepted and make good friends. Some cling to their national identities and socialize with fellow athletes from their homelands, while others develop more global identities unrelated to one national or cultural background. In some cases, teams and clubs expect foreign athletes to adjust on their own, while others provide support for those who need to learn a new language or become familiar with new cultural settings (Klein, 1999; Maguire, 2004, 2005).

Athletic talent migration also has an impact on the nations involved. For example, when the top baseball players in Latin American nations are recruited by MLB teams in the United States and Toronto, it depletes the talent needed to maintain professional teams in Latin American nations and forces fans to depend on U.S.-based satellite television companies to watch players from their nations. As players from Japan and Korea sign contracts with MLB teams, some Japanese people worry that this trend could destroy professional baseball in their country. At the same time, they are proud that Japanese players excel on MLB teams (Cyphers, 2003; Nakamura, 2005). As they watch MLB games on satellite television, attendance and television ratings for Japanese baseball decline. Furthermore, as people in other countries watch sports based in the U.S. and Canada, they often are exposed to images and messages consistent with the advertising interests of corporations headquartered in North America.

There is also a reverse pattern of migration with players who are retired from or have not been recruited to the top tier of North American professional teams playing on European or Japanese teams in baseball, rugby, U.S. football, basketball, volleyball, and hockey (e.g., Maguire, 1995). It has been common at recent Winter Olympics for Canadian hockey commentators to point out how many players on teams from other countries are "actually Canadian," and who are taking the opportunity of dual citizenship to compete at the Olympics.

Similar patterns exist in connection with European soccer teams that recruit players from around the world (see the box on "Child Trafficking in Sports" on the Online Learning Centre). In fact, soccer has higher rates of talent migration than other sports, although hockey, baseball, track and field, and basketball have high rates as well. The impact of this migration on national talent pools, and on the ability of local clubs and teams to maintain economically viable sport programmes is complex. Talent migration usually benefits the nation to which athletes move more than it benefits the nation from which athletes come, but this is not always the case.

The global migration of athletes also may influence how people think about and identify themselves in connection with nation-states, but the topic has not been studied. Many people appreciate athletic talent regardless of the athlete's nationality (Cyphers, 2003), but they also may have a special affection for athletes born and raised in their own nation. Does this make people more open-minded and knowledgeable about other cultures, or does it make them more defensive and ethnocentric? This question becomes important because many teams and leagues recruit players from a wide range of national and cultural backgrounds. For example, in December of the 2007–08 season, 52 percent of NHL players were Canadian, 21 percent were from the U.S., and 27 percent were from European nations. In spring 2008, over 30 percent of the players on MLB teams were born outside the U.S. And of the 450 players on NBA rosters in the 2007–08 season, 76 players were from 31 countries other than the U.S.

These trends worry some people in the U.S., and the question has been raised in other countries where some leagues have quotas that limit the number of foreign-born or foreign-nationality players that teams may sign to contracts. For example, in the early 1990s, Japan banned U.S. female basketball players from its professional league. At the same time, professional leagues in Italy, Spain, and France allowed their teams to have up to two foreign players, many of whom were from the United States. In 1996, England lifted all quotas for both men's and women's pro basketball teams. The current CFL contract permits 19 imports and three quarterbacks (all usually from the U.S.) on a game day roster of 39; major junior hockey permits two non-North American players to play on each team; and CIS eligibility regulation 40.10.4.4 permits a maximum of three non-citizens or non-landed immigrants on Canadian interuniversity basketball teams. Currently, some people in the United States are calling for limits on the number of foreign athletes who can play on interuniversity teams—which may affect Canadian students—while many university athletic departments are recruiting more athletes from outside the United States. Non-Canadian athletes are beginning to play in increasing numbers onCanadian interuniversity teams, but this has not yet been identified as a problem.

As commercial sport organizations expand their franchise locations across national borders, and recruit athletes worldwide, talent migration will increase. The social implications of this trend are diverse and intersting to study.

Global Politics and the Production of Sports Equipment and Apparel Free trade agreements, such as GATT and NAFTA, which allow money and goods to flow back and forth across national borders without being taxed, have created a new global economic environment. This makes it even more cost-effective for large corporations selling products to people in wealthy nations to locate production facilities in labour-intensive poor nations. By closing factories in Canada and other high-income countries, corporations are able to move their production to countries where they pay lower taxes and much lower wages, and where they do not have the expense of meeting worker health and safety and environmental regulations. Thus, they can make the same product as they made in Canada for a much higher profit.

Through the first few years of this century many athletic shoes costing well over $100 a pair in Canada (where there are now fewer well-paid manufacturing workers) were cut and sewn by Chinese, Indonesian, and Vietnamese workers, some of them children, making less than US$2 per day (Enloe, 1995; Sage, 1999). Children in India and Pakistan, where working conditions and pay were reprehensible, stitched soccer balls. Outrage among people who became aware of these situations in the late 1990s led to widespread social activism, much of which was fuelled by the Internet. After years of confronting and struggling with companies such as Nike, Adidas, Reebok (now owned by Adidas), and others, human rights activists forced some of these corporations to enact anti-child labour policies and to allow their factories (often owned by subcontractors) to be monitored so that working conditions meet minimal standards of acceptance. But child labour and sweatshop conditions continue to exist, and a wide range of sporting goods and apparel consumed in wealthy nations is made by people living below poverty levels and working under conditions that are difficult to endure (Donnelly and Petherick, 2004).

Workers' rights continue to be a significant global issue. Research shows that it is possible to improve working conditions for people who produce sporting goods and other products if people in wealthy nations participate in actions that make corporations accountable and provide exploited workers with the resources they need to demand higher wages and better working conditions. Sage (1999; see also Knight and Greenberg, 2002) documented the impact of the Nike Transnational Advocacy Network, an Internet based form of political activism that mobilized people worldwide to force Nike to meet certain standards of social responsibility in the way their subcontractors treated production workers. Sage's study is heartening because it shows that change is possible, even when dealing with multibillion-dollar corporations and the autocratic governments of nations that allow corporations to exploit their people. The study is also provocative because it indicates that unless consumers in wealthy nations are concerned about how their products are made, there is little to stop transnational corporations that operate in an underregulated global marketplace from pursuing profits in whatever way they wish.

Students in North America have been very involved in these workers' rights campaigns, and organizations such as United Students Against Sweatshops have been particularly effective in their campaigns to ensure that university athletics department uniforms and shoes, and licensed products sold at university stores, are produced under fair working conditions. This has led to a situation where many universities in Canada and the U.S. now publish, and make efforts to enforce, codes of conduct for licensees. For example, the University of Toronto's Code states: "The University will do business only with licensees whose workers are present to work voluntarily, are not at undue risk of physical harm, are fairly compensated, and are not exploited in any way." The Code goes on to list specific guidelines that must be followed in terms of wages and benefits, working hours, overtime compensation, the non-use of child labour or forced labour, health and safety conditions, worker freedom from discrimination, harassment and abuse, and the freedom to organize. Many corporations still seek the cheapest labour they can find to manufacture products. Human rights and social justice groups have fought these battles for many years, but they need help. See, for example, the "Play Fair 2008" campaign to encourage the IOC, Beijing Olympic organizers, NOCs, and IFs to require fair labour practices for their products and services (www.playfair2008.org).

Making Sense of Political Realities

It is not easy to explain all the changes discussed in this chapter. Are sports simply a part of general globalization processes through which various forms of sport come together in many combinations? Are we witnessing the modernization of sports? Are sports being Americanized? Europeanized? Asianized?

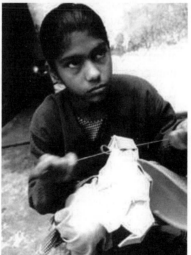

In the mid-1990s, many people became aware of the exploitive labour practices used to produce sports equipment and apparel. These photos, provided by the Global March Against Child Labour, show a twelve-year-old girl in India sewing a soccer ball. The ball is stamped with the claim that it is made with "Child Free Labour." Sweatshop labour is still used to produce sport products consumed by people in wealthy nations, but global social activism has stopped some companies from using child labour. [Global March Against Child Labor]

Do global processes involve the diffusion of sports throughout the world, with people in some countries emulating the sports played in other countries, or do they involve the use of sports in connection with capitalist expansion, new forms of cultural imperialism, and colonization? Are sports used to make poorer nations dependent on wealthier ones, or do they provide emerging nations with opportunities to establish cultural and economic independence. As globalization occurs, will traditional sports and folk games around the world be replaced by the competitive sports favoured by wealthy and powerful nations?

Those who study sport in society are increasingly concerned about these and related questions. The best work on these issues involves data collected at global *and* local levels (Bale and Christensen, 2004; Bale and Cronin, 2003; Ben-Porat and Ben-Porat, 2004; Denham, 2004; Donnelly, 1996a; Foer, 2004; Harvey et al., 1996; Hastings et al., 2005; Maguire, 1999, 2004, 2005; Okubu, 2004). This work indicates that powerful people do not simply impose certain sport forms on less powerful people around the world. Even when sports from powerful nations are played in other parts of the world, the meanings given to them are grounded in the local cultures in which they are played. Global trends are important, but so are the local expressions of and responses to those trends. Power is a process, not a thing; it is always exercised through relationships and current forms of social organization, so our understanding of power must take into account the ways that societies are organized and the ways that people determine what is important as they live with one another. This is true in connection with sports, and in all dimensions of social life.

POLITICS IN SPORTS

The term *politics* usually is associated with the formal government entities in the public sphere. However, politics include all processes of governing people and administering policies, at all levels of organization, public and private. Therefore, politics are an integral part of sports, and many local, national, and international sport organizations are referred to as "governing bodies."

One thing that characterizes sport organizations, is fragmentation. There are so many different organizations, clubs, leagues, multi-sport and service organizations, and ethical and judicial bodies dealing with issues of doping and dispute resolution, that they have an extremely difficult time ever speaking with one voice in order to lobby effectively for the sport community. Table 13.2 attempts to capture the diversity and complexity of the sport community in Canada.

Most sport organizations provide and regulate sport participation opportunities, establish and enforce policies, control and standardize competitions, and acknowledge the accomplishments of athletes. This sounds like a straightforward set of tasks, but they seldom are accomplished without opposition, debate, and compromise. Members of sport organizations agree on many things, but conflicts often arise as decisions are made in connection with the following questions:

1. What qualifies as a sport?
2. What are the rules of a sport?
3. Who makes and enforces the rules in sports?
4. Who organizes and controls sport events?
5. Where do sport events take place?
6. Who is eligible to participate in a sport?
7. How are rewards distributed to athletes and others associated with sports?

These questions are inherently political because the answers affect different people in different ways. Most people understand this, but they complain about politics in sports only when the answers are not the ones they want to hear. This becomes clear in the following sections.

What Qualifies as a Sport?

As noted in chapter 1, there is no universal agreement on the definition of *sports*. What is considered a sport in a society or in a particular event such as the Olympics, is determined through political processes (Donnelly, 1996b). The criteria used to identify sports reflect the ideas and interests of some people more than others. In the Summer Olympics, for example, a competitive activity or game for men played in at least seventy-five countries on four continents may be considered for inclusion in the Olympic Games; an activity or a game for women must be played in at least forty countries on three continents. It also must have an officially designated international governing body, a requisite number of national governing bodies, and a history of international championships before the IOC will consider recognizing it as an Olympic sport. The qualifications for entry to the Winter Olympics are necessarily less restrictive, but they are preventing women's ski jumping from inclusion at the 2010 Vancouver Olympics. IOC decisions about what qualifies as a sport may be changed, as seen in 2005 when baseball and softball were eliminated from the programme for the 2012 London Olympics,[7] and when new sports have been included despite barely meeting the qualifying requirements.

In these days of multibillion-dollar media contracts, an activity or a game is more likely to be recognized as a sport if it is attractive to viewers, who will bring new advertisers and corporate sponsors to the Olympics and the television coverage of the games. It also helps if women play the activity, because more women than men watch the Olympics and the IOC knows it must highlight gender equity if it is to avoid bad publicity for the Olympics as a whole.

This method of determining what qualifies as sport favours the nations that historically have had the resources to export their games around the world. Former colonial powers are especially favoured because they used their national games to introduce their cultural values and traditions to peoples in the regions they colonized. Wealthy and powerful nations today not only have their national sports broadcast on satellite channels around the world, but also have the resources to subsidize the development of these sports worldwide. Therefore, when the IOC uses its method of recognition, the sports from wealthy nations are at the top of the list. When these sports are recognized as official Olympic sports, the cultural values and traditions of wealthy and powerful nations are reaffirmed. In this way, the sports in wealthy and powerful nations become part of an emerging global culture that favours their interests.

This is also why native games in traditional cultures are not a part of the Olympic Games. Games played only in limited regions of the world do not qualify for recognition as sports. However, if they met the criteria outlined above (younger viewers, television friendly, female participation), or if they have substantial political support at the IOC, the criteria are easily waived. This was the case with curling and tae kwan do, which have been included at several Olympics since 1988. Therefore, if people from nations with traditional cultures want to participate in the Olympics, they must learn to play sports as they are done in wealthy nations. If people in traditional cultures lack access to the equipment and facilities needed to train in their homelands, they must depend on support from people and organizations in wealthy nations to become international athletes in recognized "international" sports. In this way, sports enable people and organizations in wealthy nations to gain a cultural foothold in other nations and use it to promote changes that foster their interests.

This type of political process also occurs in other contexts. For example, for well over one hundred years, the men who have controlled athletic departments in North American high schools and universities have used a power and performance model to designate certain activities as interschool or interuniversity sports. They have organized these sports to emphasize competition and physical dominance, so that they

---

[7]Baseball and softball are applying for re-entry at the 2016 Olympics, and golf, rugby, squash, karate, and roller sports are also applying to participate at those Games. The IOC will select two of these sports in 2009.

reaffirm male notions of character and excellence. This way of defining and organizing sports seldom has been questioned, but if power and performance sports attract fewer girls and women than boys and men, it may be time to ask critical questions about what qualifies as an interschool or interuniversity sport, and why. When we ask these questions, we become sensitive to the politics of sports that have long worked to the advantage of men in sports. Trying to change taken-for-granted political realities always creates resistance among those who have benefited from them. Ironically, many men say that people who challenge traditional realities are slaves to "political correctness." What they mean, however, is that they do not want to change the insensitive and self-interested ways of doing things that allow them to ignore the needs of others.

The development of the criteria underlying the meaning and organization of sports also occurs on a global scale. Donnelly (1996b) illustrates this in his analysis of how the ideologies of "Olympism" and "professionalism" have been combined to form a global sport monoculture, which he calls "prolympism." Prolympism is now the model for determining what qualifies and is funded as "sport" in nations around the world. This occurs even in nations where prolympism is clearly inconsistent with traditional games. In this way, the politics of defining *sports* are both local and global in impact.

What Are the Rules of a Sport?

Sports are social constructions because people create them as they interact with one another within the constraints of culture and society. The rules that govern sports are also social constructions created through political processes. Why should the penalty spot in field hockey be located 6.4 metres from the goal line? Why should soccer goals be 7.23 metres wide? Why should the top of volleyball nets be 2.24 metres off the ground in international women's volleyball? Why are pole-vaulters not able to use any type of pole they want? Why are tournament golfers

prevented from using any type of golf club or golf ball they want? Why is 6 centimetres the maximum height for the sides of bikini bottoms worn by women in beach volleyball, when men wear long shorts? This list of questions could go on and on. The point is that the rules of sports can be based on many concerns, and this makes them political. Because sports have more rules than many human activities, they are especially political.

Who Makes and Enforces the Rules in Sports?

The rules of an "official" sport are determined by a recognized governing body that makes decisions affecting the sport and its participants. The process of becoming recognized as the *sole* governing body of a sport clearly involves politics (Sugden and Tomlinson, 1998, 1999). Governing bodies have power, status, and control over resources, so it is common for more than one organization to claim that it is the rightful rule-making body for a sport. The simultaneous existence of various governing bodies creates confusion for athletes and spectators. Professional boxing, for example, has had at least four governing bodies (the WBO, the WBU, the WBF, and the IBO), each with its own weight categories and championships and each claiming to be the official rule-making body for boxing. "New" sports, such as skateboarding snowboarding, in-line skating and BMX (biking), each have had at least two organizations vying to be official governing bodies. As organizations seek power over sports and the athletes who participate in them, they battle one another to recruit dues-paying members and to sponsor competitive events, especially national and international championships. In the process, their policies confuse athletes and limit participation opportunities. When this occurs, people clearly see the politics in sports.

When rules exist, there is also a need for rule enforcement. This adds another political dimension to sports. Anyone who has ever refereed or

Table 13.2   The Canadian sport community[a]

INTERNATIONAL

Major Games Federations	International Sport Federations (IFs)	Governments and NGOs
• International Olympic Committee (IOC) • Commonwealth Games Federation (CGF) • International Paralympic Committee (IPC) • FISU (World Student Games)	• FIFA (soccer) • IAAF (track and field) •FIS (skiing)	• General Assembly of International Sport Federations (GAISF) •World Anti-Doping Agency (WADA)

REGIONAL

• North American Indigenous Games Council • PASO (Pan-Am Games)	•CONCACAF (soccer)	• Council of Europe

NATIONAL

	National Sport Organizations (NSOs)	
• Canadian Olympic Committee (COC) • Canadian Interuniversity Sport (CIS) • Commonwealth Games Canada • Canada Games Council • Canadian Colleges Athletics Association • Special Olympics Canada • Canadian Paralympic Committee • Arctic Winter Games	• Badminton Canada • Skate/Patinage Canada • Rowing Canada Aviron • Patinage de Vitesse Canada • Swimming/Natation Canada	• Canadian Heritage (Sport Canada) • Coaching Association of Canada • Canadian Centre for Ethics in Sport • Canadian Academy of Sport Medicine • Canadian Sport Centres • AthletesCAN • CAAWS • Aboriginal Sport Circle • Sport Dispute Resolution Centre

PROVINCIAL

	Provincial Sport Organizations (PSOs)	
• Provincial Games Organizations • Provincial Special Olympics • Provincial Disability Sports	• Hockey Québec • Newfoundland Rugby Union • Dancesport BC	• Provincial and Territorial Ministries Responsible for Sport • Provincial Sport Administration Centres

MUNICIPAL

	• Sport clubs • Youth sport organizations	• Municipal Parks and Recreation Departments

[...] [...] s of organizations/institutions at each level

[...] from Department [...] Heritage. Reproduced with the permission of the Minister of Public Works officiated a game or match will tell you that rule violations are seldom clear-cut. Identifying violations is difficult, and few people see violations the same way. Rule violations occur on a regular basis in many sports, but the best referees learn when to call fouls or penalties in connection with these violations. In fact, referees and officials discuss when they should or should not call fouls during games and matches. They realize that it is a political challenge to make sports appear to be fair to athletes and spectators.

Enforcing off-the-field rules is also a political challenge. The process of investigating rule violations, determining innocence or guilt, and punishing rule violators involves judgment based on ideas about fairness, moral principles, economic interests, personal reputations, organizational prestige, or other factors. How these factors are considered and which ones prevail in the rule enforcement process are political matters.

We also see the politics of rule enforcement in the policies of sport organizations. For example, CIS, the primary governing body for interuniversity sports in Canada, is made up of representatives of member universities located across Canada. Because university sports mean different things from one region of the country to another, these representatives often have contradictory ideas about what is legitimate conduct and what is not. Developing a set of rules and enforcement procedures under these conditions involves intensely political processes. Rule enforcement inevitably creates dissent among the members whose ideas about legitimate conduct are not consistent with what CIS has determined to be "right and official." When this occurs, political processes become heated, as was the case recently with the issue of scholarships.

Who Organizes and Controls Sport Events?

Representatives of official governing bodies usually organize and control sport events. Standards emerge when the governing body is stable, but standards do not exist once and for all time. For example, even though governing bodies devise formal standards for judging performances in figure skating, diving, and gymnastics, research shows that judges' votes are influenced by political loyalties, personal connections, coercion, and bribes (Jennings, 1996a; Jennings and Sambrook, 2000; Seltzer and Glass, 1991). This has been a serious issue in many Olympic Games, and became widely publicized in 2002 as "Skategate," the Salé and Pelletier judging scandal at the Salt Lake City Olympics. The ISU changed its rules to discourage unfair judging, but the changes were widely criticized and were revised several times between 2003 and 2006.

When international politics influence judges, it is disheartening to athletes, but it should be no more disheartening than the knowledge that "cuteness," "hairstyles," "body build," and "eye colour" can also influence judges when it comes to female athletes in certain events. This is a form of cultural politics that forces some athletes to spend thousands of dollars on everything from braces to straighten their teeth to plastic surgery if they wish to be successful. Politics comes in many forms.

Now that sports are heavily commercialized, official governing bodies and a combination of corporate sponsors and media production people organize and control events. The location and timing of events, event schedules, the awarding of press credentials, and the choices of which television companies will broadcast the events and which corporate logos will be displayed are resolved through political processes. The participants in those processes and their interests change from one event to the next; this means that the politics in sports never end.

Where Do Sport Events Take Place?

Site selection decisions have become increasingly political recently because more "places" now bid to host teams and events.

The selection of Olympic sites has always been political, as clearly demonstrated by the site selection, vote-buying scandal involving the IOC and the Salt Lake Olympic Organizing Committee during the 1990s. As the stakes for hosting the Olympic Games have increased, bid committees have been willing to wine, dine, bribe, and pressure IOC members, whose votes determine which city hosts a particular Games (Jennings, 1996a; Jennings and Sambrook, 2000; Simson and Jennings, 1992). The politics of site selection also work in other ways. For example, when Atlanta was selected to host the 1996 Games, it was clear to many people that the selection process was influenced by the television rights fees anticipated from NBC, and the location of Coca-Cola's international headquarters in Atlanta. Coca-Cola had a long history of paying millions of dollars to support the IOC and sponsor the Olympics, and IOC members felt indebted to the corporation. During the Games, the red-and-white Coke logo was so evident in Atlanta that many observers described them as the "Coca-Colympics."

The selection of Beijing, China, for the 2008 Summer Olympics involved political considerations and complex political processes. China was desperate to host the Games because it wanted to showcase its culture, encourage tourism and business investments, and claim political legitimacy as a global power. Despite widespread concerns about China's human rights record, members of the IOC selection committee were influenced to select Beijing by many considerations: China was home to nearly 20 percent of the world's population, it had never hosted an Olympic Games, bringing Olympism to China would strengthen the Olympic Movement, and the potential economic benefits of awarding the Games to China were very high because corporate sponsors would see China as a prime site for capitalist expansion. NBC, the U.S. network with the rights to televise the 2008 Games, saw China as an attractive site for marketing its coverage. The network knew that by 2008 many Americans would be very interested in China because of its size, power, culture, and economic growth potential. NBC also knew it could use that interest to boost ratings and sell high-priced advertising time to transnational corporations.

Site bids for events such as the Grey Cup; All-Star games; CIS championships in (men's) basketball and football; world championships in cycling, swimming, and track and field; as well as other international events, may not cost as much as bids to host the Olympics, but they are just as political.

Sports and the politics of place in many parts of the world also reflect environmental issues (Chernushenko, 1994). For example, the use of open space or agricultural land for golf courses now is being contested in Europe, Japan, and even North America. The Global Anti-Golf Movement (GAG-M; www.antigolf.org) has developed in connection with widespread objections to the use of chemical fertilizers, pesticides, and massive water resources to keep grass soft and green for golfers representing the economic elite in societies. GAG-M is a loosely organized collection of lobbying groups, often focused on environmental issues in densely populated regions of India and Southeast Asia.

Ski resort expansion in North America, Europe, and Japan also has been resisted for environmental reasons. The organizers of the 2000 Sydney Olympics faced severe criticism when they failed in important ways to live up to the environmental principles developed by the original bid committee (Lenskyj, 2002). Such examples highlight the fact that the politics of place in sports often involve local opposition to the hosting of events and the building of facilities.

Who Is Eligible to Participate in a Sport?

Cuban born Yamilé Aldama is a Sudanese citizen; she lives in London and has also taken British citizenship. Let us imagine that she married a Jamaican and gave birth to a child in Canada. As a high-performance athlete, Ms. Aldama wants to compete at the Olympics, but which is her national team? Such questions are increasingly common today as athletes have parents from different nations and a birthplace that is different from the nations where they live, train, attend university, or get married (Layden, 2005; Wertheim, 2004).

Who plays and who does not play is often a hotly contested issue in sports. As people in governing bodies make eligibility decisions, they use criteria such as gender, age, weight, height, ability (and disability), place of residence, citizenship, educational affiliation, university grades, social status, income, religion, or even race and ethnicity to determine participation eligibility. Although eligibility policies often are presented as if they are based on unchanging truths about human beings and sports, they are grounded in political agreements. This is true in local youth sport programmes and the Olympics.

People often debate the seeming arbitrariness of eligibility rules. For example, in CIS, disputes about eligibility rules have resulted in Policy No. 40 (Eligibility) being one of the longest and most complex to administer. Lawsuits sometimes follow unsuccessful appeals, because people feel they have been excluded unfairly from participation. High school students have made similar challenges when their families have moved from one school district to another and they have found that they are ineligible to play interschool sports. Even in youth sports, there are frequent debates about the age and weight rules used to determine eligibility. Athletes with a disability regularly have challenged rules prohibiting their participation in certain sports. Within events such as the Paralympics, the international event held immediately following the Olympic Games, there are frequent debates about disability classifications and eligibility (see the Breaking Barriers box on p. 453).

There are literally hundreds of other noteworthy cases of eligibility politics in amateur and professional sports. Sikh boxers in British Columbia and Ontario have challenged boxing regulations that stipulate that boxers who wear a beard are ineligible to box; and female participants in soccer and tae kwan do have challenged regulations in Québec that prevent them from wearing the *hijab*. As global mobility increases, there will be more debates about eligibility as it relates to citizenship, nationality, and place of residence. Amateur sports have been the scene for debates over the meaning of *amateur* and who qualifies as an amateur athlete. Because these meanings are socially determined, they change over time and from place to place. This is another reason why politics will always be a part of sports.

How Are Rewards Distributed to Athletes and Others?

The distribution of rewards is an issue at all levels of sport participation. Coaches, league administrators, sportswriters, judges, team owners, arbitrators, tournament committees, and parents decide who will receive special commendations, certificates of accomplishment, trophies, scholarships, contracts, pay increases, and so on. "Who gets what?" is a political question, and the answers are not always clear-cut. People discuss and sometimes argue about rewards. As the level of competition increases, so do the stakes associated with decisions. At the highest levels of competition, these decisions can involve massive amounts of money and status.

With the increased commercialization of sports, there are heated debates about how revenues should be distributed among sport organizations, organization officials, owners and promoters, athletes, and others connected with sports. As noted in chapter 11, the political processes associated with the distribution of revenues in commercial sports are complex and never ending. These processes take various forms and come to different resolutions in different countries and sports.

Other debates revolve around questions such as these: Why should professional sport team owners make more money than the best players on their teams? What percentage should agents receive when they negotiate player contracts? Why should Olympic athletes not be paid for their participation when they collectively

Breaking Barriers

Political Barriers
I Think… This Opens Some Doors for People

When we talk about sports and people with a disability, we must talk politics; there is no way around it. Take Casey Martin as an example. In 1994 as a junior at Stanford University in the U.S. he was voted captain of the golf team. He responded by leading them to the interuniversity championship. Tiger Woods joined the team in 1995, and Martin was his roommate when Stanford played tournaments away. Martin won the U.S. Intercollegiate Golf Championship that year and led Stanford to the NCAA finals.

But all was not well with Martin. He was born with a congenital defect in his right leg. It prevented normal blood circulation and was gradually eroding his bone and causing him increasingly severe and chronic pain. There were times when he could barely walk, so his coach convinced him to use a golf cart, permissible under NCAA rules, given his medical condition. After graduating, Martin played professional golf and by 1997 found that there were times when he could not walk and needed a motorized cart to complete eighteen holes. But the PGA ruled that Martin had to walk or quit. Martin sued and won an injunction allowing him to use a cart. The PGA appealed and the case eventually went to the U.S. Supreme Court. In a split decision, the court ruled in 2001 that, under the Americans with Disability Act of 1990, Martin must be allowed to use a cart because it did not force the PGA to make an unreasonable accommodation in his case.

Playing politics with the PGA for four years cost Martin well over $100,000. His pain and fatigue continued to increase and he played only nine tournaments between 2001 and late 2005. At thirty-six years old (in 2008), he knows that a leg amputation is a certainty.

In the meantime, Nike has established the Casey Martin Nike Award that honours an individual with a disability who has taken a public stand and engaged in political battles to inspire or expand sport participation rights for people with a disability. Nike's position is that, "If you have a body, you are an athlete."

The Casey Martin story is not unique. People with a disability have always fought political battles to avoid being invisible in the world of sport (DePauw, 1997). For example, even in 2005 as representatives of London, Madrid, Moscow, New York, and Paris gave detailed presentations in the hope of being chosen by the IOC to host the 2012 Olympics and Paralympics, only Madrid mentioned the Paralympics in their overall plan. Invisibility was in plain sight.

After the Supreme Court decision in 2001, Casey Martin said, "I"m thrilled… I think in the future this opens some doors for people." However, in the real world of sport where decisions are made about everything from eligibility and the rules of the game, to where events are played and the distribution of rewards, people with a disability know that if they do not play politics, eventually, they will not play at all.

Politics are related to sports for people with a disability in many ways. War, land mines, and dangerous working conditions continue to be leading causes of disabilities worldwide. Elliot Mujaji of Zimbabwe lost his arm when he was electrocuted in an accident at work. He won gold medals in the 100-metre race in both Sydney and Athens. [David Biene; photo courtesy of Ossur]

generate several billion dollars during a Summer Olympics? Why should the IOC receive 35 percent of the revenues for the Olympic Games,[8] when it does little other than award the Games to a particular city, and the members are wined and dined in lavish style in the process? Should athletes receive compensation when their images and uniform numbers are used in video games? These and hundreds of similar questions show that the "politics of rewards" is an integral part of sports.

Sometimes rewards involve status or prestige, rather than money. For example, debates over status occur in connection with the selection of professional athletes for Halls of Fame and All-Star games. And, when combined with athlete migration, they may produce "odd" status awards such as the award for the Outstanding Canadian player in the CFL (an award separate from one for the league's Outstanding Player). Even youth league teams have "politics of status" awards for "the most improved player of the year," "the most valuable player," "the most dedicated player," and so on. When people agree on the players who should receive these awards, they forget that the selection process is political. It is only when they do not agree with the selection that they talk about politics in sports.

SUMMARY

HOW DO GOVERNMENTS AND GLOBALIZATION INFLUENCE SPORTS?

Sports and politics are inseparable. Government involvement in sports is generally related to the need for sponsorship, organization, and facilities.

---

[8]Olympic Marketing revenue for 2001–04 was US$4.2 billion; approximately 65 percent of this is returned to the Summer and Winter Olympics Organizing Committees, the IOC keeps 8 percent, and the remainder is distributed to IFs and NOCs (including the Canadian Olympic Committee); the NOCs received US$319.5 million during this period.

The fact that sports are important in people's lives and can be sites for social conflict often leads to government regulations and controls. The forms of government involvement in sports vary by society, but they generally occur to (1) safeguard the public order, (2) maintain health and fitness among citizens, (3) promote the prestige and power of a group, community, or nation, (4) promote a sense of identity, belonging, and unity among citizens, (5) reproduce values consistent with dominant ideology, (6) increase support for political leaders and government structures, and (7) promote economic development.

The rules, policies, and funding priorities set by government officials and agencies reflect the political struggles among groups within any society. This does not mean that the same people always benefit when government involvement occurs, but involvement seldom results in equal benefits for everyone. For example, when funds are dedicated to the development and training of high-performance athletes, fewer funds are available to support general participation programmes. Funding priorities could favour mass participation instead of high-performance sports, but the point is that the priorities themselves are subject to debate and negotiation. This political process is an inevitable part of sports.

History shows that government intervention in sports usually favours groups with the greatest resources, organization, and outside support, and with goals that support the ideological orientations of public officials. The groups least likely to be favoured are those that fail to understand the connection between sports and politics, or lack the resources to effectively influence political decisions. As long as people believe the myth that sports and politics are unrelated, they are unlikely to be pleased when officials develop policies and allocate funds.

The connection between sports and global political processes is complex. Ideally, sports bring nations together in contexts supportive of peace and friendship. Although this occurs, the reality is that most nations use sports to foster their own interests. Displays of nationalism have been and continue to be common at international events. The Olympic Games are a good case in point. People who work with, promote, or follow the Olympics often focus on national medal counts and use them to support their claims for national superiority.

Powerful transnational corporations have joined nation-states as major participants in global political processes. As a result, sports are used increasingly for economic as well as political purposes. Nationalism and the promotion of national interests remain a part of global sports, but consumerism and the promotion of capitalist expansion have become more important since 1991 and the end of the Cold War. Within the context of global relations, athletes and teams now are associated with corporate logos as well as nation-states. Global sport events are now political *and* economic. They are sites for presenting numerous images and narratives associated with the interests of nation-states and corporate sponsors. The dominant discourses associated with sports are clearly consistent with the interests of corporate sponsors, and they promote an ideology infused with the capitalist values of individualism, competition, achievement, and consumption.

Global political processes also are associated with other aspects of sports, such as the migration patterns of elite athletes, and the production of sporting goods. Political issues are raised when athletes cross national borders to play their sports, as well as when transnational corporations produce sports equipment and clothing in labour-intensive poor nations and then sell those items in wealthy nations. These and other issues associated with global political processes are best understood when they are studied at both global and local levels. Data from these studies help to determine when sports involve reciprocal cultural exchanges leading to mutual understanding among people, and when they involve processes through which powerful nations and corporations exercise subtle influence over social life and political events in less powerful nations.

Politics are also part of the very structure and organization of sports. Political processes exist because people in sport organizations must answer questions about what qualifies as a sport, what the rules of a sport should be and how they should be enforced, who should organize and control sport events, where sport events should occur, who is eligible to participate, and how rewards will be distributed. This is why many sport organizations are described as governing bodies: they are responsible for making decisions that affect people connected with sports. This demonstrates that sports are inseparable from politics and political processes.

Visit *Sports in Society*'s Online Learning Centre at <ins>www.mcgrawhill.ca/olc/coakley</ins> for additional information, website resources, and study tools for this chapter.

Sports in High School and University

Do interscholastic sport programmes contribute to education?

The primary reason...for the existence of school sport is the educational value it imparts to the students.

> —Colin Hood, executive director, Ontario Federation of School Athletic Associations (1999)

High school sports was the key that opened up a new series of doors for me.... [They] showed me the importance of attitude, motivation, competition, and teamwork, and allowed me to understand that as years went by, if you were still thinking about what you did yesterday you probably haven't done much today.

> —Chris Walby, retired athlete, Winnipeg Blue Bombers, CBC commentator; St. John's High School, Winnipeg, Football

Ninety-two percent of Canadians believe that sport *can* positively influence the development of youth and communities. Less than 1 in 5 Canadians believe that sport is living up to its potential.

> —True Sport survey, 2003

Education through school sport.

> —OFSAA slogan

The emergence of modern organized sports is closely tied to education in the U.K., the Commonwealth, and North America. However, few high schools outside these countries and parts of Japan sponsor and fund interschool sport programmes. Organized sports for adolescents and young adults in most developed countries are tied to community-based athletic clubs funded by members or a combination of public and private sources.

Interscholastic sports have become an accepted and important part of Canadian high schools, colleges, and universities. The term **interscholastic** is used here to refer in a broad sense to *organized competitive sports carried out between educational institutions*. In general, Canada has three levels of competition:

- Interschool sports, between high schools, governed by the Canadian School Sport Federation (CCSF) and ten provincial school athletic associations; primary and middle schools often have interschool competitions—e.g., track and field and cross-country meets, basketball games, and so on;
- Intercollegiate sports (between community colleges and, in Québec, CEGEPs) governed by the Canadian Colleges Athletic Association and five regional conferences (Atlantic, Québec, Ontario, Alberta [includes Saskatchewan], and B.C.);
- Interuniversity sports governed by Canadian Interuniversity Sport (CIS) and four regional conferences (Atlantic, Québec, Ontario, and Canada West).[1]

There are no essential differences between private and public institutions in Canada with regard to interscholastic sports, except that many of the more established private schools have a clear expectation that their students and staff will be involved in extracurricular activities.

Interscholastic sports are distinguished from *intramural* sports, played within an educational institution and organized in various ways. University intramural programmes may have teams organized to represent residences, academic departments, or even ethnocultural communities, as well as teams organized on a more *ad hoc* basis. School intramurals, if they exist at all, are often organized on an *ad hoc* basis by the student athletic association, although some schools (often private schools) echo the British "house" system in which the whole school is divided into four (usually) named "houses" that compete against one another in a variety of ways, including sports (this system will be familiar to those who know Hogwarts School). There are many variations on these forms of intramural organization. We know of one Ontario elementary school that had a dynamic lunchtime activity programme (organized by an itinerant physical education teacher) in which all the teams were named after vegetables—school announcements would sound like this: "In the gym at lunchtime today, the 'Potatoes' will be playing the 'Cauliflowers,' and the 'Zucchinis' will be playing the 'Carrots' at broomball." The Canadian Intramural Recreation Association (CIRA), which, in 2003, became part of the Canadian Association for Health, Physical Education, Recreation and Dance (CAHPERD), provides leadership in school intramural sports, while many Canadian universities are affiliated with the U.S.-based National Intramural-Recreational Sports Association (NIRSA).

This chapter is organized around five major questions related to interscholastic sport programmes:

1. How do interscholastic sport programmes in Canada compare with those in the United States?
2. What are the arguments for and against interscholastic sports?
3. How are the programmes related to the educational experiences of athletes and other students in high schools and universities?

---

[1]This chapter focuses on universities and schools; colleges are excluded because we are not aware of any research on college sports and physical activity in Canada.

4. What effects do the programmes have on the organization of schools and universities and the quality of educational programmes?
5. What are the major problems associated with the programmes, and how might they be solved?

COMPARISON BETWEEN CANADIAN AND U.S. INTERSCHOLASTIC SPORTS[2]

Perhaps more than any other aspect of Canadian sports, interscholastic sports, and particularly interuniversity sports, stand in relation to and in comparison with the U.S. system of interscholastic sports. While there are striking similarities between the two systems, the differences have become the object of focus. The differences are primarily a question of scale. For example, in many parts of the U.S., high school sports—especially sports such as football and (boys') basketball—are seen as a significant part of the development system for U.S. interuniversity sports. High schools may have an intense focus on basketball, for example, or, in states such as Texas, Michigan, and Ohio, on football. Some of the U.S. programmes may have full-time coaches—we are not aware of any full-time teacher-coaches in Canada. Large paying crowds may attend the games, and a great many school resources are focused on specific (usually male) teams (cf., Foley, 1990; Grey, 1992). This so-called "hothousing" system certainly produces athletic excellence, but critics suggest that such focused excellence is achieved at the cost of failing to provide interschool sport experiences for many other students in a variety of sports (Grey, 1992). While some athletes, and their coaches, at Canadian high schools may have a similar focus in terms of attempting to achieve a U.S. university scholarship or, increasingly, a Canadian

university scholarship, in general, Canadian schools seem to offer a greater diversity of sports and a less intense level of competition. Students may be encouraged to play several sports, and teacher-coaches may encourage individuals who are unsure of their athletic abilities to participate on teams.

Interuniversity sports represent even more of a contrast in terms of scale. While many U.S. universities have interuniversity sport programmes on a scale quite similar to that in Canada, the NCAA (National Collegiate Athletic Association) Division I programmes tend to command attention in Canada, especially in sports such as football, basketball, and, to a lesser extent, hockey. With the widespread availability of U.S. networks on Canadian television, Canadians are exposed to network broadcasts of Division I football and basketball games, including the New Year's Day bowl games in football and the Final Four championships in basketball. Many Canadians also bet on the outcomes of those games. However, the similarity between the two systems is most evident at the National Association of Intercollegiate Athletics (NAIA) level, which is comprised of some 350 small universities in the U.S. Cross-border competitions occur with CIS universities, mostly in Alberta and British Columbia but also other Canadian universities such as Windsor and Laval. These competitions are often in sports (e.g., tennis, softball) that do not have CIS national championships. Cross-border tournaments and exhibition games also extend beyond the NAIA level, but at this time there are no formal arrangements between CIS and the NCAA.[3]

The vast majority of research on interscholastic sport issues has been carried out in the United States—an indication of the concerns associated with the far greater investment in and intensity of

---

[2]For more details on the U.S. system of interscholastic sports, particularly interuniversity, and a review of the research and problems, see the Online Learning Centre.

[3]In 2008, the NCAA voted to invite Canadian universities to join Division II conferences in the United States. Although two universities west of the Rockies are considering the invitation, no decisions have been made at the time of writing (Christie, 2008).

some U.S. programmes. The majority of research concerns the benefits of interscholastic sports, and they have produced equivocal results. Some studies show clear benefits, while others find no such benefits and point to actual negative aspects of the programmes. The majority of studies also have the same concerns as this chapter—to determine whether there are educational benefits associated with interscholastic sports. Studies of equity in interscholastic sports are also indirectly concerned with educational benefits. In Canada, a few studies in the 1970s and 1980s addressed similar issues to the U.S. studies, but because there were no significant issues evident in Canadian interscholastic sports, the line of research was dropped. More recently, some research has been concerned with determining how to maintain interschool sports in the face of significant budget cuts to education and poor relations between teachers and provincial governments. No research has yet been carried out on the disparities in Canadian interuniversity sports over the issue of scholarships.

The comparison between the two systems is evident throughout this chapter. However, because of the pervasiveness and presumed knowledge of the NCAA Division I system in Canada; because comparisons with, and the attractions of that system in terms of producing athletic excellence and revenue have resulted in some disagreements in Canadian interuniversity sports (see the section, "Interuniversity Sports: Problems and Recommendations," near the end of this chapter); and because most readers of this book are students at Canadian universities, we conclude this section with an examination of the development and organization of organized sports in Canadian universities.

From 1906 to 1965, the original Canadian Interuniversity Athletic Union (CIAU), which changed its name to Canadian Interuniversity Sport (CIS) in 2001, was known as CIAU Central; it involved only male sports in universities from Ontario and Québec. During that period, other regional university athletic associations were formed in western Canada and in the Maritimes, and CIAU Central provided common rules and regulations. Women's regional university athletic associations were also developed.

The rapid growth of universities, and university athletics, in Canada after World War II saw CIAU Central grow to nineteen universities, "each of which had diverse enrolment, philosophy [sic], and practices both academically and athletically"; this collapsed in 1955 because "there was no forum…to adjudicate conflicts within the organization" (www.cisport.ca). The various regional university athletic associations were brought together under a pan-Canadian CIAU formed in 1961. The women's university athletic associations came together to form the Canadian Women's Intercollegiate Athletic Union in 1969. The two organizations amalgamated under the CIAU in 1978.

The primary purpose of the CIAU, and the former CIAU Central, was to ensure standardized rules of play, determine eligibility to play, and organize championship tournaments. However, when the first pan-Canadian CIAU was organized in 1961, it was in part a response to:

- A recognized need for the formulation of consistent and acceptable sport rules and regulations for all teams represented at national championships;
- Mutually beneficial agreements with other national sport organizations (NSOs);
- Coordination of national and international competition; and
- A need to assist in developing leadership and citizenship of athletic staff (www.cisport.ca).

The re-formation of the CIAU coincided with the passage of Bill C-131, the 1961 Fitness and Amateur Sport Act, which was to have a major impact on Canadian sports, and which also came to have implications for university athletics. In return for some federal funding to the CIAU, and its relocation to the National Sport Centre in Ottawa (Gloucester) in the 1970s, university athletics became implicated in the development of Canada's high-performance sport system. As a part of the professionalization of that system, the Minister of State for Fitness and Amateur Sport, Iona Campagnolo (1977) declared that "growing demands for sophisticated administration and technical programs tend to be beyond the capacity of dedicated volunteers and...the universities and indeed all the educational system are the natural delivery systems for sport in Canada." Federal financial commitments to the CIAU increased in the 1970s to support travel equalization (for example, there are a great many more travel costs associated with competing in western Canada in comparison to Ontario university athletics), national championship travel, and involvement in the World University Games. As federal budgets for sports began to decline, especially in the 1990s, the CIAU shifted to a more corporate basis, seeking sponsorships and negotiating television contracts for university sports (see the direct link between the CIS-SIC website and TSN-RDS). The change in name from CIAU to CIS was intended to be more appealing for marketing purposes. Most recently, the CIS has been involved in establishing gender equity and negotiating the terms and conditions of awarding athletic scholarships across Canada. CIS also mandates performance-enhancing-drug education for all interuniversity athletes in Canada and carries out random drug testing.

While the structure of the CIS is quite similar to other national sport organizations and multi-sport organizations (MSOs) in terms of a voluntary board of directors and a paid staff housed at a central office in Ottawa, the directors of this MSO are somewhat different in that they are all salaried directors (e.g., managers, coordinators) of athletics at their respective Canadian universities. Thus, they function somewhat like a professional association, and all Canadian directors of athletics are involved in the annual general meetings of CIS. In addition to the CIS main office in Ottawa, the CIS International Programs Office is housed at the University of Alberta, and the Vanier Cup (national university football championships) also has an

office. Because the CIS represents university athletics, there are no individual members—the CIS represents forty-nine Canadian universities organized into the four conferences. According to the CIS website, over 12,000 athletes participate in the eleven sports that have national championships—women only in rugby and field hockey, men only in football, and eight sports for both men and women (www.cisport.ca).

The peak interest in interuniversity sport in Canada seems to have been in the 1950s and 1960s. Associated with the rapid growth of universities at that time, and a significant increase in student numbers, crowds filled the stadia and arenas for games. Competition was especially intense between the four oldest universities in CIAU Central—McGill, Queen's, Toronto, and Western Ontario. Large numbers of students would travel by train to away football games, and an informant recently told us that, for males at the University of Toronto, the single best way to get a date was to obtain a hard-to-find pair of tickets for a Varsity Blues hockey game. By the late 1960s, the counterculture with its critique of authoritarianism, and the anti-(Vietnam) war movement was widespread on university campuses in Canada. Interuniversity sports represented a "school spirit" that was no longer fashionable, and they were seen as a part of the "establishment." Although participation did not decline, the crowds did and it was no longer possible to fill the 20,000 seats at the University of Toronto's Varsity Stadium or the 16,000 seats at McGill University's Molson Stadium on Saturday afternoons in the fall. Interestingly, although the same movements and changes were evident on U.S. university campuses, they had little impact on interuniversity sports.

Some sports on some campuses (e.g., Bishop's University football) were able to retain their spectators, but the long decline continued until the 1990s. Recently, there has been a growing interest. Participation has continued to grow, with new sports being added to the schedules, and gender-equity requirements creating new opportunities and new teams for female student-athletes. Television contracts to broadcast inter-university games, and well-publicized national championships in football and men's basketball, have revived interest in interuniversity sports, and there have even been some surprises, such as the rapid growth of participation and interest in football at francophone universities in Québec. However, this growing interest has raised some difficult issues about scholarships that began to polarize Canadian universities (see the section, "Interuniversity Sports: Problems and Recommendations," near the end of this chapter).

ARGUMENTS FOR AND AGAINST INTERSCHOLASTIC SPORTS

Most people in Canada see interscholastic sports as an expected part of life at school and university. However, budget cutbacks and a few problems in certain high school and university programmes (for example, students extending their high school careers in order to play sports, some incidents of crowd violence at Toronto high school basketball games, and some hazing incidents in university sports) have raised questions about the relation-ship between these sports, the development of young people, and the achievement of educational goals. Responses to these questions are varied. Programme supporters claim that interscholastic sports support the educational mission of schools and universities and the development of young people, while critics claim that they interfere with that mission and distract students from what they should be learning to be responsible citizens. The main points made on both sides of this debate are summarized in table 14.1.

When people enter this debate, they often exaggerate the benefits or the problems associated with interscholastic sport programmes. Supporters emphasize glowing success stories, critics empha-size cases of excess and abuse, and some have

suggested that other agencies (e.g., community youth sports programmes) should be given the responsibility of organizing competitive sports for young people. The most accurate descriptions probably lie somewhere in-between. Nonetheless, both the supporters and the critics call attention to important issues in the relationship between sports and education. This section focuses on some of those issues.

INTERSCHOOL SPORTS AND THE EXPERIENCES OF HIGH SCHOOL STUDENTS

Do interschool sport programmes affect the educational and developmental experiences of high school students? This question is difficult to answer. Education and development occur in connection with many activities and relation-ships. Even though sport programmes are imp-ortant in some schools and for some students, they constitute only one of many potentially influential experiences. Quantitative research on this issue, usually based on functionalist theory, has focused primarily on the characteristics of athletes and how they compare with the characteristics of other students. Qualitative research, often guided by interactionist and critical theories, has focused on how interschool sports are connected with school culture and the everyday lives of high school students.

High School Athletes[4]

Studies carried out in the U.S. have shown consistently that, when compared with students

---

[4]We do not use the term *student-athlete* because all members of school teams are students, as are band members and debaters. Using the term *student* is redundant. The NCAA has promoted the use of this term in the United States as a political strategy to deflect the criticism that "big-time" university athletic programmes are overcommercialized, overprofessionalized, and generally unrelated to the academic mission of universities. We do not wish to be co-opted by the NCAA's political goals.

who do not play interschool sports, high school athletes, *as a group*, generally have better grades, more positive attitudes toward school, more interest in continuing their education after graduation, lower rates of absenteeism, more years of post-secondary education completed, more career success, and better health (see Barber et al., 2001; Broh, 2002; Carlson et al., 2005; Curtis et al., 2003; Eitle, 2005; Eitle and Eitle, 2002; Guest and Schneider, 2003; Hunt, 2005; Marsh and Kleitman, 2002; Miller et al., 2000, 2005; Miracle and Rees, 1994; Rees and Miracle, 2000; Videon, 2002). These differences usually have been modest, and it has been difficult for researchers to separate the effects of sport participation from the effects of social class, family background, support from friends, identity issues, and other factors related to educational attitudes and achievement.

Membership on a school team is a valued status in many U.S. schools, and it seems to go hand in hand with positive educational experiences for some students, reduced dropout rates, and increased identification with the school (Marsh, 1993; McNeal, 1995). However, research has not told us what it is about sport participation that actually *causes* these outcomes (Carlson et al., 2005).

Are Athletes Different? The most logical explanation for differences between athletes and other students is that interschool sports, like other extracurricular activities, attract students who already have characteristics that lead to academic and social success in high school. Most studies have not been able to test this explanation because researchers do not actually follow students during their high school careers to keep track of how and why changes occur in their lives. Usually, people do studies in which they collect data at one point in time and simply compare students who play on sport teams with students who do not. These studies are not very helpful because they do not allow researchers

Table 14.1 Popular arguments for and against interscholastic sports

Arguments for	Arguments against
1. They involve students in school activities and increase interest in academic activities.	1. They distract students' attention from academic activities.
2. They build the self-esteem, responsibility, achievement orientation, and teamwork skills required for occupational success.	2. They perpetuate dependence, conformity, and a power and performance orientation that is no longer appropriate in postindustrial society.
3. They foster fitness and stimulate interest in physical activities among students.	3. They turn most students into spectators and cause too many serious injuries to athletes.
4. They generate the spirit and unity necessary to maintain the school/university as a viable organization.	4. They create a superficial, transitory spirit, that is unrelated to educational goals.
5. They promote parental, alumni, and community support for all school/university programmes.	5. They deprive educational programmes of resources, facilities, staff, and community support.
6. They give students opportunities to develop and display skills in activities valued in society and to be recognized for their athletic skills.	6. They create pressure on athletes and can support a hierarchical status system in which athletes may be given excessive privilege.
7. They are an important part of non-classroom education, creating opportunities for less formal relationships with teacher-coaches outside the classroom and providing other educational, learning, and leadership opportunities.	7. At a time of declining public sector budgets that have seriously affected public education, it is difficult to justify public expenditure on interscholastic sports when more "core" educational programmes are suffering.

to say whether playing interscholastic sports really changes young people in systematic ways or whether students who try out for teams, are selected by coaches, and choose to remain on teams are simply different from other students *before* they ever become athletes.

The mere fact that young people grow and develop during the same years that they play interschool sports does not mean that sport participation *causes* the growth and development. Fourteen- to eighteen-year-olds grow and develop in many ways whether they play sports or do other things. Most studies do not distinguish among all the different activities and experiences that might explain changes that occur in students' lives during high school. This is crucial because research in the U.S. shows that young people who play on school sport teams are more likely to come from *economically privileged* backgrounds and have *above-average* cognitive abilities, self-esteem, and past academic performance records, including grades and test scores (Child Trends, 2005; Carlson et al., 2005; Eitle, 2005; Fejgin, 1994; Hunt, 2005; Rees and Miracle, 2000; Spreitzer, 1995). This means that students who try out for, make, and stay on teams are different from other students *before* they become high school athletes.

This type of *selection-in process* is common in most extracurricular activities, not just sports. Students who choose to participate in official, school-sponsored activities tend to be slightly different from other students. These differences are greatest in activities in which student self-selection is combined with formal tryouts and eligibility requirements, whereby teachers or coaches select students for participation, *if* the students are academically eligible to be involved. In the case of sports, this combination of self-selection, coach selection, and eligibility is especially powerful because it is an extension of a long-term selection-in process, which begins in youth sports and continues through junior high school. Gradually, students with lower grades and poor disciplinary records decide they do not want to be involved in school activities, including

sports, or they are simply told that they are not eligible to participate.

Research in the U.S. also suggests that students who play school sports for three years during high school are different from those who are cut from or quit teams. Those who are cut or quit are more likely to come from less advantaged economic backgrounds and have lower cognitive abilities, lower self-esteem, and lower academic averages than those who remain on teams (Spreitzer, 1995). Furthermore, athletes who receive failing grades, possibly due to an overemphasis on sports, are declared ineligible and become "nonathletes." This guarantees that nonathletes will have lower grades when researchers do studies in which their grades are compared with the grades of eligible athletes! Therefore, in addition to a selection-in process, there also is a *filtering-out process* that occurs in interschool sports. These processes combine to make athletes different from those who do not play on school teams. This means that if we want to determine if there are important educational or developmental consequences of playing sports, we must take into account that athletes are already a unique collection of students and then follow them over time so that we can measure and track changes in their lives that are primarily related to their participation in school sports. (See the box, "Are Canadian High School Athletes Different?" on the Online Learning Centre.)

Studying Athletes in Context Research over the past half century has produced confusing findings about the effects of playing interschool sports. This is because most researchers assume that playing on a school team has the same meaning in all contexts for all athletes in all sports and therefore must have the same consequences. But this is not true. Meanings vary widely depending on three factors:

1. The ways that athletes and sports are defined by people in particular contexts
2. The identities that young people develop in connection with sport participation

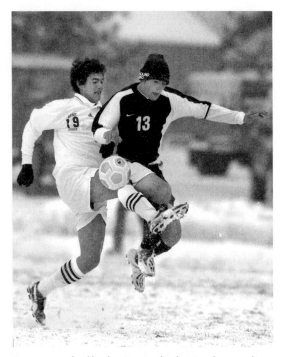

Processes of self-selection and selection by coaches ensure that students who become high school athletes often have different characteristics than other students *before* they play on interschool teams. Athletes may learn positive and/or negative things in sports, but it is difficult to separate them from general learning and developmental processes that occur during adolescence. [Marc Piscotty, *Rocky Mountain News*]

3. The ways that young people integrate an athlete identity into their lives

For example, playing on a junior varsity team or being a mediocre player on the school badminton team has different identity implications for a young man than being a provincial record holder or the captain of a successful high school basketball team. Similarly, being a young woman who is the provincial champion tennis player would be given different meaning and have different identity implications than being a young woman who leads her weight class in the provincial wrestling tournament, or plays on a junior varsity rugby team.

When researchers at the University of Chicago used data collected over four years from two large samples of high school students, they found that interschool athletes at schools located in low-income areas were more likely to be identified as good students than were athletes playing at schools located in upper-middle-income and wealthy areas (Guest and Schneider, 2003). Additionally, having an athlete identity was positively associated with grades in schools located in lower-income areas but negatively associated with grades in wealthier areas, where taking sports too seriously was seen as interfering with preparing for university and careers. Therefore, the academic implications of being an interschool athlete depended on the meaning given to playing sports and having an athlete identity in a particular social class context during the 1990s in U.S. society.

Research by Kathleen Miller and her colleagues (1998, 1999) indicates that the meanings given to playing interschool sports also vary by gender. For example, young women on school teams had *lower* rates of sexual activity (fewer sex partners, lower frequency of intercourse, and later initiation of sexual activity) than their female counterparts who did not play sports, whereas young men on school teams had *higher* rates of sexual activity than other young men in the schools. The authors suggest that playing on interschool teams enhances the social status of young people and gives them more power to regulate sexual activity on their own terms. During the 1990s, many young women used this power to resist sexual relationships that they defined as inappropriate or exploitive, whereas young men used their power to gain sexual favours from young women (Risman and Schwartz, 2002).

In a more recent study, Miller and her colleagues (2005) suggest that identifying oneself as a "jock" in some schools connects an interschool athlete with other students who are socially gregarious and like to engage in risky actions such as heavy and binge drinking. This needs to be studied further, but it seems that playing on some interschool sport teams puts students in a position where they can choose how to align themselves with various cliques or social groups in their schools. The choices made by athletes are very likely to influence how others identify them and where they fit into the overall culture of the school. In some cases, this "positions" them so that they are likely to take their academic work more seriously, whereas in other cases, it positions them so that they focus on social activities with other jocks rather than academic work.

Tracking the influence of sport participation in a person's adult life and occupational career is more challenging than tracking it over a few years in high school. The meanings people give to participation change over time and vary with social and cultural forces related to gender, race and ethnicity, and social class. For example, when we hear that many CEOs of large corporations played one or more high school sports, it tells us nothing about the effects of sport participation. The occupational success of these people, most of whom are white men, is related strongly to their family backgrounds, social networks, and the gender and ethnic relations which have existed in postindustrial societies during the past sixty years. This does not mean that these men have not worked hard or that sport participation is irrelevant to who they are and what they do, but the importance of playing sports cannot be understood apart from other social factors related to occupational success.

Several Canadian studies shed light on the effects of involvement in extracurricular activities (including sports), and on tracking these changes into adult life. Norman Okihiro (1984), now a sociologist at Mount Saint Vincent University in Nova Scotia, surveyed over 1,500 Ontario grade 12 students in 1973, and contacted them again in 1979. He found that both "athletic and social involvement in extracurricular activities play an important role in the process of educational and early job attainment" (p. 346). It is interesting to note that there were no significant differences between those who were involved in sports and other extracurricular activities, and those who were not, in terms of the prestige of their jobs or their incomes six years later. But those who were involved in high school were much more likely to be in jobs that involved spending time with people, and to have a self-concept as an active person; those who were active in high school were also likely to be active six years later. Thus, "the major influence of athletic and social involvement on educational and occupational outcomes has something to do with a facility and preference for dealing with people" (p. 346), and although this had not translated into greater job prestige and income after six years, Okihiro pointed out that such qualities would be a long-term career benefit in the new economy.

Okihiro's work was developed by Jim Curtis (who taught at the University of Waterloo), Bill McTeer (Wilfrid Laurier University), and Phil White (McMaster University), who used a theoretical framework developed by Pierre Bourdieu. Bourdieu argued that an important part of socialization is the acquisition of various forms of "capital" that are of value in later life. Canadians who participated in high school sports were more likely to participate in sports in later life (Curtis et al., 1999), and "have higher annual incomes as adults than those who did not participate" (Curtis et al., 2003, p. 60). They interpret these results not only in terms of the acquisition of economic capital, but also of physical, social and cultural capital. It is important to note that none of the authors are claiming that sports *caused* these effects, but the studies reaffirm Okihiro's (1984) conclusion:

> To the extent that high school athletic and social [extracurricular] participation carry over into adult activities, add enjoyment to our lives, and constitute potential occupational career assets, the prognosis on their value is favourable. This study suggests that the saying, "It's not the winning that counts, but playing the game," may have more sociological significance than one might expect. (p. 347)

Overall, we cannot make any conclusions about the effects of playing interschool sports without knowing about the context in which sport participation occurs. Playing basketball in a small, private school where grades are all important means something very different than playing in a large, socially diverse public school where athletes often identify with a "jock subculture" that has a strong emphasis on creating memorable social occasions and little emphasis on excelling in the classroom.

Student Culture in High Schools

Sociologists in the U.S. have long recognized that interschool sports are among the most important *social* activities sponsored by high schools (Rees and Miracle, 2000). Being on a school team may bring a student prestige among peers, formal rewards in the school, and recognition from teachers, administrators, and even people in the community. Athletes, especially males in high-profile sports, may be accorded recognition that enhances their popularity in student culture.

From a sociological perspective, it is important to ask what sports contribute to student culture in high schools. Because sports and sport events are socially significant activities in the lives of many students, they have the potential to influence students' values and actions. For example, do sports influence how students evaluate one another or how they think about social life and social relations? The cultural and structural implications of school sports are discussed in the box, "Bullying: Status and Privilege in Student Culture," which appears on the Online Learning Centre.

Sports and Popularity For many years, student culture in the U.S. was studied simply in terms of the factors that high school students use to determine popularity. These studies were all prompted by James Coleman's classic study of *The Adolescent Society* (1961), in which male high school students in the U.S. were found to value athletics over academics. In a Canadian example, David Friesen (1967) surveyed high school students in cities across Canada, hypothesizing that

Sport participation often gives young women opportunities to establish personal and social identities based on skills respected by peers and the community at large. However, playing sports, for girls such as these New Brunswick field hockey players, may not bring as much status and popularity to girls in high schools as it does to boys. [CP(Viktor Pivovarov), *Moncton Times & Transcript*]

he would find similar results to the U.S. studies. He was therefore surprised to find that Canadian students did not fit what he assumed was a North American stereotype. High school boys ranked academics over athletics and popularity, while high school girls ranked academics over popularity and athletics.

More recent research indicates that many young men in high school prefer to be known as "scholar-athletes," while young women prefer to be known as "scholars" *and* "members of the leading social group" (Chandler and Goldberg, 1990). Therefore, the link between being popular and being an athlete has traditionally been stronger for male students than for female students. When it comes to popularity for young women in high school, being in the in-group is crucial, and being an athlete does not by itself put a female student in the in-group.

What do these research findings mean? Are young men in the U.S. more concerned with being athletes than with being scholars? Are young women unconcerned about sports? The answer to both these questions is no. In fact, most high school students *are* concerned with academic achievement. They are aware of the importance of going to college or university, and their parents usually remind them regularly of how important school should be in their lives. However, in addition to academic achievement, high school students in both Canada and the U.S. are concerned with four things: (1) social acceptance, (2) personal autonomy, (3) sexual identity, and (4) growth into adults. They want to be popular enough to fit in with peers and have friends they can depend on; they want opportunities to control their lives; they strive to feel secure about their own sexual identity; and they want to show others that they are mature enough to be taken seriously.

This means that the *social* lives of adolescents revolve around a wide range of important factors. Because males and females in North America are still treated and evaluated in different ways, adolescents use different strategies for seeking acceptance, autonomy, sexual development, and recognition as young adults. As things are now, sport participation is an important basis for popularity for some young men, as long as they do not completely neglect their academic lives. In fact, young men who do not act tough may be marginalized in student culture, so they may put a premium on playing sports, especially contact sports (Eder, 1995).

Sport participation is also important for young women, but being an athlete usually must be combined with other things for a young woman to be popular within the student cultures of most high schools. Young women do not have to be traditionally feminine to be popular, but they usually must show they are something other than tough, competitive athletes; physical

attractiveness remains a key factor for a young woman's popularity in student culture, whether she plays sports or not (Eder, 1995). Thus, it seems that the visibility and status gained by high school athletes have different implications for young men than for young women in high school student culture (Carlson et al., 2005).

Additional Effects of High School Sports

In one sense, everything that we do and experience (both positive and negative) is "educational"— we learn from it, and it adds to who we are as human beings. Thus, interschool sports are always "educational" in a general sense. Since school sports are frequently justified in terms of their contribution to the educational mission of schools in a more specific sense, we have to conclude that, in and of themselves, sports are not educational. However, if sports are organized and played in certain ways, they do support educational goals, and represent an important component of experiential education, or, in other words, education outside the classroom.

Being Noticed and Rewarded Research indicates that sports support educational goals when they are organized and played in certain ways. For example, when sports are organized so that young people are taken seriously as human beings and valued by those who are important in their lives, sport participation can contribute to their educational development (Mahiri, 1998). However, if school sports are organized in ways that lead young people to think that adults are controlling them for their own purposes, they are developmental dead ends, and students, whether they play sports or not, will become cynical about school and society.

Positive adolescent development is most likely when students (1) are active participants in their schools, (2) have a range of opportunities to develop and display competence in settings where they are noticed and rewarded, and (3) have chances to prove that they are becoming valued adults in their communities. If interschool sports and other school activities are organized to do these things, they will contribute to education and to the development of students as citizens.

Attracting Adult Advocates Interschool sports are valuable when they provide young people with opportunities to meet adults who can be advocates in their lives. This is especially important when adolescents attend schools in areas where there are few adults who have the resources to help young people make important decisions and expand their awareness of the larger world in which they live. When adult advocates are scarce in the local neighbourhood, sports can provide young people with the "hook-ups" they need to gain access to opportunities that are simply taken for granted by young people in middle- and upper-class families and neighbourhoods.

Providing Occasions for Learning Sports are valuable educationally if teacher-coaches take them seriously as learning experiences (Mahiri, 1998). For example, in the U.S., Jomills Braddock and his colleagues (1991) have studied the importance of sports to young black males and have argued that sports in middle schools could be used to spark a commitment to education among many young people ready to give up on classroom learning by the time they are seventh-or eighth-graders. Carl James (2005), of York University, has shown that for some African-Canadian high school students, high school sport participation provides exactly the experiences that are usually claimed for all students—opportunities to extend one's circle of friends and interact with teachers in non-classroom settings, and increased desire and confidence to achieve academically.

Sports may be used as part of a larger process of giving students responsibility, including them in activities that will help them develop skills, rewarding them for their competence, and connecting them with adults who can exert positive influence in their lives.

The notion of deliberately designing sports to give students responsibility has been emphasized in applied research on moral and social development (Martinek and Hellison, 1997; Shields and Bredemeier, 1995). This research indicates that sport participation may take forms that actually subvert moral development and responsibility among young people, unless coaches and others make explicit attempts to prevent this. For example, some high school athletes may feel that playing sports is more important than anything they do and that they are entitled to special treatment, even if they fail to complete schoolwork or follow rules. When this occurs, interschool sports undermine student development and the academic goals of high schools.

School Sports and Ideology Research suggests that the most important social consequences of interschool sports may be their effects on ideas about social life and social relations, rather than their effects on grades, on attitudes toward school, or on student popularity (Foley, 1990a, 1999b). Sports usually have a vocabulary that emphasizes individualism and competition, and they may encourage certain views about gender, race, and social class relations. As we noted in chapter 4, many people believe that "the road to the board room leads through the locker room," and some of the arguments for gender equity in sports are based on the idea that participation will give girls the same ideas, attitudes, and "advantages" that were for so long exclusively for boys.

INTERUNIVERSITY SPORTS AND THE EXPERIENCES OF STUDENTS

Does interuniversity sport participation affect the educational and developmental experiences of university athletes? It seems that this question is only asked in Canada when budget cuts are being considered for athletic programmes, or when there is another hazing incident. For the most part, interuniversity sports are a normal, but not highly significant part of student life. There are no parallels with the highly-publicized U.S. universities where, in "big-time" sport programmes that are like professional sport cartels in every way except the age and income of the players, there is often a failure to take the education of athletes seriously. However, there are parallels with other levels of university sport in the U.S., such as the NAIA level of competition. CIS eligibility regulations determine that "[a]ll athletes must be demonstrating progress towards furthering their education and maintaining academic success." Athletes take at least nine credit hours during the term in which they are competing, and they must achieve passing grades in at least three full/six half (eighteen credit hours) courses in a year. For the most part, "scholarship athletes" in Canada are precisely that—students first and athletes second (or equal first). Thus, there is very little research in Canada on the educational and developmental experiences of university athletes. Surprisingly, since there is frequently concern about the conflict between athletics and academics, research on this issue is also relatively scarce in the United States.

The Diversity of Athlete Experiences

In the U.S., many entertainment-oriented interuniversity sport teams are characterized by chronic problems, shamefully low graduation rates, and hypocrisy when it comes to education.[5] However, there are many other teams in a variety of sports in the U.S., and most university sports in Canada, that are organized in ways that allow athletes to combine sport participation

The Vanier Cup is one of the biggest events on the interuniversity sport calendar in Canada. In order to develop the media and sponsorship opportunities, CIS maintains a separate office exclusively for the Vanier Cup. Here, the Manitoba Bisons celebrate their victory over the Saint Mary's Huskies in November, 2007. [CP(John Woods)]

with academic and social development. This combination is most likely when athletes enter university with positive attitudes about the value of a university education, and then receive support for academic involvement and the formation of academic identities (Meyer, 1988, 1990; Neinas, 2003; Shulman and Bowen, 2001).

Athletes on teams that support academic success may train very hard and define athletic success as important, but most of them take their education seriously. Those athletes who

---

[5]A number of Canadian students attending U.S. universities on athletics scholarships have experienced these conditions. Little research has been conducted on the experiences of Canadian scholarship athletes in the U.S., and an important new study compares the experiences of those who return to Canada after one or two years with those who stay to complete their scholarship eligibility (Wells, 2008).

do best are the ones who have the following: (1) past experiences that consistently reaffirmed the importance of education, (2) social networks that support academic identities, (3) perceived access to career opportunities following graduation, and (4) social relationships and experiences that expand confidence and skills apart from sports.

Many coaches in programmes that actively support academic success schedule practices and games, where possible, that do not interfere with coursework. Athletes may miss games and meets because they must study for or take exams, write papers, or give presentations. Team members may discuss academic issues and support one another when it comes to academic performance. In other words, these *are* sport programmes and teams that support the educational mission of higher education.

Grades and Graduation Rates: How Do Athletes Compare with Other Students?

Concerns about the lack of emphasis on education in some U.S. "big-time" university athletics programmes has led to the production of a great deal of data about the graduation rates of U.S. athletes. These are published annually by the NCAA, as well as by watchdog agencies such as the Institute for Diversity and Ethics in Sport at the University of Central Florida. Because there is somewhat less emphasis on sports and a greater focus on education at most Canadian universities, there has not been the same concern in Canada about athlete graduation rates. McTeer (1987), using data from the 1970s and 1980s, showed that there was no reason for concern, as athletes and non-athletes had similar grades and graduation rates. However, two more recent studies (Danylchuk, 1995; and an update by McTeer and Curtis, 1999) found lower grades and lower graduation rates for athletes, suggesting that there may now be some reasons to monitor this issue carefully.

DO SCHOOLS AND UNIVERSITIES BENEFIT FROM INTERSCHOLASTIC SPORT PROGRAMMES?

High school and university sports affect more than just athletes. In this section, we examine the influence of these programmes on schools and universities as organizations. In particular, we examine "school spirit" and budgets.

School Spirit

One of the benefits often claimed for school and university sports is that they generate "school spirit." What this means, and how it contributes to the institutions and the education of students is never fully explained. It is associated with a sense of community, belonging, and pride in one's place of education. Of course, this does *not* happen with all sport teams, nor does it happen in all schools or universities. Teams in low-profile sports usually play games with few, if any, student spectators. Teams with long histories of losing records seldom create a spirited response among more than a few students. Many students do not care about the teams that represent their institution, and some are hostile to sports, and the attention and resources received by some teams and athletes. However, in some cases, sports provide spirited social occasions, and some students use those occasions to express feelings about their teams, schools, and universities.

Proponents of interscholastic sports say that displays of school spirit strengthen student identification with their places of learning and create the feelings of togetherness needed to achieve educational goals. Critics say the spirit created by sports is temporary, superficial, and unrelated to the achievement of educational goals. A high school principal in Texas said, "Look, we don't get 10,000 people showing up to watch a math teacher solve X" (McCallum, 2003, p. 42)—a statement that may be used to support both sides of the argument.

Being a part of any group or organization is more enjoyable when feelings of togetherness accompany the achievement of goals. However, there is nothing magical about sports. Schools in other countries have used many methods to bring students together and provide enjoyable, educational experiences revolving around recreation, student-controlled clubs, and community service.

Critics of interscholastic sports, especially high school sports, are particularly concerned when these sports become elitist activities that destine most students to be passive spectators, which produces little in the way of educational experiences. They note that the resources devoted to sports might be used to fund other integrative activities that would involve more than cheering for teams, while providing experiences that actually make young people feel they are valued as contributing members of their communities. A Canadian study pointed out that good schools provide a range of extracurricular experiences for students (King and Peart, 1990). In response to the belief that sports "keep kids off the streets," critics say that, instead of inter-school sports, there should be programmes through which young people can make "the streets" into safe, vibrant public spaces in their communities.

The spirit associated with high-profile interuniversity sports is exciting for some students, but only a small proportion of the student body attends most games. Either the students are not interested or the athletic department limits student tickets because they can sell seats at a higher price to nonstudents. There is no doubt that the games of high-profile sport teams in the U.S., and, to a lesser extent, in Canada, often are major social occasions that inspire displays of spirit on university campuses, but does this spirit foster educational goals or simply allow students to drink, paint their faces, and yell for three hours? if the latter, then many universities may be wasting their money if their goal is education.

Budget cuts to interuniversity sports have made it difficult for new sports to become established on the interuniversity schedule. "Club status" is one way that students are able to introduce new sports and establish participation and competition opportunities. While they involve financial costs for students, as in this interuniversity mountain biking event, they also provide leadership opportunities for athletes that may not be so available in more established sports. [Kara Dillon and Nick Burdan. Reproduced with permission from the Faculty of Physical Education and Health, University of Toronto, www.utoronto.ca/physical]

If the spirit created by interscholastic sport is to have educational significance, it must be part of an overall programme in which students are treated as valued participants and given a sense of ownership in the institution and its activities. Unless students are actively involved in what happens every day at school or university, their cheering at weekly games is usually no more than a superficial display of youthful energy with little educational relevance.

School Budgets

High Schools Most school sport programmes are funded in partnership with the local school board, which provides from 5 percent to 80 percent of the school sport budget, depending on the province/board:

> In Ontario it is not unusual to see boards only providing 20–35% of the total funds required.

> Students often pay a participation fee and there is considerable fund raising by teachers and students. Corporate sponsorship is now an important part of school sport. (Hood, 1998)

Participation fees make sport participation less accessible to students from low-income families and, at a time when many students are already not participating because of a need, or desire, to work in their after-school hours, add to the elitist profile that high school sports already have. Sponsorships connect the future of sport programmes with the advertising budgets and revenue streams of private companies. This creates serious problems when advertising budgets are cut or when profits decline. Businesses may then withdraw their support, and programmes are left with even less funds. Other problems occur when the interests of sponsors do not match the educational goals of schools and school sports. For example, promoting the consumption of candy, soft drinks, and fast foods through ads and logos on gym walls, or through vending machine sales, often directly contradicts the health and nutrition principles taught in school classes. This clearly subverts education and makes students cynical about learning and education. If interschool sports are valuable educational experiences, they should be funded by taxes, including taxes paid by corporations, without noneducational strings attached.

Universities The relationship between sports and budgets is much more complex at the university level. Interuniversity sports in Canada are funded from a whole range of sources, with student fees being the primary source. Smaller amounts may come from gate receipts; from a share of the television income negotiated by the various conferences; and from concessions, logo licence fees, sponsors, alumni, and various other forms of fundraising. For example, a number of universities in Canada have funding campaigns to raise endowments for each of their interuniversity teams in order to reduce their dependency on student fees. No university teams in Canada make a profit, and, despite claims to the contrary, there is little evidence that athletics in many "big-time" university programmes in the U.S. make a profit.

The critiques of business and corporate sponsorships of high school sport programmes also apply to similar sponsorships of university sport programmes. Universities may have guidelines restricting alcohol or tobacco sponsorships, and some Canadian universities have joined coalitions to ensure fair labour practices in the manufacture of their licensed logo products, and uniforms. However, sponsorships may still produce dependency relationships and subvert the educational mission of the university.

Capital projects and infrastructure are a major concern at a time of restricted budgets in higher education. How are universities to maintain aging facilities, and construct new facilities, when the budgets are rarely adequate for existing programmes? Sometimes, universities may benefit from provincial donations, corporate sponsorships, or the selling of naming rights to their facilities; or they may be as lucky as McGill University, where the refurbishing of Molson Stadium was paid for by the CFL's Montréal Alouettes in their move from Olympic Stadium. In many cases, universities benefit from their city hosting major games or championships. Examples include the Olympic Oval at the University of Calgary, the refurbished Thunderbird Arena at the University of British Columbia (for the 2010 Olympics), the 2001 World Championships in Athletics and upgrading University of Alberta facilities, and the new TD Waterhouse stadium at the University of Western Ontario built for the Canada Summer Games in 2001.

HIGH SCHOOL SPORTS: PROBLEMS AND RECOMMENDATIONS

High school sport programmes generally enjoy community support, and many people have vested interests in keeping them the way they are. Many high school sport programmes are doing a good job of providing students with opportunities to develop and display physical skills in ways that have educational relevance. A few seem to have lost direct connections with education and may have subverted the educational process for some students. Problems vary from one high school programme to the next, but the most serious problems include the following: (1) restricted budgets, (2) an overemphasis on "sports development," and (3) limited participation access for students.

Restricted Budgets

The Problem The significant reductions in public expenditure that occurred across Canada in the 1990s and early 2000s had impacts that are still being felt in areas such as health and education. The effects on school sports were insidious and widespread. Education budget cuts in many provinces resulted in a reduction in the number of teachers, with most reductions coming in those areas of the curriculum designated as ancillary, such as physical and health education, art, and music. This was most evident at the elementary school level where, in many parts of the country, there are few physical education specialist positions. The consequences, which vary from province to province, and even from school board to school board, are as follows:

- Physical education programmes have been reduced, and a significant part of the required physical education curriculum is not being taught. An international survey (Hardman and Marshall, 2000) found that 43 percent of required physical education classes in Canada were not taught, compared to 26 percent in the U.S., 13 percent in western Europe, and 7 percent in northern Europe.
- Some sports have been cut from interschool programmes.

- There has been a reduction in athletic facility maintenance.
- Budget cuts have affected community sports and recreation as school boards radically increased their facility rental fees.
- Participation fees were introduced or increased; a great deal of time and effort is devoted to fund raising; and corporate sponsors now enjoy a far greater presence in school sports (see the box on "The Privatization of School Sports and Physical Education," p. 475).
- Teacher-coaches, who are always reluctant to cut sports, have experienced burnout in their attempts to raise funds and maintain programmes.
- In some provinces (e.g., Ontario), the budget cuts came at a time of major curriculum and workload changes, which led to tense labour relations and job action, with school sports being implicated in teacher work-to-rule campaigns.
- Some provincial governments have proposed turning school sports over to the community, and merging them with community sport programmes. This has been resisted by provincial school athletic associations in various ways (e.g., requiring the presence of a teacher at all practices and games if the coach is not a teacher).

Recommendations for Change The Centre for Sport Policy Studies at the University of Toronto held a conference to develop recommendations for resolving the crisis in high school sports (Donnelly et al., 2001). The delegates, representing all parties interested in school sports, made two key points:

- Better funding of school sports must go hand in hand with enhanced physical education and widely accessible intramural and student activity programmes (see the section, "Limited Participation Access," later in this chapter).

• Increased funding only to school sports would be a problem, and would be seen as elitist if other forms of extracurricular activity (e.g., music programmes, student theatre, etc.) did not also receive increases.

Thus, increased budgets must be part of a broad-based increase in access to extracurricular activities. This will only occur when there is a commitment to public education, combined with the recognition that good schools have a wide range of extracurricular activities that are an important part of student life (King and Peart, 1990). This is certainly the case in many private schools.

Overemphasis on "Sport Development"

The Problem Since Canada failed to win any gold medals at the 1976 Montréal Olympics, and the federal government embarked on a strategy to develop high-performance sports, there have been frequent attempts to incorporate sports in high schools and universities in that strategy. As Iona Campagnolo, the first Minister of State for Fitness and Amateur Sport, noted, "the universities and indeed all the educational system, are the natural delivery systems for sport in Canada" (1977). Over twenty years later, Dennis Mills pointed out that schools are the root of sport development in Canada (1998). Because education in Canada is a provincial rather than federal jurisdiction, this has been a difficult strategy to implement, and has been far more successful at the university than at the high school level (see below).

There are two ways to interpret federal government statements on this issue. In the first, schools may be seen as the ideal places to develop a physically literate population by having a wide range of physical education, intramural, exercise, and interschool programmes. A healthy, active population forms an ideal basis for identifying and selecting talented individuals for high-performance programmes, and such a population

is more likely to identify with, and be sympathetic to, investing in high-performance sports. In the second interpretation, school sports become part of the elite sport development programme, focusing their resources on individuals who are already talented athletes. These interpretations may be replicated in the increasing interest in developing sports high schools (e.g., in Alberta). In one model, the sports schools are similar to arts high schools, where students have an opportunity to pursue a variety interests, and where sports are integrated into the curriculum in various ways (e.g., sport science as part of the science requirements). In the other model, the schools recruit elite athletes and become centres for the development of athletic excellence in a limited number of sports. Unfortunately, the latter interpretation seems to be more likely.

Some high school administrators think that the best way to organize high school sports is to model them after intense sport development programmes. This leads to excessive concerns with achieving winning records, and building high-profile programmes that become the focus of attention in the school and community. These programmes often focus on football or boys' basketball, but other teams may be highlighted depending on local traditions. Building and maintaining high-profile programmes often leads to administrative decisions that overlook the educational needs of all the students.

People who focus on sport development often give lip service to keeping sports in proper perspective, but many forget their own words when it comes to the programmes at their schools. In fact, they may even encourage students to specialize in a single sport for twelve months a year, even though this may restrict overall social, educational, and athletic development (Wolff, 2002).

These problems sometimes occur in Canada when community coaches rather than teachers are involved in school sports, and sometimes with young teacher-coaches anxious to establish a reputation as a "winning coach." Older, more

REFLECT ON SPORTS

The Privatization of School Sports and Physical Education

The Canadian Teachers' Federation (2006) produced a report titled: *Commercialism in Canadian Schools: Who's Calling the Shots* (www.ctf-fce.ca). The report collected data from primary and high schools across Canada. The following outlines some of the findings related to school sport and physical education:

- Advertising in schools:
  - 55 percent of high schools reported advertising in schools—Coke and Pepsi most prominent—on scoreboards, clocks, beverage machines, banners, school signs, and gym equipment.
  - 8 percent of high school teams carried advertising (other than the manufacturers' brand) on their uniforms.
- User fees:
  - 70 percent of high schools charge user fees for sport teams.
- Fundraising:
  - 69 percent of high schools engage in various forms of fundraising for school teams (which, along with school trips, were the most common item for fundraising).
- Total funds raised per school / year:
  - Average for high schools is $38,747
- Advice given to businesses by an Alberta entrepreneur about marketing to "tweens":
  - Affiliate your business with a sports program or team."
  - Sponsor programs at school like... Athlete of the Year.

- What can you learn from the fast-food industry? Think incentives, playgrounds, contests, clubs, games.

The report also makes the following points:

- "Children from wealthier families and in wealthier neighbourhoods will have better access to a richer variety of [school] experiences, experiences that have a positive impact on a child's education" (p. 24).
- Creeping commercialism and privatization: "What role should private interests including corporations play in public education?" (p. 25).
- "A McDonald's-sponsored fitness program (the "Go Active! Olympic Fitness Challenge," which has the blessing of the Canadian Olympic Committee [McDonald's is a major sponsor of the Olympics]) has the burger corporation partnered with 445 schools (nearly 150 in Ontario) involving some 50,000 students in nearly every province and territory except Québec (where there are strict regulations about advertising to children and sponsorships in schools) and Newfoundland/Labrador. McDonald's is offering a $200 credit toward the purchase of gym equipment (to a maximum of $500 per school) for participating schools (McGregor, 2005); not surprisingly, fast- and junk-food companies are quick to blame *inactivity* for rising obesity levels among children, rather than an unhealthy diet (Robertson, 2004, p. 22)."

experienced teacher-coaches often grow to recognize the cycle of competition in which some years your teams will win, and some years they will lose; and they begin to see themselves as teachers first. Most of the issues that have to be dealt with by provincial schools athletic associations—coaches playing ineligible players, transfers between schools that seem to be motivated by athletics rather than academics, and parents petitioning school boards and suing the

athletic associations for preventing their child from a perceived opportunity to be awarded an athletic scholarship to the United States—result from an overemphasis on sport development. In fact, it has been the proximity and lure of U.S. NCAA Division I athletics programmes, and their function as professional farm systems for sports such as football and basketball, and, to a lesser extent, baseball, hockey, golf, and track and field, that has been connected to some of the problems in high school sports. This becomes even more significant for students (and their parents) who have made a major investment in sport participation, sometimes at the expense of academics, and/or who are from less affluent families. They are aware that it is possible to enter some U.S. universities with lower grades than would be required in Canada, and they often believe exaggerated stories about the number of students who receive full scholarships.

Recommendations for Change Interschool sports should be critically assessed on a regular basis. Younger teacher-coaches need to learn more about the ways sports can be made into educationally relevant activities. Coaching education programmes should emphasize student development rather than sport development.

In some cases, teacher-coaches and provincial schools athletic associations might look to students themselves for signs about the directions they might take. Are students paying to participate in private or nonprofit fitness programmes off campus when there are often adequate fitness facilities in the schools? Are lots of students in-line skating, or playing hacky sack, pick-up basketball, and Frisbee outside during breaks from classes, but not participating in school-sponsored activities? Ultimate Frisbee is a growing sport in high schools, but it is an informal, intramural, and interschool activity usually run by students. Why not give higher priority to sports involving active participation rather than just being a spectator? For example, there could be more combined male/female teams in sports such as long-distance running, doubles tennis and badminton, and so on. If sport participation produces important educational outcomes, high school sport programmes should be organized so that more students can play on teams and compete against similarly skilled students from other schools. If only 30 percent of all students play on teams, and more than one-third of students never play in games, the educational benefits of sports are reserved for the few. If playing sports is educationally

valuable, over half of the student body should not be relegated to the sidelines. Schools are the *only* place where the vast majority of the population in a certain age group, and at an important age for learning and development, have the opportunity to learn and play sports for very little cost. This is the most democratized opportunity for sport participation and, if sport participation is important, it should not be wasted.

Limited Participation Access

The Problem Across Canada, approximately 30 percent of the student body participates in interschool sports: "Most schools have the traditional sports programs such as basketball, soccer, hockey, volleyball, track, etc. but there are schools with programs such as fencing, snowboarding, rowing, and boxing" (Hood, 1998). Pan-Canadian participation statistics are difficult to compile; provincial schools athletic associations count participation in different ways (e.g., some count all students participating, while others provide a total of the number participating in each sport—those playing more than one sport are counted more than once). The Canadian School Sport Federation (CSSF/FCSS), which is the umbrella organization for school sport in Canada (10 provinces, and two territories—Nunavut is not listed) calculates that there are more than 750,000 athletes in 3,200 schools, in sports supervised by 52,000 teacher-coaches (www.schoolsport.ca). However, only Ontario has detailed statistics on participation readily available (www.ofsaa.on.ca), having tracked participation for the last 30 years. Participation has increased steadily, from approximately 70,000 girls and 118,000 boys in 1979–80 to 131,600 girls and 158,600 boys in 2004–05 (the last year for which data are available). The increase in boys' participation, expected in part because of a growing population, is matched by more rapidly increasing girls' participation. Increasing concerns about gender equity, which has led to new teams in sports such as soccer, rugby, hockey, and wrestling help to account for the increasing number of girls involved in high school sports. Figure 14.1 shows this increase for the last 10 years; and it also shows the dramatic effects on sport participation of budget cutbacks and tense labour relations in Ontario schools, with sharp declines in participation in 1998 and 2000.

The major advantage of interschool sports is that they provide students with opportunities to develop and test their skills, especially physical skills, outside the classroom. However, when high school programmes emphasize power and performance sports, they discourage participation by many males and many females who prefer sports emphasizing pleasure and participation. In fact, this may be the major factor that prevents schools from meeting their gender-equity goals, despite persistent attempts to make sure opportunities are available for females: females may not be as

eager to play sports that are built around the idea of "proving who the better man is." Most high schools have not achieved gender equity when it comes to sport participation. The situation is even worse when it comes to disability equity. Some athletes with a disability play on standard teams, and some of the provincial championships provide open competition in, for example, some track events where wheelchair racers may use the outer lane. In general, however, able-bodied students miss opportunities to see their peers with disabilities compete, and to share sport experiences with them. This represents a missed educational opportunity for able-bodied students *and* students with a disability.

Budget cuts also have interfered with changing or expanding programmes in creative ways. One of the biggest threats to more open participation in school sports is participation fees. These fees

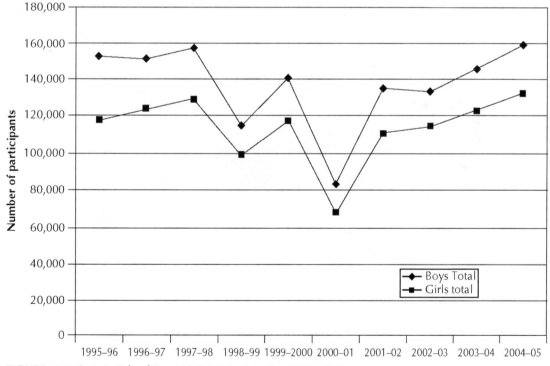

FIGURE 14.1 Ontario School Sport (OFSAA) Participation 1995–2005
Reproduced with the permission of Ontario Federation of School Athletic Associations (OFSAA).

limit access to participation, as does much of the time and energy devoted to fundraising—resources that could be better spent on participation.

Recommendations for Change Many students are not interested in playing interschool sports, especially sports based on a power and performance model. Those who do not measure up to their bigger, faster, taller, and stronger classmates need participation alternatives. There is no reason only one team should represent a school in competition. Why not have two or more teams? Why not have a football league with players under 65 kilograms, or a basketball league with all players under 1.70 metres tall, or track meets with height and weight breakdowns for certain events? In places where this has been tried, it has been successful.

There should be efforts to develop new interschool sports in which size and strength are not crucial for success. Too often, the focus is on football and basketball rather than a variety of sports suited for a variety of participants. Why not have teams in Frisbee, flag football, softball, in-line skating, skateboarding, or any sport for which there is enough local interest to field teams? With guidance, students themselves could administer and coach these teams and coordinate meets and games with teams from other schools. If responsibility builds autonomy and decision-making skills, why not let students direct their own teams, so that more of them would have opportunities to participate? This has been done with success in some countries, and it cuts costs dramatically.

The growth of women's rugby in high schools and universities led to CIS introducing national championships for women, but not for men's rugby. This helps to establish gender equity to some extent in CIS, given the cost and number of athletes involved in men's football. [Kara Dillon and Nick Burdan. Reproduced with permission from the Faculty of Physical Education and Health, University of Toronto, www.utoronto.ca/physical]

Students with a disability have been largely ignored by some school sport programmes. More schools should develop sport participation opportunities for these students. This could occur in a combination of creatively designed programmes or by including athletes with dis-abilities on existing school teams, as has sometimes been the case in track and field. This would not work in all sports, but there are certain sports in which competitors with a disability could be included in games, meets, and matches. If there are not enough athletes with disabilities in one school, then combine schools or have one team from an entire school board. This issue is discussed in the Breaking Barriers box on page 481.

Girls' sports still do not have the support that boys' sports enjoy. Of course, this problem has a history that goes far beyond the high school. But the result is that girls still participate at somewhat lower rates than boys, although the gap has closed considerably in recent years. In some areas, there is still an emphasis on boys' teams as the most important teams in the school. Gender equity in school sports could be achieved in some schools through such gender-mixed sports as those recommended in the previous section.

More schools are now using participation fees to save interschool sports. This strategy may work, but it may also limit participation among students from low-income families, even when fee waivers are available. If fees are necessary to save programmes, there should be attempts to enable students to work for the money to pay fees, and there should be ways to encourage community organizations to establish scholarship funds to pay fees for students in need of assistance.

INTERUNIVERSITY SPORTS: PROBLEMS AND RECOMMENDATIONS

Issues in Canadian interuniversity sports are not new. They were summarized by Macintosh (1986), and three of the issues—athletic scholarships, relationships with high-performance sports, and gender equity—were discussed by Hall, et al. (1991). These three, together with budget issues, are still a concern.

Athletic Scholarships

The Problem   Athletic scholarships in the U.S., as noted previously, offer both advantages and disadvantages to Canadian students. They provide financial assistance, more flexible admission standards, and a potential track to professional/high-performance sports. However, athletes may find that they have semi-professional status as "employees" of athletics departments, that the demands of sports may conflict with the demands of education, and that the (usually) partial scholarships do not nearly cover the costs of their (out-of-state/foreign student) tuition and expenses.

Many Canadian university coaches believe that athletic scholarships in Canadian univer-sities will keep athletes in Canada who would normally have gone to the U.S., and that a scholarship system will lead to improved standards in Canadian interuniversity sports and add significantly to the Canadian system of sport development. However, others believe that these scholarships will lead to the end of the traditional Canadian emphasis on academics over athletics, that their cost could lead to a limitation of the number of sports available to athletes, and that they could create the types of problems and corruption experienced by many U.S. universities. CIS recently funded a study to compare university costs between Canada and the U.S. The study found that, apart from the very few athletes who receive a "full scholarship," the costs for Canadian students, and the likelihood of graduating with a signi-ficant amount of debt, are far higher from accepting a U.S. athletic scholarship than from attending a Canadian university (Krukowska et al., 2007).

Since CIS accepted unlimited athletic scholarships at Canadian universities in 2000, they have been divisive. As universities in Ontario and several in other provinces argued for academic standards and limitations on awards, some universities in western Canada threatened to secede from CIS competitions. A compromise was agreed to, but Ontario universities im-mediately established more restrictive rules—a limit of C$2,500 per year for an athlete, a mini-mum academic average of 70 percent required to receive an award, and no entry (first-year) awards. Universities outside Ontario made awards that amount to full tuition and mandatory fees, and they can overcame the entry-level limitation by making an award at the end of an athlete's first year (an award that may therefore become part of a recruitment offer). Ontario universities discussed whether they might secede from CIS national competition, at least in football, arguing that their philosophy of more restrictive awards placed them at a competitive disadvantage.

The situation with Athletic Financial Awards (AFAs as athletic scholarships are known in Canada) has been quite dynamic. AFAs across Canada are limited to the total amount of tuition and compulsory fees. Ontario and the other CIS conferences now offer AFAs to entering students with a high school academic average of 80 percent or better. Students in Ontario must achieve a university academic average of 70 percent in order to receive an AFA in second and subsequent years, while the other CIS conferences require an academic average of 65 percent. The number of awards in CIS sports is capped at 70 percent of the Championship Roster for each sport (e.g., of the 40 players for football that constitute the Championship Roster for football, only 28 may receive full AFAs), although the CIS reviews this annually. However, a team may elect to distribute its awards more widely (e.g., football may take the total amount of 28 × tuition and compulsory fees, and distribute that amount among all 40 players). In order to reward academic excellence, Academic All Canadians (university average of 80 percent or better) are not counted in the AFA cap.

Recommendations for Change   Both sides in the AFA debate have legitimate arguments, and the problem is clearly difficult to resolve. Academic standards are important if Canada is to avoid the U.S. problems, and some universities have argued that, in order to be eligible for an AFA, athletes should have the grades that would at least make them eligible for consideration for an academic scholarship. As Jack Drover, the athletic director at Mount Allison University, noted, "We have students on the dean's list here who aren't getting anything, while athletes can get full tuition for just passing their courses" (cited by Sokoloff, 2002). Murray Sperber, a Canadian professor at the University of Indiana who was forced into hiding following death threats after he criticized the behaviour of basketball coach, Bobby Knight, warned against the slippery slope of athletic scholarships: "Athletes in the U.S. are the only group brought to campuses for entertainment, not academic purposes. It's like paying for rock stars" (cited by Sokoloff, 2002).

AFAs should be considered in the same category as other non-academic scholarships in, for example, music, art, and drama. They should be adjudicated on the basis of excellence in a non-academic area, but athletes should also have grades that make them eligible for academic scholarships. This would also help to counter the "dumb jock" stereotype. Athletic scholarships should also be funded in a way that does not lead to athletic departments cutting sports in order to fund scholarships in just a few sports.

	Inclusion Barriers
Breaking Barriers	*How Can I Wear Shoes if I Don't Have Feet?*

Seventeen-year-old Bobby Martin says, "I stand 3 foot 1 inch but I've got the soul of a 6-foot-4 person"(Grossfeld, 2005). Martin played backup noseguard and on special teams for Dayton's (Ohio) Colonel White High School football team in 2005. He was born without legs, but he wrestles, bowls, dances, and moves around school hallways and classrooms on a custom skateboard.

On the football field, Martin moves with his hands and hips. "I love the reaction people have when I make a tackle," he says. "People don't believe I can play, and I love to prove them wrong." But he was stopped from playing when a referee told his coach that the Ohio high school rules stated that all players had to wear shoes, knee pads, and thigh pads. Martin had all the necessary permissions to play, but the referees were not aware of them. As Martin pleaded his case, he asked, "How can I wear shoes if I don't have feet?"(in Reilly, 2005, p. 90) During subsequent games, Martin's coach presented referees with a letter in which the Dayton Public Schools declared his eligibility.

Bobby Martin's experiences received media coverage, widespread but none of the coverage mentioned that no U.S. or Canadian high school has a varsity team in any sport for students with disabilities. Nor was it noted that only a handful of universities field even one "paravarsity team" or that the NCAA and CIS do not recognize any championships in sports for athletes with disabilities. The Universities of Illinois, Alabama, and Arizona are the only campuses that have women's wheelchair basketball teams, and disability services rather than athletic departments fund them. Paid coaches are rare for paravarsity teams, and the only scholarships for athletes with a disability are given by the president's office at the University of Alabama. All of this perpetuates the (in)visibility of(dis)ability and the resultant lack of opportunities in Canada and the U.S.

Bob Szyman teaches at the Chicago High School of Agricultural Sciences. He left his position as secretary general of the International Wheelchair Basketball Federation (IWBF) so that he could return to teaching special education and physical education. His goal is to establish a wheelchair basketball league in Chicago public schools, but his biggest challenge has been finding people who are excited about such a league. He explains that "there is no wheelchair sport culture" in the schools, so students with disabilities have no expectations and make no demands, especially in lower-income and ethnic minority communities; nor do administrators, teachers, and coaches ask why there are no paravarsity teams. When Szyman organizes wheelchair sports camps and competitions, the students who participate go out of their way to thank him, but they do not ask why their schools have no sports programmes for them. They are accustomed to being ignored when it comes to sports.

There is no clear legal mandate to provide or fund paravarsity sports or to encourage teachers, administrators, and coaches to think creatively about developing opportunities—such as organizing co-op teams representing two or more high schools as is done in rural areas when there are not enough athletes in a school to field a particular team.

Few students are as assertive and determined as Bobby Martin, and this means that mainstreaming athletes with disabilities does not provide real access to the learning experiences available through high school and university sports. Some (dis)abilities require games, rules, and equipment adapted to physical characteristics. Public schools are traditionally where able-bodied young people develop and display their sports skills, but the myth that people with a disability are not interested in sports continues to subvert opportunities for them. Therefore, if Bobby Martin were speaking to educators about this issue, he might ask, "How can students with a disability play sports if we don't have teams?" This is a question begging for an answer.

Relationships with High-Performance Sports

The Problem   Sport Canada has shown ongoing interest in incorporating university sports into Canada's high-performance development system, and has been an advocate of athletic scholarships. Universities are involved in the high-performance development and training system in several ways. For example:

- Canadian Sport Centres (CSCs) are located at universities (e.g., Calgary, Manitoba), or maintain close links with local universities (e.g., Vancouver).
- Sport Canada provides bursaries, through the Athlete Assistance Programme, for national team athletes to attend Canadian universities.
- Sport Canada assists in the funding of Canadian teams to the Winter and Summer Universiade (World University Games).

Sport Canada and some NSOs are interested in greater involvement, and there have been proposals for "super leagues" in some sports to provide competition and development opportunities for the best "student" athletes. The CSCs have the advantage, from Sport Canada's perspective, of bringing the best athletes together with a leading coach whose salary is sometimes shared by a university and an NSO, in a location where good facilities and services (e.g., sport science, sports medicine) already exist.

The funding from hosting or linking with CSCs is attractive to cash-strapped university athletic departments, and the presence of high-profile athletes brings publicity to the departments and

As noted in chapters 8 and 10, the number of women in interuniversity coaching and administration remains disproportionately low. This is one of the gender inequities that has not been addressed very assertively in most universities, although it is a high priority in those with a Gender Equity Plan. [Lewko Hryhorijiw. Reproduced with permission from the Faculty of Physical Education and Health, University of Toronto, www.utoronto.ca/physical]

Table 14.2   CIS sports for males and females

Male sports	Female sports
Basketball	Basketball
Cross Country	Cross Country
Football	Field Hockey
Hockey	Hockey
	Rugby
Soccer	Soccer
Swimming	Swimming
Track & Field	Track & Field
Volleyball	Volleyball
Wrestling	Wrestling

the universities. National team athletes who are students may be on modified course loads, or may receive special consideration from professors for absences due to international competitions. Such athletes are also eligible for CIS competitions if they meet eligibility requirements.

However, blending the high-performance and university sport systems may mean losing some of the educational principles of university sports (a parallel may be drawn here with attempts to combine community sports with high school sports). It can also lead to a focus on high-performance athletes, and directing resources to a more limited number of sports. This has the effect of depriving many non-elite student-athletes of the interuniversity sport experience.

Recommendations for Change There is a clear need to negotiate the relationship between university sports and high-performance sports. The negotiations must recognize the mutual advantage that is possible from supporting the needs of high-performance sports, while maintaining and even improving the established "student first, athlete second" interuniversity sport system. This is a balancing act—too much emphasis on high-performance sports can damage the principles of university sports. However, the high-performance system can become a part of the educational environment of university sports.

Gender Equity[6]

The Problem Because of the focus on gender equity in the CIAU/CIS in the last ten years, there are now more national championships for females than males as women's sports have been added to the national championship roster in order to create equity (see table 14.2). However, in most universities across the CIS, there are fewer female athletes than male athletes, often fewer female sports available than male sports, and lower budgets for female sports than male sports. Some 54 percent of CIS athletes are male, and 46 percent are female.

Often, the cause of lower budgets and fewer female athletes is football—the sport is expensive and has large rosters of athletes—it is almost impossible to match it in female sports. Even with the additional sport for women (rugby), the rosters for football are so large as to make achieving equity difficult. Some universities (e.g., Dalhousie) have achieved gender equity without football.

When the University of Toronto was grappling with this problem in the 1990s (*Gender Equity Report*, 1994), the university found that

---

[6]It should be noted that concerns about language equity have been an ongoing issue in CIS; however, significant steps have been taken to increase French language capacity and communications in recent years (Donnelly et al., 2001).

the only way to achieve equity in budgets was to take football out of the equation. Serious consideration was given to dropping the sport, a problem given the long history of tradition of the Varsity Blues football team, which, in the past, was a Grey Cup–winning team. Their resolution was to establish an alternative source of funding for football, provided by the most outspoken group in favour of keeping the team—the alumni of the team.

The *CIAU Comparative Study* (www.universitysport.ca), which compared changes in gender equity between 1992–93 and 1998–99, found that although there had been an increase in the number of female athletic dire-ctors and female head coaches, women were still significantly underrepresented in those positions. More recent data, from the 2005 analysis of male and female coaches (see chapter 8) show continuing underrepresentation. Disparities are also evident in the distribution of AFAs. Although the gap has decreased since 2001–02, the most recent data available (2006–07) shows that, although males constitute 54 percent of athletes in CIS sports, they receive almost 62 percent of the AFAs. Thus, of the almost $7 million of AFA funding, male athletes received over $4.3 million.

Recommendations for Change Athletics departments at many Canadian universities need to recognize that more than half of the student body is female, and that student fees are their primary source of funding. Departments that do not provide equity for male and female students need to conduct serious gender-equity exercises to ensure fairness in funding of interuniversity sports, and other recreation and intramural programmes on campus, before a student organization brings a human-rights/gender-equity suit against them. Departments that wish to maintain traditional and expensive male sports, and

> Football is the SUV of the college campus: aggressively big, resource-guzzling, lots and lots of fun and potentially destructive of everything around it.
>
> —Michael Sokolove, journalist (2002)

which are unable to provide comparable funding for female sports, need to consider alternative sources of funding for the male sports. Equity exercises also need to consider the availability of coaching and administrative positions, and the distribution of athletic scholarships.

Restricted Budgets

The Problem Budgetary constraints are at the root of several of the issues described above, but they also have another consequence—that of providing fewer participation opportunities (interuniversity, intramural, and recreational) for the students who are paying the fees. In terms of interuniversity sports, athletic departments have gone through a number of budget exercises in recent years that have resulted in sports being cut. The decisions usually involve one of the following:

- "Going with your strengths," that is, putting all of the funding towards the few sports in which the university has been most competitive, and/or in which the university employs a full-time coach
- Ranking exercises in which sports are assigned to different categories of funding; for example, several years ago the University of Western Ontario assigned sports to four categories:

  - 1: Sports receive full funding and full services
  - 2: Sports receive basic funding and services
  - 3: "Varsity clubs" are self-funded and receive limited services
  - 4: "Sport clubs" involve sports that do not compete in the OUA or the CIS, and receive no athletic department funding or services

While there were attempts to establish gender equity in the Western exercise, it produced some extraordinary inequities. For example, all of the most expensive men's sports—football, hockey, and basketball—were ranked in Category 1. However, women's wrestling was ranked in Category 1, while men's wrestling was ranked Category 2; men's hockey was ranked 1, while women's hockey was ranked 2; women's swimming was ranked 2, while men's swimming was ranked 3—and these latter two teams have to travel together (Kernaghan, 2002; Pyette, 2002).

Recommendations for Change Students, who are paying the fees, must be at the table when budgets are being discussed. The first priority should be to provide interuniversity (and other participation) experiences to as many students as possible. If these experiences—interuniversity, intramural, and recreational—are considered to be valuable, which they are at every university, then they should be available to as many students as possible. Some of the recommendations for extending interschool sport experiences (multiple teams, new sports, etc.) should be considered at universities.

Careful negotiations and planning are necessary in order to determine which expenses are necessary and which are not. For example, at a time when sports are being cut, is it necessary for some teams to travel to play in expensive exhibition tournaments? Who should pay the cost when 120 football players show up to training camp? These are difficult questions, but it is necessary to ask them, and to negotiate their answers in a manner that provides equitable and accessible opportunities to participate in these educational environments.

SUMMARY

ARE INTERSCHOLASTIC SPORTS EDUCATIONAL?

Generalizing about high school and university sport programmes is difficult. There are differences among and between them. However, interscholastic sports have no place in high schools or universities unless they are organized to achieve educational outcomes for athletes in particular and all students in general. At a minimum, if the programmes do not benefit athletes educationally, they cannot be justified as school- or university-sponsored activities.

There is no consistent evidence that high school sports produce negative consequences for those who participate in them. However, it is clear that some schools, coaches, parents, and athletes lose sight of educational goals in their pursuit of competitive success. Sports can be seductive, and people connected with high school teams sometimes require guidance to keep their programmes in balance with the academic curriculum. It is up to school superintendents and principals to make sure that sport teams are organized to achieve legitimate educational goals. When many people assume that sport participation always is educational because "sports build character" automatically, it is likely that little attention will be given to the need to carefully organize sport programmes to foster education.

A main theme in this book is that sports are social constructions; that is, they are organized and played in many ways, and people give meanings to sports and sport experiences and integrate them into their lives in many ways. However, most people associated with interscholastic sports simply have assumed that sports and sport participation *automatically* produce positive results, regardless of how they are organized and the contexts in which they are played. This subverts the necessary process of critically examining sports in student culture as a whole.

The possibility that sport participation interferes with the education of athletes is greatest in U.S. big-time interuniversity programmes. The status and identity of athletes in big-time interuniversity sports may be so highly publicized and organized that it can distract students from academic work. In some cases, it can make coursework nearly irrelevant in the lives of impressionable young people, especially young men who see their destinies being shaped by sport achievements, not academic achievements.

Interscholastic sport programmes can create school spirit. But it is not known if that spirit contributes to the achievement of educational goals or interferes with the development of a learning-oriented school culture. Although nonsport activities could be used to unite students and link them with community and society, sports often are used as the central activities that make schools more interesting places to be. Although sports are included in everyday discourse covered by the media, we do not know much about their educational consequences because many studies of school sports have not taken into account the contexts in which they are played, given meaning, and integrated into people's lives. When there is a body of research that takes context into account, we will be able to say with more certainty when sports and sport participation are likely to have particular educational and developmental outcomes.

Most high school sport programmes do not seriously cut into budgets for academic programmes. The money they require is well spent if it provides students with opportunities to learn about their physicality, develop physical and interpersonal skills, and display their skills in ways that lead them to be recognized and rewarded by others. At the interuniversity level, the funding situation is complex and confusing, and needs to be carefully negotiated in order to maintain the educational goals of university sports.

High school and university sports in Canada are in a time of transition. Careful consideration needs to be given to the educational goals of interscholastic sports, and how they might be maintained. The involvement of students in these negotiations is important.

Interscholastic sport programmes never will be perfect. There always will be a need for critical evaluation and change, just as there is in any part of the curriculum. This means that the educational relevance of these programmes depends on constant evaluation and assessment. A critical approach is the only approach that will enable people to produce and reproduce sports as meaningful activities in the everyday lives of students and in the social organization of the schools and universities that sponsor them.

Visit *Sports in Society*'s Online Learning Centre at www.mcgrawhill.ca/olc/coakley for additional information, website resources, and study tools for this chapter.

Sports in the Future

What can we expect?

The primary goal of futurists is not to predict the future but to uncover images of possible, probable, and preferable futures that enable people to make informed decisions about their lives.

—W. Bell, futurist (1997)

All national and international sports federations will be disbanded and competitive "amateur" tournaments and spectacles beyond the civic level will be prohibited. The Olympic Games, in particular, will be discontinued on the grounds that they have become a hazard to public mental health and to the health of individual competitors.

—Brian Fawcett, author (1990)

Sport is the most dynamic activity in the world today, with the potential to contribute powerfully to a better world . . . . The power and influence of sport is only just being understood.

—Robert Davies, chief executive, International Business Leaders Forum (2002)

Predicting the future, especially of the multiplicity of sports, is a notoriously difficult task.

—Fred Coalter, sport policy researchers (2004)

Discussions of the future often involve exaggerations. Predicting dramatic changes is always more exciting than predicting that tomorrow will look much like today. Therefore, people often describe the future in science fiction terms and emphasize extreme hopes and fears. This sparks our interest and sometimes leaves us temporarily awestruck, but such images of the future are rarely helpful.

For better or worse, the future seldom unfolds as rapidly or dramatically as some forecasters would have us believe. Instead, changes occur in combination with emerging social conditions and the efforts of people to create a future that fits their visions of what life should be like. Of course, some people have more power and resources to create the future than others. And they seldom want revolutionary changes because their privileged positions depend on stability and controlled change. This often slows the rate of progressive cultural and structural transformations, and focuses attention on growth in the production and distribution of consumer goods.

As you read this chapter, it is important to remember two things:

1. Sports are social constructions, and many aspects of sports are contested as people integrate them into their lives.
2. People will create the future of sport; fate, computer forecasts, supernatural forces, or the predictions of sociologists will not determine the future.

The future of sports cannot be separated from general social and cultural factors, but neither can it be separated from the visions that we have for sport. It is those visions that influence the choices that we make about the kinds of physical games that we include in our lives, and the conditions under which we play and/or watch them. Sports will take many forms in the future, and each will be produced through the collective actions of human beings. Therefore, the goal of this chapter is to describe and evaluate the various models of sports that we might use to envision possibilities

for the future and make informed choices as we participate in social worlds.

MAJOR SPORT FORMS IN THE FUTURE

Sports are social constructions. This means that the dominant sports at any particular place and time are constructed with the values and ideas of those who have power in a group or society. However, dominant sports are not universally accepted in many social worlds. History shows that people often modify them, or develop alternative sports that challenge current power relations and promote ideas that resist or oppose people with power.

Through much of history, dominant sports in societies have been grounded in the values and experiences of men concerned with military conquest, political control, and economic expansion. As noted in previous chapters and explained in chapter 4, these sports are based on a *power and performance model*.

Although many people have used the power and performance model as the standard for determining the meaning, organization, and purpose of sports, not everyone accepts it. Some people have developed and maintained sport forms grounded more directly in their unique values and experiences. As noted in chapter 4, many of these sports are based on a *pleasure and participation model*.

These two models do not encompass all the possibilities for defining and playing sports. But they represent two popular conceptions of sports in contemporary societies, so they are a practical starting point for envisioning and thinking about what we would like sports to be in the future. Even with analyses such as these, we will always be surprised. For example, who would have predicted that football, formerly a power and performance sport associated with anglophones in Québec, would become so popular with francophones as both participants and spectators? Only a little less surprising on the pleasure and participation side was the decision by Vancouver City

Council to change its by-laws and open the city's streets to skateboarders.

Power and Performance Sports

Power and performance sports will continue to be highly visible and publicized sport forms in the near future. They are based on key aspects of dominant ideologies in many postindustrial societies as demonstrated by their emphasis on strength, power, speed, and a competitive quest for victories and championships.

Although power and performance sports take many forms, they are based on the idea that excellence is proved through competitive success and achieved through dedication, hard work, and a willingness to take risks. They stress setting records, pushing human limits, using the body as a machine, and defining technology as a performance aid. According to many athletes in power and performance sports, the body is to be disciplined and monitored, preparing it to meet the demands of sports. Sports are defined as battles in which the goal is to defeat opponents. Power and performance sports are exclusive in that participants are selected for their physical skills and abilities to achieve competitive success. Those who lack these "qualities" are cut or relegated to "developmental" programmes. Organizations and teams have hierarchical authority structures in which athletes are subordinate to coaches and coaches are subordinate to owners and administrators. It is widely accepted that coaches can humiliate, shame, and derogate athletes when motivating them to excel. Athletes are expected to endure these motivational tactics and show that they are willing to give all of themselves in the quest for excellence.

The sponsors of power and performance sports want to be associated with people and activities that stress competition, hard work, and the endurance of pain for the sake of productivity and progress (Hoberman, 1994). Being endorsed by winning athletes and teams is important when promoting and selling products. Sponsors assume that

Some pleasure and participation sports become incorporated into power and performance sports. However, in the case of snowboarding, this is not occurring without a struggle. The sport still has many pleasure and participation elements, including a service component. Instructors Liz Christy and James Roelofsen teach snowboarding to low-income youth. [CP(Bonny Makarewicz)]

being connected with winning athletes and teams makes them special in the eyes of people in a society or even around the world. As long as the sponsors reward those who excel in power and performance sports, the future of those sports are secure and the athletes who play them will be cultural celebrities paid to endorse the values of the sponsors. Power and performance sports will remain dominant for the foreseeable future in most societies, mostly because people who possess power and influence will use their resources to make it so.

Pleasure and Participation Sports

Although power and performance sports are highly visible, many people realize that there are other ways to organize and do sports that more closely match their values and experiences. Over the last century, this realization has led to the creation of sport forms that differ from the sports usually covered in the major media. This will continue to occur in the future.

A sport form that often coexists with power and performance sports is organized around a combination of *pleasure and participation*. It involves physical activities in which participants value freedom, authenticity, and personal connections—connections between people, mind and body, and physical activity and the environment.

Although pleasure and participation sports take many forms, they generally emphasize an ethic of personal expression, enjoyment, growth, good health, support for others including opponents, and respect for the environment. They focus on personal empowerment and the notion that the body is to be experienced and enjoyed rather than trained and used as a machine to dominate others. People who play pleasure and participation sports tend to see their bodies as inseparable from the experiences rather than as tools or weapons to be used to achieve rewards and then repaired when they break down.

Pleasure and participation sports are inclusive. The process of involvement is valued over competitive success. Skill differences among participants often are accommodated by using handicaps so that players can enjoy together the challenges associated with an activity. Sport organizations and teams based on this model have democratic decision-making structures characterized by cooperation, power sharing, and give-and-take relationships between coaches and athletes. Humiliation, shame, and derogation are inconsistent with the spirit underlying these sports.

The sponsorship of pleasure and participation sports generally is based on the beliefs that it is socially useful to promote widespread participation in a wide range of physical activities and sports, and that it is important to emphasize health and enjoyment in sports. This is why public and non-profit organizations rather than corporations sponsor many pleasure and participation sports. Corporations seek exposure to mass audiences that are inclined to consume their products when they identify with elite athletes or teams. However, some corporations sponsor pleasure and participation sports as part of an overall emphasis on social responsibility or because it will help them boost sales with clearly identified categories of consumers.

FUTURE TRENDS IN SPORTS

It is likely that power and performance sports will grow faster than pleasure and participation sports although social, economic, and demographic factors support growth in both sport forms. An emphasis on power and performance will pervade most sport spheres in the future, but future developments in all sports will be influenced by technology, the media, a cultural emphasis on rationalization and consumerism, a continuing commitment to gender equity, increasing concerns about the environment, and growing racial and ethnic diversity in most societies worldwide.

The following discussion of trends and the factors that will influence them is meant to be a guide for making informed choices about sports and what we want them to be over the next generation. As many futurists explain, "there are no future facts" and "the best way to predict the future is to create it" (in Bell and Mau, 1971).

The Growth of Power and Performance Sports

Power and performance sports will be the most visible and publicized sport forms in the foreseeable future. Vested interests in these sports are very strong, and those who benefit from them have considerable power and influence. For example, the popularity of these sports is tied to dominant forms of gender relations. When the goal is to push physical limits, men are the centre of attention, especially when limits are tied to strength, power, and speed. This means that many sports reaffirm sex differences and the superiority of men over women. When cultures highlight sex in terms of *difference*, dominant sports are usually based on a power and performance model.

A continued emphasis on power and performance sports also rests on maintaining corporate sponsorships. American football, the classic embodiment of these sports, has become the most popular spectator sport in the U.S. because it attracts billions of dollars in television rights fees and other revenues. Athletes in the NFL and other power and performance sports are portrayed in the media as heroic figures and exemplars of corporate images emphasizing productivity, efficiency, and dedication to performance despite pain and injury. Spectators are encouraged to identify with these athletes and express their identification through the consumption of licensed merchandise and other products. As long as this dynamic persists, these sports will remain dominant in the future.

Because power and performance sports often involve pushing human limits and normative limits, they are exciting and seductive. This makes them relatively easy to market and sell if they are combined with storylines that resonate with the experience of consumers. This is why the media now emphasize the personal lives of athletes and their families. Dedicated, life-long fans may be satisfied with coverage focused on games, scores, and statistics, but attracting the attention of new and less knowledgeable fans depends on presenting tabloid-style information about players' lives.

The Growth of Pleasure and Participation Sports

Through history, many physical activities and sports have embodied characteristics of the pleasure and participation model. The primary reason for this is that sports have always been social occasions in people's lives, and people incorporate into them the things that give them pleasure or reaffirm their values. Pleasure and participation sports continue to be popular to the extent that people define them as attractive alternatives to the more culturally dominant power and performance sports. Factors that fuel this search for alternatives today are concerns about health and fitness, concerns about energy and the environment, participation preferences among older people, values and experiences brought to sports by women, and groups seeking alternatives to highly structured competitive sports that constrain the range of their experiences.

Growing Concerns about Health and Fitness As health-care policies and programmes around the world emphasize prevention rather than expensive cures, people become more sensitive to health and fitness issues. In North America, for example, health-care programmes and insurance companies now encourage strategies for staying well as they seek to cut costs (cf., Health Canada's new *Physical Activity Guide*), and increase profits in the private sector. This encourages people to more actively seek alternatives to power and performance sports and increase participation in pleasure and participation sports for which health benefits are much higher (Waddington, 2000b, 2007).

In Canada, where physical education classes are often voluntary after grade 9, and where many of the scheduled required classes are never taught (for a variety of reasons), new concerns about health, fitness, and obesity are reviving interest in forms of physical education that focus on lifetime activities, noncompetitive challenges, inclusive participation philosophies, respect and support for other participants, and responsible attitudes towards the environment—all of which are characteristics of pleasure and participation sports. Many schools have introduced daily physical education or activity sessions, and there are increasing demands to re-introduce outdoor education to the curriculum in provinces where it has been cut.

If these concerns continue to grow, they will influence the sport preferences of people through the life course. As a consequence, people will begin to demand reasonable membership costs for publicly funded local recreation complexes rather than season tickets to NHL games or expensive cable packages allowing them to sit in a Laz-E-Boy and watch hundreds of hours of sports each year. If people realize that healthy exercise can be organized to create family fun and a sense of community, there will be powerful incentives for them to give priority to a wide array of pleasure and participation sports in their lives. But this depends on how people choose to create the future.

Growing Concerns about Energy and the Environment With increasing energy costs, and growing concerns about the environment, some people are seeking alternative sports that are energy efficient and do little damage to the environment. Thus, human-powered activities such as bicycling, in-line skating, and roller skating are becoming increasingly popular. The idea of "green games" is becoming more prominent (Chernushenko, 1994), and activities such as hiking, birding, power walking, and rock climbing are all becoming increasingly popular with the "greening" of the population.

Participation Preferences among Older People As the median age of the population in many societies increases, as people live longer, and as older people represent an increasingly larger segment of the world's population, there will be a growing interest in sports that do not involve intimidation, the use of physical force, the domination of opponents, and the risk of serious injuries. As people age, they are less likely to risk their physical well-being to establish a reputation in sports. Older people are more likely to see sports as social activities and are more interested in making sports inclusive rather than exclusive. Older people also realize that they have but one body, and it can be enjoyed only if it is cultivated as though it were a garden, rather than driven as if it were a machine.

Young people seeking alternatives to organized competitive sports will increase the diversity of pleasure and participation sports in the future. Mountain boarding is a good example. [Jason Lee, Mountain Board Sports]

The baby boomers in Canada who grew up playing competitive sports are not likely to completely abandon their interest in those sports as they age, but they will avoid participation in power and performance sports that have high injury rates. Many will play modified versions of competitive activities (e.g., senior leagues, "beer leagues") in which rules emphasize the pleasure of movement, connections between people, and controlled challenges. But there also will be increased participation in yoga, tai chi, walking, hiking, weight training, and other activities, which will be taken seriously but done in settings where the focus is on health, fitness, and social connections, rather than setting records, using the body to dominate opponents, or bragging about who sweats the most in Bikram yoga session.

Pleasure and participation sports will be sites where older people challenge dominant ideas about aging. Aging has often been seen as a process that involves increasing dependency and incapacity, but the sport participation of older people supports the idea that aging does not automatically mean becoming weak and incapacitated. "Seniors" and "masters" sport programmes will increase as people demand them. As a result images of older people who are fit, healthy, and accomplished athletes[1] will become more visible and serve as models for others.

Values and Experiences Brought to Sports by Women As women gain more power and resources in sports, many will reject the culture that accompanies traditional power and performance sports. In the process, they will challenge the very gender ideology on which such sports are organized. A possible outcome of this will be new norms and structures that emphasize dimensions of pleasure and participation sports. For instance, when women play sports such as rugby, soccer, and hockey, there are indications that they often emphasize inclusiveness and support for teammates and opponents in explicit ways that are seldom present in the men's versions of these sports. The "in-your-face" power and performance orientation exhibited by some men is replaced by an orientation that is expressive of the joy and connections resulting from participation. A case in point occurred recently in NCAA Division II softball. Sara Tucholsky of Western Oregon hit the first home run of her university career, but badly injured her knee while rounding first base. While the umpires and coaches discussed what to do, opposing player Mallory Holtman of Central

Washington inquired whether it would be "OK" if she and her teammates carried Sara around the bases. Which they did, showing that some things in sports are far more important than the outcome of the game.

Women face difficulties when recruiting sponsors for sports, such as ringette, that differ from men's power and performance sports. Without an emphasis on physical domination, the women's sports often are seen as second rate or not "real" enough to attract the attention that sponsors seek. However, if women choose such sports in greater numbers, sponsors may respond if they see benefits for their bottom lines. If they do, pleasure and participation sports will receive increased support.

Groups Seeking Alternative Sports People who reject power and performance sports, or certain dimensions of them, also will contribute to the growth of sports organized more closely around the pleasure and participation model. For example, high school students will continue to form their own sport groups and play games on their own, rather than put up with the constraints of playing on interschool teams, on which coaches sometimes try to control their lives and on which the emphasis on competition and win-loss records may be given priority over enjoyment and the experience of participation. The fastest growing sport in Ontario high schools, was not administered by the OFSAA and had no teacher-coaches.[2]

Unique sport subcultures have developed around many alternative sports. Studies of skateboarders and snowboarders show that some young people resist attempts to turn their sport into a commercialized, competitive form (Beal, 1995; Honea, 2005). Even in official formally sponsored contests, skaters have deliberately subverted the power and performance dimensions of

---

[1]It should be pointed out, however, that master's competitions in a number of sports retain many *power and performance* characteristics. Nonetheless, Seniors Games in many Canadian provinces include many sports and activities based in pleasure and participation principles (e.g., disk golf, bowling, card games, and darts).

[2]OFSAA now has a sanctioned an Ultimate tournament, but the sport is still largely run by the players, which conforms with the Ultimate ethic.

the event. Registered skaters pinned competition numbers on their shirts, so that they were upside down or difficult to read. "Competitors" have focused on expressing themselves rather than out-doing opponents, and they prearranged patterns for warming up and competing. In some cases, mass protests have stopped events after non-conforming athletes were disqualified for their actions. Of course, none of this appears on tele-vision broadcasts that are edited to attract young viewers (Crissey, 1999). As illustrated in figure 15.1, the athletes often feel frustrated when they are pressured by sponsors to say things that do not represent their experiences.

People sometimes resist attempts to change the pleasure and participation emphasis in their activi-ties. They do not want competition and the domi-nation of opponents to replace the expression and support of fellow participants. For example, when a twelve-year-old snowboarder was asked about adding his sport to the Olympics, he said, "Don't kill the ride, dude. Let us be free." Even at age twelve, he knew that the ideology of power and performance would subvert elements of pleasure and participation in his sport. After snowboard-ing was added to the 1998 Olympics Norwegian Terje Haakonsen, reputedly the best boarder in the world, refused to compete in Nagano. He said, "Snowboarding is about fresh tracks and carving powder and being yourself and not being judged by others; it's not about nationalism and politics and money" (in Perman, 1998, p. 61).

Male athletes in alternative-action sports are more likely than others to resist a traditional power and performance model, even though they have a reputation for taking risks and marginal-izing girls and women. They know that losing control of their sports means that an emphasis on pleasure and participation will be given low priority. This led skateboarder Tony Hawk to declare that "it's about time the riders took the competitions into their own hands—the only ones who truly know the sport are the ones who are actively doing it and pushing the limits along the way" (in Higgins, 2005). Hawk organized

Athletes with a disability will participate in sports in greater numbers. Creatively designed equipment will permit new forms of sports involvement for both the able-bodied and the disabled, as shown in this photo of trail riders. [Rob Schoenbaum]

his Boom Boom Huck Jam tour to preserve the spirit of snowboarding and other action sports in a format that would generate revenues and media coverage. Similarly, Terje Haakonsen and other snowboarders created "Ticket to Ride" (TTR), a series of events designed to preserve the plea-sure and participation ethos of their sports. They describe TTR events in this way:

> [It's] a movement connected to the core of snowboarding's identity.... The sense of fun and friendship, the appreciation of nature, the travel and the unique experiences, the freedom and creativity—this is snowboarding. This is what hap-pens every time you strap in, stand up and drop in. (www.the-arctic-challenge.com/)

People with a physical or intellectual disability have developed alternative sports and adapted dominant sports to fit their interests and needs. Although some of these sports emphasize power and performance, others emphasize pleasure and participation. Concern and support for

"I love the X Games . . . because they are all about . . . freedom and individual expression."
....

FIGURE 15.1 Some athletes in alternative sports are uneasy about what happens when their sports become commercialized and represented in terms that fit the interests of sponsors.

teammates and opponents, as well as inclusiveness related to physical abilities, characterize these latter sports. When people with a disability participate with able-bodied people in sports organized around a power and performance model, it presents an opportunity for all athletes, regardless of age or ability, to deal with the reality that human relationships always involve accommodating difference and uniqueness. Dealing with this reality involves a choice: maintain power and performance sports as they are and marginalize those with a disability, or revise them with features from the pleasure and participation model to be inclusive. It is difficult to predict how people in different situations and at different points in their lives will handle this choice, but it is certain that their decisions will create at least part of sports' future.

The Gay Games and the EuroGames provide additional examples of alternative sport

form emphasizing participation, support, inclusiveness, and the enjoyment of physical movement (Pronger, 1999). The sixth quadrennial Gay Games, held in Sydney, Australia, in 2002, involved more than 11,000 competitors from eighty-two nations. Although the Gay Games resemble dominant sports in some ways, they explicitly challenge the gender ideology that underlies dominant sports, and they are free of the homophobia that permeates them. But they are not free of internal politics as demonstrated in 2004 when the Federation of Gay Games (FGG) had a dispute with the organizers planning the 2006 Games in Montréal. The FGG wanted to focus almost exclusively on sport events, whereas the Montréal organizers wanted to also make the Games a cultural festival, with other events for gay men, lesbians, bisexuals, and transsexuals (GLBTs). Thus, there were two events in 2006: The Gay Games in Chicago and the OutGames in Montréal, both of which integrated inclusion and other aspects of the pleasure and participation model into their sports. At the community level, GLBTs organize sports to provide enjoyable experiences in their social lives. A gay man explains:

> The nice thing about playing gay sports is...to interact with gay people...[so you] don't have to be on guard. You can joke around, you can play. That's a good feeling. It's also the sense of community that comes from it....It's not that I didn't fit in [when I played volleyball at work, but it] is probably more relaxed in gay sports. (Pronger, 1990a, p. 238)

The range of sports that incorporate elements of the pleasure and participation model—from kickball to shinny—will grow if more people realize that sports are social constructions that can be created to fit even temporary interests and passing situations.

Although it is often a challenge to find corporate sponsors, forms of pleasure and participation sports usually survive because people are creative enough to find the resources to maintain them. Furthermore, corporate or media sponsors are needed only when a sport hires administrators, focuses on national and international tournaments, and requires equipment and travel expenses. When a sport is done simply for pleasure and participation, the primary resource needed is people wishing to play it. This resource has existed through human history.

Trends in Sport Spheres

Those who attempt to predict the future often use current trends and demographic data. Demographers may tend to overemphasize the effects of, for example, age cohorts, at the expense of other factors that influence social change (e.g., economics, international relations, technology, and so on), but their arguments should not be ignored, For example, University of Toronto demographer, David Foot (Foot and Stoffman, 1998) offered predictions about adult participation in sports from a demographic perspective— i.e., what effect an aging ("greying") population will have on patterns of sport and recreation. Using tennis as an example, he traced the lifecycle of a participant sport. Baby boomers, who, in 2008, range in age from 43 to 62, represent almost a third of the Canadian population. A boom in tennis, which started in the early 1970s, peaked in the mid-1980s when there were waiting lists for memberships in tennis clubs in Canada. By themid-1990s there were no more waiting lists, and clubs were advertising for members. Of course, there are still many tennis players of all ages but, Foot argues, the age group most likely to participate grew older. He also suggests that the boomers' children, the "echo generation," will reach peak tennis playing age during the next five years, so we should see a mini-boom in the sport.

The boomer generation is probably fitter, and more aware of the benefits of physical activity than any previous age cohort, but the evidence seems to indicate their declining interest in competitive sports. Curling, swimming, and walking are activities that appear to be increasing in participation. Others have pointed to the growing environmental awareness ("greening") of the Canadian population, and the implications of the greening and greying of a major cohort of the populations seems to suggest an increase in participation in activities such as hiking, snowshoeing, cross-country skiing, gardening, and birding (birdwatching). These activities also produce a major demand for appropriate clothes and equipment, putting businesses such as Mountain Equipment Co-op into a major period of expansion (helped also by the growth in adventure and outdoor sport participation among younger cohorts in the population). Foot reports that 65 million birders in the U.S. spend US$5 billion each year on birding products (cameras, binoculars, bird feed, and so on). At 10 percent of the U.S. population, but a somewhat more outdoor-oriented and "green" population, it is possible to estimate that there are more than 6.5 million birders in Canada, spending a great deal of money on their recreation.

Predicting the future is less important than knowing about current trends and using that knowledge to participate in creating the future. For instance, some people study trends so that they can more effectively plan strategies to create sports that are humane, accessible, inclusive, and democratically organized. Others have different goals, but in any case, our knowledge of current trends in various sport spheres is useful. If the result is *multiple futures*, that's ideal.

Professional Sports Current trends in professional sports involve the following:

- Profit-driven national and global expansion
- Staging expensive total entertainment events
- Dependence, to a greater or lesser extent, on public funds to build facilities designed as shopping malls
- Contentious negotiations between players and leagues/owners over working conditions

Although people think they have little control over these trends, most professional sports exist in democratic societies where citizens are sometimes in a position to vote on the use of public funds to build sport stadiums and arenas (including Olympic facilities). They also elect political representatives who determine the legal environment in which businesses, including professional sports and the Olympics, operate. This means that people could organize and pressure local legislators to impose ceilings on ticket prices in facilities built with public money, or to ensure that a number of low cost tickets are available to local citizens (cf., the Vancouver Olympics; www.vancouver2010.com). Legislators could also mandate that a lottery be used to sell tickets to major events rather than letting corporations buy all the good seats and cause ticket prices to increase. If people learn to act as citizens before professional leagues, team owners, and Olympic organizers convert them into consumers, they will create futures more in line with their interests and resources.

Interuniversity Sports Current trends in interuniversity sports in Canada involve the following:

- Concerns about scholarships, and the increasing "Americanization" of Canadian university sport
- Increasing professionalization (e.g., many university hockey teams have a large number of former Major Junior players), and the increasing isolation of university sport from the educational institution (e.g., a number of university football teams are sponsored by businesses unconnected to the university)
- Struggles over gender equity
- Student fees, and the use of athletics budgets to provide more money for fewer sports

Knowing about and understanding these trends is important. Students, administrators, and provincial legislators make decisions about the use of student fees and university sport facilities. Faculty and administrators should determine how to organize interuniversity sports so that students experience educational benefits at reasonable cost.

The possibilities for students to create futures in connection with these trends are many. Students at large universities are like citizens in small cities who can influence the use of local resources to support their sport interests—if they are organized and insist that community decisions are made democratically. If students do not do this, it will be administrators, athletic directors, alumni/ae and other donors who create the future for them.

High School Sports Current trends in high school sports involve the following:

- Limited budgets, and the increasing use of participation fees and fundraising
- Struggles over gender equity
- The need for different sports associated with an increasingly diverse population (e.g., the current growth of cricket in Toronto area schools)
- A declining school age population in parts of Canada
- The effects on school sport of the emergence of specialist sport high schools
- A reduction in the number of teacher-coaches, and the increasing use of "coaches" from the community

Debates about the meaning, purpose, and organization of high school sports often are contentious. However, they provide opportunities for students, parents, teachers, and local citizens to present their visions of what school sports should be in the future. Those who want high school sports to be a system to prepare athletes for U.S. university scholarships are often very vocal on these issues, but they do not represent the majority of citizens in most communities. Therefore, the future of high school sports depends on who participates in the debates, and how prepared they are to argue their cases. School sports are still funded in large part by tax money, and their stated goal is education. There is no justification for spending public money on school sports if they do not have an educational purpose for as many students as are interested in participating.

Youth Sports Current trends in organized youth sports involve the following:

- Continuing concerns about coach, parent, and athlete (mis)behaviour
- Continuing concerns about the treatment of talented athletes as young athletic "workers" without any of the protections enjoyed by adult workers
- Segregation of programmes by socioeconomic status, race, and ethnicity
- Decreasing opportunities for children in low-income families and communities
- More children seeking alternatives to adult-controlled organized sports

These trends mimic trends in society as a whole. An ideology that emphasizes individualism and individual achievement sometimes focuses on the achievements of one child at the expense of other children. Individualism also encourages a form of "family values" that calls for every family to provide for itself; those who have resources will use them to create playgrounds and ice rinks in their fenced backyards and to buy access to private programmes and facilities for their sports. They do not need public parks or publicly funded programmes, and seldom vote to support them. As a result, public services, including parks and recreation, are cut back and subject to user fees. The future of youth sports will involve escalating social class divisions unless people decide they want something different. Decisions similar to this will determine many aspects of our collective futures, not just youth sports.

Sports for People with a Disability Current trends in sports for people with a disability involve the following:

- Increasing numbers of people in the world disabled by war, land mines, lack of medical care, and poverty
- Increasing recognition that people with a disability want to play sports and have a right to do so (cf., the 2007 UN Convention

on the Rights of Persons with Disabilities, Article 30 of which deals specifically with sport; www.un.org/disabilities/convention/conventionfull.shtml)
- Continuing use of sport participation as therapy
- More visible examples of sports for elite athletes with a disability
- New technologies that facilitate sport participation
- Emerging ideas, vocabularies, and orientations that support people with a disability and their participation in sports

Disability is so multifaceted that there are many needs. In postindustrial societies, this is a crucial time for envisioning possibilities and working to create desired futures. In developing nations, where poverty rates frequently surpass 50 percent, possibilities are limited unless people from wealthier nations provide requested assistance. Believing or hoping that new technologies will eliminate disabilities is unrealistic and subverts actions that could create futures in which people recognize the abilities rather than the disabilities of others. To do this, we need a vocabulary to imagine a future in which ability exists on a continuum and cannot be classified in two boxes, one able and one disabled. When people think outside these two boxes, many futures become possible. This is illustrated in the Breaking Barriers box (p. 499).

Spectators and Spectator Sports Current trends related to spectators and spectator sports involve the following:

- Continuing commitment to watching sports as a central leisure activity
- Increasing use of the Internet and other technologies that provide spectator experiences
- Defining spectators as consumers who are receptive to advertising messages

Spectator sports are deeply embedded in many cultures. However, people can decide how

---

Breaking Barriers	**Vision Barriers**
	I Have to Believe

In 1997, a five-year-old youth baseball player in Conyers, Georgia, came to every practice and game with his seven-year-old brother. The seven-year-old loved baseball, but there were no teams for a child in a wheelchair. So the coach invited him to play.

The coach's action precipitated a series of events. The following season, Dean Alford and others organized the Conyers "Miracle League" for children with a disability. It was the first baseball league of its kind, so creative rules were made: every player on a team would bat each inning, all base runners were safe, and every player scored a run. Able-bodied young people and volunteers served as buddies, assisting players when the need arose.

During the first year there were thirty-five players on four teams. Watching them play inspired Alford. He saw that a conventional ball field with grass, dirt, and elevated bases created barriers for players who were blind, in wheelchairs, or using walkers and crutches. Alford worked with two Rotary Clubs to raise the money needed to design and construct a rubberized turf playing field combined with restrooms, a concession stand, and picnic area—all accessible. Three grass fields were included and designed so that they could be converted to synthetic surfaces as the Miracle League grew.

The field opened in 2000. It attracted national media attention and interest among families of children with a disability.* By 2008 there were Miracle League organizations throughout the United States, each in different stages of development. Some 172 rubberized turf playing surfaces are currently under construction in the U.S., and the first one in Canada is planned to open in 2010 in Amherstberg, Ontario.

When people hear of the Miracle League, visit websites, and watch games, their idealism often pushes them to think further outside the box of traditional parks and playing fields. For example, some communities have built a universally accessible playground adjacent to the smooth-surface baseball fields. Playground designers eliminate barriers and create an environment that is attractive to children with varying physical (dis)abilities. This enables families and friends to play

safely as they encounter physical challenges and have fun regardless of (dis)abilities.

Idealists in other communities have envisioned and organized similar play environments and sport programmes for adults with a disability. When people see a Miracle League baseball field combined with a universally accessible playground they often think, "This makes so much sense," and then they ask, "Why doesn't my community have one of these?" This is heartening to those who know one of the almost 600,000 children in Canada who, due to a (dis)ability, cannot play in existing youth baseball leagues and other sport programmes.

It is also heartening to Canadian veterans returning from Afghanistan with amputated limbs, sight and hearing impairments, and injuries that impair walking. Making sports accessible to them would seem to be a no-brainer, even among those who lack idealism. As veterans return to communities, universities, gyms, parks, trails, and workplaces, idealism is essential if barriers are to be broken.

Jayne Craike, who competes on the New Zealand Equestrian Federation national dressage circuit and also represents her country in the Paralympics, encourages people to be idealistic as they envision and work to create the future. She says, "*I have to believe* that there is still more to come in a world that is continually changing, and that we can make a difference" (Joukowsky and Rothstein, 2002b, p. 55, emphasis added; see also, http://www.lupus. org.nz/PersonalExperiences.htm). Craike knows that sports are more than therapeutic tools for people with (dis)abilities. In cultures where sport participation is highly valued, they are normalizing activities; they enable people to establish important identities; and they are sites for meeting others and forcing everyone who watches to acknowledge that (dis)abilities are a normal part of the human condition. It may be idealistic to envision and work for universal accessibility, but who wants to settle for the alternative?

---

*See and hear some of this media coverage at www.miracleleague.com/index.htm

much they will pay in terms of money, time, and effort to be spectators; what meanings they will give to their experiences; and how they will integrate those experiences into their lives. They also can envision futures that deviate from those envisioned by corporate sponsors and media executives. For example, if people voted to bring free or low-cost wireless (Wi-Fi) access to their communities, the future would involve incredibly diverse spectator experiences. But if people allow giant cable and telecom corporations to control the conditions of broadband access, their futures as spectators will be limited and expensive. Imagine futures in which broadband access is publicly provided like other essential services, such as roads and schools, and available to people around the world. Such futures would enable people to be interactive spectators with access to sports they would not otherwise see.

Sports for Development and Peace (SDP) The trend toward using sport in international development and conflict resolution initiatives is so new that even what it is called has changed several times as people try to find the best way to describe what is happening. It has been called, among others, *development through sport*, and *international development through sport*; however, the name *sports for development and peace* appears to be more widely accepted at this time (www.sportanddev.org). Current trends related to sports for development and peace involve the following:

- An almost exponential increase in the number of NGOs involved in SDP
- Increasing concerns that SDP initiatives represent a new form of colonization
- Concerns about the training and cultural sensitivity of volunteers in the NGOs
- Concerns about the sustainability of such programmes, and about the ways that NGOs may discourage actual structural changes in the countries where they are working (e.g., the introduction of government mandated physical and health education)

SDP initiatives, whether they are organized by established NGOs, churches, travel agencies (volunteer tourism initiatives), or individuals and small groups, are well meaning endeavours. They are often started by athletes intending to "give something back to the community," or who have seen the need as part of their travels as an athlete. However, they are often based on rather naïve assumptions about poverty, international development, cultural differences, and the ability of sport to "make a difference." Often, the initiatives are so short of money that no systematic evaluations of the programmes are carried out—anecdotes are used to justify the effectiveness of the programme and to raise funds. Also, so rapid has been the rise of this trend that it has almost caught researchers by surprise. There is little research on SDP, and less than a handful of university courses. However, the research that is being carried out (e.g., Darnell, 2008; Kidd, 2008) is beginning to determine what works and what does not work, and how best to use sports and physical activities to bring about progressive changes in peace, health and communities.

Factors Influencing Trends

When creating futures it is useful to know about factors that influence current trends. This enables us to anticipate possibilities, avoid resistance, and make more informed decisions as we participate in social worlds.

Many factors influence trends in sports, but the discussion here is limited to six: technology, environment and energy, telecommunications and electronic media, a widespread commitment to organization and rationalization, a cultural emphasis on commercialism and consumption, and the demographic characteristics of communities and societies.

Technology Technology is *the application of scientific or other organized knowledge to solve problems, expand experiences, or alter the conditions of reality.* It is used to make sports safer, detect and treat injuries more effectively, assess physical limits and potential, expand the experiences available in sports, train bodies to perform more efficiently, provide athletes with more control of their bodies, increase the speeds at which bodies move and the risks involved in sports, enhance the size and strength of bodies, alter bodies to match the demands of particular sports, identify rule infractions and enforce rules more accurately, measure and compare performances with precision, and improve the durability and functionality of equipment.

The major issue related to technology is when and how to use it and regulate it. The governing bodies of sports try to regulate the technologies used by coaches, officials, trainers, and athletes, but the number of new technologies has made this difficult. Assessing technology is not easy, as explained in the discussion of performance enhancing substances in chapter 6. Technologies are a part of sports, and we can make consistent and sensible suggestions about them only when we know what we want sports to be in the future. Consider genetic-enhancement technologies. They can be used to improve human performance, heal injured bodies, and correct certain physical impairments. If we want to create a future in which sports are organized around the power and performance model, the framework and criteria for assessing genetic enhancement would be different than if we want sports organized around a pleasure and participation model. This is why it is important to have a clear sense of the place of sports in society and the purpose we want sports to serve in our lives and the world as a whole.

Environment and Energy Sports have been slow to pay attention to global warming, the use of energy and resources, and the effects of sports as we now organize them on the environment. The cost of fuel is currently making travel by air or road significantly more expensive than it was just a few years ago. Professional, high-performance, university, and even many high

school and youth sports involve a great deal of air or road travel. Costs will certainly increase, and the two options available to sports on limited budgets will be to cut participation opportunities, or cut travel.

Many sports are quite intensive, to the point of being wasteful, in their use of resources. Consider the following statistics from one team in one small league—the 2008 Hamilton Tiger-Cats football team training camp (Peters, 2008). The camp involved nine coaches and 68 players in 24 practices over 20 days in order to fill 46 positions on the team. The camp used:

- 1,000   rolls of tape
- 120   football helmets
- 200   face masks
- 100   jerseys
- 36   footballs
- 250   towels per day
- 75   loads of laundry

This is not to single out football—sports waste resources whenever hockey players deliberately break a stick in anger; whenever poorly made equipment and clothing are given away at games; whenever huge stadia are used for ten football games and ten rock concerts each year and spend the rest of the time empty; whenever golf courses use large amounts of fresh water, pesticides, herbicides, and fungicides in order to function; whenever motorized sports are run without developing technological innovations to promote fuel efficiency; whenever cities bid for sports mega-events; and in so many other ways.

In order to meet their responsibility with regard to global warming and other environmental concerns, and in order to manage budgets effectively while maintaining opportunities to participate in sports, sport organizations will have to engage in some extraordinarily creative thinking on everything from scheduling to snowmaking, from refrigeration to laundry, and from new uniforms every season to their use of showers and towels. Working closely with environmental scientists and the new "green" technology companies would be a good start. It would be ideal if the wealthiest sports organizations in the world led the way on these changes, but we suspect that change will, as it so often does, begin at the bottom of the sports hierarchy.

Telecommunications and Electronic Media
Television, computers, the Internet, wireless phones, PDAs, and other devices are technologies, but they have special implications for sports. Television and the Internet, for instance, provide visual images and narratives that many people use to imagine future possibilities for sports. Some people even use them to make choices about participation and to formulate standards for assessing their sport experiences (see figure 15.2). Therefore, those who control electronic media around the word have considerable power to create the future. Media do *not* control what people *think*, but they certainly influence what people *think about* when it comes to sports. The events, athletes, and stories re-presented in the media provide topics and issues that people *think about* and discuss in their relationships. In this way, media content influences the everyday discourse out of which people form their ideas about what sports could and should be in the future.

To understand this process, imagine that hockey was the only sport that you ever saw on television. Your sense of what sports are and could be would be limited. This is what occurs in our experience as media companies select for coverage only those sports that generate profits on commercial television. As a result, those are the sports we see and talk about. For example, when the media do not cover women's sports, people are less likely to talk about them, learn about the athletes and teams, and incorporate them into the experiences they use to envision the future.

Electronic media can expose us to new worlds, but when market forces shape media content those worlds look much the same after a while. If

"Oh, Mom! Why go outside to play when I can be on my own virtual World Cup Team right here?"

FIGURE 15.2   The future of sports is difficult to predict. Will children prefer video games and virtual sports over the dominant sport forms of today? Will there ever be a video soccer game based on women players?

we realize this, we can seek images and narratives about sports that are not represented exclusively through commercial media. This expands our experience and enables us to think more creatively about the present and future. The more versions of sports we see and talk about, the more we can invent and modify sports to match our interests and circumstances today and tomorrow.

Organization and Rationalization   All sports contain the element of play. But sports today focus so much on purpose, planning, and productivity that play has been pushed to the sidelines. "Fun" in organized, purpose-driven sports is associated with achieving goals rather than emotional expression and joy. Process is now secondary to product, and the journey is secondary to the destination.

People in postindustrial cultures live with the legacy of industrialization. They emphasize organization according to rational principles based, whenever possible, on systematic research. Being organized and making plans to accomplish goals is so important that spontaneity, expression, creativity, and joy—the elements of play—are given low priority or may even be considered frivolous.

When this orientation is used in sports, it allows for standardization so that scores and performance data can be objectively and rationally compared from one event and year to the next. But it limits possibilities for play. For instance, legendary snowboarder Terje Haakonsen decided against participating in the Olympics because he felt that it was a form of sport in which organization and rationalization had subverted play. His thoughts about this are summarized in his description of snowboarding:

> That was a fun time . . . I was always learning new tricks, figuring out ways to get better. When I'm having fun snowboarding, it's like meditation. I'm not thinking about anything but what I'm doing right now. No past, no future. . . . [But today, too many] people get stuck and all they do the whole year is pipe, and that's too bad for them. They do the same routine over and over, get the moves down. It becomes like this really precise, synchronized movement, like they're little ballerinas or something. It's no longer this spontaneous sport, like when you're a kid screwing around. (in Greenfeld, 1999)

Haakonsen knows that fun, seriousness, effort, and discipline often go together. He explains that he would be exhausted after a day of fun and effort, and when he missed a trick, he would focus, get serious, and try it again and again. But he was doing it for himself on his terms rather than for judges on terms he did not control.

When creating sports, these are important things to keep in mind because there is a tendency in postindustrial cultures to organize them

Trying to improve skills on your own terms is different than doing a routine over and over to meet someone else's idea of technical perfection. Once we "feel" this distinction in our own sport participation, we become much more creative as we think of how to do sports and incorporate them into our lives. [McGraw-Hill]

so that they make sense for the purposes of rationally assessing skills and performances. Wanting to improve physical skills so that you have more opportunities to engage in different forms of play is one thing, but spending years to improve a single skill to conform to someone else's idea of technical perfection is another. Once we "feel" this distinction in our own sport participation, we become much more creative when thinking about and creating the future, not only for ourselves but also for our children and grandchildren.

Commercialism and Consumption We have become so deeply embedded in commercial culture than many people think of themselves as customers instead of citizens. We even hear students say that they are customers at the university. Instead of learners and citizens of a university community, they see themselves as consumers who buy courses. When this form of commercialism pervades our lives, it changes the way we think about others, our experiences, and ourselves. We measure everything in terms of material criteria such as dollars, profits and losses, and bottom lines.

When commercial ideology pervades sports, play becomes secondary to play-offs and payoffs. As discussed in chapter 11, commercialization influences sports in the sense that games, athletes, and even experiences become commodities— things to be bought and sold for bottom-line purposes. Sports become "sportainment" created for profit and played for external rewards. Participation revolves around the consumption of equipment, lessons, clothing, nutritional supplements, gym and club memberships, and other things. Status becomes associated with where you do sports, the equipment that you use, and the clothing that you wear.

Some people are turned off by this approach, but unless they have experienced alternatives, they may struggle to think about sports devoid of commercialism and consumption. This is why it is important to have public spaces where people can play sports that do not require fees, permits, or memberships. Creativity thrives in such spaces. But when they are not widely available, people who can afford to do so play sports in commercial spaces. In this sense, public policies at all levels of government can create or subvert possibilities for noncommercial sport futures.

Demographic Characteristics of Communities and Societies Demographics were mentioned at the beginning of this section in terms of age cohorts and participation. However, because sports are social constructions, some of the richest sport environments are those in which people have diverse cultural backgrounds and sport experiences.

Even when people play the same sport, strategies and styles often vary with their cultural backgrounds. For example, Canadians created a secular and rationalized version of lacrosse that was different from the traditional, sacred game invented and played by Native Peoples in North America (King, 2007).

Since the power and performance version of the game emerged in Montréal, it is fitting that "intercrosse," an international pleasure and participation version of the game, using softcrosse equipment, is represented in Canada mostly by Québec.[3] People in the United States, Canada, and Australia took the sport of rugby as played in England and adapted it to fit their preferences to create the American (Riesman and Denny, 1951) and Canadian gridiron versions of the game, and Australian Rules football.

Although demographic diversity presents challenges, it also presents possibilities for creating new forms and versions of sports. As geographical mobility, labour migration, and political turmoil

---

[3]At the World Games of intercrosse, players from different countries divide themselves into mixed teams as a social celebration of internationalism rather than nationalism. However, the pull of power and performance sport is such that there is now an intercrosse World Cup played every two years by the best players of every country on national teams.

push and pull together people from different backgrounds, there will be many opportunities to borrow and blend different sports, styles of play, and game strategies. If people take advantage of those opportunities without systematically privileging games from one culture and marginalizing games from other cultures, it is possible to envision and create sports that fit a wide range of interests and abilities. As a multicultural society, Canada presents an ideal laboratory for examining these opportunities. As issues regarding the wearing of the *patka* or the *hijab* are resolved in mainstream sports, the enormous variety of new sports and physical activities being introduced by new Canadians presents unimaginable opportunities.

ENVISIONING POSSIBILITIES AND CREATING FUTURES

The International Business Leaders Forum is an organization dedicated to promoting corporate social responsibility (CSR) around the globe. The chief executive, Robert Davies, tells corporate leaders worldwide that the visibility and popularity of sports at the local and global levels provides opportunities to improve health, develop communities, boost education and literacy, and empower girls and women. He says that "the power and influence of sports is only just being understood" by people concerned with CSR (Davies, 2002a).

The same message, at the same time, came from the United Nations. Speaking at the World Economic Forum, Kofi Annan, then Secretary General of the UN, (2006) said:

> [Sport] is a global language capable of bridging social, cultural and religious divides. It can be a powerful tool for fostering understanding, tolerance and peace... it teaches us teamwork and fair-play. It builds self-esteem and opens up new opportunities. This in turn can contribute to the wellbeing of whole communities and countries.

Leading up to the International Year of Sport and Physical Education (2005), sport became one of the tools for attempting to achieve the Millennium Development Goals (MDGs). The International Working Group for Sport for Development and Peace has outlined the ways in which sport and development initiatives can be involved in achieving the MDGs by the target date of 2015. The eight goals are:

- Eradicate extreme poverty and hunger
- Achieve universal primary education
- Promote gender equality and empower women
- Reduce child mortality
- Improve maternal health
- Combat HIV/AIDS, malaria, and other diseases
- Ensure environmental sustainability
- Develop a global partnership for development

As Davies and Annan think about the future from the perspectives of international development and CSR, they see possibilities for changing sports, and using them to facilitate changes beyond playing fields and locker rooms. These messages about making social changes have stimulated many young Canadians to volunteer for one of the many sport for development and peace initiatives now under way around the world. Sport and physical education clearly have a place in achieving the MDGs relating to health, education, gender equity, and the environment.

Other perspectives alert us to even more possibilities. To assess them, and to convert selected possibilities into realities, there is a need to understand connections between sport and the rest of the world. This is why social theories are especially useful; they provide frameworks to identify and explain those connections. In turn, this enables people to develop focused and consistent strategies for creating the future.

Using Social Theories to Create Futures

Each of the theories discussed in chapter 2 provides a different perspective for understanding connections between sports and social worlds, identifying problems, and selecting approaches to create sports in terms of their anticipated consequences in people's lives. The following sections provide only brief summaries of how those theories may be used for these purposes.

Functionalist Theory Functionalist theory continues to be used to envision sports in the future. For example, when Robert Davies talks to corporate leaders, he bases many of his ideas on a functionalist approach. This appeals to those leaders and to others with power and influence because such an approach takes the existing social system for granted and explains how sports help to preserve and improve that system. A functionalist approach to the future emphasizes that existing sport forms should be supported and maintained through the use of *conservative* and *reformist* strategies.

A **conservative strategy** is *based on the belief that sports reaffirm traditional values and established forms of social organization and therefore should be strengthened and expanded rather than transformed.* The focus is on management issues designed to make sports and sport organizations more efficient while maintaining the culture and structure of sports as they are. Conservative strategies are very common in sports because few people view sports in critical terms and because the people who control sports and have the resources to influence them in the future are advocates of growth, not social and cultural transformation.

A **reformist strategy** *is based on a similar belief about the merits of sports, but it focuses on eliminating problems, promoting fairness, controlling cheating and drug use, urging athletes to be positive role models, and making sport organizations more efficient.* In this way, more people will have access to sport participation and experience its benefits. In other words, eliminate problems but keep the culture and structure of sports as they are. For example, women, people with disabilities, and others who have lived on the margins of mainstream sports and wish to be included in existing structures,

programmes, and organizations frequently use reformist strategies. Reformers focus mostly on issues such as equality of opportunity and social justice.

The Canadian Association for the Advancement of Women and Sport (CAAWS) is an example of an organization that often uses reformist strategies based on a functionalist approach. CAAWS lobbies for gender equity so that girls and women have equal opportunities to participate in sports, and it calls attention to the need for more women in decision-making positions in existing sport organizations. Because CAAWS depends on national fundraising to survive, it is very careful when it uses more radical strategies based on critical and feminist theories. It does not want to alienate the majority of their donors who favour a functionalist approach and want sports to be maintained much the way they are today.

Conflict Theory Conflict theory is seldom used when many Canadians think about sports and society. Although some intellectually oriented people today think that it is fashionable to discuss injustices related to race and gender, they avoid discussing injustices related to social class and class relations (hooks, 2000). Conflict theory, with its explicit focus on social class, makes them uncomfortable. It challenges the very ideologies on which their class privilege rests and forces them to think about problems inherent in a capitalist economy that survives on profits made by paying workers as little as possible.

Conflict theory focuses attention on class relations in sports and the ways that sports are used to preserve and disguise basic social-class divisions in society. People using conflict theory to create sports adopt a particular form of **radical strategy** *in which the goal is to transform the economic organization of society so that class differences fade away.* This would make possible forms of sport in which there are no constraints on freedom, creativity, and enjoyment. The profit motive would be gone, so there would be no reason to exploit or oppress people.

Nearly everyone who uses conflict theory in Canada understands that eliminating capitalism is unrealistic at this point in history. Therefore, they favour specific strategies through which citizens, athletes, and spectators organize themselves and challenge those who have used wealth and economic power to shape sports in ways that maintain their privilege. Over the last half century, people using conflict theory have worked with like-minded reformers and people using other radical strategies to reduce racism, sexism, nationalism, and militarism in sports. Additionally, they have inspired athletes to form players' associations to bargain for their rights with leagues and team owners. In a few cases, people who used conflict theory during the 1960s and 1970s continue to work in and with those associations.

Outside North America, conflict theory remains popular among many people. In cultures where people are less devoted to consumption as a form of status expression, class-related and economic ideologies are more open and widely discussed. This makes them more sensitive to the social and political implications of extreme gaps between the very wealthy and powerful and everyone else. It also makes them less resistant to using conflict theory to envision possibilities that do not depend on commercialism and the use of large amounts of capital.

Critical Theory People who use critical theory are concerned with the processes through which culture is produced, reproduced, and changed. Therefore, they focus their attention on issues related to ideologies, representation, and power in society. They are especially interested in the ways that people use power to maintain cultural practices and social structures that represent their interests and the ways that people resist or oppose those practices and structures.

Critical theory helps people to envision possibilities for sports that are free of exploitation and oppression; organized to be inclusive in connection with age, gender, race, ethnicity, religion,

and (dis)ability; and used to empower people to participate actively in the social worlds in which they live. Reformist and radical strategies are used because the goal is to transform sports so that a diverse range of participation opportunities is available to all people. For example, radical strategies are used to disrupt and transform the structure and dynamics of social relations related to gender, race, class, sexuality, and (dis)ability so that previously marginalized or underrepresented categories of people have equal opportunities to create and participate in sports that fit their interests and needs.

The radical strategies favoured by people using critical theory emphasize eliminating inequities, creating democratic forms of participation, and making ideological and structural changes in sports and society as a whole. These strategies usually involve efforts to redistribute power, and they give voice to previously disenfranchised segments of the population in social worlds.

People with power and wealth usually strongly oppose radical strategies because they are designed to transform the ideas, beliefs, and forms of social organization on which their power and wealth depend. Privileged people dislike radicals because privilege depends on preserving the ideologies that legitimize elitist lifestyles and maintain the structures through which power is exercised over others. Their success in opposing radical strategies depends primarily on convincing most other people in society that the current, dominant ways of thinking and doing things are natural, normal, and supportive of everyone's interests in society. This is a primary reason why radical strategies are seldom used in sports; they are very risky because those who use them become targets of those who have power and influence in society. Furthermore, most people who favour radical strategies dedicate all their attention and resources to issues of poverty, homelessness, universal health care, quality education for children, accessible public transportation, full employment, and guaranteed minimum standards of living. However, a few radicals who are

Motorized sports impact the environment and the experiences of hikers, cross-country skiers, and other wilderness users. As more people incorporate technology into their sports and leisure, critical theories provide a useful basis for asking questions and doing research on these issues. [Jay Coakley]

concerned with ideological issues have used sports as sites for the following purposes: challenging dominant definitions of *masculinity* and *femininity*, raising questions about the meaning of race, highlighting the difficulties of preserving democracy in the face of a growing gap between the haves and have-nots in society, destroying long-held stereotypes about (dis)abilities, and encouraging people to think critically about the antidemocratic features of the exclusive and hierarchical structures that characterize most organized sports today.

Critical Feminist Theory People who use critical feminist theory are concerned with gender, gender relations, and gender ideology. They see sports as sites where dominant forms of masculinity and femininity may be reproduced or transformed. Therefore, much of their attention is focused on struggles over gender equity and issues related to changing sports.

Critical feminist theory focuses on transforming sports and gender ideology so that women are not systematically disadvantaged. It helps people to envision what sports could be if there were no sexism, misogyny, heterosexism, or homophobia. People guided by critical feminist theory use reformist and radical strategies—reformist strategies to promote equity and radical strategies to resist and transform the dominant gender ideology, which privileges men and gives high priority to all sports based on the values and experiences of men, especially those in positions of power. Both strategies are used to push the boundaries of gender and expand accepted ways of "doing gender" in sports and everyday life.

The International Working Group on Women and Sport (IWG) is grounded primarily in critical feminist theory. Its members around the world use many strategies, including radical strategies aimed at changing ideologies and institutions that systematically exclude women from sports and disadvantage women when they do play sports. Strategies vary from nation to nation because the problems faced by women are different in various societies (Hargreaves, 2000). The IWG uses reformist strategies to increase opportunities for girls and women to play sports and to advance women into positions of power in society and in sport organizations. Radical strategies are used to transform the gender ideologies on which male privilege is based and female disadvantage is guaranteed in many cultures around the world.

> **My Puritan soul burned with indignation at injustice in the sphere of sport. . . . Cricket had plunged me into politics long before I was aware of it. When I did turn to politics I did not have much to learn.**
>
> —C. L. R. James, writer/activist from Trinidad (1963)

Interactionist Theory When people use interactionist theory, they focus on social processes through which social worlds are created. They view those worlds, including the ones created around sports, through the eyes of the participants themselves. They assume that socialization occurs in and through sport experien-ces, that people give meaning to sports and sport participation as they interact with each other, and that people form identities as they integrate their experiences into their sense of who they are and how they are connected with the rest of the world.

Social transformation does not occur without a struggle. Producing transformation is always a challenging and tedious process. It requires dedication and long-term commitment, just as some sports require dedication and commitment. Never ever, ever, ever cease to be a critical citizen. [Jay Coakley]

Interactionists view the future in terms of the possibilities for social interaction associated with sports. They may use *conservative, reformist*, or *radical* strategies to facilitate the creation of sports in which participants have representative control over the meaning, purpose, and organization of the sports they play. For example, reformist or radical approaches have been used to create sports and sport organizations that are democratic and inclusive (Birrell, 2000; Donnelly, 1988a, b; Donnelly and Coakley, 2002). As this has been done, ideas have often been borrowed from other theories, especially critical and critical feminist theories.

Vantage Points for Creating Futures

Creating futures is a never-ending process. Being a change agent in this process is always challenging, regularly frustrating, and sometimes rewarding. For those interested in creating futures related to sports and social life, strategies can be initiated from four vantage points (Hall et al., 1991):

1. *Work within the system of sports*. You can become involved in sports and sport organizations and then use your position or power to influence and initiate changes. Having an "insider" vantage point can be very effective; sometimes, you can use it even to promote changes in society as a whole. However, becoming an insider often involves adopting the existing values of the organization where you work. This means that, even though you may favour certain reforms or transformations, your commitment to actively promoting change may decrease as you move up the organization into positions of power. Once you reach a position that enables you to make changes, you often develop an interest in keeping things as they are and using a conservative strategy to slowly make things bigger and more efficient. This is not inevitable, but it is customary. Although an insider vantage point can be a good place from which to create futures, it is important to be realistic about what insiders can do. This is highlighted when we consider "Athletes as Change Agents" in the box on pages 511–512.

2. *Join "opposition" groups*. You can become a change agent by forming or joining political groups that challenge unjust or exploitive sport policies, and put pressure on sport organizations that have antidemocratic policies and programmes. For example, opposition groups would lobby for the building of a community sport centre in a low-income neighbourhood, or lobby against using public funds to build a stadium that would serve primarily the interests of already privileged people in a community. Opposition groups would apply pressure, so that hosting a major sport event such as the Olympics would involve long-term legacies for the community, e.g., building low-cost housing for low-income community residents, and ensuring that the facilities built and equipment acquired for the Games are also a legacy, available for all of the community to use once the Games are over. The possibilities for opposition are many.

3. *Create alternative sports*. You can reject or ignore dominant power and performance sports, and the organizations that sponsor them, and develop new sports grounded in the values and experiences of a wide array of different groups of people. This is often difficult because resources are seldom available when you choose this vantage point

> What started as a 31-day attempt by two people to better understand the ordeal of the children of northern Uganda, has now grown into an impassioned worldwide movement for peace.
>
> —Adrian Bradbury and Kieran Hayward (2006), GuluWalk/Athletes for Africa (athletesforafrica.com)

REFLECT ON SPORTS

Athletes as Change Agents
Does It Ever Happen?

Athletes are visible and popular. Some have the highest name and face recognition of any human beings in history. This puts them in good positions to be change agents in society—or does it?

The visibility and popularity of athletes depends heavily on media coverage and overall public image. Leagues, teams, and corporations use athletes' images to promote events and products, but this does not mean that athletes can readily convert their celebrity status into power related to serious social, political, or economic issues.

The "context of sport celebrity" limits the extent to which athletes can be effective agents of change. If their words and actions do not match the interests of those who control their images, they risk losing the coverage and support that sustains their visibility and popularity. Team owners and corporate sponsors shy away from players who speak out on social issues; owners do not want to anger fans, and corporations do not want to anger consumers—since many fans and consumers take the same conservative approach as owners and corporations, athletes should "shut up and play!" and are not permitted the right to express a critical opinion.

Tiger Woods was widely condemned for saying that "Golf has shied away from [racism] for far too long, [and] I hope… [to] change that" (*Time*, 1997). He discovered that his influence was limited to selling clothes and golf balls, not changing golf clubs run by powerful white men. Since 1997 Woods has publicly supported only conservative approaches to changes, if he talks about change at all.

Canadian NBA player Steve Nash had a similar experience when he was selected to play in the 2003 All-Star game. While the U.S. was embroiled in war in Iraq and Afghanistan, he wore a T-shirt saying, "No War. Shoot for Peace," to media day interviews, and was widely criticized by journalists, players, and coaches (Candaele and Dreier, 2004). Nash has since been selected as MVP, and he has quietly maintained his support for progressive causes.

It is not surprising that athletes use conservative approaches based on functionalist theory when they become involved in their communities. They are strongly encouraged by their agents, sponsors,

Tommy Smith and John Carlos used this gesture to protest U.S. racism and global poverty during the 1968 Olympics. They were stripped of their medals, expelled from the Olympic village, and sent back to the United States amid widespread criticism and condemnation. In 2005, they were awarded honourary doctorates from San Jose State University in recognition of their courageous actions. If you look carefully at the photograph, you will see that Peter Norman, the Australian sprinter who won the silver medal, is wearing an Olympic Project for Human Rights button (also worn by Smith and Carlos), showing his support for his two African-American competitors. Norman was not sanctioned.[AP/Wide World Photos]

and teams to focus on reaffirming dominant social values and strengthening the *status quo* by building playgrounds, visiting children in hospital, promoting

Continued

REFLECT ON SPORTS
Athletes as Change Agents
continued

literacy, and delivering antidrug messages to high schools. Even when retired athletes enter politics, they generally represent conservative political positions aligned with preserving the *status quo*. They do not usually advocate *reforms* or *radical* changes to the structures that intensify poverty and other social problems. Starting a foundation to help children from low-income neighbourhoods is great, as are the other actions noted above. But they do not call attention to the need to change a social system that is failing children from low-income neighbourhoods.

Perhaps the most effective way for athletes to be agents of change is to work in or through established organizations. For example, Canadian-based organizations such as Right to Play, the Canadian Sport Leadership Corps, and GuluWalk/Athletes for Africa are all headed by former athletes and/or physical educators—Johann Koss (Olympic speed skater), Bruce Kidd (Olympic track athlete), and Adrian Bradbury (University of Ottawa basketball player) and Kieran Hayward (University of Toronto physical education student) respectively. Former athletes, coaches, students and recent graduates all receive the opportunity to spend time in villages,

refugee camps, and *barrios*/slums associated with major cities; they provide equipment, organize and help to run programmes, and teach skills to community members so that they can continue to run sport and physical activity programmes.

Recent history shows that, with few exceptions,[1] even suggesting the need for ideological or structural changes to combat racism, sexism, economic exploitation, or violence can create problems for athletes. When Cassius Clay (Muhammad Ali) spoke out against racism in the 1960s and, as a Muslim, refused induction into the military during the Vietnam War, he was stripped of his boxing title and sentenced to five years in prison. When 400 m champions Tommy Smith and John Carlos protested racism and global poverty on the victory podium during the 1968 Olympics in Mexico City, they encountered over twenty years of contempt and rejection in the U.S. Is this why so many athletes today choose to act as corporate shills instead of agents of change? *What do you think?*

---

[1]A major exception in Canada is the case of Sheldon Kennedy speaking out in order to help prevent the sexual abuse of other young athletes.

for making change. However, working from this vantage point can be effective even when it does not lead to concrete institutionalized changes, because it provides clear-cut examples of new ways to look at and play sports as well as new ways to look at and interact with other people. These examples then may inspire others to envision how they can create alternative sports in their own lives and communities. Former Olympian and current physical and health educator Bruce Kidd reminds us, "The effort to create alternatives to the commercial sport culture will continue to be an uphill fight. But such

alternatives do exist. They have a long, rich, and proud history" (1997, p. 270).

4. *Focus on transforming culture and social relations*. You can ignore sports and work directly on producing changes in the ideologies and structures that support and legitimize the current organization of sports in society. For example, groups that work to lower sexual assault rates in the United States: they have pressured the NFL, the NCAA, and other sport organizations to support policies that increase awareness of the problem and encourage progressive changes in gender relations.

Regardless of the vantage point for creating futures, significant social transformation always requires a combination of the following three things:

1. Visions of what sports and social life *could* and *should* be like
2. Willingness to work hard on the strategies needed to turn visions into actions
3. Political abilities to rally the resources that will make strategies effective

The future of sports and the impact of sports in society will be created as people combine vision, hard work, and politically effective strategies. Doing this is seldom easy, but if we do not create the future, it will be created for us on terms that will continue to privilege some people over others.

SUMMARY

WHAT CAN WE CREATE?

Sports are social constructions; they change as ideas and relationships change in sports and society. Although the meaning, organization, and purpose of sports will become increasingly diverse in the future, power and performance sports will remain dominant. They will receive continued funding and sponsorship from those with resources and power in society. Pleasure and participation sports will grow in connection with demographic trends and ideological changes, but they will not receive the funding and support enjoyed by sports organized around the power and performance model.

Sports at all levels will be sites for struggles over who should play and how sports should be organized. Major trends at all levels of sports are influenced by many factors including technology, environment and energy issues, telecommunications and electronic media, values supportive of organization and rationalization, a cultural emphasis on commercialism and consumption,

and the demographic characteristics of communities and societies.

Futures come to be as people envision possibilities for what sports could and should be. Social theories are important in this process because they explain the connections between sports and social worlds, identify problems, and help in the selection of strategies to turn visions of the future into realities.

Most people, especially those who are advantaged by the status quo, do not want to change sports as much as they want to expand them and make them more efficient. This conservative strategy fits with the assumptions and goals of functionalist theory. Reformist and radical changes are more apt to be inspired by conflict theory, and combinations of interactionist, critical, and critical feminist theories.

Changes in sports can be made from any one of four vantage points: within sport itself, in connection with opposition groups, through efforts to create new and alternative sport forms, and by working to transform those aspects of culture and social structure that support current forms of sports.

Regardless of the vantage point, change and transformation depend on clear visions of what sports could and should be, a willingness to work hard to turn those visions into reality, and the political abilities to initiate and maintain strategies that produce results. Unless we work to create the sports we want in the future, sports will represent the interests of those who want us to play on their terms and for their purposes.

This leaves us with an interesting choice: we can be consumers who accept sports as they are, or we can be citizens who use sports as contexts for actively making the world a better place. The goal of this book has been to prepare you to be informed citizens.

Visit *Sports in Society*'s Online Learning Centre at <u>www.mcgrawhill.ca/olc/coakley</u> for additional information, website resources, and study tools for this chapter.

Credits

PHOTOGRAPHS

Chapter 1

p. 1, © CP(Steve White);
p. 6 (all), © Jay Coakley; p. 8,
© CP(Brendon Dlouhy)/*Edmonton Sun*; p. 13, © Peter Donnelly;
p. 15, © David Biene, photo courtesy of Ossur, www.ossur.com; p. 19, © M. MacNeill; p. 21 (right), © Peter Donnelly.

Chapter 2

p. 25, © CP(Ryan Remiorz);
p. 27, © CP(Adrian Wyld);
p. 38, © CP(Crombie McNeil);
p. 43 (top), © Jay Coakley; p. 43 (bottom), © Wally Santan, AP/Wide World Photos.

Chapter 3

p. 47, Credit unknown; p. 63,
© David Biene, photo courtesy of Ossur, www.ossur.com; p. 65,
© McGraw-Hill; p. 69,
© City of Toronto Archives, Fonds 1244, item 477; p. 77,
© USOC Archives.

Chapter 4

p. 79, © Anne-Marie Webber/Taxi/Getty Images; p. 83,
© Photomondo/Taxi/Getty Images; p. 88, © Robert E. Daemmrick/Stone/Getty Images; p. 89, © CP(Preston Brownschlaigle)/*Edmonton Sun*;
p. 92, © CP(Adrian Wyld); p. 93, © CP(Jeff Stokoe)/*Red Deer Advocate*; p. 101, © Jay Coakley;
p. 104, © CP/AP(Ng Han Guan);

p. 106, © David Biene, photo courtesy of Ossur, www.ossur.com.

Chapter 5

p. 110, © Ron Chapple/Taxi/Getty Images; p. 128,
© M. MacNeill; p. 140, © Jay Coakley.

Chapter 6

p. 144, © CP(Jonathon Hayward);
p. 147, © *Colorado Springs Gazette*;
p. 156, © CP(Sean Kilpatrick);
p. 165, © Peter Cosgrove, AP/Wide World Photos; p. 169,
© Jake Schoellkopf; AP/Wide World Photos; p. 182, David Biene, photo courtesy of Ossur, www.ossur.com.

Chapter 7

p. 186, © AP Photo/Tom Olmscheid; p. 193, © CP(Jeff McIntosh); p. 197 (both), © Jason E. Kaplan Photography, Portland, Oregon; p. 200, © Derek Lang;
p. 203, © AP Photo/Jason Babyak;
p. 206, © CP(Ted Jacob); p. 211,
© CP(Ryan Remiorz); p. 213,
© CP(Tim Smith).

Chapter 8

p. 220, © CP(Andrew Vaughan);
p. 223, © AP Photo/Vincent Yu;
p. 230, © M. MacNeill; p. 233,
© CP(Aaron Harris); p. 236,
© CP(Lehtikuva, Jussi Nukari)/AP; p. 246, Photo courtesy of The Hunger Project; www.thp.org/;
p. 250, © CP(Jacques Boissinot);
p. 255, © CP(Frank Gunn).

Chapter 9

p. 259, © Arthur Tiley/Taxi/Getty Images; p. 264, © Mark J. Terrill, AP/Wide World Photos; p. 268,
© CP(Paul Chiasson); p. 279,
© CP(Frank Gunn); p. 286,
© CP(Brian Thompson)/*Brantford Expositor*; p. 287, © CP(Hans Deryk); p. 289, © John Terence Turner/Taxi/Getty Images;
p. 297, Mike Collins, Irish Football Association, Northern Ireland.

Chapter 10

p. 299, © Laura Robinson; p. 302 (both), © Jay Coakley; p. 312,
© Jay Coakley; p. 315, © CP(Chuck Stoody); p. 323, Karel Prinsloo, AP/Wide World Photos;
p. 324, © CP(Bill Sikes)/AP.

Chapter 11

p. 332, © Alison Derry; p. 335,
© Efren Lukatsky, AP/Wide World Photos; p. 340 (all), © 1988 SPOC; p. 345, © Luca Bruno, AP/Wide World Photos; p. 354,
© CP(Frank Gunn); p. 357,
© CP(Scott MacDonald).

Chapter 12

p. 373 (both), © M. MacNeill;
p. 383, CP(Chuck Stoody); p. 389,
© M. MacNeill; p. 398, © Rodolfo Gonzalez, *Rocky Mountain News*;
p. 406, © CP(Phill Snel)/*Maclean's*.

Chapter 13

p. 418, © Peter Donnelly; p. 421,
© Peter Donnelly; p. 426,
Canadian Paralympic Committee/

Benoit Pelosse; p. 434, USOC Archives; p. 445 (both), © Global March Against Child Labour; p. 453, David Biene, photo courtesy of Ossur, www.ossur.com.

Chapter 14

p. 456, St. Thomas Times Journal; p. 464, © Marc Piscotty, *Rocky Mountain News*; p. 466, © CP(Viktor Pivovarov)/*Moncton Times & Transcript*; p. 469, © CP(John Woods); p. 471, © Kara Dillon and Nick Burdan. Reproduced with permission from the Faculty of Physical Education and Health, University of Toronto, www.utoronto.ca/ physical; p. 478, © Kara Dillon and Nick Burdan. Reproduced with permission from the Faculty of Physical Education and Health, University of Toronto, www. utoronto.ca/physical; p. 482, © Lewko Hryhorijiw. Reproduced with permission from the Faculty of Physical Education and Health, University of Toronto, www. utoronto.ca/physical.

Chapter 15

p. 487, Credit unknown; p. 489, © CP(Bonny Makarewicz); p. 492, © Jason Lee, Mountain Board Sports; p. 494, © Rob Schoenbaum; p. 503, © McGraw-Hill; p. 508, © Jay Coakley; p. 509, © Jay Coakley; p. 511, © AP/Wide World Photos.

TEXT AND ART CREDITS

Chapter 3

p. 60, Adapted from Metcalfe (1989); p. 61, Adapted from Redmond (1989) and Kidd (1997); p. 62, Adapted and amended from Redmond (1989); p. 64, Modified version of table 2 in Guttmann (1978); p. 67, Adapted from Redmond (1989).

Chapter 5

p. 124, FIFA Regulations for the Status and Transfer of Players (2003).

Chapter 6

p. 158, Press release, "Governor General to launch Canadian Figure Skating Championships and present Elvis Stojko with Meritorious Service Cross," issued by the Government House Press Office, January, 1999 [www.gg.ca]; p. 172, World Anti-Doping Agency (WADA). World Anti-Doping Code (v. 3; WADA, 2003).

Chapter 8

p. 234, www.olympic.org/uk/ games/index_uk.asp; p. 240, Adapted from Analysis of Male and Female Coaches in CIS Sports, January 2005. Available online at http://www.cisport.ca/e/research/ documents/analysisofmensandwo menscoachesinCIS_000.pdf.

Chapter 9

p. 272, Data from Statistics Canada "Ethnocultural Portrait of Canada" (2006 Census). Accessed online at: http://www12. statcan.ca/english/census06/ data/highlights/ethnic/index. cfm?Lang=E; p. 273, Data from Statistics Canada "Ethnocultural Portrait of Canada" (2006 Census). Accessed online at: http://www12.statcan.ca/english/ census06/data/highlights/ethnic/ index.cfm?Lang=E.

Chapter 10

p. 305, Houston, William. "Power players of 2007." *The Globe and Mail*, Dec. 18, 2007, p. S1. Reprinted with permission from *The Globe and Mail*.; p. 306, CAAWS Press Release, 17 Jan 2008; Retrieved from www.caaws. ca/influentialwomen/e/index.htm; p. 311, Statistics Canada. *The Daily National Longitudinal Survey of Children and Youth: Participation in activities* (1998/99), May 30, 2001. http://www.statcan.ca/Daily/ English/010530/d010530a.htm (accessed May 4, 2008). Also adapted from *The Progress of Canada's Children and Youth 2006*, published by the Canadian Council on Social Development. Supplementary web data (www. ccsd.ca). Reprinted with permission.; p. 319, Team Marketing Report Inc., 2007 (www.teammarketing.com).

Chapter 12

p. 396, Based on material in Koppett (1994); p. 415, Adapted from Koppett (1994).

Chapter 13

p. 431–2, Adapted from Green (2003); p. 449, Department of Canadian Heritage. Reproduced with the permission of the Minister of Public Works and Government Services Canada, 2008.

Chapter 14

p. 477, Reproduced with the permission of Ontario Federation of School Athletic Associations (OFSAA).

References

AAA. 1998. Statement on "race." Washington, DC: American Anthropological Association. Online: www.aaanet.org/stmts/racepp.htm (retrieved June 2005).

Abdel-Shehid, G. 2000. Writing hockey through race: Rethinking black hockey in Canada. In R. Walcott, ed., *Rude: Contemporary Black Canadian cultural criticism* (pp. 69–86). Toronto: Insomniac Press.

Abdel-Shehid, G. 2002. Raptor morality: Blacks, basketball and national identity. In S. Fogel and L. Thoman, eds., *Changing identities: Reading and writing ourselves* (pp. 131–38). Toronto: Canadian Scholars Press.

Abdel-Shehid, G. 2005. *Who da man?: Black masculinities and sporting cultures.* Toronto: Canadian Scholars' Press.

Acosta, R. Vivien, and Linda Jean Carpenter. 2004. Women in intercollegiate sport: A longitudinal, national study twenty-seven-year update, 1977–2004. Online: http://webpages.charter.net/womeninsport/

Adler, Patricia A., and Peter Adler. 1998. *Peer power: Preadolescent culture and identity.* New Brunswick, NJ: Rutgers University Press.

Agence France-Press. 2008. Now that's online shopping—28,000 fans buy a soccer club. *Globe and Mail*, 20 February, p. B9.

Albert, Edward. 2004. Normalizing risk in the sport of cycling. In Kevin Young, *Sporting bodies, damaged selves: Sociological studies of sports-related injury* (pp. 181–194). Amsterdam: Elsevier.

Alesia, Mark. 2004. Lawmaker to the NCAA: Get tougher or be taxed. *Indianapolis Star* (May 19). Online: www.indystar.com/articles/0/147733-6820-036.html

Alfred University. 1999. *Initiation rites and athletics: A national survey of NCAA sports teams.* Online: www.alfred.edu/news/html/hazing_study.html

Allain, K. 2004. In other words: An examination into the experiences of non-North Americans in the Canadian hockey league. Unpublished Master's thesis, Queen's University, Kingston.

Allison, Lincoln. 2000. Sport and nationalism. In J. Coakley and E. Dunning, eds., *Handbook of sports studies* (pp. 344–355). London: Sage.

Allison, Lincoln. 2004. *The global politics of sport: The role of global institutions in sport.* London/New York: Routledge.

American Academy of Pediatrics. 2000. Intensive training and sports specialization in young athletes. (RE9906). Pediatrics 106, 01: 154–157. Online: http://www.aap.org/policy/RE9906.html

Anderson, Eric. 1999. *Comparing the black and gay male athlete: Patterns of oppression.* Paper presented at the annual conference of the North American Society for the Sociology of Sport, Cleveland, OH (November).

Anderson, Eric. 2000. *Trailblazing: America's first openly gay track coach.* Hollywood, CA: Alyson.

Anderson, Eric. 2002. Gays in sport: Contesting hegemonic masculinity in a homophobic environment. *Gender and Society* 16, 6: 860–877.

Anderson, Eric. 2004. Exploitation of the scholarship athlete. Unpublished manuscript.

Anderson, Eric. 2005. *In the game: Gay athletes and the cult of masculinity.* Albany: State University of New York Press.

Anderson, Jason. 2005. Most dangerous game. Online: www.eye.net/eye/issue/issue_04.21.05/film/murderball.html (retrieved November 2005).

Anderson, Sarah, and John Cavanagh. 2000. *The top 200.* Washington, DC: Institute for Policy Studies.

Andrews, David L. 1996a. The fact(s) of Michael Jordan's blackness: Excavating a floating racial signifier. *Sociology of Sport Journal* 13, 2: 125–158.

Andrews, David L., ed. 1996b. Deconstructing Michael Jordan: Reconstructing postindustrial America. *Sociology of Sport Journal* 13, 4. Special issue.

Andrews, David L. 2001. Sport. In R. Maxwell, ed., *Culture works: The political economy of culture* (pp. 131–162). Minneapolis: University of Minnesota Press.

Andrews, David L. 2003. Sport and the transnationalizing media corporation. *Journal of media economics*, 16 (4), 235–251.

Andrews, David L. 2007. Sport as spectacle. In George Ritzer, ed., *Encyclopedia of sociology* (in press). London/New York: Blackwell.

Andrews, David L., and Steven J. Jackson. 2001. *Sport stars: The cultural politics of sporting celebrity.* London/New York: Routledge.

Andrews, David L., and Michael Silk. 1999. Football consumption communities, trans-national advertising, and spatial transformation. Paper presented at the annual conference of the North

American Society for the Sociology of Sport, Cleveland, OH (November).

Annan, K. 2006. "Can a ball change the world?" World Economic Forum, Davos. Online: http://psdblog.worldbank.org/psdblog/2006/01/can_a_ball_chan.html (retrieved June 2007).

Anonymous. 1999. Confessions of a cheater. *ESPN The Magazine* (November 1): 80–82.

Armstrong, Gary. 1998. *Football hooligans: Knowing the score*. Oxford: Berg.

Armstrong, Gary. 2007. Football hooliganism. In George Ritzer, ed., *Encyclopedia of sociology* (in press). London/New York: Blackwell.

Armstrong, Jim. 2000. Coors Field is not the patient's place. *Denver Post* (April 24): 3D.

Armstrong, P. 1984. *Labour pains: Women's work in crisis*. Toronto: Women's Press.

Arnold, E. 2002. *Whose puck is it anyway?: A season with a minor novice team*. Toronto: McClelland & Stewart.

Assael, Shaun. 2003. Cut and run. *ESPN The Magazine* 6.14 (July 70): 40–49.

Assael, Shaun. 2005. Shape shifter. *ESPN The Magazine* 8.09 (May 90): 88–96.

Athletics Administration, April 1993, p. 22.

Atkinson, M. 2000. Brother can you spare a seat?: Developing recipes of knowledge in the ticket scalping subculture. *Sociology of Sport Journal* 17 (2), 151–70.

Atkinson, M. 2002. Fifty-million viewers can't be wrong: Professional wrestling, sports-entertainment, and mimesis. *Sociology of Sport Journal* 19, 1: 47–66.

Atkinson, M. 2004. It's still part of the game: Dangerous masculinity, crime, and victimization in professional ice hockey. In L. Fuller, ed., *Sexual sports rhetoric and violence: Teaming up gender with the language of sport*. New York: The Haworth Press.

Atkinson, M., and K. Young. 2002. Terror games: Media treatment of security issues at the 2002 Winter Olympic Games. *Olympika* 11, 53–78.

Bacon, Victoria L., and Pamela J. Russell. 2004. Addiction and the college athlete: The Multiple Addictive Behaviors Questionnaire (MABQ) with college athletes. *The Sport Journal* 7, 2. Online: www.thesportjournal.org/2004Journal/Vol7-No2/

Bairner, Alan. 2001. *Sport, nationalism, and globalization: European and North American perspectives*. Albany: State University of New York Press.

Bairner, Alan, ed. 2005. *Sport and the Irish. Histories, identities, issues*. Dublin: University College Dublin Press.

Baker, G. 2003. White Jays. *Toronto Star*, 28 June, S1.

Baker, William J. 1988. *Sports in the Western world*. Urbana: University of Illinois Press.

Bale, John, and Mette Christensen, eds. 2004. *Post-Olympism: Questioning sport in the twenty-first century*. Oxford/New York: Berg.

Bale, John, and Mike Cronin, eds. 2003. *Sport and postcolonialism*. Oxford/New York: Berg.

Bale, John, and Joseph Maguire, eds. 1994. *The global sports arena: Athletic talent migration in an interdependent world*. London: Frank Cass.

Ball, D. 1973. Ascription and position: A comparative analysis of "stacking" in professional football. *Canadian Review of Sociology and Anthropology* 10, 97–113.

Ballard, Chris. 2004. Fantasy world. *Sports Illustrated* 100, 25 (June 21): 80–89.

Bandow, Doug. 2003. *Surprise: Stadiums don't pay after all!* Cato Institute Report (October 19). Washington, DC: Cato Institute.

Barber, Bonnie L., Jacquelynne S. Eccles, and M. R. Stone. 2001. Whatever happened to the jock, the brain, and the princess? Young adult pathways linked to adolescent activity involvement and social identity. *Journal of Adolescent Research* 16, 5: 429–455.

Bartimole, Roldo. 1999. The city and the stadia (panel). Presentation at the annual conference of the North American Society for the Sociology of Sport, Cleveland, OH (November).

Bast, Joseph L. 1998. *Sports stadium madness: Why it started, how to stop it*. Heartland Policy Study, No. 85. Chicago: Heartland Institute.

BBC Sport Academy. 2005. Rugby league—Disability. Online: http://news.bbc.co.uk/sportacademy/hi/sa/rugby_league/disability/newsid_4019000/4019549.stm (retrieved November 2005).

Beal, Becky. 1995. Disqualifying the official: An exploration of social resistance through the subculture of skateboarding. *Sociology of Sport Journal* 12, 3: 252–267.

Beal, Becky. 1999. Skateboarding: An alternative to mainstream sports. In J. Coakley and P. Donnelly, eds., *Inside sports* (pp. 139–145). London: Routledge.

Beal, Becky, and Lisa Weidman. 2003. Authenticity in the skateboarding world. In Robert E. Rinehart and Synthia Sydnor, eds., *To the extreme: Alternative sports, inside and out* (pp. 337–352). Albany: State University of New York Press.

Beal, Carol R. 1994. *Boys and girls: The development of gender roles*. New York: McGraw-Hill.

Beals, Katherine A. 2000. Subclinical eating disorders in female athletes. *Journal of Physical Education, Recreation and Dance* 71, 7: 3–29.

Beamish, R. 1988. The political economy of professional sport. In J. Harvey and H. Cantelon, eds., *Not just a game: Essays in Canadian sport sociology* (pp. 141–157). Ottawa: University of Ottawa Press.

Beamish, R., and J. Borowy. 1988. *Q. What do you do for a living? A. I'm an athlete*. Kingston, Ontario: Sport Research Group.

Beamish, R. and I. Ritchie. 2006. *Fastest, highest, strongest: A critique of high-performance sport*. London: Routledge.

Beauchesne, L. 1990. *The Dubin Inquiry's political purpose*. Paper presented at the conference, "After the Dubin Inquiry: Implications for Canada's High-Performance Sport System." Queen's University, Kingston, ON, September.

Bechtel, Mark, and Stephen Cannella. 2005. Scorecard: Cable ready. *Sports Illustrated* 103, 8 (August 29): 16–17.

Becker, Debbie. 1996. Nothstein: "I enjoy the pain." *USA Today* (July 24): 14E, 17E.

Bell, Jack. 2005. M.L.S. has a wide range of salaries. *New York Times* (July 11). Online: www.nytimes.com/2005/07/11/sports/soccer/11mls.html (retrieved July 14, 2005).

Bell, Wendell, and James Mau. 1971. Images of the future: Theory and research. In W. Bell and J. Mau, eds., *The sociology of the future* (pp. 6–44). New York: Russell Sage Foundation.

Bellefleur, M. 1986. *L'Église et le Loisir au Québec avant la Revolution Tranquille*. Sillery: Presses de l'Université du Québec.

Bellefleur, M. 1997. *L'Évolution du Loisir au Québec*. Sillery: Presses de l'Université du Québec.

Belson, Matthew. 2002. Assistive technology and sports. In Artemis A. W. Joukowsky III and Larry Rothstein, eds., *Raising the bar* (pp. 124–129). New York: Umbrage Editions.

Benedict, Jeff. 1997. *Public heroes, private felons: Athletes and crimes against women*. Boston: Northeastern University Press.

Benedict, Jeff. 2004. *Out of bounds: Inside the NBA's culture of rape, violence, and crime*. New York: HarperCollins.

Benedict, Jeff, and A. Klein. 1997. Arrest and conviction rates for athletes accused of sexual assault. *Sociology of Sport Journal* 14 (1): 86–94.

Benedict, Jeff, and Don Yaeger. 1998. *Pros and cons: The criminals who play in the NFL*. New York: Warner Books.

Bennhold, K. 2006. Soccer dreams and reality. Online: www.playthegame.org

Ben-Porat, Guy, and Amir Ben-Porat. 2004. (Un) bounded soccer: Globalization and localization of the game in Israel. *International Review for the Sociology of Sport* 39, 4: 421–436.

Berck, P. 2003. Personal communication. 20 March.

Berlage, G. 1982. Are children's competitive team sports socializing agents for corporate America? In A. Dunleavy, A. Miracle, and R. Rees, eds., *Studies in the sociology of sport* (pp. 309–24). Fort Worth: Texas Christian University Press.

Bernstein, Alina, and Neil Blain, eds. 2003. *Sport, media, culture: Global and local dimensions*. London: Frank Cass.

Berra, Lindsey. 2005. This is how they roll. *ESPN The Magazine* 8.24 (December 5): 104–111.

Best, J., M. Blackhurst, and L. Makosky. 1992. *Sport: The way ahead*. Ottawa: Fitness and Amateur Sport.

Bibby, R. 2006. Project Canada Press Release #3: CFL Interest in Canada. University of Lethbridge, June 9.

Bilger, Burkhard. 2004. The height gap. *New Yorker* (April 5): 38–45.

Birrell, Susan. 2000. Feminist theories for sport. In J. Coakley and E. Dunning, eds., *Handbook of sport studies* (pp. 61–76). London: Sage.

Birrell, Susan, and Diana M. Richter. 1994. Is a diamond forever? Feminist transformations of sport. In S. Birrell and C. L. Cole, eds., *Women, sport, and culture* (pp. 221–244). Champaign, IL: Human Kinetics.

Bjerklie, David, and Alice Park. 2004. How doctors help the dopers. *Time* 164, 7 (August 16): 58–62.

Blain, Neil, Raymond Boyle, and Hugh O'Donnell. 1993. *Sport and national identity in the European media*. Leicester, England: Leicester University Press.

Blake, Andrew. 1996. *The body language: The meaning of modern sport*. London: Lawrence and Wisehart.

Blinde, Elaine M., Diane E. Taub, and Lingling Han. 1994. Sport as a site for women's group and societal empowerment: Perspectives from the college athlete. *Sociology of Sport Journal* 11, 1: 51–59.

Block, Martin E. 1995. Americans with Disability Act: Its impact on youth sports. *Journal of Health, Physical Education, Recreation and Dance* 66, 1: 28–32.

Bloom, Gordon A., and Michael D. Smith. 1996. Hockey violence: A test of the cultural spillover theory. *Sociology of Sport Journal* 13, 1: 65–77.

Bloom, Marc. 1998. Slower times at American high schools. *New York Times* (January 29): C27.

Blumenthal, Ralph. 2004. Texas tough, in lipstick, fishnet and skates. *New York Times*, section 1 (August 1): 14.

Blumstein, Alfred, and Jeff Benedict. 1999. Criminal violence of NFL players compared to the general population. *Chance* 12, 3: 12–15.

Boileau, R., F. Landry, and Y. Trempe. 1976. Les Canadiens-français et les Grands Jeux Internationaux. In R. Gruneau and J. Albinson, eds., *Canadian Sport: Sociological Perspectives* (pp. 141–69). Don Mills, ON: Addison Wesley.

Bolin, Anne. 1992. Beauty or beast: The subversive soma. Unpublished manuscript.

Bolin, Anne. 1998. Muscularity and femininity: Women bodybuilders and women's bodies in culturo-historical context. In K Volkwein, ed., *Fitness as cultural phenomenon* (pp. 187–212). Munster: Waxmann.

Bolin, Anne. 2003. Beauty or the beast: The subversive soma. In A. Bolin and J. Granskog, eds., *Athletic intruders: Ethnographic research on women, culture, and exercise* (pp. 107–130). Albany: State University of New York Press.

Bonilla-Silva, Eduardo. 2001. White supremacy and racism in the post-civil rights era. Boulder, CO: Lynne Rienner.

Bonilla-Silva, Eduardo. 2003. *Racism without racists: Color-blind racism and the persistence of racial inequality in the United States.* Lanham, MD: Rowman and Littlefield.

Booth, D., and J. Loy. 1999. Sport, status and style. *Sport History Review* 30: 1–26.

Bouchier, N. 2003. *For the love of the game: Amateur sport in small-town Ontario, 1838–1895.* Montreal and Kingston: McGill-Queen's University Press.

Bourdieu, Pierre. 1986. *Distinction: A social critique of the judgment of taste.* London: Routledge.

Braddock, Jomills Henry, et al. 1991. Bouncing back: Sports and academic resilience among African-American males. *Education and Urban Society* 24, 1: 113–131.

Braddock, Jomills Henry, Jan Sokol-Katz, Anthony Greene, and Lorrine Basinger-Fleischman. 2005. Uneven playing fields: State variations in boys' and girls' access to and participation in high school interscholastic sports. *Sociological Spectrum* 25, 2: 231–250.

Brady, Erik. 1996. Some legislators say Baltimore's money misspent. *USA Today* (September 6): 19C.

Bray, C. 1984. Gender and the political economy of Canadian sport. In N. Theberge and P. Donnelly, eds., *Sport and the Sociological Imagination* (pp. 104–24). Fort Worth: Texas Christian University Press.

Bray, C. 1988. Sport and the Canadian state: Gender and class issues. *Resources for Feminist Research* 17 (3), 75–77.

Bredemeier, Brenda Jo Light, Ellen Brooke Carlton, Laura Ann Hills, and Carole Ann Oglesby. 1999. Changers and the changed: Moral aspects of coming out in physical education. *Quest* 51, 4: 418–431.

Bridges, Lee. 2003. Out of the gene pool and into the food chain. In Robert E. Rinehart and Synthia Sydnor, eds., *To the extreme: Alternative sports, inside and out* (pp. 179–189). Albany: State University of New York Press.

Briggs, Bill. 2002. A heavy burden: Way of life leads to early death for many NFL linemen. *Denver Post* (October 20): 1J, 8J.

Briggs, Bill. 2004. Crowds gone wild. *Denver Post* (November 28): 1B.

Brittain, Ian. 2004. Perceptions of disability and their impact upon involvement in sport for people with disabilities at all levels. *Journal of Sport and Social Issues* 28, 4: 429–452.

Broh, Beckett A. 2002. Linking extracurricular programming to academic achievement: Who benefits and why? *Sociology of Education* 75, 1: 69–95.

Brookes, Rod. 2002. *Representing sport.* New York: Oxford University Press.

Brown, Adam, ed. 1998. *Fanatics! Power, identity and fandom in football.* London/New York: Routledge.

Brown, Gary T. 2000. Beating the odds. *NCAA News*, extra section (December 18): A1, A4.

Brown, Matthew, Mark Nagell, Chad McEvoy, and Daniel Rascher. 2004. Revenue and wealth maximization in the National Football League: The impact of stadia. *Sport Marketing Quarterly* 13, 4: 227–236.

Brown, Michael K., et al., eds. 2005. *Whitewashing race: The myth of a color-blind society.* Berkeley: University of California Press.

Brownell, Susan. 1995. *Training the body for China: Sports in the moral order of the People's Republic.* Chicago: University of Chicago Press.

Bruce, Toni. 2007. Media and sport. In George Ritzer, ed., *Encyclopedia of sociology* (in press). London/New York: Blackwell.

Bryant, Adam. 1999. Shock treatment. *Newsweek* 134, 18 (November 1): 58–59.

Bryshun, Jamie, and Kevin Young. 2007. Hazing as a form of sport and gender socialization. In Philip White and Kevin Young, eds., *Sport and gender in Canada* (pp. 302–327). Don Mills, ON: Oxford University Press.

Bull, Chris. 2004. The healer. *ESPN The Magazine* 7, 04 (February 16): 90–95.

Burstyn, Varda. 1999. *The rites of men: Manhood, politics, and the culture of sport.* Toronto, ON: University of Toronto Press.

Butler, Judith. 2004. *Undoing gender.* New York: Routledge.

Bylsma, D., and J. Bylsma. 1998. *So your son wants to play in the NHL?* Toronto: McClelland & Stewart.

CAAWS-ACAFS news release. 1997. Coverage of women's sports plummets despite strike, lockout. In P. Donnelly, ed., *Taking sport seriously: Social issues in Canadian sport* (pp. 289–90). Toronto: Thomson Educational Publishing.

CAAWS (Canadian Association for the Advancement of Women and Sport). 1998. *A Media Guide for Athletes and their Coaches.* Ottawa: CAAWS.

CAAWS. 2002. Presentation to the sub-committee on the study of sport in Canada: Bill C-54, *The Sport and Physical Activity Act.* 22 May.

CAAWS Press Release, 2008. CAAWS's 20 most influential women in sport and physical activity. Retrieved from www.caaws.ca/influentialwomen/e/index.htm

Cagan, J., and N. deMause. 1998. *Field of schemes: How the great stadium swindle turns public money into private profit.* Monroe, ME: Common Courage Press.

Campagnolo, I. 1977. *Toward a national policy on amateur sport: A working paper.* Ottawa: Ministry of State, Fitness and Amateur Sport.

Campbell, M. 1995. Tense clash of cultures surrounds Mann Cup. *Globe and Mail*, 14 September, p. C8.

Campbell, M. 2003. Join the dots on politics, fitness, sports and schools. *Globe and Mail*, 13 May, p. A9.

Campbell, M. 2007. Amateur sports: To score big, Ontario athletes need new facilities. *Globe and Mail*, 10 April, p. A12.

Canadian Council on Social Development (CCSD). 2006. Frequency of participation in recreation by children, 2000. *Progress of Canada's Children and Youth*. Ottawa: CCSD.

Canadian Press. 1994. Équipe canadienne de hockey aux Jeux: un seul francophone à Lillehammer. *Le Devoir*, 24 January.

Canadian Teachers' Federation (CTF), Canadian Centre for Policy Alternatives (CCPA) and Fédération des syndicates de l'enseignement 2006. *Commercialism in Canadian schools: Who's calling the shots?* Online: www.ctf-fce.ca; www.policyalternatives.ca; www.fse.qc.ca

Candaele, Kelly, and Peter Dreier. 2004. Where are the jocks for justice? *The Nation* 278, 25 (June 28). Online: www.thenation.com/doc.mhtml?i=20040628&s=candaele

Cantelon, H. 2006. Have skates, will travel: Canada, international hockey, and the changing hockey labour market. In D. Whitson and R. Gruneau (eds.), *Artificial ice: Hockey, culture, and commerce*. Peterborough, ON: Broadview Press, pp. 215–235.

Cantelon, M. 2001. *The Canadian Football League: Radically Canadian?* Unpublished master's thesis, University of Ottawa.

Carlson, Deven, Leslie Scott, Michael Planty, and Jennifer Thompson. 2005. *Statistics in brief: What is the status of high school athletes 8 years after their senior year?* Washington, DC: U.S. Department of Education, Institute of Education Sciences, National Center for Educational Statistics (NCES 2005-303). Online: http://nces.ed.gov/pubs2005/2005303.pdf

Carnegie, H. 1997. *A fly in a pail of milk: The Herb Carnegie story*. Oakville, ON: Mosaic Press.

Carpenter, Linda Jean, and R. Vivian Acosta. 2005. *Title IX*. Champaign, IL: Human Kinetics.

Carrington, Ben. 2004. Cosmopolitan Olympism, humanism and the spectacle of race. In John Bale and Mette Christensen, eds., *Post-Olympism: Questioning sport in the twenty-first century* (pp. 81–98). Oxford/New York: Berg.

Carrington, Ben, and John Sugden. 1999. Trans-national capitalism and the incorporation of world football. Paper presented at the annual conference of the North American Society for the Sociology of Sport, Cleveland, OH (November).

Cashmore, Ellis, 2007. Gambling and sports. In George Ritzer, ed., *Encyclopedia of sociology* (in press). London/New York: Blackwell.

Caudwell, Jayne. 2003. Sporting gender: Women's footballing bodies as sites/sights for the (re) articulation of sex, gender, and desire. *Sociology of Sport Journal* 20, 4: 371–386.

CCES. 2004. Canadian Anti-Doping Program. Ottawa, ON: Canadian Centre for Ethics in Sport (cces.ca).

Chafetz, Janet, and Joseph Kotarba. 1999. Little League mothers and the reproduction of gender. In J. Coakley and P. Donnelly, eds., *Inside sports* (pp. 46–54). London: Routledge.

Chalip, Laurence, and B. Christine Green. 1998. Establishing and maintaining a modified youth sport program: Lessons from Hotelling's location game. *Sociology of Sport Journal* 15, 4: 326–342.

Chandler, T. J. L., and A. D. Goldberg. 1990. The academic all-American as vaunted adolescent role-identity. *Sociology of Sport Journal* 7 (3): 287–93.

Chapin, Tim. 2002. *Identifying the real costs and benefits of sports facilities*. Cambridge, MA: Lincoln Institute of Land Policy. Online: www.lincolninst.edu/pubs/dl/671_chapin-web.pdf

Chastain, Brandi. 2004. *It's not about the bra*. New York: Harper Resource.

Chernushenko, D. 1994. *Greening our games: Running sports events and facilities that won't cost the earth*. Ottawa: Centurion Publishing.

Child Trends. 2005. Participation in school athletics. Child Trends Data Bank. Online: www.childtrendsdatabank.org (retrieved September 5, 2005).

Christenson, Marcus, and Paul Kelso. 2004. Soccer chief's plan to boost women's game? Hotpants. *The Guardian* (United Kingdom) (January 16). Online: http://football.guardian.co.uk/News_Story/0,1124460,00.html (retrieved December 1, 2005).

Christie, J. 1998. Limpert won't create Commonwealth flap. *Globe and Mail*, 14 August, p. S1.

Christie, J. 2008. "CIS executive plays down possible defections to NCAA." *Globe and Mail*, 16 January.

Clark, C. 2000. National sport programs weak in French, report says. *Globe and Mail*, 15 June, p. S2.

Clarke, A. 2003. Picturing diversity through wrong eyes. *TVO*, 8, 10 February.

Clement, W. 1975. *The Canadian corporate elite: An analysis of economic power*. Toronto: McClelland & Stewart.

Cluer, S., P. Donnelly, M. MacNeill, and G. Knight. 2001. *Lessons learned: A case study of CBC coverage of men's and women's diving at the Sydney Olympics*. Paper presented at the North American Society for the Sociology of Sport Annual Conference, San Antonio, TX, 31 October–3 November.

Clutterbuck, P. and Howarth, R. 2002. "Toronto's quiet crisis: The case for social and community infrastructure investment." Research Paper 198. Toronto: Centre for Urban and Community Studies.

Coakley, Jay. 1983. Leaving competitive sport: Retirement or rebirth? *Quest* 35, 1: 1–11.

Coakley, Jay. 1992. Burnout among adolescent athletes: A personal failure or social problem? *Sociology of Sport Journal* 9, 3: 271–285.

Coakley, Jay. 1993. Sport and socialization. *Exercise and Sport Science Reviews* 21: 169–200.

Coakley, Jay. 1994. Ethics in coaching: Child development or child abuse? *Coaching Volleyball* (December–January): 18–23.

Coakley, Jay. 1998. *Sport in society: Issues and controversies* (6th ed.). New York: McGraw-Hill.

Coakley, Jay. 2002. Using sports to control deviance and violence among youths: Let's be critical and cautious. In M. Gatz, M. A. Messner, and S. J. Ball-Rokeach, eds., *Paradoxes of youth and sport* (pp. 13–30). Albany: State University of New York Press.

Coakley, Jay. 2006. The good father: Parental expectations and youth sports. *Leisure Studies* 25, 2: 153–163.

Coakley, Jay. 2007. Socialization and sports. In George Ritzer, ed., *Encyclopedia of sociology* (in press). London/New York: Blackwell.

Coakley, Jay, and Peter Donnelly, eds. 1999. *Inside sports*. London: Routledge.

Coakley, Jay, and Peter Donnelly. 2004. *Sports in society: Issues and controversies* (First Canadian edition). Toronto: McGraw-Hill Ryerson.

Coakley, Jay, and Anita White. 1999. Making decisions: How young people become involved and stay involved in sports. In J. Coakley and P. Donnelly, eds., *Inside Sports* (pp. 77–85). London: Routledge.

Cochrane, J., A. Hoffman, and P. Kincade. 1977. *Women in Canadian life: Sports*. Toronto: Fitzhenry & Whiteside.

Cohen, Greta L. 1994. Media portrayal of the female athlete. In G. L. Cohen, ed., *Women in sport: Issues and controversies* (pp. 171–184). Newbury Park, CA: Sage.

Cohen, Leah Hager. 2005. *Without apology: Girls, women, and the desire to fight*. New York: Random House.

Colchester, M. 2008. How to own a soccer club: Online with 26,000 others. *Globe and Mail*, 2 January, p. B5.

Cole, Cheryl L. 2000a. Body studies in the sociology of sport. In J. Coakley and E. Dunning, eds., *Handbook of sport studies* (pp. 439–460). London: Sage.

Cole, C. L. 2000b. The year that girls ruled. *Journal of Sport and Social Issues* 24, 1: 3–7.

Coleman, J. 1961. *The adolescent society: The social life of the teenager and its impact on education*. Westport, CT: Greenwood Press.

Collins, Michael F., and James R. Buller. 2003. Social exclusion from high-performance sport: Are all talented young sports people being given an equal opportunity of reaching the Olympic podium? *Journal of Sport and Social Issues* 27, 4: 420–442.

Collins, Patricia Hill. 2004. *Black sexual politics: African Americans, gender, and the new racism*. New York/London: Routledge.

Comité sur la place du Québec dans le système sportif Canadien. 2001. *Le Québec dans le système sportif Canadien*. Report presented to the Ministre délégué au Tourisme, au Loisir et au Sport.

Conroy, Pat. 1986. *The prince of tides*. Boston: Houghton Mifflin.

Cooky, Cheryl. 2004. Raising the bar? Urban girls' negotiations of structural barriers in recreational sports. Paper presented at the annual conference of the American Sociological Society, San Francisco (August).

Cotton, Anthony. 2005a. Pain in the grass. *Denver Post* (October 16): 1J.

Coulombe, S., and M. Lavoie. 1985. Les francophones dans la Ligue nationale de hockey: Une analyse économique de la discrimination. *L'Actualité économique* 61 (1), 73–92.

Couser, G. Thomas. 2000. The empire of the "normal": A forum on disability and self-representation— introduction. *American Quarterly* 52, 2: 305–310.

Coventry, Barbara. 2004. On the sidelines: Sex and racial segregation in television sports broadcasting. *Sociology of Sport Journal* 21, 3: 322–341.

Cox, Barbara, and Shona Thompson. 2000. Multiple bodies: Sportswomen, soccer and sexuality. *International Review for the Sociology of Sport* 35, 1: 5–20.

Crawford, Garry. 2004. *Consuming sport: fans, sport, and culture*. London/New York: Routledge.

Creedon, Pamela J. 1998. Women, sport, and media institutions: Issues in sports journalism and marketing. In Lawrence A. Wenner, ed., *MediaSport* (pp. 88–99). London/New York: Routledge.

Crissey, Joy. 1999. *Corporate cooptation of sport: The case of snowboarding*. Ft. Collins, CO: Master's thesis, Colorado State University.

Crist, Steven. 1998. All bets are off. *Sports Illustrated* 88, 3 (January 26): 82–92.

Crosset, Todd. 1995. *Outsiders in the clubhouse: The world of women's professional golf*. Albany: State University of New York Press.

Crosset, Todd. 1999. Male athletes' violence against women: A critical assessment of the athletic affiliation, violence against women debate. *Quest* 52, 3: 244–257.

Cunningham, George B., and Michael Sagas. 2005. Access discrimination in intercollegiate athletics. *Journal of Sport and Social Issues* 29, 2: 148–163.

Curry, Timothy. 1991. Fraternal bonding in the locker room: A profeminist analysis of talk about competition and women. *Sociology of Sport Journal* 8, 2: 119–135.

Curry, Timothy. 1993. A little pain never hurt anyone: Athletic career socialization and the normalization of sports injury. *Symbolic Interaction* 16, 3: 273–190.

Curry, Timothy. 1996. *Beyond the locker room: Sexual assault and the college athlete*. Presidential Address, North American Society for the Sociology of Sport Conference (Birmingham AL).

Curry, Timothy. 1998. Beyond the locker room: Campus bars and college athletes. *Sociology of Sport Journal* 15, 3: 205–215.

Curry, Timothy J., Kent P. Schwirian, and Rachael Woldoff. 2004. *High stakes: Big time sports and downtown redevelopment*. Columbus: Ohio State University Press.

Curry, Timothy, and R. H. Strauss. 1994. A little pain never hurt anybody: A photo-essay on the normalization of sport injuries. *Sociology of Sport Journal* 11, 2: 195–208.

Curtis, J. and Ennis, R. 1988. Negative consequences of leaving competitive sport?: Comparative findings for former elite hockey players. *Sociology of Sport Journal* 5: 87–106.

Curtis, J., and P. White. 1992. Toward a better understanding of the sport practices of francophone and anglophones Canadians. *Sociology of Sport Journal* 9 (4), 403–22.

Curtis, J., W. McTeer, and P. White. 1999. Exploring effects of school sport experiences on sport participation later in life. *Sociology of Sport Journal*, 16(4) 348–65.

Cyphers, Luke. 2003. Next. *ESPN The Magazine* 6.26 (December 22): 58–66.

Dacyshyn, Anna. 1999. When the balance is gone: The sport and retirement experiences of elite female gymnasts. In J. Coakley and P. Donnelly, eds., *Inside sports* (pp. 214–222). London: Routledge.

Dallaire, C. 2000. At the Alberta Francophone Games. In P. Donnelly, ed., *Taking sport seriously: Social issues in Canadian sport*, 2nd Edition (pp. 126–27). Toronto: Thomson Educational Publishing.

Dallaire, C., and C. Denis. 2000. "If you don't speak French, you're out": Don Cherry, the Alberta Francophone Games, and the discursive construction of Canada's Francophones. *Canadian Journal of Sociology* 25.

Danylchuk, K. 1995. Academic performance of intercollegiate athletes at a Canadian university. Comparisons by gender, type of sport and affiliated faculty. *Avante* 1 (2): 78–93.

Darby, P., Akindes, G. and Kirwin, M. 2007. Football academies and the migration of football labour to Europe. *Journal of Sport and Social Issues*, 31 (2), 143–161.

Darnell, S. 2008. *Changing the world through sport and play: A post-colonial analysis of Canadian volunteers in the "Sport for Development and Peace" movement*. Unpublished doctoral thesis, Toronto: University of Toronto.

Dater, Adrian. 2005. Female boxer, 34, dies after Golden Gloves bout. *Denver Post* (April 5): 1D.

Davies, Robert. 2002a. Sports, citizenship and development: Challenges and opportunities for sport sponsors. Presentation at the World Sports Forum Lausanne (September). Online: www.iblf.org

Davies, Robert. 2002b. Media power and responsibility in sport and globalisation. Presentation made to the Third International Conference for Media Professionals in a Globalised Sport World, Copenhagen (November). Online: www.iblf.org

Davis, Caroline. 1999. Eating disorders, physical activity, and sport: Biological, psychological, and sociological factors. In Philip White and Kevin Young, eds., *Sport and gender in Canada* (pp. 85–106). Don Mills, ON: Oxford University Press.

Davis, Laurel, and Othello Harris. 1998. Race and ethnicity in U.S. sports media. In L. A. Wenner, ed., *Media sport* (pp. 154–169). London/New York: Routledge.

Day, R. 1981. Ethnic soccer clubs in London, Canada: A study in assimilation. *International Review for the Sociology of Sport*, 16 (1): 37–52.

Delaney, Kevin J., and Rick Eckstein. 2003. *Public dollars, private stadiums: The battle over building sports stadiums*. Piscataway, NJ: Rutgers University Press.

Denham, Bryan E. 2004. Hero or hypocrite?: United States and international media portrayals of Carl Lewis amid revelations of a positive drug test. *International Review for the Sociology of Sport* 39, 2: 167–185.

Denver Post Wire Services. 1998. "Pain" isn't in players' vocabularies. *The Denver Post* (May 5): 7D.

Department of Athletics and Recreation. 1994. Report of the Task Force on Gender Equity. University of Toronto.

Department of Canadian Heritage. 2003. Reproduced with the permission of the Minister of Public Works and Government Services Canada.

DePauw, Karen. 1997. The (in)visibility of disability: Cultural contexts and "sporting bodies." *Quest* 49, 4: 416–430.

Desrosiers, H., and H. Eid. 2007. Physical activity outside of class hours among children six years of age. Institute de la Statistique du Québec. Online: www.stat.gouv.qc.ca

Devereaux, E. 1976a. Backyard versus Little League baseball: The impoverishment of children's games. In D. Landers, ed., *Social Problems in Athletics* (pp. 37–56). Urbana: University of Illinois Press.

Devereaux, E. 1976b. "Two Ball Games" (30 min.). Consortium of University Films Centre, Cornell University, Ithaca, NY.

Dewhirst, Timothy, and Robert Sparks. 2003. Intertextuality, tobacco sponsorship of sports, and adolescent male smoking culture: A selective review of tobacco industry documents. *Journal of Sport and Social Issues* 27, 4: 372–398.

DiPasquale, Mauro G. 1992. Editorial: Why athletes use drugs. *Drugs in Sports* 1, 1: 2–3.

Doaks, Clinton. 2004. We can handle the truth. *Mile High Sport Magazine* (November): 10.

Doane, Ashley W., and Eduardo Bonilla-Silva. 2003. *White out: The continuing significance of racism.* New York/London: Routledge.

Dobie, Michael. 1987. Facing a brave new world. *Newsday* (November 8): 13.

Domhoff, G. William. 2002. *Who rules America?* New York: McGraw-Hill.

Domi, Tie. 1992. Tough tradition of hockey fights should be preserved. *USA Today* (October 27): C3.

Donnelly, P. 1981. Four fallacies, III: Climbing is character building. *Mountain* 82:20–23.

Donnelly, P. 1988a. Sport as a site for "popular" resistance. In R. Gruneau, ed., *Popular cultures and political practices* (pp. 69–82). Toronto: Garamond Press.

Donnelly, P. 1988b. Subcultures in sport: Resilience and transformation. In A. Ingham and J. Loy, eds., *Sport and social development: Traditions, transitions, and transformation* (pp. 119–46). Champaign, IL: Human Kinetics.

Donnelly, P. 1993a. Democratization revisited: Seven theses on the democratization of sport and active leisure. *Loisir et société/Society and Leisure* 16 (2): 413–434.

Donnelly, P. 1993b. Problems associated with youth involvement in high-performance sports. In B. R. Cahill and A. J. Pearl, eds., *Intensive participation in children's sports* (pp. 95–126). Champaign, IL: Human Kinetics.

Donnelly, P. 1996a. The local and the global: Globalization in the sociology of sport. *Journal of Sport & Social Issues* 20 (3): 239–57.

Donnelly, P. 1996b. Prolympism: Sport monoculture as crisis and opportunity. *Quest* 48 (1): 25–42.

Donnelly, P. 1997. Child labour, sport labour: Applying child labour laws to sport. *International Review for the Sociology of Sport* 32, 4: 389–406.

Donnelly, P. 2000. Youth sport in Canada: Problems and resolutions. In R. Jones and K. Armour, eds., *Sociology of sport: Theory and practice* (pp. 167–86). Harlow, England: Pearson Education.

Donnelly, P. 2002. George Herbert Mead and the development of an interpretive sociology of sport. In J. Maguire and K. Young, eds., *Theory, sport and society* (pp. 83–102). London: Elsevier.

Donnelly, P. 2004. "It's not rocket science: The last word on media marginalization and trivialization of women's sports." Public lecture given in the "Gender, Sport and Mass Media" series at the University of Copenhagen, 25 March.

Donnelly, P. 2006. Who's fair game?: Sport, sexual harassment and abuse. In P. White and K. Young, eds., *Sport and gender in Canada*, 2/e (pp. 279–301). Toronto: Oxford University Press.

Donnelly, P. 2008. Sport and social theory. In B. Houlihan, ed., *Sport and society: A student introduction*, 2/e (pp. 11–32). London: Sage.

Donnelly, P., and J. Coakley. 2002. *The role of recreation in promoting social inclusion.* Toronto: Laidlaw Foundation Working Papers on Social Inclusion. Online: www.laidlawfdn.org

Donnelly, P. (with J. Coakley). 2004. Recreation and youth development: What we know. In B. Kidd and J. Phillips, eds., *From enforcement and prevention to civic engagement: Research on community safety* (pp. 156–167). Toronto: Centre of Criminology, University of Toronto.

Donnelly, P. (with Sarah Cluer, Candice Skelton, Margaret MacNeill & Graham Knight) 2004. It's not rocket science: The last word on media marginalization and trivialization of women's sports. Public lecture given in the "Gender, Sport and Mass Media" series at the University of Copenhagen, 25 March.

Donnelly, P., and J. Harvey. 1996. *Overcoming systemic barriers to access in active living.* Ottawa: Fitness Branch, Health Canada, and Active Living Canada.

Donnelly, P., and J. Harvey. 2007. Class and gender: Intersections in sport and physical activity. In P. White and K. Young, eds., *Sport and gender in Canada* (pp. 40–64). Don Mills, ON: Oxford University Press.

Donnelly, P., and Y. Nakamura. 2006. Sport and multiculturalism—A dialogue: Final Report. Canadian Heritage.

Donnelly, P., and LeAnne Petherick. 2004. Workers' playtime?: Child labour at the extremes of the sporting spectrum. *Sport in Society* 7, 3: 301–321.

Donnelly, P., and Kevin Young. 1999. Rock climbers and rugby players: Identity construction and confirmation. In J. Coakley and P. Donnelly, eds., *Inside sports* (pp. 67–76). London: Routledge.

Donnelly, P., and R. Sparks. 1997. Child sexual abuse in sport. In P. Donnelly, ed., *Taking sport seriously: Social issues in Canadian sport* (pp. 200–05). Toronto, Ontario: Thomson Publishing, Inc.

Donnelly, P., B. Kidd, J. Harvey, S. Laberge, and G. Rail. 2001. Plus ça change…: Patterns of association in Canadian Hockey. Report for the project, *Patterns of Association in Canadian Civil Society: Linguistic Relations in Non-Governmental Organizations.*

Doping for Gold. 2008. A Firefly Production for Thirteen/WNET New York and ITVS International in association with Five, Channel Four International, and History Channel (UK).

Downward, Paul, and Alistair Dawson. 2000. *The economics of professional team sports*. London/New York: Routledge.

Drahota, Jo Ann T., and D. Stanley Eitzen. 1998. The role exit of professional athletes. *Sociology of Sport Journal* 15, 3: 263–278.

Drakich, K. 2002. Personal communication.

Dubin, C. 1990. *Commission of inquiry into the use of drugs and banned practices intended to increase athletic performance*. Ottawa: Ministry of Supply and Services.

Dukes, Richard L., and Jay Coakley. 2002. Parental commitment to competitive swimming. *Free Inquiry in Creative Sociology* 30, 2: 185–197.

Duncan, Margaret Carlisle, and Michael A. Messner. 2005. *Gender in televised sports: News and highlights shows, 1989–2004*. Los Angeles: Amateur Athletic Foundation. Online: www.aafla.org/9arr/ResearchReports/tv2004.pdf

Duncan, M., and C. Hasbrook. 1988. Denial of power in women's televised sports. *Sociology of Sport Journal,* 5 (1), 1–21.

Dunn, Katherine. 1994. Just as fierce. *Mother Jones* (November–December): 35–39.

Dunn, Robert, and Christopher Stevenson. 1998. The paradox of the Church Hockey League. *International Review for the Sociology of Sport* 33, 2: 131–141.

Dunning, Eric. 1999. *Sport matters: Sociological studies of sport, violence and civilization*. London: Routledge.

Dunning, Eric, Patrick Murphy, Ivan Waddington, and Antonios E. Astrinakis, eds. 2002. *Fighting fans: Football hooliganism as a world phenomenon*. Dublin: University College Dublin Press.

Dunning, Eric, Patrick Murphy, and John Williams. 1988. *The foots of football hooliganism: An historical and sociological study*. London: Routledge and Kegan Paul.

Dunning, Eric, and Kenneth Sheard. 1979. *Barbarians, gentlemen and players: A sociological study of the development of rugby football*. New York: University Press.

Duquin, M. 1993. One future for sport: Moving toward an ethic of care. In G. Cohen, ed., *Women and sport: Issues and controversies* (pp. 289–96). Newbury Park, CA: Sage.

Duquin, Mary. 2000. Sport and emotions. In J. Coakley and E. Dunning, eds., *Handbook of sports studies* (pp. 477–489). London: Sage.

Dworkin, Shari L. 2001. "Holding back": Negotiating a glass ceiling on women's muscular strength. *Sociological Perspectives* 44, 3: 333–351.

Dworkin, Shari L. 2003. A woman's place is in the … cardiovascular room? Gender relations, the body, and the gym. In Anne Bolin and Jane Granskog, eds., *Athletic Intruders: Ethnographic research on women,* *culture, and exercise* (pp. 131–158). Albany: State University of New York Press.

Dyck, N. 2001. *Immigration, integration and sport in Canada*. Paper presented at the Policy Research Seminar on Identity, Halifax, NS.

Early, Gerald. 1998. Performance and reality: Race, sports and the modern world. *The Nation* 267, 5: 11–20.

Eccles, Jacquelynne S., and Bonnie L. Barber. 1999. Student council, volunteering, basketball, or marching band: What kind of extracurricular involvement matters? *Journal of Adolescent Research* 14, 1: 10–43.

Eckstein, Rick, and Kevin Delaney. 2002. New sports stadiums, community self-esteem, and community collective conscience. *Journal of Sport and Social Issues* 26, 3: 236–248.

Eddington, B. 2000. Lacrosse: Little brother of war. *The Beaver*, October–November, pp. 8–14.

Eder, D. (with C. C. Evans and S. Parker). 1995. *School talk: Gender and adolescent culture*. New Brunswick, NJ: Rutgers University Press.

Edwards, Harry. 1973. *Sociology of sport*. Homewood, IL: Dorsey Press.

Edwards, Harry. 2000. The decline of the black athlete (as interviewed by D. Leonard). *ColorLines* 3, 1: 29–24.

Eitle, Tamela McNulty. 2005. Do gender and race matter? Explaining the relationship between sports participation and achievement. *Sociological Spectrum* 25, 2 (March–April): 177–195.

Eitle, Tamela McNulty, and David J. Eitle. 2002. Just don't do it: High school sports participation and young female adult sexual behavior. *Sociology of Sport Journal* 19, 4: 403–418.

Elias, Norbert. 1986. An essay on sport and violence. In N. Elias and E. Dunning, eds., *Quest for excitement* (pp. 150–174). New York: Basil Blackwell.

Elias, Norbert, and Eric Dunning. 1986. *Quest for excitement*. New York: Basil Blackwell.

Elkind, D. 1981. *The hurried child: Growing up too fast too soon*. Don Mills, Ontario: Addison Wesley.

Elling, Agnes, Paul de Knop, and Annelies Knoppers. 2003. Gay/lesbian sport clubs and events: Places of homo-social bonding and cultural resistance? *International Review for the Sociology of Sport* 38, 4: 441–456.

Engh, Fred. 1999. *Why Johnny hates sports*. Garden City Park, NY: Avery.

Enloe, C. 1995. The globetrotting sneaker. *Ms.* 5 (5), March/April: 10–15.

ESPN. 1999. High school athletes: Do jocks rule the school? *Outside the Lines* (June 20–June 24) (edited by T. Farrey). Online: www.espn.com/gen/features/jocks

ESPN The Magazine. 2005. Special report: Turning a blind eye to steroids—The inside story of baseball's open secret. *ESPN The Magazine* 8.23 (November 21): 69–84.

Evans, R.G., M. Barer, and T. Marmor. 1994. *Why are some people healthy and others not?* New York: Aldine de Gruyter.

Ewald, Keith, and Robert M. Jiobu. 1985. Explaining positive deviance: Becker's model and the case of runners and bodybuilders. *Sociology of Sport Journal* 2, 2: 144–156.

Falk, William B. 1995. Bringing home the violence. *Newsday* (January 8): 12–13.

Farber, Michael. 2004. Code red. *Sports Illustrated* 100, 12 (March 22): 56–60.

Farrey, Tom. 2005. Baby you're the greatest: Genetic testing for athletic traits. *ESPN The Magazine* 8.03 (February 14): 80–87. Online: http://sports.espn.go.com/espn/news/story?id=2022781

Fasting, Kari. 1996. 40,000 female runners: The Grete Waitz Run—Sport, culture, and counterculture. Paper presented at International Pre-Olympic Scientific Congress, Dallas (July).

Fausto-Sterling, Anne. 2000. *Sexing the body: Gender politics and the construction of sexuality.* New York: Basic Books.

Fejgin, Naomi. 1994. Participation in high school competitive sports: A subversion of school mission or contribution to academic goals? *Sociology of Sport Journal* 11, 3: 211–230.

Fenstermaker, Sarah, and Candace West, eds. 2002. *Doing gender, doing difference: Inequality, power, and institutional change.* New York: Routledge.

Ference, Ruth, and K. Denise Muth. 2004. Helping middle school females form a sense of self through team sports and exercise. *Women in Sport and Physical Activity* 13, 1: 28–35.

Ferguson, Andrew. 1999. Inside the crazy culture of kids sports. *Time* 154, 2 (July 12): 52–61.

Feschuk, S. 1998. COA chastised for language faux pas. *Globe and Mail*, 18 March, p. A4.

Fish, Mike. 1993. Steroids riskier than ever. *Atlanta Journal-Constitution* (September 26): A1, A12–A13 (part one of four parts).

Florey, Brennen. 1998. Snow job. *Independent* (Colorado Springs) (January 28–February 4): 9–14.

Foer, Franklin. 2004. *How soccer explains the world: An unlikely theory of globalization.* New York: HarperCollins.

Foley, D. 1990. The great American football ritual: Reproducing race, class, and gender inequality. *Sociology of Sport Journal* 7 (2): 111–35.

Foley, D. 1999. High school football: Deep in the heart of south Tejas. In J. Coakley and P. Donnelly, eds., *Inside sports* (pp. 133–38). London: Routledge.

Foot, D., and D. Stoffman. 1998. *Boom, bust & echo 2000: Profiting from the demographic shift in the new millennium.* Toronto: Macfarlane Walter & Ross.

Forsyth, J. 2007. The Indian Act and the (re)shaping of Canadian Aboriginal sport practices. *International Journal of Canadian Studies*, 35, (pp. 95–111).

Fosty, G., and D. Fosty. 2004. *Black ice: The lost history of the Colored Hockey League of the Maritimes, 1895–1925.* New York: Stryker-Indigo Publishing.

Foucault, Michel. 1961/1967. *Madness and civilization.* London: Travistock.

Franseen, L., and S. McCann. 1996. Causes of eating disorders in elite female athletes. *Olympic Coach* 6, 3 (Summer): 15–17.

Fredrickson, Barbara L., and Kristen Harrison. 2005. Throwing like a girl: Self-objectification predicts adolescent girls' motor performance. *Journal of Sport and Social Issues* 29, 1: 79–101.

Friedman, Vicki A., Linda G. Martin, and Robert F. Schoeni. 2004. An overview of disability in America. *Population Bulletin* 59, 3 (special issue, "Disability in America").

Friesen, D. 1967. Academic—athletic—popularity syndrome in the Canadian high school society. *Adolescence* 3 (1), 39–52.

Frisby, W., S. Crawford, and T. Dorer. 1997. Reflections on participatory action research: The case of low income women accessing local physical activity services. *Journal of Sport Management* 11, 8–28.

Frisby. W., C. Reid and P. Ponic. 2007. Levelling the playing field: Promoting the health of poor women through a community development approach to recreation. In K. Young and P. White, eds., *Sport and gender in Canada* (pp. 120–136). Toronto: Oxford University Press.

Fusco, C. 1995. Lesbians and locker rooms. In P. Donnelly, ed., *Taking sport seriously: Social issues in Canadian sport* (pp. 91–94). Toronto: Thomson Educational.

Galasso, P. 1988. *Philosophy of sport and physical activity.* Toronto: Canadian Scholars' Press.

Gard, M. and J. Wright. 2005. *The obesity epidemic: Science, morality and ideology.* London: Routledge.

Garrett, Robyne. 2004. Negotiating a physical identity: Girls, bodies and physical education. *Sport, Education and Society* 9, 2: 223–237.

Gavora, Jessica. 2002. *Tilting the playing field: Schools, sports, sex and Title IX.* San Francisco: Encounter Books.

George, John. 1994. The virtual disappearance of the white male sprinter in the United States: A speculative essay. *Sociology of Sport Journal* 11, 1: 70–78.

Giddens, A. 1989. *Sociology.* Cambridge: Polity Press.

Gilbert, D. 1976. *Little giant in the world of sport: Sports comparison study, GDR—Canada.* Toronto: Kontakt Press.

Gillett, J., P. White, and K. Young. 1996. The prime minister of Saturday night: Don Cherry, the CBC, and the cultural production of intolerance. In H. Holmes and D. Taras, eds., *Seeing ourselves: Media, power and policy in Canada* (pp. 59–72). Toronto: Harcourt, Brace & Jovanovich.

Giordano, Rita, and Kristen A Graham. 2004. An early leg up. *Philadelphia Inquirer* (February 24): D1, D3.

Giulianotti, R. 1994. "Keep it in the family": An outline of Hibs' football hooligans' social ontology. In R. Giulianotti and J. Williams, eds., *Game without frontiers: Football, identity, and modernity* (pp. 327–58). Aldershot, England: Arena (Ashgate).

Giulianotti, R. 2005. *Sport: A critical sociology*. Cambridge: Polity.

Giulianotti, R., N. Bonny, and M. Hepworth, eds. 1994. *Football, violence, and social identity*. London: Routledge.

Giulianotti, R., and Gary Armstrong. 2002. Avenues of contestation: Football hooligans, running and ruling urban spaces. *Social Anthropology* 10, 2: 211–238.

Glock, Allison. 2005. The look of love. *ESPN The Magazine* 8.12 (June 20): 66–74.

Goffman, Erving. 1963. *Stigma: Notes on the management of spoiled identities*. Englewood Cliffs, NJ: Prentice-Hall.

Gordon, M. 1964. *Assimilation in American life*. New York: Oxford University Press.

Gorman, Christine. 2005. Why more kids are getting hurt. *Time* 165, 23 (June 6): 58.

Gramsci, Antonio. 1971. *Selections from the prison notebook* (Q. Hoare and G. N. Smith, Trans). New York: International Publishers (original work published in 1947).

Gramsci, Antonio. 1988. Selected writings: 1918–1935 (D. Forgacs, ed.). New York: Shocken.

Grant, Alan. 2002a. Body shop. *ESPN The Magazine* 5.03 (February 4): 50–54.

Grant, Alan. 2002b. A painful reality. ESPN Mag.com (January 30). Online: http://espn.go. com/magazine/ grant_20020130.html (retrieved June 2005).

Green, Mick. 2003. An analysis of elite sport policy change in three sports in Canada and the United Kingdom. Unpublished doctoral thesis, Loughborough University, UK.

Green, Mick. 2004. Power, policy, and political priorities: Elite sport development in Canada and the United Kingdom. *Sociology of Sport Journal* 21, 4: 376–396.

Green, Mick, and Barrie Houlihan. 2004. Advocacy coalitions and elite sport policy change in Canada and the United Kingdom. *International Review for the Sociology of Sport* 39, 4: 387–403.

Greendorfer, S. L. 1993. Gender role stereotypes and early childhood socialization. In G. L. Cohen, ed., *Women in sport* (pp. 3–14). Newbury Park, CA: Sage.

Greenfeld, Karl Taro. 1999. Adjustment in mid-flight. *Outside* (February). Online: http://outside.away.com/ magazine/0299/9902terje_2.html

Grenfell, Christopher C., and Robert E. Rinehart. 2003. Skating on thin ice: Human rights in youth figure skating. *International Review for the Sociology of Sport* 38, 1: 79–97.

Grenier, G., and M. Lavoie. 1992. Discrimination and salary determination in the National Hockey League: 1977 and 1989 compared. In G. Scully, ed., *Advances in the Economics of Sport*, volume 1 (pp. 153–77). Greenwich: JAI Press.

Grey, M. 1992. Sports and immigrant, minority and Anglo relations in Garden City (Kansas) High School. *Sociology of Sport Journal* 9 (3), 255–70.

Grey, M. 1999. Playing sports and social acceptance: The experiences of immigrant and refugee students in Garden City, Kansas. In J. Coakley and P. Donnelly, eds., *Inside Sports* (pp. 28–36). London: Routledge.

Griffin, Pat. 1998. *Strong women, deep closets: Lesbians and homophobia in sport*. Champaign, IL: Human Kinetics.

Grossfeld, Stan. 2005. New spin on rugby: Quadriplegic athletes take sport to the extreme with wheelchair version. *Boston Globe* (May 31): D1.

Gruneau, R. 1988. Modernization or hegemony: Two views of sports and social development. In J. Harvey and H. Cantelon, eds., *Not just a game* (pp. 9–32). Ottawa, Ontario: University of Ottawa Press.

Gruneau, R. 1989. Making spectacle: A case study in television sports production. In Lawrence Wenner, ed., *Media, sports & society* (pp. 134–54). London: Sage.

Gruneau, R. 1999. *Class, sports, and social development*. Champaign, IL: Human Kinetics.

Gruneau, R. 2006. 'Amateurism' as a sociological problem: Reflections inspired by Eric Dunning. *Sport in Society*, 9 (4): 559–582.

Gruneau, R., and J. Albinson. 1976. *Canadian sport: Sociological perspectives*. Toronto: Addison-Wesley.

Gruneau, R., and David Whitson. 1993. *Hockey night in Canada: Sport, identities, and cultural politics.* Toronto: Garamond Press.

Guest, Andrew, and Barbara Schneider. 2003. Adolescents' extracurricular participation in context: The mediating effects of schools, communities, and identity. *Sociology of Education* 76, 2 (April): 89–09.

Guilbert, Sèbastien. 2004. Sport and violence: A typological analysis. *International Review for the Sociology of Sport* 39, 1: 45–55.

Guttmann, Allen. 1978. *From ritual to record: The nature of modern sports*. New York: Columbia University Press.

Guttmann, Allen. 1986. *Sport spectators*. New York: Columbia University Press.

Guttmann, Allen. 1998. The appeal of violent sports. In J. Goldstein, ed., *Why we watch: The attractions of violent entertainment* (pp. 7–26). New York: Oxford University Press.

Guttmann, Allen. 2004. *Sports: the first five millennia*. Amherst: University of Massachusetts Press.

Hall, A. 1999. Creators of the lost and perfect game?: Gender, history, and Canadian sport. In P. White and K. Young, eds., *Sport and gender in Canada* (pp. 5–23). Toronto: Oxford University Press.

Hall, A. 2002. *The girl and the game: A history of women's sport in Canada*. Peterborough, ON: Broadview Press.

Hall, A., T. Slack, G. Smith, and D. Whitson. 1991. *Sport in Canadian society*. Toronto: McClelland and Stewart.

Haney, C. Allen, and Demetrius W. Pearson. 1999. Rodeo injuries: An examination of risk factors. *Journal of Sport Behavior* 22, 4: 443–467.

Hannigan, J. 1998. *Fantasy city: Pleasure and profit in the postmodern metropolis*. London and New York: Routledge.

Hansell, Saul. 2005. More people turn to the web to watch TV. *New York Times* (August 1): C1.

Hardman, K., and J. Marshall. 2000. The state and status of physical education in schools in international context. *European Physical Education Review* 6 (3), 203–29.

Hargreaves, Jennifer, 1994. *Sporting females: Critical issues in the history and sociology of women's sport*. London: Routledge.

Hargreaves, Jennifer. 2000. *Heroines of sport: The politics of difference and identity*. London: Routledge.

Hargreaves, J., and P. Vertinsky, eds. 2007. *Physical culture, power, and the body*. London: Routledge.

Harney, R. 1985. Homo ludens and ethnicity. *Polyphony*, 7 (1): 1–12.

Harp, Joyce B., and Lindsay Hecht. 2005. Obesity in the National Football League. *Journal of the American Medical Association* 293, 9 (March 2): 1061–1062.

Harris, C. 2005. *Breaking the ice: The Black experience in professional hockey*. Toronto, ON: Insomniac Press, 2005.

Harrison, C. Keith, and Suzanne Malia Lawrence. 2004. College students' perceptions, myths, and stereotypes about African American athletes: A qualitative investigation. *Sport, Education and Society* 9, 1 (March): 33–52.

Harrison, Louis, Jr. 1995. African Americans: Race as a self-schema affecting physical activity choices. *Quest* 47, 1: 7–18.

Harrison, Louis, Jr., Laura Azzarito, and Joe Burden, Jr. 2004. Perceptions of athletic superiority: A view from the other side. *Race Ethnicity and Education* 7, 2: 149–166.

Harrison, Louis, Jr., Amelia M. Lee, and Don Belcher. 1999. Race and gender differences in sport participation as a function of self-schema. *Journal of Sport and Social Issues* 23, 3: 287–307.

Hart, M. Marie. 1981. On being female in sport. In M. M. Hart and S. Birrell, eds., *Sport in the socio-cultural process* (pp. 291–301). Dubuque, IA: Brown.

Hartmann, Douglas. 2001. Notes on midnight basketball and the cultural politics of recreation, race, and at-risk urban youth. *Journal of Sport and Social Issues* 25, 4: 339–371.

Hartmann, Douglas. 2003a. The sanctity of Sunday afternoon football: Why men love sports. *Contexts* 2, 4: 13–21.

Hartmann, Douglas. 2003b. Theorizing sport as social intervention: A view from the grassroots. *Quest* 55, 2: 118–140.

Harvey, J. 1988. Sport and the Quebec clergy, 1930–1960. In J. Harvey and H. Cantelon, eds., *Not just a game: Essays in Canadian sport sociology* (pp. 69–84). Ottawa: University of Ottawa Press.

Harvey, J. 1999. Sport and Quebec nationalism: Ethnic or civic identity? In J. Sugden and A. Bairner, eds., *Sport in divided societies* (pp. 31–50). Aachen: Meyer & Meyer Sport.

Harvey, J. 2006. Whose sweater is this?: The changing meanings of hockey in Québec. In D. Whitson and R. Gruneau, eds., *Artificial ice: Hockey, culture, and commerce* (pp. 29–52). Peterborough, ON: Broadview Press.

Harvey, J., and F. Houle. 1994. Sports, world economy, global culture and new social movements. *Sociology of Sport Journal* 11 (4), pp. 337–55.

Harvey, J., Alan Law, and Michael Cantelon. 2001. North American professional team sport franchises ownership patterns and global entertainment conglomerates. *Sociology of Sport Journal* 18, 4: 435–457.

Harvey, J., and R. Proulx. 1988. Sport and the state in Canada. In J. Harvey and H. Cantelon, eds., *Not just a game* (pp. 93–120). Ottawa, Ontario: University of Ottawa Press.

Harvey, J., G. Rail, and L. Thibault. 1996. Globalization and sport: Sketching a theoretical model for empirical analysis. *Journal of Sport & Social Issues* 20 (3): 258–77.

Hasbrook, Cynthia A. 1999. Young children's social constructions of physicality and gender. In J. Coakley and P. Donnelly, eds., *Inside Sports* (pp. 7–16). London: Routledge.

Hasbrook, Cynthia A., and Othello Harris. 1999. Wrestling with gender: Physicality and masculinities among inner-city first and second graders. *Men and Masculinities* 1, 3: 302–318.

Hastings, Donald W., Sherry Cable, and Sammy Zahran. 2005. The globalization of a minor sport: The diffusion and COM modification of masters swimming. *Sociological Spectrum* 25, 2: 133–154.

Haut Commissariat à la Jeunesse, aux Loisirs et aux Sports. 1978. Situation des Québécois dans le secteur du sport sur l'échiquier canadien: Rapport final. Québec: Gouvernement du Québec.

Hawes, K. 1999a. Dangerous games: Athletics initiation—Team bonding, rite of passage, or hazing? *The NCAA News*, 13 September, 1, 14–16.

Hawes, K. 1999b. Weighing in. *The NCAA News*, 36 (24), 22 November, 1, 24–25.

Hawes, K. 2001. Mirror, mirror. *NCAA News*, special report (September 24): A1–4.

Heckert, Alex, and Druann Heckert. 2002. A new typology of deviance: Integrating normative and reactivist definitions of deviance. *Deviant Behavior* 23: 449–479.

Heckert, Alex, and Druann Heckert. 2004. Using a new typology to analyze ten common norms of the American middle class. *Sociological Quarterly* 45: 209–228.

Heckert, Alex, and Druann Heckert. 2007. Positive deviance. In George Ritzer, ed., *Encyclopedia of sociology* (in press). London/New York: Blackwell.

Heine, M. 1995. Gwich'in Tsii'in: A history of Gwich'in Athapaskan Games. Unpublished doctoral thesis, University of Alberta.

Henry, F., and C. Tator. 2002. *Discourses of domination: Racial bias in the Canadian English-language press*. University of Toronto Press.

Heywood, Leslie. 1998. *Bodymakers: A cultural anatomy of women's bodybuilding*. New Brunswick, NJ: Rutgers University Press.

Heywood, Leslie, and Shari Dworkin. 2003. *Built to win: The female athlete as cultural icon*. Minneapolis: University of Minnesota Press.

Hiestand, Michael. 2002. Security tighter, more costly for teams, venues. *USA Today* (September 11): 3C.

Higgins, Matt. 2005. A sport so popular, they added a second boom. *New York Times* (July 25). Online: http://query.nytimes.com/mem/tnt.html?emc=tnt&tntget =2005/07/25/sports/othersports/25boom.html

Higgins, Paul C. 1992. *Making disability: Exploring the transformation of human variation*. Springfield, IL: Thomas.

Hilliard, Dan C., and J. M. Hilliard. 1990. Positive deviance and participant sport. Paper presented at the annual conference of the North American Society for the Sociology of Sport, Las Vegas (April).

Hoberman, John M. 1992. *Mortal engines: The science of performance and the dehumanization of sport*. New York: Free Press.

Hoberman, John M. 1994. The sportive-dynamic body as a symbol of productivity. In T. Siebers, ed. *Heterotopia: Postmodern utopia and the body politic* (pp. 199–228). Ann Arbor: University of Michigan Press.

Hoberman, John M. 1995. Listening to steroids. *Wilson Quarterly* 19, 1 (Winter): 35–44.

Hoberman, John M. 2004. *Testosterone dreams: Rejuvenation, aphrodisia, doping*. Berkeley: University of California Press.

Hoffman, S. 1992. *Sport and religion*. Champaign, IL: Human Kinetics.

Hoffman, S. 1999. The decline of civility and the rise of religion in American sport. *Quest* 51, 1: 69–84.

Holton, K. 2008. IOC updates Internet rights rules for Olympics. Reuters, April 2.

Honea, Joy. 2005. *Youth cultures and consumerism: Sport subcultures and possibilities for resistance*. Ft. Collins: Ph.D. dissertation, Colorado State University.

Honea, Joy. 2007. Alternative sports. In George Ritzer, ed., *Encyclopedia of sociology* (in press). London/New York: Blackwell.

Hood, C. 1998. *The status of high school sport in Canada*. Report presented to the International School Sport Federation.

Hooks, Bell. 2000. *Where we stand: Class matters*. New York/London: Routledge.

Houlihan, B. 2000. Politics and sport. In J. Coakley and E. Dunning, eds., *Handbook of sport studies* (pp. 213–227). London: Sage.

Houlihan, B. 2005. Securing the Olympic legacy. *Parliamentary Brief*, 9 (11): p. 16.

Houston, W. 2007. Power players of 2007. *Globe and Mail*, 18 December, p. S1.

Houston, W. 2008. Internet makes it a whole new game. *Globe and Mail*, 12 November, p. S5.

Hovden, J. 2000. Gender and leadership selection processes in Norwegian sporting organizations. *International Review for the Sociology of Sport* 35, 1: 75–82.

Howe, P. David. 2003. Kicking stereotypes into touch: An ethnographic account of women's rugby. In Anne Bolin and Jane Granskog, eds., *Athletic intruders: Ethnographic research on women, culture, and exercise* (pp. 227–246). Albany: State University of New York Press.

Howe, P. David. 2004. *Sport, professionalism and pain: Ethnographies of injury and risk*. London/New York: Routledge.

Howell, C. 2001. *Blood, sweat and cheers: Sport and the Making of Modern Canada*. Toronto: University of Toronto Press.

Howell, J. 2005. Manufacturing experiences: Urban development, sport and recreation. *International Journal of Sport Management and Marketing*, 1 (1/2), 56–68.

Hudson, Ian. 2001. The use and misuse of economic impact analysis: The case of professional sports. *Journal of Sport and Social Issues* 25, 1: 20–39.

Huey, J. 1996. The Atlanta game. *Fortune* 134 (2): 22 July, 43–56.

Hughes, C., and S. Griffiths. 1992. *No level playing field: Recreation and poverty in Scarborough—A community report.* Toronto: Laidlaw Foundation.

Hughes, Robert, and Jay Coakley. 1991. Positive deviance among athletes: The implications of overconformity to the sport ethic. *Sociology of Sport Journal* 8, 4: 307–325.

Hughson, John. 2000. The boys are back in town: Soccer support and the social reproduction of masculinity. *Journal of Sport and Social Issues* 24, 1: 8–23.

Hui, Stephen. 2004. Transexual Olympiads. Online: www.alternet.org/rights/19525/ (retrieved December 1, 2005).

Humber, W. 1983. *Cheering for the home team: The story of baseball in Canada.* Erin, Ontario: Boston Mills Press.

Humber, W. 2004. *A sporting chance: Achievements of African-Canadian athletes.* Toronto: Natural Heritage Books.

Hunt, H. David. 2005. The effect of extracurricular activities in the educational process: Influence on academic outcomes? *Sociological Spectrum* 25, 4: 417–445.

Ingham, Alan G., B. J. Blissmer, and K. W. Davidson. 1999. The expendable prolympic self: Going beyond the boundaries of the sociology and psychology of sport. *Sociology of Sport Journal* 16, 3: 236–268.

Ingham, Alan G., Melissa A. Chase, and Joanne Butt. 2002. From the performance principle to the developmental principle: Every kid a winner? *Quest* 4, 4: 308–332.

Ingham, Alan, and Alison Dewar. 1999. Through the eyes of youth: "Deep play" in peewee ice hockey. In J. Coakley and P. Donnelly, eds. *Inside sports* (pp. 7–16). London: Routledge.

Ingham, Alan, and Mary McDonald. 2003. Sport and community/communitas. In R. Wilcox, D. L. Andrews, R. L. Irwin, and R. Pitter, eds., *Sporting dystopias: The making and meaning of urban sport cultures* (pp. 17–34). Albany: State University of New York Press.

Irwin, Katherine. 2003. Saints and sinners: Elite tattoo collectors and tattooists as positive and negative deviants. *Sociological Spectrum* 23, 1: 27–57.

Jackson, Susan A., and Mihaly Csikszentmihalyi. 1999. *Flow in sports.* Champaign, IL: Human Kinetics.

Jackson, Steven J. 1998. Life in the (mediated) Faust lane: Ben Johnson, national affect and the 1988 crisis of Canadian identity. *International Review for the Sociology of Sport* 33 (3), 227–38.

Jackson, Steven J., and David L. Andrews, eds. 2004. *Sport, culture and advertising: identities, commodities and the politics of representation.* London/New York: Routledge.

Jackson, Steven J., and B. Hokowhitu. 2002. Sport, tribes and technology: The New Zealand All Blacks Haka and the politics of identity. *Journal of Sport and Social Issues* 26 (1): 125–39.

Jackson, Steven J., and J. Scherer. 2002. *Screening the nation's past: Adidas, advertising and corporate nationalism in New Zealand.* Paper presented at the North American Society for the Sociology of Sport Conference, Indianapolis.

James, C. 1984. *Beyond a boundary.* New York: Pantheon Books.

James, C. 2005. Race in Play: *Understanding the socio-cultural worlds of student athletes.* Toronto: Canadian Scholars Press.

Janson, G. 1995. Emparons-nous du sport: les canadiens-français et le sport du XIXe sie`cle. Montréal: Guérin.

Jayson, Sharon. 2004. On or off the field, it's a "civility" war out there. *USA Today* (November 30): 9D.

Jenkins, Chris. 2000. Caught in gambling's web. *USA Today* (March 13): 1C–2C.

Jennings, A. 1996. *The new lords of the rings.* London: Pocket Books.

Jennings, A. 2006. *Foul!—The secret world of FIFA: Bribes, vote rigging and ticket scandals.* London: Harper Collins.

Jennings, A., and Clare Sambrook. 2000. *The great Olympic swindle: When the world wanted its games back.* New York: Simon and Schuster.

Jerome, W., and J. Philips. 1971. The relationship between academic achievement and interscholastic participation: A comparison of Canadian and American high schools. *Journal of the Canadian Association for Health, Physical Education and Recreation* 37, 18–21.

Jhally, S. 1984. The spectacle of accumulation: Material and cultural factors in the emergence of the sports/media complex. *The Insurgent Sociologist* 12 (3), 41–57.

Johns, David. 1992. Starving for gold: A case study in overconformity in high performance sport. Paper presented at the annual conference of the North American Society for the Sociology of Sport, Toledo (November).

Johns, David. 1996. Positive deviance and the sport ethic: Examining weight loss strategies in rhythmic gymnastics. *Hong Kong Journal of Sports Medicine and Sport Science* 2 (May): 49–56.

Johns, David. 1997. Fasting and feasting: Paradoxes in the sport ethic. *Sociology of Sport Journal* 15, 1: 41–63.

Johns, David P., and Jennifer S. Johns. 2000. Surveillance, subjectivism and technologies of power. *International Review for the Sociology of Sport* 35, 2: 219–234.

Johnson, J. 1999. *Sport hazing experiences in the context of anti-hazing policies: The case of two Southern Ontario universities.* Unpublished master's thesis. Toronto: University of Toronto.

Johnson, J., and M. Homan, eds. 2004. *Making the team: Inside the world of sport initiations and hazing.* Toronto: Canadian Scholars' Press.

Jones, B., D. Cowan, and J. Knapik. 1994. Exercise, training and injuries. *Sports Medicine*, 18, 202–214.

Joukowsky, Artemis A. W. III, and Larry Rothstein, eds. 2002a. *Raising the bar.* New York: Umbrage Editions.

Joukowsky, Artemis A. W. III, and Larry Rothstein. 2002b. New horizons in disability sport. In Artemis A. W. Joukowsky III and Larry Rothstein, eds., *Raising the bar* (pp. 8–17). New York: Umbrage Editions.

Joyce, G. 1997. White rules. In P. Donnelly, ed., *Taking sport seriously: Social issues in Canadian sport* (pp. 325–35). Toronto: Thomson Educational.

Jutel, Annemarie. 2002. Olympic road cycling and national identity: Where is Germany? *Journal of Sport and Social Issues* 26, 2: 195–208.

Katz, Jackson. 2003. When you're asked about the Kobe Bryant case. Online: www.jacksonkatz.com/bryant.html

Kay, Joanne, and Suzanne Laberge. 2003. Oh say can you ski? In Robert E. Rinehart and Synthia Sydnor, eds., *To the extreme: Alternative sports, inside and out* (pp. 381–398). Albany: State University of New York Press.

Kay, T. 2000. Sporting excellence: a family affair? *European Physical Education Review*, 6 (2): 151–169.

Kay, T. 2001. *Children in high-performance sport: Family issues.* Paper presented at the 3rd Annual Colloquium of the Centre for Sport Policy Studies: "Talented children in sport, music and dance: How can we nurture talent without exploiting or abusing children?" University of Toronto, 27–29 September, 2001.

Kay, T., ed. 2006. Special issue: Fathering through leisure. *Leisure Studies*, 25(2).

Kearney, Jay. 1999. Creatine supplementation: Specifics for the trained athlete. *Olympic Coach* 9, 2: 3–5.

Keating, Peter. 2004. Insurance run. *ESPN The Magazine* 7.14 (July 5): 70–73.

Keating, Peter. 2005. Baseball has solved its steroid problem—at least that's what they want you to believe. *ESPN The Magazine* 8.24 (December 5): 16.

Kellner, Douglas. 2003a. Toward a critical theory of education. *Democracy and Nature* 9, 1 (March): 51–64. Online: www.gseis.ucla.edu/faculty/kelllner/

Kellner, Douglas. 2003b. *Media spectacle.* London/New York: Routledge.

Kellner, Douglas. 2004. The sports spectacle, Michael Jordan, and Nike. In Patrick B. Miller and David K. Wiggins, eds., *Sport and the color line* (pp. 305–326). New York/London: Routledge.

Kennedy, S. 2006. *Why I didn't say anything: The Sheldon Kennedy story.* Toronto: Insomniac Press.

Keown, Tim. 2004. World of hurt. *ESPN The Magazine* 7.16 (August 2): 57–77.

Keri, M. G. 2000. Take me out of their ball game. *Utne Reader*, No. 97, January/February, 55.

Kernaghan, J. 2002. Search for equity leads to unequal teams. *London Free Press*, 17 May.

Kesterton, M. 2002. Social Studies. *Globe and Mail*, 14 June, p. A24.

Kidd, B. 1980. *Tom Longboat.* Toronto: Fitzhenry & Whiteside.

Kidd, B. 1983. In defense of Tom Longboat. *Sport History Review* 14, 1: 34–63.

Kidd, B. 1984. The myth of the ancient games. In A. Tomlinson and G. Whannel, eds., *Five-ring circus* (pp. 71–83). London: Pluto Press.

Kidd, B. 1987. Sports and masculinity. In M. Kaufman, ed., *Beyond patriarchy: Essays by men on pleasure, power, and change* (pp. 250–265). New York: Oxford University Press.

Kidd, B. 1988. The philosophy of excellence: Olympic performance, class power, and the Canadian state. In P. Galasso, ed., *Philosophy of sport and physical activity: Issues and controversies* (pp. 11–31). Toronto: Canadian Scholars Press.

Kidd, B. 1992. The culture wars of the Montreal Olympics. *International Review for the Sociology of Sport* 27 (2), 151–63.

Kidd, B. 1995. Inequality in sport, the corporation, and the state: An agenda for social scientists. *Journal of Sport and Social Issues* 19, 3: 232–248.

Kidd, B. 1996a. Taking the rhetoric seriously: Proposals for Olympic education. *Quest* 48 (1): 82–92.

Kidd, B. 1996b. Worker sport in the New World: The Canadian story. In A. Kruger and J. Riordan, eds., *The story of worker sport* (pp. 143–56). Champaign, IL: Human Kinetics.

Kidd, B. 1997. *The struggle for Canadian sport.* Toronto: University of Toronto Press.

Kidd, B. 2008. A new social movement: Sport for development and peace. *Sport in Society*, 11 (4): 370–380.

Kidd, B., and P. Donnelly. 2000. Human rights in sports. *International Review for the Sociology of Sport*, 35 (2): 131–148.

Kidd, B., and M. Eberts. 1982. *Athletes' rights in Canada.* Toronto: Ministry of Tourism and Recreation.

Kilvert, Gwen. 2002. Missing the X chromosome. *Sports Illustrated Women* 4, 4: 21–22.

King, A. J. C., and M. J. Peart. 1990. *The good school: Strategies for making secondary schools effective.* Toronto: Ontario Secondary School Teachers' Federation.

King, C. Richard. 2007. Sport and ethnicity. In George Ritzer, ed., *Encyclopedia of sociology* (in press). London/New York: Blackwell.

King, Kelley. 2002. The ultimate jock school. *Sports Illustrated* 97, 21 (November 25): 48–54.

King, Peter. 2004. Painful reality. *Sports Illustrated* 101, 14 (October 11): 60–63.

Kinkema, Kathleen M., and Janet C. Harris. 1998. MediaSport studies: Key research and emerging issues. In L. A. Wenner, ed., *MediaSport* (pp. 27–54). London/New York: Routledge.

Kirby, S., L. Greaves, and O. Hankivsky. 2000. *The dome of silence: Sexual harassment and abuse in sport*. Halifax, NS: Fernwood Publishing.

Kjeldsen, E. 1984. Integration of minorities into Olympic sport in Canada and the USA. *Journal of Sport and Social Issues* 8 (2), 29–44.

Klein, A. 1991. *Sugarball: The American game, the Dominican dream*. New Haven, CT: Yale University Press.

Klein, A. 1993. *Little big men: Bodybuilding subculture and gender construction*. Albany: State University of New York Press.

Klein, A. 1997. *Baseball on the border: A tale of two Laredos*. Princeton, NJ: Princeton University Press.

Klein, A. 1999. Coming of age in North America: Socialization of Dominican baseball players. In J. Coakley and P. Donnelly, eds., *Inside sports* (pp. 96–103). London: Routledge.

Klein, A. 2006. *Growing the game: Globalization and Major League Baseball*. New Haven, CT: Yale University Press.

Knight, G., and J. Greenberg. 2002. Promotionalism and subpolitics: Nike and its labor critics. *Management Communication Quarterly* 15 (4): 541–70.

Knight, G., M. MacNeill, and P. Donnelly. 2005. The disappointment game: Narratives of Olympic failure in Canada and New Zealand. *International Review for the Sociology of Sport*, 40 (1), 25–51.

Knoppers, Annelies, and Agnes Elling. 2004. "We do not engage in promotional journalism": Discursive strategies used by sport journalists to describe the selection process. *International Review for the Sociology of Sport* 39, 1: 57–73.

Knudson, Mark. 2005. The Mark: The whole IX yards. *Mile High Sports Magazine* 3, 9 (May): 21–23.

Kohn, A. 1992. *No contest: The case against competition*. Boston: Mariner Books.

Koppett, Leonard. 1994. *Sports illusion, sports reality*. Urbana: University of Illinois Press.

Koukouris, Konstantinos. 1994. Constructed case studies: Athletes' perspectives of disengaging from organized competitive sport. *Sociology of Sport Journal* 11, 2: 114–139.

Kozol, Jonathan. 1991. *Savage inequalities*. New York: Crown.

Krane, Vikki, Precilla Y. L. Choi, Shannon M. Baird, Christine M. Aimar, and Kerrie J. Kauer. 2004. Living the paradox: Female athletes negotiate femininity and muscularity. *Sex Roles* 50, 5/6: 315–329.

Krukowska, L. et al. 2007. Canada vs. USA: The financial implications of choice. Ottawa: CIS. Online: www.universitysport.ca

Laberge, S. 1986. *Rapport de l'Enquéte sur le 'Fait Français.'* Présenté à La Direction du Sport d'Élite, Ministere du Loisir, de la Chasse at de la Peche.

Laberge, S. 1995. Sports et activités physique: modes d'aliénation et pratiques émancipatoires. *Sociologie et Sociétés* 27 (1), 53–74.

Laberge, S., and Mathieu Albert. 1999. Conceptions of masculinity and of gender transgressions in sport among adolescent boys: Hegemony, contestation, and social class dynamic. *Men and Masculinities* 1, 3: 243–267.

Laberge, S., and Y. Girardin. 1992. Questioning the inference of ethnic differences in achievement values from types of sport participation: A commentary on White and Curtis. *Sociology of Sport Journal* 9 (2), 295–306.

Laberge, S., and David Sankoff. 1988. Physical activities, body *habitus*, and lifestyles. In J. Harvey and H. Cantelon, eds., *Not just a game* (pp. 267–286). Ottawa: University of Ottawa Press.

Lafferty, Yvonne, and Jim McKay. 2004. "Suffragettes in satin shorts"? Gender and competitive boxing. *Qualitative Sociology* 27, 3: 249–276.

LaFlamme, A. 1977. The role of sport in the development of ethnicity: A case study. *Sport Sociology Bulletin* 6 (1), 47–51.

Lamb, L. 2000. Can women save sports? An interview with Mary Jo Kane. *Utne Reader* 97: 56–57.

Lance, Larry. M. 2005. Violence in sport: A theoretical note. *Sociological Spectrum* 25, 2: 213–214.

Landry, F., C. St-Denis, and C. Turgeon. 1966. Les Canadiens-français et les Grands Jeux Internationaux. *Mouvement* 1 (2), 115–32.

Landry, F., R. Boileau, and Y. Trempe. 1972. Les Canadiens-français et les Grands Jeux Internationaux. *Mouvement* 7 (1–2), 81–92.

Lapchick, Richard. 2004. *Racial and gender report card, 2003*. Orlando: Institute for Diversity and Ethics in Sports, University of Central Florida.

Lapchick, Richard. 2005. *2004 racial and gender report card*. Orlando: Institute for Diversity and Ethics in Sports, University of Central Florida.

Laqueur, Thomas. 1990. *Making sex*. Cambridge, MA: Harvard University Press.

Lareau, A. 2000. *Home advantage: Social class and parental intervention in elementary education*. Lanham, MD: Rowman & Littlefield.

Laurendeau, Jason. 2004. The "crack choir" and the "cock chorus": The intersection of gender and sexuality in skydiving texts. *Sociology of Sport Journal* 21, 4: 397–417.

Lavoie, M. 1989. Stacking, performance differentials, and salary discrimination in professional ice hockey: A survey of the evidence. *Sociology of Sport Journal*, 6 (1): 17–35.

Lavoie, M. 1998. *Désavantage numérique: Les Francophones dans la LNH*. Hull: Vent D'Ouest.

Lavoie, M. 2000. Economics and sport. In J. Coakley and E. Dunning, eds., *Handbook of sports studies* (pp. 157–170). London: Sage.

Law, A., J. Harvey, J. and S. Kemp. 2002. The Global Sport Mass Media Oligopoly: The three usual suspects and more." *International Review for the Sociology of Sport*, 37 (3/4), 277–300.

Lawler, Jennifer. 2002. *Punch: Why women participate in violent sports*. Terre Haute, IN: Wish Publishing.

Layden, T. 1995a. Better education. *Sports Illustrated* 82, 13 (April 3): 68–90.

Layden, T. 1995b. Book smart. *Sports Illustrated* 82, 14 (April 10): 68–79.

Layden, T. 1995c. You bet your life. *Sports Illustrated* 82, 15 (April 17): 46–55.

Layden, T. 2005. I am an American. *Sports Illustrated* 103, 17 (October 31): 60–69.

Le Batard, Dan. 2005b. Open look: So you're tired of the Barry Bonds act? *ESPN The Magazine* 8.07 (April 11): 18.

Lefkowitz, Bernard. 1997. *Our guys: The Glen Ridge rape and the secret life of the perfect suburb*. Berkeley: University of California Press.

Lehrman, Sally. 1997. *Forget men are from Mars, women are from Venus*. Stanford Today. Online: www.stanford.edu/dept/news/stanfordtoday/ed/9705/9705fea401.shtml (retrieved December 1, 2005).

Leland, J. 2000. Why America's hooked on wrestling. *Newsweek* 135, 6 (February 7): 46–55.

Lenskyj, H. J. 1986. *Out of bounds: Women, sport and sexuality*. Toronto: Women's Press.

Lenskyj, H. J. 1999. Women, sport, and sexualities: Breaking the silences. In P. White and K. Young, eds., *Sport and gender in Canada* (pp. 170–181). Don Mills, ON: Oxford University Press.

Lenskyj, H. J. 2000. *Inside the Olympics industry: Power, politics, and activism*. Albany: State University of New York Press.

Lenskyj, H. J. 2002. *The best Olympics ever? The social impacts of Sydney 2000*. Albany: State University of New York Press.

Lenskyj, H. J. 2003. *Out in the field: gender, sport and sexualities*. Toronto: Women's Press. Online: http://www.womenspress.ca/

Lenskyj, H. J. 2004. Making the world safe for global capital: The Sydney 2000 Olympics and beyond. In John Bale and Mette Christensen, eds., *Post-Olympism: Questioning sport in the twenty-first century* (pp. 135–146.). Oxford, England/New York: Berg.

Levy, Don. 2005. Fantasy sports and fanship habitus: Understanding the process of sport consumption. Paper presented at the annual conference of the American Sociological Society, Philadelphia (August).

Lewis, Amanda E. 2003. *Race in the schoolyard: Negotiating the color line in classrooms and communities*. New Brunswick, NJ: Rutgers University Press.

Ligutom-Kimura, Donna Ann. 1995. The invisible women. *Journal of Physical Education, Recreation and Dance* 66, 7: 34–41.

Lindberg, K. 2006. The man who traced 442 soccer slaves. *PlaytheGame Magazine*, p. 3.

Lipsyte, Robert. 1996. Little girls in a staged spectacle for big bucks? *New York Times*, 4 August, 28.

Lipsyte, Robert. 1998. A step in the healing process. *New York Times* (March 5): C22.

Longman, J. 1996. Slow down, speed up. *New York Times* (May 1): B11.

Longman, J. 2001. Getting the athletic edge may mean altering genes. *New York Times* (May 11). Online: http://www.nytimes.com/2001/05/11/sports/11GENE.html

Lopiano, Donna. 1991. Presentation at the Coaching America's Coaches Conference, United States Olympic Training Center, Colorado Springs, CO.

Loveless, Tom. 2002. *The 2002 Brown Center report on American education: How well are American students learning?* Washington, DC: Brookings Institution.

Lowe, Maria R. 1998. *Women of steel: Female bodybuilders and the struggle for self-definition*. New York: New York University Press.

Lowe, P. 1998. Rodeo women over a barrel, champion racer says. *The Denver Post*, 24 January: F-01.

Lowes, Mark Douglas. 1999. *Inside the sports pages: Work routines, professional ideologies, and the manufacture of sport news*. Toronto: University of Toronto Press.

Loy, J. W. 1995. The dark side of agon: Fratriarchies, performative masculinities, sport involvement and the phenomenon of gang rape. In K. H. Bette and A. Rutten, eds., *International Sociology of Sport: Contemporary Issues* (pp. 263–282). Stuttgart: Verlag SN.

Loy, J., and D. Booth. 2001. Emile Durkheim, structural functionalism and the sociology of sport. In J. Maguire and K. Young, eds., *Theory, sport and society* (pp. 41–62). Oxford: Elsevier Science.

Lupton, Deborah. 2000. The social construction of medicine and the body. In G. Albrecht, R. Fitzpatrick, and S. Scrimshaw, eds., *The handbook of social studies in health and medicine* (pp. 50–63). London: Sage.

Luxton, M. 1980. *More than a labour of love: Three generations of women's work in the home*. Toronto: The Women's Press.

Lyons, B. 2002. Fallen legends were beset by life's frailties. *Denver Post* (September 29): 4C.

MacAloon, J. 1990. Steroids and the state: Dubin, melodrama, and the accomplishment of innocence. *Public Culture* 2, 41–64.

Macintosh, D. 1986. Intercollegiate athletics in Canadian universities: An historical perspective. In *The role of interuniversity athletics: A Canadian perspective* (pp. 3–7). London, ON: Sports Dynamics.

Macintosh, D., T. Bedecki, and C. Franks. 1987. *Sport and politics in Canada: Federal government involvement since 1961*. Kingston and Montreal: McGill-Queen's University Press.

MacMillan, H. L., et al. 1997. Prevalence of child physical and sexual abuse in the community: Results from the Ontario Health Supplement. *The Journal of the American Medical Association* 278:131–135.

MacNeill, M. 1996. Networks: Producing Olympic ice hockey for a national television audience. *Sociology of Sport Journal* 13 (2): 103–24.

MacNeill, M. 1998a. Sex, lies and videotape: The political and cultural economics of celebrity fitness videos. In G. Rail, ed., *Sport and postmodern times*. Albany, NY: State University of New York Press.

MacNeill, M. 1998b. Sports journalism, ethics, and Olympic athletes' rights. In L. Wenner, ed., *MediaSport* (pp. 100–15). London: Routledge.

MacNeill, M. 1999. Social marketing, gender, and the science of fitness: A case-study of ParticiPACTION campaigns. In P. White and K. Young, eds., *Sport and gender in Canada* (pp. 215–231). Don Mills, ON: Oxford University Press.

MacNeill, M. 2004. *Wrestling with identity: A case study of competing nationalisms mediating Olympic, media, sponsor, athlete, and audience relations*. Paper presented at Pre-Olympic Congress, Thessaloniki, Greece, 6–11 August.

MacNeill, M. In press. Remote control: Canadian youth, access to physical activity, and contradictory relationships with the media. In P. Donnelly and B. Kidd, eds., *Sport for all in Canada: Building on the European experience*. Toronto: Canadian Scholars' Press.

MacNeill, M., G. Knight, and P. Donnelly. 2001. Corporate training: Identity construction, preparation for the Sydney Olympic Games, and relationships between Canadian media, swimmers and sponsors. *Olympika*, 10, 1–32.

Macpherson, A., L. Rothman, and A. Howard. 2006. Body-checking rules and childhood injuries in ice hockey. *Pediatrics*, 117 (2): e143–e147.

Madison, James K., and Sarita L. Ruma. 2003. Exercise and athletic involvement as moderators of severity in adolescents with eating disorders. *Journal of Applied Sport Psychology* 15, 3: 213–222.

Maguire, Brendan. 2005. American professional wrestling: Evolution, content, and popular appeal. *Sociological Spectrum* 25, 2: 155–176.

Maguire, J. 1988. Race and position assignment in English soccer: A preliminary analysis of ethnicity and sport in Britain. *Sociology of Sport Journal* 5, 3: 257–269.

Maguire, J. 1990. More than a sporting touchdown: The making of American football in England, 1982–1990. *Sociology of Sport Journal* 7 (3): 213–37.

Maguire, J. 1994. Globalisation, sport and national identities: "The Empires Strike Back?" *Society and Leisure* 16: 293–323.

Maguire, J. 1995. Blade runners: Canadian migrants and global ice hockey trails. *Journal of Sport and Social Issues* 20 (3), 335–60.

Maguire, J. 1999. *Global sport: Identities, societies, civilizations*. Cambridge, England: Polity Press.

Maguire, J., 2004. Sport labor migration research revisited. *Journal of Sport and Social Issues* 28, 4: 477–482.

Maguire, J., ed. 2005. *Power and global sport: Zones of prestige, emulation and resistance*. London/New York: Routledge.

Maguire, J., Grant Jarvie, Louise Mansfield, and J. Bradley. 2002. *Sport worlds: A sociological perspective*. Champaign, IL: Human Kinetics.

Maguire, J., and E. Poulton. 1999. European identity politics in Euro '96: Invented tradition and national habitus codes. *International Review for the Sociology of Sport*, 34 (1): pp. 17–29.

Maguire, J., and David Stead. 2005. "Cricketers of the Empire": Cash crops, mercenaries and symbols of sporting emancipation? In Joseph Maguire, ed., *Power and global sport: Zones of prestige, emulation and resistance* (pp. 63–86). London/New York: Routledge.

Mahany, Barbara. 1999. Parents drive free time from lives of kids. *Chicago Tribune* (May 27): LIFE1.

Mahiri, Jabari. 1998. *Shooting for excellence: African American youth culture in new century schools*. New York/London: Teachers College Press (Columbia University).

Majors, Richard. 1998. Cool pose: Black masculinity and sports. In G. Sailes, ed., *African Americans in sport* (pp. 15–22). New Brunswick, NJ: Transaction.

Malcomson, Robert. W. 1984. Sports in society: A historical perspective. *British Journal of Sport History* 1, 1: 60–72.

Malloy, D. C., and Dwight H. Zakus. 2002. Ethics of drug testing in sport—an invasion of privacy justified? *Sport, Education and Society* 7, 2 (October): 203–218.

Mangan, J. A., ed. 2003. Militarism, sport, Europe: War without weapons. London/New York: Routledge.

Mannon, James M. 1997. *Measuring up: The performance ethic in American culture*. Boulder, CO: Westview Press.

Marchie, A. and D. Cusimano. 2003. Bodychecking and concussions in ice hockey: Should our youth pay the price? *Canadian Medical Association Journal*, 169 (2), pp. 123–127.

Markula, Pirkku. 1995. Firm but shapely, fit but sexy, strong but thin: The postmodern aerobicizing female bodies. *Sociology of Sport Journal* 12, 4: 424–453.

Marple, D. 1975. Analyse de la discrimination que subissent les Canadiens-français au hockey professionnel. *Mouvement* 10 (1), 7–13.

Marriott, M. 2004. Your shot, he said, distantly. *New York Times*, circuits (August 26): 1.

Marriott, M. 2005. Cyberbodies: Robo-legs. *New York Times* (June 20): F1.

Marsh, Herbert W. 1993. The effect of participation in sport during the last two years of high school. *Sociology of Sport Journal* 10, 1: 18–43.

Marsh, Herbert W., and Sabina Kleitman. 2002. Extracurricular school activities: The good, the bad, and the nonlinear. *Harvard Educational Review* 72, 4: 464–511.

Marsh, Herbert W., and Sabina Kleitman. 2003. School athletic participation: Mostly gain with little pain. *Journal of Sport and Exercise Psychology* 25, 2: 205–228.

Marsh, Peter. 1982. Social order on the British soccer terraces. *International Social Science Journal* 34, 2: 247–256.

Marsh, Peter, and A. Campbell, eds. 1982 *Aggression and violence*. Oxford, England: Basil Blackwell.

Martin, Randy, and Toby Miller, eds. 1999. *SportCult*. Minneapolis: University of Minnesota Press.

Martinek, Thomas J., and Donald R. Hellison. 1997. Fostering resiliency in underserved youth through physical activity. *Quest* 49, 1: 34–49.

Martzke, Rudy, and Reid Cherner. 2004. Channeling how to view sports. *USA Today* (August 17): 1C–2C.

Marvez, Alex. 2002. Steroid abuse grips wrestling, too. *Rocky Mountain News* (July 19): C8.

Mayeda, David Tokiharu. 1999. From model minority to economic threat: Media portrayals of major league baseball pitchers Hideo Nomo and Hideki Irabu. *Journal of Sport and Social Issues* 23, 2: 203–217.

McAll, C. 1992. English/French Canadian differences in sport participation: Comment on White and Curtis. *Sociology of Sport Journal* 9 (2), 307–13.

McCallum, Jack. 2003. Thank God it's Friday. *Sports Illustrated* 99, 12 (September 29): 40–42.

McCarthy, D., R. L. Jones, and P. Potrac. 2003. Constructing images and interpreting realities: The case of the black soccer ptelevision. *International Review for the Sociology of Sport* 38, 2: 217–238.

McChesney, Robert W. 1999. The new global media: It's a small world of big conglomerates. *The Nation* 269, 18: 11–15.

McClelland, J. 2006. *Body and mind: Sport in Europe from the Roman Empire to the Renaissance*. London: Routledge.

McCloy, C. 2002. Hosting international sport events in Canada: Planning for facility legacies. Proceedings of the Sixth International Symposium on Olympic Research, London, ON: pp. 135–142.

McCloy, C. 2006. The role and impact of Canadian federal sport hosting policies in securing amateur sport legacies: Case studies of the past four decades. Unpublished doctoral thesis. Toronto: University of Toronto.

McClung, Lisa R., and Elaine M. Blinde. 1998. Negotiation of the gendered ideology of sport: Experiences of women intercollegiate athletes. Paper presented at the annual conference of the North American Society for the Sociology of Sport, Las Vegas (November).

McCormack, Jane B., and Laurence Chalip. 1988. Sport as socialization: A critique of methodological premises. *Social Science Journal* 25, 1: 83–92.

McCullagh, Ciaran. 2002. *Media power*. New York: Palgrave.

McGarry, Karen. 2005. Mass media and gender identity in high performance Canadian figure skating. *The Sport Journal* 8, 1. Online: www.thesportjournal.org (retrieved July 14, 2005).

McGregor, R. 2003. Temples of gloom: Big arenas haven't been the panacea hockey clubs had hoped for. *Globe and Mail*, 9 January, p. A2.

McGregor, R. 2005. An unexpected partner helps Canada's students improve their fit ness. *Globe and Mail*, October 7.

McHale, James P., Penelope G. Vindon, Loren Bush, Derek Richer, David Shaw, and Brienne Smith. 2005. Patterns of personal and social adjustment among sport-involved and noninvolved urban middle-school children. *Sociology of Sport Journal* 22, 2: 119–136.

McKay, Jim. 1997. *Managing gender: Affirmative action and organizational power in Australian, Canadian, and New Zealand sport*. Albany: State University of New York Press.

McKay, Jim. 1999. Gender and organizational power in Canadian sport. In P. White and K. Young, eds., *Sport and gender in Canada* (pp. 197–215). Don Mills, ON: Oxford University Press.

McKenzie, Bette. 1999. Retiring from the sideline: Building new identities on new terms. In J. Coakley and P. Donnelly, eds., *Inside sports* (pp. 232–236). London: Routledge.

McNeal, Ralf B., Jr. 1995. Extracurricular activities and high school dropouts. *Sociology of Education* 64, 1: 62–81.

McShane, Larry. 1999. Winner take all (Associated Press). *Colorado Springs Gazette* (July 4): LIFE4.

McTeer, W. 1987. Intercollegiate athletics and student life: Two studies in the Canadian case. *Arena Review*, 2: 94–100.

McTeer, W., and J. Curtis. 1999. Intercollegiate sport involvement and academic attainment: A follow-up study. *Avante* 5 (1), 39–55.

Meisel, J., and V. Lemieux. 1972. Amateur hockey associations. In *Ethnic relations in Canadian voluntary associations* (pp. 55–70), Documents of the Royal Commission on Bilingualism and Biculturalism—13. Ottawa: Supply and Services.

Mendelsohn, Daniel. 2004. What Olympic ideal? *New York Times Magazine* (August 8). Online: www.nytimes.com/2004/08/08/magazine/WLN130551.html

Mennesson, C. 2000. "Hard" women and "soft" women. *International Review for the Sociology of Sport* 35 (1): 21–33.

Merrill, Dave. 2002. Skateboarding grinds out urban revival. *USA Today* (July 30): 6C–7C.

Merron, Jeff. 1999. Running on empty. *SportsJones* 3 (June). Online: www.sportsjones.com/running.htm

Messner, M. A. 1990. When bodies are weapons: Masculinity and violence in sport. *International Review for the Sociology of Sport* 25 (3): 203–19.

Messner, M. A. 1992. *Power at play*. Boston: Beacon Press.

Messner, M. A. 1996. Studying up on sex. *Sociology of Sport Journal* 13, 3: 221–237.

Messner, M. A. 2002. *Taking the field: women, men, and sports*. Minneapolis: University of Minnesota Press.

Messner, M. A., Darnell Hunt, and Michele Dunbar. 1999. *Boys to men: Sports media messages about masculinity*. Oakland, CA: Children Now.

Messner, M. A., and Mark A. Stevens. 2002. Scoring without consent: Confronting male athletes' violence against women. In M. Gatz, M. A. Messner, and S. J. Ball-Rokeach, eds., *Paradoxes of youth and sport* (pp. 225–240). Albany: State University of New York Press.

Metcalfe, A. 1978. *Working class physical recreation in Montreal*, 1860–1895. Working papers in the sociological study of sports and leisure 1 (2): 1, 12–14002E

Metcalfe, A. 1987. *Canada learns to play: The emergence of organized sport, 1807–1914*. Toronto: McClelland and Stewart.

Metcalfe, A. 1989. The evolution of organized physical recreation in Montreal, 1840–1895. In M. Mott, ed., *Sports in Canada: Historical readings* (pp. 130–155). Toronto: Copp Clark Pittman.

Meyer, Barbara B. 1988. The college experience: Female athletes and nonathletes. Paper presented at the North American Society for the Sociology of Sport Conference, Cincinnati.

Meyer, Barbara B. 1990. From idealism to actualization: The academic performance of female collegiate athletes. *Sociology of Sport Journal* 7, 1: 44–57.

Meyer, Jeremy. 2002. Ward's fire within. *Denver Post* (July 14): 1C, 12C.

Midol, N., and G. Broyer. 1995. Toward an anthropological analysis of new sport cultures: The case of whiz sports in France. *Sociology of Sport Journal* 12, 2: 204–212.

Mihoces, Gary. 2005. Injured skaters struggle in world championships. *USA Today* (March 15): 7C. Online: www.usatoday.com/sports/olympics/winter/2005-03-14-skating-worlds_x.htm

Miller, Kathleen E., Grace M. Barnes, Donald F. Sabo, Merrill J. Melnick, and Michael P. Farrell. 2002. Anabolic-androgenic steroid use and other adolescent problem behaviors: Rethinking the male athlete assumption. *Sociological Perspectives* 45, 4: 467–490.

Miller, K., G. Barnes, J. Hoffman, M. Melnick, M. Farrell, and D. Sabo, D. 2003. Jocks, gender, race, and adolescent problem drinking. *Journal of Drug Education*, 33 (4): 445–462.

Miller, K., M. Melnick, G. Barnes, M. Farrell, and D. Sabo. 2005. Untangling the links among athletic involvement, gender, race, and adolescent academic outcomes. *Sociology of Sport Journal*, 22 (2): 178–193.

Miller, K., D. Sabo, M. Farrell, G. Barnes, and M. Melnick. 1998. Athletic participation and sexual behavior in adolescents: The different world of boys and girls. *Journal of Health and Social Behavior* 39, 108–123.

Miller, K., D. Sabo, M. Farrell, G. Barnes, and M. Melnick. 1999. Sports, sexual behavior, contraceptive use, and pregnancy among female and male high school students: Testing cultural resource theory. *Sociology of Sport Journal* 16, 4: 366–387.

Miller, K., D. Sabo, M. Melnick, M. Farrell, and G. Barnes. 2000. *The Women's Sports Foundation report: Health risks and the teen athlete*. East Meadow, NY: Women's Sports Foundation.

Miller, Toby, Geoffrey Lawrence, Jim McKay, and David Rowe. 2001. *Globalization and sport: Playing the world*. London: Sage.

Miller, Toby, David Rowe, Jim McKay, and Geoffrey Lawrence. 2003. The over-production of U.S. sports and the new international division of cultural labor. *International Review for the Sociology of Sport* 38, 4: 427–440.

Mills, D. 1998. *Sport in Canada: Everybody's business—leadership, partnership and accountability*. Report of the Standing Committee on Canadian Heritage, Sub-Committee on the Study of Sport in Canada.

Mills, James, and Paul Dimeo. 2003. "When gold is fired it shines": Sport, the imagination and the body in colonial and postcolonial India. In John Bale and Mike Cronin, eds., *Sport and postcolonialism* (pp. 107–122). Oxford, England/New York: Berg.

Miracle, Andrew W., and C. Roger Rees. 1994. *Lessons of the locker room: The myth of school sports*. Amherst, NY: Prometheus Books.

Moore, David Leon. 2002. Parents pay dearly to coach kids for stardom. *USA Today* (July 26): 1A–2A. Online: www.usatoday.com/educate/college/firstyear/casestudies/20040106-coaching.pdf

Morris, G. S. D., and James Stiehl. 1989. *Changing kids' games*. Champaign, IL: Human Kinetics.

Morris, Jenny. 1996. Introduction. In J. Morris, ed., *Encounters with strangers: Feminism and disability* (pp. 1–12). London: Women's Free Press.

Morrow, D. 1986. A case study in amateur conflict: The athletic war in Canada, 1906–1908. *British Journal of Sports History* 3: 173–90.

Morrow, D. 1988. The Knights of the Snowshoe: A study of the evolution of organized sport in nineteenth century Montreal. *Journal of Sport History*, 15 (1): 5–40.

Morton, D. 1983. *A short history of Canada*. Edmonton: Hurtig Publishers.

Mrozek, D. 1987. Games and sport in the Arctic. *Journal of the West* 26 (1), 34–46.

Munro, J. 1970. *A proposed sport policy for Canadians*. Ottawa: Queen's Printer.

Murphy, Geraldine. M., Al J. Petipas, and Britton W. Brewer. 1996. Identity foreclosure, athletic identity, and career maturity in intercollegiate athletics. *The Sport Psychologist* 10, 3: 239–246.

Murphy, Patrick, John Williams, and Eric Dunning. 1990. *Football on trial: Spectator violence and development in the world of football*. London: Routledge.

Murphy, Shawn. 1999. *The cheers and the tears: A healthy alternative to the dark side of youth sports today*. San Francisco: Jossey-Bass.

Myers, J. 2000. *Afraid of the dark: What whites and blacks need to know about each other*. Chicago: Lawrence Hill Books.

Nack, William, and Lester Munson. 1995. Sports' dirty secret. *Sports Illustrated* 83, 5 (July 31): 62–75.

Nack, William, and L. Munson. 2000. Out of control. *Sports Illustrated* 93, 4 (July 24): 86–95.

Nack, William, and Don Yaeger. 1999. Every parent's nightmare. *Sports Illustrated* 91, 10 (September 13): 40–53.

Nakamura, Y. 2002. "Beyond the hijab: Female Muslims and physical activity". *Women in Sport and Physical Activity Journal*, 11 (2), 21–48.

Nakamura, Y. 2005. The Samurai sword cuts both ways: A transnational analysis of Japanese and US media representations of Ichiro. *International Review for the Sociology of Sport*, 40 (4), 467–480.

Nash, B., and A. Zullo. 1986. *The baseball hall of shame* (2). New York NY: Simon and Schuster.

National Forum on Health. 1997. *Canada health action: Building on the legacy*. Ottawa: Public Works and Government Services.

Naughton, J. 1996. Alcohol abuse by athletes poses big problems for colleges. *The Chronicle of Higher Education* 43 (4): A47–A48.

Nauright, J., and P. White. 1996. Nostalgia, community, and nation: Professional hockey and football in Canada. *Avante* 2 (3), 24–41.

Naylor, D. 2002. CFL strike is going nowhere. *Globe and Mail*, August 15, p. S3.

NBC/USA Network. 2005. Homosexuality and sports. Full-survey results online at http://sportsillustrated.cnn.com/2005/magazine/04/12/survey.expanded/; discussion and partial results in Wertheim, 2005 and Smith, 2005.

Neinas, Chuck. 2003. *2003 AFCA player survey*. American Football Coaches Association. Online: www.afca.com/lev1.cfm/88 (retrieved September 10, 2005).

Nelson, M. B. 1991. *Are we winning yet?* New York: Random House.

Nelson, M. B. 1994. *The stronger women get, the more men love football: Sexism and the American culture of sports*. New York: Harcourt Brace.

Nelson, M. B. 1998. *Embracing victory: Life lessons in competition and compassion*. New York: Morrow.

Newbery, Liz. 2004. Hegemonic gender identity and outward bound: resistance and re-inscription? *Women in Sport and Physical Activity Journal* 13, 1: 36–49.

Newfield, Jack. 2001. The shame of boxing. *The Nation* 273, 15: 13–22.

Newsweek. 2004. Perspectives: Entertainment. *Newsweek* 143, 1 (December 29–January 5): 122.

Neyer, Rob. 2000. A matter of size. *Scientific American* 11, 3: 14–15.

NHANES—National Health and Nutrition Examination Survey. 2002. *Prevalence of overweight and obesity among adults: United States, 1999–2000*. Hyattsville, MD: National Center for Health Statistics.

Nichol, Jon P., Patricia Coleman, and B. T. Williams. 1993. *Injuries in sport and exercise: Main report*. London: Sports Council.

Nixon, H. L. II. 1993a. Accepting the risks and pain of injury in sport: Mediated cultural influences on playing hurt. *Sociology of Sport Journal* 10 (2): 183–96.

Nixon, H. L. II. 1993b. A social network analysis of influences on athletes to play with pain and injuries. *Journal of Sport & Social Issues* 16 (2): 127–35.

Nixon, H. L. II. 1994a. Coaches' views of risk, pain, and injury in sport, with special reference to gender differences. *Sociology of Sport Journal* 11 (1): 79–87.

Nixon, H. L. II. 1994b. Social pressure, social support, and help seeking for pain and injuries in college sports networks. *Journal of Sport & Social Issues* 18 (4): 340–55.

Nixon, H. L. II. 1996a. Explaining pain and injury attitudes and experiences in sport in terms of gender, race, and sports status factors. *Journal of Sport & Social Issues* 20 (1): 33–44.

Nixon, H. L. II. 1996b. The relationship of friendship networks, sports experiences, and gender to expressed pain thresholds. *Sociology of Sport Journal* 13 (1): 78–86.

Nixon, H. L. II. 2000. Sport and disability. In J. Coakley and E. Dunning, eds., *Handbook of sport studies* (pp. 422–438). London: Sage.

Noll, R., and A. Zimbalist, eds. 1997. *Sports, jobs, and taxes*. Washington, DC: Brookings Institution.

Noonan, David. 2003. High on testosterone. *Newsweek* 142, 13 (September 29): 50–51.

NPR. 1996. Morning edition. *National Public Radio* (August 1), report from Atlanta.

O'Brien, Richard. 1992. Lord gym. *Sports Illustrated* 77, 4, (July 27): 46–52.

Office of the Commissioner of Official Languages (OCOL). 2000. *Official languages in the Canadian sports system*, vols. 1 and 2. Ottawa: Minister of Public Works and Government Services.

Office of the Commissioner of Official Languages (OCOL). 2003. *Official languages in the Canadian sport system: Follow-Up*. Ottawa: Minister of Public Works and Government Services.

Offord, D., E. Lipman, and E. Duku. 1998. *Sports, the arts and community programs: Rates and correlates of participation*. Applied Research Branch, Strategic Policy, Human Resources Development Canada. October (W-98-18E).

Oglesby, Carole, and Diana Schrader. 2000. Where is the white in the Rainbow Coalition? In D. Brooks and R. Althouse, eds., *Racism in college athletics: The African-American athlete's experience* (pp. 279–293). Morgantown, WV: Fitness Information Technology.

Okihiro, N. 1984. Extracurricular participation, educational destinies and early job outcomes. In N. Theberge and P. Donnelly, eds., *Sport and the sociological imagination* (pp. 338–49). Fort Worth: Texas Christian University Press.

Okubu, Hideaki. 2004. *Local identity and sport: Historical study of integration and differentiation*. Sankt Augustin, Germany: Academica Verlag.

Oliver, Michael. 1996. *Understanding disability: From theory to practice*. New York: St. Martin's Press.

Omi, Michael, and Howard Winant. 1994. *Racial formation in the United States*. New York/London: Routledge.

Orlick, T. 1978. *The cooperative sports & games book: Challenge without competition*. New York: Pantheon Books.

Orlick, T., and C. Botterill. 1975. *Every kid can win*. Chicago: Nelson-Hall Co.

Osterland, Andrew. 1995. Field of nightmares. *Financial World* (February 14): 105–107.

Ozanian, Michael K. 1995. Following the money. *Financial World* 164, 4 (February 14): 27–31.

Palmer, B. 1979. *A culture in conflict: Skilled workers and industrial capitalism in Hamilton, Ontario, 1860–1914*. Montreal and Kingston: McGill-Queen's University Press.

Palmer, J. 2000. Bad call. In P. Donnelly, ed., *Taking sport seriously: Social issues in Canadian sport*, 2nd Edition (pp. 155–57). Toronto: Thomson Educational Publishing.

Paraschak, V. 1982. The heterotransplantation of organized sport: A Northwest Territories Case Study. In B. Kidd, ed., *Proceedings of the 5th Canadian Symposium on the History of Sport and Physical Education*. Toronto: School of Physical Education, University of Toronto.

Paraschak, V. 1989. Native sports history: Pitfalls and promises. *Canadian Journal of History of Sport* 20 (1), 57–68.

Paraschak, V. 1995. The native sport and recreation program, 1972–1981: Patterns of resistance, patterns of reproduction. *Canadian Journal of History of Sport* (December): 1–18.

Paraschak, V. 1996. An examination of sport for Aboriginal females on the Six Nations Reserve, Ontario, from 1968 to 1980. In C. Miller and P. Chuchryk, eds., *Women of the First Nations: Power, wisdom, and strength* (pp. 83–96). Winnipeg: University of Manitoba Press.

Paraschak, V. 1997. Variations in race relations: Sporting events for Native Peoples in Canada. *Sociology of Sport Journal* 14, 1: 1–21.

Paraschak, V. 2007. Doing race, doing gender: First Nations, "sport," and gender relations. In P. White and K. Young, eds., *Sport and gender in Canada*, 2nd Edition (pp. 137–154). Don Mills, ON: Oxford University Press.

Parcels, J. 2000. *Straight facts about making it in pro hockey*. Online: www.nepeanhockey.on.ca/Docs/MakingIt.htm

Park, R. 1950. *Race and culture*. Glencoe: The Free Press.

Parrish, Paula. 2002. The height of gaining an edge. *Rocky Mountain News* (September 21): 1B, 12B–13B.

Pastore, Donna L., Sue Inglis, and Karen E. Danylchuk. 1996. Retention factors in coaching and athletic management: Differences by gender, position, and geographic location. *Journal of Sport and Social Issues* 20, 4: 427–441.

Patrick, Dick. 2002. U.S. Anti-Doping Agency willing to administer testing for baseball. *USA Today* (June 14): 6C.

Patrick, Dick. 2005. USOC lobbies for anti-doping agency funds. *USA Today* (May 25): 7C.

Patterson, O. 2002. Beyond compassion: selfish reasons for being unselfish. *Daedalus* (Winter): 26–38.

Pelak, Cynthia Fabrizio. 2002. Women's collective identity formation in sports: A case study from women's ice hockey. *Gender and Society* 16, 1: 93–114.

Pelak, Cynthia Fabrizio. 2005. Athletes as agents of change: An examination of shifting race relations within women's netball in post-apartheid South Africa. *Sociology of Sport Journal* 22, 1: 59–77.

Pennington, Bill. 2004. Reading, writing and corporate sponsorships. *New York Times*, section A (October 18): 1.

Pennington, Bill. 2005. Doctors see a big rise in injuries for young athletes. *New York Times*, section A (February 22): 1.

Peretti-Watel, Patrick, Valérie Guagliardo, Pierre Verger, Patrick Mignon, Jacques Pruvost, and Yolande Obadia. 2004a. Attitudes toward doping and recreational drug use among French elite student-athletes. *Sociology of Sport Journal* 21, 1: 1–17.

Peretti-Watel, Patrick, Valérie Guagliardo, Pierre Verger, Jacques Pruvost, Patrick Mignon, and Yolande Obadia. 2004b. Risky behaviours among young elite-student-athletes: results from a pilot survey in South-Eastern France. *International Review for the Sociology of Sport* 39, 2: 233–244.

Perman, Stacy. 1998. The master blasts the board. *Time* (January 19): 61.

Perrottet, Tone. 2004. *The naked Olympics: The true story of the ancient games*. New York: Random House.

Perrucci, Robert, and Earl Wysong. 2003. *The new class society*. Lanham, MD: Rowman and Littlefield.

Peters, K. 2008. Camp Tiger-Cat isn't for Boy Scouts. *Hamilton Spectator*, 31 May.

Petersen, Alan. 2007. *The body in question: A socio-cultural approach*. London/New York: Routledge.

Petrecca, Laura. 2005. Marketers tackle participants in fantasy football. *USA Today* (August 25): 3B.

Pettavino, P., and P. Brenner. 1999. More than just a game. *Peace Review* 11, 4: 523–530.

Picard, A. 2003. High-fees slam-dunk children's basketball. *Globe and Mail*, 13 May, p. A9.

Pike, Elizabeth C. J. 2004. Risk, pain, and injury: "A natural thing in rowing"? In Kevin Young, ed., *Sporting bodies, damaged selves: Sociological studies of sports-related injury* (pp. 151–162). Amsterdam: Elsevier.

Pike, Elizabeth C. J., and Joseph A. Maguire. 2003. Injury in women's sport: Classifying key elements of "risk encounters." *Sociology of Sport Journal* 20, 3: 232–251.

Pilz, Gunther A. 1996. Social factors influencing sport and violence: On the "problem" of football hooliganism in Germany. *International Review for Sociology of Sport* 31, 1: 49–68.

Pipe, Andrew. 1998. Reviving ethics in sports. *Physician and Sportsmedicine* 26, 6 (June): 39–40.

Pitter, R. 1996. The state and sport development in Alberta: A struggle for public status. *Sociology of Sport Journal* 13 (1), 31–50.

Pitter, R. 2004. Midnight basketball: Avoiding the hazards of assimilative reform. In B. Kidd and B. Phillips, eds., *Research on community safety: From enforcement and prevention to civic engagement* (pp. 170–181). University of Toronto: Centre of Criminology.

Pluto, Terry. 1995. *Falling from grace: Can pro basketball be saved?* New York: Simon and Schuster.

Poli, R., and Ravenel, L. 2006. *Annual Review of the European Players' Labour Market*. University of Neuchatel: Centre Internationale d'Etude du Sport. Online: www.eurofootplayers.org

Polsky, S. 1998. Winning medicine: professional sports team doctors' conflicts of interest. *Journal of Contemporary Health Law Policy* (IDD) 14, 2 (Spring): 503–529.

Ponic, P. 2000. A herstory, a legacy: The Canadian Amateur Sports Branch's Women's Program. *Avante* 6 (2), 51–63.

Pooley, J. 1981. Ethnic soccer clubs in Milwaukee: A study in assimilation. In M. Hart and S. Birrell, eds., *Sport in the sociocultural process* (pp. 430–447). Dubuque, Iowa: Wm. C. Brown.

Poppen, Julie. 2004. Pro performance. *Rocky Mountain News* (March 31): 6B.

Porterfield, Kitty. 1999. Late to the line: Starting sport competition as an adult. In J. Coakley and P. Donnelly, eds., *Inside sports* (pp. 37–45). London: Routledge.

Poulton, Emma. 2004. Mediated patriot games: The construction and representation of national identities in the British television production of Euro '96. *International Review for the Sociology of Sport* 39, 4: 437–455.

President's Council on Physical Fitness and Sports. 1997. *Physical activity and sport in the lives of girls*. Minneapolis: Center for Research on Girls and Women in Sport, University of Minnesota.

Preves, Sharon E. 2005. *Intersex and identity: The contested self*. New Brunswick, NJ: Rutgers University Press.

Price, S. L. 1997. What ever happened to the white athlete? *Sports Illustrated* 87, 23 (December 8): 31–55.

Price, S. L. 2004. Flag jumper. *Sports Illustrated* 101, 8 (August 30.): 54–56.

Price, S. L. 2005. The sprinter. *Sports Illustrated* 102, 21 (May 23): 52–61.

Pronger, B. 1990a *The arena of masculinity: Sports, homosexuality, and the meaning of sex*. New York: St. Martin's Press.

Pronger, B. 1990b. Gay jocks: A phenomenology of gay men in athletics. In M. Messner and D. Sabo, eds., *Sport, men and the gender order* (pp. 141–52). Champaign, IL: Human Kinetics.

Pronger, B. 1995. Rendering the body: The implicit lessons of gross anatomy. *Quest* 47 (4): 427–46.

Pronger, B. 1999. Fear and trembling: Homophobia in men's sport. In P. White and K. Young, eds., *Sport and gender in Canada* (pp. 182–97). Don Mills, Ontario: Oxford University Press.

Pronger, B. 2002. *Body fascism: Salvation in the technology of physical fitness*. Toronto: University of Toronto Press.

Pyette, R. 2002. Mustangs assigned their corrals. *London Free Press*, 17 May.

Raboin, S. 1998. A family torn apart. *USA Today*, 9 December, 1C–2C.

Raboin, S. 1999. Bela is back on U.S. team. *USA Today* (November 16): 1A–2A.

Rail, G., V. Gaston, and J. Harvey. 1995. *Quebec 2002 and the confrontation of nationalisms*. Paper presented at the annual meeting of the North American Society for the Sociology of Sport, Sacramento, CA.

Rains, P. 1984. The production of fairness: Officiating in the National Hockey League. *Sociology of Sport Journal* 1 (2): 150–62.

Real, Michael R. 1996. The postmodern Olympics: Technology and the commodification of the Olympic movement. *Quest* 48, 1: 9–24.

Real, Michael R. 1998. MediaSport: Technology and the commodification of postmodern sport. In L. A. Wenner, ed., *MediaSport* (pp. 14–26). London/New York: Routledge.

Redmond, G. 1989. Some aspects of organized sport and leisure in nineteenth-century Canada. In M. Mott, ed., *Sports in Canada: Historical readings* (pp. 81–106). Toronto: Copp Clark Pittman.

Rees, C. Roger, and Andrew W. Miracle. 2000. Sport and education. In J. Coakley and E. Dunning, eds., *Handbook of sports studies* (pp. 291–308). London: Sage.

Regroupement des organismes nationaux de loisir du Québec, Secteur Sport. 1983. Rapport de la Conférence de presse Dénoncant l'Unilinguisme Anglais dans les Organismes Canadiens de Sport.

Reid, E. 1997. My body, my weapon, my shame. *Gentlemen's Quarterly* (September), 361–367.

Reid, S. M. 1996. The selling of the Games. *Denver Post* (July 21) 4BB.

Reilly, Rick. 2004. The silent treatment. *Sports Illustrated* 101, 20 (November 22): 144.

Reilly, Rick. 2005. Half the size, twice the man. *Sports Illustrated* 103, 13 (October 3): 90.

Rice, Ron (with David Fleming). 2005. Moment of impact. *ESPN The Magazine* 8.11 (June 6): 82–83.

Riesman, David, and Reuel Denny. 1951. Football in America: A study of cultural diffusion. *American Quarterly* (Winter): 302–325.

Rigauer, Bero. 2000. Marxist theories. In J. Coakley and E. Dunning, eds., *Handbook of sports studies* (pp. 28–47). London: Sage.

Rinehart, R. E. 1998. *Players all: Performances in contemporary sport*. Bloomington: Indiana University Press.

Rinehart, R. E. 2000. Arriving sport: Alternatives to formal sports. In J. Coakley and E. Dunning, eds., *Handbook of sports studies* (pp. 504–519). London: Sage.

Rinehart, R. E., and C. Grenfell. 1999. *Icy relations: Parental involvement in youth figure skating*. Paper presented at the annual conference of the North American Society for the Sociology of Sport, Cleveland, OH (November).

Rinehart, R. E., and C. Grenfell. 2002. BMX spaces: Children's grass roots' courses and corporate-sponsored tracks. *Sociology of Sport Journal* 19, 3: 302–314.

Rinehart, R. E., and S. Sydnor, eds. 2003. *To the extreme: Alternative sports, inside and out*. Albany: State University of New York Press.

Rintala, Jan, and Judith Bischoff. 1997. Persistent resistance: Leadership positions for women in Olympic sport governing bodies. *OLYMPIKA: The International Journal of Olympic Studies* 6, 1–24.

Risman, Barbara, and Pepper Schwartz. 2002. After the sexual revolution: Gender politics in teen dating. *Contexts* 1, 1: 16–24.

Robertson, H.-j. 2004. Doing it daily. *Phi Delta Kappan*, 85 (5), 411–412.

Robidoux, M. 2001. *Men at play: A working understanding of professional hockey*. Montreal and Kingston: McGill-Queen's University Press.

Robidoux, M. 2006. The nonsense of Native American sport imagery: Reclaiming a past that never was. *International Review for the Sociology of Sport*, 41 (2), 201–219.

Robidoux, M., and P. Trudel. 2006. Hockey Canada and the bodychecking debate in minor hockey. In D. Whitson and R. Gruneau, eds., *Artificial ice: Hockey, culture, and commerce* (pp. 101–122). Peterborough, ON: Broadview Press.

Robinson, L. 1995. Indigenous Games offer new goal to girl athletes. *NOW*, March 9–15, p. 31.

Robinson, L. 1997. Canoe race gracefully protests Hydro devastation. In P. Donnelly, ed., *Taking sport seriously: Social issues in Canadian sport* (pp. 342–44). Toronto: Thomson Educational Publishing.

Robinson, L. 1998. *Crossing the line: Violence and sexual assault in Canada's national sport*. Toronto: McClelland and Stewart.

Robinson, L. 2000a. Games boys play. In P. Donnelly, ed., *Taking sport seriously: Social issues in Canadian sport*, 2nd Edition (pp. 79–83). Toronto: Thomson Educational Publishing.

Robinson, L. 2000b. Prairie priorities on thin ice. In P. Donnelly, ed., *Taking sport seriously: Social issues in Canadian sport*, 2nd Edition (pp. 114–15). Toronto: Thomson Educational Publishing.

Robinson, L. 2002a *Black tights: Women, sport and sexuality*. Toronto: HarperCollins.

Robinson, L. 2002b. *The nightmare of residential school: A story of ten indigenous runners in Canada*. Paper presented at the Playing the F+Game Conference, Copenhagen, Denmark, 9–14 November.

Romanow, R. 2002. *Building on values: The future of health care in Canada* (Ch. V). Ottawa: Government of Canada Publications.

Rosentraub, M. 1997. *Major League losers: The real cost of sports and who's paying for them*. New York: Basic Books.

Roth, Amanda, and Susan A. Basow. 2004. Femininity, sports, and feminism: Developing a theory of physical liberation. *Journal of Sport and Social Issues* 28, 3: 245–265.

Rowe, D. 2004a. *Sport, culture and the media: the unruly trinity* (2nd ed.). Maidenhead, Berkshire: Open University Press.

Rowe, D., ed. 2004b. *Sport, culture and the media: Critical readings*. Maidenhead, Berkshire: Open University Press.

Rowe, D., G. Lawrence, Toby Miller, and Jim McKay. 1994. Global sport?: Core concern and peripheral vision. *Media, Culture & Society* 16, 661–75.

Rowe, D., J. McKay, and T. Miller. 1998. Come together: Sport, nationalism, and the media image. In L. A. Wenner, ed., *MediaSport* (pp. 119–133). London/New York: Routledge.

Rubenstein, L. 2003. Most Canadians at U.S. colleges see dreams turn to nightmares. *Globe and Mail*, 18 January, p. S5.

Russo, R. D. 1999. Root, root, root for the home team. *Denver Post* (June 14): D1, D7.

Ryan, Joan. 1995. *Little girls in pretty boxes: The making and breaking of elite gymnasts and figure skaters*. New York: Doubleday.

Sabo, Don, and Sue Curry Jansen. 1998. Prometheus unbound: Constructions of masculinity in sports media. In L. A. Wenner, ed., *MediaSport* (pp. 202–20). London: Routledge.

Sabo, D., Kathleen Miller, Michael Farrell, Grace Barnes, and Merrill Melnick. 1998. *The Women's Sports Foundation report: Sport and teen pregnancy*. East Meadows, NY: Women's Sport Foundation.

Sabo, D., K. Miller, M. Melnick, M. Farrell, and G. Barnes. 2005. High school athletic participation and adolescent suicide: A nationwide study. *International Review for the Sociology of Sport* 40, 1: 5–23.

Sabo, D., K. Miller, M. Melnick, and Leslie Heywood. 2004. *Her life depends on it: Sport, physical activity, and the health and well-being of American girls*. East Meadow, NY: Women's Sport Foundation.

Sachs, Carolyn J., and Lawrence D. Chu. 2000. The association between professional football games and domestic violence in Los Angeles County. *Journal of Interpersonal Violence* 15: 1192–1201.

Safai, P. 2001. Healing the body in the 'culture of risk,' pain and injury: Negotiations between clinicians and injured athletes in Canadian competitive intercollegiate sport. Unpublished Master's thesis. Toronto: University of Toronto.

Safai, P. 2002. Boys behaving badly: Popular literature on the misbehaviour of male team sport athletes in North America. *International Review for the Sociology of Sport* 37 (1): 97–102.

Safai, P. 2003. Healing the body in the "culture of risk": Examining the negotiation of treatment between sport medicine clinicians and injured athletes in Canadian intercollegiate sport. *Sociology of Sport Journal* 20, 2: 127–146.

Sage, G. H. 1996. Patriotic images and capitalist profit: Contradictions of professional team sports licensed merchandise. *Sociology of Sport Journal* 13, 1: 1–11.

Sage, G. H. 1998. *Power and ideology in American sport: A critical perspective*. Champaign, IL: Human Kinetics.

Sage, G. H. 1999. Justice do it! The Nike transnational advocacy network: Organization, collective actions, and outcomes. *Sociology of Sport Journal* 16, 3: 206–235.

Sam, Michael P. 2003. What's the big idea? Reading the rhetoric of a national sport policy process. *Sociology of Sport Journal* 20, 3: 189–213.

SAMHSA (Substance Abuse and Mental Health Administration). 2002. *The 2000 national household survey on drug abuse: Team sports participation and substance use among youths*. Rockville, MD: SAMHSA. Online: http://www.DrugAbuse Statistics.samhsa.gov

Sammond, Nicholas, ed. 2005. *Steel chair to the head: The pleasure and pain of professional wrestling*. Durham, NC: Duke University Press.

Sapolsky, Robert M. 2000. It's not all in the genes. *Newsweek* 135, 15 (April 10): 68.

Saporito, Bill. 2004. Why fans and players are playing so rough. *Time* 164, 23 (December 6): 30–34.

Sato, Daisuke. 2005. Sport and identity in Tunisia. *International Journal of Sport and Health Science* 3: 27–34. Online: www.shobix.co.jp/ijshs/tempfiles/journal/3/20040072.pdf

Saunders, Patrick. 2005. NFL policy on drugs questioned. *The Denver Post* (April 12): 5D.

Scanlan, L. 2002. *Grace under fire: The state of our sweet and savage game*. Toronto: Penguin Canada.

Schaller, Bob. 2005. Toni Davis. Online: www.blackathletesportsnetwork.net/artman/publish/article_0510.shtml (retrieved December 3, 2005).

Scheerder, Jeroen, Bart Vanreusel, Marijke Taks, and Roland Renson. 2002. Social sports stratification in Flanders, 1969–1999: Intergenerational reproduction of social inequalities? *International Review for the Sociology of Sport* 37, 2: 219–246.

Schefter, Adam. 2003. Working through the pain. *Denver Post* (December 7): 1J, 6J.

Scheinin, Richard. 1994. *Field of screams: The dark underside of America's national pastime*. New York: Norton.

Scher, J. 1993. Mr. Dirty. *Sports Illustrated* 78 (8): 40–42.

Scherer, J. 2001. Globalization and the construction of local particularities: a case study of the Winnipeg Jets. *Sociology of Sport Journal*, 18 (3), 205–230.

Schilling, Mary Lou. 1997. Socialization, retirement, and sports. Online essay and links: http://edweb6.educ.msu.edu/kin866/resschilling1.htm (retrieved June 2005).

Schimmel, Kimberly S. 2000. Take me out to the ball game: The transformation of production-consumption relations in professional team sport. In C. L. Harrington and D. D. Bielby, eds., *Cultural production and consumption: Readings in popular culture* (pp. 36–52). Oxford, England: Blackwell.

Schimmel, Kimberly S. 2002. The political economy of place: Urban and sport studies perspectives. In J. Maguire and K. Young, eds., *Theory, sport and society* (pp. 335–353). Oxford, England: JAI (Elsevier Science).

Schimmel, K. 2006. Deep play: Sports mega-events and urban social conditions in the USA. *The Sociological Review*, 54 (2), 160–174.

Schimmel, K., Alan G. Ingham, and Jeremy W. Howell. 1993. Professional team sport and the American city: Urban politics and franchise relocations. In A. G. Ingham and J. W. Loy, eds., *Sport in social development* (pp. 211–244). Champaign, IL: Human Kinetics.

Schultz, B. 1999. The disappearance of child-directed activities. *Journal of Physical Education, Recreation and Dance* 70, 5: 9–10.

Seeley, Morgan, and Genevieve Rail. 2004. Youth with disabilities: Rethinking discourses of the "healthy" body. Paper presented at the annual meeting of the North American Society for the Sociology of Sport, Tucson, Arizona (November).

Seeley, J. R., R. A. Sim, and E. W. Loosley. 1956. *Crestwood Heights: A Study of the Culture of Suburban Life*. New York: Basic Books.

Seltzer, R., and W. Glass. 1991. International politics and judging in Olympic skating events: 1968–1988. *Journal of Sport Behavior* 14, 3: 189–200.

Sernau, Scott. 2005. *Worlds apart: Social inequalities in a global economy*. Thousand Oaks, CA: Pine Forge Press.

Sewart, James. 1987. The commodification of sport. *International Review for the Sociology of Sport* 22, 3: 171–192.

Sewell, J. 2000. "Hollowing out the core: How city money is flowing from downtown to the suburbs." *Eye*. Online: www.eye.ney/eye/issue/issue_03.16.00/news/citystate.php

Shakib, Sohaila. 2003. Female basketball participation: Negotiating the conflation of peer status and gender status from childhood through puberty. *American Behavioral Scientist* 46, 10: 1404–1422.

Shaw, Mark. 2002. Board with sports. Paper written in Introductory Sociology, University of Colorado, Colorado Springs, spring semester.

Sheil, Pat. 2000. Shed a tear or two . . . or else! Online: www.abc.net.au/paralympics/features/s201108.htm

Shields, David L. L., and Brenda J. L. Bredemeier. 1995. *Character development and physical activity*. Champaign, IL: Human Kinetics.

Shields, David L. L., Brenda J. L. Bredemeier, D. E. Gardner, and A. Bostrom. 1995. Leadership, cohesion, and team norms regarding cheating and aggression. *Sociology of Sport Journal* 12, 3: 324–336.

Shilling, C. 1994. *The body and social theory*. Thousand Oaks, CA: Sage.

Shilling, C. 2007. Sociology and the body: classical traditions and new agendas. Sociological Review 55, s1: 1–18.

Shogan, Debra, and Maureen Ford. 2000. A new sport ethics. *International Review for the Sociology of Sport* 35, 1: 49–58.

Shulman, James L., and William G. Bowen. 2001. *The game of life: College sports and educational values*. Princeton, NJ: Princeton University Press.

Siklos, Richard. 2005. News Corp. to acquire owner of MySpace.com. *New York Times* (July 18). Online: http://www.nytimes.com/2005/07/18/business/18cnd-newscorp.html?

Silk, Michael L. 1999. Local/global flows and altered production practices. *International Review for the Sociology of Sport* 34, 2: 113–123.

Silk, Michael L. 2004. A tale of two cities: The social production of sterile sporting space. *Journal of Sport and Social Issues* 28, 4: 349–378.

Silk, M., and J. Amis. 2000. Institutional pressures and the production of televised sport. *Journal of Sport Management* 14 (4): 267–92.

Silver, J. 1996. *Thin ice: Money, politics, and the demise of an NHL franchise*. Halifax: Fernwood.

Simson, Viv, and Andrew Jennings. 1992. *The lords of the rings: Power, money and drugs in the modern Olympics*. London: Simon and Schuster.

Slack, E. 2003. Municipal funding for recreation. Online: www.laidlawfdn.org

Smedley, Audrey. 1997. Origin of the idea of race. *Anthropology Newsletter* (November). Online: www.pbs. org/race/000_About/002_04-background-02-09.htm (retrieved October 15, 2005).

Smedley, Audrey. 1999. Review of Theodore Allen, *The Invention of the White Race*, vol. 2. *Journal of World History* 10, 1 (Spring): 234–237.

Smedley, A. 2003. PBS interview for the series, *Race—the power of an illusion*. Online: www.pbs.org/race/000_ About/002_04-background-02-06.htm (retrieved June, 2005).

Smith, Andrew, and Nigel Thomas. 2005. The inclusion of elite athletes with disabilities in the 2002 Manchester Commonwealth Games: An exploratory analysis of British newspaper coverage. *Sports, Education and Society* 10, 1: 49–67.

Smith, B. 2002. Keep courts out of sports—lawyer. *Globe and Mail*, 21 August, p. S5.

Smith, D. 1997. Score: How the millionaire owners of the Winnipeg Jets got the public to pay for their hockey team. In P. Donnelly, ed., *Taking sport seriously: Social issues in Canadian sport* (pp. 240–43). Toronto: Thomson Educational.

Smith, G. 2005a. What do we do now? *Sports Illustrated* 102, 13 (March 28): 40–50.

Smith, G. 2005b. The shadow boxer. *Sports Illustrated* 102, 16 (April 18): 58–68. Online: http:// sportsillustrated.cnn.com/2005/magazine/04/12/ griffith0418/ (retrieved July 2005).

Smith, G., and C. Grindstaff. 1972. Race and sport in Canada. In A. Taylor and M. Howell, eds., *Training: Scientific basis and application*. Springfield, IL: Charles C. Thomas.

Smith, Jason M., and Alan G. Ingham. 2003. On the waterfront: Retrospectives on the relationship between sport and communities. *Sociology of Sport Journal* 20, 3: 252–274.

Smith, Michael. 1975. Foreword. In T. Orlick and C. Botterill, eds., *Every kid can win* (pp. ix–xi). Chicago: Nelson-Hall.

Smith, M. 1983. *Violence and sport.* Toronto: Butterworths.

Smith, Ronald. E. 1986. Toward a cognitive-affective model of athletic burnout. *Journal of Sport Psychology* 8, 1: 36–50.

Smith Maguire, J. 2002. Bodies fit for consumption: The cultural production of the fitness field. Unpublished doctoral thesis, City University of New York Graduate School, New York.

Snyder, Eldon. E. 1994. Interpretations and explanations of deviance among college athletes: A case study. *Sociology of Sport Journal* 11, 3: 231–248.

Sokoloff, H. 2002. Universities spend $6.2m to aid athletes. *National Post*, 31 January.

Sokolove, Michael. 2002. Football is a sucker's game. *New York Times Magazine*, section 6 (December 22): 36–41, 64, 68–70.

Sokolove, Michael. 2004a. The thoroughly designed American childhood: Constructing a teen phenom. *New York Times*, section 6 (November 28): 80.

Sokolove, M. 2004b. In pursuit of doped excellence. *New York Times Magazine*, section 6 (January 18): 28–33, 48, 54, 58.

Sokolove, M. 2004c. Built to swim. *New York Times Magazine*, section 6 (August 8): 20–5.

Sparkes, Andrew, and Brett Smith. 2002. Sport, spinal cord injury, embodied masculinities, and the dilemmas of narrative identity. *Men and Masculinities* 4, 3: 258–285.

Sparks, R. 1992. "Delivering the male": Sports, Canadian television, and the making of TSN. *Canadian Journal of Communications* 17 (3): 319–42.

Spence, C. 1999. *The skin I'm in: Racism, sports and education*. Halifax: Fernwood Publishing.

Spence, J. and L. Gauvin. 1996. Drug and alcohol us by Canadian university athletes: A national survey. *Journal of Drug Education*, 26 (3): 275–287.

Spink, K. 1988. *Give Your Kids a Sporting Chance: A Parents' Guide*. Toronto: Summerhill Press.

Spirou, Costas, and Larry Bennett. 2003. *It's hardly sporting: Stadiums, neighborhoods, and the new Chicago*. DeKalb: Northern Illinois University Press.

Sports Québec. 1998. Brief presented to the Sub-Committee on the Study of Sport in Canada of the House of Commons Standing Committee on Canadian Heritage.

Spreitzer, Elmer A. 1995. Does participation in interscholastic athletics affect adult development: A longitudinal analysis of an 18–24 age cohort. *Youth and Society* 25, 3: 368–387.

Starr, M., and A. Samuels. 2000. A season of shame. *Newsweek* 135, 22 (May 29): 56–60.

Statistics Canada. 2000. National longitudinal survey on children and youth (NLSCY): cycle 4, 2000–2001. Online: www.statcan.ca/english/rdc/ nlscy_cycle4.htm

Statistics Canada. 2001. National longitudinal survey on children and youth (NLSCY): participation in activities. *The Daily*, 30 May.

Statistics Canada. 2003. Canada's Ethnocultural Portrait: The changing mosaic (*2001 census analysis series*). Ottawa: Minister of Industry.

Statistics Canada. 2007. *Ethnic origins, 2006 counts, for Canada, provinces and territories – 20% sample data (table). Ethnocultural Portrait of Canada Highlight Tables*. 2006 Census. Statistics Canada Catalogue no. 97-562-XWE2006002. Online: http://www12. statcan.ca/english/census06/data/highlights/ethnic/index.cfm?Lang=E (accessed August 14, 2008).

Stead, David, and Joseph Maguire. 2000. "Rite of passage" or passage to riches?: The motivation and objectives of Nordic/Scandanavian players in English Soccer League. *Journal of Sport and Social Issues* 24, 1: 36–60.

Stempel, C. 2005. Adult participation in sports as cultural capital: A test of Bourdieu's theory of the field of sports. *International Review for the Sociology of Sport*, 40 (4), 411–432.

Stempel, C. 2006. Gender, Social Class, and the Sporting Capital? Economic Capital Nexus. *Sociology of Sport Journal*, 23 (3), pp. 273–292.

Stevens, N. 1999. Stojko earns medal of different sort. Ottawa: Canadian Press, 26 January.

Stevenson, C. 1991. The Christian-athlete: An interactionist-developmental analysis. *Sociology of Sport Journal* 8, 4: 362–379.

Stevenson, C. 1997. Christian-athletes and the culture of elite sport: Dilemmas and solutions. *Sociology of Sport Journal* 14, 3: 241–262.

Stevenson, C. 1999. Becoming an elite international athlete: Making decisions about identity. In J. Coakley and P. Donnelly, eds., *Inside sports* (pp. 86–95). London: Routledge.

Stevenson, C. 2002. Seeking identities: Towards an understanding of the athletic careers of masters swimmers. *International Review for the Sociology of Sport* 37, 2: 131–146.

Stoelting, Suzanne Marie. 2004. She's in control, she's free, she's an athlete: A qualitative analysis of sport empowerment and the lives of female athletes. Paper presented at the annual conference of the American Sociological Society, San Francisco (August).

Stoll, Sharon K., and Jennifer M. Beller. 1998. Can character be measured? *Journal of Physical Education, Recreation, and Dance* 69, 1: 18–24.

Stoll, S. K., and J. M. Beller. 2000. Do sports build character? In J. R. Gerdy, ed., *Sports in school: The future of an institution* (pp. 18–30). New York: Teachers College Press (Columbia University).

Stone, Jeff, Christian I. Lynch, Mike Sjomeling, and John M. Darley. 1999. Stereotype threat effects on black and white athletic performance. *Journal of Personality and Social Psychology* 77, 6: 1213–227.

Stone, J., Zachary W. Perry, and J. M. Darley. 1997. "White men can't jump": Evidence for the perceptual confirmation of racial stereotypes following a basketball game. *Basic and Applied Social Psychology* 19, 3: 291–306.

Straits Times Interactive. 2000. In soccer bondage. 24 December. Online: http://straitstimes.asia1.com...g/mnt/html/preiership/news-dec-22.html

Strug, Kerri. 1999. Life in Romania, Texas. *Newsweek* 134, 17 (October 25): 73.

Sugden, J., and A. Tomlinson. 1998. *FIFA and the contest for world football: Who rules the peoples' game?* Cambridge, England: Polity Press.

Sugden, J., and A. Tomlinson. 1999. *Great balls of fire: How big money is highjacking world football*. Edinburgh, Scotland: Mainstream.

Sugden, J., and A. Tomlinson. 2000. Theorizing sport, social class and status. In J. Coakley and E. Dunning, eds., *Handbook of sport studies* (pp. 309–321). London: Sage.

Sundgot-Borgen, J. 2001. Eating disorders. In K. Christensen, A. Guttmann, and G. Pfister, eds., *International encyclopedia of women and sports* (pp. 352–358). New York: Macmillan Reference.

Svoboda, M. and P. Donnelly. 2005. Linguistic barriers to access to high-performance sport. Sport Canada/TSN Canadian Facts Social Policy Research/Ekos; E & F. Online: www.pch.gc.ca/progs/sc/pubs/recherches-research_e.cfm [_f.cfm]

Swain, Derek. 1999. Moving on: Leaving pro sports. In J. Coakley and P. Donnelly, eds., *Inside sports* (pp. 223–231). London: Routledge.

Sweeney, Emily. 2005. Cost of prosthetics stirs debate. *Boston Globe* (July 5): 2. Online: www.boston.com/business/globe/articles/2005/07/05/cost_of_prosthetics_stirs_debate/?page=2 (retrieved July 21, 2005).

Sweeney, H. Lee. 2004. Gene doping. *Scientific American* 291, 1 (July): 69.

Swift, E. M., and D. Yaeger. 2001. Unnatural selection. *Sports Illustrated* 94, 20 (May 14): 87–93.

Swim B.C. 2005. Swim Guide, 2005–06. Online: swim.bc.ca/admin/docs/Swim% 20Guide_Dec2005.pdf

Swoopes, Sheryl. 2005 Outside the arc (as told to L. Z. Granderson). *ESPN The Magazine* 8.22 (November 7): 120–125.

Taub, Diane E., and Kimberly R. Greer. 2000. Physical activity as a normalizing experience for school-age children with physical disabilities: Implications for legitimating of social identity and enhancement of social ties. *Journal of Sport and Social Issues* 24, 4: 395–414.

Taylor, I. 1982a. Class, violence, and sport: The case of soccer hooliganism in Britain. In H. Cantelon and R. Gruneau, eds., *Sport, culture, and the modern state* (pp. 39–97). Toronto: University of Toronto Press.

Taylor, I. 1982b. On the sports violence question: Soccer hooliganism revised. In J. Hargreaves, ed., *Sport, culture, and ideology* (pp. 152–97). Boston: Routledge and Kegan Paul.

Taylor, I. 1987. Putting the boot into a working-class sport: British soccer after Bradford and Brussels. *Sociology of Sport Journal* 4, 2: 171–191.

Temple, Kerry. 1992. Brought to you by . . . *Notre Dame Magazine* 21, 2: 29.

Tenebaum, K. 1996. *Daunted spirits, mangled bodies: Children in high-performance sport.* Unpublished paper, McMaster University.

Tewksbury, M. 2007. *Inside Out: Straight Talk from a Gay Jock.* Toronto: Wiley Canada.

Theberge, N. 1977. *An occupational analysis of women's professional golf.* Unpublished doctoral thesis, University of Massachusetts, Amherst.

Theberge, N. 1981. The world of women's professional golf: Responses to structured uncertainty. In M. Hart and S. Birrell, eds., *Sport in the sociocultural process* (pp. 287–300). Dubuque, IA: Wm. C. Brown.

Theberge, N. 1999. Being physical: Sources of pleasure and satisfaction in women's ice hockey. In J. Coakley and P. Donnelly, eds., *Inside sports* (pp. 146–155). London: Routledge.

Theberge, N. 2000a. Gender and sport. In J. Coakley and E. Dunning, eds., *Handbook of sport studies* (pp. 322–333). London: Sage.

Theberge, N. 2000b. *Higher goals: Women's ice hockey and the politics of gender.* Albany: State University of New York Press.

Theberge, N. 2002. Challenging the gendered space of sport: Women's ice hockey and the struggle for legitimacy. In S. Scraton and A. Flintoff, eds., *Gender and sport: A reader* (pp. 292–302). London: Routledge.

Thomas, Carol. 1999. Narrative identity and the disabled self. In M. Corker and S. French, eds., *Disability discourse* (pp. 47–56). Milton Keynes, England: Open University Press.

Thomas, R. 1996. Black faces still rare in the press box. In R. Lapchick, ed., *Sport in society: Equal opportunity or business as usual?* (pp. 212–233). Thousand Oaks, CA: Sage.

Thompson, R., and R. T. Sherman. 1999. Athletes, athletic performance, and eating disorders: Healthier alternatives. *Journal of Social Issues* 55, 2: 317–337.

Thompson, S. 1999a. The game begins at home: Women's labor in the service of sport. In J. Coakley and P. Donnelly, eds., *Inside sports* (pp. 111–20). London: Routledge.

Thompson, S. 1999b. *Mother's taxi: Sport and women's labor.* Albany: State University of New York Press.

Thompson, W. 1999. Wives Incorporated: Marital relationships in professional ice hockey. In J. Coakley and P. Donnelly, eds., *Inside sports* (pp. 180–89). London: Routledge.

Thomsen, Steven R., Danny W. Bower, and Michael D. Barnes. 2004. Photographic images in women's health, fitness, and sports magazines and the physical self-concept of a group of adolescent female volleyball players. *Journal of Sport and Social Issues* 28, 3: 266–283.

Thomson, Rosemarie Garland. 2000. Staring back: Self-representations of disabled performance artists. *American Quarterly* 52, 2 (June): 334–338.

Thomson, Rosemarie Garland. 2002. Integrating disability, transforming feminist theory. *National Women's Studies Association Journal* 14, 3: 1–32.

Time. 1997. *Time's* 25 most influential Americans. *Time* 149, 16: 40–62.

Tirone, S. 1999–2000. Racism, indifference, and the leisure experiences of South Asian Canadian teens. *Leisure* 24 (1–2), 89–114.

Tirone, S., and A. Pedlar. 2000. Understanding the leisure experiences of a minority ethnic group: South Asian teens and young adults in Canada. *Loisir et Société/Society & Leisure* 23 (1), 145–69.

Todd, Terry. 1987. Anabolic steroids: The gremlins of sport. *Journal of Sport History* 14, 1: 87–107.

Tomlinson, Alan. 2007. Sport and social class. In George Ritzer, ed., *Encyclopedia of sociology* (in press). London/New York: Blackwell.

Toohey, K. 2004. An Antipodean approach to rethinking the Olympics in the new Millennium: Should we turn the Games upside down? Paper presented at the Pre-Olympic Scientific Congress, Thessaloniki, Greece.

Toohey, K., and A. J. Veal. 2007. *The Olympic Games: A social science perspective.* Wallingford, U.K.: CABI Publishing.

Torbert, Marianne. 2004. A games model for facilitating a constructivist approach. In R. L. Clements and L. Fiorentino, eds., *The child's right to play: A global approach* (pp. 133–135). Westport, CT/London: Praeger.

Torbert, Marianne. 2005. *Follow me: A handbook of movement activities for children.* Eagan, MN: P.L.A.Y. (also Temple University: Leonard Gordon Institute for Human Development Through Play.)

Tracy, Allison J., and Sumru Erkut. 2002. Gender and race patterns in the pathways from sports participation to self-esteem. *Sociological Perspectives* 45, 4: 445–467.

Tracey, Jill, and T. Elcombe. 2004. A lifetime of healthy meaningful movement: Have we forgotten the athletes? *Quest* 56, 2: 241–260.

Troutman, Parke. 2004. A growth machine's plan B: Legitimating development when the value-free growth ideology is under fire. *Journal of Urban Affairs* 26, 5: 611–622.

Trulson, Michael E. 1986. Martial arts training: A novel "cure" for juvenile delinquency. *Human Relations* 39, 12: 1131–1140.

Trussell, D., and W. McTeer. 2007. Children's sport participation in Canada: Is it a level playing field? *International Journal of Canadian Studies*, 35, 113–132.

Tuaolo, Esera. 2002. Free and clear. *ESPN The Magazine* 5.23 (November 11): 72–77.

Tuggle, C. A., and A. Owen. 1999. A descriptive analysis of NBC's coverage of the centennial Olympics: The "Games of the Woman"? *Journal of Sport & Social Issues* 23 (2): 171–82.

Turner, Bryan S. 1997. *The body and society.* London: Sage.

Tymowski, G. 2001a. Rights and wrongs: Children's participation in high-performance sports. In I. R. Berson, M. J. Berson, and B. C. Cruz. eds., *Cross cultural perspectives in child advocacy* (pp. 55–93). Greenwich, CT: IAP (Information Age Publishing).

Tymowski, G. 2001b. Pain, children, and high-performance sport: A justification of paternalism. *Journal of Professional Ethics.* 9 (3–4): 121–152.

University of Toronto. 1994. Report of the Task Force on Gender Equity. Department of Athletics and Recreation.

Unwin, P. 2001. Who do you think I am?: A story of Tom Longboat. *The Beaver,* April–May, 20–26.

Upton, Jodi. 2005. Violence at games means trouble for all. *USA Today* (November 23): 11C.

USDHHS (U.S. Department of Health and Human Services). 1996. *Physical activity and health: A report of the surgeon general.* Washington, DC: USDHHS.

U.S. News and World Report. 1983. A sport fan's guide to the 1984 Olympics. *U.S. News and World Report* (May 9): 124.

USOC (U.S. Olympic Committee). 1992. *USOC drug education and doping control program: Guide to banned medications.* Colorado Springs, CO: USOC.

van Sterkenburg, Jacco, and Annelies Knoppers. 2004. Dominant discourses about race/ethnicity and gender in sport practice and performance. *International Review for the Sociology of Sport* 39, 3: 301–321.

Veblen, Thorsten. 1899. *The theory of the leisure class.* New York: Macmillan. (See also 1953 paperback edition, New York: A Mentor Book.)

Verducci, Tom. 2002. Totally juiced. *Sports Illustrated* 96, 23 (June 3): 34–48.

Veri, Maria J. 1999. Homophobic discourse surrounding the female athlete. *Quest* 51, 4: 355–368.

Vertinsky, P. A. 1987. Exercise, physical capability, and the eternally wounded woman in late nineteenth century North America. *Journal of Sport History* 14, 1: 7–27.

Vertinsky, P. A. 1990. *The eternally wounded woman: Women, exercise and doctors in the late nineteenth century.* Manchester: Manchester University Press.

Vertinsky, P. A. 1994. Women, sport, and exercise in the 19th century. In D. M. Costa and S. R. Guthrie, eds., *Women and sport: Interdisciplinary perspectives* (pp. 63–82). Champaign, IL: Human Kinetics.

Videon, Tami M. 2002. Who plays and who benefits: Gender, interscholastic athletics, and academic outcomes. *Sociological Perspectives* 45, 4: 415–435.

Vincent, John. 2004. Game, sex, and match: The construction of gender in British newspaper coverage of the 2000 Wimbledon Championships. *Sociology of Sport Journal* 21, 4: 435–456.

Vine, C., and P. Challen. 2002. *Gardens of shame: The tragedy of Martin Kruze and the sexual abuse at Maple Leaf Gardens.* Vancouver: Douglas and McIntyre.

Wacquant, L. J. D. 1992. The social logic of boxing in black Chicago: Toward a sociology of pugilism. *Sociology of Sport Journal* 9, 3: 221–254.

Wacquant, L. J. D. 1995a. The pugilistic point of view: How boxers think and feel about their trade. *Theory and Society* 24: 489–535.

Wacquant, L. J. D. 1995b. Pugs at work: Bodily capital and bodily labour among professional boxers. *Body & Society* 1 (1): 65–93.

Wacquant, L. J. D. 2004. *Body and soul: Notebooks of an apprentice boxer.* Oxford, England/New York: Oxford University Press.

Waddington, I. 2000a. Sport and health: A sociological perspective. In J. Coakley and E. Dunning, eds., *Handbook of sports studies* (pp. 408–421). London: Sage.

Waddington, I. 2000b. *Sport, health and drugs : A critical sociological perspective.* London: Routledge.

Waddington, I. 2007. Health and sports. In George Ritzer, ed., *Encyclopedia of sociology.* London: Blackwell.

Waldron, Jennifer, and Vikki Krane. 2005. Whatever it takes: Health compromising behaviors in female athletes. *Quest* 57, 3: 315–329.

Walker, Rob. 2005. Extreme makeover: Home edition—entertainment poverty. *New York Times,* section 6 (December 4). Online: www.nytimes com/ 2005/12/04/magazine/04wwin_consumed.html.

Walseth, Kristin, and Kari Fasting. 2003. Islam's view on physical activity and sport: Egyptian women interpreting Islam. *International Review for the Sociology of Sport* 38, 1: 45–60.

Wann, D. L., Gaye Haynes, B. McLean, and P. Pullen. 2003. Sport team identification and willingness to consider anonymous acts of hostile aggression. *Aggressive Behavior* 29: 406–413.

Wann, D. L., Jamie L. Hunter, Jacob A. Ryan, and Leigh Ann Wright. 2001a. The relationship between team identification and willingness of sport fans to consider illegally assisting their team. *Social Behavior and Personality: An International Journal* 29, 6: 531–537.

Wann, D. L., Merrill. J. Melnick, Gordon W. Russell, and Dale G. Pease. 2001b. *Sport fans: The psychology and social impact of spectators.* New York: Routledge.

Wann, D. L., Robin R. Peterson, Cindy Cothran, and Michael Dykes. 1999. Sport fan aggression and anonymity: the importance of team identification.

Social Behavior and Personality: An International Journal 27, 6: 597–602.

Wann, D. L., Joel L. Royalty, and A. R. Rochelle. 2002. Using motivation and team identification to predict sport fans' emotional responses to team performance. *Journal of Sport Behavior* 25, 2: 207–216.

Wann, D. L., Paula J. Waddill, and Mardis D. Dunham. 2004. Using sex and gender role orientation to predict level of sport fandom. *Journal of Sport Behavior* 27, 4: 367–377.

Wasielewski, Patricia L. 1991 Not quite normal, but not really deviant: Some notes on the comparison of elite athletes and women political activists. *Deviant Behavior: An Interdisciplinary Journal* 12, 1: 81–95.

Waterford, Robin. 2004. Athens suffers old stereotypes. *USA Today* (August 5): 15A.

Wearden, Stanley T., and Pamela J. Creedon. 2002. "We got next": Images of women in television commercials during the inaugural WNBA season. *Sport in Society* 5, 3: 189–210.

Weber, Max. 1968/1922. *Economy and society: An outline of interpretive sociology* (trans. G. Roth and G. Wittich). New York: Bedminster Press.

Wechsler, Henry, et al. 1997. Binge drinking, tobacco, and illicit drug use and involvement in college athletics. *Journal of American College Health* 45 (March): 195–200.

Wechsler, Henry, and Bernice Wuethrich. 2002. *Dying to drink : Confronting binge drinking on college campuses.* New York: Rodale and St. Martin's Press.

Wedgewood, Nikki. 2004. Kicking like a boy: Schoolgirl Australian rules football and bi-gendered female embodiment. *Sociology of Sport Journal* 21, 2: 140–162.

Weed, Mike. 2001. Ing-ger-land at Euro 2000: How "Handbags at 20 paces" was portrayed as a full-scale riot. *International Review for the Sociology of Sport* 36, 4: 407–424.

Weiner, Jay. 1999. What do we want from our sports heroes? *BusinessWeek* (February 5): 77.

Weiner, Jay. 2000. *Stadium games: Fifty years of big league greed and bush league boondoggles.* Minneapolis: University of Minnesota Press.

Weinstein, Marc D., Michael D. Smith, and David L. Wiesenthal. 1995. Masculinity and hockey violence. *Sex Roles* 33, 11/12: 831–847.

Weir, Tom. 2000. Americans fall farther behind. *USA Today* (May 3): 3C.

Weisman, Larry. 2004. Propelled to think past NFL. *USA Today* (June 16): 1C.

Weiss, Otmar. 1996. Media sports as a social substitution pseudosocial relations with sports figures. *International Review for the Sociology of Sport* 31, 1: 109–118.

Wells, C. (2008, in progress). *Getting on-track, getting off-track: Canadian student-athletes discuss their US athletic*

scholarships. Unpublished Master's thesis, University of Toronto.

Wendel, Tim. 2004. How fantasy games have changed fans. *USA Today* (September 20): 23A.

Wenner, Lawrence A., ed. 1998. *MediaSport.* London: Routledge.

Wenner, L. A., and Walter Gantz. 1998. Watching sports on television: Audience experience, gender, fanship, and marriage. In L. A. Wenner, ed., *MediaSport* (pp. 233–251). London: Routledge.

Wensing, E., and T. Bruce 2003. Bending the rules: Media representations of gender during an international sporting event. *International Review for the Sociology of Sport*, 38 (4), 387–396.

Wertheim, Jon. 2004. Globalization in sports: The whole world is watching (part 1 of 4). *Sports Illustrated* 100, 2 (June 14): 72–86.

West, Brad. 2003. Synergies in Deviance: Revisiting the Positive Deviance Debate. *Electronic Journal of Sociology* 7, 4. Online: www.sociology.org/content/vol7.4/west.html

Whannel, Garry. 2002. *Media sport stars: Masculinities and moralities.* London/New York: Routledge.

Wharnsby, T. 2008. 'I played like a girl,' Plekanec says. *Globe and Mail*, 15 April, p. S3.

Wheaton, Belinda, and Becky Beal. 2003. "Keeping it real": Subcultural media and the discourses of authenticity in alternative sport. *International Review for the Sociology of Sport* 38, 2: 155–176.

Wheeler, Garry David, et al. 1996. Retirement from disability sport: A pilot study. *Adapted Physical Activity Quarterly* 13, 4: 382–399.

Wheeler, Garry David, et al. 1999. Personal investment in disability sport careers: An international study. *Adapted Physical Activity Quarterly* 16, 3: 219–237.

White, Anita, et al. 1992. *Women and sport: A consultation document.* London: Sports Council.

White, Anita, and Ian Henry. 2004. *Women, leadership and the Olympic movement.* Loughborough, England: Institute of Sport and Policy Research, Loughborough University. Online: http://multimedia.olympic.org/pdf/en_report_885.pdf

White, Kelly. 2004. Discriminating airwaves. Online: www.womenssportsfoundation.org/cgi-bin/iowa/issues/article.html?record=999 (retrieved August 25, 2005).

White, P. 2004. The costs of injury from sport, exercise and physical activity: A review of the evidence. In, K. Young (ed.), *Sporting bodies, damaged selves: Sociological studies of sports-related injury.* Amsterdam: Elsevier, pp. 309–331.

White, P., and J. Curtis. 1990a. Participation in competitive sport among anglophones and francophones in Canada: Testing competing hypotheses. *International Review for the Sociology of Sport* 25, 125–39.

White, P., and J. Curtis. 1990b. English/French Canadian differences in types of sport participation: Testing the school socialization hypotheses. *Sociology of Sport Journal* 7, 347–68.

White, P., and B. Wilson. 1999. Distinctions in the stands: An investigation of Bourdieu's 'Habitus,' socioeconomic status and sport spectatorship in Canada. *International Review for the Sociology of Sport*, 34, pp. 245–264.

White, P., and Kevin Young. 1997. Masculinity, sport, and the injury process: A review of Canadian and international evidence. *Avante* 3, 2: 1–30.

Whitson, D. 1998. Circuits of promotion: Media, marketing, and the globalization of sport. In L. A. Wenner, ed., *MediaSport* (pp. 57–72). London/ New York: Routledge.

Whitson, D. 2004. Bringing the world to Canada: 'The periphery of the centre.' *Third World Quarterly*, 25 (7), 1215–1232.

Whitson, D., and D. Macintosh. 1996. The global circus: International sport, tourism, and the marketing of cities. *Journal of Sport & Social Issues*, 20 (3), 278–295.

Wieberg, Steve. 1994. Conley nears end of six-year career. *USA Today* (November 17): 8C.

Wieberg, Steve. 2000a. A judgment in Vermont. *USA Today* (February 3): 16C.

Wieberg, Steve. 2000b. A night of humiliation. *USA Today* (February 4): 1C–2C.

Williams, Patricia J. 2005. Genetically speaking. *The Nation* 280, 24: 10.

Willmsen, Christine, and Maureen O'Hagan. 2003. Coaches continue working for schools and private teams after being caught for sexual misconduct. *Seattle Times* (December 14). Online: http://seattletimes.nwsource.com/news/local/coaches (retrieved June 2005).

Wilmore, Jack H. 1996. Eating disorders in the young athlete. In O. bar-Or, ed., *The child and adolescent athlete* (pp. 287–303). Vol. 6 of the *Encyclopaedia of sports medicine* (IOC Medical Commission). London: Blackwell Science.

Wilson, B. 1997. "Good Blacks" and "Bad Blacks": Media Constructions of African-American Athletes in Canadian Basketball. *International Review for the Sociology of Sport* 32 (2), 177–89.

Wilson, B. 1999. "Cool pose" incorporated: The marketing of black masculinity in Canadian NBA coverage. In P. White and K. Young, eds., *Sport and gender in Canada* (pp. 232–253). Don Mills, ON: Oxford University Press.

Wilson, B. 2002. The "anti-jock" movement: Reconsidering youth resistance, masculinity, and sport

culture in the age of the Internet. *Sociology of Sport Journal* 19, 2: 206–233.

Wilson, B., and R. Sparks. 1996. "It's Gotta Be the Shoes": Youth, Race, and Sneaker Commercials. *Sociology of Sport Journal* 13 (4), 398–427.

Wilson, B., and R. Sparks. 2001. Michael Jordan, Sneaker Commercials, and Canadian Youth Cultures. In D. Andrews, ed., *Michael Jordan Inc.: Corporate sport, media culture, and late modern America* (pp. 217–55). Albany, NY: State University of New York Press.

Wilson, Thomas C. 2002. The paradox of social class and sports involvement: The roles of cultural and economic capital international. *Review for the Sociology of Sport* 37, 1: 5–16.

Winant, Howard. 2001. *The world is a ghetto: Race and democracy since World War II*. New York: Basic Books.

Wittebols, James H. 2004. *The soap opera paradigm: Television programming and corporate priorities*. Lanham, MD: Rowman and Littlefield.

Wolfe, Tom. 1979. *The right stuff*. New York: Farrar, Strauss, Giroux.

Wolff, Alexander. 2002. The vanishing three-sport star. *Sports Illustrated* 97, 20 (November 18): 80–92.

Wolff, Alexander. 2003. The American athlete: Age 10. *Sports Illustrated* 99, 13 (October 6): 59–67.

Wolff, Eli A. 2005. The 2004 Athens Games and Olympians with disabilities: Triumphs, challenges, and future opportunities. Presentation at the Forty-Fifth International Session for Young Participants International Olympic Academy. Athens, Greece.

Wood, Skip. 2004. Leftwich's job skills include pain tolerance. *USA Today* (October 22): 15C.

Woog, Dan. 1998. *Jocks: True stories of America's gay male athletes*. Los Angeles: Alyson Books.

Young, I. M. 1990. *Throwing like a girl and other essays in philosophy and social theory*. Bloomington and Indianapolis: Indiana University Press.

Young, I. M. 1998. Situated bodies: Throwing like a girl. In D. Welton, ed., *Body and flesh: A philosophical reader* (pp. 259–273). Oxford, England: Blackwell.

Young, K. 1993. Violence, risk, and liability in male sports culture. *Sociology of Sport Journal* 10, 4: 373–396.

Young, K. 2000a. Sport and violence. In J. Coakley and E. Dunning, eds., *Handbook of sport studies* (pp. 382–407). London: Sage.

Young, K. 2000b. *Toward a more inclusive sociology of sports-related violence*. Paper presented at the North American Society for the Sociology of Sport, San Antonio, TX.

Young, K. 2002a. From "sports violence" to "sports crime": Aspects of violence, law, and gender in the sports process. In M. Gatz, M. A. Messner, and S. J. Ball-Rokeach, eds., *Paradoxes of youth and sport* (pp. 207–224). Albany: State University of New York Press.

Young, K. 2002b. Standard deviations: An update on North American crowd disorder. *Sociology of Sport Journal* 19, 3: 237–275.

Young, K., ed. 2004a. *Sporting bodies, damaged selves: Sociological studies of sports-related injury*. Amsterdam: Elsevier.

Young, K. 2004b. The role of the courts in sports injury. In Kevin Young, ed. *Sporting bodies, damaged selves: Sociological studies of sports-related injury* (pp. 333–353). Amsterdam: Elsevier.

Young, K. 2007a. Violence among athletes. In George Ritzer, ed., *Encyclopedia of sociology* (in press). London/New York: Blackwell.

Young, K. 2007b. Violence among spectators. In George Ritzer, ed., *Encyclopedia of sociology* (in press). London/New York: Blackwell.

Young, K., and P. White. 1995. Sport, physical danger, and injury: The experiences of elite women athletes. *Journal of Sport and Social Issues* 19, 1: 45–61.

Young, K., P. White, and William McTeer. 1994. Body talk: Male athletes reflect on sport, injury, and pain. *Sociology of Sport Journal* 11, 2: 175–195.

Zeman, B. 1988. *To run with Longboat: Twelve stories of Indian athletes in Canada*. Edmonton: GMS Ventures.

Zhang, J. J., et al. 1997a. Impact of broadcasting on minor league hockey attendance. *Research Quarterly for Exercise and Sport* 68, March Supplement, A117.

Zhang, J. J., Dale G. Pease, and E. A. Jambor. 1997b. Negative influence of market competitors on the attendance of professional sport games: The case of a minor league hockey team. *Sport Marketing Quarterly* 6, 3: 31, 34–40.

Zhang, J. J., D. G. Pease, and Dennis W. Smith. 1997c. Relationship between broadcasting media and minor league hockey game attendance. *Sport Management Quarterly* 12, 2: 103–122.

Zhang, J. J., and D. W. Smith. 1997. Impact of broadcasting on the attendance of professional basketball games. *Sport Marketing Quarterly* 6, 1: 23–29.

Zimmer, Martha Hill, and Michael Zimmer. 2001. Athletes as entertainers. *Journal of Sport and Social Issues* 25, 2: 202–215.

Zorpette, Glenn. 2000. The chemical games. *Scientific American* 11, 3: 16–23.

Name Index

Subject Index